STRATEGIC MANAGEMENT

A CANADIAN CASEBOOK

FIFTH EDITION

MARY M. CROSSAN
Richard Ivey School of Business
The University of Western Ontario

JOSEPH N. FRY
Richard Ivey School of Business
The University of Western Ontario

J. PETER KILLING
International Institute for Management Development

ALLEN J. MORRISON
Richard Ivey School of Business
The University of Western Ontario

RODERICK E. WHITE
Richard Ivey School of Business
The University of Western Ontario

PRENTICE HALL INC., SCARBOROUGH, ONTARIO

Canadian Cataloguing in Publication Data

Main entry under title:

Strategic management
5th ed.

Previously published under title: Business policy: a Canadian casebook.

ISBN 0-13-083681-8

1. Business planning—Canada—Case studies. 2. Business planning—Case studies. 3. Industrial management—Canada—Case studies. 4. Industrial management—Case studies. I. Crossan, Mary M. II. Title: Business policy: a Canadian casebook.

HF5351.F79 2000   658.4'01'0971   C98–932951–8

Prentice-Hall, Inc., Upper Saddle River, New Jersey
Prentice-Hall International (UK) Limited, London
Prentice-Hall of Australia, Pty. Limited, Sydney
Prentice-Hall Hispanoamericana, S.A., Mexico City
Prentice-Hall of India Private Limited, New Delhi
Prentice-Hall of Japan, Inc., Tokyo
Simon & Schuster Southeast Asia Private Limited, Singapore
Editora Prentice-Hall do Brasil, Ltda., Rio de Janeiro

ISBN 0-13-083681-8

Publisher: Patrick Ferrier
Acquisitions Editor: Mike Ryan
Associate Editor: Sherry Torchinsky
Senior Marketing Manager: Ann Byford
Marketing Assistant: Elsa Passera
Production Editor: Nicole Mellow
Copy Editor: Catharine Haggert
Production Coordinator: Jane Schell
Permissions: Susan Wallace-Cox
Art Director: Mary Opper
Cover Design: Carole Knox
Cover Image: Phototone
Page Layout: Steve Eby

1 2 3 4 5   04 03 02 01 00

Printed and bound in the United States of America.

Visit the Prentice Hall Canada Web site! Send us your comments, browse our catalogues, and more at **www.phcanada.com**. Or reach us through e-mail at **phcinfo_pubcanada@prenhall.com**.

CONTENTS

PART ONE: Introduction to Strategic Management

1   London Telecom Network   1

Joseph N. Fry and John Bogert

London Telecom Network (LTN) is a fast-growing reseller of long distance telephone services. The company has survived where many have failed and is starting to generate significant profits. Now management is beginning to look at a range of initiatives to further build the business. The situation raises some interesting questions for Rob Freeman, the founder and owner of the business. Are the circumstances right for LTN to be pursuing new ideas? If so, which of several proposals deserves priority attention?

2   Gametronics   15

Allen J. Morrison, Jan Visser, Andres Maldonado and Heather Leonard

After several years of steady growth and healthy profits, Gametronics, a manufacturer of video game software, has recently seen its growth flatten out. Martin Fueller, the controlling shareholder of the company, has just received a call from a friend on Wall Street reporting the rumour that Sony Corp. is contemplating a takeover offer. Fueller has asked the new CEO, Tom Katz, to put together an action plan.

PART TWO: Strategy—Environment

3   Aikenhead's   25

Mary M. Crossan and Katy Paul-Chowdhury

Stephen Bebis, the CEO of Aikenhead's, is opening the first warehouse home improvement centre in Toronto, which will radically alter the competitive landscape. He must assess how he should roll out the business given competitive pressures.

4   The Diaper War: Kimberly-Clark versus Procter & Gamble   37

Allen J. Morrison and Kerry S. McLellan

The management of Kimberly-Clark watched with great interest and concern as Procter & Gamble announced the appointment of a new CEO, Edwin Artzt. Artzt had considerable international experience in the disposable diapers industry, and Kimberly-Clark management wondered if his appointment signaled a new phase of competition in the industry.

Deregulation of the airline industry has been fiercely competitive. During the 1990s neither of the two major Canadian players has been profitable. But Canadian Airlines' situation is the most desperate. Its board of directors has set a target date to reach agreement with its unions to achieve lower costs as the basis for growth (Plan A). The alternative is to dramatically shrink the airline (Plan B). By the deadline, only one-third of the target was negotiated. Senior management must prepare a recommendation for the Board on how to proceed.

Top management at the Bank of Montreal is considering a proposal for a pilot launch of a direct banking venture. (Direct banking bypasses the traditional branch network and deals directly with the customers by phone, fax, personal computer and ABM). At issue are such matters as the nature, scope and independence of the venture and the pace of introduction.

In early 1996, Vincor was Canada's largest wine company. It had grown rapidly, largely through acquisition. It is now looking at the prospect of an Initial Public Offering (IPO) in order to reduce debt and fund further growth. But what specifically is the case to be put before the investment community? Could a compelling case be built for a reasonably priced IPO?

PART THREE: Strategy—Resource/Capabilities

Harlequin, the world's largest and most successful publisher of romantic fiction, is ending a decade of solid growth and profitability. What should be the firm's strategy to sustain this performance?

For 20 years Imasco has been diversifying from its core cigarette business to encompass other major operations in financial services, drug store chains and fast-service restaurant chains. A new proposal has just been received from its Hardee's restaurant business to spend almost $400 million on the acquisition of the Roy Rogers restaurant chain in the United States. How should the proposal be assessed? Indeed, how should Imasco's now well-developed diversification program be assessed?

Starbucks must decide how it should leverage its core competencies against various opportunities for growth. Some options include introducing its coffee in McDonalds, pursuing further expansion of its retail operations, and leveraging the brand into other product areas.

PART FOUR: Strategy—Organization

Mary M. Crossan and Ariff Kachra

Service Corporation International, the world's largest funeral home consolidator, has just made a formal takeover bid for the Loewen Group, its key competitor. The offer is approximately 50 per cent above the price that Loewen Group stock traded at 30 days ago. Should Loewen Group fight the takeover or accept it?

PART FIVE: Strategy——Management Preferences

Roderick E. White

Jim Dunlop is an entrepreneur with a record of successful turnarounds, the latest of which is the Designer Classics Carpet business. Rapid sales increases have created some internal problems, but Dunlop is intent on moving ahead. He has just acquired a spinning mill to produce yarn for the carpet business, and he is considering related investments in importing, manufacturing and distribution.

J. Peter Killing

Aer Lingus, the Irish National Airline, has been remarkably successful in diversifying from its reliance on the airline industry. This case is about the pursuit of a new initiative in robotics which has led to a potential acquisition of a promising Canadian software company. The owner would remain as general manager and 25 per cent shareholder of the firm, but concerns are growing over how well he will take direction from Aer Lingus.

Mary M. Crossan and Nick Bontis

Diane McGarry, Chairman, CEO and President of Xerox Canada has been meeting with her leadership team since eight o'clock in the morning to craft the organization's new vision statement. Three and a half hours into the meeting the team hits a road block. With 30 minutes left in the session, McGarry must decide whether and how to proceed.

Joseph N. Fry and Stephen Jack

Charles Douglas is a recent business school graduate and a new employee of Archimax Systems. Archimax is a small company with big aspirations in the fast changing virtual reality market. Douglas is soon caught up in the pace and uncertainty of work in such a company. At the time of the case, he is facing a particularly difficult set of decisions that call for him to integrate the interest of the company, his boss and himself.

Allen J. Morrison and Detlev Nitsch

In 1992, senior management of Hydro-Quebec were faced with the problem of how to avoid the possible cancellation of its multibillion-dollar hydroelectric development project. Highly publicized opposition had arisen from aboriginal rights groups and environmental activists both in Quebec and the United States on socio-political, economic and ecological grounds. This situation was jeopardizing a major export contract by the New York Power Authority.

PART SIX: Competing in Foreign Markets

PART SEVEN: Managing Strategic Change

Joseph N. Fry

Hiram Walker is a very profitable business, but it is not growing. Cliff Hatch, Jr., its president for two years, is becoming concerned. There is a lot of talk about growth but little action. What action should be taken to address this seeming malaise?

Mary M. Crossan and Detlev Nitsch

Phil McLeod had been appointed as the editor of The London Free Press (LFP) with a mandate to make changes. Like most other North American daily newspapers, the LFP had been gradually losing readership, and its share of advertising revenues in the community was shrinking. Despite its ability to remain profitable, McLeod thought that it was not living up to its potential, especially since it was the only daily newspaper in London. He wondered if it would be possible to stop the slow decline of the newspaper, or if its shrinkage was an inevitable consequence of broader trends in the information industry and Canadian society.

Joyce Miller and Terry Deutscher

ICI Colours is a large, complex, global business. It is experiencing performance problems on several fronts, but particularly in providing timely and reliable service to its widespread and diverse customer base. The commercial director is considering the launch of a new initiative to establish a service agreement with key customers that commits ICI to monitoring and correcting service deficiencies at their source. There are mixed views in the company about the wisdom of such a move.

Mary M. Crossan and Julian Birkinshaw

Murray Wallace has just taken over as CEO and President of Wellington Insurance, a "company without hope" according to a recent consultant's report. Wallace is faced with the challenge of effecting a complete revitalization at Wellington when the prospects for the industry and the company look bleak.

PART EIGHT: Strategic Analysis and Personal Action

Mary M. Crossan and Katy Paul-Chowdhury

Taco Bell Background Note describes recent dramatic changes in the fast-food restaurant industry, the emergence of Taco Bell as a major company and the situation Sanjiv Yajink faces as a new market manager. The Taco Bell series of cases establishes the link between strategic analysis and personal action, and illustrates the incremental, emergent nature of strategy formation and implementation.

34 Sabena Belgian World Airlines (A)   499

Mary M. Crossan and Barbara Pierce

When Pierre Godfroid took over as Sabena's CEO, Sabena was in crisis and facing imminent bankruptcy. On the strength of a restructuring plan developed by Godfroid and his staff, the Belgian government had agreed to bail out the airline in return for assurances that this would be the last time government assistance would be requested. Godfroid's task was to transform the company into a viable private enterprise. The case provides the opportunity to evaluate the viability of Godfroid's strategy. More importantly, it sets the stage for a sequence of follow-on cases dealing with the implementation of the strategy.

35 Delta Agrochemicals, Inc.   512

J. Peter Killing and Joyce Miller

A senior manager in a large agrochemical company considers transferring to a sister division, which is deciding what strategic and organizational changes it needs to improve profitability.

36 The GE Energy Management Initiative (A)   521

Joseph N. Fry and Julian Birkinshaw

Raj Bhatt, Business Development Manager for GE Canada, met with executives from GE Supply, a U.S.-based distribution arm of GE. The purpose of the meeting was to discuss new business opportunities in Energy Efficiency. Bhatt had identified some opportunities for business development in Canada, while GE Supply had just put together an energy-efficiency joint venture in the U.S. Bhatt was keen to work with GE Supply and retain a high level of operating autonomy. The challenge was to put together an appropriate organizational structure.

PART NINE: Comprehensive

37 Nestlé-Rowntree (A)   529

James C. Ellert, J. Peter Killing and Dana G. Hyde

Nestlé is the world's largest food company. For some time it has been attempting, without success, to develop a link with Rowntree PLC, one of the world's top chocolate companies. As a matter of policy, Nestlé does not make hostile takeovers, but now its hand seems to be forced by the sudden purchase of 14.9 per cent of Rowntree by Jacobs Suchard, one of Nestlé's keenest rivals in the European chocolate business. Rowntree is preparing to fight all comers; the stakes are enormous.

PREFACE

Appropriate for Strategic Management and Business Policy courses at Canadian universities, this fifth edition continues to effectively present the concept of strategy and the high quality, class-tested cases that have made it the premier strategic management casebook in Canada. The underlying theme of the cases remains that of a general manager facing issues of strategy formulation and implementation, strategic change and personal action.

NEW TO THIS EDITION

Twelve new cases have been introduced, adding to a collection of perennial favourites. Several of these new additions are supplemented with video segments from the classroom or on the job site. For example, the video segment that accompanies Sabena Belgian World Airlines presents the head of catering describing staff, union and cultural problems that were addressed in order to implement the airline bail-out. The Vincor: IPO Roadshow clip features the presentation that was made to senior brokerage officials at the time of the initial public offering of stock in Canada's largest winery conglomerate. To obtain a copy of this video, please contact your Prentice Hall Canada sales representative.

IMPROVED STRUCTURE

Cases from the Competing in the North American Market section have been incorporated into the Competing in Foreign Markets section. Furthermore, the cases from the Business Scope and Competitive Advantage section have been incorporated into the Strategy—Resource/Capabilities section. In both instances, the intent was to reduce the artificial separation and increase the case selection in each area.

Mirroring the structure of *Strategic Analysis and Action* by Fry and Killing, the first five parts cover each of the elements in the Diamond-E Framework. These elements are then extended to an international context in Part Six. The cases in Part Seven can be used to examine strategy formulation, but they offer the added benefit of a detailed assessment of managing strategic change. It has become increasingly important to us over time to anchor concepts of strategy formulation and implementation in the personal action of the manager and, where possible, recent graduates of business schools. The cases in the Strategic Analysis and Personal Action section are designed to make the concept of strategy more meaningful to the business school graduate. Several of the cases in this section also reinforce the real-time nature of strategy by requiring students to respond in the moment to a variety of situations. The cases in this section also provide a strong closing to the book by integrating all strategic management aspects learned in the course.

SUPPLEMENTS

The following supplements have been carefully prepared to accompany this new edition:
- a video featuring managers in the classroom and on the job, helping to bridge the gap between theory and practice.
- an Instructor's Resource Manual containing detailed teaching notes for all of the cases, including suggestions for case sequencing, assignments, teaching approach and supplementary readings and references.
- a Transparency Resource package containing electronic slides prepared in PowerPoint 7.0 as well as black-and-white transparency masters.

ACKNOWLEDGMENTS

The cases in this book were prepared with the generous cooperation and assistance of a large number of executives. One of the continuing delights of the case writing process is the opportunity for us to meet and to learn from these individuals. We owe them a great, collective vote of thanks.

Case writing is an expensive process. It would not be possible without continued support from the general coffers of the Fund for Excellence at the Richard Ivey School of Business. Some of the businesses that we were studying also helped us indirectly by contributing to the Fund and others, directly, by picking up expenses ranging from airline tickets to the proverbial free lunch. Thank you all. We would also like to thank the International Institute for Management Development (IMD) in Lausanne, Switzerland and Thunderbird, the American Graduate School of International Management, for permission to use their cases.

The encouragement that is essential in sustaining a case development program comes from a supportive administrative context and from the help of our immediate colleagues. Ken Hardy, the Associate Dean of Research, has been a consistent supporter, as have our Deans past and present: Bud Johnston, Al Mikalachki, Adrian Ryans and Larry Tapp. We have been greatly assisted by our teaching colleagues and former colleagues who have contributed cases and who have been an essential part of the work of testing, refining and, indeed, figuring out how to teach the cases. We have also had the opportunity of working with a cooperative and skilled group of PhD candidates and research assistants, whose names and individual contributions are acknowledged in the cases on which they worked. We are also grateful to the following reviewers for their comments and suggestions: Neil Abramson, Simon Fraser University; Robert Gephart, University of Alberta; Gordon Holmes, Mohawk College; Terry Seawright, McMaster University; and Francis Tapon, University of Guelph.

We are indebted to our publisher, Prentice Hall Canada, and in particular Mike Ryan, Sherry Torchinsky, Nicole Mellow, Catharine Haggert, Ann Byford and Elsa Passera for their help in editing, producing and promoting this book. At our school we are, in particular, obliged to Sue O'Driscoll, Dorothy Zavitz, and Shirley Koenig for their diligent and industrious effort in bringing everything together.

Mary M. Crossan
Joseph N. Fry
J. Peter Killing
Allen J. Morrison
Roderick E. White

London, Ontario

INTRODUCTION

All of the cases in this book deal with problems facing general managers. Although some are disguised, all are based on real situations and raise issues that are in some way related to a firm's strategy. We have presented the cases in a logical and orderly progression—from analysis (what are the key elements in this firm's situation?) through desired action (what should be done?) to detailed implementation (how should it be done?). However, we do not recommend that the casebook be used alone. It should be employed in conjunction with either a policy textbook or an organized set of readings that present the basic concepts of strategy formulation and implementation and the management of strategic change.

Our preferred text is *Strategic Analysis and Action*, Fourth Edition, and the Diamond-E model on which it is based. This model links the firm's strategy with its environment, its resources, the preferences of its managers and its organization. We have used it for a number of years, and have found that it permits useful insights not only into the cases presented in this book but also into a wide variety of other general management situations.

The key to using the Diamond-E model is to begin by identifying the firm's existing or proposed strategy. In *Strategic Analysis and Action*, Fourth Edition, we suggest that a description of a firm's strategy should include its goals, product-market focus, competitive premise, and business system focus. The Diamond-E model can then be used to assess methodically the new or existing strategy by means of the following questions:

1. Is the strategy internally consistent?
2. Is the strategy consistent with the environment?
3. Is the strategy consistent with present or obtainable resources?
4. Is the strategy consistent with the firm's organizational attributes?
5. Is the strategy consistent with the personal preferences and beliefs of top management?

We have grouped the cases according to the strategy relationships in the Diamond-E model that they emphasize. This is a rough cut as strategic issues do not come in neat packages, but it does provide for a flow of emphasis over the progression of a course. The first five sections of the casebook correspond to the Diamond-E framework. Part Six provides the opportunity to examine all elements of the Diamond-E in the context of foreign markets.

THE DIAMOND-E FRAMEWORK

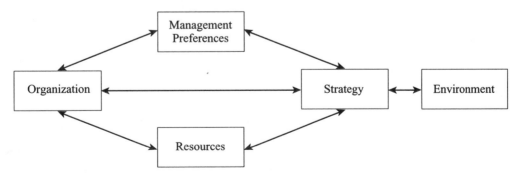

SOURCE: J.N. Fry and J.P. Killing, *Strategic Analysis and Action*, Fourth Edition. Scarborough, Ontario: Prentice Hall Canada Inc., 2000.

The five cases that comprise Part Seven, Managing Strategic Change, are the most difficult in the book. In these, the questions of what must be done and how it should be done need to be addressed simultaneously. The section in *Strategic Analysis and Action* dealing with this topic considers three variables: the pace at which the general manager should attempt to effect change, the targets to focus efforts on, and the tactics that should be employed. Each issue deserves close examination in these cases.

Part Eight, Strategic Analysis and Personal Action, presents four cases that accomplish three objectives: 1) to present strategic analysis from the perspective of a new manager rather than a CEO or senior manager; 2) to demonstrate the incremental and emergent nature of strategy as a "pattern" of decisions; and 3) to challenge students to understand and internalize the personal attributes required to think and act strategically.

The Nestlé-Rowntree Series in Part Nine is a comprehensive case series. The (A) case provides a vehicle to do a thorough assessment of a global industry. The follow-on cases require the students to decide and act.

We hope that you find these cases enjoyable as well as instructive. The new cases as well as our favourites give us a great deal of satisfaction, provoke dialogue among us and give us new insights.

LONDON TELECOM NETWORK

case

1

John Bogert and
Joseph N. Fry

On a snowy Thursday in December, 1995, Rob Freeman, chairman and sole owner of London Telecom Network Inc. (LTN), was driving to Hamilton for his bi-weekly meeting with senior management. LTN was one of Canada's more prominent long distance resellers, servicing over 22 000 customers and generating annualized revenues of $23 million. Profits had improved in the past year from a break-even in the first five months to a cumulative $1 million forecast by the end of December. (See Exhibit 1 for further financial information.)

IVEY

John Bogert prepared this case under the supervision of Professor Joseph N. Fry solely to provide material for class discussion. The author does not intend to illustrate either effective or ineffective handling of a managerial situation. The author may have disguised certain names and other identifying information to protect confidentiality.

Rob and his management team were encouraged by the developing profitability of the business. They were now turning their attention to longer-term issues, and particularly to opportunities for further growth. The problem here was not one of generating new ideas, but rather of deciding which ideas made sense. Rob's aims were high—to pursue the prospect of offering "flat rate long distance to everyone" and becoming a billion dollar, debt-free telecommunications corporation.

THE CANADIAN LONG DISTANCE TELECOMMUNICATIONS INDUSTRY

Overview

The 1995 Canadian market for telephone telecommunications services was estimated at $16 billion per year. Of this amount, $8 billion was for local service and $8 billion was for long distance. The local service market included local phone service and phone equipment. The long distance market—including phone calls, data transmission, and fax—encompassed all calls that originated and terminated in Canada and the Canadian portion of calls that originated or terminated outside Canada. Overall, the long distance market was growing at a rate of 5 to 10 per cent per year.

Background

Until the mid 1980s, Canadian telecommunications services had been controlled by a series of regulated provincial monopolies. A notable exception to this situation was Bell Canada, which was a public company that operated as a regulated monopoly in southern Ontario and southern Quebec (60 per cent of the total market). Bell and the provincial monopolies were organized into a consortium called the Stentor Alliance, which provided a unified front for them to lobby on regulatory matters and other industry-wide issues. The Stentor Alliance was comprised of: BCTel (British Columbia), SaskTel (Saskatchewan), AGT (Alberta), MTS (Manitoba), Bell Canada (Ontario and Quebec), Quebec-Tel (northern Quebec), IslandTel (Prince Edward Island), MT&T (New Brunswick and Nova Scotia), NewfoundlandTel (Newfoundland), and NorthwestTel (Northwest Territories and Yukon).

The CRTC

Radio, television and telecommunications in Canada were controlled by the Canadian Radio-television and Telecommunications Commission (CRTC). In the late 1980s the CRTC had come under immense pressure from industry to deregulate the long distance market. Canadian industry, which had watched long distance rates in the U.S. drop some 40 per cent in the five years since U.S. deregulation, wanted the same opportunities in Canada. In addition, some companies were using technical and legal loopholes to enter the long distance market. This practice undermined the CRTC's control. As a result, the CRTC passed Ruling 90-3 in the spring of 1990, deregulating 90 per cent of all long distance services, and Ruling 92-12 in late 1992, deregulating the remaining 10 per cent. These revisions forced the Stentor Alliance to rent long distance lines and time to registered resellers.

The CRTC's mandate had thence become one of ensuring the smooth deregulation of the telecommunications market. In this passage, rate re-balancing became a major issue. Under regulation, the Stentor Alliance companies had been charged with providing all Canadians with "affordable" local phone service. As a result residential users paid $11–$15 per month for a service that cost $38 to deliver. Long distance charges subsidized local service costs. As lower prices and competition cut into the Stentor Alliance's long distance income, it became difficult to continue to cross-subsidize local residential service. Therefore, the CRTC decided to allow the Stentor Alliance to phase in rate re-balancing. Over a five-year period, long distance charges would drop 35–50 per cent, while local residential line charges would go up 30 to 40 per cent.

It was thought that the CRTC's increase in local access charges would pave the way for deregulation of the local loop (lines that run from individual houses to the main switch). Local charges needed to reflect actual costs if competition was to be successful. Most recently, the CRTC had ruled to allow the Stentor Alliance to deliver cable television and the cable companies to deliver local telephone service. Experts were curious as to what would happen to phone charges as local loops were privatized. If the cable companies could deliver an individualized movie to a house for $5, how would they justify charging $0.20/minute for a phone call that used 1/10 000 of the bandwidth?

The Canadian Long Distance Market

There were three basic ways in which a company could provide long distance service:

Buy time on a per minute basis:	Renting the use of another carrier's network, one call at a time.
Rent lines and switch space:	Stentor Alliance companies and alternative carriers had excess capacity on their switches and fibre optic lines. Alternative carriers rented a dedicated amount of capacity for a flat monthly fee, to supplement their dedicated networks.
Build a dedicated network:	Buying lines and switches was very capital intensive, but resulted in the lowest cost per minute, once capacity was filled.

There were three types of companies that provided long distance service to end-users: the Stentor Alliance, the alternative carriers, and the resellers. The Stentor Alliance controlled 82 per cent of the $8-billion long distance market, with the remaining 18 per cent divided among 270 resellers and the alternative carriers.

Stentor Alliance

The Stentor Alliance companies had traditionally controlled 100 per cent of the long distance market. With the advent of deregulation, however, they had lost 18 per cent of the market to resellers and alternative carriers. The Alliance continued to control 100 per cent of the market for local phone service, however, and were the only providers of long distance that reached into all the small towns and cities across Canada. Therefore, many resellers and alternative carriers bought long distance services from the Stentor Alliance.

Resellers

There were 265 resellers of long distance in Canada, which had collectively captured about 9 per cent of the end-user market. They were called resellers because they rented time from Bell or the alternative carriers. Take, for example, a reseller that buys time from Bell. When a customer places a long distance phone call, Bell carries the call, tracks the fact that this was a customer of the reseller, and invoices the reseller instead of the customer. Bell forwards individualized call data to the reseller when invoicing, so that the reseller could repackage it to the customer's needs. Typically, the reseller bought time at a 50 per cent discount and then resold it at a 35 per cent discount. These businesses, with low overheads and low advertising, focused on capturing mid-size businesses, which were looking for additional services such as calling cards, data lines, and customized billing.

Resellers lived in a constant cash crunch. They often had to pay their provider in advance for service (at least until they built up a credit history), and had to wait 30–60 days to collect from their customers. It was easy to enter the industry, and easy to fail as well.

Alternative Carriers

There were four major alternative long distance carriers in Canada: Sprint, fonorola, ACC and Unitel (see Table 1). These companies had all started as resellers, but over the past five years they had invested in their own dedicated networks, which were typically installed between major hubs and connected to their U.S. parent. The alternative carriers all supplemented their networks by leasing lines and space on switches from the Stentor Alliance companies. Each firm had its own discount plan, often complicated by different discounts for specific areas and customers. Although competition was stiff, customers could generally expect to receive up to 25 per cent off Bell rates. (See Exhibit 2 for an example of discounts.)

TABLE 1   Canadian Alternative Carriers—Revenue and Performance

1995 Data	Sprint	fonorola	ACC	Unitel
Revenue ($ MM)	457	209	109	1118E
Profits ($ MM)	-65	-7.2	0.6	-181E

Source: Company financial statements, Unitel figures are estimates.

Alternative carriers had financed their network expansion with equity and debt issues (see Exhibits 3 & 4 for financial data on ACC and Sprint Canada). These funds were spent to install fibre optic cable between major hubs and switches. The expectation was that lower costs per unit would result once the network was filled. All of these companies (with the exception of Unitel) were expected to start turning a profit in 1996.

LONDON TELECOM NETWORK

History

In 1988, Rob Freeman, a real estate broker living in Strathroy, Ontario, was bothered by the $0.35/minute charge for calling London, only 12 miles away. Rob knew something about telecommunications (telecom) switches, having studied two years of electrical engineering at the University of Waterloo, and having toyed with telecom as a hobby for years.

Through a friend who worked at Bell Canada, he inquired about the legality of setting up a phone in Mount Bridges, halfway between Strathroy and London, to forward phone calls. He could then make a local call to Mount Bridges from Strathroy. The phone in Mount Bridges would forward a second local call from Mount Bridges to London. The net effect was that a long distance call would be converted into two local calls, and no long distance charges would apply.

Bell, of course, claimed that such a system was illegal. Rob disagreed; his research had not revealed any preventative regulations. He decided to proceed without Bell's permission. Selling long distance was illegal in 1988, so he started a sharing group, and convinced 100 Strathroy residents to join. Because he had no money, he asked the members to prepay two months. He then set up a switch in Mount Bridges with 10 lines in and 10 lines out. Later, he added Exeter and St. Thomas.

Bell filed a complaint with the CRTC. The ruling came out in Rob's favour: as long as the call was forwarded only once, he could continue. However, call forwarding more than once was ruled to be illegal.

In 1990, when the CRTC deregulated the Canadian long distance market, Rob acquired the interests of the other members of the sharing group, and formed London Telecom. Rob knew that, to survive, LTN had to grow. Therefore, he established a line through Oakville to link Burlington to Toronto, and rented his first trunk line to carry long distance calls. In the first week LTN signed up 400 customers. By the end of 1991, the company had 1 000 customers. From this starting point LTN grew rapidly, and by December, 1995, the company provided services to over 22 000 customers.

The Organization

LTN was a flat organization. A group of six managers—Jim Weisz, president; Rob Belliveau, vice president, sales and marketing; Gary Campbell, vice president, finance and information services; Greg Cope, manager, regulatory issues and special projects; Maureen Merkler, manager, human resources; and Randy Patrick, vice president, network services—handled virtually all the business operating decisions and the supervisory activities for a roster of about 100 employees. Rob Freeman, as chairman, confined his involvement primarily to policy issues and to developing the management group. Jim Weisz explained the management approach:

> We try to keep ourselves lean. We need to keep costs down in this market and at the same time we need to be able to make decisions quickly. The CRTC keeps us on our toes. That's why I have Greg Cope keeping an eye on the CRTC for us.
>
> The organization is growing and Rob Freeman would like LTN to hire from within whenever possible. Maureen Merkler was hired a year ago to help in this area. We are working to get job descriptions down for all positions, and have sent a few employees who were not performing out for training.

LTN's Product Offering

As of late 1995 LTN operated a network connecting 41 Canadian cities (see Exhibit 5). LTN rented all of its equipment and lines at flat monthly rates from the Stentor Alliance companies. Between different cities, depending on call traffic, LTN could vary the amount of bandwidth rented on lines and switches. There were significant economies of scale in renting long distance bandwidth. For example, a DS-0 line could carry 12 calls at a time at a cost of $4 100 per month, while a DS-3 line could carry 504 calls at a cost of $37 800 per month. To ensure customer service levels, LTN had an agreement with fonorola to carry overflow calls.

LTN had been rapidly increasing the scope and capacity of its network. Randy Patrick commented:

> "We had a problem last January with growth. The network was growing faster than marketing could keep up. Bell requires that we give them two months' notice on changes to the network, so we have to order the lines before we know for sure if the sales are going to materialize. Up until then, we had been growing at a rate of one city a week. We have cut back to one city every three weeks. Of course, our network still has a lot of empty space on it, but unfortunately our technology doesn't allow us to pin down exactly where very easily.
>
> We are Bell's second largest customer. None of the long distance resellers get the kind of discounts we do. While Bell's sales guys might not like us because we are stealing business from them, they realize that losing a sale to us is better than losing a sale to Unitel."

Unlike its competitors, LTN charged a flat rate for its long distance service: $74.95 per month to residential customers and $94.95 per month to business customers. For this customers received 40 hours of long distance covering calls placed anytime of the day. If they exceeded the 40 hours, customers were automatically sold time in additional five hour blocks. LTN's service included a reverse calling feature; for example, relatives could call the customer using the customer's LTN account.

There were regulatory and economic reasons why few companies charged a flat rate like LTN. Until recently, the Stentor Alliance, Sprint and Unitel had not been allowed to do so; as inter-exchange carriers they had been limited by the CRTC in the way in which they could bill for services. In September, 1995, the CRTC decided to allow Sprint and Unitel to charge in whatever way they pleased, leaving only the Stentor companies strictly controlled by pricing tariffs. Resellers, which could legally sell flat rate services, usually sold on a per-minute basis because they bought their services on a per-minute basis and avoided the risk associated with fixed-cost line rentals.

LTN also departed from industry norms in not offering direct access service. To use LTN, customers first had to call the LTN network using a local access number, and then dial the number of the party they wanted to reach (see brochure—Exhibit 5). LTN had configured its network this way to take advantage of the lower rates set by the CRTC for non-direct access service.

The net result of buying services on a flat rate and operating a non-direct access network meant that LTN's costs were lower than a reseller buying time on a per-minute basis, providing LTN could achieve a minimum utilization of 40 per cent.

Rob Belliveau summed up how the customers felt about the flat rate, and the extra dialing:

> Our product is simple to understand. The flat rate concept sets us apart from the other resellers. We offer the security of a constant long distance phone bill and we don't try to force our customers to make their calls in the middle of the night if they want to save money. In fact, our nights are full. We wish more customers would call during the day.
>
> Customers don't mind dialing the extra numbers. With speed dialing it's just not a big deal. As far as I'm concerned, it's actually a bonus. A customer can sign up with Unitel for overseas calls and still keep us for Canadian calls.

Billing

Since the inception of the call-sharing group, Rob had always required that customers pay first and last month when joining. As the business grew, he saw no reason to change this system, although recently LTN had been hearing complaints about the high up-front cost to join. For example, a residential customer joining LTN would have to pay $150 in advance ($75—first month, and $75—last month).

LTN billed every day of the month, based on the day the customer signed up. This helped the accounting staff to smooth the workload. Billing was further simplified by the fact that all customers received a one-line invoice for either $74.95 or $94.95. The occasional customer who used more than 40 hours in a month received a second invoice. This procedure was quite different from the industry standard of multi-line invoices detailing the length and cost of every call.

Marketing

LTN relied heavily on advertising through direct mail. As each new city was added to the network, LTN would blanket the area with brochures. More recently, Rob Belliveau had begun experimenting with focused mailing efforts directed at certain demographic pockets and had run a 30 second TV spot in the World Series. LTN used sales representatives to follow up on leads:

Sales Agents: 10 sales agents across the country went door to door, cold calling residential and small business customers.

Inside Sales: LTN had 15 people in its call centre who answered inquiries and received a commission for customers that they closed.

Direct Sales: Two full time sales representatives handled inquiries from business prospects and made site visits to close sales.

Most of LTN's customers fell into three categories (see Table 2):

- residential customers, calling primarily within Canada;
- small and medium sized businesses, especially home-based businesses and outbound tele-marketers; and
- large businesses, willing to use more than one company to minimize costs.

TABLE 2   LTN's Current Canadian Market Segmentation and Share

	High Use Residential	Med. Use Residential	Low Use Residential	Small/Med. Business	Large Business	Total
Total Market						
% Accounts (residential only)	5%	35%	60%			
Spending per month	>$100	$10–100	<$10			
Total $ (mil.)	$750	$1 680	$432	$2 000	$3 138	$8 000
% Market	9.4%	21.0%	5.4%	25%	39.1%	100%
LTN						
# Customers	14 000	0	0	9 300	1	23 300
Revenue ($ mil.)	$12.6	0	0	$10.2	$0.2	$23.0
Current Market Share	1.7%	0.0%	0.0%	0.5%	0.01%	0.3%

Source: Consultant estimates.

The Call Centre

The 15 employees in LTN's call centre handled all inbound calls, with customers often waiting 10–15 minutes for service. Monday mornings were especially busy because potential customers would be calling after seeing advertisements on the weekend. Simultaneously, customers with billing problems would be calling, wondering why they had received two, and sometimes three, invoices. When call loads were especially heavy, the call centre would forward calls related to invoices to the accounting department.

Gary Campbell, vice-president finance and information systems, commented:

> We are still using the ACCPAC accounting package. It was designed for a few thousand customers at most, and we have 22 000. We figure that 50 per cent of the calls received by the call centre are related to billing problems. We are hoping to have a new accounting system in place in the next few months. Once that is done, call centre traffic should drop substantially.
> Confounding the problem, was that we are adding 1 000 customers a month. The computer system can't handle it. Call centre staff trying to add a new customer over the phone typically wait five minutes to pull up a file on the computer.

Wintel

Wintel was a separate company controlled by LTN management that was established in the summer of 1995 to deal with start-up competitors in the Toronto area. These companies were using the call forwarding technique that Rob Freeman had originally developed. LTN had been looking for a way to compete effectively with these new competitors without cannibalizing its own product line. The Wintel start-up provided the solution by offering a package of $29.95 flat rate for 40 hours, covering a limited area around Toronto. By December, 1995, Wintel had 600 customers of its own.

LOOKING AHEAD

The LTN senior management team had several ideas for continued expansion. The options included:

1. Going public,
2. Expanding into the U.S.,
3. Expanding the Canadian product offering,
4. Introducing new products, and
5. Building a permanent network.

Going Public

LTN senior management had approached Rob Freeman with the idea of going public. They felt that this option would provide funding for some of the ideas they were considering. One plan, which had been discussed in a preliminary way with an investment banker, involved issuing $10 million worth of shares: $5 million would be new issue, with funds to be used by the company, while $5 million would be sold by Rob Freeman. After the issue, Rob Freeman would retain 46 per cent of the shares, the public would hold 46 per cent, and the remaining 8 per cent would be divided equally among the senior managers.

Expanding into the U.S.

The management team had been working on and off on this expansion possibility for months. Originally, they had been interested in the possibility of providing Canadian customers with access to the U.S.; however, they had been looking more recently at full entry into the U.S. market.

The $80 billion U.S. long distance market had been deregulated five years longer than the Canadian market. Twenty-eight per cent of all long distance traffic was carried by 150 alternative carriers, 7 per cent by the 3 800 resellers, and the remainder by AT&T. The regulatory aspects of the long distance market were controlled by the Federal Communications Commission (FCC). This body was similar to the CRTC in mandate; but unlike the CRTC, its rulings had to be passed by Congress before they became law.

LTN had two potential plans for entry. The first was to ease into the market, growing slowly as it had in Canada, by starting in upstate New York, or around Chicago, and expanding outward. Advertising would be primarily by direct mail, and word of mouth. The second possibility was to go after traffic between the major centres by connecting the six biggest cities in the U.S. The advantage of this option was that LTN would immediately cover 30 per cent of the population of the U.S. The network would gradually expand out to the smaller centres.

In either case, LTN expected to offer a flat rate service. Although some competitors were already offering flat rates per minute, none was offering a flat monthly rate. LTN hoped to manage the network from Canada, but realized it would need a U.S. call centre to give customers service with a local feel. Randy Patrick (network) and Greg Cope (regulatory) had been working hard to determine whether FCC regulations would allow LTN to set up a low cost network similar to the one in Canada. Even without favourable FCC regulations, LTN was optimistic. With over 100 alternative carriers in the U.S., the competition to sell to resellers was intense. LTN had been quoted a cost of five cents a minute for nationwide coverage, and anticipated that it would be able to sell time for eight cents a minute.

Expanding the Canadian Product Offering

The average customer used only 20 of the 40 hours available. Management was concerned that they might lose some customers who decided that they were not getting their money's worth. Therefore, they were considering two new products:

- five hours for $29.95
- ten hours for $49.95

Rob Freeman, who was concerned about cannibalization, was also excited about the prospect of expanding the customer base by offering packages with more universal appeal. Rob Belliveau (marketing) had inquired with marketing research companies, but data on new customer potential were not available. Management was also considering automatic billing for the new products. Customers who submitted their credit card numbers would be billed automatically once a month.

Introducing New Products

Jim Weisz had recently been in contact with Calldex Inc., the manufacturer of a new technology: a calling card with a digital display that showed a new PIN number every minute. The advantage of this system was that the calling card number could not be stolen by someone looking over the shoulder of a caller entering the code.

LTN intended to use this new technology to target the cellular market. LTN could not offer cellular long distance service with their current network setup. Regular phone calls carried with them the number from which they had originated, which was used for services like call-display. LTN used this number to verify that calls into their network came from registered customers. Unfortunately for LTN, cellular calls did not carry this number. LTN planned to reconfigure the network so that customers could input a calling card number, in this way solving the cellular problem.

LTN wanted to charge flat rate for long distance calls placed with the calling card. The Calldex card was perfect for this, because the user could not pass the number around to friends or coworkers; the customer had to have the card in hand to place a call. LTN's proposal was that customers would use the Calldex cards to circumvent per minute long distance charges by using the local access numbers to call the LTN network. Once connected, they would input their calling card number, the PIN number currently being displayed, and the number they want to reach. Customers would pay a flat amount in advance, as well as an additional $160 to buy the card.

An alternative idea was to sell disposable calling cards with a fixed amount of long distance time pre-loaded with amounts of $10, $25, or $50. Disposable cards were popular in Europe, where people paid a per-minute charge for local calls. LTN hoped to sell the cards directly to current customers, as well as to packaged-goods companies, which might want to put $2 worth of long distance credit into every cereal box as a promotion.

Building a Permanent Network

With the growth of the business base and the possibility of going public, management felt LTN should plan on building a permanent network. To transmit calls, the company was considering using microwave towers, which, although susceptible to weather, were much cheaper than fibre optic cable. Rob Freeman thought that LTN could easily arrange a contract with one of the alternative carriers to carry calls when the weather was bad.

DECISION

Rob Freeman had almost reached the Hamilton office, where he would be meeting with his management team to discuss the options at 10 a.m. Although each option had potential, he was uncertain about how to make a choice and unwilling to take any big risks.

EXHIBIT 1 London Telecom Networks: Financial Statements 1992–1995

Income Statement

	Jan 31,1992	Jan 31,1993	Jan 31,1994	Jan 31,1995	*11 month ending* Dec 31, 1995
Revenue	253 387	1 625 012	5 899 065	12 368 252	20 036 062
Line costs	127 987	860 832	3 919 194	8 836 132	13 273 814
Gross Margin	125 400	764 180	1 979 871	3 532 120	6 762 248
Sales, General & Admin	117 678	906 566	1 820 178	4 007 550	5 305 266
Amortization	9 514	49 785	100 428	704 110	456 725
Operating Profit	(1 792)	(192 170)	59 265	(1 179 540)	1 000 257
Other Income	2 240	0	0	92 465	0
Unusual Item (1)	0	0	0	(1 000 000)	0
Taxes	0	0	0	0	0
Net Profit	448	(192 170)	59 265	(2 087 075)	1 000 257

Balance Sheet

Assets

Cash	17 948	0	354 037	299 450	1 675 700
Accounts Receivable	32 716	471 915	1 330 838	1 983 534	3 138 090
Prepaids	0.00	3 273	13 348	51 660	560 004
Due from Shareholders	0	0	31 233	96 630	201 980
Total Current Assets	50 664	475 188	1 729 456	2 431 274	5 575 774
Capital Assets (net)	69 944	296 663	509 452	772 134	1 469 330
Due from Related Companies	0	0	15 487	286 465	908 358
Other Assets	63 058	56 591	50 123	43 657	0
Total Assets	183 666	828 442	2 304 518	3 533 529	7 953 462

Liabilities

Short-term Debt	0	48 162	0	0	0
Accounts Payable	139 278	198 184	614 073	1 069 528	2 672 297
Deferred Revenue	45 268	456 014	1 163 008	2 043 873	3 393 849
Customer Deposits	0	313 810	658 343	1 638 109	2 105 040
Shareholders Advance	(2 880)	2 443	0	0	0
Non-competition A/P	0	0	0	1 000 000	1 000 000
Total Liabilities	181 666	1 018 613	2 435 424	5 751 510	9 171 186

Equity

Capital Stock	2 000	2 000	2 000	2 000	2 000
Retained Earnings	0	(192 170)	(132 906)	(2 219 981)	(1 219 724)
Total Liabilities and Equity	183 666	828 442	2 304 518	3 533 529	7 953 462

Notes: (1) Unusual item in 1995: non competition agreement paid to past shareholder.

Source: LTN internal documents.

EXHIBIT 2   Comparison of Competitive Long Distance Prices and Costs

	cost/min. (cents)
1. Bell Canada: Prices	
Base rate (Quebec-Windsor corridor):	37.0
Residential	
Evening discount (6–11 p.m.)—35%	24.1
Late night (after 11 p.m.)/weekend discount—60%	14.8
Business	
Large business (over $300 000/month)	
day rate	14.8
late night rate	10.4
Medium business (over $2 500/month)	
day rate	16.7
late night rate	11.7
Bell Canada: Costs	
Cost per MOU (minute of use)—average	8.0

2. Large Alternative Carriers (ACC, fonorola, Unitel, Sprint): Prices	
Business and Residential	
Best discount—25% off Bell rate	
day rate	27.8
evening	18.0
late night/weekend	11.1
Large Alternative Carriers: Costs	
Cost per MOU (minute of use)—average	12.0–16.7

3. Small Resellers: Prices	
Business and Residential	
Best discount—35% off Bell rate	
day rate	24.1
evening	15.6
late night/weekend	9.6
Small Resellers: Costs	
Cost per MOU (minute of use)	77% of selling price

Source: Discount rates based on literature search. Better discounts may be available to key clients.

EXHIBIT 3   ACC TelEnterprises Overview and Financial Statements 1994/1995

Overview

ACC TelEnterprises was a subsidiary of ACC Corp. of Rochester, New York. ACC rented all of its long distance equipment, but had invested in switching technology and frame relay equipment to ensure that it was able to offer a full range of services to its customers. As a part of this, the Canadian ACC network was interconnected with ACC's networks in the U.S. and in the U.K. In 1995, ACC TelEnterprises spent $4.2 million on switches and equipment.

ACC's motto was to be "all things to some people". ACC ended 1995 with 136 000 residential and 25 000 commercial customers, an increase of 58 000 over December, 1994. ACC had exclusive marketing rights at 30 universities in Canada, provided private label services to The Bay, and had recently introduced internet services.

Income Statement

(Amounts in 000s)

	Dec. 31, 1994	Dec. 31, 1995
Revenue	95 511	120 002
Network Costs	65 482	76 130
Operating Expenses	36 729	40 231
EBITDA	(347)	10 005
Net Profit	(11 002)	631

Balance Sheet

Assets

Current	17 350	23 147
Fixed	13 604	16 017
Other	10 997	20 317
Total Assets	41 951	59 481

Liabilities & Equity

Accounts Payable	15 350	20 612
Debt	354	3 437
Due to Affiliates	20 440	28 167
Other	185	1 008
Capital Stock	22 990	22 994
Deficit	(17 368)	(16 737)
Total	41 951	59 481

Source: ACC TelEnterprises Annual Report.

EXHIBIT 4 Call-Net (Sprint Canada) Overview and Financial Statements 1994/1995

Overview

Call-Net Enterprises (Sprint Canada) was 25 per cent owned by Sprint U.S., and had signed special distribution agreements with Sprint U.S. that ensured Call-Net exclusive Canadian rights to Sprint U.S.'s switched voice network and trademarks. Sprint Canada had over 700 000 circuit miles of company-owned fibre optic cable, and state-of-the-art switching equipment in Vancouver, Toronto, Calgary, and Montreal. Call-Net had spent $110 million on network expansion over the last two years and had planned an additional $50 million for 1996.

Sprint Canada was involved in all areas of the Canadian long distance market, including residential and business long distance services, toll free services, bill analysis software, global frame relay (for interconnecting LANs), private line, data packet switching, and internet access services.

Over the past two years, most of Sprint's new revenues had come from residential and small/medium business clients, but in 1996 Sprint had planned to focus more effort on large business clients, and on the cellular market.

Income Statement

(Amounts in 000s)

	Dec. 31, 1994	*Dec. 31, 1995*
Revenue	176 287	457 461
Network costs	125 093	302 016
Operating Expenses	82 382	171 238
EBITDA	(31 188)	(15 793)
Net Profit	(55 359)	(64 751)

Balance Sheet

Assets

Cash	157 730	179 626
Other Current	41 507	92 643
Fixed	85 290	132 008
Other	115 446	120 481
Total Assets	399 973	524 758

Liabilities & Equity

Accounts Payable	53 498	104 367
Debt	139 634	164 853
Due to Affiliates		
Other	2 587	5 900
Capital Stock	262 638	372 593
Deficit	(58 384)	(123 135)
Total Liabilities	399 973	524 578

Source: Call-Net Enterprises Annual Report.

EXHIBIT 5 LTN Network and Network Access

HOW TO DIAL

Welcome to London Telecom,™ Canada's flat rate long distance company.

Here's the fast and simple way to start using our flat rate service and start saving money. For easy reference, keep this brochure and your London Telecom™ Directory by your phone.

If you're at work, select the line designated for London Telecom's™ flat rate service. At home, just pick up your receiver.

Dial your local seven digit access number _____, and wait for a continuous dial tone. It's best to set this number up in speed dial.°

Enter the area code and the seven digit number you are calling.
(Never dial 1 or 0 before the area code).

Talk without worrying about per minute charges.

The London Telecom Network™ uses only the latest technology. All your calls will be placed with fast, clear connections, quickly and with no lengthy numbers to call and without delays for authorization. All you need is London Telecom's™ service and a touch tone phone. If you do not dial your local London Telecom™ access number, you will be calling long distance through your regular long distance carrier.

° Note: Write your access number in the space provided. If your telephone service does not provide call identity on your line, London Telecom™ flat rate services can not be accessed.

OUR FLAT RATE COVERAGE AREA

Your Local London Telecom™ Office

ONTARIO

ALLISTON	(705) 435-3450
BARRIE	(705) 734-1017
BELLEVILLE	(613) 966-7373
BRANTFORD	(519) 751-9410
BROCKVILLE	(613) 342-4885
CAMBRIDGE	(519) 658-6667
CHATHAM	(519) 352-2900
COBOURG	(905) 377-0750
COLLINGWOOD	(705) 446-2575
CORNWALL	(613) 933-3242
GEORGETOWN	(905) 873-6060
GUELPH	(519) 766-4997
HAMILTON	(905) 570-8700
KITCHENER	(519) 741-5990
KINGSTON	(613) 544-7212
LINDSAY	(705) 324-0001
LONDON	(519) 646-3131
MIDLAND	(705) 526-5445
NEWMARKET	(905) 895-3020
NORTH BAY	(705) 474-5095
ORANGEVILLE	(519) 940-4400
ORILLIA	(705) 327-5117

OSHAWA	(905) 404-6666
OTTAWA	(613) 567-4881
OWEN SOUND	(519) 371-4213
PETERBOROUGH	(705) 743-2382
ST. CATHARINES	(905) 685-5155
SARNIA	(519) 337-1060
SLT. STE. MARIE	(705) 256-7718
SIMCOE	(519) 428-2600
STEVENSVILLE	(905) 382-4448
STRATFORD	(519) 273-4910
SUDBURY	(705) 669-1300
TORONTO	(416) 777-2600
WINDSOR	(519) 257-2900
WOODSTOCK	(519) 537-1000

QUÉBEC

MONTRÉAL	(514) 879-8502
QUÉBEC CITY	(418) 694-2500

WESTERN CANADA

KELOWNA	(604) 470-4999
VANCOUVER	(604) 606-4949
VICTORIA	(604) 953-9449

Our Coverage Area is Constantly Expanding

COMING SOON

Cobourg, Ontario	Nov. 20, 1995
Sault Ste. Marie, Ontario	Nov. 27, 1995
Calgary, Alberta	Dec. 11, 1995

OUR COVERAGE AREA

LOCAL CALLING AREAS OF ALL CITIES SHOWN ARE ALSO INCLUDED IN LONDON TELECOM'S™ FLAT RATE NETWORK.

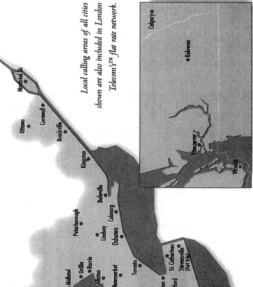

Local calling areas of all cities shown are also included in London Telecom's™ flat rate network.

WESTERN CANADA

Source: LTN promotional brochure

GAMETRONICS

case

2

Allen J. Morrison,
Jan Visser,
Andres Maldonado
and Heather Leonard

Early Wednesday morning, August 10, 1994, Tom Katz, the new CEO and President of GAMETRONICS (a manufacturer of video game software), settled into his chair at his office in San Jose, California, and began to scan the morning newspaper. The phone rang. It was Martin Fueller, a controlling shareholder and Chairman of the Board of GAMETRONICS. Fueller told Katz that he had just received a call from a close friend in New York with some troubling news. Rumours were circulating in the arbitrage department of one of the large securities firms that Sony Corp. was planning a hostile takeover of GAMETRONICS. Fueller said that he did not believe a takeover could be achieved without his consent since he held 42.5% of GAMETRONICS' shares. He also told Katz that while he had not yet been contacted by Sony, if the rumours proved correct, he probably would receive a call within the next week or two.

THUNDERBIRD
The American Graduate School
of International Management

Thunderbird Case Series. 15249 N. 59th Ave., Glendale, AZ 85306-6000 USA (602) 978-7385, cases@t-bird.edu

As the conversation progressed, Fueller acknowledged that over the past year he had grown increasingly concerned about the company's lacklustre performance. "Of course you know, Tom," he said, "you have my full support. But we have to act. I am giving you one week to put together a plan. One that we can live with, not only now, but into the future." After Katz hung up the phone, he called his secretary and cancelled all meetings for the day. Then he sat staring out his fourth-story window, wondering why only two months earlier he had been so happy to assume his new position as president.

THE VIDEO GAME INDUSTRY

The video game industry was composed of a wide range of small, medium and large companies in both software and hardware segments. Both sides of the industry were closely tied together through their mutual dependence on technological innovation and an often fickle market. Over its short twenty-year life, the industry suffered cycles of enormous prosperity followed by often significant downturns. In the early 1970s, the industry sprang to life with Pong as well as several derivative products. During the late 1970s and early 1980s, the industry experienced a major boom led by upstart Atari. After 1982, the bottom fell out of Atari's sales as a consequence of its inability to come up with newer, more interesting and more appealing video games. In 1985, the industry began recovering and during the late 1980s and early 1990s, video game hardware and software sales and profits boomed.

The industry's recovery in the late 1980s was led by Japan-based Nintendo, which offered an array of innovative games based on 8-bit technology. To entice parents to purchase their machines, Nintendo sold hardware at prices close to its costs. Only after the machines were purchased did parents learn that an enormous investment would be required in new software to maintain their children's interests. Nintendo's strategy of squeezing most of its profits out of the software side of the business became a model for other competitors. To maximize returns, only the most critical hardware and software design and marketing functions were kept in-house. In 1992, Nintendo employed just 892 people and generated sales of $5.5 billion.

In 1989, Sega, a medium-sized Japanese video game manufacturer, entered the market with Genesis. Genesis employed superior 16-bit technology, which resulted in more realistic and complex graphics compared to the Nintendo system. Sega also attracted consumers with rock-bottom hardware prices. It combined this approach with lower licensing fees for software suppliers. Lower fees attracted some of the best software developers in the industry, and the resulting line of new games led to soaring sales. In 1992, Sega's sales topped $4 billion.

By 1994, worldwide video game hardware and software industry revenues topped $11.3 billion. The industry was effectively controlled by Nintendo with 46% market share and Sega with 36% market share. The remaining 18% share was split among several other minor players. By 1994, both Nintendo and Sega had an installed base of approximately 65 million machines across the United States, Europe and Asia-Pacific.

Despite an enormous boom in sales during the late 1980s and early 1990s, the industry in 1994 was starting to show signs of another downturn. Beginning in early 1993 and continuing through mid-1994, Sega and Nintendo had been engaged in an ongoing price war that emerged from the growing software inventories that the two firms had been unable to sell. The failure of both companies to keep introducing innovative new games appeared to be a major problem. As Mike Anderson, account manager at one major retail outlet indicated:

> Consumers are tired of having to pay large amounts of money for the same games; both Sega and Nintendo thought lowering prices was the way to get rid of inventories by stealing market share from each other or by attracting new consumers. This has not been the answer.... What customers want is new technology The current generation of video games is losing steam; consumers are waiting for a new line of video games that should be ready for late 1994 or for the beginning of 1995.

Exacerbating the problems for both Sega and Nintendo was the arrival of several new competitors. The evolution of video games into virtual reality capabilities attracted the interest of other high-tech companies seeking a place on the new information superhighway. Sony, for example, announced that it would be entering the market in late 1994 in Japan and early 1995 in the U.S. with compact disc (CD) technology. Sony's new machine, called the Playstation, was equipped with 32-bit chips that could support more complex software and sophisticated graphics programs. In bringing CD games to the market, Sony planned to tap its enormous Hollywood movie library. Atari also re-entered the market with a new hardware game system called Jaguar. Commodore and Phillips were also getting ready with CD-based game systems.

Beyond these dedicated video game competitors was the growing threat of personal computer (PC) based games. While in 1994 it was estimated that about 85% of video games were sold in cartridge format, the rapidly escalating graphics and sound quality of PCs suggested that the PC-based video game sales would grow at a disproportionate rate. The movement towards PC-based games was also attracting a variety of new software entrants. For example, in the fall of 1994, Walt Disney entered the software fray by introducing two interactive, multimedia PC-based games: *Aladdin Activity Center* and *Disney's Animated Storybook: The Lion King*.

NINTENDO AND SEGA STRIKE BACK

Motivated by fear of fleeing sales, both Sega and Nintendo began developing their own CD-based systems in the early 1990s. To cut development time and incorporate the most advanced technology available, Sega established a series of collaborative agreements with leading technology companies. Agreements were made with AT&T to develop telephone communication capabilities for the games, with Hitachi to manufacture microprocessor chips, with Yamaha to produce greater sound capabilities, and with JVC to assemble the machines. Sega was also holding discussions with Microsoft to develop a range of new software products. The result was a prototype 3-D, combination CD and cartridge system called Saturn. By mid-1994, Sega was reported to have a $200 million annual research and development budget, much of it going towards Saturn. While the company hoped to have the system on the market by late 1994, the coordination of software and hardware development was proving to be a significant challenge.

Nintendo's strategy for the mid- and late-1990s centred on Project Reality, which was intended as a 32-bit replacement for Super Nintendo. In proceeding with Project Reality, the company announced it would be sticking to cartridges as opposed to CD technology. According to one company spokesperson:

> CD technology takes longer than cartridges to seek out and display images on the screen and, therefore, does not test hard trigger reflexes. The format is very complex and that is why there are so few good CD games.[1]

Despite this concern, CD-ROM games were cheaper to manufacture than cartridge games—roughly two dollars to make one CD-ROM game, compared with ten dollars to make a cartridge. For consumers, however, cheaper games were offset by significantly more expensive CD-ROM hardware.

Not surprisingly, many in the industry debated the attractiveness of CD-ROM technology. Even within companies, opinions differed. For example, at Electronic Arts Inc., a major manufacturer of game software, Bing Gordon, an Executive Vice President, argued that "although the whole industry believes CD-ROM is the wave of the future, there is reason to believe that the mass market is not going to understand the value of the improved play as justification for the higher price CD-ROM-equipped console."[2] This view

---

[1] "Sega Trying Video Component Strategy," *Television Digest*, 21 March 1994, p. 11.

[2] "Sega Trying Video Component Strategy," *Television Digest*, 21 March 1994, p. 11.

was not shared by his boss, Lawrence Probst, Chairman of Electronic Arts, who actually set company strategy. According to Probst, "Our strategy is to get there (CD-ROM-based games) early, be prolific and carve out market share."[3] Even Nintendo seemed to be hedging its bets. Despite its public statements of disinterest in CD-based games, the company was negotiating a partnership with Silicon Graphics Inc. to develop unspecified multimedia (PC/CD-ROM-based) applications.

SOFTWARE DEVELOPERS

Individual software companies developed from as few as one to as many as fifteen or more games per year. Games were typically for either Nintendo or Sega. Once developed, game manufacturers would approach the target company for licensing opportunities. If a game was not accepted, the approval process began all over again after repackaging in an alternate format. With few exceptions, Nintendo and Sega insisted that outside software developers sign exclusive contracts and pay royalties that could amount to as much as 30% for the privilege of writing games for Nintendo and Sega systems. Even in cases where developers were not required to sign exclusivity contracts, they risked losing all future sales if either Nintendo or Sega found out they had been double-dealing.

Software played a major role in determining the fate of the major hardware vendors. Of the software used by Nintendo, approximately 65% was developed externally; for Sega, the figure was 55%. With software development costs soaring due to increasingly complex operating systems, many industry observers predicted that both Nintendo and Sega would promote fewer, more expensive games in the future.

In many cases, both Nintendo and Sega relied on the same software development companies. Sega's growing market share was generally well-received by software companies because it meant less reliance on Nintendo. In 1994, Nintendo had begun changing its rigid licensing stance in the face of increased competition. In exceptional circumstances, Nintendo had even begun paying development fees to certain software companies plus royalties that ranged between 2% and 12%.

In 1994, only about 30% of the games developed were accepted by Sega and Nintendo. Part of the problem was that software companies had to consider the constantly changing tastes of end users who were, as Bobby Kotick, CEO of Activision, defined, "boys from six to sixteen and guys who can't get a date on Saturday night."[4] Terry Munson, a Nintendo employee who answered telephone questions from stumped players, believed that a really successful title was one that kids enjoyed for a month. The impact of a fickle market was perhaps best summed up by Nintendo of America President Minoru Arakawa: "If we don't supply kids with interesting new products all the time, we get killed and buried."[5]

A combination of both design talent and an eye for ever-changing market demands was essential in developing winning software. Many industry observers were increasingly convinced that market research was producing too many me-too games and that true blockbusters could only come from design genius. While market research could indicate an insatiable demand for hit games like Mortal Kombat and Street Fighter II, many copycat games had only limited appeal. Totally new game concepts frequently came from within the mind of the designer. This view was expressed by Sigeru Miyamoto, the chief developer of Nintendo's Super Mario Brothers: "I am not creating a game, I am in the game. The game is not for children, it is for me.[6]

---

[3] Jim Carlton, "Electronic Arts Shifts Focus to CD-ROM Video Games," *The Wall Street Journal*, 7 September 1994, p. B6.

[4] V. Rice and B. Snyder, "Busy Going Hollywood," *PC Week*, 29 November 1993, p. A6 (1).

[5] Ibid., p. A7.

[6] As quoted in David Sheaf, *Game Over: How Nintendo Zapped an American Industry, Captured Your Dollars, and Enslaved Your Children* (New York: Random House, 1993), p. 51.

Despite the demand for highly innovative software designers, in many cases these individuals were difficult to work with. Many designers were perfectionists who became so obsessive in the design process that they had enormous problems getting up to speed on new projects. In addition, top designers often lacked interpersonal skills and had a difficult time working in teams. Finally, good designers commanded top salaries but reciprocated with limited company loyalty.

GAMETRONICS

GAMETRONICS manufactured and developed video game software that was distributed throughout the United States and several European and Asian countries. In 1993, net company sales reached $58.34 million and operating profits topped $7.98 million. (See Exhibits 1, 2, and 3 for a review of GAMETRONICS' performance.) The company had 156 employees worldwide, divided primarily between software development, operations, sales and service. In 1994, all GAMETRONICS video game software was licensed or sold to Sega and Nintendo. These companies, in turn, added their own labels and distributed the product worldwide

GAMETRONICS was started in 1980 as a wholly owned affiliate of Fueller Corp. Fueller was begun by Martin Fueller in 1963 with inheritance money received from his grandfather, who had built a sizeable fortune in the 1920s and 1930s in the textile industry. During much of the 1960s and 1970s, Fueller was engaged in plastic production with plants in West Virginia, New York and Illinois. In 1978, the company started manufacturing plastic floppy disk covers for the computer industry and became a principal supplier for Apple II computers. At the end of the same year, Fueller's floppy disk business was incorporated under the name of Protoinfo, Inc. This company operated with relative success until heightened competition in the mid-1980s pushed Protoinfo out of the floppy disk cover business. Protoinfo then refocused its efforts on the manufacturing of plastic parts for computer components. In 1994, Protoinfo had sales of $32 million in plastic computer keys, laptop computer casings, and floppy disk storage and carrying cases.

With growing contacts in the computer industry, Martin Fueller had become convinced that the real profits in the industry lay in software development. Concern that the giant computer companies would be hard to work with, combined with Atari's spectacular profits in the late 1970s, convinced Fueller that niche, game-based software would offer the easiest avenue to success. In 1979, a separate software development division was created at Protoinfo. Six software engineers were hired, each a recent graduate in computer science. One of these engineers, Harold Green, age 26, was appointed general manager of software operations. After nine months of development, the company entered the market with its first video game, Martian Invasion. Within six months, 320 000 copies had been sold with an average retail price of $19.95. Protoinfo received about $7.00 for each game cartridge.

With this initial success, the video game business at Protoinfo was spun off into GAMETRONICS, a wholly owned affiliate of Fueller. Harold Green was appointed President. By 1983 the engineering staff had tripled to eighteen people. An additional fifteen people had been hired in manufacturing and shipping, and an additional six employed as full-time sales representatives.

In 1985, after several years of good returns, Martin Fueller took GAMETRONICS public, selling some 57.5% of his shares in the process. At the time, net sales were near $12.8 million, and operating profits were almost $2.5 million. In looking back on the events surrounding the public offering, Martin Fueller commented:

> We decided to take it public because the industry had such a promising future. Prices were going wild. At the time of the initial offering, the stock was trading at 32 times earnings. My other businesses weren't doing anywhere near that well. In retrospect, it was almost certainly a mistake. Back then, Microsoft

only had sales of $140 million. Look at Bill Gates today. I actually thought that I needed the money. A friend had me convinced of a great opportunity to buy into an under-utilized plastics resin plant that Monsanto had put on the block. I thought it would be a great fit with Protoinfo. I ended up buying a 20% share. Yet resin prices have been very volatile and I have never been satisfied with its performance.

In taking GAMETRONICS public, Fueller was able to maintain effective control because no other single shareholder held more than 2% of the stock.

Sales climbed each year during the next eight years. They were helped by highly favourable industry conditions and a string of software hits including Alligator Warrior, Super Racer, Cliff Diver and Jungle Warfare. As performance picked up, Martin Fueller devoted more and more of his time to outside interests, although he would visit every month to check the books. Harold Green was left to make critical decisions.

CHANGES IN TOP MANAGEMENT

In May 1994, Harold Green announced that he would be stepping down as President of GAMETRONICS to assume a senior management position at a major Utah-based software development company. One month later, Martin Fueller appointed 42-year-old Tom Katz to the vacated position of President and CEO of GAMETRONICS. Katz, who was at the time serving as Vice President of Sales and Marketing, assumed his new duties on June 6.

Tom Katz was raised in the New York City borough of Queens and in 1975 graduated from City University of New York with an undergraduate degree in Computer Science. Upon graduating, he immediately entered the MBA program at Fordham University and placed in the top 5% of his 1977 graduating class. Interested in working in the computer industry, Katz accepted an offer from a major Boston-based software manufacturer. Over the next three years, Katz became the top performer at the company where his responsibilities included selling pre-installed software packages to large accounts including Wang, IBM, Toshiba, and COMPAQ.

Katz first became acquainted with GAMETRONICS and Green at a software trade show in Las Vegas in 1983. Over the next two years both men kept in contact, and in November 1985 Green asked whether Katz would ever be interested in working for GAMETRONICS. One month later, Katz joined the company in the newly created position of Vice President of Sales. When Green left the company, Fueller turned to Katz as the obvious replacement: "He has the experience and the results behind him to successfully lead the company through the changing future of the video game manufacturing industry."

The majority of employees were also delighted at the news. Gerry Oswald, head of production, was quoted at the time as saying:

> This is the right decision. The president needs to be someone who will move GAMETRONICS towards the future of the video game industry. Tom is the person who will initiate changes and listen to the ideas of not only customers, but employees as well.

EMERGING CHALLENGES

In assuming his new position, Katz was aware of several challenges facing the company. One problem was that sales increases seemed to be much more a function of title proliferation than of market hits. The company's best-selling game, Jungle Warfare, accounted for 18% of GAMETRONICS' sales, representing approximately 700 000 units at $15 each. While this resulted in a solid market position, it was not a blockbuster. True blockbuster games generated sales of over one million cartridges and provided enormous cash flow. Cash flow was essential for funding new games. Development costs in the industry averaged well over $1 million for each new game; in some well-publicized cases, game development costs exceeded $3 million. Of GAMETRONICS' library of 138 games, only six had been introduced within the last twelve months.

GAMETRONICS was also having internal problems with production and inventory control. All sales of video games to Nintendo and Sega were subject to extensive performance parameters, and rejected games became the sole financial burden of GAMETRONICS. In 1993 rejection rates were twice that of industry averages. The rejections were primarily the result of packaging and labelling problems. In addition, company managers felt that GAMETRONICS' prototype games were often rejected on the apparent whims of Nintendo and Sega purchasing agents. When a decision was made to buy from GAMETRONICS, Nintendo and Sega demanded almost overnight deliveries. The result was that GAMETRONICS often over-produced batches of cartridges in expectation of escalating demand that in many cases never materialized.

Internal friction mounted when sales did not materialize. In most cases, the sales staff blamed the software developers for producing inferior games. Software developers, in turn, blamed the sales and marketing staff for ineffective research and for weak customer contacts. The production department was often blamed for either over-producing or not having the right products available when needed. When Katz met individually with managers to discuss possible solutions, he was disappointed with their responses. Gerry Oswald argued:

> Pressure from the sales staff to have new products developed or production increased is unrealistic. I don't think they understand what goes into developing the product and preparing it for distribution. Even if some of them do, they don't seem to care.

Paul Frierson, Vice President of Development, argued:

> We are falling behind on R&D compared with the others. The budget isn't there to hire the new talent coming on the market. Furthermore, whatever we do doesn't seem to be good enough. A lot of my people are getting demoralized.

Before Fueller's call on June 1, Katz had intended to focus his short-term efforts on the mounting internal problems facing GAMETRONICS. This priority now seemed to fade.

WEIGHING OPTIONS

As Katz considered where to turn, his thoughts shifted to an initiative that Green had explored but which had been cut short by his departure. It was the option of moving the company into educational software. The idea had come to Green quite unexpectedly during the summer of 1993 when Green heard his neighbours complain that their children spent too much time playing video games. This comment made Green realize that a movement to educational games could represent a good business opportunity for the company. Green called Fueller early the next day and told him the idea. Fueller agreed:

> This sounds great. It could be the solution that would help us offset the weak demand for video games that we seem to be facing. It would also help diversify some of the risk involved in being in a particular segment of the industry. Education seems like a low-risk option.

Green started researching the educational software industry and found that it had an entirely different structure than the video game business. A number of small companies had been able to survive in the market, thanks to very specialized software development. While most educational software was distributed through medium- and large-sized companies, these small firms were able to deliver the product directly to end consumers, typically through mail order distribution. Since the late 1980s, the industry had expanded, fueled in large part by a surge in home computer sales. After reviewing the files prepared by Green, Katz determined that the cost of developing educational software capabilities from scratch would require a capital investment of approximately $4 million over two years.

Another alternative was to buy an existing educational software company. Green had already done some preliminary research into this possibility. About three months before he left GAMETRONICS, Green had taken a trip to Bombay, India, to follow up on a lead to buy a small educational software development company called Educomp. Educomp's software was developed by four Indian nationals who shared ownership of the company. Total sales for Educomp were approximately $5.2 million, with about $1 million coming from exports to the U.S. and England. After-tax profits had averaged between 20% and 25% for the last three years. These returns were significantly higher than industry norms for educational software companies, which averaged between 17% and 18%. While Katz had not had any direct contact with Educomp, he had been in recent phone contact with Green who indicated that he would be happy to make formal introductions. In their telephone conversation, Green also offered some additional commentary:

> Tom, although it has now been a couple of months since I left, one of my big disappointments was in not getting closure on Educomp. Things just got too busy at the end. They are good people with world-class talents. I am sure they would still be happy to talk. I was also impressed with the abundance of inexpensive, talented programmers in India... It is obviously your call. My guess is that with the right arguments, you could quite easily get Fueller to go along.

In addition to considering a move into educational software, Katz was weighing an option to sell the company's game library. This option was the result of a recent inquiry by a software distributor who was interested in buying GAMETRONICS' library of cartridges in order to turn them into PC-based games. Under the proposal, GAMETRONICS would receive $2.6 million in cash for the library with additional annual royalty payments of 4%. Only existing games would be covered; new titles would not be included. Katz estimated that royalty payments might amount to as much as $400 000 in the first year, declining each year thereafter.

Another option was to focus efforts on strengthening the existing development team at GAMETRONICS. It was clear that the company needed a constant stream of winning software titles and that pressure to do so would only increase. By focusing on the engineering core and investing in new computing facilities and manpower, GAMETRONICS could maximize its chances of staying at the forefront of software development. Katz figured that if he increased the R&D budget by 20% and allocated one-half of the additional money to new benefits such as bonuses and other incentives to the designers, morale, and quite possibly output, would improve significantly. The remaining new money could also fund the hiring of possibly four new software designers.

A final solution would be to attempt to form an alliance with some as-yet-to-be-determined large company in the industry. GAMETRONICS was dwarfed in sales by some of its larger software game competitors such as Virgin Interactive Entertainment (a unity of Viacom, Inc.), Acclaim Entertainment Co., and Electronic Arts Inc., which had sales that ranged from $100 million to $1 billion. By working with a company like NEC or Microsoft, GAMETRONICS would have access to the latest technologies and benefit from their distribution channels. Katz was uncertain whether an ideal partner would be one in the software side or one in the hardware side of the industry. He was also aware of a number of instances where alliances led to a significant loss of autonomy on the part of the smaller company and wondered how Martin Fueller might perceive this risk.

With so many options, Katz was uncertain how to proceed. He realized that involving his top managers in a discussion of the options was highly risky. If word of the potential acquisition of GAMETRONICS slipped out, the impact on employee morale might be disastrous. In the back of his mind, Katz wondered whether being acquired would not be such a bad idea for him personally. New investment would lead to more responsibility and expanded career options. However, Katz knew that such thoughts could not be shared with Fueller, who was certain to fight any appearance of an acquisition. As he sat at his desk, Katz realized that Fueller expected a plan of action. He had maybe a week to put it all together.

EXHIBIT 1 GAMETRONICS Income Statement

(In $ Millions)

	1985	*1990*	*1991*	*1992*	*1993*
Net Sales	12.81	39.09	47.81	54.02	58.34
Costs of Goods Sold	6.40	19.74	24.29	27.50	30.12
Gross Profit	6.41	19.35	23.52	26.52	28.22
Selling & Admin Expenses	2.31	7.94	9.75	11.07	12.26
R&D Expenses	1.26	3.91	5.88	6.64	6.87
Depreciation, Amortization	0.35	0.72	0.80	1.07	1.12
Operating Profit	2.49	6.78	7.09	7.74	7.97
Total Interest	0.12	0.43	0.48	0.70	0.76
Non-op Income/Expenses	0.21	1.13	1.27	1.43	1.50
Pretax Income	2.16	5.22	5.34	5.61	5.71

EXHIBIT 2 GAMETRONICS Unit and Dollar Sales

(In $ Millions)

	1985	*1990*	*1991*	*1992*	*1993*
Unit Sales	1.42	3.55	4.20	4.16	3.89
Sales	13.26	41.32	50.68	58.13	63.01

EXHIBIT 3 GAMETRONICS Balance Sheet, 1993

(In $ Millions)

Assets

Cash and Equivalents	3.70
Accounts Receivable	3.52
Inventories	7.12
Other Current Assets	6.56
Total Current Assets	**20.90**
Gross Plant	6.74
Accumulated Depreciation	1.75
Net Plant	4.99
Deferred Charges	0.46
Intangible Assets	36.49
Other Long-Term Assets	0.32
Total Assets	**63.16**

Liabilities

Notes Payable	1.20
Accounts Payable	4.96
Accrued Expenses	3.96
Taxes Payable	1.81
Other Current Liabilities	1.21
Total Current Liabilities	**13.14**
Deferred Taxes	0.90
Long-Term Debt	8.20
Other Long-Term Liabilities	0.62
Total Liabilities	**22.86**

Equity

Preferred Stock	27.00
Common Stock	7.00
Retained Earnings	5.70
Other Liabilities	0.60
Total Equity	**40.30**
Total Liabilities and Equity	**63.16**

AIKENHEAD'S

case

3

Mary M. Crossan and
Katy Paul-Chowdhury

When Stephen Bebis placed his business plan in front of Molson Companies Ltd. in 1991, the landscape of Canadian companies in the home improvement industry did not include any warehouse stores. His proposal for the first in a series of home improvement warehouses (HIW) would change the face of Canadian retailing.

IVEY

Professor Mary Crossan and Katy Paul-Chowdhury prepared this case solely to provide material for class discussion. The authors do not intend to illustrate either effective or ineffective handling of a managerial situation. The authors may have disguised certain names and other identifying information to protect confidentiality.

WAREHOUSE CONCEPT

Having its origins in U.S. retailing, the warehouse concept was burgeoning, and impacting on almost every area of retailing. In the U.S., Wal-Mart, Kmart, Toys "Я" Us, Home Depot, Circuit City Stores, Office Depot, Target Stores, and Costco were among the giant power retailers who were expected to put 50% of retailers out of business by the year 2000.

Every megaretailer had its own formula. Some focused solely on price, while others attempted to combine the traditional advantages of large volume discount stores, in terms of price and selection, with the customer service of its smaller competitors. Doing so meant gaining the maximum benefit out of every aspect of operations.

The megastores sought more than volume discounts and low prices from their suppliers, although this was clearly one of their major strengths. For example, Wal-Mart and Kmart both abandoned the brand named "Totes" slippers in favour of a manufacturer who was able to knock-off the concept at a 25% discount. Their strengths, however, extended beyond the clout they wielded to obtain preferential pricing. They worked with their suppliers to develop products that customers wanted, often getting exclusives on some merchandise. One of the areas in which they had made their greatest gains was in inventory management, which enabled them to substantially reduce costs. From electronic hook-ups with suppliers to mandatory bar-coding, the megaretailers had been able to hold operating and selling expenses to as low as 15% of sales versus 28% for their counterparts. As a result they needed only operating margins in the low teens to cover their costs as opposed to traditional retailers who required margins around 30%.

In-store management of merchandise was also critical. Products that didn't move were quickly identified and replaced. While a number of the chains varied on the degree of in-store customer service, some of the more successful warehouses actually provided more in-store service than traditional retailers.

Marketing costs were significantly reduced, since most of the megaretailers promised "everyday low prices," often with some associated guarantee of having the lowest prices. The focus was, therefore, placed on advertising the store concept, as opposed to a myriad of individual products.

AIKENHEAD'S CONCEPT

The Aikenhead's name had a rich history in the Toronto market. Founded in 1830 as Canada's first hardware chain, it grew into a major wholesaling operation with 19 retail stores when it was purchased by Molson's in 1971. The Molson companies, which also owned Beaver Lumber, were very interested in the warehouse concept since they had witnessed the impact of the concept in the U.S. market on mid-level home centres, like Beaver. They believed that in order to protect and strengthen their market share in Canada, they would have to pursue warehouse retailing early in the game. The proposed Aikenhead's concept would be radically different from the original flagship store in downtown Toronto, which had recently undergone a name change to "Armoury Hardware" to reflect the difference in concept.

The proposed Aikenhead's concept was intended to mirror the very successful U.S. Home Depot chain, which was founded in 1978. Home Depot was the largest home improvement retailer with sales of $5.1 billion from 178 outlets in 15 states. Given the higher margins and lower operating expenses of Home Depot, it was estimated that its EBIT of 6.4%, and its return on net assets of 27.5% in 1988 were double that of competitors who followed a traditional retail format. As stated in Aikenhead's business plan:

> The high sales volumes, better buying techniques, focused advertising, intense customer service, everyday low pricing and deep and wide assortments combine to make warehouse home centre retailing one of the fastest growing success stories in terms of sales, profit and investment.

Table 1 provides a comparison of the proposed Aikenhead's home improvement warehouse (HIW) concept and the typical home centre as identified in the Aikenhead's business plan. Table 2 provides a comparison of the sales and profitability of the two concepts. Examples of some of the special customer services to be offered by Aikenhead's, including computerized deck and kitchen designs, and free "how to" videos, can be found in Exhibit 1.

TABLE 1   Comparison Between HIW and Typical Home Centre

	HIW	Typical Home Centre
Size	100 000 sq. ft.	40–60 000 sq. ft.
	22–26′ ceilings	10–14′ ceilings
SKUs	30–40 000 SKUs	10–20 000 SKUs
Asst/Mix	In-depth assortment of all HI products including professional quality	Limited to the best-sellers of each category
Fixtures	All pallet racking and cantilever racking	Gondola with some pallet and cantilever
Display Format	Bulk oriented Goods are cut cased and massively displayed	Most goods are hung on pegs, hooks or displayed neatly on shelves
Staffing	90% full time	Split to mostly part timers with full-time management
Service	Knowledgeable tradespeople committed to customer service Teach customers to do it themselves Knowledgeable tradespeople on staff in all departments	Most employees are utilized to stock away merchandise Limited service
Supply & Logistics	Worldwide manufacturers Purchase direct from the manufacturers Large quantity, bulk buying, solid trucks, container loads, rail cars 2–4 week leadtime	Worldwide manufacturers Purchase through distributors, wholesalers and brokers Small quantities, common carriers, mixed trucks 7–10 day leadtime
Capital Requirements	$6–7 million/store (excluding real estate)	$3–4 million/store (excluding real estate)
Pricing	Everyday low pricing	Higher pricing with sales
	Always the best price on every item, everyday; pricing driven by the market Negotiate special buys from vendors on key products with savings passed onto the customer The price leader on key commodity items	Selectively sharp on some items, others are based on the store margin budget Run sales on items and absorb profit loss Follows behind the warehouse stores or ignores them
Customer Mix	Do-it-yourselfers Buy-it-yourselfers Professional business customer Customer profile is determined by store placement; insures store will be heavily oriented to the homeowner Over 50% of the customers are female	Not focused on any particular type of customer; some have strong contractor orientation Customer profile varies depending on store location; could be mostly contractors Mostly men with women a smaller minority

TABLE 2 **Comparative Sales and Profitability**

Performance	HIW	Typical Home Centre
Sales	$24.2 million	$10–12 million
Operating exp.	20.6%	25.9%
EBIT	6.4%	3.4%
RONA (before tax)	27.5%	12.9%

MARKET STUDIES

While the HIW concept had been extremely successful in the U.S., there was no Canadian precedent to test the viability of the concept in the new market. However, Price Club and Toys "Я" Us had already successfully penetrated the Canadian market. To probe the level of receptivity of Canadians to the HIW concept, $1 million was spent on market studies in the Toronto area, which is where the "roll-out" would begin. Focus groups in the Toronto market indicated that consumers were not particularly loyal as shown by the following types of comments on their shopping habits:

> I drove around until I found the best deal.
> We shop through catalogues in advance.
> I make up a list and look for sales over the next two to three weeks.

While customers perceived that the HIW concept might provide value in terms of convenient shopping, they indicated some scepticism about whether it would provide a high level of service, low prices, convenient location and a wide assortment of branded products. Further research showed that over 80% of shoppers in metropolitan markets were willing to drive 30 minutes to a store with competitive prices. Most consumers would be attracted to the store for its large selection of products and competitive prices.

As well, the research indicated that Canada's 14 largest urban areas, representing one third of its population, could support close to 40 stores with an estimated market size of $3.6 billion.

COMPETITION

Aikenhead's would be stepping into a market with well-established and successful competitors. In 1990, Canadian Tire dominated the industry with sales of $3.1 billion through 418 outlets. Beaver Lumber, which was also owned by Molson's, generated sales of $1.1 billion through 158 outlets. While Canadian Tire and Beaver Lumber characterized the retailing format of the larger retailers, there were chains of independent retailers such as Home Hardware that generated significant sales volumes. Through 985 outlets, Home Hardware generated sales of $850 million. A synopsis of Canadian Tire, Beaver Lumber and Home Hardware is provided in Exhibit 2.

In the Toronto market, with estimated sales for retail home improvement of $482 million, Canadian Tire was the dominant player with a market share of 37% from a base of 33 stores. Beaver Lumber had a 14% market share with 11 stores. Lansing Buildall, Lumber City and Pascal Hardware each had less than 10% of the market. Many smaller retailers such as Home Hardware or other independents made up the remainder of the market. While Bebis viewed every retailer or contractor who sold home improvement products as a competitor, he was confident that Aikenhead's concept would provide it with a superior competitive position in the Canadian context. His primary concern was to establish Aikenhead's before Home Depot entered the market. Molson's believed it would have a few years before Home Depot entered the

Canadian market, since in early 1990, when Molson approached Home Depot to form a joint venture, Home Depot indicated they were more interested in pursuing growth opportunities in the U.S.

However, Aikenhead's expected to expand the market, not just to divide the pie a little differently. It viewed itself competing for the consumer's discretionary dollars, and not just for the existing amount spent on home improvement. By making home improvement projects easier and more affordable, it was felt that the entire market had much more room to grow.

In spite of the success U.S. retailers had enjoyed, and the potential that existed in the market according to the research conducted, Bebis was concerned about implementation. The most difficult aspect of the plan was its execution. One of the first things Bebis discovered about the Canadian market was the general lack of pride in the retail sector. He suggested that "in the U.S., individuals do an MBA to get into retail, while in Canada they do an MBA to get out of retail." Executing the Aikenhead's concept would require a revolution in the way retail was conducted; but, more importantly, what was needed was a revolution in the way people thought of retail.

PHILOSOPHY/EXECUTION

Execution would go far beyond the words on the page of the business plan that attempted to capture the Aikenhead's corporate philosophy:

> Aikenhead's believes that performing to a standard of excellence in everything we do will optimize the earnings potential of the enterprise.

Fundamental to this standard of excellence are the following philosophical underpinnings:

> Our customers will decide our destiny. We work as a team in which every transaction must convey integrity, value and satisfaction.
>
> Our employees are our greatest resource. Each is an individual who must be treated with dignity and respect. This will be achieved through providing a work environment which embraces open communications, opportunity, equality and individual fulfillment.

At the outset, the plan tried to identify some of the behaviours that would support the philosophy of a high level of customer service, including getting a carriage for the customer, walking a customer to a product location rather than pointing, and helping the customer carry products to the checkout.

A critical part of the plan was to employ knowledgeable salespeople, and to provide even further training on the culture of the company and the products offered. However, candidates would have to be more than just knowledgeable. Aikenhead's would be looking for individuals who were self-starters, had a high degree of energy, were social, confident, ambitious and could communicate well. Since the organizational structure would be very flat, it was important that all individuals be capable of making decisions. The 200 people to be recruited for the first store opening in March 1992 would swell to 1500, with nine stores, by 1994.

Aikenhead's would have no commissions, or associate (Aikenhead's referred to employees as associates) discounts, as it was felt that they got in the way of customer service and were costly to track. However, associates would be well compensated. Aikenhead's expected to be one of the highest paying retailers in Canada. As well, associates would be provided with the opportunity to earn a financial stake in the business, and bonuses based on store performance. Bebis stated this philosophy:

> In order to get high calibre people, we must: a) pay well; b) offer benefits which are equal to if not better than those offered elsewhere in the industry; c) treat the associates like human beings; d) offer them an environment in which they can grow as individuals; e) encourage them to use their creativity and intelligence; and f) listen to them.

Bebis stated that he would rather hire one associate at $10 per hour than two associates at $6 per hour. With motivated and knowledgeable associates, Bebis saw the benefits of a higher level of sales turnover, arising from the extra care and attention provided to customers and to merchandising products. Training would be used extensively to aid in the development of a new retail mindset. Many of the associates would be coming from traditional retail backgrounds in which the standard was that "there was never enough time to do something right the first time, but enough time to do it over." At Aikenhead's, associates would be encouraged to seek out labour-saving devices to free up the time required to do things right in the first place. Information systems would play a major role in executing the strategy. Systems would be used to reduce costs and to enhance service throughout the organization.

Bebis envisioned that systems would tie Aikenhead's into its supplier network in order to garner efficiencies in ordering, shipping, receiving and billing. If Aikenhead's could reduce a supplier's operating expenses, it was expected that these savings would be passed on to Aikenhead's in the form of lower product costs. Aikenhead's expected to have a partnership relationship with its suppliers that, for many, would require dramatic changes to their business, including selling directly to Aikenhead's. Selling directly meant that manufacturers would have to learn how to service a retailer, while absorbing the additional costs of acting as a warehouse and distribution centre that delivers directly to individual stores. A synopsis of two major suppliers is provided in Exhibit 3.

As well, Aikenhead's would use the same information systems to reduce its own operating expenses and to enhance service. For example, systems designed to track products could be used to manage inventory levels, respond to customer inquiries, establish sales patterns to support decisions about product mix, staffing levels, and to provide information on performance levels.

The company would be organized along functional lines as outlined in Exhibit 4. Each of the vice-presidents had already been recruited. Their profiles are provided in Exhibit 5. Given the flat structure, and the close proximity of the Aikenhead's "home office," which would be adjacent to their first store, executives would be able to stay close to the customer and to remain aware of the cross-functional challenges in running the business.

LEADERSHIP

When Molson's decided to pursue the HIW business, they decided that they needed a CEO who was knowledgeable about warehouse retailing, was an entrepreneur, a self-starter and one who could "make it happen." They hired Bebis as their first employee. Bebis described his view of the business as follows:

> I always wanted to open and operate my own business as an entrepreneur but never had the money. The opportunity to come to Canada and to open the first full size warehouse store in the industry and to run the show from scratch using someone else's money was a dream come true. The reasons I chose Canada were that it was virgin territory for our concept; we would blaze new trails and this was very exciting. I was with Home Depot for six years. I was a small fish in a big pond. By coming to Canada, I was able to become the number one guy and to create a new company from the ground up. This opportunity only comes around once in a lifetime and I wanted to take advantage of it.

When Bebis joined Aikenhead's, Molson's had bought into the concept and had agreed to one store. At that time the name had not even been selected. Bebis described his introduction to the business:

> The one thing I remember fondly is showing up for work the first day and not having a phone or a pencil and certainly not an office. It truly was a greenfield start. I worked out of a hotel room and had to rent office space for myself and buy office furniture. Bob Wittman and I also designed the first store.

Bebis described his leadership role in implementing the concept:

It was a matter of setting high goals, demanding excellence in the execution of achieving those goals and never wavering from our focus. I have an unwavering commitment to customer service. I am focused and never let up. I believe that constant hammering, constant retraining, constant reinforcement of our mission and why we are here are critical to our success. Being able to go through brick walls to make things happen is definitely one of my strong points.

Bebis knew that to execute the concept, leadership would be required at every level of the organization. Teeth were put into the concept of "empowerment" through the design of the systems and the structure of the organization. The flat organizational structure meant that associates would be required to make key decisions. Training provided them with the knowledge to make the decisions, and the tools were put in place to aid in the process. For example, information systems and in-store terminals enabled them to advise customers on the status of products. Furthermore, each of the 200 store associates would be authorized to contact suppliers as needed, in an industry in which supplier contact had previously only been made at the most senior levels of the organization. Résumés were already pouring in for the first store. While many people questioned opening the store during a recession, Bebis suggested that it was an ideal time to establish a new business. Deals could be made on real estate, suppliers were hungry for business, and Bebis had his pick of some of the best people in the industry. With construction at a standstill, there were hundreds of professional plumbers, electricians and carpenters who would jump at the chance to supplement their sporadic business with the opportunity for steady work. As Bebis submitted the business plan to Molson's, the question in his mind was not whether the Aikenhead's concept would work, but how big and how fast he should grow the business.

E X H I B I T 1 Special Customer Services

- Computerized Kitchen Design
- Computerized Deck Design
- Product Fairs
- Department Demos
- Multiple Credit Plans
- Lock Keying/Duplicate Keys
- Glass Cutting
- Lumber Cutting—Mini Blinds Cutting
- Delivery
- Special Orders—Kitchen, Bath, Millwork
- Free Project Advice
- Computerized Colour Matching/Mixing
- Short/No Wait Checkouts
- Cash Only Lines
- Scanning
- Free Use of How To Videos
- Use of Car Carrier Racks
- Free Use of Insulation Blower With Purchase
- Sprinkling System Design
- Assistance in Loading Cars
- Equipment Rentals, i.e., Post Hole Digger; Insulation Blower; File Cutter

EXHIBIT 2 Competitors

Beaver Lumber

Beaver Lumber was owned by The Molson Companies Limited, Aikenhead's parent. With 158 locations across Canada, Beaver Lumber was a retailer of building and lumber supplies. As well, it carried a full range of home improvement merchandise. The company served two distinct sets of customers: individuals and, in rural areas, contractors. It was billed as "Canada's largest do-it-yourself retailer." The chain had sales of $1 074 million in 1991, down from $1 129 million in 1990. Operating profit was $29.1 million in 1991, down from $44.8 million in 1990.

Beaver Lumber had a mixture of corporate-owned and franchised stores. Stores were free to purchase products either from a Beaver Lumber distribution centre or from other distributors. The corporation earned its return partly on the sale of goods through the distribution centre, but mainly from the 50–50 split of net income from the franchised stores. The typical Beaver Lumber store was 30 000 square feet in size, with approximately 50 employees. Over 50% of the stores were in secondary urban or rural markets.

Traditionally, the urban stores had performed poorly. They had higher prices and limited product breadth and depth compared to their competitors. Stores in the smaller centres, however, profited from extensive high-margin business with building contractors. Beaver Lumber differentiated itself from its competitors by offering credit to contractors. For this reason, the stores typically had unusually high levels of accounts receivable. Indeed, it was the infrastructure required to support these financing activities which contributed to Beaver Lumber's higher costs and prices.

Beaver Lumber introduced a number of strategic and operating initiatives in 1991. It began to move toward a more centralized organizational structure, in order to exercise greater control over inventories. The company announced plans to increase the number of products carried by its stores by up to 5 000 stocking units. It introduced six different standardized store layouts, and doubled the number of hours of training for store managers. The information system at Beaver Lumber had been in place for approximately 15 years.

Canadian Tire

Canada's largest hardgoods retailer, Canadian Tire had sales of $3.0 billion in 1991, down from approximately $3.1 billion the year before. Net earnings were $127 million, a 12% drop from 1990 levels. Sales of hardware represented 25% of Canadian Tire's revenues, while sales of automotive and sporting goods comprised the remaining 75%.

Canadian Tire had two operating divisions: the Merchandise Business Group, representing 80% of revenues, which supplied goods and services to the company's Associate stores, and the Diversified Business Group comprised mainly of the Petroleum Division and Canadian Tire Acceptance, the financial services division.

The company employed approximately 3 800 full-time and 1 500 part-time workers across the country, in addition to those hired by the firm's Associate Dealers. The Associate Dealer stores were not franchises. Instead, they functioned much like auto dealerships, with five-year contracts to purchase their products from Canadian Tire's Merchandise Business Group. The corporation wielded significant power in its relationship with the Associated Dealers. Margins had traditionally been evenly split between the Corporation and the Dealer, but in the mid-1980s Canadian Tire forced up its share by several percentage points. Canadian Tire earned its return from selling goods and services to its Associated Dealers, and required that Dealers purchase all but the most specialized products from the Corporation.

Canadian Tire had identified the trend toward an increasingly competitive marketplace. It saw its challenge as balancing short-term seasonality and business cycle fluctuations with longer-term changes in buying behaviour, demographics and technology. The company described their customers as demanding low-cost distribution of commodity products, as well as better quality, service and selection.

Canadian Tire considered its competitive advantages to be its entrepreneurial Associate Dealers, convenience of location (77% of the Canadian population lives within a 15-minute drive of a Canadian Tire store), and consumer awareness. Its interrelated business units allowed synergies in cross-merchandising, marketing and information management. Traditionally, information systems played a crucial role in the company's development and competitive positioning. It invested heavily in information technology, resulting in inventory control and management systems at both corporate and store levels which were far superior to those of competitors. Investment in IS was ongoing, with individual stores upgrading their systems every couple of years.

Canadian Tire stores varied widely in size, from 2 500 to 40 000 square feet. Approximately 25 000 products or product sizes were sold.

In summary, the distribution channels at both Beaver Lumber and Canadian Tire were as follows:

| Manufacturer | → | Company Distributor | → | Dealer |

Home Hardware

Home Hardware, with 985 outlets, was Canada's largest dealer-owned chain. Approximately 80 of these stores were located in the Metro Toronto area. The dealers were independents who had organized themselves into a buying group. In 1990, Home Hardware generated $850 million in sales.

Home Hardware considered its competitive advantage to be convenient location. It believed that, while customers might be willing to drive across town for a lower price on big-ticket items, they would choose the closest store for smaller purchases.

Because Home Hardware dealers did not have the backing of a large corporation, they sometimes had difficulty securing bank financing. As a result, the stores tended to be understocked compared to their competitors. The outlets varied greatly in size, but tended to be smaller overall than their competitors.

E X H I B I T 3 Suppliers

Suppliers of products to the Canadian home improvement industry operated within similar distribution channels. Manufacturers sold to distributors, who in turn serviced retail outlets. Distributors were responsible for meeting the demands of the retailer which included on-time delivery, in-store merchandising and servicing, and "hands on" product knowledge and training. They were also responsible for dealing with special shipping instructions, EDI requirements, UPC packaging requirements and the handling of any problems with product quality.

Suppliers did, however, differ from each other along at least three dimensions. The first dimension was the degree of perceived elasticity of demand for their products. For example, Manco, a major manufacturer of a fairly standard product for the home improvement industry, believed that the overall demand for their products was relatively inelastic; a lower price would not result in an increase in demand. In general, it was felt that demand was reasonably fixed and a change in distribution would not impact purchase decisions to a great extent. On the other hand, Hardco, a major manufacturer of tools for the home improvement industry, believed that the overall demand for its product was affected by the efforts on the part of retailers to market their product in ways that expanded the home improvement industry's share of customer's discretionary dollars.

The second way that suppliers differed was the degree to which they dominated distribution channels and shelf space. For example, given Manco's market dominance, it was extremely difficult for new competitors to enter the business. Customers did not demand a wide selection in the product category and therefore retailers were not willing to give a lot of shelf space to the product. Similarly, distributors carried only a few products, and therefore Manco dominated the channel.

Finally, suppliers differed in terms of their geographic market focus and the degree of integration of their operations. For example, Manco Canada was part of Manco Worldwide, which was amongst the largest manufacturers of the product line in the world. However, there was little integration between the Canadian company and its parent. This meant that the Canadian operation had not closely observed other parts of the organization, which were responding to dramatic industry change. At Hardco, however, international operations were well integrated. The Canadian operation had watched its U.S. counterpart deal with radical changes in the U.S. industry, and had been waiting for the same pressures to be exerted on the Canadian market.

EXHIBIT 4 Organizational Chart 1991

Home Improvement Warehouse—Corporate

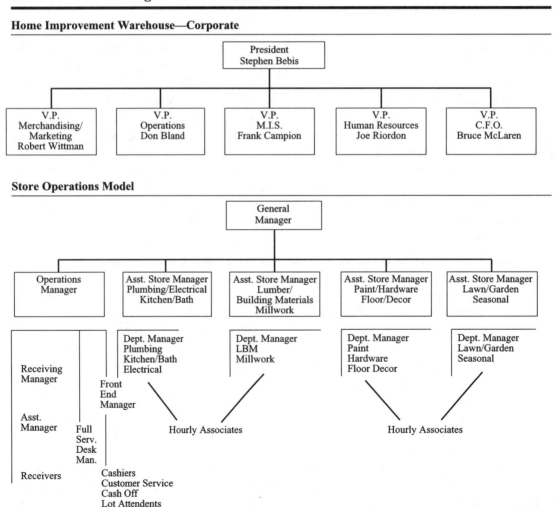

Store Operations Model

EXHIBIT 5 The Management Team

Stephen Bebis (President)

Steve is a superbly qualified retailing executive. His 20 years of experience have given him a clear understanding of the synergies required to keep all components of an enterprise functioning optimally for the achievement of superior results. His increasingly significant marketing and merchandising responsibilities with Sears Roebuck & Co., Grossman's and, most recently, Home Depot have provided him with the cross-category knowledge necessary to guarantee merchandising success and customer acceptance.

Robert J. Wittman (Vice-President, Merchandising and Marketing)

Bob has a wide range of business experience acquired through 25 years in retailing. He has served in various merchandising capacities with such organizations as Supermarkets General, Loblaws (Canada), Grossman's, Bradlees Department Stores, Somerville Lumber and Home Quarters Warehouse Inc. Bob is an intuitive marketer with a thorough understanding of the categories, assortments and presentations essential to the success of a warehouse home improvement store.

Donald C. Bland (Vice-President, Operations)

Don is a seasoned specialist with 25 years of experience. His progressively increased responsibilities in both merchandising and operations with such companies as Target Stores, Montgomery Ward, The J.L. Hudson Division of Dayton Hudson Corporation, Lechemere Inc. and Home Quarters Warehouse Inc. have provided him with top-flight retail executive credentials. His strategic as well as operational management competence will contribute a great deal to the success of this enterprise.

Frank D. Campion (Vice-President, Information Systems)

Frank is an Information Systems specialist whose experience in the United States Navy, Haines Furniture, Camellia Food Stores and Home Quarters Warehouse Inc. have given him the superb qualifications needed to provide this organization with state-of-the-art systems support. Frank understands the systems needs and the solutions essential to enhancing warehouse store operations through systems that optimize both customer and management information services.

Joseph P. Riordon (Vice-President, Human Resources)

Joe is the epitome of the consummate retailing Human Resources executive. His experience with the Allstate Insurance Company, Royal Trust, Boots Drugstores (Canada) Ltd. and F.W. Woolworth Company Ltd. have provided him with a broad operational and human resource base. He has a thorough understanding of all the component aspects of people management and will be a highly effective link in the cross-functional optimization of people in our company.

EXHIBIT 5 (continued)

Bruce W. McLaren (Vice-President, Finance)

Bruce McLaren is a highly competent financial executive who has, during his career, designed and implemented virtually every type of financial system and/or process relating to the retail sector. His progressive experience with Thorne Riddell, Sears Canada and Kmart has provided Bruce with a profound understanding of the retail environment, and the role of the finance function in it, which will allow him to be a strong contributor to the organization's success.

Source: Aikenhead's Business Plan.

THE DIAPER WAR: KIMBERLY-CLARK VERSUS PROCTER & GAMBLE

Kerry S. McLellan and Allen J. Morrison

On November 1, 1989, the management of Kimberly-Clark (K-C) watched with great interest and concern as Procter & Gamble (P&G) announced the appointment of a new CEO, Edwin Artzt. Artzt had considerable international experience in the disposable diapers industry and management at K-C wondered if his appointment would signal a new phase of competition within the industry. Six months earlier, prior to Artzt's appointment, P&G had introduced gender-specific disposables with designer colours. While a

IVEY

significant product improvement, gender-specific disposables were not in the tradition of the technological competitive breakthroughs of the past. K-C had responded with test marketing of a similar product, but a national roll-out would still be several months away. The decision to proceed with a national roll-out was tempered by concern that such a move would acknowledge P&G's leadership in the marketplace. Furthermore, K-C managers questioned whether a move into gender-specific disposables would distract the company from important research and development efforts aimed at the environmental concerns now confronting the industry. In considering options, K-C management was faced with significant financial constraints and they wondered if greater opportunities would be available outside the increasingly competitive North American industry. International opportunities in Europe and Japan merited greater attention, particularly given recent moves by overseas competitors to enter the North American diaper industry. Also of interest to K-C management were the company's ongoing efforts to build a market position for its adult incontinence products. As K-C faced the 1990s, managers braced for heightened competition and wondered how and when to respond.

THE NORTH AMERICAN DIAPER INDUSTRY

The Development of Disposable Diapers

The disposable diaper, invented in postwar Sweden, was introduced to America by Johnson & Johnson in the late 1940s. Kendall and Parke Davis entered the market a decade later. At that time, marketing efforts were focused on travelling parents with infants. Research and development efforts tried to increase product effectiveness by improving the methods of matting the absorbent tissue. These early diapers, used with fastening pins and plastic pants, were generally perceived as ineffective in keeping either babies or parents dry. With slow sales, prices for the product remained high (10¢ each for disposables versus 3¢–5¢ for cloth diaper services and 1¢–2¢ for home laundered diapers). As a result, most firms remained uninterested in making significant investments in this market segment.

Procter & Gamble's Entry: Pampers

There are several stories surrounding the motivation for P&G's initial interest in disposable diaper products. One version cited the frustration of a senior engineer with the state of disposable diaper technology in the 1950s. The engineer was a new grandfather who felt a strong motivation to develop a better product. The other popularized story involved the complaints of a nun in charge of the nursery at a Cincinnati Catholic Hospital. She complained to company personnel regarding the sanitary problems of cloth diapers. Her comments spurred action at the firm to develop a product that would meet the needs of her nursery.

While P&G's initial interest in disposable diapers was surrounded by stories of chance, the firm's commercialization of the product was clearly motivated by shrewd analysis. By the late 1950s, the firm was beginning to recognize elements of opportunity in this dismally viewed market sector. Although the industry was fragmented and the market undeveloped, the conditions fit well with P&G's strategy of trying to introduce products into markets where there was a reasonable expectation that a premium segment niche could be created by effective marketing and superior product characteristics. In 1957, cellulose fibre research began in earnest, spurred on by P&G's purchase of the Charmin Paper Company.

In 1961, P&G announced its entry into the disposable diapers industry with the introduction of Pampers; test marketing began a year later. Pampers provided a clear technological breakthrough from previous products as it was the first disposable diaper to use a plastic back-sheet coupled with absorbent wadding and a porous rayon sheet facing the baby's skin. Despite these advantages, however, the product did not achieve P&G's sales targets, and thus Pampers was not distributed nationally. This early market failure was blamed on the product's high price of 10¢ per diaper which was similar to that charged by other firms and reflected the underlying manufacturing cost structure of Pampers. The cost problem reflected P&G's production approach of purchasing partially completed components to be assembled later. This manufacturing process, while the norm in the industry, was both expensive and time-consuming.

Recognizing production inefficiencies, P&G concentrated research efforts on reducing the manufacturing costs of the disposable product. In 1964, the firm's engineers developed a continuous process technology that allowed the manufacture of diapers at speeds of 400 per minute. This process proved many times faster than the previous manufacturing method and allowed the use of minimally processed raw materials. This advance, as well as changes in purchasing, allowed P&G to cut costs significantly. As a result, Pampers was reintroduced into a second test market site at a price of 5.5¢ per diaper. The test was very successful and a national introduction followed in 1966. Full national distribution was achieved by 1969.

Kimberly-Clark's Entry: Kimbies

Diaper research at K-C also began in earnest in the mid-1960s, focusing primarily on new product technology. The firm used its experience with feminine napkins to develop a product that used fluff pulp in place of tissue. The pulp provided cheaper and better absorbency. These advantages, coupled with the introduction of adhesive tabs and an improved shape, were incorporated into a new product, called Kimbies, introduced by K-C in 1968. The use of fluff pulp as the primary absorbent material provided competitive cost savings. Kimbies was parity priced with Pampers but competitive cost savings were not passed through to consumers. Rather, K-C reinvested the excess profit into further product improvements. This strategy fit with industry market research that showed a strong relationship between improved product features and market and sales growth. The cost of product improvements could be passed on, as many consumers seemed to show a high degree of price indifference.

Other competitors active during the late 1960s included Scott Paper, Borden, and International Paper. All three were experimenting with a two-piece disposable diaper system in the mid-1960s. This system, which relied on technology developed in Europe, involved a disposable inner liner and a reusable plastic outer shell. The product also had a distinct advantage over Pampers in that the diapers used snaps instead of pins.

By 1970, a competitive pattern had begun to emerge in the industry. Rivalry was increasingly focused on product innovation. However, these improvements were not always translated into market share gains for reasons that appeared to be two-fold: poor marketing communication of product benefits, and the inability of some firms to reduce manufacturing costs to P&G's level. In spite of what some regarded as an inferior product, Pampers appeared unstoppable. By 1970, P&G peaked with an estimated market share of 92%. Observers began recognizing that technology alone was not enough and that many of the large industrial-focused paper companies might be in an untenable position in the industry.

Industry Shake-Out

There was a rapid shake-out of the disposable diaper industry in the early 1970s. The restructuring was hastened by a constant series of modifications undertaken by P&G to further strengthen its Pampers line. For example, the company converted from tissue to fluff pulp in 1972 and to adhesive tabs in 1973. As a result of the heightened competition, Borden exited the industry in 1970, Scott left the U.S. market in 1971, International Paper stopped U.S. production in 1972, and Johnson & Johnson's Chicopee discontinued its brand in 1972. Other competitors retreated slowly as continuous costly improvements upped the ante. P&G's dominant position was maintained until K-C's Kimbies began to gather steam in the 1972–74 period.

In 1971, Darwin Smith was appointed as the new president of K-C. Smith's objective was to reduce K-C's reliance on core newsprint and paper operations and to strengthen its position in consumer products.

This transformation took several years to complete and involved the selling off of various mills and wood-lands, and the strengthening of the company's market leading Kleenex and Kotex brands. This strategic refocusing produced a war-chest of $350 million that was to be used for further expansion into consumer products. K-C's Kimbies was an early benefactor of this shift in strategy. Buoyed by increased marketing expenditures, Kimbies' market share peaked in 1974 at 20%. However, as the decade progressed, management did not pay enough attention to Kimbies' performance and sales began to decline. In spite of the transformation in the industry, disposable diapers were only used regularly on about 35% of babies in 1976. Total market growth remained flat. To most parents, the benefits of disposables were still not large enough to support their added cost.

THE COMPETITION INCREASES

Procter & Gamble Introduces Luvs

In 1976, P&G announced the test marketing and selected regional introduction of a premium diaper product, Luvs. This diaper offered several improvements over Pampers, including a fitted, elasticized shape and a more effective absorbent structure. Luvs was priced 25–30% above Pampers. This introduction was intended to create a new premium market segment, moving Pampers into a middle segment. P&G continued regional market testing for more than two years but seemed indecisive on a national rollout decision. Many observers believed that this hesitation was related to test market results indicating a large negative impact on Pampers.

Kimberly-Clark Introduces Huggies

By 1978, K-C's corporate transformation was nearly complete and attention was refocused on the diaper sector. That year, K-C introduced Huggies to replace Kimbies. The product was superior to both Pampers and Luvs. It was better fitting, more absorbent, and offered an improved tape fastening system. In support of the new product, K-C hired top marketing talent and backed the introduction with large promotional and advertising investments.

At the time of Huggies' introduction, Luvs was still available only on a limited regional basis. P&G's indecision provided K-C with a tremendous opportunity to develop a product with characteristics superior to Luvs. Because of the introduction of Huggies, P&G was forced to complete the national rollout of Luvs. Luvs, suffering from inferior performance relative to that of Huggies, was unable to gain control of the premium segment. K-C continued to produce Kimbies for the market's middle segment, but concentrated resources on Huggies, allowing Kimbies to die a slow death. National distribution of Kimbies was discontinued in 1983.

Huggies' sales grew rapidly as consumers discovered the diaper's superior characteristics. Sales growth came not only through market share growth, but also as a result of the increased usage of disposable diapers. With Huggies, consumers could now see the benefit of switching from traditional cloth diapers to disposable products. Market penetration of disposables increased rapidly.

Procter & Gamble Responds

P&G initially did little to respond to K-C's new market entry. Part of the reason for the slow response was that K-C had introduced Huggies after upgrading its manufacturing processes and P&G had large investments in older diaper machines. P&G was clearly hesitant to make the huge investments necessary to match K-C production processes. This older technology limited P&G's ability to match K-C's product modifications and put the company at somewhat of a cost disadvantage. To avoid this expense, P&G

aggressively promoted Pampers; however, sales continued to slump. Brand market share fluctuated widely during the 1981–89 period, with the early 1980s being the most difficult period for P&G (Exhibit 1).

By 1983, market research began to convince P&G management that the middle sector was disappearing. Consumers either wanted the best products for which they seemed willing to pay a premium price or they wanted low priced—typically private label—products, regardless of performance. Pampers appeared to be stuck in the middle.

It was not until late 1984, when Huggies had captured 30% of the market, that P&G upgraded its products with comparable features and fought to regain market share. There were two elements in the strategy. First, P&G decided to reposition Pampers as a premium product, comparable to Luvs. The repositioning was accomplished through improvements in Pampers' shape and fastening system, and a major improvement in absorbent structure. Also, to improve cost structure and offer the improved features, P&G made major investments in its production system. The competitive upgrade of P&G's diaper lines was very expensive, costing an estimated $500 million for a new plant and equipment. A further $225 million in additional advertising and promotion support was used to re-launch P&G's slumping brands.

The technological leap-frog competition was on. In the first half of 1986 alone, seven of P&G's 19 patent searches involved diaper product improvements (Exhibit 2). These searches were the subject of great interest to K-C researchers.

New Technology Results in Super-Thin Diapers

During 1986, the competition entered a new stage of intense technological rivalry with both P&G and K-C introducing super-thin, super-absorbent disposables. The new diapers contained polyacrylate, a powder crystal that absorbed 50 times its weight in liquid. By using polyacrylate, diapers could be manufactured that were 30% thinner. The two firms had to re-educate consumers into not associating absorbency with thickness. The campaign was a success and parents seemed to like the new diaper's sleek profile and improved performance. P&G and K-C were able to achieve transportation cost savings and retailers were pleased with improved shelf utilization.

P&G introduced the new technology into the U.S. early in 1986. K-C's introduction followed nine months later. P&G's competitive leadership in North America, however, did not come from development work in the U.S., but rather from access to technology developed in Japan, where the company had considerable operations. Because K-C lacked a significant presence in the Japanese market, the company had been forced to follow P&G's introduction in North America. Initially, P&G and K-C were dependent on Japanese suppliers for polyacrylate and neither was able to obtain the North American licence. After two years, however, Cellanese, a U.S. chemical firm, was given a licence to manufacture the product in North America.

The introduction of super-thin technology clearly hastened the demise of the mid-market segment. Super-thin technology was regarded as so unique that its use would automatically position a product at the high end of the market. The repositioning of Pampers in 1984 and the withdrawal of Kimbies in 1983 represented an effective abandonment of the mid-price segment of the market by the major industry players. During the later half of the 1980s, neither P&G nor K-C attempted to introduce products to fill the now largely unserved mid-price market segment. During the early 1980s, however, P&G and K-C had continued to test products aimed at the low-priced segment. K-C tested Snuggems, and P&G experimented with Simply Pampers. Neither product received national distribution, although regional testing continued until the later part of the 1980s. The inability of P&G and K-C to place products in the low-priced segment was primarily the result of the reluctance of mass merchandisers to give Snuggems or Simply Pampers adequate shelf space. The retailers were able to earn much higher margins from their private label brands, targeted at the same segment.

HEAD-TO-HEAD COMPETITION

By the Fall of 1989, the industry had effectively evolved into a duopoly dominated by K-C with a 32% market share, and P&G with a 49% market share. Both companies sold super-thin diapers exclusively. In 1989, total retail sales of disposable diapers exceeded $4.5 billion in the United States and $400 million in Canada. The disposable diaper market appeared saturated with little growth in total market size expected.

As a duopoly, competition between P&G and K-C was intense. Given the huge fixed costs involved in the production of disposable diapers, it was estimated that each percentage gained in market share resulted in $6–10 million in additional annual profit. As a result, competition extended beyond research and development to marketing and promotion, and to manufacturing.

Marketing and Promotion

The war between P&G and K-C started with ads in the magazines that appealed to expectant mothers. The fight entered a more open, intense phase when the companies fought to get their products into maternity wards and pediatricians' offices, where their use carried an implied endorsement by the medical community. Only a handful of promotional firms were allowed to distribute samples in hospitals and both K-C and P&G paid for their services.

Once the free samples had been used, mothers realized just how expensive disposables would be. In 1989, at a price of 18¢–36¢ each, depending on size, it would cost $1 400–1 700 to diaper one child for 2.5 years in brand-name disposables. It was estimated that the cost of cloth diapers supplied by diaper services was comparable, but could be up to 20% lower depending on the type of service provided. Generic or private label disposables were about 30% cheaper than national brands, but most suffered from distressing performance problems. Cloth diapers washed at home would cost $600 or less.

Increasingly, however, price was being discounted as a purchasing criterion. With up to 75% of new mothers working outside the home, many families often valued time and convenience more than money. Similarly, as family size diminished, parents showed an increased willingness to spend money on outfitting babies. This trend meant that more and more families were prepared to pay for quality disposable diapers.

In North America, P&G and K-C were each estimated to spend a total of more than $110 million annually on diaper promotion. This promotion primarily involved commercials and coupons. Retailers often used diapers as loss leaders and the companies supported these activities through volume rebates based upon the number of tons of diapers sold. Couponing potentially saved a consumer 10–15%, but the unwritten rule was that neither firm would undercut the other.

In addition to traditional means of promotion, both firms had successfully tried other innovative measures. P&G had used Pamper Care Vans, staffed by nurses, visiting malls and fairs. The firm had also sponsored childbirth classes and infant communication literature. K-C had countered with a public relations and advertising campaign showing Huggies as the diaper used by baby Elizabeth in the movie *Baby Boom*. After the firms had found these innovative promotional methods effective, they began diverting increased resources to their use.

Both firms had a record of using extensive test marketing prior to national introduction. In the 1960s and 1970s, it took three to five years from test market to complete national distribution. P&G and K-C had cut this time down to months. Despite the pressures on rapid market launch, both firms had continued to conduct extensive test market research.

Manufacturing

The production of disposable diapers was capital intensive. The process was a continuous flow of assembly using large, complex, high speed machines. The machines were several hundred feet long with a cost range of $2–4 million, depending on speed and features. Usually several machines were grouped at each plant location. As a result of the high capital costs, capacity planning and utilization were essential to profitability. Both P&G and K-C attempted to operate their diaper machines 24 hours a day, seven days a week.

Additions to manufacturing capacity required a lead time of 12–18 months, slowing the national roll-out of new products. In addition, most facilities needed several months to work the bugs out of new equipment. In the past, uncertain market share forecasts and fluctuations had led to capacity surpluses and product shortages for both firms. The competition between P&G and K-C had resulted in a history of wide swings in market share. Ironically, manufacturing costs for both firms would have benefited from reasonable industry stability.

Despite technological improvements, diapers were still a bulky product and transportation costs were estimated to comprise at least 7% of the retail value. To minimize transportation costs, both K-C and P&G had traditionally built regional plants. Transportation costs had been 50% higher prior to the introduction of super-thin, super-absorbent technology.

THE FUTURE BASIS OF COMPETITION

As the rivalry between P&G and K-C heated up, it was uncertain whether the principal focus of the competitive battle would remain fixed on technological innovation and strong promotional support. Some observers thought that consumers would likely pay for only so much technology. Yet the stakes were high and both companies were very intent on winning the battle. It was estimated that K-C and P&G both enjoyed net profit margins of 15% on diapers, as compared to less than 10% on most of their other consumer paper products. In determining the future basis of competition, both P&G and K-C had different resource bases and corporate interests. These are described in the following two sections.

Procter & Gamble Company

In 1989, P&G was a leading competitor in the U.S. household and personal care products industries with $13.3 billion in U.S. sales. For detailed financials, see Exhibit 3. P&G's products held dominant positions in North America in a variety of sectors including detergents (Tide, Cheer), bar soap (Ivory), toothpaste (Crest), shampoo (Head and Shoulders), coffee (Folgers), bakery mixes (Duncan Hines), shortening (Crisco), and peanut butter (Jiff). Disposable diapers were an important product group that comprised approximately 17% of the firm's total sales in North America.

Historically, most of P&G's annual growth had come from the expansion of existing brands where the company's marketing expertise was well known. In building these brands, P&G typically followed a strategy based on developing a superior consumer product, branding it, positioning it as a premium product, and then developing the brand through advertising and promotion. The strategy was consistent with the company's objectives of having top brands and highest market shares in its class. The company strongly believed that profitability would come from dominant market positions.

P&G's marketing strengths were supported by core competencies in research and development. With shorter product lifecycles for many non-food consumer products, R&D was becoming increasingly important to the company. Much of the company's R&D efforts were focused on upgrading existing products. However, in the late 1980s, the firm was devoting large amounts of R&D resources towards several new products, such as Olestra, a fat substitute. In 1989, total P&G research and development expenditures were $628 million, approximately $100 million of which diapers were estimated to have received. Some industry observers had suggested that the slowdown of innovations in the diaper wars may have been partially a result of P&G channelling R&D resources to new product areas.

In addition to being a dominant competitor in the U.S. household products and personal care products industries, P&G also had a strong position in several key international markets. In 1989, international sales surpassed $8.5 billion and income from international operations soared to $417 million, up almost 37% from the previous year. Sales growth in Europe and Japan was particularly impressive, with European sales up almost 15% and Japanese sales up more than 40% over 1988 figures. Performance in international markets was led by strong showings in diapers and detergents.

Kimberly-Clark

In 1989, K-C was a leading manufacturer and marketer of personal, health care and industrial products made primarily from natural and synthetic fibres. In 1989, the firm had revenues of $5.7 billion with a net income of $424 million. Detailed financials are found in Exhibits 4 and 5. Well-known products manufactured by K-C included Kleenex facial tissues, Kotex and New Freedom feminine care products, Hi-Dri household towels and Depend incontinence products. For product analysis, see Exhibit 6. Huggies disposable diapers were K-C's largest single product, contributing $1.4 billion to 1989 sales and an estimated 37% of net income.

K-C was organized into three divisions. By far the largest of these was the personal, health care and industrial products division. Personal products included disposable diapers, feminine care products, disposable hand towels and various incontinence products. Health care products included primarily surgical gowns, packs and wraps. Industrial products included cleaning wipers made of unwoven materials. Together, the division's products contributed 77% of K-C's 1989 sales and 78% of its net income.

K-C also manufactured newsprint and groundwood printing papers, premium business and correspondence papers, cigarette papers, tobacco products and specialty papers. These operations were part of the firm's second division that represented 19% of corporate sales and net income. The importance of the woodlands-related products to K-C had diminished throughout much of the 1970s and 1980s as the company shifted resources into consumer products. The two divisions were, however, closely linked to the degree that many of K-C's consumer products relied on cellulose fibres supplied by the company's woodlands operations. It was estimated that 65% of the wood pulp needs for consumer products were supplied in-house, a level considered high in the industry. It was thought that vertical control provided the advantage of flexibility and security under rapidly changing competitive conditions.

Observers noted that prices for newsprint and paper products had been highly cyclical during much of the 1980s. In 1989, there was an indication that prices were softening and would likely remain depressed as large amounts of capacity were expected to be added to the industry in the early 1990s.

The company's smallest division (4% of revenues and 3% of net income) operated a business aircraft maintenance and refurbishing subsidiary, and Midwest Express Airlines, a commercial airline based in Milwaukee, Wisconsin.

K-C's international operations provided 29% of company sales and 30% of the operating income in 1989. The company's major markets, on a consolidated basis, were Canada, the United Kingdom, France, the Philippines and Brazil. K-C had several international equity investments; the largest, in Mexico, provided $36 million in net income. In 1989, K-C manufactured disposable diapers in nine countries and had sales in more than 100 countries. Outside North America and Europe, however, sales of disposable diapers were very low, largely because of undeveloped markets. Also, after K-C had abandoned the Japanese market, its potential for expansion into growing Asian markets was weakened.

INTERNATIONAL OPPORTUNITIES AND THREATS

After the introduction of super-thin technology from Japan, it became increasingly apparent that the competitive conditions in North America could not be viewed in isolation. By the late 1980s, competitive conditions in both Europe and Japan were having a significant influence on opportunities and threats facing North American competitors.

Japan

Historically, Japanese consumers had enjoyed better quality cloth diapers than consumers in other countries, thus slowing the acceptance of disposables. After World War II, the new Japanese government appointed a special commission to examine the national supply of diapers. The commission came up with a unique system involving a cloth diaper liner and a woven, absorbent cotton overpanty. This system received the approval of the Japanese Medical Society, significantly increasing its acceptance in traditional Japanese society. In recent years, however, the consumer benefits provided by disposables have become more apparent. Changing roles of women in Japanese society have also led to a rapid growth in the demand for disposable diapers.

P&G's competitive experiences in Japan's diaper industry were remarkably similar to its experiences in North America. In the early 1970s, P&G enjoyed a market share greater than 90% of the Japanese disposable market. However, as in North America, the product had performance problems and total market penetration was weak. P&G's biggest problem was complacency. In 1982, P&G was making its diapers with old-fashioned wood pulp. In the same year Japan's Uni-Charm Corp. (1989 Sales: $600 million) introduced a highly absorbent, granulated polymer to soak up wetness and hold it in the form of a gel, keeping babies dry longer. In 1984, KAO Corporation, a Japanese soapmaker (1989 Sales: $4 billion) launched a similar brand of super-thin diapers under the brand name Merries. P&G did not begin selling its polymer-packed Pampers in Japan until January 1985. By that time P&G's share of the Japanese market had fallen below 7%. In 1985, Uni-Charm controlled almost half the market and KAO about 30%.

In recommitting to the Japanese market, P&G recognized that Japanese product technology was years ahead of U.S. levels. Being well positioned in Japan meant that P&G would have greater access to Japanese technology, which could be exported back to the U.S to use in its battle with K-C. Because K-C had sold its interest in its Japanese equity company in 1987, it was not a major competitor in this market.

By 1989, the Japanese market had not yet reached the same level of maturity demonstrated in the U.S. While the market was worth over $1 billion in 1989, the penetration estimates varied from 35% to 50%. However, Japanese parents changed their babies twice as often as North American parents and therefore used many more diapers. Industry estimates indicated that the Japanese market, if developed to the same degree as the U.S. (85–90% penetration), would be almost as large as the U.S. This result was despite a population size of less than half. As a result, there was tremendous opportunity for growth in the Japanese market.

Faced with intense domestic competition, Japanese firms historically showed little interest in moving internationally. However, there was growing concern in North America that Japanese preoccupation with domestic competition might not last. When in 1988 KAO acquired Jergens Ltd., the U.S. producer of personal care products, several analysts speculated that this move was the beachhead for a major Japanese thrust into the North American market for personal products, including disposable diapers. There was also speculation in the press that Uni-Charm had begun negotiations with Weyerhauser to set up joint production-distribution operations in the U.S. Weyerhauser was a large, integrated U.S. forest products company that held a 50% share of the low-priced, private label market for disposable diapers. It was known that Weyerhauser had been considering a major move into the mid-priced segment for disposables.

Europe

The development of the disposable diapers industry in Europe was decidedly different from that in North America. Europeans began producing disposable diapers using a two-piece system in the early 1960s. Unlike the North American industry, however, the European industry did not experience a high degree of rationalization. There were two main reasons for this. First, Europe was composed of very different, often protected national markets. As a result, production, marketing, and distribution economies were limited. Second, no large European industry leaders emerged and foreign competitors from North America and Japan were preoccupied with domestic competitive battles. As a result, several strong country-specific firms emerged. Beginning in the mid-1980s, both P&G and K-C began to refocus attention on Europe, achieving some success. However, by 1989 the market was still fragmented with neither firm enjoying the dominant position experienced in their domestic market. The use of super-thin technology, pioneered in Japan and promoted in North America, was gradually becoming the industry norm in Europe.

Penetration of disposable diapers varied widely across Europe. In Scandinavia, the market had been saturated at least five to ten years prior to the North American market. Consumer demand appeared to be entering a new phase, becoming increasingly preoccupied with environmental concerns. Many consumers were experimenting with a variety of alternatives to disposables. Other countries were undergoing similar experiences. In France, 98 out of 100 diaper changes were done using disposables. However, in southern Europe, penetration levels were much lower and the market less sophisticated. Here, the percentage of women employed outside the home was lower, and many observers felt that these markets offered significant growth opportunities. The development of a unified internal market for Europe promised potential industry rationalization opportunities.

By 1989, P&G had established a strong presence in the fragmented European market with a major plant in Germany. At this time, K-C had not moved aggressively into this market. An issue faced by both companies was whether limited investment capital for expensive market development would be better spent at home or overseas; and if overseas, in which market? Also of concern was the potential reaction of European firms, both overseas and in North America, to the perceived aggressiveness of U.S. firms.

ADDITIONAL ISSUES

The Environment

In 1989, almost 19 billion disposable diapers were sold in North America. This produced an estimated 4–5.5 billion pounds of discarded diapers. In some residential landfills, tests showed that disposable diapers constituted almost 5% of the total volume (industry studies showed a much lower estimate of 1–2%), leading to widespread criticism of the industry for the non-biodegradable nature of the plastics in the product. (It took an estimated 250 years for a plastic disposable diaper to biodegrade.) Environmental groups had highlighted concerns about potential health risks for sanitation workers and the threat to ground water. As the environmental movement gathered steam, many industry experts feared that unless more environmentally friendly disposable diapers were introduced, consumers would increasingly seek out alternative diapering systems.

Additional regulatory pressures were also appearing because of the perceived environmental problem. By 1989, legislation taxing, regulating or banning the sale of disposable diapers had been introduced in eleven U.S. states. It was expected that most other states would consider similar legislation during the early 1990s. However, the legislation had not yet impacted the diaper industry, as most punitive measures were not scheduled to come into effect until 1992–94.

There were signs that the seriousness of the environmental problem had not fully reached either P&G or K-C. For example, Sue Hale, associate director of P&G's public relations was quoted in 1989 as defending the firm's disposable diapers as being 60–70% biodegradable. Richard R. Nicolosi, vice-president in charge of P&G's worldwide diaper operations, was quoted as saying, "We don't think mothers are willing to give up one of the greatest new products of the postwar era."

Although K-C had a note in its 1989 annual report citing the potential seriousness of the threat, the company had been reticent about specific plans for dealing with the issue. According to Tina Barry, vice-president of corporate communications at K-C, "We're working with our suppliers to find a reliable plastic that is biodegradable. But we haven't come across any plastic material that breaks down and maintains product performance and reliability."

By 1989, no promising technologies had been introduced to address these rising environmental concerns. This situation was in contrast to the Japanese market where the market leaders had avoided or minimized the use of non-biodegradable plastics. It was also recognized that Japanese firms had considerable technological experience with biodegradable external retaining fabrics. Both P&G and K-C had yet to adopt such technology.

Both firms were trying to divert criticism by testing small-scale recycling projects. The diapers were washed and the components separated. Then the pulp was sanitized and sold to paper mills. The plastic was recovered for use in flower pots and garbage bags. However, the cost of recycling was much higher than the value of the components recovered. Added to this problem were the difficulties associated with collection of soiled diapers.

It was believed that unless environmentally friendly disposables were introduced, cloth diapers would be the main benefactor of the environmental movement. In the late 1980s, both Fisher-Price and Gerber had begun to re-examine this market and had introduced form-fitting, two-piece diaper systems. Claims that cloth diapers were environmentally friendly were countered by the industry with studies showing that the laundering of cloth diapers used six times the amount of water as was used in the manufacture of disposables and the laundering created ten times as much water pollution.

Product Diversification

As the North American disposable diaper market became saturated, both P&G and K-C sought other market opportunities that might utilize the technological expertise gained from their diaper rivalry. One avenue that seemed particularly attractive was increased development of incontinence products for adults. Incontinence products appeared to be an ideal product extension for the super-thin technology used in disposable diapers. With the improvement in incontinence product performance, sales and market penetration had exploded. Some estimated that sales in the U.S. would be as high as $1 billion in 1990, and that the potential size of this market could eventually exceed that of diapers. Of the 31 million North Americans over 65, it was estimated that about 10% had a problem with incontinence. An aging population would allow total market growth opportunities as well as growth through increased penetration.

The fight for the incontinence market was shaping up to be a replay of the disposable diaper war, with the same players. A difference in this competition was the contrasting strengths possessed by each firm in the distribution network. P&G dominated the institutional distribution channel while K-C was the leader in the commercial-retail channel. K-C had broken important new ground in this market and strengthened its distribution position by successfully developing a television advertising program that tastefully promoted the benefits of its incontinence products.

In May 1989, K-C also began the rollout of its new Huggies Pull-Up Training Pants. This product would extend the length of time children would use Huggies through months of toilet training. By November, national distribution had not yet been achieved but early market results in Western states were promising. Although P&G was watching the product carefully and had registered trademarks suitable for a similar line, the company had not yet responded with its own introduction.

Recent Events

On November 1, 1989, P&G announced the appointment of Edwin Artzt as the company's new CEO. Artzt, who was chosen for the position over an heir apparent, had directed P&G's international operations since 1984. In that capacity he had been responsible for the company's spectacular recovery in Japan, particularly in diapers, and its double digit growth in Asia and Europe.

K-C was particularly concerned about the possible impact that Artzt's appointment might have on its intense competition with P&G in the North American diaper industry. Managers at K-C wondered whether the appointment of Artzt signalled a shift in P&G's emphasis away from the U.S. marketplace. They also speculated whether his appointment was designed to strengthen P&G's access to new Japanese technology that could produce more environmentally friendly diapers. In response to these concerns, K-C managers wondered what sort of action to take, either internationally or in North America.

As a backdrop to the technological challenges that lay ahead, there had been ongoing litigation between P&G and K-C over the use of proprietary technologies. P&G had sued K-C for patent infringement on technology developed for elastic waistbands. K-C countersued, claiming P&G had unlawfully monopolized the market for disposable diapers and was in violation of antitrust laws. While industry observers did not expect significant damages to be awarded in either suit—indeed, neither firm had noted material reserves on its financial statements—both P&G and K-C remained very interested in and suspicious of the other's research activities.

With external pressures mounting, the nature of the competition in the North American disposable diaper industry showed signs of change in 1989. For the first time, neither of the two competitors had introduced major product improvements; instead, each made style changes. In the summer of 1989, P&G had introduced His and Hers diapers with designer colour patterns and special absorbent pads strategically placed for boy and girl babies. P&G had backed the introduction with a huge advertising and promotional campaign, which made it difficult to gauge the true market share impacts of the new products. In response, K-C had introduced mild product line extensions and had developed a similar product, which was in test marketing phase. It was estimated that a similar national product introduction for K-C would cost $50–75 million.

In responding to mounting competitive pressures, both K-C and P&G recognized that balance between short-term and long-term perspectives was essential. The focus of this balance was, however, the basis of considerable uncertainty.

EXHIBIT 1   Market Share Data

(% of U.S. retail shipments)

Brand	1980	1981	1982	1983	1984	1985	1986	1987	1988	1989
K-C Huggies	7.1	11.7	12.3	18.1	24.0	33.0	31.0	31.3	31.7	32.0
P&G Pampers	55.7	48.0	44.7	40.0	35.0	30.5	34.0	38.0	35.6	31.6
P&G Luvs	9.8	17.2	18.0	17.7	17.5	18.4	20.0	17.0	16.1	17.4
Other	27.4	23.1	25.0	24.2	23.5	18.1	15.0	13.7	17.6	19.0

Source: Various publicly available documents on product shipments.

EXHIBIT 2   Procter & Gamble U.S. Patent Searches

(first half 1986)

Patent	Title
4 562 930	Easy-Open Laminated Container with Optional Re-closing Means and Method of Making
* 4 563 185	Disposable Diaper Having Elasticized Waistband with Non-Linear Severed Edge
4 564 633	Compositions and Methods Useful for Producing Analgesia
4 566 884	Ether Polycarboxylates
4 568 556	Margarine Product and Process
4 571 391	Chromium Acetylacetonate as a Dietary Supplement and Pharmaceutical Agent
* 4 571 924	Method and Apparatus of Manufacturing Porous Pouches Containing Granular Product
* 4 573 966	Disposable Waste-Containment Garment
* 4 576 962	Prostaglandin Analogues
* 4 578 068	Absorbent Laminate Structure
* 4 578 071	Disposable Absorbent Article Having an Improved Liquid Migration Resistant Perimeter Construction
* 4 578 073	Composite Waste-Containment Garment Having Disposable Elasticized Insert
4 578 200	Fabric Softeners
4 582 216	Easy Open-Reclosable Container with Pouring Lip/Drain Surface
4 584 203	Dough Rolling Process for Laminated Cookies
4 589 676	Sanitary Napkin
4 590 006	Oral Compositions
4 591 533	Coffee Product and Process
4 594 184	Chlorine Bleach Compatible Liquid Detergent Compositions
4 596 714	Process for Making a Baked Filled Snack

* Patents related to Disposable Diaper Research.

Source: First Boston Equity Research, August 1986.

EXHIBIT 3   Procter & Gamble Consolidated Statement of Earnings

(millions of dollars except per share amounts)

	Year Ended June 30		
	1989	*1988*	*1987*
Income			
Net sales	$21 398	$19 336	$17 000
Interest and other income	291	155	163
	21 689	19 491	17 163
Costs and Expenses			
Cost of products sold	13 371	11 880	10 411
Marketing, administrative and other expenses	5 988	5 660	4 977
Interest expense	391	321	53
Provision for restructuring	—	—	805
	19 750	17 861	16 546
Earnings Before Income Taxes	1 939	1 630	617
Income Taxes	733	610	290
Net Earnings	1 206	1 020	327

Segment Information (millions of dollars)

Geographic Areas		*U.S.*	*Inter-national*	*Corporate*	*Total*
Net Sales	1987	$11 805	$5 524	$ (329)	$17 000
	1988	12 423	7 294	(381)	19 336
	1989	13 312	8 529	(443)	21 398
Net Earnings*	1987	329	120	(122)	327
	1988	864	305	(149)	1 020
	1989	927	417	(138)	1 206

* Net earnings have been reduced by $357 million in the U.S. and $102 million in International by the provision for restructuring.

E X H I B I T 3 (continued)

(millions of dollars)

Consolidated Balance Sheet

	June 30	
	1989	*1988*
Assets		
Current assets	6 578	5 593
Property Plant and Equipment	6 793	6 778
Goodwill and Other Intangible Assets	2 305	1 944
Other Assets	675	505
Total	$16 351	$14 820
Liabilities and Shareholders' Equity		
Current liabilities	4 656	4 224
Long-Term Debt	3 698	2 462
Other Liabilities	447	475
Deferred Income Taxes	1 335	1 322
Shareholders' Equity	6 215	6 337
Total	$16 351	$14 820

Source: Procter & Gamble, 1989 *Annual Report.*

EXHIBIT 4 Kimberly-Clark Corporation and Subsidiaries Consolidated Income Statement

(millions of dollars except per share amounts)

	Year Ended December 31		
	1989	*1988*	*1987*
Net sales	$5 733.6	$5 393.5	$ 4 884.7
Cost of products sold	3 654.1	3 404.2	3 065.9
Distribution expenses	195.8	185.2	181.2
Gross profit	1 883.7	1 804.1	1 637.6
Advertising promotion and selling expense	813.4	784.1	674.9
Research expense	118.0	110.9	110.5
General expense	278.9	268.5	266.1
Operating profit	673.4	640.6	586.1
Interest income	19.3	11.2	7.2
Other income	24.2	24.2	26.2
Interest expense	(68.2)	(80.6)	(65.6)
Other expense	(17.9)	(11.5)	(19.8)
Income before income taxes	630.8	583.9	534.1
Provision for income taxes	242.4	229.8	230.5
Income before equity interests	388.4	354.1	303.6
Share of net income of equity companies	49.3	46.0	35.3
Minority owners' share of subsidiaries' net income	(13.9)	(21.5)	(13.7)
Net income	$ 423.8	$ 378.6	$ 325.0

EXHIBIT 4   (continued)

Consolidated Balance Sheet (millions of dollars)

	1989	1988
Assets		
Total current assets	$1 443.2	$1 278.3
Net fixed assets	3 040.9	2 575.3
Investments in equity companies	296.6	291.7
Deferred charges and other assets	142.3	121.8
	$4 923.0	$4 267.6
Liabilities		
Total current liabilities	$1 263.2	$ 925.7
Long-term debt	745.1	743.3
Other non-current liabilities	79.9	53.7
Deferred income taxes	643.5	585.0
Minority owners' interests in subsidiaries	105.5	94.3
Total stockholders' equity	2 085.8	1 865.5
	$4 923.0	$4 267.6

Source: Kimberly-Clark, 1989 *Annual Report*.

EXHIBIT 5 **Kimberly-Clark Corporation and Subsidiaries Analysis of 1989 Consolidated Operating Results**

(millions of dollars)

Geographic Areas	1989	% Change vs. 1988	% of 1989 Consolidated
Sales			
North America	$4 664.0	+ 6.4%	81.3%
Outside North America	1 087.1	+ 6.0	19.0
Adjustments	(17.5)		(.3)
Consolidated	$5 733.6	+ 6.3%	100.0%
Net Income			
North America	$ 316.7	+ 12.1%	74.8%
Outside North America	107.1	+ 11.3	25.2
Consolidated	$ 423.8	+ 11.9%	100.0%

Source: Kimberly-Clark, 1989 *Annual Report.*

EXHIBIT 5 (continued)

Segment Breakdown 1981–89 (millions of dollars)

	1981	1982	1983	1984	1985	1986	1987	1988	1989
Net Sales									
Consumer Products Division	$2 103	$2 205	$2 464	$2 734	$3 172	$3 370	$3 809	$4 165	$4 481
Forestry Division	$ 781	742	795	845	856	876	1 001	1 121	1 096
Aviation Division	44	61	75	97	118	99	125	166	211
Subtotal	$2 928	$3 008	$3 334	$3 676	$4 146	$4 345	$4 935	$5 452	$5 788
(Interclass)	(42)	(62)	(60)	(60)	(73)	(42)	(50)	(59)	(54)
Total	$2 886	$2 946	$3 274	$3 616	$4 073	$4 303	$4 885	$5 393	$5 734
Operating Income									
Consumer Products Division	$ 171	$ 173	$ 221	$ 263	$ 361	$ 363	$ 434	$ 435	$ 535
Forestry Division	120	109	118	139	162	145	177	204	129
Aviation Division	3	7	8	11	2	9	13	23	26
Subtotal	$ 294	$ 289	$ 347	$ 413	$ 525	$ 516	$ 624	$ 662	$ 690
Corporate	(16)	(19)	(31)	(38)	(39)	(32)	(38)	(21)	(17)
Total	$ 278	$ 270	$ 316	$ 375	$ 486	$ 485	$ 586	$ 641	$ 673
Return on Average Assets									
Consumer Products Division	11.4%	10.5%	12.0%	12.7%	15.3%	14.0%	15.9%	14.2%	15.0%
Forestry Division	22.5	19.6	20.4	23.9	27.1	22.8	26.0	27.7	15.7
Aviation Division	5.0	10.8	12.3	15.0	2.8	12.3	17.0	17.4	6.5
Subtotal	14%	12.7%	13.9%	15.1%	17.4%	15.7%	17.9%	12.0%	11.9%
Unallocated/Interclass	N.M.	N.M.	N.M.	N.M.	N.M.	N.M.	N.M.	N.M.	N.M.
Total	11.7%	10.6%	11.3%	12.3%	14.6%	13.5%	15.5%	11.9%	11.7%

Source: "Duff & Phelps Research Report," Kimberly-Clark, *Annual Report*, November 1988.

EXHIBIT 6   Kimberly-Clark Consumer, Health Care Industrial Products

(millions of dollars)

Domestic Categories	1987 Est. Sales	1987 Est. Oper. Profit	1988 Est. Mkt. Share	Est. Rank of Brands	Major Competitors/Mkt. Share
Disposable Diapers	$1 220	$220	32%	2	Pampers 35% Luvs 16% (PG); Private Label 17%
Facial Tissue	450	52	45%	1	Puffs 17% (PG); Scotties 10% (Scott Paper)
Feminine Pads	270	21	26%	2	J&J 37%; Always 20% (PG); Maxithins 5%; Private Label 12%
Tampons	30	2	6%	4	Tambrands 58%; Playtex 26%; J&J 8%
Paper Household Towels	170	10	10%	4	Scott Paper 23%; PG 20%; James River 11%
Bathroom Tissue	35	0	N.M.	N.M.	PG 30%; Scott Paper 19%; James River 13%
Table Napkins	30	2	N.M.	N.M.	Scott Paper 23%; James River 8%
Consumer Incont. Products	60	3	49%	1	Attends 28% (PG); Serenity 8% (J&J); Private Label 15%
Inst./Ind. Tissue Products	170	5			
Inst. Healthcare	180	4			
Other Non-wovens	176	4			
Medical	30	2			
Total Domestic	2 821	325			
Canada	250	20			
Sub-Total North America	3 071	345			
Outside North America	738	89			
Total Consumer Division	3 809	434			

Source: "Duff & Phelps Research Report," Kimberly-Clark, *Annual Report*, November 1988.

case

5

CANADIAN AIRLINES CORP.

Nick Bontis,
Joseph N. Fry and
Roderick E. White

In early 1995, the senior management of Canadian Airlines Corp. (CA) set a June 30 deadline for the completion of plans and negotiations aimed at improving the airline's cost position by some 14% per available seat mile, or approximately $325 million on an annualized basis. This initiative, they anticipated, would improve profitability and cashflow enough to allow the airline over time to renew its fleet and take advantage of new transborder and international markets. The alternative, in their view, was bleak. The company

IVEY

would have to downsize, which meant focusing operations on currently profitable international routes, exiting many markets and implementing major layoffs.

The cost savings were being pursued by an unprecedented joint management-labour group called the Strategic Planning Steering Committee (SPSC). The SPSC, which included representatives from five of six of CA's unions, had worked to achieve a mutual understanding of CA's performance and to clarify its basic strategic options. The SPSC had concluded that change was necessary—simply continuing on an "as is" basis left the airline exposed to the next industry downturn and insufficiently profitable in the good years to support the necessary fleet renewal program. On these grounds the SPSC had created alternative growth/cost-cut versus downsize scenarios, referred to respectively as Plan A and Plan B. They had then initiated projects and negotiations aimed at achieving the cost improvements deemed essential for the success of Plan A.

As June 30 approached it was becoming increasingly apparent that the SPSC, in spite of substantial progress in which improvements amounting to some $110 million (of the $325 million target) had been agreed, was not going to be able to complete in time all the necessary negotiations and arrangements. An immediate issue for senior management was whether to continue with Plan A negotiations, or to honour the self-imposed deadline and take steps to implement Plan B.

CA was no stranger to critical situations. Its development, from a profitable regional carrier in the mid-1980s to one of Canada's two national airlines in 1995, was marked by a series of difficult challenges. The airline industry had proven to be a tough environment in which to profit and survive. Management was abundantly aware of this, and understood that the history of the airline, and in parallel, that of the industry, was important in shaping perceptions of the current situation, and of the possibilities for dealing with it.

BEGINNINGS TO 1985: THE INDUSTRY UNDER REGULATION

The path of development of the airline industry had been dominated by two basic federal government policies—government ownership and regulation. Under the first, the government chose in 1937 to form Trans Canada Airlines, the predecessor of Air Canada (AC), as a crown corporation and as its chosen instrument for the development of a domestic and, subsequently, an international air transportation infrastructure. Under the second, the government chose to regulate the industry, establishing agencies, most latterly the Canada Transport Commission (CTC), with the authority to pursue "public convenience and necessity" in approving, for example, licences for new routes, exit from established routes, fares, schedules, and mergers and acquisitions.

Over the 50-plus years preceding the early 1980s the industry grew, under regulation, from a host of early operators into a loose, three-tiered structure of scheduled national, regional and commuter/short-haul carriers (see Exhibit 1). Charter, or non-scheduled service, was a fourth segment.

The National Carriers

By the early 1980s, there were two major Canadian-based carriers, AC and privately owned CP Air (Canadian Pacific Air Lines). Though both airlines operated domestic and international services, AC was, by a factor of three, the dominant carrier (see Table 1). Domestically, AC's trunk or long haul network covered Canada's major cities. This network was supported by AC's own regional service, which was particularly strong in the East and was bolstered in the West by cooperation with a regional carrier, PWA (Pacific Western Airlines). Relatively speaking, CP Air (Canadian Pacific Air Lines) had a thin national network, having been constrained by regulation to a secondary role behind AC. CP Air was quite strong regionally in the West but relied very heavily on interline arrangements with regional carriers for coverage and feed in the East.

The international services of the two airlines were split by government policy. International air traffic was controlled by a series of bilateral agreements between countries. In setting up these agreements and designating the Canadian carrier, the Canadian government had followed a policy referred to as "division of the skies." AC was made the primary and almost exclusive carrier on routes to Europe, the U.S. and the Caribbean while CP Air was favoured over the Pacific and to South America.

The Regional Carriers

Prior to deregulation there were a number of "independent" regional airlines—Pacific Western Airlines (PWA), Nordair, Québecair and Eastern Provincial Airlines—flying jet aircraft on mid-length, domestic routes and feeding traffic to the transcontinental and international carriers. For the most part the regional airlines operated in cooperation with the national carriers, providing feed from, and distribution to, points that the latter were not vitally interested in. Where routes overlapped there was competition, but always within the moderating context of regulation. And, at the margin, the regionals were constrained from expansion into long-haul by their equipment, which was typically small jets such as Boeing 737s, and again, by regulation.

Among the regionals, PWA (see Table 1) was notable for the success of its operations in the West and North and for its apparent expansion ambitions as and when regulatory limits were relaxed. PWA owned a modern fleet of 737s and was pressing these into extensions of its regional service, including a Calgary to Toronto flight, which was legitimized by a stop in Brandon, Manitoba. At the same time, PWA served in an important feeder role to AC for Western Canada. In anticipation of deregulation, AC had started looking for more secure feed and thus, closer ties with PWA. So in 1985 for example, AC and PWA purchased equal equity positions in Air Ontario (a short-haul carrier).

The market value of PWA common shares in 1985 equalled about $150 million versus a book value of $200 million and a liquidation value (before severance and other costs) of $420 million. The high liquidation value according to industry analysts was due to the market value of PWA's 737 aircraft being 100% higher than book value.

T A B L E 1   Profiles of AC, PWA and CP Air

Measure	AC (1982)	AC (1985)	PWA (1982)	PWA (1985)	CP (1982)	CP (1985)
Revenue ($ million)	2 305.9	2 772.5	318.7	352.7	862.8	1 119.2
Operating Income	–25.8	1.5	25.3	6.2	–26.2	34.7
Net Income	–35.6	–14.8	6.3	13.4	–34.6	–23.5
RPM* (billions)	13.6	14.1	1.3	1.5	5.5	7.0
Number of Employees	23 300	22 100	3 046	2 873	7 994	8 578

*Refer to Appendix A for definitions.

Source: Company Reports.

The Commuter/Short-Haul Carriers

By 1984 there were 700 smaller Canadian carriers that operated one or more propjet aircraft on short and often remote routes. It was uneconomical to fly larger jet aircraft on low traffic routes of less than 250 kilometres. These services seldom overlapped those of the nationals and regionals. In spite of their numbers the short-haul carriers accounted for only 8% of the passengers flown.

The Charter Carriers

Prior to deregulation charter service was entirely separate from regularly scheduled service. Charters began by carrying planeloads of vacationers to international tourist destinations. By the 1980s a domestic charter business had developed. No mixing of charter and scheduled service was allowed and certain "fences" were imposed: membership in a group, minimum stays, no change in itinerary or cancellation, full prepayment, etc. In order to improve their equipment utilization, all of Canada's scheduled carriers operated charter services, but these were of minor importance to their total revenues—about 3% in the case of AC and CP Air, and 17% for PWA. Wardair was the foremost of the purely charter operators and had built up a solid business and a remarkable reputation for fine service.

Anticipating Deregulation

In the late 1970s and early 1980s dissatisfaction had built among consumer groups and industry participants. Regulation was variously thought to limit service, increase prices, and stifle innovation, and to be increasingly irrelevant to the purposes for which it was created, such as safety, reasonable cost and national accessibility. National governments had a history of using their airline(s) to achieve social and technological objectives, and undeniably, the motives influencing government engagement in an airline overlapped into an expression of national pride. Governments had, among other things, restricted ownership, controlled prices, set operating and safety standards, and allocated routes and frequencies.

However, regulation had not guaranteed carriers' monopolies on all routes. If traffic between two cities could support an additional carrier, or the incumbent carrier was deemed not to be providing adequate service, than a competitor's licence application might be approved. However, the incumbent, as part of the approval process, had the opportunity to object. The nature of this competitive process was characterized by orderly arrangements of "give and take" between the CTC and the airlines as well as among the airlines themselves, where allied relationships were the norm (e.g., PWA as a regional feeder for AC).

The national carriers were not exactly prospering in this regulated context either. After taking a profit hit in the 1981 recession, neither AC nor CP Air was able to report more than marginal profits and losses as the economy improved through 1985. Critics of regulation also lashed out at AC, claiming that its status as a crown corporation had allowed it to become dominant, but not particularly driven by concerns for cost, service and profits.

As the disenchantment with a regulated industry grew, the federal government started to "liberalize" regulation and give notice of impending deregulation. By 1985, the honourable Don Mazankowski, the Minister of Transport at the time, introduced a paper entitled "Freedom to Move" which criticized the economic regulation of air transport and proposed future steps toward a deregulated regime.

With deregulation looming, AC seemed to be courting PWA in order to face CP Air head-on in Western Canada. At one point it was rumoured that AC and PWA were discussing an arrangement under which AC would fly all the trunk routes using wide-bodied aircraft and PWA would fly shorter hauls in narrow-bodied aircraft. Furthermore, there was talk of the pending privatization of AC, as federal officials and airline analysts realized that only a private AC— removed from the grasp of the government—would survive an industry shakedown expected from post-deregulation.

Lessons from the U.S. Deregulation Experience

The U.S. experience with deregulation was traumatic. Deregulation was introduced in late 1978 with no provisions for a transitional phase. Airlines were no longer required to apply for route licensing or fare changes. Any carrier was able to fly any route provided it was "fit, willing and able." Many carriers expanded rapidly by expanding their route structures, increasing flight frequencies, purchasing new equipment, and acquiring other carriers. The resulting overcapacity led to an almost continuous series of price wars. These in turn made cost a critical variable for survival. But under regulation, costs had been of secondary importance and most carriers were poorly prepared for this dramatic change.

In the inevitable industry shakeout some long-standing airlines were put out of business or onto the ropes (e.g., Braniff, PanAm, Eastern), some new operators went in and out of business (People Express), and the remaining healthy carriers pressed to find elements of competitive advantage and security. The carriers that survived developed strategic tools such as frequent flyer plans (FFPs) and computerized reservation systems (CRSs)—see Appendix A for an elaboration of these and other industry terms. They also moved to establish hub and spoke networks and to attempt to dominate particular hubs. But the wars continued nonetheless in what observers called "the pursuit of Pyrrhic victories in market share."

1985-90: DEREGULATION AND RESTRUCTURING

As deregulation proceeded the Canadian airline industry started into a period of rapid consolidation. By 1990 there would be just two vertically integrated carrier groups, Air Canada and Canadian Airlines (see Exhibit 1 for a genealogy of major Canadian air carriers). The major events of the 1985–90 period were the emergence of CA, the privatization of AC, the absorption of the second and third level carriers into the major groups, and the emergence of a bitter rivalry between the AC and CA camps.

The Emergence of Canadian Airlines

CA emerged in the 1985–90 period as the consequence of an aggressive and unexpected acquisitions program by PWA of first CP Air and later Wardair.

THE CP AIR ACQUISITION
With the door to unregulated expansion opening, CP Air moved in 1985–86 to acquire three eastern regional carriers—Eastern Provincial Airways (EPA), Nordair, and Québecair—and seemed to be rising to pose a serious challenge to AC's dominance in Eastern Canada. But CP Air's parent, the railway-based conglomerate CP Ltd., was ambiguous about airline expansion, and when a chance came in 1987 to sell CP Air, it did. The buyer, in a move that shocked the industry, was the much smaller PWA. The purchase price was $300 million, some of which was funded by a previously arranged major fleet refinancing on the part of PWA.

To help fund expansion, PWA had earlier entered into a major financing transaction involving the forward sale and sale-leaseback of 16 of its Boeing 737-200 aircraft. The market for new and used aircraft had been very buoyant through the 1980s. Aircraft in use were appreciating in value; positions for delivery of new aircraft were traded as a valuable commodity. Gains in the purchase and sale of aircraft had become a major element in airline profit and cash flow. For PWA, the fleet sale generated net cash infusions of $24 and $67 million for 1985 and 1986.

THE WARDAIR ACQUISITION
By January 1988, Wardair was straining to stay in flight. Through its history it had been a successful charter operator, but with deregulation, it had launched an aggressive and, in retrospect, foolhardy campaign to become a major scheduled domestic carrier. Wardair triggered a fierce round of price wars that it had neither the financial capacity nor the operating abilities to sustain. So once again, in April 1989, CA surprised the airline industry by announcing the purchase of Wardair, including its brand new fleet of Airbus aircraft.

By late 1989, fuel prices began to rise quickly as a result of significant increases in the price of crude oil. Faced with these economic trends, CA made the decision to amalgamate its operations with Wardair as quickly as possible. A new fleet plan was announced. The plan included the sale of the Wardair Airbus A310 aircraft for a projected $900 million in proceeds. This money would be used to substantially reduce the company's debt and assist in the funding of replacement aircraft.

PWA had begun the period of deregulation as a regional carrier flying one type of aircraft (Boeing 737). Following the CP Air and Wardair acquisitions it was a major international and domestic carrier flying a mixed fleet of aircraft from Europe in the East to China in the West, from Resolute Bay in the North to Buenos Aires in the South. The new operating entity bore the name Canadian Airlines but in the beginning it was actually an amalgam of its six precursor companies—PWA, CP Air, EPA, Nordair, Québecair and Wardair. Operational and cultural integration was underway but still incomplete.

The new CA had emerged as AC's major competitor. All inter-relationships between PWA/CA and Air Canada were severed. Interline agreements were terminated and PWA's interest in Air Ontario was sold to AC. While still smaller than AC there was a feeling at CA that AC was vulnerable; they believed that years of regulation and government ownership had left AC with high costs and stodgy management.

The Privatization of Air Canada

With deregulation in the horizon, AC and others had argued that its status as a crown corporation would hold back its ability to compete effectively. The arguments prevailed and in 1988 AC announced a planned public offering of treasury common shares, proceeds to be used for the acquisition of aircraft and other operational needs. The initial offering yielded $234 million. Full privatization of the airline occurred in July 1989, when the Federal Government offered its remaining 57% interest for $474 million. The privatization of AC represented a recognition by the federal government that it did not require a state-owned airline to fulfill its public policy goals. AC was now free to pursue a purely commercial strategy.

The Decade Ends

The structure of the airline industry had changed dramatically during the 1980s. By the end of the decade two major integrated carriers had emerged. Each ranged from short-haul through regional, transcontinental and international service. While broadly similar there were important differences.

The outcome of the formation of CA was a faltering airline. AC posted better earnings in 1989 and 1990. The Wardair purchase had created financial pressures because the cashflow from the sale of Wardair's aircraft did not materialize as expected. Furthermore, CA's profits were under pressure from the price war, first initiated by Wardair but continued sporadically by AC and CA.

The restructuring of the industry had left the two carriers battling in a very competitive, deregulated environment. CA and AC, once allies, now faced off in a new era of competitive rivalry (see Table 2 for relative positions and Exhibit 3 for financial data).

1990-95: COMPETITIVE RIVALRY

The intense rivalry between CA and AC continued into the 1990s—price and capacity battles for market share were commonplace. Both airlines experienced substantial losses but CA, partly because it had entered the battle in a weakened state, verged on bankruptcy. Because of its dire circumstances CA reluctantly considered merger proposals from AC. But these discussions in no way diminished the continued rivalry in the marketplace.

TABLE 2   Relative Positions in 1990

Measure	Canadian Airlines	Air Canada
Cashflow from Operations	–$ 43 million	$ 41 million
Interest and Lease Coverage	0.60 X	1.01 X
Current Ratio	0.74 to 1	1.47 to 1
Debt to Equity	2.47 to 1	3.63 to 1
Total Fleet	88	115
Average Passenger Journey	2 479 km	1 405 km
Personnel Cost per ASK	2.3¢	3.0¢
Canadian Destinations	109 cities	74 cities
United States Destinations	7 cities	19 cities
International Destinations	24 cities	25 cities
Frequency: Toronto–Montréal	15 per day	20 per day
Frequency: Toronto–Vancouver	6 per day	6 per day
Frequency: Vancouver–Calgary	14 per day	7 per day

Source: Company Reports.

Capacity Wars

AC and CA were unable, through the marketplace, to achieve capacity and fare levels that allowed either airline to be profitable. During this period AC aggressively added capacity even when confronted by declining load factors. In late 1992 CA had announced a 15% reduction in domestic capacity. AC did not follow suit. CA claimed that AC was flooding the market with excess capacity and driving down fares and load factors. It launched a $1 billion lawsuit against its rival for alleged damages. The capacity situation continued to be so problematic that Rhys Eyton, chairman of CA at the time, appealed to the federal Transport Minister to take action. Eyton said CA

> desperately wants to avoid 'reregulation' of the airline industry but it may be necessary on a temporary basis if AC refuses to cut its capacity, something CA has been willing to do.

He went on to say

> Canada's airline industry is being 'decimated' because of an estimated 20% overcapacity in the domestic industry (a figure also quoted by AC). We'll both be out of business if we allow this to go on.[1]

There was no direct response by the government to this appeal. As a result of the intense rivalry (and poor market conditions) CA lost over $500 million in 1992, effectively eliminating the company's accumulated equity. This opened the door to merger proposals from AC which CA's board could not ignore.

Merger Proposals

AC made various merger and purchase offers to CA beginning in 1992. In September 1992 the boards of the two companies reached an agreement to pursue a merger. The reaction by CA employees was immediate and vociferous, as suggested by the following report:

> "Better dead than red," said a pilot in the uniform of Canadian Airlines. With those four words he expressed the depth and emotion that surrounds the proposed merger of Canadian Airlines and Air Canada and illustrated just how difficult it will be to meld the blue and red cultures if the deal goes

---

[1] *Globe and Mail*, February 19, 1993.

through. "We don't understand this hatred," an Air Canada pilot said. "It doesn't seem reasonable. As it is we work together now, sharing information, like what the ride is like." But whether it's reasonable or not, many Canadian Airlines employees dread the thought of working in an Air Canada environment, and their dread grows as merger of the two carriers comes closer to reality.... if the airlines are merged, at least 6 000 and possibly many more employees will lose their jobs. That has emotions running high at both airlines but especially at Canadian Airlines. Many employees believe that because theirs is the younger company, it will bear the brunt of the layoffs.[2]

AC dropped their merger proposal two months later stating that the consolidation would not produce a single, viable merged airline and would not be in the best interests of its shareholders. At the same time, the federal government reluctantly agreed to loan CA $50 million to aid in its restructuring plan—an amount much smaller than the company had requested. Soon after, CA temporarily ceased payments to its creditors.

During the failed merger proposal from AC, CA had also been negotiating with AMR Corp., the parent company of American Airlines. In November 1992 they announced a comprehensive strategic alliance which included a $246 million equity infusion from AMR, a marketing arrangement whereby each airline would participate in the other's FFP and a "services agreement" between the airlines. But several hurdles remained before the alliance could be consummated.

The deal required a restructuring of CA's financial arrangements with shareholders, lenders and lessors. It involved a substantial debt to equity conversion. A continuation and expansion of the $200 million Employee Investment Plan was also needed. Substantially all of CA's employees were participating in a payroll reduction plan whereby employees received a portion of their wages, to a maximum of $200 million over a four-year period, in the form of rights to acquire common shares of the company. Last but not least, the completion of the services agreement involved the withdrawal by CA from its Gemini CRS and the transfer of those activities to AMR's Sabre system. In the financial press AMR Corp. pointed out that, among other things, its investment in CA was justified by the incremental contribution to its Sabre system.

Gemini was a joint venture between CA, AC and the Covia[3] group. In order to withdraw CA needed the approval of the other partners. This was something AC was not willing to provide. CA, in a precedent setting legal manoeuvre, appealed to the Competition Tribunal to set aside the Gemini partnership agreement.

In November 1993, CA was released by the Competition Tribunal from Gemini. AC promptly appealed this decision. AC then offered to purchase CA's international routes for $250 million in cash and the assumption of $800 million in obligations. CA's international routes—specifically the Pacific Rim destinations—were a sought after asset. Since AC was traditionally precluded by the government for these highly profitable routes, it felt that the only alternative was to purchase them outright. Not willing to give up its lucrative routes, but desperately short of cash, CA rejected the deal and pursued its partnership with AMR Corp.

In January 1994 AC changed its tactics and dropped its appeal of the Gemini decision, clearing the way for the CA–AMR alliance. The next day AC was awarded the right to fly to Osaka, Japan by the federal government. Speculation about a "deal" was later confirmed when a disgruntled Hollis Harris (Chairman, President and CEO of AC) declared:

> Some members of the cabinet looked at me right in the eye and said that if I would pull the appeal on the Gemini issue and let them go with American Airlines they promised I would have Osaka, Hong Kong, and the People's Republic of China negotiated. I said "you've got a deal."[4]

However, AC was not immediately given rights to Hong Kong or China as reportedly promised.

---

[2] *Globe and Mail*, October 13, 1992.

[3] Controlled by United Airlines.

[4] *Globe and Mail*, December 22, 1994.

The Global Perspective

While AC and CA were locked in their intense rivalry the world of global air travel was changing. Total international traffic would grow at 5.6% a year, while world-wide domestic traffic would increase by 4.7% a year.[5] In particular, the Pacific Rim and Latin America were growing faster than any other region. Global networks were emerging to exploit this growth. It was predicted that eventually air travel would be dominated by less than a dozen global airline consortia. Four of the most imposing groups were: British Airways–US Air–Quantas; KLM–Northwest; Delta–Swissair–Singapore Airlines; and Lufthansa–United Airlines. Neither AC or CA was part of a significant global consortia although both had established links to carriers outside of Canada.

During the early 1990s AC had pursued an ownership position with USAir. Its route structure had a good fit with AC's network. However, British Airways eventually secured an ownership position with USAir, further developing its global network while taking AC out of the equation.

AC was eager to find a large American partner. In April 1993, AC completed a $450 million investment in Houston-based Continental Airlines. Continental had just emerged from Chapter 11 bankruptcy protection (under which it had operated since December 1990). AC's equity interest was equal to 19.6%. Continental was three times AC's size based upon capacity (see Exhibit 2). But their route structures had few points of interconnection; only Houston and Newark.

With the Gemini dispute settled, CA established a strong alliance with American Airlines (AA). AA was the largest domestic U.S. carrier (see Exhibit 2). The link with CA made a strong North American alliance. In 1995, after the ratification of the Canada–U.S. "open skies" agreement, CA and AA integrated their transborder flight schedules and set up extensive code-sharing. However, AA was less dominant internationally. In particular, the Pacific Rim was a weak area. CA's Far East routes offered some help in addressing this shortcoming.

Canada–U.S. Open Skies Treaty

The weakest link in CA's route structure relative to AC was in its limited number of destinations to the U.S. In 1990, CA had only one-third the number of U.S. destinations of AC. By 1995, the disparity was slightly diminished. But what CA really needed was a new air travel agreement between Canada and the U.S. Eventually they got it.

In February 1995 a new "open-skies" agreement was signed. It allowed Canadian carriers immediate access to United States destinations without restrictions on capacity, frequency or aircraft, with the exception of Chicago's O'Hare airport and New York's La Guardia airport, which both had restrictions on takeoff and landing slots. American carriers had similar rights, except their unlimited access to Toronto was postponed for three years, and to Montréal and Vancouver for two years. The deal did not provide for cabotage rights within each country's domestic market (see Appendix A for glossary of terms and Appendix C for further description on U.S. carriers).

Competitive Threat from the Charters

While the country's dominant scheduled carriers, CA and AC, jockeyed for position in the marketplace, other contenders emerged to occupy a significant and expanding position. The growth of domestic charter airlines over the past few years had been substantial. Domestic traffic on charter carriers had swelled from 19 700 passengers in 1989 to almost 789 000 in 1993.[6] Table 3 from Statistics Canada shows how the rising contenders have grown in importance.

---

[5] Boeing Commercial Airline Group, *Current Market Outlook*, May 1994.

[6] Statistics Canada.

TABLE 3   **Charters Increase of Market Share on Key City Pairs**

City Pair	1989	1993
Vancouver–Toronto	5.5%	31.4%
Montréal–Vancouver	3.0%	28.3%

A CA executive shed some further insight on the remarkable growth of the charters:

> Charters' ability to reallocate capacity to suit demand is one reason for their competitive edge. The key factor to their success, however, is their numerous cost advantages—lower ownership costs, lower administration costs, a simplified fleet and lower unit-labour costs [both wages and productivity], to name a few. All of this adds up to an average cost per ASM ranging from four and a half to seven cents, compared to ours at twelve and a half cents.

CA and AC still offered many advantages over chartered carriers, especially for business travellers, who desired frequency, consistency and service and wanted to associate themselves with the scheduled carriers' FFPs. Charters, on the other hand, had minimal service and did not own their own CRSs. Although charters had been limited by their "non-scheduled service" status under regulation, they had since been freed from that constraint. Nevertheless, they chose to keep many features of charter service after the policy change, and continued to provide the lowest priced service. The presence of low-cost domestic charter carriers made it difficult for AC and CA to raise fares and manage capacity.

With the new "open skies" agreement in place, it was possible for CA to increase its exposure to the U.S. Furthermore, CA was strategically better positioned for a future as an international carrier given its foothold on key international routes to the Pacific Rim and Latin America (two of the fastest growing regions in the world) and its alliance with American Airlines (one of the largest carriers in the world). Given its weak financial position, CA still continued to seek ways to increase its customer base and thus raise its load factors and yields (see Appendix A for these and other definitions and Appendix B for a review of industry revenue and cost structure).

PRESENT SITUATION

After several dismal years, both of Canada's airlines announced improving financial performance by early 1995. Each was attempting to reposition itself to build market position, respond to cost pressures, and rehabilitate their balance sheets.

Airline employees and analysts watched the recent developments south of the border closely. Wages for equity swaps, wage reductions and productivity concessions became the norm in the U.S. industry. Wage for equity packages had been granted at United, Northwest, America West, TWA, and most recently, at Southwest, which was already the lowest cost carrier in the U.S. Southwest's pilots agreed to a ten-year contract with no wage increases in years one through five. This effectively "lowered the limbo bar" for all other North American airlines as they went through their cost reduction dance.[7]

AC had improved its financial performance in virtually every financial and operating category and markedly improved its operating statistics (see Exhibit 3). Compared with other major airlines, AC had the most modern and efficient fleet of airplanes in the world.[8] Notwithstanding this positive news, Hollis Harris warned:

---

[7] Tony Hine, Scotia McLeod Inc., *Transportation and Environment Services Outlook*, December 8, 1994.

[8] Tony Hine, Scotia McLeod Inc., *Globe and Mail*, June 10, 1994.

If AC is to survive as an independent entity, and not become a branch plant of a foreign airline, growth must be our destiny—not unbridled or unfocussed growth, but sustainable growth which enhances the security of all AC stakeholders. Despite AC's return to profitability last year [1994] at near record levels, I challenge the notion that we have accomplished our mission.[9]

Senior management at AC declared that the purpose for their $500 million equity issue in the spring of 1995 was: (1) to open new international routes to Hong Kong, Madrid and Israel, (2) to buy new aircraft, (3) to improve airport facilities, and (4) for general corporate purposes. CA was still smaller than its main adversary but somewhat leaner (lower unit costs, see Exhibit 4 for a comparative graph on revenue and cost management). Although CA and its employees had already suffered through numerous challenges and concessions in the last few years, senior management understood that the recent AMR Corp. capital infusion was for debt refinancing and not any new strategic developments. The airline also recognized that its domestic operations were still not as profitable as its international routes. In order of operating income per ASM, the regions of Japan and South East Asia made the most profit for CA, while flights to Continental Europe, Northern Canada and within the Eastern Triangle (Toronto, Montréal, Ottawa) were still struggling.

Fundamental change was required if the company was going to survive in the future. Since the unionized employees had recently become partial owners, it was only logical that they should also help decide the fate of their airline (see Table 4 for a company profile). This resulted in the forming of a new joint labour–management committee to decide upon CA's new strategic options and direction.

T A B L E 4 CA Employee Profile

Period	February 1988 (Post PWA/CP Air Merger)	December 1989 (Post Wardair Acquisition)	March 1995 (Pre SPSC Target Date)
Union members	10 525	12 375	12 060
Non-union employees	2 712	2 671	2 179
Total	13 237	15 046	14 239

Strategic Planning Steering Committee (SPSC)

Senior management realized that if any solutions were to be found by the SPSC, they would have to involve all of the key stakeholders of the airline, including the union members who had steadily been investing in the company since late 1992. The role of the SPSC was to join labour and management together to help reduce costs, improve productivity, expand customer loyalty, and establish a viable future for the airline. This new joint endeavour began a process of fundamentally rewriting the rules of traditional labour-management relations. All unions participated with the exception of CUPE (the union representing the flight attendants), which had declined the invitation to get involved until their contract was renegotiated in December 1995. CUPE's absence, although noticeable, did not inhibit the SPSC's progress.

The process was totally "open book," with management and labour sharing all of the operational and financial information about the airline. The urgency of CA's financial requirements was driving the SPSC's agenda. Information sharing between unions and management did not have an impeccable history. Union members had often felt that management figures were not truly reflective of the operations. However,

---

[9] Air Canada 1994 *Annual Report.*

communications in this particular process showed much improvement because management's view of the dire financial situation was reiterated by two external parties. First, the pilot's union had an opportunity to audit the figures themselves and they agreed with management's view of the unstable financials. In addition, the Boston Consulting Group came in and reviewed the organization's position with the parties concerned and again reiterated CA's precarious situation. Exhibit 5 is a copy of the letter sent to all employees of CA identifying the target date of June 30, 1995, and detailing the two broad alternatives that the SPSC believed the airline faced, namely Plan A and Plan B.

Plan A: A Blueprint for Growth

Plan A entailed achieving and using a lower cost-base to increase market share in key domestic markets, especially transcontinental routes. The airline would pursue growth only on its more profitable international, transcontinental and transborder routes, while maintaining scope and improving the profitability of selected centres in its domestic system.

This plan would allow CA to achieve financial strength and generate enough cash to finance growth (to new Pacific Rim and U.S. destinations), revitalize the fleet (to meet Stage 3 noise requirements), ward off any competitors (to compete successfully with AC and the charters), and sustain any economic recession anticipated in the late 1990s. Plan A also offered the employment stability that could only be provided by working for a financially healthy company.

The SPSC believed that the long-term impact of Plan A would be to increase revenue and capacity dramatically. Schedules would be improved to offer greater frequency to the most popular destinations. Reducing costs per ASM would improve the competitive position of CA against AC and low-cost carriers, such as Canada 3000, Royal Air and Air Transat. Further, the SPSC also hoped that this particular plan would allow for broadened employee involvement in all aspects of the decision-making process for the future.

As a prototype for Plan A, the 1995 Summer Initiative Program was proposed on the basis that a growth strategy founded on higher productivity and greater revenues could succeed. The $27 million in performance improvements identified by the program would permit the addition of three widebody aircraft—and 12% capacity—to key domestic routes. As the early summer results accumulated, however, speculation mounted as to whether the $27 million in projected contribution would be fully realized since traffic gains had been hard to come by.

One difficulty with Plan A was that in order to get the required $325 million in savings for the airline, over $125 million in concessions from the union members would have to be realized. These concessions were to be primarily in the form of productivity improvements; significant wage cuts and layoffs were not part of the plan. Employees at CA had been quite cooperative in the past, but were pessimistic about the future given that they perceived the AMR deal had not saved them as was envisioned. The tumultuous past of CA had left many employees sceptical and had strained management–union relations. If Plan A were to work, a whole new corporate-wide attitude in strategic renewal would have to take place.

Plan B: A Pattern for Reduction

The objective of Plan B was to downsize and restructure the airline. The result would be an airline that was eventually a fraction of CA's current size. The plan required exiting all unprofitable routes and routes that were not essential to support the international network. The non-core routes would be transferred to Canadian Regional and those that could not be transferred would be abandoned. Commercial alliances would be established with regional carriers to maintain domestic feed and support for Canadian Airline's FFP. In addition, all transborder routes (U.S.–Canada) would be flown largely by AA under code sharing with CA.

The SPSC envisioned a code-sharing agreement with American Airlines in order to feed CA's international and remaining domestic network. By streamlining the domestic network, CA hoped that the domestic fleet could be simplified to one wide-body aircraft type in order to maximize fleet utilization. The rest of the non-core airline components would be sold off to generate short-term cash flow.

Under this scenario, massive layoffs would affect all areas of operation. The majority of the 737 fleet would be eliminated and all heavy maintenance would be contracted out. The difficulty with Plan B was the risk of losing security on domestic feed for CA's international flights. Also, the selling-off of unwanted equipment and space might involve significant write-offs.

Besides the two publicized alternatives that had been voiced by the SPSC, there was always the possibility of following a hybrid plan. CA could very well start with Plan A and eventually resort back to Plan B. This was considered a "stall tactic." In other words, the airline would continue with business as usual—except for a 14% lower cost base—and move later (maybe in 12 months) to drastically restructure. Conversely, if CA were to follow Plan B and become a smaller and more efficient operator, it may eventually want to grow from that position and attempt to increase its feed by further developing and expanding its route structure.

White Water at Canadian Airlines

The future of CA would entail as much "turbulence" as had been traversed in the past. For CA, the stakes were high because the carrier had said that within five years it would be the leader in all the markets in which it served.[10]

CA's Board of Directors had targeted June 30, 1995, to reach a new agreement with its unions. This mammoth task involved an unprecedented team effort among management, consultants and unions. The education campaign associated with these negotiations had created confusing and largely negative press coverage which, in turn, hurt CA's stock price on the market.

In the minds of many of those associated with CA, especially the exasperated union members, were the thoughts, "Is this just another restructuring task disguised as a management gimmick, or could this truly be the end of my job as I know it?"

Senior management was now preparing a recommendation for their Board on how to proceed in the immediate period ahead.

---

[10] PWA Corporation (Canadian Airlines) 1994 *Annual Report*.

EXHIBIT 1 Genealogy of Major Canadian Air Carriers

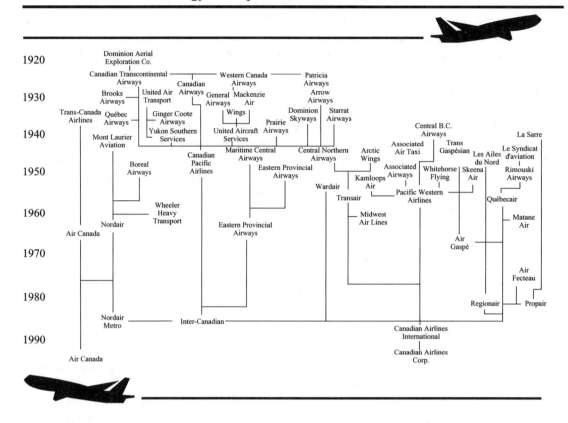

Industry Structure Before Deregulation (1983)—Three Tiered Levels

Level I—national carriers	Air Canada, CP Air
Level II—regional carriers	Eastern Provincial Airways, Nordair, Pacific Western Airlines, Québecair
Level III—commuters and charters	Air BC, Air Ontario, First Air, Northwest Territories Airways, Time Air, Air Maritime, Norcanair, Regionair, Austin Airways, Wardair

Industry Structure After Deregulation (1989)—An Emerging Duopoly

Group I	*Group II*
Air Canada	Canadian Airlines
Air Nova, Air Alliance, Air Ontario, Air Toronto,	Ontario Express, Air Atlantic, Wardair,
NWT Air, Air BC, First Air, City Express	Calm Air, Time Air, Nationair, Worldways, Crown Air

Source: Casewriter's illustration and analysis (data taken from industry reports).

EXHIBIT 2   Comparative of Key Operating Statistics for Selected Airlines

(Calendar Year 1993)

Rank	Airline	Revenue	Airline	Expenses	Airline	Income	Airline	Margin
1	AA	14 737	AA	14 173	AA	564	SI	14.7%
2	UA	14 354	UA	14 059	SI	548	KO	11.5%
3	LU	9 540	LU	9 786	KO	384	AA	3.8%
4	CO	5 775	CO	5 793	UA	295	AC	2.1%
5	AL	4 349	AL	4 406	AC	58	UA	2.1%
6	SI	3 737	SI	3 189	CO	–18	CO	–0.3%
7	KO	3 342	KO	2 958	CA	–48	AL	–1.3%
8	AC	2 699	AC	2 641	AL	–57	CA	–2.3%
9	CA	2 066	CA	2 114	LU	–246	LU	–2.6%

Rank	Airline	RPK	Airline	ASK	Airline	Load	Airline	Y/RPK
1	UA	162 527	AA	258 805	SI	71.5%	LU	18.1¢
2	AA	156 302	UA	242 052	CA	68.3%	AL	15.3¢
3	CO	68 114	CO	107 843	UA	67.1%	AC	13.2¢
4	LU	52 658	U	79 727	KO	67.1%	KO	13.1¢
5	SI	41 265	SI	57 738	LU	66.0%	CA	10.4¢
6	AL	28 377	AL	43 337	AL	65.5%	AA	9.4¢
7	KO	25 588	KO	38 125	AC	64.3%	SI	9.1¢
8	AC	20 491	AC	31 891	CO	63.2%	UA	8.8¢
9	CA	19 935	CA	29 171	AA	60.4%	CO	8.5¢

Rank	Airline	Y/ASK	Airline	C/RPK	Airline	C/ASK	Airline	p/ASK
1	LU	12.0¢	SI	7.7¢	CO	5.4¢	KO	1.01¢
2	AL	10.0¢	CO	8.5¢	AA	5.5¢	SI	0.95¢
3	KO	8.8¢	UA	8.7¢	SI	5.5¢	AA	0.22¢
4	AC	8.5¢	AA	9.1¢	UA	5.8¢	AC	0.18¢
5	CA	7.1¢	CA	10.6¢	CA	7.2¢	UA	0.12¢
6	SI	6.5¢	KO	11.6¢	KO	7.8¢	CO	–0.02¢
7	UA	5.9¢	AC	12.9¢	AC	8.3¢	AL	–0.13¢
8	AA	5.7¢	AL	15.5¢	AL	10.2¢	CA	–0.16¢
9	CO	5.4¢	LU	18.6¢	LU	12.3¢	LU	–0.31¢

Note: Currency figures in US$; statistics include both international and domestic travel.

AA	American Airlines	Revenue	Operating Revenue (US$ millions)	Load	Passenger load factor (%)
UA	United Airlines	Expenses	Operating Expenses (US$ millions)	Y/RPK	Revenue Yield per RPK (¢)
LU	Lufthansa	Income	Operating Income (US$ millions)	Y/ASK	Revenue Yield per ASK (¢)
CO	Continental Airlines	Margin	Income divided by Revenue (%)	C/RPK	Operating Expense per RPK (¢)
AL	Alitalia	RPK	Revenue passenger kilometres (millions)	C/ASK	Operating Expense per ASK (¢)
SI	Singapore Airlines	ASK	Available seat kilometres (millions)	p/ASK	Income divided by ASK (¢)
KO	Korean Air Lines			
AC	Air Canada			
CA	Canadian Airlines			

Source: Casewriter's analysis (data taken from IATA World Air Transport Statistics).

EXHIBIT 3 Financial and Operating Results (1985–1994)

Canadian Airlines	1994	1993	1992	1991	1990	1989	1988	1987	1986	1985
Financial results										
Revenue	2 954	2 754	2 709	2 730	2 625	2 668	2 301	1 946	362	361
Expenses	2 883	2 819	2 818	2 843	2 636	2 678	2 223	1 782	336	354
Income	71	–65	–109	–112	–12	–10	78	164	25	6
Net Income	–38	–296	–547	–166	–19	–63	23	21	30	6
Total Assets	2 353	2 265	2 462	2 811	2 964	2 912	2 125	1 989	946	453
S/H's Equity	298	–267	25	570	605	622	495	472	321	290
Financial ratios										
Revenue Growth	7.3%	1.7%	–0.8%	4.0%	–1.6%	15.9%	18.2%	438%	0.3%	8.7%
Margin	2.4%	–2.4%	–4.0%	–4.1%	–0.4%	–0.4%	3.4%	8.4%	6.9%	1.7%
ROE	–123%	deficient	–184%	–28%	–3%	–2%	5%	5%	10%	2%
Operating statistics										
RPM	14.0	13.4	13.3	12.7	13.9	14.7	12.1	10.5	1.7	1.5
ASM	20.1	19.4	19.9	19.8	21.4	21.9	17.7	15.1	2.8	2.6
Load Factor (%)	69.3	69.2	66.9	64.1	64.8	67.3	68.8	69.6	59.9	58.3

Air Canada	1994	1993	1992	1991	1990	1989	1988	1987	1986	1985
Financial results										
Revenue	4 024	3 598	3 501	3 485	3 939	3 650	3 404	3 114	2 872	2 723
Expenses	3 780	3 521	3 646	3 649	3 950	3 547	3 296	3 011	2 759	2 721
Income	244	77	–145	–164	–11	103	108	103	113	2
Net Income	129	–326	–454	–218	–74	149	89	43	37	–15
Total Assets	4 997	5 039	4 810	4 921	4 579	4 121	3 437	3 084	2 923	2 545
S/H's Equity	365	230	316	770	988	1 062	913	590	548	513
Financial ratios										
Revenue Growth	11.8%	2.8%	0.5%	–11%	7.8%	7.2%	9.3%	8.4%	5.5%	9.0%
Operating Margin	6.1%	2.1%	–4.1%	–4.7%	1.3%	2.8%	3.2%	3.3%	3.9%	0.1%
ROE	47%	–238%	–86%	–25%	–7%	15 %	14%	8%	7%	–3%
Operating statistics										
RPM	14.9	13.8	14.4	13.7	16.6	16.3	15.6	14.4	14.4	14.1
ASM	23.7	21.2	21.6	20.0	23.2	23.3	21.8	20.2	21.3	21.7
Load Factor (%)	63.2	65.1	66.5	68.4	71.4	69.7	71.4	71.1	67.7	65.2

Note: Results in C$ million, Operating Statistics include Canadian Airlines International and Air Canada (not consolidated) RPMs and ASMs in billions.

Source: Company Annual Reports.

E X H I B I T   4   **Canadian Airlines versus Air Canada (Revenue and Cost Management)**

Selected Statistics	1994	1993	1992	1991	1990
Canadian Airlines					
Yield per RPM	15.6¢	14.9¢	14.9¢	15.8¢	15.2¢
Yield per ASM	10.8¢	10.3¢	10.0¢	10.1¢	9.8¢
Operating Cost (excl. fuel) per RPM	17.8¢	18.1¢	18.5¢	19.1¢	15.8¢
Fuel Cost per ASM	1.97¢	1.99¢	1.79¢	2.13¢	2.11¢
Air Canada					
Yield per RPM	19.6¢	19.2¢	18.1¢	19.2¢	18.0¢
Yield per ASM	12.4¢	12.5¢	12.0¢	13.1¢	12.8¢
Operating Cost (excl. fuel) per RPM	18.0¢	18.7¢	18.1¢	19.0¢	16.9¢
Fuel Cost per ASM	2.00¢	1.86¢	2.18¢	2.58¢	2.74¢

Note: Selected statistics include Canadian Airlines International and Air Canada (not consolidated).

Source: Casewriter's illustration (data taken from company reports).

EXHIBIT 5   Copy of Letter Sent to All Employees of Canadian Airlines

May 15, 1995

Canadian

Dear Fellow Employee:

The Strategic Planning Steering Committee (SPSC) has had many successes to date. Achievements of this joint strategy process have been excellent. Joint labour and management teams met between January and March and identified $78 million in annualized cost savings and revenue enhancements which will now be built into our growth plan. These improvements will be in all areas of operation. Examples include fuel efficiencies, better weighing and measuring of cargo, and consistently collecting excess baggage charges.

Through a process of negotiations, joint teams of CALDA, CALPA, CAST, CAW and IAM representatives along with management, developed the Summer 1995 Initiative adding three new wide-body aircraft (two DC10s and a B767) to our summer fleet. These negotiations resulted in annualized savings of $27 million in work rules, scheduling and other productivity measures with no additional labour costs.

These successes to date, while substantial, are only the beginning of what we must achieve. We are now at a crossroad and it is time to choose: Plan A or Plan B.

Plan A: The Growth Plan

This plan will result in significant improvements to our profitability and consumer loyalty while building cash to buy new aircraft and renew our fleet. Plan A would allow us to take full advantage of new opportunities in the transborder and international markets. We would be able to add significantly more new aircraft and modernize or replace our B737 fleet to meet Stage 3 noise requirements. To achieve this growth, service new routes and rebuild our cash reserves, we must IMPROVE OUR COST POSITION BY 14% per available seat mile. Based on 1994 costs, this would total $325 million. Even with the savings identified to date, there is still some distance to go in closing the gap.

Performance Improvements	$ 78
1995 Summer Initiative	$ 27
Overhead (unrelated to Union)	$ 29
Amendments to Union Agreements	$125
Remaining gap yet to be allocated	$ 66
Total Required	$325

All of the unions and management in the SPSC process are working together to close the gap. We are stretching to save all monies possible from non-labour costs. Over the next two months, negotiations will also be proceeding using a mutual interest-based process that identifies how the long-term interests of workers are to be safeguarded, while at the same time improving the productivity of the airline.

EXHIBIT 5 (continued)

Plan B: Downsizing

If we are unable to achieve the cost-savings required for growth, the company will be forced to address its unprofitable routes by downsizing and retrenching to its more profitable international flying. Plan B is being developed by the company as an alternative if Plan A fails. Under Plan B, Canadian would exit many cities, and massive layoffs would be anticipated.

The Choice

The SPSC clearly does not support Plan B but recognizes that the STATUS QUO IS UNACCEPTABLE. All of us will be faced with making a choice in the next **six weeks** between Plan A and Plan B. Plan A can mean increased security for our employees and the opportunities for personal and professional development that come with being part of a growing company. However, it will require sacrifices from each of us and these will be equitably distributed. Canadian's employees have proven we are willing to make sacrifices for a healthy and growing airline.

E X H I B I T 6   **Historical Stock Price Trend**

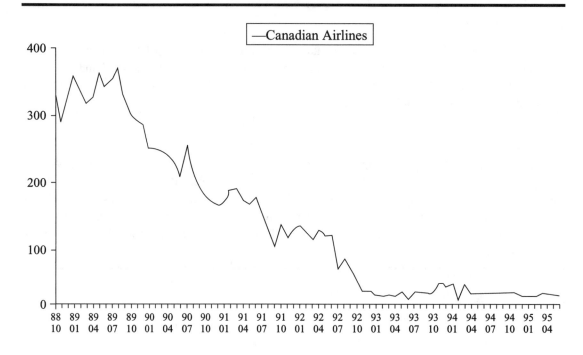

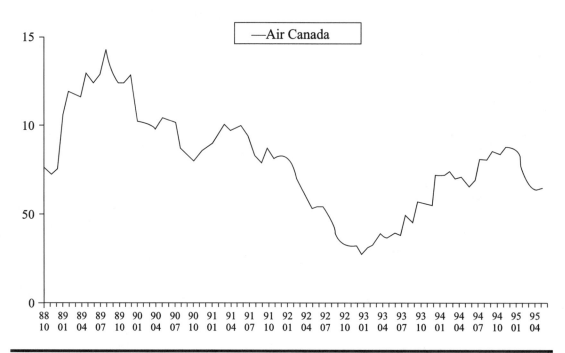

Note: Monthly close stock prices used for illustration.

Source: Casewriter's illustration (data taken from Bloomberg).

APPENDIX A   Glossary of Terms and Abbreviations

ASM

Available seat miles—the number of seats an airline provides times the number of miles they are flown; a measure of airline capacity.

Cabotage

The right of an airline to carry local traffic in a foreign market. As a general rule, cabotage is strictly prohibited. For example, Lufthansa is unable to board passengers originating in Atlanta for Dallas on its Frankfurt-Atlanta-Dallas service.

CRSs

Computerized Reservation Systems began with the American Airlines Sabre System. Originally used to track seat availability, it had expanded to include the booking of other travel services (e.g., car rental, hotels, etc.) and was critical to yield management and airline operations.

FFPs

Frequent flyer programs rewarded passengers with free trips and other benefits based on kilometres flown. First introduced by American Airlines, this marketing innovation favoured large carriers with extensive route systems on which customers could more readily accumulate mileage and select desirable reward destinations. Most larger airlines had initiated their own FFPs.

Load Factor

Revenue passenger miles divided by available seat miles; a measure of aircraft utilization.

RPM

Revenue passenger miles—the number of passengers times the number of miles they fly.

Six Freedoms

Each contracting state in a bilateral air agreement can grant to the other contracting state or states the following Six Freedoms in respect of scheduled international services:

1. The privilege to fly across the territory of another country without landing. For example, Olympic Airways flies from Montreal to Athens over Spain.

2. The privilege to land in another country for technical and other non-traffic purposes. For example, Aeroflot stops for a technical stop (take on fuel and food) in Gander, Newfoundland during its flight from Moscow to Havana.

3. The privilege to put down passengers, mail and cargo in another country. For example, Delta lets passengers off in Lisbon during its New York to Rome flight.

4. The privilege to take on/board passengers, mail and cargo in another country destined for Canada. For example, CA picks up passengers in Zurich and flies them into Calgary.

5. The privilege to take on passengers, mail and cargo in one foreign country for carriage to another foreign country. For example, CA on its Toronto to Frankfurt route can land in Ireland and pick up Irish passengers and carry them to Frankfurt and vice versa.

6. The privilege of carrying traffic between two foreign countries via one's own country. For example, an American passenger can board a CA flight in Los Angeles and go via Vancouver to Ho Chi Minh, Vietnam.

Unit Costs   Operating costs from scheduled operations divided by scheduled available seat miles.

Yield   The revenue per passenger mile an airline receives; it represents an aggregate of all the airfares and airline charges and is measured on a per mile basis.

APPENDIX B   Industry Revenue and Cost Structure

Four basic factors affect airline profitability: (1) the load factor; (2) the yield or ticket revenue; (3) the unit cost of operating the aircraft, and (4) other on-the-ground costs (i.e., ticketing, terminal operations, etc.). Profits can be enhanced by increasing yields and load factors or by lowering costs. Typically, an airline followed one of these three strategies: (1) a greater load factor for a constant revenue yield, (2) higher fares and hence greater revenue yield for a constant load factor, or (3) lower costs while maintaining yield and load factors.

PROFIT DYNAMIC

The operating profits from passenger traffic were determined by a simple relationship:

$$\text{operating profit} = \text{revenue} - \text{costs}$$

but revenue and aircraft costs can be re-stated in unit terms (per kilometre):

$$\text{operating profit} = ((\text{revenue} / \text{RPK} * \text{RPK}) - (\text{costs} / \text{ASK} * \text{ASK}))$$

Revenue / RPK is called yield, or unit revenue (how much the average passenger pays for one kilometre flown). Cost / ASK is called unit costs (the cost of flying an average airline seat (empty or full) one kilometre). So:

$$\text{operating profit} = (\text{yield} * \text{RPK}) - (\text{UC} * \text{ASK})$$

This can be re-stated as:

$$\text{operating profit} = ((\text{yield} * \text{RPK} / \text{ASK}) - \text{UC}) * \text{ASK}$$

Remember that RPK / ASK = Load Factor (LF), therefore:

$$\text{operating profit} = ((\text{yield} * \text{LF}) - \text{UC}) * \text{ASK}$$

Dividing both sides by ASK results in:

$$\text{operating profit} / \text{ASK} = \text{yield} * \text{LF} - \text{UC}$$

In simple terms, operating profit per available seat kilometre flown is equal to yield times load factor minus unit costs. While the basic formula is simple, the factors affecting revenue yields, load factors and units costs are more complex.

REVENUE STRUCTURE

Revenues were the result of the number of passengers flown times the fare, or price paid. About 90% of airline revenue was derived from passengers and 10% from cargo. The price passengers paid for an airline seat differed dramatically. Price varied by class of service, as well as within the same class. Airlines differentiated class of service by segmenting the aircraft cabin. Typically two classes of service were offered both domestically and internationally. AC and CA have economy and business class on all routes. Most American carriers call their products economy and first class.

First and business classes of service provided a separate cabin, larger seats, more personalized service, better food and other amenities. For these enhancements first-class fares were more than double full fare economy and business class carried a 15–30% premium.

Fares also differed dramatically in the economy cabin. Airlines created certain fences, or restrictions such as staying over a Saturday night, minimum stays, advanced booking and payment, penalties for cancellation and itinerary changes, etc. Passengers prepared to meet some or all of these restrictions could save up to 60% off full fare economy. In 1994 discounted fares accounted for 61% of domestic travel. Most of the fences were designed to prevent business travellers, who desired flexibility and convenience, from taking advantage of discounted fares. These fares (and the accompanying restrictions) accommodated the travel needs of the so-called VFR segment (vacationers, friends and relatives).

Share of passengers on any specific route (city pair) were disproportionate to frequency on that route (i.e., 60% of available departures often translated to 70% market share). This is because passengers tend to travel with the carrier that has the most frequent number of flights.

COST STRUCTURE

The airline industry was characterized by a high level of fixed costs. The major operating costs for airlines were wages and fuel. The proportion of operating costs varied substantially between the major carriers. Route structures contributed to some of the discrepancy. Shorter routes, and smaller and older aircraft tended to burn more fuel per available seat mile. However, once route structure and the aircraft type were selected, little could be done to affect fuel efficiency.

Fuel was significantly cheaper in western Canada and most expensive in Atlantic Canada (about a 50% premium), with central Canada costs falling midway between. As a result, because CA concentrated more of its activity in Alberta and British Columbia, it was able to fuel at an average rate cheaper than AC. However, any substantial regional advantage was mitigated by the need to fuel where you flew and by AC's ability to access that fuel as well. On-the-ground costs like airport gate fees, check-in, travel agent commissions, advertising, administration, etc. accounted for slightly less than half of total costs.

YIELD AND COST MANAGEMENT

Actually balancing an optimal pricing and cost strategy was complicated. Load factors could be improved by offering seasonal promotions and discounts, but cutting fares eroded revenue yield. Skillful balancing of this trade-off was vital to airline competitive advantage and profitability. Unit cost reductions were dependent upon increasing productivity of labour and equipment without diminishing passenger service and safety. A large proportion, 82% of airline operating costs were fixed or semi-variable; only 18% were truly variable—travel agency commissions, ticketing fees and meals. Semi-variable costs could be varied only by large and expensive "steps" over the medium- and long-term. The implications were that once an airline determined its route structure (the combination of destinations, frequencies and aircraft) fuel, crew and ground staff costs were largely fixed. Almost the same amount of fuel was used whether a plane flew empty or full; crew size was determined by the type of aircraft, not the passenger load.

The objective of yield management was to optimally balance load factor and yield to maximize operating profit. This task was entrusted to sophisticated computer software that was resident in each airline's CRS. All of the largest airlines had proprietary CRSs to coordinate booking and ticketing activity, yield and cost management, and accounting. Smaller airlines cooperated in joint systems, or licensed another airline's CRS. Sophisticated algorithms forecasted demand and attempted to optimize final load factor and yield.

Typically, Asian carriers had the lowest costs in the industry, followed in increasing order by the U.S., Canadian and European operators. An airline's comparative costs were heavily influenced by its unit and wage costs and by the productivity of its support operations. Exhibit 2 compares key operating statistics among several airlines. Airline executives learned to be cognizant of the sensitivity of these and other important variables. For example, management at CA studied the effects of certain important industry variables and their financial impact on operating income before tax.

Variable	*Financial Impact ($ millions)*
Increase of $1 per barrel of crude oil	$ – 11
Increase in passenger load factor by 1%	$ + 28
Domestic market growth of 1%	$ + 9
Domestic market share increase of 1%	$ + 20
A 1¢ increase in yield per RPK	$ + 185

APPENDIX C   Open Skies and U.S. Carriers

The advent of "open skies" would raise the prospects of increased competition between Canadian and U.S. airlines. In the short run, this competitive rivalry would be moderated by the current alliances in place (Canadian Airlines–American Airlines and Air Canada–Continental Airlines). However, in the long run, Canadian Airlines and Air Canada would feel strong pressure to establish links with one of the global airline consortiums. The following list describes the major U.S. carriers in the airline industry. The ultimate threat to Air Canada and Canadian Airlines will be when these carriers start demanding cabotage rights into Canada.

- American Airlines:
  largest carrier in the world (revenue and capacity)
  primary hubs include Dallas/Fort Worth and Chicago
  strong base of North Atlantic service

- United Airlines:
  largest carrier in the world (RPKs—revenue passenger kilometres)
  primary hubs include Chicago and Denver
  number one U.S. carrier in the Pacific market

- Delta Airlines:
  member of global consortium with Swissair and Singapore Airlines
  primary hubs include Atlanta and Cincinnati
  has conservative management with good operating record

- Northwest:
  member of global consortium with KLM
  primary hubs include Minneapolis/St. Paul and Detroit
  biggest U.S. challenger in the Pacific

- USAir:
  alliance with British Airways
  primary hubs include Pittsburgh and Washington
  focuses on domestic medium-haul traffic

- Southwest:
  considered the industry renegade
  lowest unit costs in the U.S. industry
  concentrates on specific city pairs.

case

6

FIRST BANK DIRECT

Joseph N. Fry

Late in August 1996, senior management of the Bank of Montreal (the Bank, BMO) were reviewing the development of the Bank's direct banking services and, specifically, plans for the pilot launch of a comprehensive direct banking venture in Calgary in mid-October under the name of First Bank Direct. An air of urgency had been added to the discussions by recent announcements from Vancouver City Savings, a relatively small but progressive credit union, and ING, the giant Dutch insurance group, that they were

IVEY

Joseph N. Fry prepared this case solely to provide material for class discussion. The author does not intend to illustrate either effective or ineffective handling of a managerial situation. The author may have disguised certain names and other identifying information to protect confidentiality.

each preparing to launch "virtual banking" concepts, and by rumours that the Royal Bank, another of Canada's large financial institutions, was considering a similar move.

THE BANK OF MONTREAL

The Bank of Montreal group of companies ranked third (as measured by total assets) in 1995 among Canadian chartered banks and ninth in scale among North American banks. The Bank was unique among Canadian banks in the extent of its involvement in the United States, through its Harris Bank operating unit, and in Mexico, through a 20 per cent stake in Bancomer, a large Mexican bank. In the fiscal year 1995, the Bank marked its sixth consecutive year of earnings growth and of return on equity above 14 per cent. The fiscal year 1996 promised to be a banner year for the Bank and for its Canadian competitors as well. There were expectations that the earnings of a number of banks, including BMO, would, for the first time, exceed $1 billion.

The Changing Environment of Banking

In spite of the record earnings there was a distinct sense of concern among senior management in the Bank, and throughout the industry for that matter, that the current prosperity of the industry was masking basic changes in the banking environment and slowing the pace of adaption to new realities. This view was reflected, for example, in an address by Matthew Barrett, CEO of the Bank, to bank executives in June 1996, in which he highlighted six drivers of change: globalization; the democratization of information; demographic patterns; alienation; the new workplace; and the restructuring of the financial services industry. Excerpts are presented below:

GLOBALIZATION

...The financial services industry... (has been)... in many, although not all, ways the leader in economic globalization. Major banks are competing at home and abroad with rivals whose competitive advantages are hard to match. They are fighting back by investing heavily in technology, by upgrading their human resources, by adopting sophisticated techniques for the management of risk, and by seeking economies of scale and a global presence through mergers, acquisitions and alliances. Often they are trying to do all these things at once. Not all will succeed.

DEMOCRATIZATION OF INFORMATION

...Far more information is more readily accessible to far more people than ever before. Few, if any, sectors are more affected by this revolution than the financial services industry. It is not simply that banks have become utterly dependent on vast computer and communications networks. Information technology has brought a massive shift in power to the customer and thereby made banking far more competitive and responsive.

A dynamic spiral has been set in motion whereby new technology creates new products and new standards of service; customers welcome these, quickly take them for granted, and demand the next wave of greater convenience and choice. Perhaps more important, abundant information is eroding the bankers' traditional arbitrage that sprang from superior knowledge of the available means and opportunities for lending and investing money. To keep ahead or even abreast of their customers' rising expectations and complex demands, banks are being forced to train staff to far higher levels of expertise than ever before. Paradoxically, while information technology is eliminating many traditional human careers in banking, it is greatly increasing the value of others. It follows that banks that fail to invest in people will not be with us long.

DEMOGRAPHICS

...Shifting (demographic) patterns are...reinforcing the effects on financial institutions of the democratization of information. In the short and medium term they are moving banks from an emphasis on lending products to one on savings products, and from transaction-based customer relationships to more complex partnerships. Products and services are being re-designed to meet the higher expectations of a more educated, experienced and diverse customer base.... In the longer term, banks will evolve into essentially professional institutions, whose core product is advice, backed up by access to capital, processing capability, and skill at marshalling and analyzing information...

ALIENATION

Sweeping...(social and economic)...discontinuities have left many people in North America and around the world increasingly alienated from their social and political institutions, or even actively hostile to them.... Such a mood will breed protest movements, internal withdrawal and attempts to return to a real or imaginary past when life was simpler.... Since banks are among the most conspicuous institutions in any modern society, they are prime targets and can expect rather more than their fair share of public resentment. Given the degree to which banks everywhere are subject to regulation, this is grounds for serious concern, and nowhere more so than in Canada. Banks are among the few institutions present in every part of this country and a tenacious Canadian myth paints them as a protected and monopolistic cartel.

THE NEW WORKPLACE

... For those awake to (trends in the workplace)...a secure career is more and more perceived to flow from constant investment in oneself.... A lifetime may see service with many different employers, but the true employers will always be the employees themselves. Increasingly the employees are entrepreneurs, in partnership with a larger entrepreneur who supplies the framework for their skills.

The implications for large commercial banks are potentially nothing less than earth-shattering. They have tended to be textbook models of the traditional corporation: strongly hierarchical, bureaucratic, rule-based and driven from the top down. The real and continuing need for stability, prudence and customer confidence has legitimized the hierarchy, and indeed tends to validate all established procedures simply because they have stood the test of time thus far.... Adopting the new model of the workplace, while retaining the old model's advantages of continuity and employee loyalty, will amount to a revolution in banking...

RESTRUCTURING

All these trends together are bringing about a sweeping restructuring of the world's financial services industry...and all the more rapidly because many developed country markets suffer from overcapacity in traditional distribution channels.

Canada, in particular, is over-banked. We have too many major banks, so that none of them is large enough to compete globally. They, in turn, have too many branches, which saddle them with high distribution costs. This situation is aggravated by the rapid growth of alternate, low-cost, convenient distribution channels such as ABMs, telephone banking and soon the Internet, too. So-called niche players—specialized, focused non-banks—are capturing an increasing share of their chosen markets, while political pressures prevent the banks using their costly branch networks to compete effectively. Those same pressures will delay a major restructuring of the Canadian industry, but no serious observer doubts that it will come sooner or later. Some branches will close, others will be transformed as new distribution channels grow in importance. Expect to see major mergers between Canadian banks, or yes, even between Canadian and U.S. banks. We are living in the last years of the Big Five, and of the street corner with up to five different bank branches competing head to head.

Notes on Technology

New technologies were creating new channels of distribution for the handling of traditional banking transactions. These technologies offered dramatically lower costs. According to McKinsey consultants: "It is roughly 40 to 50 per cent cheaper to process a cash withdrawal at an ATM than at a branch teller window, up to 90 per cent cheaper to deal with an electronic payment, and 70 per cent cheaper to employ an automated telephone response unit."[1] A further illustration of the economics of typical transactions is given in Table 1.

TABLE 1 Example Transaction Costs by Channel

Transaction Type	Channel	Cost Per Transaction ($)
Withdrawals	Branch	2.00
	ABM (Bank-Owned)	.40
	Other ABM	.75
Deposits	Branch	2.00
	ABM	2.00
Bill Payments	Branch	2.00
	Telebanking—Agent	1.25
	Telebanking —AVR*	.40
	ABM	.40
	Direct Debit	.04
	PC	.04
Account Transfers	Branch	2.00
	Telebanking —Agent	1.25
	Telebanking —AVR	.40
	ABM	.04
	PC	.04

* AVR: Automatic Voice Response

Source: Bank of Montreal, Industry Sources.

The new technologies, in tandem with relaxed legislation and more knowledgeable customers, were also facilitating the entry of new competitors into traditional bank markets. For example, in the U.S., "four main product areas—mortgages, savings, personal loans and credit and life insurance—account for almost 65 per cent of total industry profitability. A number of companies focusing on these areas have recently emerged, notably Countrywide in mortgages, AT&T, GM, Ford, and many others in credit cards, and mutual fund companies such as Vanguard specializing in high return money market funds in deposits."[2]

A good example of parallel developments in Canada was in mutual funds. According to CIBC Wood Gundy Securities: "… investors dissatisfied with low interest rates have flocked into mutual funds in force, applying pressure on banks to sweeten the rates offered to clients…since 1992, Canadian bank deposits have increased by 38 per cent while mutual fund assets under management have jumped 160 per cent.

---

[1] Lenny Mendonca and Gordon D. McCallum, "Battling for the Wallet," *The McKinsey Quarterly*, Number 2, 1995, p. 76–92.

[2] Mendonca and McCallum, "Battling for the Wallet," p. 80.

Mutual fund assets in Canada represent approximately half the amount of bank deposits, while in the U.S. they are equal to bank deposits. Consequently, we believe that the mutual fund growth will continue."[3] And to pursue this potential, mutual fund companies were moving to offer bank-like services, such as cheque-writing privileges on money market accounts, and in the case of Trimark Mutual Fund's purchase of Bayshore Trust, integrating forward into the ownership of trust companies.

But there was even more to the new technology. It also offered unique opportunities for capturing customer information, storing and assembling it, and "mining" it to create new and specifically targeted marketing strategies. This was not yet common. According to McKinsey: "Few providers have yet developed a significant sales capability through these channels, especially for complex products, but things are likely to change rapidly in the next decade with growing acceptance of electronic and remote channels among younger consumers."[4] There was little question, however, that sophisticated marketing, based on sophisticated customer data bases, was just around the corner.

THE BANK'S BUSINESSES

The Bank managed its operations through four operating groups, each with its own distinct market, product and geographic mandate. These units were the:

1. Personal and Commercial Financial Services group (PCFS), which provided financial services to individuals and commercial businesses in the Canadian market.
2. Corporate and Institutional Financial Services (CIFS), which provided financing, treasury and operating services to large corporate and institutional customers throughout North America and selectively abroad.
3. Harris Bank (HB), which provided banking, trust and investment services to individuals, as well as small and mid-market businesses in the Chicago area; corporate banking services throughout the Midwest United States; and trust, cash management, investment management and private banking card services throughout the United States.
4. Investment Banking (IB) included Canada's largest investment dealer, Nesbitt Burns, and offered full-service brokerage, mutual funds, investment management, discount brokerage and various planning and advisory services to corporate, government, institutional and private clients in Canada and the United States and selectively in other markets.

The operating groups were provided with technology, transaction processing and professional services by two support groups—Operations and Corporate Services. The relative scale and contribution of the operating groups to the Bank as a whole are summarized in Table 2.

T A B L E 2   1995 Net Income and Average Assets by Operating Group

($ millions)	*PCFS*	*CIFS*	*HARRIS*	*IB*	*OTHER*	*TOTAL*
Net Income	571	301	213	55	(198)	986
Average Assets	54 493	42 514	22 229	22 068	2 811	144 115

Source: Bank of Montreal *Annual Report*, 1995.

---

[3] CIBC Wood Gundy, "The Canadian Chartered Banks," August 23, 1996.

[4] Mendonca and McCallum, "Battling for the Wallet," p. 85.

PCFS

PCFS was the Bank's traditional core business, and notwithstanding significant diversification moves by the Bank in the past 15 years, still its largest operating group. It was this group that, arguably, had been facing and would continue to face the brunt of changes in the industry environment.

PCFS had been responding to these changes with a wide range of initiatives. It had adopted a community banking structure under which bank executives in 230 communities across Canada were given the authority to make significant decisions to meet the unique needs of each local community. It had invested in new technology, including the expansion of its ABM network and telephone service channels, the development and initial introduction of Pathway, a software product that put a range of information about the Bank's products at the fingertips of sales representatives, and extensive employee training. These kinds of investments had helped PCFS to improve its revenues, earnings and productivity (Table 3), to maintain its position with respect to facilities (Table 4), and to improve its market share (Table 5).

Bank executives took some satisfaction in these results. But there was also a sense that they were achieved by doing the same things better rather than transforming the thrust of the Bank. As Ron Rogers, vice-chairman and head of PCFS put it: "Even if we continue to run full out, even if we stick with the strategies that made us the success we are today, we are not going to increase our rate of growth. We flatline— and that is a danger sign flashing bright red." Tony Comper, president and chief operating officer, spoke about the Bank as a whole: "We can't do the job by 'keeping on keeping on' and hoping that our competitors won't rise to the challenge either."

The task set by senior management for PCFS, and for the Bank generally, was one of reinvention and reinvention in a hurry. As Tony Comper put it: "We must reinvent our relationship with customers. Which means we must reinvent our relationships with the employees we count on to create and nurture our relationships with customers. Both of which require us to reinvent our business processes and tools—in other words, the way we do business…(and to change fast we must)…become very adept at continuously reshaping our corporate structure…(at making)…fundamental and ongoing realignments to increase sales origination and efficiency. In some cases we need to reorganize by line of business rather than geography, which is the only way to operate efficiently from an enterprise-wide perspective. Right now, for example, we provide cash management services through CIFS and Harris Bank. We need to integrate them. And the same can be said for our credit, debit, and smart card lines of business." Matthew Barrett added a note of impatience: "We have a beaver on top of our coat of arms, but in many ways a tortoise would be far more appropriate."

DIRECT BANKING

Direct banking, virtual banking, branchless banking, multimedia banking, whatever the term, referred to a wholly new form of banking created by clustering previously separate technical developments. Its features were described by McKinsey consultants as follows:

> A multimedia bank looks nothing like a traditional financial institution. It need have neither branches nor tellers…it gives customers easy access to a wide variety of financial services—credit cards, bill payment, insurance, investments, and brokerage—in a single integrated account. It offers products from many different providers: a bond fund from Fidelity, a credit card from Visa, a mortgage from Countrywide.
>
> Consumers communicate with the multimedia bank through a range of devices including phones, PCs, faxes and ATMs. All the information on their accounts is automatically downloaded and updated in real time as the transactions take place.

TABLE 3   BMO PCFS Financial Record

($ millions except as noted)

As at or for the year ended October 31	1996 (E)	1995	1994	1993	1992
Net interest income	2 281	2 234	2 139	1 914	1 881
Other income	640	608	581	578	529
Provision for credit losses	123	88	108	140	144
Non-interest expense	1 736	1 752	1 666	1 552	1 534
Income before taxes	1 062	1 002	946	800	732
Income taxes	452	431	416	344	308
Net income	610	571	530	456	424
Average assets	57 870	54 539	50 892	49 277	46 412
Average current loans	52 764	49 380	45 050	42 770	39 231
Average deposits	53 159	50 723	47 893	46 492	44 040
Full-time equivalent staff (number)	15 782	16 363	17 233	17 162	17 165
Expense-to-revenue ratio (%)	59.4	61.6	61.2	62.3	63.7

Source: BMO Annual Reports, Internal Files.

TABLE 4   BMO PCFS: Selected Facilities Comparisons

	BMO		Royal		CIBC		TD		BNS		NA	
	1992	1996	1992	1996	1992	1996	1992	1996	1992	1996	1992	1996
Branches*	1 176	1 148	1 471	1 262	1 464	1 352	895	910	1 081	1 137	643	614
ABMs**	1 293	2 017	3 828	4 215	2 596	3 032	1 663	1 991	1 190	1 526	482	713

* Excludes: Corporate/Independent Business Centres/Student Loan Centres/Private Banking, etc. (e.g., Royal Trust's 99 branches are excluded).
** ABMs: Automated Banking Machines

Source: Bank Annual Reports, BMO Internal Files.

TABLE 5   BMO PCFS: Market Share by Selected Business LINRS

	Bank Market* (%)	
Product/Service	1992	1996
Total Personal Deposits	13.9	14.4
Personal Loans	14.3	15.0
Residential Mortgages	12.9	14.4
Small Business Loans	14.0	16.0

* Bank Market includes credit unions and trust companies.

Source: BMO Annual Reports, Internal Documents.

The advantages over conventional banking are numerous. Clearly, multimedia banking offers customers real convenience. It also gives financial institutions the opportunity to use information residing in the new integrated accounts to carry out highly tailored marketing. But the most compelling—and least understood—advantage derives from cost.

The multimedia bank…(avoids)…both the expense of branches and, in the long run, the processing costs associated with paper transactions. By carefully targeting its customers and service offerings, a phone-based direct bank can secure a 30 percentage point cost advantage over traditional banks, thus redefining cost-effectiveness for the entire industry. (Table 6)

T A B L E 6   Traditional Retail vs. Multimedia: Comparative Business Models

Expense Category	Expense/Revenue (%)	
	Large Retail	*Multimedia*
Salaries	25	9
Rent	11	2
Transaction Related	10	8
Systems/Communication	4	5
Marketing/Advertising	3	4
Other	12	5
Total	65	33

Source: John H. Ott, Jack M. Stephenson, Paul K. Weberg, "Banking on Multimedia", *The McKinsey Quarterly*, 1995, Number 2, p. 97.

The savings come from three sources:

- A smaller, leaner staff with a greater focus on marketing. To serve a customer base of one million, a multimedia bank will have a total headcount of 2 000 compared with approximately 3 000 to 3 500 for a traditional bank. Despite paying higher wages to its more skilled employees, the multimedia bank will have a total salary bill less than half that of its conventional rival.
- Occupancy costs that are 80 per cent lower than for a traditional institution. The multimedia bank will have centralized customer service and processing centers located in low rent areas, in direct contrast to the geographically dispersed retail bank operating a high cost branch network largely in urban areas.
- Lower transaction processing costs, due to the lower volume of cash, cheques, and personal transactions. As technology continues to develop, the economic advantage of the multimedia bank will grow. With the introduction of electronic cash, processing costs should decline even further.

Through its emphasis on electronic payment, the multimedia bank will also acquire many opportunities to capitalize on information…(enabling)…highly customized marketing approaches and a flurry of new product innovation…finally, the multimedia bank will reduce transaction times and expand the number of consumer access options available 24 hours a day.[5]

---

[5] Brian A. Johnson, John H. Ott, Jack M. Stephenson, and Paul K. Weberg, "Banking on Multimedia," *The McKinsey Quarterly*, Number 2, 1995, p. 94–106.

Experience with Direct Banking

The traditional banks had adopted two modes of entry for introducing direct banking services, commonly referred to as complementary direct banking and standalone direct banking.

COMPLEMENTARY DIRECT BANKING

Under complementary direct banking, traditional banks offered "extended telephone service and ATM access and mimicked many of the attributes of direct banks, but positioned…(these services)…under the core brand of the parent bank as a supplement to the branch system. Often, …(these services)…are priced at premiums to branch-based transactions, creating incentives curiously at odds with the underlying economics."[6]

Complementary direct banking was the dominant practice in the industry in North America and in Europe. The banks were clearly fearful of the consequences of a standalone approach for their traditional systems and had chosen what McKinsey called a "wait and see" response. Under this approach banks "take marginal costs out of the branch system while focusing the bulk of marketing and other activities on supporting the branches…and they make ad hoc investments in new distribution systems like phones or PCS, and participate in industry alliances and consortia without taking a clear leadership role."[7]

McKinsey goes on to note that the "wait and see" approach seems "at first sight conservative…(but)…actually is far more costly than it seems. It actually layers on additional costs as channels multiply and the cost of complexity rises…(and)…it overlooks the cost-reduction and skill-building programs that are required to compete in the new environment…(and it risks)…lockout as key alliances are formed and the industry consolidates."[8]

A further limiting consequence of layering in new direct bank channels was that it typically failed to realize the potential for consolidating customer information. Most banks had built their formidable information systems to facilitate transactions and capture revenues and costs by products, services, branches and other organizational entities, but not by customer. The reality of millions of customers, multiple product and organizational entities and complex systems constituted an enormous barrier to reworking the systems to track and assemble information by customer. But this was quite feasible from a fresh start if the direct banking services were handled on a standalone basis.

STANDALONE DIRECT BANKING

Standalone direct banks sought to build a separate entity—internally, in terms of organization, and externally in terms of independent services and brand identity. Several European banks had moved in this direction and it also tended to be favoured by U.S. banks for expansion outside their established territory. Wells-Fargo was using a standalone concept, for example, to reach out to small and medium business accounts outside their branch coverage in the U.S. and was attempting to secure approval to move into Canada.

There appeared to be a tremendous opportunity with standalone banking to pick off and target specific customer segments and to try to capture their business across a wide range of traditional banking services. There was a rule of thumb in the industry, for example, that about 20 per cent of retail customers accounted for 120 to 140 per cent of retail profitability. These customers were an obvious target for new standalone entries.

---

[6] Johnson et al, "Banking on Multimedia," p. 100.

[7] Johnson et al, "Banking on Multimedia," p. 100.

[8] Johnson et al, "Banking on Multimedia," p. 98.

Midland's First Direct[9]

Perhaps the most successful example of standalone banking was in the United Kingdom—Midland Bank's First Direct.[10] First Direct was launched in October 1989. At the time, telephone banking was largely untested and a completely new idea to the public at large. Midland proceeded on the premise that a viable alternative to branch banking had to put the customer first and that this would require an autonomous banking service with its own systems, culture and operating philosophy. It set a young development team to work on what would become an independent person-to-person banking service available over the phone, 24 hours a day, seven days a week, 365 days a year.

First Direct engaged in very heavy introductory promotion, with a television budget alone estimated at £6 million. By the end of its first year it had enlisted over 60 000 customers. By 1994 First Direct broke even with approximately 450 000 customers, and in 1995 announced its first full year of profitability with over 500 000 customers and a growth rate of over 10 000 customers per month.

By 1996 First Direct employed about 2 000 full-time equivalent workers and offered checking accounts, credit cards, savings products, mortgages, personal loans, brokerage, travel and insurance services. Customer satisfaction was high; 87 per cent of First Direct customers were extremely/very satisfied with their service compared with an average of 51 per cent for high street banks. Customers split roughly evenly between male and female, were predominantly in the age range of 25–44 and from the higher socioeconomic categories. In common, these customers reported that they valued speed and efficiency *and* human contact and interaction. Among new customers, about 73 per cent came from Midland's competition and 41 per cent reported that word-of-mouth was critical to their decision.

First Direct handled about 26 000 telephone calls a day with an average duration of three minutes. To support this requirement First Direct operated a dedicated call center with some 330 miles of cabling in a totally flexible, open plan environment, purposely built to adapt to new technology. Banking representatives (BR) each worked with a Davox intelligent terminal which allowed them to access several systems simultaneously, providing a total picture of the caller's personal details, business with the bank and previous transactions. By 1992, First Direct was working to develop special software that would build customer profiles identifying characteristics such as price, service and time sensitivity and even to forecast the next major product purchase that the customer was going to make.

Five years after the launch of First Direct, the four other leading retail banks in the U.K. had moved to offer telephone and other direct banking channels. These, however, were add-on units, designed to remove the need for a branch visit for standard transactions, rather than clones of Midland's unique, branded operation. The Bank of Scotland had launched a similar direct bank, but the major banks had yet to launch standalone competitors.

The official view inside Midland was that the traditional branch system and First Direct were partners, providing service in a different, albeit similar, market. Further, they emphasized that First Direct was not about cutting costs, but about finding a better way to serve customers. Nevertheless, Midland had had to defend First Direct against complaints that it was skimming the bank's most profitable customers, and magnifying job losses in the conventional structure.

---

[9] This section is drawn from Virginie Lagoutte, "The Direct Banking Challenge", Middlesex University, April, 1996.

[10] Johnson et al, "Banking on Multimedia," p. 100.

FIRST BANK DIRECT

In Canada, through to the summer of 1996, BMO and the major Canadian banks had adopted, implicitly at least, the complementary direct banking strategy. New access channels and services had been and were being offered as technology permitted, but always within the context of the traditional branch systems. At BMO, however, there had been a growing concern that this approach was not moving costs down fast enough and that it was not proving particularly effective in building revenues (as compared to sustaining them). For some time a line of thought had been developing that the Bank should move in the direction of a more comprehensive direct banking initiative. Specifically, work had been proceeding on the development of a new and distinct business entity that would offer its customers an integrated range of direct banking services while operating under the umbrella of the PCFS infrastructure and side-by-side with the traditional system.

The new initiative was to be called First Bank Direct, an extension of the Bank's existing brand lineup, and plans had been laid for a pilot launch in Calgary in mid-October. Then, as PCFS refined the marketing and operational aspects of the new business, and as results justified, the concept would be rolled out across the country. The recent announcements by ING and Vancouver City Savings of their intentions to launch "virtual" banks and the rumours that the Royal Bank was considering a similar move were focusing increasing attention on the First Bank Direct project. Was this a sufficient response to a changing environment and impending direct bank competition?

VINCOR
INTERNATIONAL INC.

*Darren Roberts
and Joseph N. Fry*

In early January, 1996, Donald Triggs, CEO of Vincor International Inc., of Mississauga, Ontario, was reviewing the merits of taking Vincor public. Vincor was the largest wine company in Canada, with a 21 per cent share of the market, and the sixth largest wine company in North America. The company had grown rapidly, largely through acquisitions, and in the process had accumulated substantial debt. The limits of financial capacity were now threatening to constrain growth. In addition, Vincor's two largest shareholders had indicated an interest in realizing on their positions. There were a number of questions on the

IVEY

Darren Roberts prepared this case under the supervision of Professor Joseph N. Fry solely to provide material for class discussion. The authors do not intend to illustrate either effective or ineffective handling of a managerial situation. The authors may have disguised certain names and other identifying information to protect confidentiality.

table. Was the timing right for an initial public offering (IPO)? What amounts and pricing should be contemplated? What would be an appropriate distribution of the total issue, as between corporate purposes and the selling shareholders?

THE ORIGINS OF VINCOR

Vincor was the outcome of the combination of a number of Canadian wineries—Barnes Wines, Brights Wines, Cartier Wines and Beverages, Inniskillin Wines and most recently Dumont Vins et Spiritueux Inc. (Dumont)—over a period from 1989 through early 1996. Forecast net sales for the year ending March 31, 1996 (including Dumont results from January 10, 1996) were $126 million with a net income of $4 million.

Ridout Wines

The beginning of Vincor, in terms of the continuity of management, was with Ridout Wines in 1989. Ridout's owner, John Labatt Ltd, decided to sell the winery as part of a strategy of consolidating its operations in the brewing business. The Ridout management team, led by Allan Jackson, Peter Grainger and John Hall undertook to put together a management buyout, and sought out Donald Triggs to lead the purchase and become CEO. At the time, Triggs was Chairman of Fisons PLC's International Horticultural Business in the U.K., but he had had prior experience in the wine industry in Canada and the U.S. Triggs saw promise in the company and in the industry and joined the effort to arrange financing and negotiate the deal. The management team subsequently raised over $2 million in equity, largely from personal resources, and borrowed $25 million. They were successful in acquiring Ridout and named their new company Cartier Wines and Beverages.

With a starting debt to equity ratio of over 10 to 1, the new owners faced some tense situations. They went to work, however, to sell off unnecessary assets, to reduce capital requirements by increasing inventory turns, and to improve profitability by streamlining operations and marketing. By 1992, Cartier had reduced the bank debt to a more comfortable $11 million level.

Inniskillin Wines Inc.

Cartier management was well aware of the growing strength of high quality wines in Canada, and in the fall of 1991 had initiated discussions with Inniskillin Wines Inc., which had strong management and well-established brands in the premium wine market segments. These discussions resulted in the formation, in September, 1992, of Cartier and Inniskillin Wineries Ltd. (CIV), Canada's third largest winery. The purchase price was 13 times earnings, and was paid 75 per cent in stock and 25 per cent in cash in a deal structured to keep the Inniskillin management team of Donald Ziraldo and Karl Kaiser as part of the ongoing CIV management group. Management interpreted the successful combination of the Cartier and Inniskillin businesses as an indicator of the significant opportunities for synergy that existed by bringing together firms in the fragmented Canadian wine industry.

Brights Wines

Meanwhile, in 1991, the T.G. Bright Company (Brights) of Niagara Falls, the largest Canadian winery, had been put up for sale. While the situation was of interest to Cartier management they remained on the sidelines as a contest for Brights emerged between a new company, Wine Acquisitions Inc. (WAI) and Andrés Wines Ltd. (Andrés), the second largest winery in Canada. WAI was successful in acquiring Brights and after a short period of consolidation approached CIV, in early 1993, with a proposal to merge the two companies. An agreement was worked out, and after a number of transactions and name changes a new combined company, Vincor International Inc., emerged in late 1993. The largest shareholders were American Farm Investment Corporation, with 27.4 per cent, and the Ontario Teachers Pension Plan Fund, with 23.9 per cent. After the consideration of options, senior management of Vincor collectively held about 23 per cent of the company.

The Vincor merger resulted in significant synergies totalling approximately $4.7 million annually through plant closures, salesforce consolidation, administrative efficiencies and overhead reductions. In addition, the combined business benefited from complementary product lines, which resulted in leading brands in virtually all segments of the wine market in Canada. Brights retail presence in Ontario communities complemented CIV's retail presence in the metropolitan Toronto area. Finally, the integration of wineries in Ontario, British Columbia and Atlantic Canada, together with the integration of sales, marketing, accounting and administrative functions, enabled the combined company to significantly improve operating efficiencies and production capacity utilization.

Dumont

On January 10, 1996, Vincor purchased all of the outstanding shares of Dumont, the second largest winery in Quebec. Dumont had become a leader in the development of negotiant brands—based on wines imported in bulk to Canada for domestic bottling and sale. The acquisition of Dumont almost doubled Vincor's business in Quebec with a market share of over 26 per cent.

The acquisition of Dumont was completed for $14.9 million in cash plus the issuance of preferred shares valued at approximately $0.8 million. In addition, $6.0 million for acquisition and rationalization costs with respect to combining operations were expected to be reflected in the company's balance sheet. The fair value of the tangible net assets acquired approximated $8.8 million. Vincor expected to save $3 million annually through further rationalization of wine production and sales.

For Vincor management, the eight-year odyssey from the relative obscurity of Ridout to the prominence of running the largest winery in Canada had been one of recognizing and capitalizing on the opportunities presented by a changing Canadian wine industry. In large part, their future opportunities would also be shaped by continuing industry developments.

THE CANADIAN WINE INDUSTRY

The Canadian wine and refreshment beverage market, of some 26.7 million cases in 1995, had, in the aggregate, been growing quite slowly in recent years. Beneath the aggregate, however, there were substantial swings of preference toward red wines and higher quality wines. The competitive structure of the industry was evolving towards two groups: a small handful of reasonably large wineries and importers on the one hand, and hundreds of small "estate" wineries and importers, on the other hand. Government support and regulation had been a dominant factor in industry development from early in the century through to the late 1980s. In recent years, however, the forces of trade liberalization had been increasingly limiting government support. The industry, nevertheless, remained heavily regulated and heavily taxed.

Demand

Aggregate trends in the quantity and origin of wine and refreshment beverages consumed in Canada are presented in Table 1. Consumption was essentially flat at between 26 million and 27 million nine-litre-equivalent cases. Within the aggregate, imported wines were showing a slow but steady increase in popularity at the expense of domestically produced wines.

Wine Types

Trends in consumption nationally, by various wine classifications, are presented in Table 2. Within the overall table wine category, red wine was growing, essentially at the expense of white wine. Some of this growth was attributed to the changing tastes of a more sophisticated wine market, some to widespread reports of health benefits from the moderate consumption of red wine.

T A B L E 1 Wine Sales in Canada[1]

(000, 9-litre cases)

	1995	1994	1993	1992	1991
National	26 700	26 400	25 800	26 000	26 400
Domestic[2]	12 300	12 200	12 100	12 800	13 300
Imported	14 400	14 200	13 700	13 200	13 100

[1] Includes wine, wine and spirit coolers and cider sold in liquor and private winery stores.
[2] Encompasses all wine manufactured in Canada by licensed wineries using domestic and/or imported grapes and grape juice.

Source: Vincor files.

T A B L E 2 Wine Sales in Canada by Type, Price[1]

(000, 9-litre cases)

	1995	1994	1993	1992	1991
Wine	19 700	19 700	19 400	19 600	19 200
White	11 200	11 700	12 000	12 400	12 800
Red	6 800	6 300	5 700	5 400	4 900
Rosé	400	400	300	300	300
Sparkling	1 300	1 300	1 400	1 500	1 200
Coolers	2 100	2 100	2 300	2 700	2 200
Cider	1 200	900	800	700	600
Wine Varietal	4 700	4 000	3 500	n/a	n/a
%	23.8	20.3	18.0	n/a	n/a
Wine Premium	6 800	6 400	5 800	5 600	n/a
%	34.5	32.5	30.0	28.6	n/a

[1] Sales through winery owned retail stores not included.

Source: Vincor files, casewriter estimates.

Varietal wine is labelled after the principal variety of grape used to make the wine as distinct from wines identified by the region from which they originated or simply by a producer brand name. Varietal wine labelling had been pioneered in the late 1970s by the emerging wine industries in Australia and California to counter the traditional "geographic origin" strengths of European producers. The consumption of varietal wines in Canada had grown to the point where it represented 24 per cent of the total table wine market in Canada in 1995.

Consumption trends by price classification reflected two quite different developments. The consumption of popular priced wines (less than $7 per bottle) was falling at between two and three per cent per year. It was thought that this trend was in large part the result of the growth of so-called grey market production—wine produced by do-it-yourselfers at home or at specialty retail outlets. A growing number of retailers, particularly in Ontario, provided ingredients and assistance that made it possible for individuals to "produce" a drinkable wine of their own, and in the process, bypass the high taxation and distribution markups that applied to traditional channels of wine production and distribution. It was estimated that the grey market was in the order of 25 per cent of the conventional market by volume.

Premium wine, however, was growing at a healthy rate, and in 1995 accounted for 39 per cent of all wine purchased. The growth in premium wines was a testament to the development of more complex and specialized tastes among wine consumers.

Finally, the cider market had been growing rapidly from a small base. Similar growth in the cider market had been experienced in the U.S. and U.K. The cooler segment was considered a mature market and was not expected to grow.

Geography

Trends in the consumption of wine by geographic area are presented in Table 3. In 1995, approximately 90 per cent of wine consumption was concentrated in Ontario, British Columbia and Quebec, with Ontario being the largest producer of wine products and the largest market for these products. There were 36 wineries licensed to manufacture wine in Ontario, and 35 in British Columbia.

Competition

The competitors in the Canadian wine industry ranged from large, well-established national and multinational corporations to small "estate" wineries and importers. The market share positions and trends for the most notable domestic producers and importers are presented in Table 4.

T A B L E 3   Wine Sales in Canada by Geography [1]

(000, 9-litre cases)

	1995	1994	1993	1992	1991
National	26 700	26 400	25 800	26 000	26 400
Ontario	9 700	9 300	9 000	9 000	9 000
Quebec	7 600	7 700	7 700	7 800	7 900
British Columbia	5 000	4 900	4 700	4 800	5 000
Prairies	3 400	3 400	3 300	3 300	3 300
Atlantic	1 100	1 100	1 100	1 100	1 200

[1] Includes wine, wine and spirit coolers and cider sold in government liquor and private winery stores.

Source: Vincor files.

In 1995, the top five wine companies—Vincor, Andrés, Mission Hill, Cellier du Monde, all Canadian producers, and Seagrams, an importer—accounted for approximately 43.9 per cent of the wine, cooler and cider market. Thereafter, the structure of competition became increasingly fragmented with the next 15 suppliers accounting for a further 21.7 per cent of the market. The remaining 34.4 per cent of the market was supplied by dozens of small Canadian wineries and hundreds of small import agencies.

Most of the major wine companies had national scope, but their sales emphasis varied substantially by geographic area as shown in Table 5. Vincor's geographic sales mix, for example, most closely mirrored the national pattern, while Mission Hill was primarily a British Columbia company. The major importing houses, with the exception of Gallo, did the majority of their business in Ontario. Gallo, a very large U.S. producer, in fact, the largest producer in the world, was a relative newcomer to the Canadian market and had been slowly building its share position across the country.

Andrés was Vincor's most significant national competitor. Andrés was founded in 1961 in British Columbia by the Peller family. It was now a public company, based in Ontario, but the family still owned about 60 per cent of the voting shares. Andrés had broken into the ranks of the major wineries in the early 1970s as an innovator in marketing, most notably in the creation of Baby Duck, a sweet, sparkling, low-alcohol wine. Baby Duck was a great success and became the largest selling wine brand in the country. But Baby Duck and similar products faded in the 1980s as tastes turned to conventional table wines. Andrés adapted, moving its emphasis into the promotion of branded popular priced wines featuring a new four litre bag-in-a-box package. Subsequently, Andrés seemed to run out of steam, with sales flat at about $55 million from 1986 through 1994, albeit with equivalently steady and reasonable profitability (see Table 6). Through this period Andrés had also missed some acquisition opportunities, but in 1994 it did move to acquire Hillebrand Estates Winery, an intermediate producer located in Ontario. Hillebrand's sales were on the order of $15 million; the acquisition price was $10.8 million plus the assumption of $9.8 million in liabilities for assets of $20.6 million, including $3.6 million in goodwill. Coincident with the purchase of Hillebrand, Andrés appeared to be getting more aggressive in the premium segments of the wine market.

T A B L E 4 Wine Company Market Shares (% by volume)[1]

	1995	*1994*	*1993*	*1992*	*1991*
Major Domestic Producers					
Vincor	19.9	20.8	22.0	23.4	22.5
Andrés	8.6	8.6	8.8	9.4	9.5
Mission Hill	5.3	4.4	3.9	3.7	2.2
Cellier du Monde	3.5	3.7	3.8	3.5	3.0
Intermediate Domestic Producers					
Calona	3.0	3.1	3.0	3.2	3.2
Geloso	1.4	1.6	1.6	1.2	1.3
London	0.6	0.7	0.9	0.9	0.9
Major Estate Wineries					
Pelee Island	0.5	0.4	0.5	0.4	0.3
Colio	0.3	0.3	0.3	0.3	0.2
Kittling Ridge	0.2	0.0	0.0	0.0	0.0
Major Import Suppliers					
B&G/Seagrams	5.2	4.9	5.4	5.7	3.5
Gallo	3.4	3.0	2.9	2.5	2.1
Piat	2.2	2.3	2.4	2.6	2.8
Kressman	1.6	1.7	1.8	1.9	1.9
Roux/Tarride	1.0	1.1	1.1	1.0	0.8

[1] Includes wine, coolers and cider. Does not include winery store data.

Source: Company files.

TABLE 5 Wine Company Sales Mix by Geographic Area (% Volume)[1]

	Ontario	Quebec	B.C.	Prairies	Atlantic
Sales as % National	36.3	28.5	18.7	12.4	4.1
Major Domestic Producers Sales Mix					
Vincor	33.0	35.5	16.9	9.1	5.5
Andrés	39.9	20.4	17.0	15.1	7.6
Mission Hill	7.2	1.0	78.6	13.2	0.0
Calona	12.2	0.0	59.1	28.7	0.0
Major Import Suppliers Sales Mix					
B&G/Seagrams	63.5	4.0	4.7	22.0	5.8
Gallo	33.3	11.1	22.5	23.7	9.4
Piat	58.1	2.1	10.5	22.6	6.7
Kressman	62.9	10.0	17.0	6.1	4.0
Roux/Tarride	93.3	0.0	2.6	2.9	1.2

[1] Includes wine, wine and spirit coolers, cider sold in government liquor and private winery stores.

Source: Vincor files.

In specific geographic areas Vincor met regional companies such as Cellier du Monde, Barton and Guestier/Seagrams, Mission Hill and Calona. While these companies were relatively small on a national base, they were very significant competitors in their home market regions.

TABLE 6 Andrés Wines Ltd. Summary of Results

($000,000)

	1995	1994	1993	1992	1991
Net Sales	70.6	55.8	56.4	55.8	52.6
EBIT	7.7	6.8	7.7	8.0	7.8
Net Earnings	4.2	4.0	4.4	4.6	4.5
Working Capital	21.7	31.9	41.1	39.3	37.4
Total Assets	54.5	49.9	57.2	55.5	54.2
Shareholders Equity	42.4	41.0	49.0	46.9	44.9

Source: Andrés *Annual Report.*

Supply

The primary split in the supply of wines in Canada was between those wines produced in Canada and those imported for sale. As Table 1 shows, imported wines accounted for slightly more than half of Canadian consumption and were growing at the expense of domestically produced products. A number of factors were thought to be contributing to this trend, including a lingering perception on the part of some consumers that imported wines were of higher quality; a continuing expansion of the variety of imported products offered by the import houses and the provincial distribution channels; and subsidization and aggressive marketing by the exporting countries.

Domestic producers, except in Ontario, could participate directly in the import sector by importing wine in bulk and bottling it for sale under their own "negotiant" brands. It was expected that Ontario would soon allow this practice.

Grape growing in Canada was focused on the Niagara Peninsula in Ontario and the Okanagan Valley in British Columbia. Niagara grapes accounted for over 95 per cent of the Ontario crop and accounted for about 20 per cent of the grape requirements of domestic producers. The Okanagan accounted for over 95 per cent of British Columbia's grape production and about six per cent of domestic producer needs. Aside from minor quantities from other Canadian growing areas, the balancing 70 per cent plus of domestic winery requirements was made up from grapes and must (unfermented grape juice) imported from grape-growing areas around the world. Given the economics of grape growing in Canada and the advantages of foreign supply in terms of variety, price and four-season availability, there was little encouragement to increase Canadian supply.

To sustain and enhance a uniquely Canadian presence in the industry, the vineyards and wineries in Canada had adopted an Appellation of Origin system similar to that used by traditional wine-producing countries. Under this system, the designation VQA (for Vintners Quality Alliance) could be used in connection with wines that were produced exclusively from grapes grown within specified Canadian growing areas and met agreed high standards of quality. VQA wines were seen as a way at once of establishing a credible presence for Canadian wines in the premium wine categories and of encouraging improvements in the supply system from grape growing through vinification.

One remaining issue for the VQA was establishing national standards that transcended the two somewhat different requirements for Ontario and British Columbia wines. In December 1995, the vintners moved closer to approving such standards. Once the national regulations were approved, it was expected to be easier to gain access to export markets, particularly the European Union (EU). The EU did not recognize Canada's viticultural areas and, with the exception of Britain, did not allow Canadian wines to be imported and sold. The lack of national quality standards had been the biggest barrier to entry into the EU.

Government Support and Regulation

SUPPORT For several decades leading to the mid-1980s, the federal, Ontario and British Columbia governments had attempted to protect the domestic wine industry, primarily to support grape growers but inevitably in the interest of winery operators, too. The programs and devices adopted over the years were many and intricate, but they boiled down to a relatively simple proposition: in return for purchasing the Canadian grape crop, which was high in price and often indifferent in quality, the wineries would be provided with protection from import competition.

A favourite device for protecting domestic producers, given government control of distribution, was to apply differential markups to imported and domestic wines. This arrangement ultimately ran afoul of the General Agreement on Tariffs and Trade, however, and after a ruling against Canadian wine-pricing policy, Canada and the EU reached an agreement under which Canada was to phase out the Canadian markup differentials over the period 1989 to 1998. Coincidentally, the Free Trade Agreement between Canada and the U.S. limited markup differentials on U.S. wine to the actual cost of service differences between domestic and U.S. wines. And it further mandated the phase out of the non-cost-related markups by the end of 1995.

As Canadian grape growers and wine producers became increasingly exposed to international competition, the provincial governments of Ontario and British Columbia, in cooperation with the federal government implemented grape and wine adjustment programs to assist their industries in adapting to the new trading environment. At a cost of about $100 million from 1988 to 1995, these programs provided incentives for growers to remove surplus and undesirable grape vines ($50 million), income stabilization subsidies to grape growers, which allowed wineries to access more competitively priced domestic grapes ($27 million) and marketing assistance to wineries ($15 million). Separately, the Ontario Winery Adjustment Program was launched in 1988 by the Ontario government with $45 million in forgivable loans for wineries, tied to their volume of Ontario grape purchases. By 1996, however, with subsidy programs of one kind or another running down, and governments facing international pressure, on the one hand, and internal financial stress, on the other hand, the days of generous support seemed surely to be coming to an end.

REGULATION The Canadian wine industry was regulated by the provinces, who issued licences for the manufacture and sale of beverage alcohol, and established rules for pricing, packaging, labelling, advertising and the production and distribution of products manufactured by licensed wineries.

Traditionally, in Canada, the provincial governments had used their licensing, taxing and distribution powers as vehicles to meet their not necessarily consistent objectives of maximizing revenues, policing the industry and moderating the consumption of alcohol. Taxes typically accounted for about 30 per cent of the retail price of a bottle of wine and distribution markups about 40 per cent. In some provinces, the government had relaxed its hand to allow significant private distribution of at least beer and wine, but even in these cases the controlling (and collecting) hand was quite evident. A brief review of the major consuming provinces follows.

ONTARIO In Ontario, the Liquor Control Board of Ontario (LCBO), a government owned agency, was the primary distributor of wine. The LCBO operated a province-wide system of 601 retail stores and 86 agency outlets across the province and distributed, as well, to licensed bars and restaurants. The LCBO was the largest purchaser of wine and spirits in the world. From time to time, the possibility of privatizing all or part of the LCBO had come up in public debate, but various governments had chosen not to pursue the matter. However, a new Progressive Conservative government elected in June 1995 had promised to review, and possibly reform, beverage alcohol distribution.

Wineries in Ontario were also allowed to sell through stores located on the winery premises and through about 300 licensed winery-controlled retail outlets. All of these outlets were restricted to the sale of products produced by the controlling winery. A moratorium on the issue of new off-winery retail licences had been imposed with the advent of the FTA, although existing licences could be traded with government approval.

QUEBEC All shipments from wineries and agents had to go through the Société des Alcools du Quebéc (SAQ). The SAQ operated 350 retail outlets. The SAQ also sold wine to 4 000 grocery and 6 000 convenience stores. Grocery and convenience stores could only sell wine bottled in Quebec and brand trademarks that originated in Quebec. Grocery store markups were dictated by the SAQ.

BRITISH COLUMBIA The distribution situation in British Columbia was less constrained. The British Columbia Liquor Board operated 233 outlets and, in addition, licensed wine sales through 277 privately owned beer and wine retail outlets. These private outlets ordered directly from the wineries and agents who arranged distribution directly to the retailer. The B.C. government, nevertheless, had created a tax structure that ensured that the private outlets sold at prices at least equivalent to those charged in the Liquor Board stores.

ALBERTA All beverage alcohol was channelled through the government-owned exclusive distributor. The distributor then sold to the 620 privately owned retail locations in the province, who were free to set the ultimate retail price. There were no provincially owned retail stores.

OTHER PROVINCES The other provinces in Canada operated, for the most part, through traditional government-owned distribution systems, augmented where necessary for remote locations, by agency stores.

FEDERAL GOVERNMENT The Canadian government was reviewing legislation that would require the marketers of beverage alcohol products to put health warning labels on the bottles. These labels would warn, for example, of the risks of drinking and driving, and drinking during pregnancy. This legislation was opposed by the industry on the grounds that it would cost millions of dollars and would be far less effective than using advertising and other more targeted tactics to discourage alcohol abuse.

THE UNITED STATES WINE INDUSTRY

Industry sales of wine in the U.S. in 1994 amounted to 192.7 million nine-litre-equivalent cases, up about 2 per cent from 1993, but down about 4 per cent from 1992. Per capita consumption was stable at about 6.8 litres. Imported volumes were significant, amounting to about 30 million nine-litre-equivalent cases in 1994.

The U.S. industry was fragmented, but it was going through a process of consolidation that was similar to that being experienced in Canada. Under U.S. legislation, wine producers were required to distribute through wholesalers, who held exclusive rights to distribute wine to licensed retail operators. The particular system of distribution, in terms of government ownership and control, varied by State, but in general the U.S. system was more open to private ownership, particularly at the retail level.

An important feature of the three tiered distribution system in the U.S. was that the major wineries worked very hard to build close ties with their wholesale distributors. In this context, the major wineries were not beyond reminding their distributors of their mutual dependence, and this created some difficulties of access and expansion for small wineries and importers.

VINCOR'S FUTURE

With the completion of the Dumont acquisition, Vincor management felt that they were in a strong position to continue their growth pattern. They pointed, in particular, at Vincor's leading market position, portfolio of brands, sales and marketing capacity, efficient supply arrangements and depth of management experience. Selected financial information on the company is given in Table 7; further details are provided in Exhibits 1 through 3.

TABLE 7   Vincor: Selected Consolidated Financial Information

(thousands of dollars)

	Nine months ended December 31		Fiscal year ended March 31	
	1995	1994	1995	1994[1]
	(unaudited)		*(audited)*	
Operating Results				
Net sales	$102 064	$97 307	$114 522	$81 316
Cost of goods sold	56 857	55 728	66 693	44 378
Gross margin [2]	45 207	41 579	47 829	36 938
Selling and administration [3]	29 244	28 333	35 400	30 058
EBITDA [4]	15 963	13 246	12 429	7 053
Depreciation and amortization	2 680	2 633	3 383	3 200
Interest	4 475	4 748	6 149	4 441
Income (loss) before income taxes and minority interest	8 808	5 865	2 897	(606)
Net income (loss)	5 094	3 485	1 677	(928)
Wine volume (thousands of cases)	3 284	3 277	3 842	3 017
Average net selling price per case	$ 27.17	$ 25.98	$ 26.25	$ 25.03
Refreshment volume (thousands of cases)	843	812	924	438
Average net selling price per case	$ 15.25	$ 15.01	$ 14.79	$ 13.25

	As at December 31,	As at March 31,	
	1995	1995	1994
	(unaudited)	*(audited)*	
Balance Sheet Data			
Fixed assets net	$ 28 357	$ 28 907	$ 29 315
Total assets	118 815	112 370	125 576
Long-term debt	46 870	51 070	63 370
Shareholders' equity	24 026	19 202	14 995

T A B L E 7 (continued)

Forecast Consolidated Statement of Operations

(thousands of dollars)

	Year ending March 31, 1996 (unaudited)
Net sales [5]	$126 174
Gross margin [2]	54 933
EBITDA [4]	16 801
Income before income taxes	6 962
Net income	4 063

[1] Results of operations for the year ended March 31, 1994, include 11 months of operations of Brights from May 1, 1993 and five months of operation of CIV from November 1, 1993. EBITDA for the 12 months ended March 31, 1994 aggregating 12 months of Brights and CIV was $9 492.

[2] Net sales less cost of goods sold.

[3] For fiscal year ended March 31, 1994 includes $155 gain on sale of assets held for resale.

[4] Earnings before interest, taxes, depreciation and amortization.

[5] Net sales for Dumont included from January 10, 1996.

Market Position

Vincor held over 21.0 per cent of the Canadian market, putting it well ahead of its nearest competitors, Andrés, with about 9 per cent, and Seagram's with about 5 per cent (Table 4). Vincor had national scope, with a sales profile across the country that roughly paralleled consumption (Table 5). Vincor, furthermore, was represented in all segments of the market and was pushing for growth in the expanding categories such as red wine and varietals, where it currently held, respectively, a 16 per cent and 12 per cent market share. A concurrent shift in emphasis to higher price point categories had resulted in an increase in Vincor's net selling price per case as shown in Table 7.

Vincor's principal customers were the various provincial and territorial government liquor boards, which represented 75 per cent of Vincor sales. The remainder of sales were generated through direct sales to the public via Vincor's retail chains in Ontario where Vincor owned 128 Wine Rack Stores and four Inniskillin Boutiques. Approximately 87 per cent of Vincor sales to the government liquor boards was eventually sold through the retail channel to the public. The remainder was sold by the liquor boards to licensees.

Approximately 1 per cent of Vincor sales were through exports, but Vincor management believed that excellent opportunities existed to increase exports, particularly to countries that did not have an indigenous wine industry. There was, in particular, a huge export demand for Inniskillin icewine, a dessert wine produced from frozen grapes. Approximately 7 000 cases were produced annually, but this level of production could not satisfy the demand. Inniskillin icewine sold at wholesale for $300/case.

Brand Portfolio

The wine industry in Canada had evolved from regional competitors, and as a result there were few well-established national brands. With falling provincial barriers, however, Vincor and some of its competitors had moved to broaden their geographic scope and to develop national brands. A partial listing of Vincor's brands is presented in Table 8. Some of the more notable brands in the portfolio were as follows.

TABLE 8   **Partial Listing of Vincor Brand Portfolio**

Beverage Category	Brand	Distribution	Price Points
Popular Price Table Wine			
	L'Ambiance	National	<$7.00
	Notre Vin Maison	Quebec	
	Entre-Lacs	National except Quebec	
	Le Villageois (N)[1]	National	
		(Bottled in France for Ontario)	
	California House (N)	Quebec, Western Canada	
	Sawmill Creek	Ontario, moving national	<$7.00
Premium Price Table Wine			
	Jackson-Triggs	Primarily Ontario	$7.00–$10.00
	Inniskillin		$7.00–$15.00
			$7.00–$20.00
	Santa Reina (N)	Quebec	
	Santa Isabella (N)	National	>$7.00
			>$7.00
Sparkling Wine			
	Spumante Bambino	National	
	President		
	Canadian Champagne	National	
Refreshment			
	Canada Cooler	National, except Quebec	
	Growers Cider	National, except Quebec	

[1] (N) Negotiant brand

The Sawmill Creek brand covered a family of wines and was positioned as an introduction to the varietal wine and premium wine segments. Sawmill Creek was benefitting from the growth of varietal sales and included the third-largest selling Chardonnay in Canada and the number one Chardonnay in Ontario.

The Jackson-Triggs brand was launched in 1993 and was dedicated to offering exceptional quality and value in the premium and super premium wine category. In the latter category, Jackson-Triggs offered a broad selection of prize-winning VQA wines from both the Niagara Peninsula and the Okanagan Valley.

Vincor regarded Inniskillin as the premier vintner of estate wines in Canada. Wines produced by Inniskillin had won many international awards and had established founders Donald Ziraldo and Karl Kaiser as leaders in the Canadian industry. Inniskillin products were focused in the premium through super premium segments. Inniskillin's sales base was largely in Ontario.

Sales and Marketing

Vincor had the largest sales and marketing force in the Canadian wine industry with 100 professionals. This force was more than 50 per cent larger than the size of any other wine competitor in Canada.

The salesforce was divided into two divisions. The retail division was responsible for sales by individual retail locations including government liquor board stores. The licensee division was focused on sales to licensed establishments such as restaurants, clubs, hotels and bars.

Vincor aggressively supported its wines with direct advertising and promotions. This included television, print and event promotions such as the sponsorship of Whistler/Blackcomb Ski Resort. Vincor management had worked particularly hard to develop a comprehensive marketing data system that provided them with highly detailed and timely information on industry sales trends by product category, geographic area and channel.

Supply

The Canadian grape crop contributed about 19 per cent of Vincor's annual requirements. In this respect, Vincor purchased approximately 50 per cent of the wine grape crop in the Niagara Peninsula in Ontario and 8 per cent of the Okanagan Valley crop in British Columbia. The balance of the company's requirements was met by importing grapes, must and bulk wine. Vincor had developed an extensive network of long-term relationships with growers and suppliers worldwide to ensure a secure four season flow of imported requirements.

Glass bottle costs were one of the largest components of cost of goods sold. The glass bottle industry was highly concentrated, with only a small number of producers in North America and only one commercial glass supplier in Canada. Although there had been no supply problems, Vincor supplemented its glass purchases with imported glass for use in some super premium wines.

Management

Donald Triggs believed that Vincor had assembled a highly capable and committed management team, and that this was evidenced in the success of the company's acquisition program and in the strength of its resulting marketing and operations. Brief biographies on selected senior managers are presented in Table 9.

T A B L E 9 Brief Biographies—Selected Vincor Corporate Management

Donald L. Triggs

Mr. Triggs has been the President and Chief Executive Officer of Vincor since the completion of the New Brights/CIV merger in November 1993. In 1989, with Allan Jackson, Peter Grainger and other senior executives, he purchased the Canadian wine operations of John Labatt Limited and became the Chairman, President and Chief Executive Officer of Cartier Wines & Beverages Corp. (which became CIV after its purchase of Inniskillin Wines Inc. in 1992). Mr. Triggs was the President in the North American horticultural operations of Fisons PLC, an international company in the horticulture, pharmaceutical and scientific equipment industries, from 1982 to 1989 and became Chairman of its international horticulture division in 1989. From 1973 until 1979 Mr. Triggs held senior officer positions with Chateau-Gai Wines and from 1979 until 1982 was the President of John Labatt Limited's Canadian Wine Group, and subsequently, Labatt's United States wine operations. Mr. Triggs is currently a Director and the Chairman of the Canadian Wine Institute and an Honourary Director of the Public Policy Forum. Mr. Triggs holds a BScA (Honours) from the University of Manitoba and an MBA from the University of Western Ontario.

Allan H. Jackson

Mr. Jackson is the Executive Vice-President, Production of Vincor. Prior to November 1993, he held the same position with CIV. Mr. Jackson has been involved in the wine industry for 25 years commencing with his bachelor and doctoral theses involving the study of the flavour components that determine the specific taste character of different grape and wine varietals. In 1977, Mr. Jackson joined John Labatt Limited to initiate its wine research program in association with the National Research Council. Mr. Jackson has been responsible for all technical and production matters for Vincor and for CIV and its predecessors. Mr. Jackson holds a BSc (Honours) and a PhD in Chemistry from McMaster University.

Richard G. Jones

Mr. Jones was appointed Executive Vice-President Finance and Administration of Vincor in June 1995. Prior thereto, he was the Vice-President, Finance and Administration of Beatrice Foods Inc. (food manufacturer). From 1987 until 1989, Mr. Jones was

Controller of the Food Products Division of Beatrice. From 1974 until 1987, Mr. Jones worked in corporate finance, business analysis, operations and acquisitions at General Foods. Mr. Jones holds an Honours Business Administration degree from the University of Western Ontario and is a Certified Management Accountant.

Donald J.P. Ziraldo

Mr. Ziraldo has been the President of Inniskillin Wines Inc. since its inception in 1975. Mr. Ziraldo was the Chairman of the Vintner's Quality Alliance from its inception in 1988 until 1995 and is a Director of the Wine Council of Ontario. He has won numerous awards for his innovative and entrepreneurial contributions to the wine industry in Ontario. Mr. Ziraldo holds a BSc in Agriculture from Guelph University and was awarded an Honourary Doctor of Laws Degree from Brock University in 1994, along with the co-founder of Inniskillin, Karl Kaiser.

Gordon Munroe

Mr. Munroe joined Vincor as Vice-President, Marketing in May 1995. Prior thereto, he was Vice-President, Sales and Marketing for Alberta Distillers in 1993 and 1994, Director of Marketing, Retail Beverages and Marketing Manager of A&W Foodservices from 1985 to 1993, an Account Director of McCann Erickson in 1984 and 1985 and held various sales and marketing positions with the Nabisco Brands Wines and Spirits Group from 1979 to 1984. Mr. Munroe holds a BA in Commerce from Simon Fraser University.

Source: Company files.

Vincor management had maintained a significant level of ownership of the company. In total, 44 senior and middle managers were shareholders. This represented all senior executives and 70 per cent of middle management.

Vincor had 1 037 employees of which 222 full- and part-time employees were unionized. Unionized employees were represented by five different unions, and relations with employees had been good. There was no union representation in Western or Atlantic Canada.

Considerations for an IPO

Donald Triggs recognized that there were a number of background factors that had to be integrated into his consideration of initiating the pursuit of an IPO.

Vincor's financial position subsequent to the completion of the Dumont acquisition was significantly leveraged. This was a situation that management had worked through before and was not particularly nervous about in the present circumstances. But there was a possibility that some growth opportunities might have to be passed over as a result of the heavy debt load.

The market for IPOs seemed to be picking up. After a distinctly slow beginning in 1995, with just four new offerings in the first quarter, the year finished with 29 companies having gone public on the Toronto Stock Exchange. Among these, notably, was a small Ontario winery, Magnotta, which started trading on the TSE in October of 1995. Basic financial information on Magnotta and other selected publicly traded wine companies, is presented in Exhibit 4. Looking ahead, there was some anticipation that the Canadian economy and the TSE would shake off their lethargic recent performance. Growth in real GDP for 1995 was 2.2 per cent; growth for 1996 and 1997 was forecasted at 1.6 and 2.6 per cent respectively. Inflation for 1995 was 2.1 per cent; inflation levels for 1996 and 1997 were forecasted at 1.7 and 2.0 per cent respectively. The 10-year Canadian government bond rate was 7.14 per cent. The 91-day treasury bill was at 5.52 per cent.

Vincor's two largest shareholders, American Farm Investment Corporation (AFIC) and the Ontario Teachers Pension Plan Fund (Teachers) had indicated an interest in realizing on their investments when the time and price were right. AFIC was controlled by Mr. Gerald Schwartz, perhaps better known as the CEO of the Onex Corporation, an investment company that bought businesses with the goal of improving their operations, and then selling them at a profit. At 54, Schwartz was one of Canada's foremost practitioners of leveraged buyouts, and Onex was his prime vehicle. Schwartz had partnered in other situations with Teachers.

Given the interests of AFIC and Teachers, Triggs thought that any plan for an IPO should include a primary offering to raise funds for company use and a secondary offering to accommodate the desires of AFIC and Teachers.

E X H I B I T 1 Summary of Consolidated Balance Sheets[1]

(In thousands of dollars)

	December 31 1995 (Unaudited)	March 31 1995	1994
Assets			
Current Assets			
Accounts receivable	$ 13 823	$ 6 222	$ 8 120
Inventories	38 386	37 622	44 490
Prepaid expenses	694	1 022	619
Assets held for resale	2 075	2 075	5 075
	54 978	46 941	58 304
Fixed assets	28 357	28 907	29 315
Other assets (note 1)[2]	13 134	13 733	14 577
Goodwill net of amortization (note 2)	22 346	22 789	23 380
	$118 815	$112 370	$125 576
Liabilities and Shareholders' Equity			
Current Liabilities			
Bank indebtedness—secured	$ 20 707	$ 19 379	$ 24 121
Accounts payable and accrued liabilities	16 798	15 795	17 015
Income and other taxes payable	687	279	570
Deferred income taxes	1 384	1 466	1 664
Current portion of long-term debt	10 400	9 400	9 100
	49 976	46 319	52 470
Long-term debt (note 3)	36 470	41 670	54 270
Deferred income taxes	8 343	5 179	3 841
Shareholders' equity:			
Capital stock (note 4)	19 650	19 493	16 422
Retained earnings (deficit)	4 376	(291)	(1 427)
	24 026	19 202	14 995
	$118 815	$112 370	$125 576

[1] Summarized by casewriter from company records.
[2] See Notes attached as Exhibit 3.

Source: Vincor files.

EXHIBIT 2 Summary of Consolidated Statements of Operations and Retained Earnings (Deficit)[1]

(in thousands of dollars)

	Nine months ended December 31		Year ended March 31	
	1995	1994	1995	1994
	(Unaudited)			
Net sales	$102 064	$97 307	$114 522	$81 316
Cost of goods sold	56 857	55 728	66 693	44 378
	45 207	41 579	47 829	36 938
Operating Expenses:				
Selling and administration	29 244	28 328	35 400	30 058
Depreciation and amortization	2 680	2 638	3 383	3 200
Interest	4 475	4 748	6 149	4 441
Gain on sale of assets held for resale	—	—	—	(155)
	36 399	35 714	44 932	37 544
Income (loss) before income taxes and minority interest	8 808	5 865	2 897	(606)
Income taxes	3 714	2 380	1 220	(33)
Minority interest	—	—	—	(289)
Net income (loss)	$ 5 094	$ 3 485	$ 1 677	$ (928)
Income (loss) per common share	$ .39	$ .28	$ .10	$ (.16)
Deficit beginning of period	$ (291)	$(1 427)	$ (1 427)	$ —
Net income (loss)	5 094	3 485	1 677	(928)
Preferred share dividends (note 4)[2]	(427)	(401)	(541)	(499)
Retained earnings (deficit) end of period	$ 4 376	$ 1 657	$ (291)	$(1 427)

[1] Summarized by casewriter from company records.
[2] See Notes attached as Exhibit 3.

Source: Vincor files.

EXHIBIT 3 Notes to Consolidated Financial Statements

(In thousands of dollars)

1. Other Assets

	December 31	March 31	
	1995	1995	1994
	(unaudited)		
Deferred financing costs net of amortization	$ 2 448	$ 3 047	$3 869
Deferred pension costs	3 481	3 481	3 481
Preferred shares BW Loanco Inc.	3 223	3 223	3 223
Preferred shares BW Finco Inc.	3 895	3 895	3 895
Other investments	87	87	109
	$13 134	$13 733	$14 577

The preferred shares of BW Loanco Inc. and BW Finco Inc., affiliates of the company, are 10 per cent non-cumulative redeemable preferred.

2. Goodwill

The cost of acquired businesses is allocated first to identifiable assets and liabilities based on estimated fair values. The excess of cost over identifiable assets and liabilities is recorded as goodwill and amortized over a period of up to 40 years. The company continually re-evaluates the propriety of the carrying amount of goodwill, as well as the related amortization period, to determine whether current events and circumstances warrant adjustment to the carrying values or estimate of useful life. This evaluation is based on the company's projection of the undiscounted future operating results. At this time, the company believes that no impairment of goodwill has occurred and that no reduction of the estimated useful life is warranted.

3. Long-Term Debt

	December 31	March 31	
	1995	1995	1994
	(unaudited)		
Bank term loans with fixed interest rates from 7.42% to 7.68%	$ 33 500	$ 37 700	$ 50 000
Subordinated debentures with interest at 10%	12 500	12 500	12 500
Senior subordinated note with interest at 12.5% and principal due October 1998	870	870	870
	46 870	51 070	63 370
Less current portion	10 400	9 400	9 100
	$36 470	$41 670	$54 270

Bank operating and term loans are secured by assignments of accounts receivable and inventories, a fixed and floating charge on fixed assets and a security interest in all other assets. Bank term loan repayments for the years ending March 31 are as follows: 1996—$9 400, 1997—$10 400, and 1999—$7 500.

The subordinated debentures were issued to BW Loanco Inc. and BW Finco Inc. Subordinated debenture repayments for the years ending March 31 are as follows:
2000—$1 250, 2001—$2 500, 2002—$8 750.

EXHIBIT 3   (continued)

Interest on long-term debt amounted to:

	Nine months ended December 31		Year ended March 31	
	1995	*1994*	*1995*	*1994*
	(unaudited)			
Bank term loans	$1 983	$2 688	$3 441	$2 444
Subordinated debentures	1 043	1 024	1 370	984
	$3 026	$3 712	$4 811	$3 428

4. The authorized share capital consists of unlimited preferred shares issuable in series and unlimited common shares. Details of the issued share capital are as follows:

	December 31 1995	March 31	
		1995	*1994*
	(unaudited)		
Class A preferred shares Series 1	$ 3 901	$ 3 744	$ 3 559
Common shares	15 749	15 749	12 863
	$19 650	$19 493	$16 422

In May 1993, 1 702 602 Class A preferred shares were issued at $2.00 per share. These shares are redeemable and retractable at $3.00 per share on December 31, 1999. The difference between the issue and retraction price is being amortized over the period to December 31, 1999 using the effective interest method. Such amortization is included in preferred share dividends.

In May 1993, 8.5 million common shares were issued at $1.00 per share to finance the acquisition of Brights. An additional 2.125 million common shares were issued as part of the acquisition of Cartier & Inniskillin Vintners Inc. for an aggregate consideration of $4 363. In August 1994, the company issued 1.443 million common shares for cash consideration of $2 886.

Source: Vincor files.

E X H I B I T 4 **Publicly Traded Wine Companies**

The following is a list of publicly traded wine companies and was prepared for comparative purposes. Canandaigua Wine Inc. and the Robert Mondavi Corporation were U.S. companies. Andrés was a major Canadian wine producer and traded on the Toronto Stock Exchange. Magnotta is another very small Canadian wine producer that nevertheless underwent an IPO in October 1995.

Canandaigua Wine Inc. produced and marketed more than 125 national and regional beverage alcohol brands, which included table, dessert and sparkling wine, imported beer and distilled spirits.

Andrés Wines Ltd. produced and sold a full range of wines to Liquor Control Boards across Canada, and to the public through retail stores in Ontario and grocery stores in Quebec. The Peller family controlled approximately 59.3 per cent of the voting shares.

Robert Mondavi Corporation produced and marketed ultra-premium, super premium and popular premium wines worldwide under the following labels: "Robert Mondavi", "Napa Valley", "Vichon California" and "Bryon Vineyards and Winery". Through a partnership, the winery also produced and marketed "Opus One" and is involved in several joint ventures.

	Canandaiqua[1] (US$)	Mondavi[2] (US$)	Magnotta[3]	Andrés[4]
Net earnings per share	2.46	.83	0	1.02
Price per share	32.625	27.625	1.45	11.50
Number of shares (millions)	16.61	14.75	9.3	4.59
P/E ratio based on				
previous year's earnings	13.3	16.74	–	14.02
Market capitalization	541.97	407.5	13.49	52.79
Price/book value	2.22x	2.36x	1.93x	–
Price/EBITDA	7.30x	7.26x	7.25x	5.64x
Beta	.70	.55	–	.70
Sales (millions)	906	116.35	6.8	70.60 (3/95)
Net income (millions)	41	12.62	.9	4.74
Total assets (millions)	1099	339.9	7.0	51.11 Total
Liabilities (millions)	507.85	166.7	4.4	11.87
Current ratio	1.74	2.73	1.08	2.9
Total debt/total cap.	.58	.37	.78	.2

[1] Canandaiqua fiscal year is September to August.
[2] Mondavi fiscal year is July to June.
[3] Magnotta's figures are as of 31 January 1995.
[4] Andrés fiscal year is April to March.

HARLEQUIN ENTERPRISES LIMITED—1979

case

8

J. Peter Killing

In 1979 Harlequin Enterprises was the largest publisher of romance novels in the world and was judged by many to be North America's most profitable publishing company. Harlequin's sales and profits had increased every year since 1970 and in 1979 were forecasted at $180 million and $20 million respectively. Harlequin romances were produced in nine languages and sold in more than 90 countries.

As the 1970s drew to a close, the pace of change at Harlequin seemed to be quickening. In 1978, for example, Harlequin had produced its first feature film, based on one of its romance novels, and opened its

IVEY

first retail store, designed to sell educational material produced by the company's "Scholar's Choice" division. In 1979 the company was launching its romance novels in Japan, Scandinavia, Mexico, Venezuela and Greece, as well as adding new romance series in North America, Germany and Holland. As Larry Heisey, Harlequin's president, looked ahead, he stated:

> Strategies that served us well in the 1970s will be continued into the 1980s. We will work to develop our present resources, to make use of those growth channels that have been established, and to pursue the flexibility that will enable us to react to market opportunities.... We look to the 1980s as a time of great promise for this company.

THE PUBLISHING INDUSTRY

Apart from educational material, publishing a book is typically a high-risk venture. Each book is a new product with all the risks attendant on any new product introduction. The risks vary with the author's reputation, the subject matter and the predictability of the market's response. Among the numerous decisions facing the publisher are selecting manuscripts out of the thousands submitted each year, deciding how many copies to print and deciding how to promote the book.

Insiders judged that the key to success in hardcover publishing was the creative genius needed to identify good young authors among the hundreds of would-be writers, and then publish and develop them throughout their careers. Sol Stein of Stein and Day Publishers commented that

> Most successful publishers are creative editors at heart, and contribute more than risk capital and marketing expertise to the books they publish. If a publisher does not add value to what he publishes, he's a printer, not a publisher.

Successful hardcover authors and their publishers could profit greatly from the sale of paperback publishing rights and film rights. In the 1970s, prices paid for paperback rights had skyrocketed, as softcover publishers bid astronomical amounts, frequently more than $1 million, for books they judged would sell the numbers necessary for paperback success.

These high prices raised the already high break-even volumes for paperback publishers. Publishers generally received about 50% of the retail price, of which about 13% (15¢ per book) would pay for printing costs, 10% for distribution, 10% for selling expenses, 5–7.5% for advertising and promotion, and the remainder would cover rights and overheads. If the publisher failed to sell enough books, the loss could be substantial. One result was that the mass paperback publishers in the United States earned only about 2% on sales of new releases, whereas Harlequin, using a distinctly different approach to the business, earned in the 15% range. Harlequin's financial results are summarized in Exhibit 1.

HARLEQUIN'S FORMULA: STANDARDIZATION

Harlequin's formula was fundamentally different from that of traditional publishers: content, length, artwork, size, basic formats and print were all standardized. Each book was not a new product, but rather an addition to a clearly defined product line. The consequences of this uniformity were significant. The reader was buying a Harlequin novel, and advertising promoted the Harlequin line, rather than a particular book or author. The standardized size made warehousing and distribution more efficient. A comparison of Harlequin's formula and the operations of traditional "one-off" publishers is presented in Table 1.

Because all its novels were aimed at the same target market—"any and all female readers over the age of 15"—Harlequin could afford to do a significant amount of market research, identifying its customers and their likes and dislikes. The average Harlequin reader was 35.5 years old, was married, had 2.5

children, was equally likely to be working or a housewife, and had probably finished high school. Harlequin described the relationship between its books and its readers as follows:

> The world of romantic fiction offers the reader delights of a kind which are absent from her every-day life. Identifying herself with the heroine, the romance reader can meet the strong, masterful hero of her dreams and be courted by him. Without stirring from her fireside, she can travel to other countries, learn about other ways of life, and meet new people. After the vicarious enjoyment provided by such literature, the reader can return to safe reality, where domineering males seldom have to be confronted and trips to exotic parts of the world never happen, so that illusion is always preserved. The romance provides compulsive reading and leaves a feeling of satisfaction and pleasure.

T A B L E 1   The Harlequin Formula

	Harlequin	*One-Off Publisher*
Editorial	Emphasis on consistency with established guidelines	Requires separate judgement on potential consumer demand for each manuscript
Rights	Standardized process, usually for established amounts	Can be a complex process, involving subrights, hard/soft cover deals and tying up authors for future books
Author Management	Less dependent on specific authors	Vulnerable to key authors changing publisher
Marketing	Builds the imprint/series	Builds each title/author
Selling	Emphasis on servicing, rack placement and maintaining distribution	Sell on strength of author, cover, critical reviews, special promotional tactics
Production Distribution/order regulation/information systems	Consistent format, focus on efficiency Very sophisticated shipping and returns handling procedures	Emphasis on cover design, cost control secondary Traditionally has not received much attention and hence is not as sophisticated

Source: Adapted from a Canada Consulting Group report.

Harlequin's view that its novels could be sold "like other branded consumer products" perhaps explained why employees hired from mass-marketing companies such as Procter and Gamble had skills and aptitudes that led them to do well at Harlequin. The company's 1974 Annual Report documented its mass market focus, its use of sampling techniques, and its entry into television advertising, which in many cities increased sales by as much as 80%.

> We are selling branded literature which can be promoted like other branded consumer products. Sampling techniques, the costs of which are prohibitive to the general publisher because of the variety of books published, are being used by Harlequin to expand its market. For example, several million books were distributed free to the trade in 1973 and 1974 for use in introducing our products to new consumers. Since September 1974, a television advertising campaign has been tested in ten cities in Canada and the United States. Expansion of this advertising will begin in 1975.

Responsibility for the development of Harlequin novels lay with the company's British editorial staff and stable of more than 100 writers, most of whom were also British. Harlequin had acquired this editorial expertise in 1971 when it purchased Mills and Boon, a long established British publisher of romance novels. The genius of the Mills and Boon editors, according to one observer, was that they were able to produce a consistency in the final product, even though many authors were contributing. Readers always knew what they were getting and were satisfied again and again. In addition to the work of its regular writers, Mills and Boon received approximately 5 000 unsolicited manuscripts per year. Typically, about 50 of these were accepted.

Harlequin's editorial process did not generate or even encourage best-sellers. "Best-sellers would ruin our system," stated Bill Willson, Harlequin's vice-president of finance. "Our objective is steady growth in volume. We have no winners and no losers." All Harlequin books published in any month sold about the same number of copies. Unsold paperback books could be returned to the publisher for credit; a consequence of Harlequin's even and predictable sales was that its rate of return of unsold books was much lower than that of its competitors, 25–30% of sales versus 40–50%.

One industry analyst commented on Harlequin's approach to the industry as follows:

> You've got to realize that these guys at Harlequin revolutionized the North American book industry. They brought professional marketing and business techniques to an industry that seems to publish "for love rather than money." At retail, for instance, they ignored the bookstores. This was a good move because most people never enter bookstores. Instead they built Harlequin book racks and placed them in supermarkets, mass merchandisers and drug stores where women are. They made each of the books 192 pages by changing the type size. This allowed for standard packaging and six books would fit into each pocket on the rack. Once the books were accepted by the trade they went on a monthly standing order system like magazines. This allowed for uniform print runs, shipping containers, and so on. Everything was done for efficiency, prices were kept low and volumes skyrocketed.

Distribution

In late 1977, Harlequin established a national retail sales organization in Canada, ending a joint venture agreement with another publisher in which a single sales force had represented both companies. By early 1979 Harlequin executives declared themselves well satisfied with the new arrangement, which allowed the sales force to focus solely on Harlequin products.

In the U.S. Harlequin was represented by the Pocket Books Distribution Corporation, a wholly owned subsidiary of Simon and Schuster. Pocket Books' 120-person sales force was responsible for dealing with the 400 or so independent regional distributors who distributed Harlequin's books and the major chains who bought direct, and for ensuring that Harlequin books were properly displayed and managed at the retail level. In addition to handling the Harlequin romance series, the sales force carried Simon and Schuster's own pocket books which were "one-offs" issued monthly.

Harlequin did not print any of its own books. Harlequin novels that were sold in the U.S. were printed by a major American printer of mass market books and distributed through a distribution centre in Buffalo, New York. Harlequins sold in Canada were printed in Canada and distributed through the company's Stratford, Ontario, warehouse.

HARLEQUIN'S PRODUCTS AND MARKETS

The Romance Novel

The backbone of Harlequin's business was its two major series, Harlequin Presents and Harlequin Romances, which consistently produced over 90% of the company's sales and earnings. Originally Harlequin had published only the Romances line, consisting of very chaste conservative stories selected from the Mills and Boon line by the wife of one of Harlequin's founders. After a period of time, however, Mills and Boon executives suggested to Harlequin that they were not publishing Mills and Boon's most popular books. Arguing that the British and North American markets were not the same, Harlequin nevertheless tried a blind test—two of its choices and two of the slightly more "racy" Mills and Boon choices—on 500 of its North American customers. To the company's amazement the Mills and Boon selections were very popular and, bowing to its customers' wishes, Harlequin created the Presents line to offer Mills and Boon's less chaste romance stories. In early 1979 the still growing Presents line was increased from four titles per month to six in North America, and sales rose by 50%. At the same time the Romances line was cut back from eight titles per month to six, with the net result that in North America the two lines were selling very similar quantities of books.

Both the Presents and Romances lines were sold at retail and, since 1970, through Harlequin's "Reader Service" book club. This direct mail operation offered heavy Harlequin readers the possibility of purchasing every book the company published, delivered right to the front door. The book club was an important source of profit, as in the U.S. six books were sold through the book club for every ten sold at retail. Furthermore, a book sold through the book club yielded Harlequin the full cover price, whereas a book sold at retail netted the company approximately half the retail price, and required advertising, distribution costs, the acceptance of returns from retailers and so on. As one observer put it, "No wonder the company is willing to pay the mailing costs for its book club members!"

Competition

No other publisher concentrated as heavily as Harlequin on the romance novel although, attracted by Harlequin's profit margins, most of the majors had made attempts to penetrate the market. Bantam Books, the largest, and generally considered the best-run conventional paperback publisher in North America, had tried to enter Harlequin's market in the early 1970s with a series titled Red Rose Romances. The line was a failure and had been phased out of existence by 1977. Four or five other major publishers had also attempted to penetrate the romantic novel market in the late 1960s and early 1970s. Consumers were offered Valentine Romances from Curtis Publishing, Rainbow Romances from New American Library, Hamilton House from Fawcett, and Candlelight Romances from Dell. The only one of these series selling in 1979 was Dell's, offering one or two new titles per month. Willson explained that the problem faced by all of these firms was their editorial content. The stories simply weren't good enough. Heisey agreed, adding:

> We are good managers and good marketers, I admit, and those things make us more profitable than we otherwise would be, but the essence of this firm is the editorial department and our group of more than 100 authors. It is these resources which make us unique, and it is precisely these resources which our competition cannot duplicate.

International Markets

Commencing in 1975, Harlequin began to establish foreign language ventures for its romance novels in countries around the world. Typically, a new venture would start with two or four titles per month, translated from the Romances or Presents lines, and then expand as the market allowed. In spite of predictions from many (male) publishers that the Harlequin line would not appeal to the women of their country, virtually all of the new ventures prospered. Entry costs were not high in most countries, and profits came quickly. Harlequin's major international moves are listed in Table 2.

TABLE 2 International Expansion

1975	Harlequin Holland established. Four titles per month. Extremely successful. Second line introduced in 1976. Further expansion in 1977 and 1978. Holland, together with Canada, has Harlequin's highest per capita (women over 15) market penetration rate.
1976	Harlequin paid $2.1 million for a 50% interest in the West German company that had been publishing Mills and Boon novels for several years. The company published five romance titles per month, plus a French detective series. In spite of new competition in the romance area in 1978, the company was performing well.
1977	Harlequin France established. In 1978 a four title per month series was launched, aimed at French, Belgian and Swiss markets. Line expanded in 1979. Company became profitable in 1979.
1978	Mills and Boon's Australian operation (established in 1973) took a major step forward with the introduction of TV advertising and a new line. A successful operation.
1979	New launches in Japan, Scandinavia, Greece, Mexico and Venezuela.

Harlequin's major new romance novel venture in 1979, representing an investment of $2 million, was its entry into the Japanese market. Despite skepticism from outsiders, initial market research had indicated that the appeal of Harlequin's product would be even stronger in Japan than North America. In early 1979 the company also entered its smallest foreign-language markets to date, those of the Scandinavian countries. A Harlequin executive explained the company's rationale:

> Harlequin's operation in Stockholm is the headquarters for publishing and marketing activities in the Swedish, Finnish and Norwegian languages. We will begin publishing romance fiction in Sweden and Finland in March, at the rate of four titles per month, and in Norway in April, at two titles per month. Denmark is currently being examined as a potential new market.
>
> The four Scandinavian countries, with populations varying from 4.1 million to 8.3 million, will provide Harlequin with experience in the management of smaller markets. We also believe that, despite their size, they are potentially productive and represent a well-founded investment.

Literary Diversification

Harlequin's heavy dependence on the romance novel had been a source of concern to company executives for a number of years. In 1975 the company had attempted diversification with a line of science fiction novels for the North American market, known as the Laser series. In spite of an intense marketing effort the series was discontinued after 18 months and 58 titles. Heisey indicated that no one factor was responsible, suggesting that the problem was likely part editorial, part distribution, and part pricing (Appendix A).

Subsequent literary diversification attempts were more modest. In 1977, Mills and Boon created a series of romance stories in medical settings focusing on doctors and nurses, and these were introduced at the rate of two titles per month. In 1978 the Masquerade line of historical romances was also introduced at the rate of two titles per month. In Willson's view, these were "the same romance stories, but with long dresses." While both lines showed some initial promise, neither was expected to match the success of Harlequin Presents or Harlequin Romances.

In 1979 Harlequin took the somewhat bolder step of creating a new brand, Worldwide Library, which would act as an umbrella imprint for new products. The first of these was Mystique Books, introduced in March 1979. This romantic suspense series, adapted from a successful line of French novels, was introduced at the rate of four titles per month, with heavy television advertising. It did not carry the Harlequin name.

The importance that Harlequin placed on new series such as these was illustrated in the five-year plan of the North American book division, the company's most important business unit. This division's objective was a 30% annual increase in sales and profits throughout the early 1980s, to be achieved by increasing the U.S. penetration rate of the Presents and Romances lines closer to Canadian levels and at the same time, through the introduction of new "spin off" products, to reduce the overall dependence on those two lines to 65% of sales and profits by 1985. Harlequin's penetration rate in the U.S. (sales per woman over the age of 15) was approximately half that of the Canadian penetration rate.

Scholar's Choice

Scholar's Choice was created in the early 1970s when Harlequin acquired and merged two small Canadian companies involved in the production of educational material for school boards and teachers. Dissatisfied with what it described as "mixed results" from "less than buoyant Canadian institutional markets for educator supplies" during the mid-1970s, the company opened a retail store in Toronto in 1977. The success of this store led to a second Toronto store in 1978 and plans for seven more stores across Canada in 1979. All of these stores would sell educational material and would be wholly owned by the company.

Harlequin Films

Harlequin entered the movie-making business in 1977 with the $1.1 million film, "Leopard in the Snow." The movie featured no well-known actors, but it was based on a successful novel by one of Harlequin's established authors. The venture was a first step toward Harlequin's objective of "becoming to women what Walt Disney is to children." Willson elaborated on Harlequin's rationale:

> In the traditional film-making business there are a number of quite separate participants. The screen-play and actual creation of the movie is done by one group, financing by another group, distribution and marketing of the finished product by a variety of people. The people who actually create the product virtually lose control of it by the time it is marketed. Because so many conflicting groups are involved with different objectives and skills, the entire process is extremely inefficient.

> Harlequin could manage this process quite differently. We have the books for screen-plays—over 2 000 on our backlist—and we have the finances to make the films. We know how to market and we have far more knowledge about our target market than most moviemakers ever do. We could, once we gain confidence, use the distributors only to get the films into the theatres for a flat fee. We would do the promotion ourselves and take the financial risk.

> The other advantage to Harlequin is the same one that we have in the publishing business—consistency. For other producers, each film is a new product and new risk and the public has to be educated separately. We could advertise Harlequin films on a pretty intensive scale, and they could reinforce and be reinforced by the book sales. The potential may be tremendous.

The box office results of "Leopard in the Snow" were described by the company as "somewhat inconsistent" and further testing was to be done in 1979 to determine the feasibility of the concept.

Forward Integration

Harlequin's current three-year contract with Pocket Books was going to expire on December 31, 1979 and the company was considering ending the arrangement and establishing its own U.S. sales force. The following factors indicated that such a move might make sense:

1. *Cost.* Harlequin paid Pocket Books a set fee per book sold for the use of its U.S. sales force. As volumes continued to rise, so would Harlequin's total selling cost, even though Pocket Book's sales force costs were unlikely to increase. Harlequin executives estimated that they were already paying "well over half" the total cost of the Pocket Book sales force, even though the volumes of books it handled for Simon and Schuster and Harlequin were approximately equal. In fact, since Simon and Schuster's line consisted of "one-offs" which had to be "sold" to the distributors each month and the

Harlequin line was all on automatic reorders, there was little doubt that Harlequin received less than half of the sales force's attention. The net result was that Harlequin felt it would get better service at lower cost from its own sales force.

2. *New Products.* As new products like the Mystique line were introduced to the U.S. market with increasing frequency, the attention given to each product line by the sales force would become extremely important. If such new lines were to be a success, Harlequin felt that it would need to be able to directly control the activities of its U.S. sales force.

3. *Returns.* One of the tasks of a Harlequin sales force was known as "order regulation." This job, which was to check with individual retailers to determine their return rate, was necessary because the independent distributors, set up to handle magazines, could not accurately monitor pocket book returns by customer. If the return rate was too high, books were being printed and distributed for no gain. If it was too low, retailers were stocking out and sales were being lost.

Larry Heisey commented:

> I ran a check to see what kind of a job Pocket Books was doing for us on order regulation. We had about 400 distributors, each carrying Romances and Presents. That means we could have had up to 800 changes in order positions per month as wholesalers fine-tuned their demands to optimize our return rates. As I recall, there were only about 23 changes per month in the time period we checked. The Pocket Book's sales force simply wasn't managing the situation the way they should have been.

The only concern expressed at Harlequin about dropping Pocket Books was the possible reaction of Dick Snyder, the tough and aggressive president of Simon and Schuster. Snyder had become president of Simon and Schuster in 1975, the same year that the New York-based publisher was acquired by Gulf and Western, a large U.S. conglomerate. Snyder was interested in growth and profits, and was achieving results in both areas. *Newsweek* commented as follows:

> S&S has always been a best-seller house, but Snyder has turned it into the bastion of books-as-product—and the target of derision by other publishers who pride themselves on a commitment to good literature. He expects his editors to bring in twice as many titles per year as are required at other houses...
>
> The marketing staff is renowned for its aggressiveness—and high turnover rate. "Simon and Schuster runs a sales contest every year," former sales representative Jack O'Leary says only half jokingly. "The winners get to keep their jobs."

The Acquisition Program

In 1977, Heisey and Willson had estimated Harlequin's potential world market for romance novels (all non-communist countries) at $250 million, but as Harlequin's prices and volumes continued to rise, it became apparent that this estimate may have been too low. No matter how big the ultimate market, however, neither man felt that the company could penetrate this market any faster than it already was. They also emphasized that Harlequin's romantic fiction business could not profitably absorb all the cash it generated. As a result, Willson, with the approval of the Torstar Corporation (publisher of *The Toronto Star* newspaper) which had acquired 59% of Harlequin's shares in the late 1970s, hired several staff analysts and began a search for acquisitions. Early investigation revealed that the major U.S. paperback companies were not for sale, and the minor ones were not attractive.

Willson prepared a list to guide the search process (Exhibit 2), deciding that he was not interested in any company which would add less than 10% to Harlequin's profits. With more than $20 million in cash in 1977 and no debt to speak of, Willson had thought that $40 million would be a reasonable amount to spend on acquisitions; he visualized two major acquisitions, both in the U.S. One would be in the publishing business and the other in a related business.

By 1979, Willson and his group had made several acquisitions, but were still searching for one or two really sizeable takeover candidates. In mid-1977 they had purchased the Ideals Corporation of Milwaukee, a publisher of inspirational magazines and books, as well as greeting cards and a line of cookbooks, for $1.5 million. In 1978 Harlequin acquired a 78% interest in the Laufer Company of Hollywood, California, for $10.5 million, approximately $8 million of which represented goodwill. In the nine months ended December 31, 1977, Laufer earned US$814 000 on sales of $10 million. Laufer published eight monthly entertainment magazines including *Tiger Beat, Right On!* and *Rona Barrett's Hollywood*, for teenage and adult markets. The Laufer and Ideals businesses were subsequently combined to form the Harlequin Magazine Group. (An organization chart is presented in Exhibit 3.) During the first half of 1979 the magazine group acquired a 50% interest in *ARTnews* ("the most distinguished fine arts magazine in the United States"), a 60% interest in *Antiques World*, which was launched in 1979 as a sister publication to *ARTnews*, and a 57.5% interest in a new Toronto publication titled *Photo Life*.

THE FUTURE

As the financial results for the first six months of 1979 arrived, showing a 45% increase in sales (no doubt in part a result of the 20% and 30% price increases on the Presents and Romances lines in North America— bringing retail prices to $1.50 and $1.25 respectively) and a 23% gain in net income, Larry Heisey looked forward to the 1980s with keen anticipation.

> We believe the 1980s will be very important to Harlequin, even more so than the seventies. Our market research indicates substantial growth potential in the English-language markets. The rapid development of markets in Holland and French Canada to per capita levels nearly equivalent to those of English-speaking Canada, our most mature market, suggest the great potential of Mills & Boon romance fiction in other languages.
>
> The goals that we established for ourselves at the beginning of the seventies are being realized, generating an outstanding growth pattern. We have every reason to believe that this pattern will continue in the 1980s, for the company's financial resources are more than adequate to support an active expansion and diversification program.

EXHIBIT 1 Harlequin Summary of Financial Performance

	1978	1977	1976	1975	1974	1973	1972	1971	1970
Operating Results ($000 000s)									
Net revenues									
Publishing	n/a	n/a	44.1	35.1	24.8	16.4	11.0	4.0	3.0
Learning materials*	n/a	n/a	8.3	8.2	6.2	4.0	4.3	4.0	5.1
Total net revenues	$125.9	$80.9	$52.4	$43.2	$31.0	$20.4	$15.3	$ 8.0	$ 8.0
Net earnings	$ 16.8	$12.5	$ 5.2	$ 4.4	$ 3.5	$ 3.0	$ 1.6	$ .5	$ .1
Financial Position ($000 000s)									
Cash and securities	22.5	24.0	9.3	4.2	3.5	3.2	1.1	1.2	
Total current assets	58.4	45.8	23.6	19.2	14.3	10.0	6.1	6.2	4.0
Current liabilities	25.2	21.2	10.5	8.4	7.0	5.0	3.4	4.0	2.1
Working capital	33.2	24.6	13.1	10.8	7.2	5.0	3.0	2.5	2.0
Net fixed assets	2.3	1.7	1.0	.9	.7	.5	.2	.2	.2
Other assets	14.1	6.4	5.8	3.7	3.7	3.7	4.0	4.0	2.2
Shareholders' equity	45.2	30.5	19.4	15.4	11.7	9.1	6.8	4.3	3.9
Financial Ratios									
Net earnings on net revenues	13.3%	15.6%	10.2%	10.2%	11.4%	13.4%	10.3%	5.7%	1.4%
Net earnings on equity	37.1%	41.0%	27.5%	28.8%	30.2%	30.0%	23.2%	10.5%	2.8%
Working-capital ratio	2.3:1	2.2:1	2.3:1	2.3:1	2.0:1	2.0:1	1.8:1	1.7:1	1.7:1
Fully diluted earnings per share	$1.06	$.79	$.34	$.29	$.24	$.18	$.12	$.04	$.01
Dividends declared ($000 000s)	2.3	1.4	1.3	1.2	1.0	.4	.1	—	—
Other Data									
Share price** —low	7.75	3.83	2.75	1.33	.94	1.30	.44	.23	n/a
—high	16.00	9.00	3.79	3.25	1.72	1.83	1.67	.46	
Number of employees	980	881	584	332	313	240	201	157	188
Number of books sold (000 000s)	125	109	90	72	63	42	29	25	19

* Although exact figures were not available, learning materials were still a relatively low proportion of Harlequin sales in 1978.
** Adjusted for splits. Stock price mid-1979 was $18 to $20.

EXHIBIT 2 Harlequin's Guide for Acquisitions

Potential Areas to Look for Acquisition in Publishing Business	*Areas to Consider for Acquisition in Related Industry*
1. Trade Books —paperback fiction and non-fiction —hardcover series and partworks 2. Reference Books —text books and learned journals —professional publishing: legal, medical, accounting —reference guides and handbooks 3. Magazines —consumer magazines —trade and business publications 4. Other publishing —greeting cards, stationery —sewing patterns —diaries and albums —music publishing	1. Entertainment —movies and television films —records —video tapes —music 2. Mass-marketed low-technology consumer products —adult games —children's games —children's toys 3. Handicraft and hobby products

124

EXHIBIT 3   Organization Chart Harlequin Enterprises Limited

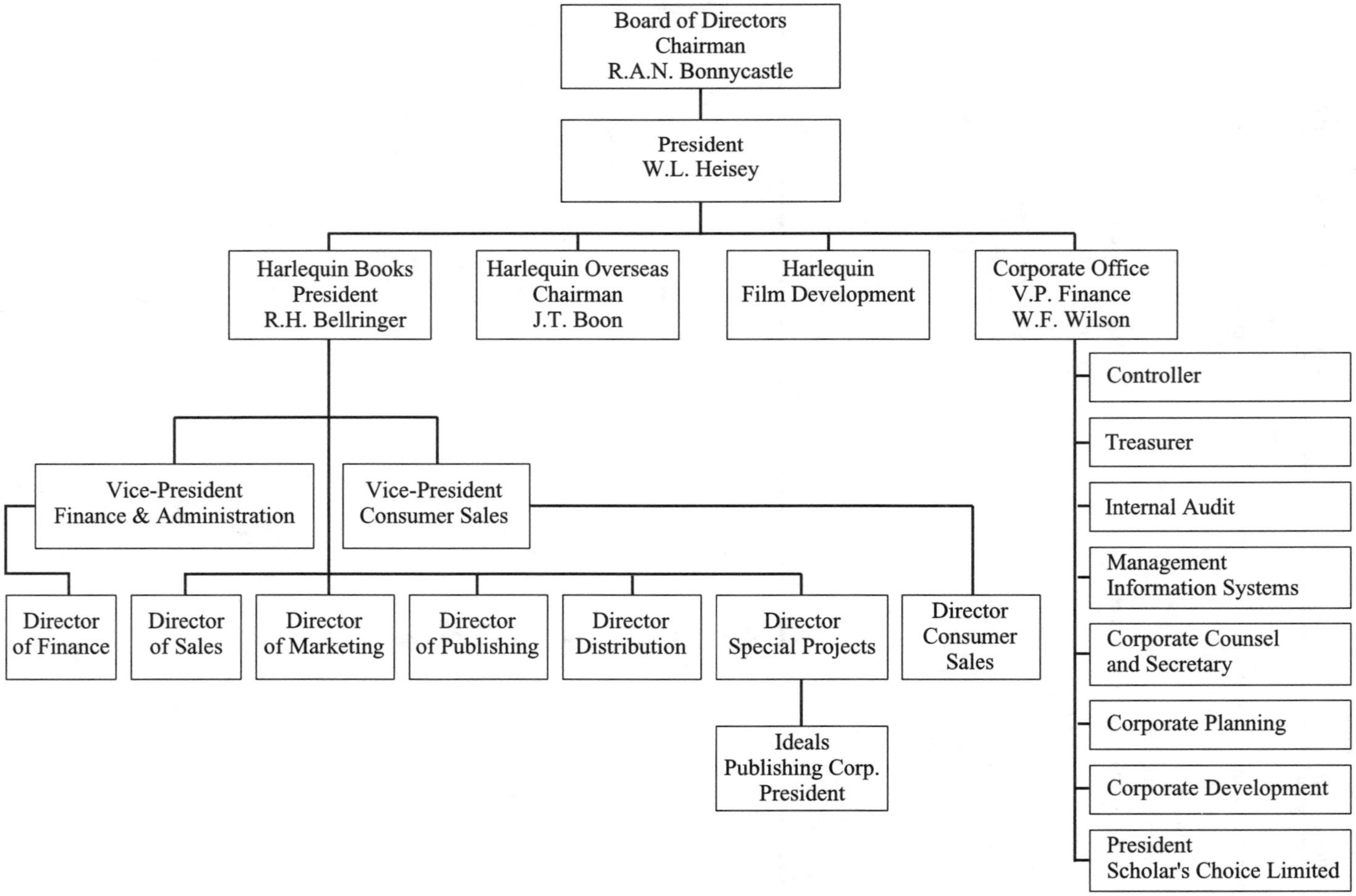

```
                    Board of Directors
                    Chairman
                    R.A.N. Bonnycastle
                           │
                       President
                       W.L. Heisey
                           │
   ┌──────────────┬──────────────┬──────────────┬──────────────┐
Harlequin      Harlequin       Harlequin      Corporate Office
Books          Overseas        Film           V.P. Finance
President       Chairman       Development     W.F. Wilson
R.H. Bellringer J.T. Boon                           │
                                            ┌───┬───┬───┬───┬───┬───┬───┐
                                        Controller
                                        Treasurer
                                        Internal Audit
                                        Management Information Systems
                                        Corporate Counsel and Secretary
                                        Corporate Planning
                                        Corporate Development
                                        President Scholar's Choice Limited

Harlequin Books:
   ┌──────────────────────┬──────────────────────┐
Vice-President         Vice-President
Finance & Administration Consumer Sales
   │                       │
Director of Finance    Director of Marketing
Director of Sales      Director of Publishing
                       Director Distribution
                       Director Special Projects ── Ideals Publishing Corp. President
                       Director Consumer Sales
```

Appendix A

Why Harlequin Enterprises Fell Out of Love with Science Fiction by Brian M. Fraser

"It didn't work," says Harlequin Enterprises President W. Lawrence Heisey. "We didn't perceive that it would be profitable in the reasonably short-term future, so we decided to abandon it. Period."

Although noncommittal on the failure, Heisey said no one factor was responsible: "I think it was a lot of problems," he said. "it wasn't any one thing. I don't think the distribution was that bad; it probably begins with editorial and ends with pricing so it was a whole collection of problems. But it didn't work."

Hard-core SF enthusiasts were against the venture from the start, fearing science fiction would be watered down into pap for the masses. And, indeed, this was essentially true: the plots of the Laser books generally took standard ideas in the genre and sketched new adventure stories, but without much depth.

Like its romances, which are mainly sold in supermarkets and drug stores, Harlequin attempted to produce a uniform product in the science fiction category. It also hoped it would prove as addictive to young male readers as the light romances are for some housewives.

Harlequin put all its marketing expertise and resources behind the new SF paperbacks, beginning with six titles plus a free novel (*Seeds of Change* by Thomas F. Monteleone) as incentive to anyone who bought a Laser book and returned a questionnaire. Like good marketers, they used these names to build a mailing list for promotional material.

An extensive publicity and advertising program was tied to the announcement. Major Canadian media carried articles, focusing on the worldwide financial success of the Harlequin Romances line.

To attract potential readers directly, full-page ads were placed in major science-fiction digest magazines, such as *Analog*, and in amateur fan magazines, such as *Locus*. And, with sage marketing skill, Harlequin also attempted to create a favourable selling environment through ads in *Publisher's Weekly* and the *West Coast Review of Books*, which are read by bookstore managers.

Harlequin even placed trial direct response ads in a girlie magazine, ran radio commercials in Toronto and U.S. test markets, and its ad agency, Compton Advertising of New York, tried out a television commercial.

These innovative merchandising techniques, not part of the repertoire of most Canadian publishers, have been used with some success on the romances.

"The failure can be attributed to a complete misunderstanding of the special appeal of science fiction and the nature of its addictive readers. Nobody in the know ever believed this venture would succeed," says veteran U.S. SF editor Donald Woolheim.

The inside-SF consensus is that Harlequin underestimated the intelligence of the science fiction reader who, unlike the devotees of Harlequin romances, looks for non-formula fiction, cerebral material with new and well-developed ideas.

It's conceivable that lack of adequate distribution may have been one of the prime reasons Harlequin pulled out. With the Romances line, Harlequin has been phenomenally successful in penetrating the grocery and drugstore markets, placing racks specifically for their interchangeable 12 titles a month. But no such breakthrough was evident with the Laser line.

Source: Original article appeared in *The Financial Post*, December 17, 1977.

case

9

IMASCO LIMITED: THE ROY ROGERS ACQUISITION

Kent E. Neupert and Joseph N. Fry

In January 1990, Purdy Crawford, the chairman, president and CEO of Imasco Limited, was reviewing an acquisition proposal from one of Imasco's operating companies, Hardee's Food Systems, Inc. (Hardee's) to purchase the Roy Rogers restaurant chain. Bill Prather, Hardee's CEO, was coming to Montreal the following day to present the proposal to the Imasco board. Prather thought the acquisition would permit Hardee's to expand rapidly into markets where they had very little presence. While Crawford was inclined

IVEY

Kent E. Neupert prepared this case under the supervision of Professor Joseph N. Fry solely to provide material for class discussion. The author does not intend to illustrate either effective or ineffective handling of a managerial situation. The author may have disguised certain names and other identifying information to protect confidentiality.

to support Prather's proposal, he wanted to carefully weigh its broader impact for Imasco as a whole. The probable price of more than $390 million represented a substantial commitment of funds, at a time when growth in the U.S. fast food business was slowing.

IMASCO BACKGROUND

Imasco was a diversified Canadian public corporation with consolidated revenues of $5.7 billion in 1989 and net profits of $366 million. Imasco's founding and largest shareholder was B.A.T Industries (B.A.T), which had maintained a relatively constant 40% equity ownership over the years. B.A.T was a very large diversified British company with roots, like Imasco, in the tobacco business. The balance of Imasco shares were widely held. In 1990, Imasco's operations were focused on four major operating companies, "the four legs of the table," as Crawford referred to them. The companies were: Imperial Tobacco, Canada's largest manufacturer and distributor of cigarettes; CT Financial, the holding company for Canada Trust, a major Canadian retail financial services business; Imasco Drug Retailing Group, made up of Shoppers Drug Mart in Canada and Peoples Drug Stores in the U.S.; and Hardee's Food Systems, Inc. in the U.S. A fifth, smaller company was The UCS Group, Canada's leading small space specialty retailer. Highlights of Imasco's operations for the years 1985–89 are shown in Table 1.

T A B L E 1 Imasco Operating Highlights

($ million unless otherwise noted)

	1989	1988	1987	1986	1985
System-wide Sales	14 715.6	13 836.5	12 951.5	11 132.2	8 371.8
Revenues	5 724.7	6 000.6	5 924.4	5 596.6	5 110.2
Operating Earnings	692.0	636.7	578.4	455.6	464.1
Total Assets	5 378.0	5 310.2	5 656.6	5 505.5	2 905.7
Earnings before Extraordinary Items	366.1	314.3	282.7	226.4	261.6
EPS before Extraordinary Items	2.87	2.51	2.24	1.92	2.40
DVDS/Share	1.12	1.04	0.96	0.84	0.72

IMASCO DIVERSIFICATION ACTIVITIES

Imasco Limited was created in 1969 as a corporate entity to encompass and oversee the tobacco, food and distribution businesses of Imperial Tobacco Limited, and to manage a program of further diversification. The aim was to build a broadly based corporation that would rely less on the tobacco business and be better received in the stock market.

Paul Paré was the first president, chairman and CEO of Imasco, and the person with prime responsibility for its diversification program up to his retirement from the chairmanship in 1987. Paré's 38-year career began in the legal department of Imperial Tobacco and led to senior positions in the marketing areas. He became president and CEO in 1969 and chairman in 1979. Except for a two-year stint with the Department of National Defence, his career was always in the tobacco industry. Paré's approach to diversification in the early years had been a conservative one. He preferred to make a number of relatively small investments, and build or divest the positions as experience dictated.

Crawford, Paré's successor, pictured the first ten years of diversification as a process of experimentation and learning. He described the evolution of thought and action: "Imperial's first attempt at diversification had been through vertical integration." Crawford explained: "Although it appeared logical that if Imperial bought a tinfoil company and made foil wrap themselves there were economies to be realized, we quickly learned that making cigarettes and making tinfoil are two different things." Imperial knew little about the highly specialized tinfoil business, and also discovered that "the competition didn't like the idea of buying tinfoil from us."

Upon reflection, management determined that they were "in the business of converting and marketing agricultural products." Crawford recounted: "It made sense then that the next acquisition was a winery. Unfortunately, we failed to take into consideration provincial liquor regulations which made it impossible to operate at a sufficient scale to be profitable."

Management then broadened its perspective and decided that they were best at marketing. This led to acquisitions that "embodied exciting new marketing concepts," such as two sporting goods companies, Collegiate and Arlington, and a discount bottler and retailer of soft drinks called PoP Shoppes. These investments were held for several years, but they failed to live up to their promise and were subsequently sold off. Other acquisitions, in food processing and distribution, for example, were quite successful, but not on a scale of importance to Imasco. These were later divested when Imasco refocused its efforts.

For the most part, these early diversification moves involved the acquisition of several small companies, and subsequent restructuring of them into a larger enterprise. Most of these acquisitions were then later divested. For example, Imasco's three food companies, which were sold in the late 1970s and early 1980s, were originally ten different companies. Amco Vending, sold in 1977, was built up from eight separate vending companies across Canada. Other businesses which were grown and later sold included wines, dry cleaning, and video tape services.

With time, Paré's team built an understanding of its capabilities, sharpened its sense of mission, and focused its acquisition criteria. The mission was to "create shareholder value as a leading North American consumer products and services company." Based on their learning, the criteria for acquisitions were formalized. Imasco would acquire companies that (1) were well positioned in the consumer goods and services sector of the economy; (2) had a capable management team in place, or were able to be smoothly integrated into an existing operating division; (3) had above average growth potential, and were capable of making a meaningful and immediate contribution to profits; and (4) were North American based, preferably in Canada. Crawford noted that "perhaps the most important end result of approximately ten years of experimentation was that we developed a clear vision of what the company was and was not."

As Imasco became more focused and confident of its skills, the acquisitions became less frequent and larger in size, and the diversification from tobacco more significant. Imasco's acquisitions and net investments are given in Exhibit 1. The most significant events of the 1980s are described below in the review of the present-day Imasco operating companies. The net result of 20 years of diversification was that Imasco increased its revenues tenfold and its earnings twentyfold. Moreover, its reliance on tobacco for corporate earnings went from 100% in 1970 to 48% in 1989. A twenty year review of Imasco performance is given in Exhibit 2.

Corporate Management

While Imasco's diversification policy was directed from the central office, its operations were not centralized. The corporate management structure was decentralized and rather flat. Only 50 people staffed the head office in Montreal. The various companies, with operations across Canada and most of the U.S., were encouraged to aggressively pursue the development of their businesses and related trademarks. Management believed that "combining the experience and expertise that flow from the individual operating companies creates a unique opportunity to add value to all of its (Imasco's) operations and assets." Accordingly,

Imasco saw its greatest strengths as the high degree of autonomy, and clear lines of authority and responsibility, which existed between Imasco's head office (the Imasco Centre) and the operating companies. While each company's CEO operated with the widest possible autonomy, they also contributed to the development of the annual and five-year plans, and "to furthering Imasco's overall growth objectives." The role of the Imasco Centre was to guide Imasco's overall growth without interfering with the operating companies. The 1988 business plan stipulated that "the role of the Imasco Centre is to be a source of excellence in management dedicated to achieving overall corporate objectives, and supporting Imasco's operating companies in the fulfilment of their respective missions and objectives."

It was very important to Imasco that any acquisition be friendly. While it was not formally stipulated in the acquisition criteria, it was evident in Imasco's actions, such as the aborted acquisition of Canadian Tire in 1983.

In June of that year, Imasco initiated an acquisition attempt of Canadian Tire, but later withdrew the offer. Imasco had outlined a proposal to the members of the Billes family, majority shareholders in Canadian Tire, and the management of Canadian Tire in which Imasco would purchase as many of Canadian Tire's outstanding common and Class "A" shares as would be tendered. Imasco stipulated the offer was conditional on family and management support. Imasco expected the cost of the acquisition to be about $1.13 billion.

Several days later, Paré issued a press release in which he stated:

> We at Imasco are obviously disappointed with the reaction of the senior management group at Canadian Tire to purchase all of the outstanding shares of the company. We stated at the outset that we were seeking both the support of the major voting shareholders and the endorsement of management. It now appears that such support and endorsement are not forthcoming. In light of this and in view of the announcement made... by the trustees of the John W. Billes estate, we have concluded that one or more of the conditions to our offer will not be satisfied. Therefore, we do not propose to proceed with our previously announced offer.

In explaining Imasco's rationale for withdrawing the offer, Paré continued:

> Throughout the negotiations, we have been keenly aware of the essential ingredients that have made Canadian Tire one of the retail success stories in Canada. These ingredients include the able leadership of the management group, the unique relationship between management and the associate-dealers, and the employee profit-sharing and share-ownership plans. As we have mentioned on several occasions, it was our intention to preserve these relationships and the formulas that have so obviously contributed to the success of the Canadian Tire organization.

OPERATING COMPANIES

Imperial Tobacco

Imperial Tobacco was the largest tobacco enterprise in Canada, with operations ranging from leaf tobacco buying and processing, to the manufacture and distribution of a broad range of tobacco products. The manufacture and sale of cigarettes constituted the largest segment of its business, representing 89.4% of Imperial Tobacco's revenues in 1989. Highlights of Imperial Tobacco's operations for the years 1985–89 are shown in Table 2.

TABLE 2   Imperial Tobacco Operating Summary

($ million unless otherwise noted)

	1989	1988	1987	1986	1985
Revenues	2 385.6	2 018.1	1 926.0	1 754.6	1 701.8
Revenues, Net of Sales and Excise Taxes	896.2	862.0	816.2	712.0	757.5
Operating Earnings	334.0	308.0	279.1	208.1	243.7
Operating Margins (%)	37.3	35.7	34.2	29.2	32.2
Market Share–Domestic	57.9	56.2	54.4	51.5	52.6
Capital Employed*	558.1	496.4	513.9	594.6†	587.0†

* Capital employed of each consolidated segment consists of directly identifiable assets at net book value, less current liabilities, excluding income taxes payable and bank and other debt. Corporate assets and corporate current liabilities are also excluded.
† Reflects fiscal year ending March 31.

Over the years, Imperial had concentrated on building its market share in Canada from a low of 36% in 1970 to 57.9% in 1989. Revenues in 1989 reached an all time high of almost $2.4 billion, in spite of a 4% decline in unit sales to 27.5 billion cigarettes. The market share gains had been achieved by focusing on the strength of Imperial Tobacco's trademarks, particularly the continued growth of its two leading Canadian brands, Player's and du Maurier. Together these two brands held 47.4% of the market in 1989.

Imperial Tobacco had production and packaging facilities in Montreal and Joliette, Quebec, and Guelph, Ontario, and leaf processing facilities in Joliette and LaSalle, Quebec, and Aylmer, Ontario. Imperial continually modernized its production facilities to the point that management claimed them to be "the most technologically advanced in the tobacco industry in Canada." The distribution and promotion of Imperial Tobacco's products to wholesalers and retailers was carried out through a nationwide sales staff operating out of the sales offices and distribution centres in St. John's, Moncton, Montreal, Toronto, Winnipeg, Calgary and Vancouver.

Imasco Enterprises (Including Canada Trust)

Imasco Enterprises Inc. (IEI) was wholly owned through Imasco Limited and three of its other companies, making it an indirect wholly owned subsidiary. In 1986, Imasco announced its intention to acquire all of the outstanding common shares of Genstar Corporation (Genstar) through IEI. At the time, Imasco's primary objective was to gain entry into the financial services sector by assuming Genstar's 98% ownership position in Canada Trust. Genstar had purchased Canada Trust in 1985 for $1.2 billion and merged it with Canada Permanent Mortgage Corporation, which Genstar had purchased in 1981. This merger created Canada's seventh largest financial institution with $50 billion in assets under administration.

Once acquired, Imasco intended to sell off all of Genstar's non-financial assets. Within the year, all of the shares were acquired at a cost of approximately $2.6 billion. This was the first acquisition orchestrated by Crawford.

In addition to Canada Trust, Genstar had holdings in an assortment of other businesses. Most of these, such as the cement and related operations, Genstar Container Corporation, and Seaspan International, were sold off. The cost of those assets retained, including Canada Trust, was about $2.4 billion, of which all but $150 million was attributed to the Canada Trust holding. The balance of the amount was accounted for by a variety of assets which included Genstar Development Company, Genstar Mortgage Corporation, a one-third limited partnership in Sutter Hill Ventures, a portfolio of other venture capital investments, and certain other assets and liabilities. Genstar Development Company was involved in land development in primary Canadian metropolitan areas, such as Vancouver, Calgary, Edmonton, Winnipeg, Toronto and

Ottawa. U.S.-based Sutter Hill Ventures had capital investments in over 43 different companies. Most of these investments were in the areas of medical research, biotechnology, communications and computer hardware and software. Highlights of investments in IEI are shown in Table 3.

TABLE 3   Investments in Imasco Enterprises, Inc.

($ million)

	1989	1988	1987*
Equity in Net Earnings of Imasco Enterprises	152.5	142.1	126.5
Investment in Imasco Enterprises	2 700.2	2 655.4	2 613.5

* Financial information is shown beginning with 1987 to reflect the acquisition of Canada Trust in 1986.

CT Financial was the holding company for the Canada Trust group of companies. In 1989, Canada Trust was Canada's second largest trust and loan company, and a major residential real estate broker. The principal businesses of Canada Trust were financial intermediary services, such as deposit services, credit card services, mortgage lending, consumer lending, corporate and commercial lending, and investments. It also offered trust services, real estate services and real estate development. Canada Trust operated 331 financial services branches, 22 personal and pension trust services offices, and 275 company operated and franchised real estate offices. Total assets under the administration of Canada Trust at the end of 1989 were $74.1 billion, comprising $32.7 billion in corporate assets, and $41.4 billion in assets administered for estate, trust and agency accounts. Total personal deposits were estimated to be the fourth largest among Canadian financial institutions. The return of common shareholders' average equity was 17.3% compared with an average of 7.7% for Canada's six largest banks. Highlights of CT Financial operations are shown in Table 4.

Imasco Drug Retailing

SHOPPERS DRUG MART Shoppers Drug Mart provided a wide range of marketing and management services to a group of 633 associated retail drug stores located throughout Canada, operating under the trademarks Shoppers Drug Mart (585 stores), and Pharmaprix in Quebec (48 stores). The Shoppers Drug Mart stores also included the extended concepts of Shoppers Drug Mart Food Baskets and Shoppers Drug Mart Home Health Care Centres.

TABLE 4   Operating Performance Data for CT Financial

($ million unless otherwise noted)

	1989	1988	1987*
Assets under Administration	74 096.0	67 401.0	60 626.0
Corporate Assets	32 666.0	29 219.2	25 514.8
Deposits	30 403.0	27 319.5	23 859.0
Loans	24 201.1	22 661.7	19 679.3
Net Earnings Attributed to Common Shares	240.2	232.0	201.0
Return on Common Shareholders Average Equity (%)	17.3	19.0	19.4

* Financial information is shown beginning with 1987 to reflect the acquisition of Canada Trust in 1986.

In 1989, Shoppers Drug Mart was the largest drug store group in Canada with about 33% of the retail drug store market. In system wide sales, it ranked first and fifth among all drug store groups in Canada and North America, respectively. In the past, competition had come primarily from regional chains and independent drug stores, but food stores with drug departments represented a growing challenge. During 1989, management had emphasized strengthening the productivity and profitability of existing stores, particularly the former Super X Drugs and Howie's stores, recently converted to Shoppers Drug Mart stores.

The Shoppers Drug Mart operating division utilized licensing and franchise agreements. Under the licensing arrangement, each Shoppers Drug Mart was owned and operated by a licensed pharmacist, called an Associate. In Quebec, Pharmaprix stores used a franchise system. In return for an annual fee, each Associate of a Shoppers Drug Mart store and Franchisee of a Pharmaprix store had access to a variety of services, such as store design, merchandising techniques, financial analysis, training, advertising and marketing. Highlights of Shoppers Drug Mart operations are shown in Table 5.

T A B L E 5 Shoppers Drug Mart Operating Summary

($ million unless otherwise noted)

	1989	1988	1987	1986	1985
System-wide Sales	2 597.7	2 355.6	2 073.4	1 775.0	1 522.3
Revenues	136.2	114.9	95.7	86.6	73.4
Operating Earnings	70.6	57.1	51.3	48.9	42.5
Operating Margins (%)	51.8	49.7	53.6	56.5	57.9
Average Sales per Store	4.1	4.2	4.1	3.9	3.6
Number of Stores	633	613	586	543	431
Capital Expenditures	24.0	28.0	27.6	23.3	16.4
Capital Employed*	204.1	209.8	194.2	117.9†	106.8†
Depreciation	26.6	20.6	17.9	13.0	11.8

* Capital employed of each consolidated segment consists of directly identifiable assets at net book value, less current liabilities, excluding income taxes payable and bank and other debt. Corporate assets and corporate current liabilities are also excluded.
† Reflects fiscal year ending March 31.

PEOPLES DRUG STORES
Peoples Drug Stores, Incorporated (Peoples) operated 490 company owned drug stores in the U.S. during 1989. The stores were primarily operated from leased premises under the trade names Peoples Drug Stores, Health Mart, and Rea and Derick. Imasco had built the Peoples operating division from several acquired drug store chains in six eastern U.S. states and the District of Columbia.

After a disappointing performance in 1986, Peoples began a comprehensive plan to revitalise the chain and focus on areas of market strength. Earnings steadily improved, with operating earnings of $8.0 million in 1989, compared with operating losses of $8.3 million in 1988 and $22.5 million in 1987. The turnaround involved restructuring, including the divestment of Peoples' Reed, Lane, Midwest, Bud's Deep Discount, and other smaller divisions. During 1989, a total of 326 drug stores were sold, 21 were closed, and 13 opened for a net decrease of 334 stores. At the beginning of 1990, only five Bud's stores remained to be sold. The result was a concentration on Peoples' strongest markets, primarily, the District of Columbia, Maryland, Virginia, West Virginia and Pennsylvania. The highlights of Peoples' operations are shown in Table 6.

T A B L E 6   Peoples Drug Stores Operating Summary

($ million unless otherwise noted)

	1989	1988	1987	1986	1985
Revenues	1 207.2	1 841.6	1 850.2	1 922.5	1 737.3
Operating Earnings	8.0	(8.3)	(22.5)	0.1	52.5
Operating Margins (%)	0.7	(0.5)	(1.2)	—	3.0
Average Sales per Store (US $)	2.1	1.8	1.7	1.7	1.5
Number of Stores	490	829	819	830	824
Capital Expenditures	12.4	41.9	29.1	32.7	58.5
Capital Employed*	369.4	523.5	703.6	819.5†	653.5†

* Capital employed of each consolidated segment consists of directly identifiable assets at net book value, less current liabilities, excluding income taxes payable and bank and other debt. Corporate assets and corporate current liabilities are also excluded.
† Reflects fiscal year ending March 31.

The UCS Group

In 1989, The UCS Group operated 531 stores in Canada from leased premises. The stores carried a wide variety of everyday convenience items, including newspapers and magazines, cigarettes and smokers' accessories, confectionary, snack foods, gifts and souvenir selections. The retail outlets were all company-operated, and included UCS newsstands in shopping centres, commercial office towers, airports, hotels, and other high consumer traffic locations. The UCS group operated 531 stores in five divisions: Woolco/Woolworth, Specialty Stores, Hotel/Airport, Den for Men/AuMasculin, and Tax and Duty Free. Highlights of The UCS Group operations are shown in Table 7.

T A B L E 7   The UCS Group Operating Summary

($ million unless otherwise noted)

	1989	1988	1987	1986	1985
Revenues	286.1	256.6	235.3	206.0	187.8
Operating Earnings	8.3	7.5	6.7	6.6	5.5
Operating Margins (%)	2.9	2.9	2.9	3.2	2.9
Average Sales per Stores ($000)	543	489	461	432	410
Average Sales per Sq. Ft. ($)	790	718	675	651	629
Number of Stores	531	525	524	494	460
Capital Employed (Est.)*	41.4	45.6	40.7	37.6 †	57.2†

* Capital employed of each consolidated segment consists of directly identifiable assets at net book value, less current liabilities, excluding income taxes payable and bank and other debt. Corporate assets and corporate current liabilities are also excluded.
† Reflects fiscal year ending March 31.

Hardee's Food Systems

Imasco's move to make a major investment in a U.S.-based company arose in part from the greater opportunity offered by the U.S. economy for potential acquisitions of an interesting nature and scale, and in part from the constraints on Canadian acquisitions posed by the Foreign Investment Review Act (FIRA). The purpose of FIRA was to review certain forms of foreign investment in Canada, particularly controlling acquisitions of Canadian business enterprises, and diversifications of existing foreign-controlled firms into unrelated businesses. For several years, Imasco came under the control of FIRA due to B.A.T's 40% ownership of Imasco. In later years, however, Imasco was reclassified as a Canadian-owned enterprise.

Imasco's involvement with Hardee's and the U.S. restaurant business developed slowly. Imasco first became acquainted with Hardee's in 1969 when its pension fund manager was on holiday in South Carolina. The manager and his family were so fond of the Hardee's hamburgers that upon returning to Montreal, he investigated Hardee's as a possible pension fund investment. The following year, Imasco made a relatively small investment in Hardee's.

Later, when Hardee's was looking for expansion capital, it approached Imasco. In March 1977, Imasco invested $18.2 million in convertible preferred shares which, if converted, would give Imasco a 25% position in Hardee's. Between March 1980 and January 1981, Imasco converted their preferred shares and purchased the outstanding common shares at a cost of $114.1 million. At this time, Hardee's was the seventh largest hamburger restaurant chain in the U.S. Later, Imasco made additional investments in Hardee's to facilitate growth and acquisition.

By 1989, Hardee's Food Systems, Inc. (Hardee's) was the third largest hamburger restaurant chain in the U.S., as measured by system-wide sales and average unit sales volume. In number of outlets, it ranked fourth. With its head office in Rocky Mount, North Carolina, Hardee's restaurant operations consisted of 3 298 restaurants, of which 1 086 were company-operated and 2 212 were licensed. Of these restaurants, 3 257 were located in 39 states and the District of Columbia in the U.S., and 41 were located in nine other countries in the Middle East, Central America, and Southeast Asia. Average annual unit sales for 1989 were $1 060 300, compared with $1 058 000 in 1988. Highlights of Hardee's operations are shown in Table 8.

TABLE 8 Hardee's Operating Summary

($ million unless otherwise noted)

	1989	1988	1987	1986	1985
System-wide Sales	4 146.7	4 058.9*	4 059.1	3 721.6	3 248.4
Revenues	1 786.5	1 756.9	1 801.7	1 642.0	1 457.0
Operating Earnings	118.6	130.3	137.3	129.0	117.1
Operating Margins (%)	6.6	7.4	7.6	7.9	8.0
Average Sales per Restaurant (US $)	922	920	877	837	801
Capital Expenditures	155.3	209.9	217.0	135.6	99.9
Depreciation	78.9	78.0	75.5	63.0	53.4
Restaurants Company Owned	1 086	1 070	995	893	876
Restaurants Franchised	2 212	2 081	1 962	1 818	1 662
Total Restaurants	3 298	3 151	2 957	2 711	2 538
Capital Employed**	618.3	587.7*	777.5	668.1†	555.4†

* Includes sale and leaseback of properties.
** Capital employed of each consolidated segment consists of directly identifiable assets at net book value, less current liabilities, excluding income taxes payable and bank and other debt. Corporate assets and corporate current liabilities are also excluded.
† Reflects fiscal year ending March 31.

Hardee's had encouraged multi-unit development by licensees. In some cases, Hardee's granted exclusive territorial development rights to licensees on the condition that minimum numbers of new licensed restaurants in the area be opened within specific periods of time. As of December 31, 1989, Hardee's had license agreements with 234 licensee groups operating 2 205 restaurants. The ten largest of these licensees operated 1 213 restaurants, representing 55% of the licensed restaurants in the chain, and the two largest operated 738 licensed restaurants, or approximately 33% of the licensed restaurants.

Hardee's restaurants were limited-menu, quick-service family restaurants, and featured moderately priced items for all meals. These products were principally hamburgers, roast beef, chicken, turkey club, ham and cheese and fish sandwiches, breakfast biscuits, frankfurters, french fries, salads, turnovers, cookies, ice cream, and assorted beverages for both take-out and on-premise consumption. Recent additions to the Hardee's menu included a grilled chicken sandwich, Crispy Curl fries, and pancakes. These new products followed a series of initiatives taken in 1988, which included being the first hamburger chain to switch to all-vegetable cooking oil in order to lower fat and cholesterol levels in fried products. Hardee's also introduced more salads and more desserts to the menu.

Fast Food Merchandisers, Inc. (FFM) was an operating division of Hardee's that furnished restaurants with food and paper products through its food processing and distribution operations. All company-operated Hardee's restaurants purchased their food and paper products from FFM. Although licensees were not obligated to purchase from FFM, approximately 75% of Hardee's licensees purchased some or all of their requirements from FFM. FFM operated three food processing plants and eleven distribution centres. FFM also sold products to other food service and supermarket accounts.

THE PROPOSED ROY ROGERS ACQUISITION

The U.S. Food Service Industry[1]

Over the past twenty years, Americans spent a rising portion of their food dollars at restaurants. More two-income families, fewer women as full-time homemakers and a decline in the number of children to feed made dining out increasingly popular. In 1989, U.S. consumers spent $167 billion at 400 000 restaurants. This excluded an estimated $61 billion spent at other food and beverage outlets, such as employee cafeterias, hospitals, ice-cream stands and taverns. Although sales growth for the restaurant industry outpaced the economy in recent years, industry analysts noted indications of outlet saturation. In 1989, franchise restaurant chains expected to have U.S. sales of $70.4 billion, up 7.4% from the year before. However, on a per unit basis, 1989 sales for franchise chain units averaged $737 000, up only 4.3% from the previous year. Analysts pointed out that this rise corresponded to increases in menu prices.

Quick service or "fast food" restaurants had led industry growth for several decades, and were expected to do so over the near term. However, industry analysts cautioned that, as the average age of the American consumers increased, a shift away from fast food restaurants toward mid-scale restaurants might occur. Increased emphasis on take-out service and home delivery would help to maintain momentum, but analysts expected that fast food sales and new unit growth would not be up to the 6.6% compound annual rate from 1985 to 1989. McDonald's 8 000 U.S. outlets had sales of $12 billion, or about 7% of total U.S. restaurant spending. Chains that emphasized hamburgers, hot dogs, or roast beef were the largest part of the U.S. franchise restaurant industry, with 1989 sales of $33.8 billion from 36 206 outlets. McDonald's U.S. market share in the segment was about 36.1%, followed by Burger King (19.2%), Hardee's (9.9%), and Wendy's (8.5%).

Nature of Operations

The large hamburger chains generated revenues from three sources: (1) the operation of company owned restaurants; (2) franchising, which encompassed royalties and initial fees from licensees operating under

---

[1] Industry figures in U.S. dollars.

the trade name; and (3) commissary, consisting of food processing and the distribution of food, restaurant supplies and equipment essential to the operation of the company and franchised outlets. Profitable operation of company-owned restaurant operations called for high unit sales volume and tight control of operating margins.

Franchising had been the major chains' initial growth strategy. This enabled them to increase revenues, establish a competitive position, and achieve the scale necessary for efficient commissary and marketing operations. In 1989, there were 90 000 franchise operations accounting for 40% of U.S. restaurant operations. In 1989, McDonald's operating profit from franchising ($1.2 billion) substantially exceeded its profit from company operated restaurants ($822 million). It was often the case that in a franchising relationship, the cost of the land, building and equipment were the responsibility of the franchisee. The franchisee also paid a royalty, typically 3–6% of sales, and were charged 1–5% of sales for common advertising expenses. In return, the franchisee got brand name recognition, training and marketing support. However, some of the larger chains had taken an alternate approach by owning the land and the building. Not only did such an approach provide lease revenue but it also allowed the company to maintain some control over the franchisee's facilities.

Competition

Fast food restaurants competed with at-home eating, other restaurant types and each other. To build and maintain unit volumes, top chains developed strategies to differentiate themselves by target market, style of operation, menu and promotional approach, among other methods.

MCDONALD'S McDonald's was the leader of the fast food restaurant business. The chain began in the early 1950s in California. The McDonald brothers discovered that a combination of assembly line procedures, product standardization and high volume made it possible to offer exceptional value, providing consistent quality food at a reasonable price. The potential of their concept was recognized by Ray Kroc, a paper cup and milkshake mixer salesman. He acquired the operations, and provided the leadership for the formation and subsequent growth of the McDonald's corporation.

McDonald's had traditionally targeted children, teens and young families, and focused its menu of products around hamburgers and french fries. Scale, experience and simplified operating procedures permitted McDonald's to operate at significantly lower costs than its competitors. In the late 1970s, the company broadened its target market to follow demographic shifts and increase unit volumes. The menu was expanded to include a breakfast line and chicken items, and the hours of operation were increased. The emphasis on simplicity and efficiency was maintained, and the company continued its rigorous dedication to quality, service and cleanliness. This strategy was supported by the largest promotional budget in the industry. McDonald's typical arrangement with franchisees was that it owned the property, which the franchisee then leased. Highlights of McDonald's operations are shown in Table 9.

BURGER KING Burger King had been a subsidiary of Pillsbury until December 1988, when Grand Metropolitan PLC acquired Pillsbury and its holdings, which included Burger King. Burger King's traditional target market had been the 25–39 age group, but it was trying to improve its appeal to the family trade. The key element of Burger King's competitive strategy had been to offer more product choice than McDonald's. Burger King's food preparation system was centred around a hamburger that could be dressed to customer specifications, with onions, lettuce, tomato, etc. Burger King had been the first hamburger chain to diversify significantly into additional hot sandwich items, but this had resulted in somewhat longer service times and higher food preparation costs.

In 1989, Burger King's profits were $48.2 million, down 49% from the previous two years. Its market share was 19.2%, down from 19.9% in 1987. Average unit sales in 1989 were $1.05 million. Burger King had four different CEOs during the past ten years, and was having problems with its marketing program, changing advertising campaigns five times in two years. Additionally, Burger King had experienced problems with their franchisees prior to the acquisition by Grand Metropolitan, but these were beginning to subside with the ownership change.

TABLE 9   McDonald's Operating Summary

(US$ million unless otherwise noted)

	1989	1988	1987
Revenues	6 142.0	5 566.3	4 893.5
Depreciation	364.0	324.0	278.9
Operating Income	1 459.0	1 283.7	1 161.9
Operating Profit Margin (%)	23.7	23.1	23.7
Interest Expense	332.0	266.8	224.8
Pretax Income	1 157.0	1 046.5	958.8
Net Income	727.0	645.9	596.5
Net Income Margin (%)	11.8	11.6	12.2
Earnings Per Share	1.95	1.72	1.45
Dividend Per Share	.30	.27	.24
Market Price Year End	34.50	24.06	22.00
Price/Earnings Ratio	17.7	14.0	15.2
Shareholders Equity	3 549.0	3 412.8	2 916.7
Total Common Shares Outstanding (million)	362	375	378

Source: Worldscope 1990.

WENDY'S Wendy's also targeted the young adult market. Like Burger King, it provided food prepared to specification, and had broadened its initial emphasis on hamburgers to cover a variety of items, including chili and a self-service buffet and salad bar. In 1989, Wendy's 3 490 restaurants had average unit sales of $.79 million. This was an increase from $.76 million and $.74 million in 1988 and 1987, respectively. Highlights of Wendy's operations are shown in Table 10.

HARDEE'S Hardee's was the third largest hamburger-based fast food chain in the U.S., in terms of total sales and unit sales volume; and fourth in outlets. Approximately 30% of Hardee's sales were at breakfast, and it was a leader in the breakfast trade. The other major sales category was hamburgers, with 34% of sales. The demographic profile of Hardee's customers was skewed slightly to males. Children and 25- to 34-year-olds were two groups that had been targeted for higher penetration. The introduction of ice cream in 1987 had spurred a 98% increase in visits by children under 13. Packaged salads and the broadening of menu selections were expected to help attract 25- to 34-year-olds. Hardee's management was highly regarded in the food service industry for taking a very shaky firm in 1972–73 and turning it into a good performer. In 1979, Hardee's was cited by *Restaurant Business* magazine as a prime example of a corporate turnaround.

TABLE 10   Wendy's Operating Summary

(US$ million unless otherwise noted)

	1989	1988	1987
Revenues	1 069.7	1 045.9	1 051.1
Depreciation	56.4	57.3	55.4
Operating Income	51.3	44.0	0.1
Operating Profit Margin (%)	4.8	4.2	NIL
Interest Expense	22.3	16.9	24.2
Pretax Income	36.9	43.8	(12.8)
Net Income	30.4	28.5	4.5
Net Income Margin %	2.8	2.7	0.4
Earnings Per Share ($)	.25	.30	.04
Dividend Per Share ($)	.24	.24	.24
Market Price Year End ($)	4.63	5.75	5.63
Price/Earnings Ratio	18.5	19.2	140.6
Shareholder Equity	428.9	419.6	412.2
Total Common Shares Outstanding (million)	96	96	96

Source: Worldscope 1990.

In 1981, Jack Laughery, Hardee's CEO through the turnaround period, was awarded the Food Manufacturer's Association gold plate award for exemplary involvement in the food service industry. In 1990, Laughery was Hardee's chairman, and Bill Prather was the president and CEO.

Hardee's Acquisition of Burger Chef

In 1981, Hardee's was relatively small in the industry, and decided it had to expand quickly just to keep pace with its larger competitors. Competition had intensified, and the ability to support heavy fixed promotional costs became increasingly critical. Hardee's viewed an acquisition as a way to build a stronger market share base to support an increased television campaign.

Burger Chef, acquired by General Foods in 1968, had 1981 sales of $391 million. General Foods had nurtured it into a profitable regional chain. However, due to management changes at General Foods and the acquisition of the Oscar Meyer company, Burger Chef was no longer important to General Foods' future plans.

Imasco and Hardee's saw this as an opportunity. The Burger Chef chain was made up of about 250 company units and 450 franchised units, located primarily in the states of Michigan, Ohio, Indiana, Iowa and Kentucky. Most of the locations complemented Hardee's markets. Imasco purchased Burger Chef in 1981 for $51.8 million. During the next three years, they converted the sites to Hardee's at a cost of about $80 000 per unit. The acquisition of Burger Chef created two more market areas for Hardee's overnight. By 1986, the stores in these areas were, and still are, the most profitable in the entire Hardee's system. Similarly, in 1972, Hardee's had expanded their market base by acquiring Sandy's Systems, a fast food chain of about 200 restaurants for $5.7 million.

The Roy Rogers Opportunity

The Roy Rogers restaurant chain was owned by the Marriott Corporation (Marriott), and was located in the northeastern U.S. In Baltimore, Washington, D.C., Philadelphia and New York, it was second only to McDonald's in number of locations. Roy Rogers restaurants were well known for fresh fried chicken and roast beef sandwiches. In 1989, Roy Rogers system-wide sales[2] were $713 million, up from the previous year's $661 million. In 1988, revenues were $431 million, up from $399 million in 1987. Operating earnings in 1988 were $43.7 million, up from $38 million the year before. The chain had 660 units, up from 610 the previous year, with average annual unit sales of $1 081 000.

Marriott was a leader in the hotel lodging industry and had extensive restaurant holdings. In 1988, Marriott began to refocus on lodging. As a result, it had reevaluated its other holdings, among these the Roy Rogers chain. In 1988, Marriott had talked to Hardee's about the possible sale of Roy Rogers. However, Marriott was not yet committed to selling the chain and the two companies were unable to agree on a sale price. In late 1989, Marriott announced it was again interested in selling Roy Rogers.

Prather contacted Marriott about the details. Marriott was offering to sell 648 of its Roy Rogers units, of which 363 were company owned and 285 were franchised. These units were in attractive market locations that would not otherwise be available. However, Marriott wanted to retain several sites located on various turnpikes and interstate highways. Additionally, Marriott had a 14-point contract to which any purchaser had to agree. The contract addressed such things as Marriott's concern for Roy Rogers franchisees and indemnification against future litigation.

Prather saw this as the opportunity he had been waiting for and began putting together an acquisition proposal. Before he could make a serious offer to Marriott, he had to first get the approval of Crawford and the Imasco board. While preparing the proposal, Prather had reflected on what it was like to work in the Imasco organization. He had built his career in the food service industry, coming up through the ranks, starting as an assistant store manager. Until 1986, he had been the Number Three man at Burger King, vice president in charge of world operations. Prather had spent 14 years with the company, when it was owned by Pillsbury. Pillsbury, a highly centralized company, had required that any expenditures over $1 million had to be authorized by the head office. He thought how much this contrasted with Imasco. For him, Imasco was "like a breath of fresh air," a decentralized organization in the best sense. He had a great working relationship with Crawford and the others at the Centre, in contact by phone every couple weeks or as required. There was easy and open access with no surprises.

Prather had received preliminary approval from Crawford to proceed with the negotiations. Marriott had structured the Roy Rogers sale in two rounds. In the first round, all those parties who were interested in the chain were interviewed, "much like a job interview," Prather recalled. It was during this first round that Marriott expressed their concerns for their franchisees, and assessed the capabilities and sincerity of those interested in buying the chain. To Prather, "the first round was a screening process just to get into the game."

Prather made it through the first round, but there were three or four other interested groups still in the running. During the next round, the terms of the sale would be negotiated. Although the rumoured price had initially been $390 million, Prather thought that it might be more. Prather felt he could convince Marriott that Hardee's offered the best means of exit, given Marriott's concern for the franchisees, and that a solid offer of $420 million would convince them to sell Roy Rogers to Hardee's.

Prather figured conversion to Hardee's outlets would cost $80 000 to $115 000 per unit, depending on local conditions. He weighed this against the average "from scratch" start-up cost of $1.2 million per

---

[2] System-wide sales reflect retail sales figures of both company-owned and franchisee stores. Revenues reflect retail sales of only company-owned stores, in addition to royalties received from franchisees.

site. Additionally, Roy Rogers' menu, which included their popular fresh fried chicken, would complement Hardee's current menu. However, he was not sure it would be an "easy sell" in Montreal. Imasco's 40% shareholder, B.A.T, was in the midst of fighting off a takeover bid from Sir James Goldsmith (see Appendix). Prather knew that Crawford and the board would be concerned about Goldsmith's run at B.A.T, but the Roy Rogers deal was just what he needed to solidify Hardee's number three industry position.

E X H I B I T 1 Imasco Acquisitions: Distinguishable Eras in Acquisition Size

1963–77

Canada Foils	
Growers Wine	
Simtel and Editel	
S&W Foods:	$18.4 million (Canadian)
Uddo & Taormina (Progresso):	$32.5 million (Canadian)
Pasquale Brothers (Unico):	$4 million (Canadian)
Grissol:	$12.2 million (Canadian)
Collegiate:	$1.4 million (Canadian)
Arlington Sports	
Top Drug Mart and Top Value Discount	
Tinderbox:	$1.4 million (US)
POP Shoppes investment:	$10.5 million (Canadian)
Canada Northwest Land Ltd. investment	
Hardee's Food Systems investment:	$15 million (US)
—Includes Imperial Tobacco Limited acquisitions	

1978–86

Shoppers Drug Mart (Koffler's):	$66.6 million (Canadian)
Further Hardee's investment:	$15 million (Canadian)
Hardee's totally acquired:	$76 million (US)
Burger Chef:	$44 million (US)
Peoples Drug Stores:	$398 million (Canadian)
Rea & Derick Drug Stores:	$114 million (Canadian)
Genstar:	$2.4 billion (Canadian)

EXHIBIT 2   20-Year Financials: Imasco Ltd. and Tobacco Business

($ millions unless noted)

	Imasco Ltd.				Tobacco Business			Imasco Ltd.		
Year	Total Revenues	Operating Earnings	Net Earnings Before Extra-ordinary Items	Earnings per Common Share[4,5]	Tobacco Operating Earnings/ Total Operating Earnings (%)	Tobacco Revenue	Tobacco Operating Earnings	Stock Price High[6]	Stock Price Low[6]	Annual Dividend[5] per Common Share
1970[1]	582.2	37.3	15.7	.20	.88	435.2	32.7	16.13	12.00	0.10
1971[1]	569.6	40.6	17.7	.22	.88	418.0	35.9	20.50	15.25	0.125
1972[1]	625.6	48.1	22.2	.28	.84	430.4	40.4	28.38	19.00	0.137 5
1973[1]	717.1	56.0	28.0	.36	.81	446.9	45.4	34.75	25.75	0.15
1975[3]	1 030.3	78.5	36.8	.47	.79	610.5	62.0	33.25	18.75	0.193 75
1976[2]	941.2	74.9	36.5	.47	.81	560.1	60.7	32.00	26.00	0.162 5
1977[2]	1 031.6	74.7	34.9	.45	.81	605.4	60.9	27.25	20.63	0.169
1978[2]	1 049.4	84.2	43.1	.55	.81	655.0	68.3	31.63	24.00	0.18
1979[2]	1 161.5	114.8	56.4	.70	.69	741.4	78.8	40.75	29.75	0.205
1980[2]	1 150.5	132.1	68.2	.83	.75	826.7	99.1	47.25	38.25	0.25
1981[2]	1 423.7	168.8	89.6	1.07	.73	952.9	123.2	38.25	21.25	0.30
1982[2]	2 190.7	247.0	124.2	1.39	.63	1 120.2	156.0	44.50	29.50	0.35
1983[2]	2 713.9	300.3	156.8	1.73	.61	1 242.9	182.3	37.50	18.00	0.40
1984[2]	2 873.2	339.6	194.2	2.03	.60	1 358.9	205.2	36.25	29.88	0.50
1985[2]	4 353.2	432.0	234.1	2.25	.52	1 451.1	224.0	28.25	17.38	0.645
1986[2]	5 325.1	465.9	261.7	2.40	.53	1 769.8	246.0	35.00	22.63	0.75
1987[1]	5 924.4	578.4	282.7	2.24	.48	1 926.0	279.1	46.00	24.25	0.96
1988[1]	6 000.6	636.7	314.3	2.51	.48	2 018.1	308.0	29.50	23.75	1.04
1989[1]	5 724.7	692.0	366.1	2.87	.48	2 385.6	334.0	40.50	27.63	1.12

[1] January – December Fiscal Year.
[2] April – March Fiscal Year.
[3] Reflects 15-month period from January 1974 to March 1975.
[4] Before extraordinary items.
[5] Prior to 1980, adjusted to reflect three stock splits; after 1980, 2 for 1 stock splits July 1980, November 1982, and March 1985.
[6] Not adjusted for stock splits.

Source: Imasco Limited.

APPENDIX IMASCO Limited, 1990

In the summer of 1989, Sir James Goldsmith formed a syndicate of investors under the name of Hoylake Investments Limited to mount a takeover attempt on B.A.T, Imasco's largest shareholder. Goldsmith's argument was that B.A.T was being valued by the market at less than the sum of its parts, and that the true value would only be realized by the "unbundling" of B.A.T. The stakes in the bid were enormous—it was estimated that Hoylake and its partners would have to put up over $25 billion to carry through on the transaction. Hoylake's intentions with respect to the block of Imasco's shares that B.A.T owned were unknown. Imasco's position was that, while it was an "interested observer," it was not directly involved in the proceedings and would only monitor developments related to the offer. While the specifics of Goldsmith's case are not pertinent here, the general arguments are. These are given below as excerpts from Goldsmith's letter to B.A.T shareholders dated August 8, 1989.

THE KEY QUESTIONS

The case for this bid must rest on the answer to simple questions. Has the existing management placed B.A.T in a position to compete successfully? Are the subsidiaries growing healthily, or are they failing relative to their competitors? Have shareholders' funds been invested in a wise and progressive way which adds value to the shares of the company? Is the conglomerate structure able to provide strength and innovation over the longer term to its diversified subsidiaries? In short, is B.A.T in a state to compete in the modern world and to face the future with confidence? Or has it been managed in a way which could lead to progressive senescence and decay? That is the crux of the argument.

CONGLOMERATION—B.A.T'S FAILURE

It is our case that B.A.T's management has sought size rather than quality or value; it has used shareholders' funds to acquire totally unconnected businesses, about which it knew little, and which are being damaged by having been brought under the control of B.A.T's bureaucratic yoke.

THE CAUSE OF FAILURE

Before presenting the case in factual detail, I would like to explain why such a state of affairs can occur. It is not that the men in charge are malevolent. Not at all. No doubt they are serious administrators. The problem originates from their belief that tobacco was a declining business, and that the company should diversify into other industries. This logic sounded compelling. The flaw was that B.A.T's management knew something about tobacco, but little about the businesses of the companies that it was acquiring. Also there exists a very natural conflict of interest between management and shareholders. Management wishes its company to be big. The bigger it is, the greater the respect, power and honours that flow to management. Shareholders, on the other hand, want value. They do not seek size for the sake of size. They want growth to be the result of excellence, and thereby to improve the short- and long-term value of their investment. Some conglomerates have performed well under the leadership of their founders. But that ceases when the flame of the founder is replaced by the dead hand of the corporate bureaucrat. That is why great conglomerates often have been well advised to de-conglomerate before they retire.

PURPOSE OF THE OFFER

1. We intend to reverse B.A.T's strategy. Instead of accumulating miscellaneous companies within B.A.T, we intend to release them and, as described below, return the proceeds to you.

    We would concentrate B.A.T's attention on running its core business, tobacco. That is the process which we have described as "unbundling."

CONSEQUENCES

Of course, you will be concerned to know the consequences for the companies being released, and for those who work within them. Will those companies suffer? Will jobs be sacrificed? Would their future be jeopardized, for example, by a reduction in the level of investment in research, development and capital equipment? That is what you may have been led to believe. The reality is the opposite. Instead of vegetating within B.A.T, those companies would either return to independence, or they would join more homogeneous companies. Such companies have the skills which would contribute to future development, and a true mutuality of interest would result. This would lead to increased opportunity for employees, greater long-term investment, productivity and growth. The real danger to employees is that they should remain trapped within B.A.T, and condemned to slow but progressive relative decline. Ultimately that would lead to employee hardship, despite the benevolent intentions of existing management.

CONCLUSION

To summarize, the flawed architecture of the tobacco-based conglomerates was exposed, first with the acquisition of Imperial Group by Hanson in 1986, and late last year when the management and directors of RJR/Nabisco recognized that shareholder values could only be properly realized by a sale of the company.

Size is often a protection against change, but these same basic structural defects have now been revealed, and the logic of unbundling B.A.T has become inescapable.

STARBUCKS

*Ariff Kachra
and Mary M. Crossan*

Mr. Howard Schultz, the Chairman and CEO of Starbucks Corporation, had just given a speech on the future of the coffee industry at a well-known business school. As he left the lecture hall, he stopped at the University's most popular coffee shop, the Brewery. The shop's sign indicated that it was "Now Serving Starbucks Coffee". As Mr. Schultz ordered the House Blend, he noticed that the Brewery was a far cry from any Starbucks coffeehouse. The shop was messy, the service was poor, and the coffee was

IVEY

Ariff Kachra prepared this case under the supervision of Professor Mary Crossan solely to provide material for class discussion. The authors do not intend to illustrate either effective or ineffective handling of a managerial situation. The authors may have disguised certain names and other identifying information to protect confidentiality.

average. As Mr. Schultz was leaving the Brewery, Orin Smith, Starbucks President and COO, called him on his cellular phone. McDonald's, whom Starbucks had turned down a number of times, was once again petitioning for a contract to serve Starbucks coffee. On the plane back to Seattle, Washington, Mr. Schultz's thoughts drifted back to his experience at the Brewery and the call from McDonald's. He asked himself two questions: Was Starbucks growing in the best way possible? Was Starbucks overextending in its quest for growth?

SPECIALTY COFFEE INDUSTRY

Coffee was the second most traded commodity next to oil. It was divided into two categories: specialty coffee and basic coffee. Specialty coffee was the highest echelon of quality coffee available in the world. Many people described it as gourmet coffee. There was no one accepted definition in the industry; however, everyone agreed that specialty coffee was of higher quality than basic supermarket-brand coffee.

It was estimated in 1994 that the specialty coffee industry was growing at a rate of 15 per cent per year and that the basic coffee industry was suffering. Although most consumers only saw this division at the retail level, specialty versus basic coffee was a concept that originated with the coffee grower.

SUPPLIERS

Specialty coffee companies did not typically deal with suppliers, i.e., coffee farmers, directly. They dealt with exporters instead. About a third of the coffee farms in the world were less than three acres. These farmers did not have the desire, the volume, the money, the expertise, or the connections to export coffee themselves because most countries regulated coffee sales. Coffee processors or exporters regularly visited smaller farmers and bought their coffee[1] either in cherry or parchment.[2] The coffee would then be moved to a mill where there would be other farmers' production from the same or different regions. After husking the parchment, the millers sold it to the exporter(s). It was common place for coffee to change hands as many as five times before it reached a specialty coffee seller. Typically, coffee was moved from the farmer, to the collector, to the miller, to the exporter, to the importer, and finally, to the specialty coffee seller.

The bean suppliers that managed this process well, typically concentrated on high quality Arabica beans for which they could command premium prices. Lower-quality bean suppliers concentrated on Robusta beans. This quality division was somewhat congruent to the way the industry was divided, i.e., lower quality beans were harvested for the commercial industry and higher quality beans for the specialty coffee industry. (Industry experts estimated that specialty coffee made up 31 per cent of the total coffee consumption. See Exhibit 1.)

The price of certain coffee was a direct reflection of the quality and quantity of coffee available at a particular time. It was very difficult to get price confirmations because a successful coffee harvest was dependent on so many different factors. These included weather conditions, health of the coffee trees, harvesting practices, disease and infection caused by insects, and the social, political, regulatory and economic environments of the coffee-producing countries. For example, the 1975 Brazilian frost drove the price of coffee up, and U.S. coffee consumption never recovered from the 18.5 per cent decline.

---

[1] This process varied by country.

[2] Once the coffee cherry had been washed and dried, what remained was the coffee bean in some sort of husk.

CONSUMERS

Coffee consumption patterns had changed in the U.S. In 1996, the per capita consumption of coffee was 1.7 cups/day/person, a significant decrease from the two to three cups daily consumption in the '60s and '70s. The National Coffee Association attributed this decrease to poor product development, packaging and position (price focused) by the industry's leading coffee producers. However, now it seemed that coffee consumption was on the rise. The following compares U.S. consumption rates to global consumption rates:

> In terms of kilograms of coffee per person consumed in 1985, the United States at 4.7 ranked tenth, behind Sweden (11.6), Denmark (11.0), Finland (10.0), Holland (9.5), Germany (6.8), France (5.5), and Italy (4.9) among the coffee-consuming nations, and behind Costa Rica (6.5) and Brazil (5.5) among the coffee-producing nations. Overall, in the decade between 1975 and 1985, Europe's levels of imported coffee rose significantly, those of Japan doubled, while those of the United States remained steady despite increased population.[3]

The recent popularity of specialty coffee was the result of four consumer trends: (1) the adoption of a healthier lifestyle had led North Americans to replace alcohol with coffee; (2) coffee bars offered a place where people could meet; (3) people liked affordable luxuries and specialty coffee fit the bill; and (4) consumers were becoming more knowledgeable about coffee.

Profile

According to *Avenues for Growth—A 20-Year Review of the U.S. Specialty Coffee Industry*,[4] 22 per cent of U.S. consumers purchased specialty coffee. This 22 per cent of the population typically lived and worked in urban areas, and had an annual income over $35 000. Research had shown that two-parent families with a stay-at-home mother purchased 41 per cent more specialty coffee than the average. Single people purchased 39 per cent more than the average and consumers with college degrees purchased 49 per cent more than the average. Females purchased slightly more specialty coffee than men and coffee consumption was higher among individuals aged 30–59 than those aged 20–29.[5] Research by many coffee companies had found that once a consumer learned to appreciate a high-quality specialty coffee, he/she did not go back to his/her favourite average quality brew.

Community Gathering Place

Consumers' patterns of socializing had changed since the eighties. While the mid-eighties were characterized by the pursuit of entertainment outside the home, in the early nineties, people wanted to stay home. There was a move away from restaurants and dance clubs.

Now, in the second part of the decade, there seemed to be a resurgence of outside-the-home entertainment. Coffeehouses were able to fill this need and were more accessible than bars. Coffee's image had changed from being purely a breakfast drink to a beverage that could be enjoyed any time and as a social catalyst. Coffee purchasers wanted more than just a place where they could get a higher quality cup of coffee. They wanted a place that answered a lifestyle need. Increasingly, coffee shops were turning into living rooms, where people sat back and enjoyed a cup of coffee or something else and relaxed with their friends or business associates. Coffeehouses had become community gathering places.

---

[3] Encyclopaedia of American Industries, Volume 1, Manufacturing Industries, SIC 2095, Roasted Coffee.

[4] Montgomery Securities, April 30, 1996, Vol. 27.

[5] *1995 Winter Coffee Drinking Study*, National Coffee Association of the U.S.A. & Montgomery Securities, Volume 27.

COMPETITION

Product-Based Competition

In retail coffeehouse sales, specialty coffee not only competed with basic coffee, it also competed with tea, juice, soft drinks, alcohol and other coffee and non-coffee-related drinks. However the consumption of all of these beverages relative to specialty coffee was declining.

Specialty coffee could be divided into flavoured coffee, which represented 25 per cent of all specialty coffee sold, and non-flavoured coffee. Flavoured coffee referred to coffee that was flavoured with a variety of essences during the roasting process. Popular flavours included hazelnut, amaretto, raspberry, etc. Flavoured coffee was not offered by specialty coffee companies like Starbucks, Peet's, Caribou Coffee and The Coffee Station, but the opposite was true for Timothy's and The Second Cup. Flavoured coffee was popular among traditionally non-coffee drinkers, younger coffee drinkers, and those interested in a low calorie substitute for desserts or snacks. For a comparison of retail sales of different types of coffee, see Exhibit 2.

Another important product substitute was specialty coffee originating from basic coffee companies in the grocery chain. To respond to the phenomenal growth in specialty coffee in the grocery chain, many large, basic coffee manufacturers were moving into more specialty brands by introducing upscale versions of already popular supermarket brands. However, industry analysts forecasted that there would be a shift in consumer purchasing of specialty coffee. Currently, grocery stores were responsible for 81 per cent of specialty coffee sales; this figure was expected to fall to 46 per cent in 1999. This shift would result in greater amounts of coffee being purchased from specialty stores: 19 per cent currently to 54 per cent in 1999.

Retail-Based Competition

The Specialty Coffee Association of America estimated there would be room for about 10 000 coffee retail outlets in the United States and Canada by 1999. But only 5 500 of those would be coffee bars and cafes; the rest would be carts.[6] The following table depicts the amount of room for growth in the retail coffee industry:

Location	Population (millions)	Number of Starbucks Stores	Current Population/ Store	Population necessary to support a coffee house	Maximum number of coffee stores supportable by market	Total Starbucks stores as a percentage of total possible stores
Top 50 U.S. Markets	144.9	914	158 581	54 470	2 661	34%
Vancouver, Toronto, Ottawa, Montreal, Calgary	11.3	113	99 611	56 000	201	56%
Top 100 U.S. & Major Canadian Markets	180.2	1 074	167 784	55 000	3 276	33%
Total U.S. & Canadian Markets	276.2	1 074	257 128	56 000	4 931	22%

Source: William Blair & Company, Starbucks Corporation, June 20, 1997.

---

[6] *Chicago Tribune*, Sunday, March 10, 1996.

Given the low barriers to entry in the retail specialty coffee market, there were more than 3 485[7] competitors in the market. However, most of these were one-store establishments with no real plans for growth. A description of those companies that had developed a strong regional and/or national presence follows.

Diedrich's Coffee	Green Mountain Coffee Inc.	Coffee People
• made with its own freshly roasted beans • sold light food items and whole bean coffee • a few wholesale customers • operated a total of 32 coffeehouses in Texas, Colorado and California • 1996 sales: $10.2 million	• primarily a wholesaler of specialty coffee (3 000 customers) • small number of retail operations with in-store roasting facilities • roasted over 25 high-quality Arabica coffees to produce over 70 varieties • 1996 sales: $38.3 million	• located in suburban neighbourhoods and business districts, averaging about 1 500 to 2 000 square feet in size • used specialty kiosks located in high traffic locations such as airports and shopping malls • hoped to have 100 locations by 1998

Al Van Houtte	Barnie's Coffee & Tea Company	Caribou
• offered 36 types of ground coffee, nine types of flavoured coffee and 54 types of whole beans • sold its coffee through restaurants, including its own network of 107 cafe bistros (only 4 corporate stores) • good reputation as a vendor of coffee to offices, hotels, etc. • 1996 sales: $164.1 million	• focused on the merchandising aspect of coffee retailing; it offered 400 different branded products • typically seated about 50 people and was located in malls • its newest innovation was a restaurant, La Venezia Cafe; seated 200 people and offered 47 different coffees	• wanted to be the 3rd place between work and home where people could socialize • implemented a very American feel to its coffeehouses rather than a European feel • offered very fast service, magazines, newspapers, free refills, and seating • had 50 stores; analysts predicted that it would be a growth leader

---

[7] "Caffeine Rush: Customers are High on Gourmet Coffee and so are Operators," *Restaurant Business*, January 1, 1996.

Coffee Beanery	Chock Full O'Nuts	Cafe Appasionato
• franchiser who operated 175 units across the U.S. • coffee beverages and food accounted for 80% of the sales and 20% came from merchandise • focus had always been on malls but it was now shifting its focus to free-standing locations • begun franchising coffee cans	• operated as a coffee supplier to the restaurant industry • enough contracts with restaurants to warrant its own fleet of 150 trucks • recently, company had begun diversifying into different coffeehouse formats like double drive throughs and sit-down retail outlets, about 3 000 square feet in size	• small but aggressive player in the industry • primarily a coffee roaster • sold its coffee in its own retail outlets, franchised stores, wholesale coffee to specialty stores and restaurants, grocery division, direct mail, exports to the Pacific Rim, private label coffee production and co-label ventures with fast food chains, such as Taco Bell

SECOND CUP

Second Cup was primarily a franchiser (90 per cent of all locations), and as a result, the company was consistently cash flow positive and had the benefit of taking little operating risk at the store level. Traditionally, the Second Cup was mall-based, but in the past few years it had moved into more stand-alone locations. These locations were established rather quickly and were not always on prime real estate. In its retail concept, the Second Cup offered specialty coffee drinks, varietals, flavoured coffee and snack items.

The Second Cup was very growth-oriented and believed strongly in growth via acquisitions. One of its major acquisitions included Gloria Jean's (247 locations) in the U.S. Including its own 243 stores, the Second Cup was the second largest player in the specialty coffee industry. Where the Second Cup's revenues came from liquid coffee and snack food items, Gloria Jean's obtained a high percentage of sales from coffee mugs, related items and coffee beans.

In recent times, the Second Cup had become quite active in developing alliances with other food service companies. Through its alliance with Cara Operations Ltd., the Second Cup hoped to gain access to a number of its partner's institutional and retail sites such as Harvey's and Swiss Chalet. The Second Cup also held a 30 per cent interest in the Great Canadian Bagel that operated 120 stores in 1996 and was planning to own 175 by the end of 1997. Finally, the company had also struck a deal to serve its coffee on Air Canada flights. Revenues for 1996 amounted to $63.3 million.

See Exhibit 3 for a comparison of the industry competitors using different financial and growth measures.

STARBUCKS' STRATEGY

Starbucks' strategy for the future was presented in the following extracts of a letter to Starbucks' shareholders. This letter, from Howard Schultz, Chairman and CEO, and Orin Smith, President and Chief Operating Officer, appeared in the company's 1996 Annual Report:

> We have firmly established our leadership position, ending fiscal 1996 with more than 1 000 retail locations in 32 markets throughout North America and two new stores in Tokyo, Japan. With more than

20 000 dedicated partners (employees), we are creating opportunities every day for millions of customers around the world to enjoy the Starbucks Experience. From selecting the finest Arabica beans to hiring the most talented people, we are committed to applying the highest standards of quality in everything we do.... When you walk into a Starbucks store, when you open a mail order package, when you drink our coffee on United Airlines, it is our goal to offer more than just a great cup of coffee—we want to offer a memorable experience.... We are excited about the global possibilities as more new customers embrace our business, and we know that we have many brand-building opportunities ahead of us. In 1994, when we entered into a joint venture agreement with Pepsi-Cola to develop ready-to-drink coffee products, we knew that we wanted to redefine the category...we look forward to the positive reception of bottled Frappuccino...but most importantly, we know that we have developed a platform for bigger product innovations. During fiscal 1996, we installed proprietary, state-of-the-art roasting and manufacturing equipment to create a world-class logistics and manufacturing organization.... Our specialty sales and marketing team has continued to develop new channels of distribution...our direct response group launched a new America Online Café Starbucks store...we continue to work towards our long-term goal of becoming the most recognized and respected brand of coffee in the world.... We believe more strongly than ever that at the heart of our continuing success lie the company's two cornerstones, coffee and our people.... Twenty-five years from now, when we look back again, if we can say that we grew our company with the same values and guiding principles that we embrace today, then we will know we have succeeded.

STARBUCKS' BUSINESS SYSTEM

Sourcing

Starbucks sourced approximately 50 per cent of its beans from Latin America, 35 per cent from the Pacific Rim, and 15 per cent from East Africa. Having a diversified portfolio allowed Starbucks to offer a greater palette of coffees to its customers while being able to maintain a hedged position.

Starbucks maintained close relationships with its exporters by working directly with them and providing them with training. Mary Williams, Senior Vice-President of Coffee at Starbucks, described what it took to be considered an official Starbucks' exporter:

> If I am working with a dealer who has sold me 5 000 bags of Guatemalan for January's shipment and he knows that he is not going to be able to deliver, I don't want to hear about it in January. I want him to call me in September and say, "Mary, we are going to have trouble with this January. What can we do? How can we work this problem out? What can I do to help you? Shall we switch it to another coffee?" If I have a quality problem, I expect to be able to call up the person I bought the coffee from and say: "Sorry, I have to reject this; it doesn't meet our standards". I expect them to say: "OK, we will take it back, no problem and we will replace it". Both the customer service and consistency are the things we look for over time.

Exporters of high quality coffee were very anxious to become Starbucks suppliers because Starbucks purchased more high quality coffee than anyone else in the world. Starbucks' relationship with its suppliers was so good that if Supplier 'A' sold to a number of different buyers and it had only one container of a certain coffee, Starbucks would be the first to get it.

To ensure quality, Starbucks extracted three different samples of coffee from every shipment of 250 bags. Sample one was an offer sample sent by an exporter trying to make a sale to Starbucks. Sample two was taken just before the shipment was due to be sent. Sample three was extracted from the shipment, which arrived at the coffee roasting plant. At every stage of sampling, Starbucks reserved the right to reject the coffee if it was not in line with its quality standards.

Starbucks hoped to double volumes over the next three years. This could make the ability to find coffees that would meet its quantity/quality requirements difficult. Starbucks needed to offer an increasing number of blends to deal with its increasing volumes, since blends provided more flexibility around components. Mary Williams explained:

> When you blend coffee, it's like baking a cake; you need to put lots of different kinds of spices in a spice cake; you don't necessarily have to have cinnamon, nutmeg and allspice. You can have other kinds of spices, and the consumers of that cake will not know the difference, because it tastes like a spice cake. So a House Blend with a particular flavour profile, can have different types of the same quality components to reach the same flavour profile. Moving towards offering more blends and revolving varietals is one of the most important things Starbucks can do to ensure the quality/quantity mix of the coffee we buy.

Despite Starbucks' large supply needs, growing its own, high-quality coffee was an option that was never seriously considered.

ROASTING AND BLENDING

Roasting was a combination of time and temperature. Recipes were put together by the coffee department once all the components had been tested and were up to standard. Despite computerized roasters that guaranteed consistency, roasting was not a complete science; it was more of a technological art. This was because the people roasting the coffee had to understand the properties of the roasting process, i.e., managing temperature and being able to roast coffees along different roast curves. Roasting was essential to Starbucks, because how a coffee was roasted could change its entire taste.

Starbucks undertook a great deal of research by roasting its coffees in many different ways, under many different temperature and time conditions to ensure that it was getting as much as possible from the bean. These trial and error sessions allowed Starbucks to build signature roasting curves. These roasting curves were then built into proprietary computer software. The method by which they were developed was as much a result of the technology as the art. This ensured that even if a roaster were to defect to another competitor, he/she would not be able to duplicate Starbucks' signature roasts.

After roasting and air cooling, the coffee was immediately vacuum-sealed in one-way valve bags. This packaging was unique in its ability to ensure freshness, since it allowed gases naturally produced by fresh roasted beans out without letting oxygen in. This one-way valve technology extended the shelf life of Starbucks coffee to 26 weeks. However, Starbucks did not keep any coffee on its shelves for more than three months and for the coffee it used to prepare beverages in the store, the shelf life was limited to seven days after the bag was opened.

SUPPLY CHAIN OPERATIONS

Starbucks Supply Chain Operations (SCO) claimed it had the best transportation rates in the industry, a complex bakery distribution model, a forecasting process for "who will need coffee when'" that was generally very accurate, strong inventory turns for the specialty coffee industry, and a fully integrated manufacturing and distribution process that protected the coffee beans from oxygen from the time beans were roasted to the time they were packaged (closed loop system). Starbucks had developed these skills and benefits because it benchmarked against its competitors, hired experts, and believed strongly in the concept of integrated supply.

Starbucks tried to build its supply chain operations in order to eliminate redundancy and maximize efficiency. Supply chain operations served four business units: the retail store units, the specialty sales and wholesale channels, the mail order business and the grocery channel. According to Ted Garcia, Starbucks' Executive Vice President, Supply Chain Operations, the phenomenal growth in these business units was posing challenges to supply chain operations:

> Supporting four business units in an integrated, effective, efficient, cost-effective method is a challenge. We are trying new and innovative things. We are not afraid to enter into agreements or challenge our suppliers such as United Parcel Service (UPS) to do things in new and innovative ways.

RETAIL SALES

The retail outlet had been Starbucks' fundamental growth vehicle. For many customers Starbucks was not only a place to drink coffee but also an experience. Howard Schultz's vision for Starbucks was a place that offered interesting coffee-related drinks in a theatrical kind of atmosphere, which pivoted around an espresso machine:

> You get more than the first coffee when you visit Starbucks. You get great people, first-rate music, a comfortable and upbeat meeting place, and sound advice on brewing excellent coffee at home. At home you're part of a family. At work you're part of a company. And somewhere in between there's a place where you can sit back and be yourself. That's what a Starbucks store is to many of its customers—a kind of "third place" where they can escape, reflect, read, chat or listen.[8]

Starbucks' formula was firmly based in its coffee, its employees, its merchandising, its ownership philosophy, its real-estate approach, its image, and its innovativeness.

Employees

Starbucks' store employees (baristas) tended to be either in college or university. They received a great deal of training and were able to talk about a variety of different coffees and processes. Having baristas that had a strong coffee education was essential because Starbucks' consumers were becoming more and more knowledgeable about coffee. Mary Williams, SVP Coffee for Starbucks, outlined the nature of the questions asked of the baristas at Starbucks:

> We have very educated consumers. They ask very interesting questions of the people who work in our stores; such as, "I am having chocolate mousse for dessert, what kind of coffee should I serve?"; or "I am having shrimp scampi for dinner and a fruit salad for dessert, what kind of coffee should I serve?" So we have to give the baristas some kind of a basis and background so that they can answer these difficult questions.[9]

Developing coffee knowledge and service expertise demanded a great deal of effort from employees and as Starbucks grew, finding enough good people that could replicate the values, culture and service experiences was an ongoing challenge.

Merchandising

Starbucks only carried the highest quality merchandise. In terms of coffee-making equipment, it purchased its machines from manufacturers like Krups, Gaggia and Bodum. It also offered accessory items bearing the Starbucks Logo such as coffee mugs, grinders, coffee filters, storage containers and other items. In terms of merchandising, Starbucks faced challenges related to the design of a nationally consistent merchandising program, since many of its stores dealt with individual suppliers.

---

[8] 1995 *Annual Report*, Starbucks Corporation.

[9] Mary Williams, SVP Coffee, Starbucks Corporation.

Real-Estate Approach

Starbucks considered itself to be real estate opportunistic. It did not always wait for the perfectly designed location, i.e., a box. It had a design team that could fit a location in many retail spaces, be it a corner, a trapezoid, or triangle. This flexibility, in addition to Starbucks' concept of store clustering, which often placed retail outlets across from one another or on the same block, allowed Starbucks to maximize its market share in given areas of a city and to begin building a regional reputation.

To meet its growth needs Starbucks had approximately 20 real estate managers across the country. These managers worked with "street sniffers", i.e., professionals who specialized in identifying the best retail locations. Their commissions were paid either by the landlord or by Starbucks. These real estate brokers were guaranteed a minimum commission per location, if the landlord's brokerage commission did not cover the minimum, Starbucks paid the difference. This engendered a very loyal relationship between Starbucks and the real estate network.

Starbucks was very disciplined about its entire approach to real estate:

> Discipline is the difference between locating a store in a targeted demographic area this year, in order to get in there and gain market share versus being disciplined enough to wait for the corner or the mid-block with a parking lot. Discipline is rooted in the ability to understand the differences and business issues involved with taking a store today that may do $750 000 versus waiting for a store that may do $1 million. Understanding and acting upon location issues such as corners, parking lots and co-tenants; that's the discipline of it.[10]

As Starbucks grew and the number of 'A' sites in 'A' markets decreased, one of the key challenges faced by Starbucks was to constantly motivate its real estate staff to continue to generate 20 to 40 solid stores per month. Starbucks had to meet this challenge if it was going to meet its goal of 2000 stores by the year 2000. Traditionally, Starbucks had been focused on the retail store on Main and Main of every major North American city. Now it was expanding to the Main and Main of different regions within a city. See Exhibit 4 for the actual and forecasted income statement of a typical store.

Another way in which Starbucks hoped to reach a new customer base was through the introduction of its new espresso carts or kiosks. By introducing Starbucks Espresso Cans, the company had succeeded in branding the coffee cart, which had always been a brandless, grassroots type of specialty coffee retailer. Starbucks called its version of the espresso cart Doppio. The Doppio was an 8x8-foot cube that unfolded into a larger stand with sides, counters, and Starbucks' trademark finishes. It would allow the company to take advantage of sales areas such as train stations, street corners, malls, etc. Starbucks was in the initial stages of its Doppio strategy.

Domestic versus International Retail Image

The retail system is the base or anchor of the brand-building strategy, the essence of the company's passion for quality coffee, and the showcase for the lifestyle that Starbucks is defining. It is this lifestyle attribute of the brand that could catapult the company beyond its roots as a specialty retailer/restaurant with a few closely associated brand extensions.[11]

Starbucks decided to enter the international marketplace to prevent competitors from getting a head start, to build upon the growing desire for Western brands, and to take advantage of higher coffee consumption rates in different countries. It focused on Asia Pacific simply because it did not have the resources to go into

---

[10] Arthur Rubinfeld, Senior Vice-President Real Estate, Starbucks Corporation.

[11] Merrill Lynch Capital Markets, Starbucks Company Report, September 16, 1996.

different areas of the globe at once and because one half of the world's population lived a five-and-a-half hour flight from the area. It was expected that in the next five to ten years, international retail's contribution would be sizeable. See Exhibit 6 for a forecast of International Retail's potential contribution to Starbucks' earnings. Also see Exhibit 5 for a forecast of Starbucks' growth in the Pacific Rim.

SPECIALTY SALES

Specialty sales were agreements with retailers, wholesalers, restaurants, service providers, etc. to carry Starbucks coffee. Specialty sales not only provided Starbucks with revenue growth potential but also with increased name recognition. Starbucks partnered with companies that were leaders in their field, companies that had stellar reputations for success and quality. Partnerships existed with many different companies, some of which included:

United Airlines	Starbucks was served on all domestic and international flights.
Nordstrom	Starbucks had developed a special blend for Nordstrom.
Barnes & Noble Bookstores	Starbucks operated individual but attached locations. Many of these locations had separate entrances that allowed them to stay open even after Barnes & Noble closed.
PepsiCo	Starbucks and PepsiCo had jointly developed the Frappuccino product, a milk-based cold coffee beverage in a bottle.
PriceCostco	Starbucks had developed a special brand name, Meridian, for PriceCostco.
Red Hook Breweries	Starbucks provided coffee concentrate as an ingredient for one of the brewery's beers, Double Black Stout.
Dreyers' Ice Cream	In this joint venture, Starbucks had its own brand of ice cream that Dreyers' promoted via its grocery channels.
ARAMARK	This was the world's leading provider of a broad range of services to businesses, reaching 10 million people a day at more than 400 000 locations. Through ARAMARK, Starbucks coffee was now being served at over one hundred of those locations, including such college campuses as the University of Florida and Boston University, corporations such as Boeing and Citicorp, and hospitals such as St. Vincent's in New York. ARAMARK also had a few licensed locations.

Some of these partnerships involved serving Starbucks coffee, some were for product development and others were for store development. Starbucks was actively increasing its participation in specialty sales contracts.

NEW VENTURES

Three of Starbucks' newest business ventures included its contract with Dreyers' Ice Cream, its bottled Frappuccino product with Pepsi and its penetration into the grocery channel.

It was estimated that Starbucks' ice cream would perhaps reach $40 million at retail and contribute at least $500 000 to earnings during fiscal 1997. Although the return was somewhat limited (see Exhibit 6), it opened Starbucks to an entirely new customer base, reinforced its premium quality image, and built its reputation with supermarket chains.

Bottled Frappuccino was Starbucks' attempt to introduce a quality ready-to-drink coffee beverage into the North American market place. Starbucks viewed this bottled beverage as a $1 billion opportunity. These estimates were from Pepsi, who said that it had never seen a product test quite as well as bottled Frappuccino, where 70 per cent of testers became repeat purchasers. Other products that had hit the billion dollar mark with less favourable test results were Ocean Spray Juices and Lipton Iced Teas. The product might even do better in countries where there was already a market for cold coffee beverages, like the Pacific Rim. Bottled Frappuccino was currently being offered in all Starbucks retail stores and had begun to be distributed via PepsiCo's national distribution channels. See Exhibit 6 for a forecast of bottled Frappuccino's contribution to Starbucks' future earnings.

In penetrating the grocery market, Starbucks met with a great deal of success when it began test marketing in the Portland area. Now it was test marketing the Chicago market. If it was successful in Chicago, then it would consider initiating a national roll out with the expectation that in five years it would be nationally available. See Exhibit 6 for an estimate of the impact of a national roll out on Starbucks' earnings. Mr. Orin Smith, Starbucks President and COO, explained how he viewed the importance of Starbucks' penetration into the grocery chain:

> Presence in supermarkets is not essential to Starbucks' survival or prosperity. However, in the interest of being a major player in coffee for the home, we have to be available in supermarkets. This is because convenience plays a key role in the decision to purchase coffee for the home. Therefore, no matter how many stores we open, we will never overcome the "convenience" advantage of supermarkets. For us, the choice is clear: Are we going to allow supermarkets to continue to capture 70 to 80 per cent of the home coffee business or are we going to join up and take our piece of that? Supermarkets are very interested in carrying Starbucks Coffee because we can offer them greater margins; we can grow their business and we will help pull consumers out of the lower priced categories into our category.[12]

Other areas of opportunity included the introduction of Starbucks coffee to the higher echelon restaurants and day-part chains. Day-part chains are retail outlets catering to the day-time trade. Examples are bagel shops, juice bars, lunch counters etc.

MAIL ORDER

For a long time, mail order had allowed Starbucks to meet the needs of its customers not located near a Starbucks retail store and its regular home users. The company had a direct mail program entitled Encore. Encore customers received a monthly shipment of a different type of either ground or whole bean coffee. This program helped boost sales by increasing transaction size, and introducing customers to a wider range of company products.

HOWARD SCHULTZ

Howard Schultz began his coffee career with Starbucks Coffee Company in 1982, when it used to be a retailer solely of whole bean coffees. On a buying trip to Italy, in 1983, the vast number of coffee bars in Milan inspired Mr. Schultz. He returned to Starbucks and presented his idea to expand the whole bean retailer into a coffee bar. The Board of Directors rejected his idea and two years later, Mr. Schultz left Starbucks to start his own coffee bar company, which he named Il Giornale. After two years of great success, Il Giornale purchased the Starbucks name and assets and changed the names of all of its retail outlets to Starbucks.

---

[12] Orin Smith, Chief Operating Officer, Starbucks Corporation.

Howard Schultz came from rather humble beginnings. He remembered how his father used to work hard for little money and no respect. He said his upbringing instilled in him "not a fear of failure but a fear of mediocrity". He was the first in his family to get a college degree and had always been an over-achiever. He was young and energetic at 45 and very hands-on in the company. "Howard is very creative, he is very inspiring, he is exceptionally demanding, he is tremendously competitive, exceptionally ambitious, and has very high standards in everything we can do and he is always ratcheting the bar up. He really cares about people; anything anyone would do to damage the culture—he would be right on it.[13]

Howard Schultz played a very important and unique role at Starbucks. "The barista's interpretation of the vision is the engine of the company, Howard is the on-board computer, and to some extent he is also the fuel that drives through it. People around here feel very much that they are following Howard up some mountain with a flag clenched under their teeth and they give 110 per cent."[14]

HUMAN RESOURCES

Starbucks had a very flat organizational structure. Everyone from the CEO to a barista was a partner and not an employee. Starbucks placed a great deal of effort into seeking the thoughts and opinions of its baristas, because they were in direct contact with Starbucks' customers. Starbucks' retail management, at headquarters, kept in regular contact with field people. Many people in the stores knew Deidra Wager, the Executive Vice-President of Retail, and would not hesitate to call her directly to talk about the retail group's decisions. The head office managers had sessions with people in the field, standard mission reviews where they collected questions from anyone about any topic and then responded, and open forums where they heard from and listened to the partner base.

The coffee service system was built on three principles: hospitality, production and education. Starbucks expected baristas to be customer-service oriented by being hospitable, effective in making exactly the type of drink the customer requested and able to answer the customers' coffee-related questions. This demanded a great deal of effort on behalf of the baristas. To prepare them for the challenge, they all underwent 24 hours of training before they were allowed to serve a cup of coffee to a Starbucks customer. Every employee, even those that were hired for executive positions, went through the same training program, which included a two-week term in a store.

In addition to training, Starbucks paid its partners a slightly higher wage than most food service companies. Also, all employees received health insurance (vision, dental, medical), disability and life insurance, and a free pound of coffee each week. All company employees also received "Bean Stock", an employee stock option plan. This was quite profitable for some employees.

From its baristas to its senior managers, Starbucks took great care in recruitment. For baristas, turnover rates were about 60 per cent; this was less than half of the industry average (150 to 300 per cent). Many of the senior managers came from companies like Taco Bell, Nike, McDonald's, Hallmark, Wendy's and Blockbuster. These managers knew how to manage a high growth retailer.

ORGANIZATIONAL CULTURE

The following six guiding principles, from the company's 1995 *Annual Report*, helped Starbucks measure the appropriateness of its decisions:

---

[13] Orin Smith, Chief Operating Officer, Starbucks Corporation.

[14] Scott Bedbury, Senior Vice-President, Marketing, Starbucks Corporation.

1. Provide a great workplace and treat each other with respect and dignity.
2. Embrace diversity as an essential component of the way we do business.
3. Apply the highest standards of excellence to the purchasing, roasting and fresh delivery of our coffee.
4. Develop enthusiastically satisfied customers all of the time.
5. Contribute positively to our community and our environment.
6. Recognize that profitability is essential to our future success.

The following statements captured employee sentiments about Starbucks' culture.

> When people ask me what I do for a living, I say: I drink coffee and talk about it. That's my job—not too shabby. I have a lot to learn, and a lot of places I can go if I wanted to leave Starbucks, but it's so interesting and I've met the neatest people that work here. I have a lot of passion for it. You know you go through bumps and grinds because we've changed a lot but it's like being in any kind of relationship. You fall in love, it's all great, everything is beautiful and then you find out that there are some things like wrinkles or bad habits. You work on those and then you're in puppy love again. I love working at Starbucks; my husband thinks it's pretty twisted. I mean I was a store manager and I lived at my store...people would say that you do such a great job and I would say that I couldn't do it without these people—I can't do it alone—none of us can. I totally rely on the wealth and depth of knowledge that other people have, the background they bring to Starbucks, their support and work ethic. And I just embrace that hugely; I can bring my weird ideas and be as goofy as I want one day or as serious as I need to be another day and it's OK. When I started at Starbucks someone told me: you tell me what you want to do and I will help you.[15]

> In a day offsite, with Jim Collins (author of *Built to Last*), the senior management team of 40 people or so was divided into 10 groups of four. First, we identified our own set of values and then we broke into groups of four people and combined our lists of values. It was absolutely mind-boggling that we all came back and had exactly the same list of values. Collins had never seen anything like that. Everyone is passionate about what they do, about life, about everything. Everybody has a sense of integrity, that we want to succeed but we want to do it in a fair, equitable, ethical way. We care about winning; you know we aren't ashamed to admit that we want to be successful, that we do care about people and do respect our partners. The fifth value was our entrepreneurial spirit. We don't want this to become a big company; we want to continually strive to be innovative and continually rejuvenate the company.[16]

FINANCIAL

Starbucks' stock price and EPS had been rapidly increasing over the last five years (see Exhibit 7). In the span of six months, from January to June 1997, four prominent investment companies had rated the company as a "BUY" in their report to investors. See Exhibit 8 for a forecast from each of these companies regarding EPS, P/E ratios and share price. One investment company that rated Starbucks as a long-term buy stated:

> Since its 1992 IPO, Starbucks has executed its strategy to near perfection, achieving its initial goal of building the country's leading branded retailer of specialty coffees. As growth in its North American retail business decelerates from unsustainably rapid rates, the company is now in the early stages of pursuing a more ambitious goal—to build the most recognized and respected coffee brand in the world. Current initiatives include the development of Starbucks stores with local partners in the Pacific Rim, domestic brand extensions into packaged ice cream and bottled beverages, and test-marketing Starbucks whole bean coffees in the supermarket channel. While greatly enhancing the company's long-term growth

---

[15] Aileen Carrell, Coffee Taster, Starbucks Corporation.

[16] Liz Sickler, Director, Special Projects, Starbucks Corporation.

potential, we believe these new pursuits also raise the risk profile of the stock. With SBUX shares trading at 33 times our estimate of calendar 1998 EPS, we believe extraordinary intermediate-term appreciation relies upon the successful execution of these ventures. Given the strength of the brand, our confidence in management, and impressive joint-venture partners, we are optimistic that these activities, in the aggregate, will contribute significantly to Starbucks' profitability over the next three to five years. We conclude that Starbucks remains a core holding for long-term growth stock investors, albeit with higher risk, as it transitions from a category-dominant domestic branded retailer into a global consumer brand.[17]

In North America, Starbucks owned all of its retail outlets other than host licensing arrangements. However, owning all of its stores, Starbucks was faced with the prospect of depending heavily on equity and debt financing to grow. Its competitors like Seattle's Best Coffee and the Second Cup were all franchised, and consequently needed less internal financing to roll out stores. For Starbucks' balance sheet, see Exhibit 9. For the income statement, see Exhibit 7.

MARKETING

Of key concern in Starbucks' marketing department was its brand equity. The retail business had historically been Starbucks' source of brand equity. This had meant that Starbucks was never just about the coffee; it was about a place, an experience.

Starbucks now wanted to develop its brand beyond being the preferred outlet from which to purchase coffee to becoming the preferred consumer brand. Scott Bedbury, Starbucks' Senior Vice-President of Marketing, explained its brand:

> We are transitioning from a very retail-centric view about the brand to a view that will allow us to say that Starbucks' role is to provide uplifting moments to people every day. I didn't say coffee! If you go beyond coffee, you can get to music, you can get to literature, you can get to a number of different areas. It can also become a licence to dilute the brand. Therefore our goal is to remain true to our core, coffee. After all we are the protectors of something that is 900 million years old. Just like when you drop a rock in a pond there will be ripples that come outside that core, Starbucks is not just a pound of coffee, but a total coffee experience.

One of the key challenges faced by Starbucks was trying concretely to define its brand image. Company executives felt that this was essential before Starbucks started mounting grand-scale, national advertising campaigns and other brand leveraging activities. Liz Sickler, Starbucks Director of Special Projects, commented:

> I don't think that we leverage our size well enough. Very often we have strong competition in local markets from Caribou, to Seattle's Best Coffee to the Second Cup in Canada: And it's always mind-boggling how they can be so competitive in their local markets despite the fact that our national brand image is so much stronger. We need to take advantage of our national presence. We need to compete on our brand recognition. I think that's why we started to do some national advertising this year to see if that's how we can leverage our size. I think going into different distribution channels and leveraging the brand is the answer.

OPTIONS

Howard Schultz and the senior management at Starbucks were committed to the company's strategy. It was felt that Starbucks' current strategic direction would allow it to sustain growth by continuing the development

---

[17] William Blair and Company on June 20, 1997.

of the Starbucks brand image and by increasing its presence in different markets. Starbucks was growing very rapidly and was consistently evaluating new opportunities in its domestic and international retail markets, new specialty sales partners, penetration in the grocery channel and the future potential of its mail order business. How the company should react to all of these opportunities was one of Mr. Schultz's key concerns.

EXHIBIT 1   Specialty Coffee Sales As a % of Total Coffee Sales

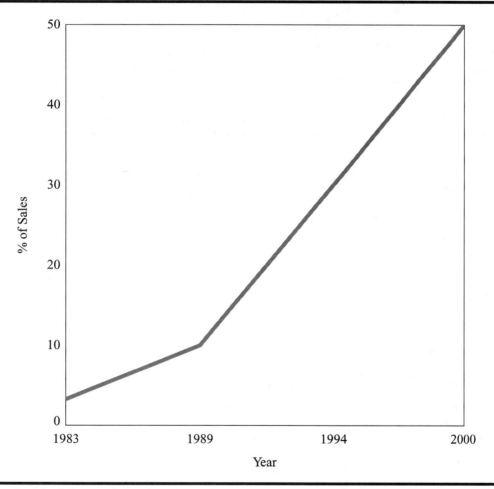

Source: Specialty Coffee Association of America, Montgomery Securities, Volume 27.

E X H I B I T 2   Comparing the Retail Sales of Coffee

(US$ millions)

	1990	1994	1998E	1990–1994 growth	1994–1998E growth
Ground Regular	2 050	1 240	800	-11.8 %	-10.4%
Ground Decaffeinated	650	575	450	-3.0%	-5.9%
Ground Specialty	810	1 315	1 635	12.9%	5.6%
Instant Regular	1 175	1 010	780	-3.7%	-6.3%
Instant Decaffeinated	385	295	170	-6.4%	-12.9%
Whole Bean	255	380	500	10.5%	7.1%
Ready-To-Drink	5	250	1 255	165.9%	49.7%
Total	**5 330**	**5 065**	**5 590**	**-1.3%**	**2.5%**

Source: Yorkton Securities Inc., March 25, 1997.

E X H I B I T 3   Coffee Chains' Stock Prices and Market Capitalizations

	Year		
Company	High ($)	Low ($)	Market Cap.($mm)
U.S. Companies			
Brothers	4.63	2.13	30.8
Coffee People	9.38	6.00	21.4
Diedrich	12.00	3.00	23.6
Green Mountain	7.50	6.88	24.8
Starbucks	40.25	21.50	2 438.5
Canadian Companies			
Cam	4.80	3.30	440.2
Van Houtte	28.35	18.50	225.6
Second Cup	13.35	9.15	137.2

Comparing the Coffee Chains

Company	TEV[1]/EBITDA[2]	Net Margin
U.S. Companies		
Brothers	6.0	−14.0%
Coffee People	8.4	1.7%
Diedrich	15.6	1.2%
Green Mountain	7.3	3.3%
Starbucks	25.1	6.0%
Average	14.5	
Canadian Companies		
Cara	7.7	5.8%
Van Houtte	7.8	4.7%
Second Cup	13.2	-3.7%
Average	17.9	

[1] TEV is total enterprise value defined as current market cap plus debt less cash. Debt and cash are as latest available balance sheet date.
[2] EBITDA for Brothers and Diedrich is trailing twelve months.

Source: Yorkton Securities Inc., March 25, 1997.

E X H I B I T 4 **Analysis of Unit Economic Trends**

(US$ thousands)

	1994	*1995*	*1996*	*1997E*	*1998E*	*1999E*
Cash Investment:						
Store Build Out[1]	330	357	315	310	305	300
Pre-opening	16	23	21	20	20	20
Beginning Inventory	17	20	24	20	20	20
Total Cash Investment	363	400	360	350	345	340
Average Sales/Store[2]	820	820	850	825	790	765
Average Sales/Investment	2.3x	2.1x	2.4x	2.4x	2.3x	2.3x
EBIT Margin[3]	18.9%	17.5%	16.5%	18.0%	17.8%	17.6%
EBIT	155	144	140	150	141	135
ROI (EBIT/Cash Invested)	43.0%	36.0%	39.0%	43.0%	41.0%	40.0%

[1] Estimated investment per store opened during the fiscal year.
[2] Estimated average sales and EBIT for units open at least one year.
[3] EBIT includes marketing and field level overhead expenses.

Source: William Blair & Company, 1997.

E X H I B I T 5 **Starbucks Corporation Projected Pacific Rim Development (a)**

(US$ millions)

	1997E	*1998E*	*1999E*	*2000E*
New units	13	30	55	100
Ending units	15	45	100	200
Average unit volume	$1.0	$1.0	$1.0	$1.0
Total sales [a]	$9	$30	$73	$150

[a] Note that total sales reflect sales of joint ventures, partnerships and licensees. We expect additional partnership agreements in the Pacific Rim to be disclosed before year-end. In fact, an executive of President Foods (the largest food company in Taiwan and a 7-Eleven franchisee) was recently quoted saying that the company expected to develop Starbucks stores in Taiwan, and perhaps China. Given the magnitude of the opportunity in the Pacific Rim, we do not anticipate development in Europe until at least 1999. Whereas the long-term potential of international development is tremendous, we expect expenses of building infrastructure and growing rapidly will be a drag on Starbucks profits at least through 1999. Depending on the structure of future international ventures, this business could become a significant consumer of Starbucks investment capital.

Source: William Blair & Company, 1997.

EXHIBIT 6 · **Projected Avenues of Growth—Estimated Contribution from Joint Ventures**

(US$ millions)	1995	1996	1997E	1998E	1999E
Annual Investment					
Ice Cream	0.0	0.9	2.0	1.0	0.5
Bottled Beverages	1.2	2.7	18.0	15.0	10.0
Whole Bean	0.0	0.0	3.0	5.0	9.5
Total	**1.2**	**6.0**	**30.0**	**33.0**	**35.0**
Retail Revenues					
Ice Cream	0.0	15.0	40.0	45.0	50.0
Bottled Beverages	0.0	0.0	65.0	250.0	300.0
Whole Bean	0.0	0.0	1.3	43.8	78.8
Total	**0.0**	**15.0**	**114.8**	**368.8**	**501.3**
Contribution to Starbucks Earnings					
Ice Cream	0.0	-0.7	0.5	2.4	3.0
Bottled Beverages	- 1.2	-0.4	-0.5	4.4	7.9
Whole Bean	0.0	0.0	-0.5	1.6	4.5
Total	**-1.2**	**-1.1**	**-1.5**	**8.4**	**15.4**
Joint Venture Contributions	-1.2	-1.1	-1.5	8.4	15.4

Source: William Blair & Company, 1997.

EXHIBIT 7 Income Statement

(US$ thousands)	1994	1995	1996	1997E	1998E	1999E
Net Revenues						
Retail	248 453	402 874	600 367	827 003	1 053 796	1 276 840
Specialty Sales	26 498	47 917	78 702	110 331	148 612	193 552
Direct Response	9 972	14 422	17 412	22 066	25 792	30 008
Total Net Revenues	284 923	465 213	696 481	959 400	1 228 200	1 500 400
Store Operating Expenses	90 087	148 757	210 693	296 200	368 700	441 800
Other Operating Expenses	8 698	13 932	19 787	24 200	31 800	40 200
Cost of Sales and Related Occupancy Costs	162 840	262 408	409 008	548 800	687 000	827 700
Operating Income	23 298	40 116	56 993	90 200	140 700	190 700
Other Expenses	-5 544	3 027	11 508	3 600	-2 600	-7 000
Earnings before Income Taxes	17 754	43 143	68 501	93 800	138 100	183 700
Income Taxes	7 548	17 041	26 373	36 100	53 200	70 700
Net Earnings	10 206	26 102	42 128	57 700	84 900	113 000
Preferred Stock Dividends Accrued	-270	0	0	–	–	–
Net Earnings Available to Common Shareholders	9 936	26 102	42 128	57 700	84 900	113 000
Net Earnings Per Share	0.17	0.36	0.47	0.70	1.00	1.30
Weighted Average Shares Outstanding	57 575	71 909	80 831	88 600	89 500	90 400
Average Share Price	25	15	24	–	–	–
Price Earnings Ratios	148	42	51	51	36	28

Note 1: The $0.47 EPS in 1996 excludes the gains from the sale of Noah's Bagels.
Note 2: The $0.17 EPS in 1994 would be $0.22 without the one-time charges associated with the acquisition of Coffee Connection.
Note 3: On December 1, 1995, the company recorded a 2 for 1 stock split to holders of record on November 1, 1995. Net earnings per share for all years have been restated to reflect the stock split.

Sources: Starbucks Annual Reports & William Blair & Company.

EXHIBIT 8 Forecast of EPS, PE Ratio and Share Price

Robinson-Humphrey Company Inc.	*1996*	*1997E*	*1998E*	
Earnings Per Share	$0.54*	$0.70	$1.00	
Price/Earnings Ratio	55.6 times	42.9 times	30.0 times	
Forecasted Share Price			$49.00	
Alex Brown & Sons	*1996*	*1997E*	*1998E*	
Earnings Per Share	$0.48	$0.70	$0.98	
Price/Earnings Ratio		39.0 times	27.8 times	
Forecasted Share Price			$45.00	
Painewebber Inc.	*1996*	*1997E*	*1998E*	
Earnings Per Share	$0.47	$0.70	$0.95	
Price/Earnings Ratio		40.5 times	30.0 times	
Forecasted Share Price			$42.00	
William Blair and Company	*1996*	*1997E*	*1998E*	*1999E*
Earnings Per Share	$0.47	$0.70	$1.00	$1.30
Price/Earnings Ratio	76.1 times	51.1 times	35.8 times	27.5 times

*Includes a one-time gain on the sale of Noah's Bagels.

E X H I B I T 9 Balance Sheet

(US$ thousands)

	1994	1995	1996	1997E	1998E	1999E
Assets						
Current Assets						
Cash and Cash Equivalents	8 394	20 944	126 215	128 900	53 200	21 000
Accounts Receivable	5 394	9 852	17 621	24 300	31 100	38 000
Inventories	56 064	123 657	83 370	122 500	149 600	178 100
Other Current Assets	14 728	50 897	112 335	12 500	16 100	19 600
Total Current Assets	84 580	205 350	339 541	288 200	250 000	256 700
Property and Equipment, Net	140 754	244 728	369 477	496 700	617 600	733 600
Other Assets	6 087	18 100	17 595	43 100	78 100	121 100
Total Assets	231 421	468 178	726 613	828 000	945 700	1 111 400
Liabilities and Shareholders' Equity						
Current Liabilities						
Accounts Payable	9 128	28 668	38 034			
Other Current Liabilities	31 290	42 378	63 057			
Total Current Liabilities	40 418	71 046	101 091	134 100	165 800	198 100
Other Liabilities	81 105	84 901	173 862			
Shareholders' Equity						
Common Stock	89 861	265 679	361 309	519 400	604 300	717 200
Retained Earnings	20 037	46 552	90 351			
Total Shareholders' Equity	109 898	312 231	451 660			
Total Liabilities	231 421	468 178	726 613	828 000	945 700	1 111 400

Sources: Starbucks Corporation Annual Reports & William Blair & Company.

case

11

MINERVA S.A.

*Allen J. Morrison
and Elpida Frantzeskarou*

In early December 1995, Theo Grigoris, Managing Director of Minerva S.A., met with Vassili Goudes, the company's newly appointed Commercial Director, to discuss the future direction of the Athens, Greece based manufacturer of edible oils and margarine. While the company was a leading producer of high quality olive oil and a significant competitor in seed oils and margarine, increasing competition from Unilever's Greek affiliate and changing buying habits were forcing the company to reassess its basic approach to business. Over the past year the company had begun a major overhaul of its operations including the announcement of a new plant and the introduction of new management practices and technologies. However, resistance to change was everywhere. Mr. Goudes presented his assessment of the challenges that lay ahead:

THUNDERBIRD
THE AMERICAN GRADUATE SCHOOL
OF INTERNATIONAL MANAGEMENT

We are far behind where we should be in terms of management depth and market position. Managing the change process has been very difficult. Yet I have no hesitation that we need to change. The big question is setting priorities.

COMPANY HISTORY

The name Minerva is steeped in Greek history. The city of Athens was named after Athena, the Greek goddess of wisdom and agriculture in Greek mythology. Athena promised the people of Athens that olive trees would flourish within the city. Athens has been closely associated with olives and olive trees ever since. With the decline of the Greek empire and the arrival of the Romans in 150 BC, the goddess Athena was renamed Minerva, its Latin translation.

Early Days

Minerva branded olive oil was first produced in 1904 through a cottage business managed by Mr. E. Giannakos on the Greek island of Lesvos. Mr. E. Giannakos passed the business to his son Mr. P. Giannakos, who later formed a partnership with another local olive oil producer, Mr. A. Sahpaloglou. The partnership focused on bulk sales of olive oil under the Minerva and Reggina brand names. The business was relatively simple and focused on the purchase of olive oil from area farmers, processing, bottling and distribution throughout Greece. In 1970, Mr. E. Giannakos retired and in 1971 the company was officially renamed "Minerva Olive Oil Manufacturing and Commercial S.A."

Selling branded olive oil was an unusual strategy in Greece where, for millennia, olive oil had been purchased by consumers directly from farmers. Buying habits were age-old and had become ingrained in Greek family traditions. Even with the increasing urbanization of Greek society, family outings to purchase olive oil from select farms were common. By the late 1970s, well over 80% of Greek olive oil was still being purchased directly from farmers.

The Company Is Sold

Over the years, Minerva emerged as the leading olive oil brand in Greece. Still, sales and profits were limited. In 1978, Mr. A. Sahpaloglou, old and suffering from cancer, sold the company to U.K.-based Paterson Zochonis for $1.5 million. Under the Paterson Zochonis Group, the company would experience significant growth.

Paterson Zochonis traced its roots to the West African country of Sierra Leone in the 1870s when George Paterson, a Scot, and George Zochonis, a Greek from Sparta, first met and established an office in England to import West African products—palm produce, groundnuts, coffee, hides and timber—while also managing the sale of European textiles and foodstuffs to Sierra Leone. Despite harsh living conditions the business flourished. In 1929, George Zochonis died and Constantine Zochonis, George's nephew, took over the reins as chief executive. George Paterson gradually sold his shares to the Zochonis family and for the next 50 years Paterson Zochonis would remain a British registered company, managed by Greeks doing almost all of its business in Africa.

From the late 1940s to the early 1970s, Paterson Zochonis invested heavily in sub-Saharan Africa. The company expanded into the manufacture and sale of soap, toiletries, sewing threads and proprietary pharmaceuticals. In 1953, Paterson Zochonis became a public company in the U.K. with its shares quoted on the London Stock Exchange. While the Zochonis family maintained controlling interest in the company, the new infusion of equity fueled further growth in Africa. In 1973, Paterson Zochonis formed a joint venture company that became the largest producer of refrigerators in Africa.

With a strong position in Africa, Paterson Zochonis management began to search for growth opportunities in Europe. In 1972, the company purchased Roberts Laboratories Limited of Bolton, England, a manufacturer of proprietary drugs, principally for markets in the Middle East, Africa and the U.K. In 1975 Paterson Zochonis purchased Cussons Group Ltd., a major British soap and toiletries manufacturer. Cussons' best-known brands were Imperial Leather soap and toiletries and 1001 household cleaning materials. This move established Paterson Zochonis as a major force in the U.K. market. With new sources of financing, Cussons constructed soap factories in Australia, Singapore, Malaysia, Indonesia, Thailand, Pakistan, Bangladesh and Kenya.

Many managers of Paterson Zochonis regarded the acquisition of Minerva S.A. as a natural move. One long-time Greek national who served as a Paterson Zochonis manager in Africa in 1978 reflected back on the thinking at that time:

> Greece was known worldwide for its olive oil. It was its one main export. Minerva was the top brand in Greece at that time. We bought the company because it was a high profile Greek company that was for sale. We also saw it as an opportunity to expand into other food products. Our ambition was for Minerva to become a major food products company in Greece.

In 1982 George Loupos, a native of Sparta, Greece and a member of the Zochonis family, was named the Managing Director of Paterson Zochonis. Turnover at Paterson Zochonis in 1995 was estimated at £287.8 million with profits over £16 million. In late 1995, Loupos was still serving as Managing Director.

Despite high ambitions for Minerva, Paterson Zochonis was reluctant to assert itself in the day-to-day operations of its new acquisitions. From 1978 until 1982 Minerva was managed by five brothers from the Athens-based Lazopoulos family. When George Loupos became Managing Director at Paterson Zochonis in 1982 he replaced the Lazopoulos brothers with Nick Foros as Managing Director of Minerva. Foros had recently retired from Paterson Zochonis where he had served in various management capacities in Africa. In 1985, Foros was replaced by Mike Kourtessis, who had also come out of retirement from Paterson Zochonis in Africa. Suffering from ill health, Kourtessis retired a second time and in March 1993 was replaced as Managing Director by Theo Grigoris. Grigoris had worked in Africa for Paterson Zochonis since 1953, rising to Chief Executive for the company's Nigerian operations—its largest and most profitable affiliate in Africa. He was a close personal friend of George Loupos and had retired from Paterson Zochonis in 1990. Grigoris commented:

> In Africa we retire at an early age, maybe 53 years old. We are typically offered a job back in England. But many don't want to go. I returned to Greece. Paterson Zochonis always takes care of its people. Those that remain with the company over the years, as I did, get hooked to the company. When they asked me to come back as Managing Director, I agreed. My mission at Minerva was to professionalize the management and move the company forward.

Minerva's Key Markets

By the early 1990s Minerva had emerged as a major player in the Greek markets for edible oils (which included both olive oil and seed oils), margarine and fats. In these key markets, Minerva faced serious competition from Elais, a Greek company purchased by Unilever in 1962. In 1995 Elais had sales revenues of approximately 60B Gr. Drs., was growing at over 15% per year and employed about 550 people.[1]

Olive Oil

Two different categories of olive oil were recognized: virgin olive oil and pure olive oil. Each category of olive oil could be further segmented according to a variety of quality factors. The flavour, aroma, and

---

[1] In December 1995, the exchange rate was approximately 235 Greek Drachmas/US$.

colour of virgin olive oils varied significantly from country to country, region to region, and even farm to farm. Factors such as soil and climate conditions, the variety of olive trees used (hundreds of varieties of trees exist), the age of the tree, harvesting methods, timing, and processing methods all impact the characteristics of virgin olive oil.

Like wine, international standards have been adopted to grade virgin oils. To be considered extra virgin olive oil, for example, the oil has to be produced from the first pressings of olives. Furthermore, the flavour, colour and aroma have to meet certain standards, and acid content cannot exceed 1%. Fine virgin olive oil cannot have an acidity level greater than 1.5%; semi-fine virgin olive oil could not have an acidity level greater than 3%. In contrast, pure olive oil is refined from the remains of pressed olives. These remains often have high levels of acidity, strong aromas and flavours. Refining lowers these levels and standardizes the colour consistent with semi-virgin olive oil. Pure olive oil is sold at a slight discount to extra virgin olive oil.

WORLD OLIVE OIL MARKETS

World production of olive oil amounted to approximately 1.75 million tons in 1995. Spain was the world's largest producer with 600 000 tons, followed by Italy with 400 000 tons, Greece with 300 000 tons and Tunisia with 200 000 tons. During the early 1990s, olive oil consumption skyrocketed on reports of its positive health benefits. From 1992 to 1995, olive oil consumption increased 20% in the U.S., 15% in Australia, and 10% in Northern Europe. Growing demand led to rising prices: from 1992 to 1995, world olive oil prices increased almost 40%.

Stathis Lempesis, Sales Director for Minerva, commented on the production of olives:

> It takes over 20 years for an olive tree seedling to grow to full production. Olive trees can live thousands of years. They recently found an olive tree in Athens that was 2 000 years old. However, as trees grow past about 100 years, the quality and quantity of olives falls. So we are constantly cutting out old trees and planting new ones. The European Union will pay farmers to grow more. However, the EU won't do anything unless the Greek government brings it to their attention. So far the Greek government doesn't have a policy. The good news is that policies applied in Italy and Spain will also be applied here as well. It just takes time to get sorted out.

GREEK OLIVE OIL MARKETS

In Greece, olives were harvested from November to the end of March. Farmers typically owned presses and managed the oil extraction process. A farm which produced 1 000 tons of oil per year would be considered large. Farmers generally avoided long-term production/pricing contracts with packaging companies. The custom for most farmers was to promote self-consumption sales while speculating on future prices with packaging companies. Once an agreement was reached to sell to a packaging company, delivery would typically be made within the week. Minerva could store about two months inventory of raw material and typically had no problem finding sellers of olive oil throughout the year. However, by August farm inventories would begin to dry up and prices rise. Some farmers would hold back inventories for several years in order to speculate on prices. (Even when properly stored, olive oil begins to deteriorate in quality after about one year.) After virgin olive oils had been received, packaging companies would clean and purify the supplies, grade and blend the oils and run a bottling operation.

Greeks prided themselves as olive oil connoisseurs and would not buy what was perceived to be lower quality Italian, Spanish or Tunisian olive oils. Although Greek olive oil had a superior reputation for quality, Greek olive oil was about 10% more expensive than Italian or Spanish oils. Almost all of the cost difference was made up in manufacturing costs. The largest Greek oil plant (run by Elais with a capacity of 60 000 tons) was perhaps one-third the size of Bertoli's largest plant in Italy. Greek plants were also used to produce both olive oils and seed oils whereas the large Italian and Spanish plants focused exclusively on olive oils. Despite cost disadvantages, Theo Grigoris asserted that "Greeks will never buy an Italian olive oil." As of 1995, olive oil from these countries had not made inroads in the Greek marketplace.

Greece exported approximately 150 000 of the 300 000 tons of olive oil it produced annually. Of the amount exported, less than 10 000 tons was branded olive oil. The rest was bulk exports. Minerva's branded export sales in 1995 were 500 tons; the company had no bulk export sales. In terms of domestic consumption, about 100 000 tons of the 150 000 tons of olive oil purchased in Greece was sold directly by farmers—typically in 16 liter tins—to either consumers or industrial customers. The remaining 50 000 tons represented pre-packaged consumer sales. Both Minerva and Elais focused their efforts on this segment. It was estimated that Elais held a 6.2% share of the Greek packaged consumer market for virgin olive oil and a 51% share of the pure olive oil market; Elais did not sell pomage.[2] A breakdown of the key market segments and Minerva's product focus is shown in Exhibit 1.

Three market trends were evident in the Greek olive oil industry. First, Greeks were increasingly shifting towards prepackaged, branded oils. Urbanization, time constraints and the loosening of relationships between farmers and urban consumers were regularly cited for this trend. Second, Greeks were moving from virgin oils to cheaper blended varieties. Increased retail stocking fees and the increased international demand for olive oil had pushed prices substantially higher. Faced with steep annual price increases, many consumers were shifting to more economical blends. Third, the demand for bulk Greek olive oil from Spanish and Italian traders was increasing. Poor harvests in Spain combined with soaring markets in North America pushed large Spanish and Italian traders and bottlers to aggressively seek new supplies of olive oil. In an effort to spur olive oil production the EU in January 1995 transferred subsidies of 400 Gr. Drs. per kilogram to Greek olive growers. However, growers did not cut prices to processors.

Seed Oils

The second major edible oil market where Minerva competed was seed oils. Common seed oils include corn oil, sunflower oils, soybean oil, cottonseed oil, palm oil and various blends. With the exception of cottonseed and some sunflower seed oils, Greece was not a seed oil producing country. Seed oils were imported from a variety of countries: palm oil was imported from Malaysia, corn and soybean oils from France and the U.S., blends from Belgium, the Netherlands and Germany. There were no duties on oils produced within the EU; duties on imports from the U.S. and Malaysia averaged 10%.

Seed oils were generally processed by large, integrated manufacturers. To be competitive, processing facilities focused on maximizing volume-based efficiencies; the average capacity of a large seed oil plant in Northern Europe was 150 000 tons/year. Output could be shipped in two basic forms, bulk or bottles. Bulk oils were usually shipped in 1 000 ton increments in the holds of ocean-going vessels. Upon arrival, the oil would be filtered to remove impurities that were commonly picked up during shipping. The oil would then be bottled for local distribution. Reprocessing and local bottling added costs to the production process. As an alternative, distributors could purchase bottled oil—either with a private or manufacturer's label—directly from one of the large processors in Northern Europe. However, shipping costs for bottled oils were much higher than for bulk oil. As a result, the cost differential for reprocessed versus bottled oil was minimal. One marketing manager at Minerva commented:

> Bulk oil has to be filtered. The hold of a ship is never clean enough. We have to make sure the oil meets our standards. Huge plants from Northern Europe are efficient not just from the economies of scale but also because they can make the bottle and fill it on the same line. But when you put a label on it, all the bottles look the same. Maybe they can deliver it in Greece 5% cheaper than we can produce it here from bulk. However, having a custom bottle is also important in the consumer's mind.

In 1995, approximately 90% of the corn oil and sunflower oil sold in Greece was bottled in Greece.

---

[2] Pomage is residual oil collected from pure olive oil storage containers. It is used for cooking and frying oils.

THE GREEK SEED OIL MARKET

In 1995, the total Greek market for seed oils was approximately 110 000 tons. Of this amount, about 50% or 55 000 tons was devoted to consumer markets; the remaining 50% represented industrial sales. Elais was actively developing the industrial market and was by far its single largest supplier. Minerva had generally ignored the industrial segment where it had only about a 2% share.

The Greek consumer seed oil market was dominated by both Minerva, which had an estimated 20.5% share of the market, and Elais, which had approximately 26.5% market share. Elais focused principally on three seed oil segments: (1) the corn oil segment where its Flora brand enjoyed a 20% market share, (2) the sunflower segment where its Sol brand had an estimated 65% market share, and (3) the blended segment where the company's Friol brand had a 3% share. Minerva did not brand its seed oils separately but promoted its products by using the Minerva name and standard company bottles. Key seed oil segments and Minerva's market share data are provided in Exhibit 2.

EXHIBIT 1   **Key Greek Olive Oil Market Segments & Minerva's Market Focus, 1995**

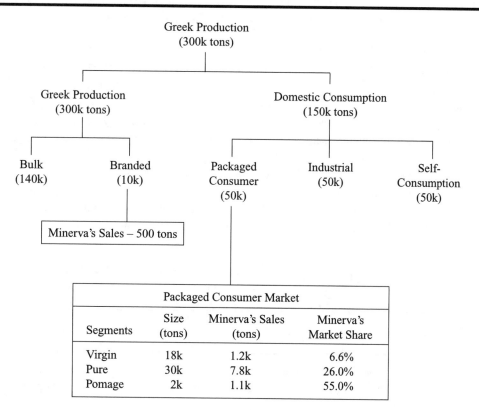

Packaged Consumer Market			
Segments	Size (tons)	Minerva's Sales (tons)	Minerva's Market Share
Virgin	18k	1.2k	6.6%
Pure	30k	7.8k	26.0%
Pomage	2k	1.1k	55.0%

EXHIBIT 2 **The Greek Seed Oil Market & Minerva's Market Focus, 1995**

Total Greek Market	110k tons
Industrial	55k tons
Consumer	55k tons
Minerva's sales	1.13k ton

Segment	Size (tons)	Minerva's Sales (tons)	Minerva's Market Share
Corn	19.0k	7.0k	36.8%
Sunflower	25.0k	2.2k	8.8%
Soybean	6.0k	0.6k	10.0%
Cottonseed	2.5k	0.3k	12.0%
Blends	2.5%	1.2k	48.0%
Totals	55.0k	11.3k	20.5%

From 1990 to 1995 the overall seed oil market had remained largely static. The main trend was a switch from cotton, sunflower and blended oils to corn oil. With olive oil prices soaring, many observers believed that a shift from olive oil to seed oils was likely during the late 1990s.

Cooking Fats and Margarines

The Greek cooking fat market was approximately 10 000 tons in 1995. Of this amount, the consumer segment was about 6 800 tons and the industrial segment was about 3 200 tons. Minerva produced about 1 000 tons (14.7% share) for the consumer cooking fats segment and 350 tons (10.9% share) for the industrial cooking fats segment. The consumer segment had been declining by 5% per year since the early 1990s. The industrial market had remained static. Elais was Minerva's only competitor in the cooking fats (industrial and consumer) market.

The Greek margarine market totaled approximately 35 000 tons in 1995, split almost evenly between consumer and industrial sales. A breakdown of market segments and Minerva's share is shown in Exhibit 3. The consumer market was split between brick (40%) and soft (60%) segments. From 1994 to 1995, the soft margarine segment grew by 2% while the brick segment declined by 6%.

EXHIBIT 3 **Greek Margarine Market and Minerva's Market Focus**

Market	Size (tons)	Minerva's Sales (tons)	Minerva's Market Share (%)
Consumer	17k	3.5k	20.5
Industrial	18k	2.1k	11.6

It was estimated that Elais enjoyed a 75% share of the consumer margarine segment and a 40% share of the industrial margarine segment. U.S.-based Kraft was number three in the Greek margarine market with the balance of the market.

Other Businesses

Minerva had minor positions as an importer and distributor of rice, soaps and detergents. Its rice business involved distributing about 260 tons per year of imported boil-in-the-bag rice. Although this represented about a 72% share of the boil-in-the-bag segment, the entire segment accounted for less than 1% of the entire Greek rice market. Minerva also had a 4.7% volume share of the Greek bar soap market. Its sales were based almost exclusively on U.K. produced Imperial Leather bar soap. Cussons was known to be dissatisfied with the limited marketing effort Minerva was placing on its bar soap sales.

MINERVA IN THE EARLY 1990s

Operations

Minerva produced all of its oils, fats and margarines in a single plant located in an industrial neighbourhood in Athens. Production capacity at the plant was approximately 22 000 tons per year for oils and 4 000 tons per year for margarine. This put the company at capacity in oils and well over capacity in margarine. The plant had been expanded numerous times over the years and covered virtually every available inch of the 5 500 square meter parcel of land it sat on. Further expansion was impossible. Total floor space was 11 000 square meters split over four stories. Raw material inventories were kept on two different floors, packaging on another and finished goods inventories on yet another. Freight elevators were used extensively to move inventory supplies causing serious bottlenecks and inefficiencies. Storage tanks and refining towers were adjacent to the main building. Some were covered from the elements while others were not.

Grigoris was troubled by the run-down state of the current factory. A tour in December 1995 revealed water and oil on floors, inconsistent use of sanitary hairnets, uniforms and gloves on the packing lines, and dirty shipping pallets located in the packaging areas. Some of the equipment used in the plant was more than 50 years old. Oil that was returned by customers was held uncovered, unprotected and outdoors for five to seven days. Some of the drums and tins were returned open and leaked oil. (The returned product would eventually be reprocessed as lower grade oil.) The state of the factory prevented the company from providing tours to prospective customers. Grigoris acknowledged that "our factory is run with old equipment and methods that are inferior to our methods in Africa."

In December 1995, the company's Manufacturing Director was P. Tokousbalides who was in his mid-60s and held a Ph.D. in physical chemistry from the University of Toledo. Tokousbalides had been in the olive oil business for over 35 years, the last 15 with Minerva. He was regarded as being technically very strong.

The factory employed 132 people in five different departments: refining; packaging, planning, quality control and maintenance. Three shifts a day were used in the factory; two shifts per day manned the packaging operations. The factory ran five days per week, 12 months per year. Over 120 of the employees were represented by a division of the National Worker's Union which was described as "very active." Salaries at the factory were estimated to be about 40% higher than for comparable jobs in Athens. While absenteeism ran high, essentially no one ever quit. Tokousbalides explained:

> Absenteeism is mostly built into the system. In Greece workers get up to three days of full pay with a doctor's certificate. It's easy to get a doctor to sign anything here. Workers can get up to 25 days off sick per year with full pay according to the law. They seem to take it and there is nothing we can do. Very few people are fired. Those who are fired want to get fired so they get extra compensation before going on government assistance.

When Grigoris joined Minerva in March 1993, a plan was under way to move the bottling and packaging functions out of the plant to a new site in Aspropyrgos, about 15 kms away. Grigoris was very uncomfortable with the added complexity this would introduce to operations and argued for an entirely new, integrated plant. In early 1994, he convinced Paterson Zochonis to provide almost $28 million in new funding to expand capacity, purchase state of the art equipment and move the plant. The money plus an additional $9 million from the Greek government would go towards buying a facility in Ritsona, Greece (about 50 kms north of Athens). Generous government incentives were provided to companies that established operations outside crowded and polluted Athens. The facility chosen was an existing yogurt factory that sat on 60 000 square meters of land. The new plant was designed to raise olive and seed oil capacity to 40 000 tons by 1997. With a third shift, capacity could reach 60 000 tons. Margarine capacity was expected to triple to 12 000 tons per year.

The move was to be carried out in stages beginning in mid-1996 and ending in March 1997. There was considerable concern that such a move would overwhelm Dr. Tokousbalides, who was planning his retirement within the next two years. To assist with the work, Paterson Zochonis seconded to Minerva Nick Mones for a period of three years starting in January 1996. Mones was in his mid-30s and was an Australian national of Greek ancestry who was running a Paterson Zochonis soap plant in Australia. Mones's assignment at Minerva was to help introduce new techniques and production practices to the processing and bottling operations. Mones spoke fluent Greek but had never actually lived in Greece nor was he completely at ease with Greek writing. Peter Dunn, the International Human Resources Director for Paterson Zochonis, commented on Mones's skills:

> The important thing is the blend of experience that Nick has. That means he is, first of all, very good at understanding business. He is a quick learner and he understands how we do things. Technically he's also extremely competent. He also has very good managerial skills. Probably his best skills were developed in Nigeria which is itself quite demanding in terms of managing labour. Unfortunately he knows nothing about making olive oil.

In December 1995, Peter Dunn traveled to Athens to assist in interviewing candidates for a new Human Resource Director position that was being created. An individual with a strong background managing Greek labour unions was being sought. According to Peter Dunn, the new HR Director would have to work very closely with Mones to "ensure that there were no surprises in the factory."

Marketing and Sales

Not only did Grigoris have to worry about the troubled state of Minerva's operations, but after arriving in 1993 he realized that the company's marketing and sales activities were in a state of disarray. He soon became committed to finding a Commercial Director for the company. A Commercial Director would be someone who could pull together and upgrade the company's marketing, sales and product development groups. One of the first places he looked for references was Sparta. Here, Grigoris met a private school teacher who strongly recommended one of his former students, Vassili Goudes. Goudes, aged 37 and educated at the University of Bath in England, was at the time working as the Market Development Manager for Mars (Trofeklekt) in Greece. Grigoris first approached Goudes in May 1994 and in May 1995 Goudes joined Minerva. Goudes commented:

> I had been at Mars for six and a half years. When I first started, Mars was a 600 million Gr. Drs. company. When I left, they were at 10 billion Gr. Drs. I helped set up their sales and marketing infrastructure. I moved up fast. Then I found myself in a position of saying, what's next? Minerva was a good opportunity. I like changing things. Mr. Grigoris was also very open. He knew things needed to change. He told me all the problems. So I knew he was serious about supporting change.

Shortly after arriving, Goudes compiled a report outlining problems in the Commercial Department. The findings included some of the following.

MARKETING AND SALES CULTURE Goudes could not find many positive aspects in Minerva's marketing and sales culture.

> There is a feeling that Minerva is like a state enterprise—employment for life with good pensions.... People who hold key positions in the structure are today obstacles to any development in terms of systems and new approaches.

About 50 people worked under Goudes in the Commercial Department. With the exception of Goudes and three others, not a single person in the company's sales and marketing operations had either a university degree or spoke English.

> They don't understand the importance of even wearing a necktie when they go visit a store manager. They also question every decision I make. It's not that they will stop me, but they just don't help. The young salespeople are with us. The old regional managers are not... People here sleep too well at night. They have never worried about deadlines or meeting budgets. We are just not sophisticated enough. [Take, for example] our promotion strategy—it too often involves off-invoice promotion or under the table money. It wouldn't be very unfair to say that promotional money was used more to transfer stock than to sell our products.

The sales group was by far the largest group in the Commercial Department. Sales activities were organized around four regions in Greece: Athens, central Greece including the Greek Isles, Western Greece and Northern Greece. The average regional manager was in his mid-40s, had worked for the company for 15 years and had no computer skills. Regional managers supervised 25 salaried sales representatives and 16 commissioned agents. While regional managers were assessed on tonnage per product category, sales representatives had no specific targets for accounts or brands.

Not surprisingly, Goudes worried that his sales representatives were not functioning up to capacity. With the arrival of larger retail chains, computer skills and greater professionalism were clearly needed. Yet according to Goudes, "people with computer knowledge could be counted on one hand." Traffic jams in Athens and Salonica also meant that many sales representatives were spending two hours or more each day stuck in traffic. All sales representatives used their own cars. Many were very old, dirty and in disrepair. Goudes worried that this could portray the company in a bad light. In mid-1995, 34 people were interviewed for three marketing management positions; 30 ended up showing no interest in Minerva. Common responses were:

> the company is too traditional, the company is not up to date, Minerva is not a school

INFORMATION SYSTEMS During late 1995, timely and accurate information was in short supply throughout the company. Lack of computers and computer skills meant that orders were being processed by hand. Sales forecasts became best guesses with over-stocking a significant concern. Another major problem was how the company handled returns. According to Goudes,

> No single department or individual is responsible for handling returns... Not surprisingly, mistakes often occur. Returned goods end up "lost" in the warehouse. The company pays sales commissions on unsold goods. Worse, retailers do not get the credit that they expect, and they become angry, which effectively undoes all our sales and marketing efforts. They... delay paying their bill, and often pay only what they think they owe after deducting the value of the return. This throws Minerva's accounts receivable department into turmoil. Eventually, we simply give up.

John Tountas, the 43-year-old Financial Manager who was charged with leading the company's computerization efforts, commented on the challenges facing the company:

We are currently changing our computer systems and have just adopted the same UNIX-based system used by Cussons International. The software works fine for manufacturing, sales, and distribution. But it doesn't work well for accounting because of unique Greek accounting and tax laws. So we are in the process of adopting a new Greek program. Overall, accounting and sales have the best computer skills. Production is weakest. We will begin training in the factory in six months. Minerva is very supportive of the new equipment. But there is some resistance to change here.

PRODUCT STRATEGY

Minerva's product strategy had evolved over time. Although in its early days Minerva had focused exclusively on olive oil, by 1995 olive oil represented only about 35% of the plant's output and 51% of the company's revenues. An overview of Minerva's product line revenues and volume is found in Exhibit 4.

EXHIBIT 4 Minerva's Manufactured Product Sales Revenues and Volumes, 1995

	Value (billions Gr. Drs.)	%	Volume ('000s tons)	%
Olive Oils	8.610	51	9.601	35
Seed Oils	5.177	31	11.271	41
Margarines	1.839	11	4.251	16
Cooking Fats	.677	4	1.297	5
Other	.423	3	.888	3
Total	16.726	100	27.308	100

Goudes summarized Minerva's product strategy:

No portfolio strategy for new products has ever been applied with the bright exception of packaging alterations. Usually Minerva follows Elais, which is considered the "safe" way to develop. No proper R&D work is taking place... No one is in charge.

Exhibit 5 reviews Minerva's cost structure for olive oil, seed oils and margarine.

EXHIBIT 5 Proportionate Costs for Minerva's Key Manufactured Products, 1995

	Olive Oil	Seed Oil	Margarine
Raw Materials	66%	49%	18%
Packaging Material	5%	19%	27%
Production Costs	7%	12%	17%
Distribution Costs	7%	7%	5%
Marketing Costs	6%	15%	15%
Interest	5%	5%	5%
Trading Profit	4%	2%	13%
Total	100%	100%	100%

FUTURE DIRECTIONS

By the end of 1995 Minerva had grown to a 17.6 billion Gr. Drs. company. (The company's income statements are shown in Appendix A.) Despite what appeared to be steady sales growth, Minerva managers often had different opinions about the future of the company. John Tountas commented:

> The big worry, in my opinion, is the decision to build the new factory. I don't know whether the Greek market is big enough for the new factory. This is a very big expense. If we don't have the sales to cover added costs we will have big problems.

Sales Director Lempesis believed that indeed the sales group was up to the task at hand.

> We are hiring new people now. In the past we did not actively seek new sales. Many times we turned down orders because of capacity shortages. The new plant will allow us to seek out new markets. I think the best opportunity for us is in the Balkans, Albania, Bulgaria, Romania, Macedonia. The area faced a lot of problems under Communism. Now they are open and they are close. It is up to them to find hard currency. If they pay up front, we have a sale.

Manufacturing Director Tokousbalides was worried that the move to the new plant would not go as smoothly as anticipated.

> The distance to the new plant is a major issue for our workers. They are worried about the longer hours on the road. For some it will mean two hours of additional travel time. Most don't have cars. Many of our older people would like an early retirement package. I think the majority of our workers will not be able to adapt and develop the new skills required for the new equipment planned. While they know they can't stop technology they feel the company should look after them with guaranteed jobs. Finding a new job is very hard these days in Athens.

In early December 1995, Grigoris and Goudes met to discuss the company's future direction. Although they shared a strong commitment to aggressively move the company forward, they differed in several key areas.

Grigoris: The added plant capacity will put a lot of pressure on managers to increase sales. When you are at capacity, managers will always tell you they are selling all we can make. Right now people buy Minerva because they like our brand and are used to our bottles. My big worry is seed oils where we all know competition will increase. Greeks are now paying a premium for seed oils. Over time prices will almost certainly fall off. In margarines I am not that worried. Refrigerated ships add a lot to transportation costs.

Goudes: Even though we face rising competition in seed oils, I think we all agree that we do not want to outsource production. Our experience is that we take too much or a quality risk. Also, what are our options? We can bring in seed oils in bulk and bottle them in our plant or we can bring them in already packed in their bottles, put our label on them and sell them in the same bottles as cheaper store brands. Bulk transportation is cheaper than bottle shipping to the point where it about offsets the production efficiencies of the big European plants.

Goudes: In margarine, the good news is that Elais is so big retailers want to support us so they can maintain some leverage over Elais. In olive oils, the good news is that store brands are not that big yet. In Greece the store brands have not had good suppliers. Retailers continue to come to us but I don't think we should ever be a private label supplier to the stores in our major products. Maybe we should look at it for start-up products where the stores could help pay for our learning.

Grigoris: My view is that growth will come as consumers buy more olive oil from supermarkets versus farmers. Also, growth will come from restaurant sales. Bulk sales to restaurants will help us fill our capacity. Elais is not very big in this sector.

Goudes: I would agree but add a few things. We also have enormous potential for olive oils in Northern Greece. In Greece, Elais is almost twice as big as Minerva in olive oils. However, in Athens we are the same size. Where they really beat us is in Northern Greece, in the provinces. During the 1980s we didn't invest in Northern Greece and we didn't advertise. Elais did. Our future growth in olive oils has to be tied much more closely to Northern Greece.

I also think there are big opportunities for us in light olive oils. If we went to light oils we could standardize the products—extra virgin looks and tastes different every year. I think we should also consider getting into bottled salad dressings. Kraft is there but it is not very strong. They have never advertised in Greece.

In seed oils, our past emphasis on one Minerva brand will, I think, be proven wrong. Let's accept the Minerva brand for olive oil. It's very old and traditional. Elais brands its seed oils. At this point we are still a market leader in corn oil but with a very small difference over Elais. Unless we do something significant we are going to lose market share to Elais.

With olive oil prices going up, Greek demand will almost certainly go down. A market shift to seed oils is going to happen. Here we are strong but Elais is stronger. And we have no competitive advantage in seed oils. As a result, the export of olive oil must now become a priority. Yet despite the opportunities, Minerva has no international connections. No ties. We have no people abroad to support the brand. But we have no choice other than to do it now. One approach I have in mind is to go after the tourist market. Greece has 10 million tourists every year. We should advertise in the airports and put Minerva bottles in duty free shops at the airport. We can position ourselves as a super-premium product for tourists.

Grigoris: Probably our biggest decision will be setting priorities. International is an area that has got to play a bigger role in the future. For olive oil, I think we can grow through exports—maybe private label. We can also use Cussons distribution. I think the more we sell their soap in Greece, the more they will be interested in selling our olive oil.

Goudes: In many countries, like the U.K., there are no stocking fees at the supermarkets. Other [olive oil] companies from Italy and Spain have developed a position without advertising. Clearly we can't afford an expensive advertising program. But we could do things like sponsor Greek nights at major supermarkets. The only thing we will have to do is buy new bottles. In margarine, our best opportunities come from exports to the Balkans. You can drive to Albania in two hours. Although the duties are 30% they do have hard currency. The potential is huge, in part because the market has been so poorly served in the past and in part because there is essentially no competition.

Grigoris: The Commercial Department needs to be expanded. We should be a food marketing and development company—not just focused on edible oils and fats. Once we get beyond edible oils and think about international sales, we need to consider new plants. We recently learned of a great opportunity to form a joint venture in Romania with another Greek firm and a Romanian government-owned enterprise. The joint venture would make yogurt and margarine. We will have all this yogurt equipment left over when we move to the new plant. Although not the most sophisticated machinery, we could essentially trade it for equity in the JV. The deal would be cheap for us—maybe, 2 million—and could provide us easy access to the Romanian market for margarine. Romania is a huge market that is being ignored. We have had other opportunities in Bulgaria to build seed oil plants that would be very good for us. These would be great opportunities for us. But Paterson Zochonis won't approve any of this until we prove ourselves. It is very frustrating.

Goudes: I don't fully agree that we should build new factories outside Greece, whether through joint ventures or not. I strongly believe that we must focus on exports. Your views are biased by your background building manufacturing plants. Paterson Zochonis has always built locally.

Grigoris: And your views are biased by your background which is in building brands.

Appendix A   Income Statements for Minerva. S.A. 1978–1995

(million Greek Drachmas)

	1978	*1980*	*1985*	*1990*	*1995*
Overall Sales				8 194	17 643
Cost of Sales				-6 650	-13 556
Gross Profit	101	131	512	1 544	4 087
Fixed Overhead	16	-15	-247	-151	-773
Selling Expense	48	-70	-228	-707	-2 433
Depreciation	3	-3	-3	-57	-5
Interest	14	-40	- 142	-335	-812
Other Income				46	96
Profit Before Tax	20	—	(108)	330	160
Taxes	-9	—	—	-101	-40
Profit after Tax	11	2	—	229	120

AB SANDVIK SAWS & TOOLS: THE ERGO STRATEGY

Roderick E. White and Julian Birkinshaw

Fifteen years ago we competed with price. Today we compete with quality. Tomorrow it will be design.
—Robert Hayes, 1991

Göran Gezelius, the president of the Sandvik Saws & Tools Business Area, looked out his office window at the serene waters of Lake Storsjön. It was early spring and the trees had not yet taken on their summer foliage. He had just returned from a two-week trip to North America a day early and had some free time in his normally hectic schedule. He thought that, overall, Saws and Tools business results for 1995

IVEY

had been adequate. Early operating results suggested that 1996 would be a challenging year. But from a strategic perspective he was not entirely satisfied with what was being accomplished with the recently introduced Ergo hand tools, especially in North America. There was a meeting of the Ergo Steering Committee later in the week and he needed to review the performance of ergonomic hand tools strategy. He reached for his Ergo file.

OVERVIEW

Over the last three years, beginning in 1993, ergonomically designed hand tools had become an increasingly important part of the strategy for the hand tools component of the Saws and Tools Business Unit. Ergonomics, the science of optimizing the interaction of the person and their work environment, had always been considered in the design process. But in 1991 Sandvik acquired Bahco Verktyg AB, a maker of spanners[1] and wrenches. Bahco had been working with an industrial design firm and they had developed an intensive methodology that set new standards for ergonomic design. In mid-1993 the Ergo Project Group was formed within Saws and Tools and created a common design philosophy and marketing statement across the range of hand tools: from handsaws to screwdrivers. A sequence was established for the conversion of existing tools to the new ergonomic standard and the changeover began. By early 1996 the process was about half completed. A considerable investment had already been made in redesign, retooling production processes and repositioning products in the marketplace. More would be required to complete the conversion.

Even though the complete line of Ergo tools would not be available for another two to three years, Göran was concerned that the initial sales of Ergo tools already introduced were not as strong as hoped. Personally he still felt very committed to the Ergo concept. However, he wondered whether the Ergo Committee should re-examine the strategy and consider alternative courses of action.

COMPANY BACKGROUND

AB Sandvik Saws & Tools was one of six global business areas within Sandvik AB. The others were: cutting tools, rock tools, hard materials, steel and process systems. Exhibit 1 provides a brief description and overview of each business area. Each operated as an autonomous business. Group management provided a few support activities (finance, legal, international sales/trading companies for less developed markets) that were drawn on by the business areas as needed.

With headquarters in Sandviken, Sweden, about 150 kilometers north of Stockholm, Sandvik began in 1862 as a manufacturer of high quality steel. Never a volume producer of steel, Sandvik specialized in applications where quality, uniformity, hardness and sharpness were important. Initially they provided steel for things like saws, fish hooks, drills for rock mining and razors. In 1886 the company started making saws. As expertise accumulated it led into other related businesses like steel tubing and cutting tools.

Although the company had evolved into different businesses there were several themes common to all of Sandvik's businesses. Sandvik products were functional. They provided the customer maximum value in terms of performance, quality, speed, productivity and flexibility. Sandvik's products usually sold at a premium price (on a per unit basis) but had higher performance and overall lower costs to the customer. The performance advantages incorporated into Sandvik products originated with its engineering and R&D efforts. Partly as a consequence of its attention to customer functionality Sandvik tended to focus on

---

[1] Called adjustable wrench in North America. The spanner had been invented by Bahco's founder.

niche markets. For example, Sandvik supplied the steel used by a leading compass manufacturer to make their magnetic compass needles (1 000 kilograms per year); or, the balls for ball-point pens (2 billion annually). In order to maintain direct contact with the customers and ensure that they understood the value of its products, Sandvik forward integrated, as far as feasible, into sales and distribution. Sandvik also manufactured most of what it sold.

The Sandvik Group's activities were global in scope. The group was active in over 60 countries. Over 90 per cent of sales were to customers outside Sweden (see Chart 1) and two-thirds of Sandvik's almost 30 000 employees were located outside Sweden. At the same time, Sandvik was the quintessential Swedish company: conservative, understated and traditional in style with a strong work ethic and a homogeneous corporate culture. As stated by chairman of the board, Percy Barnevik, "Sandvik cannot be described as a company given to excesses...put simply, the company does a darn fine job without a lot of fuss and without any particular recognition for it."

C H A R T 1 Sandvik AB: Sales by Region

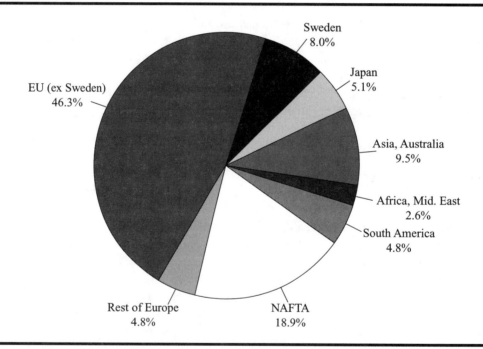

Most of the Group's businesses were industrial. Thus sales, and profits even more so, tended to follow the business cycle. (See Chart 2.) Partly as a consequence of this exposure Sandvik had a very conservative financial structure. Long-term liabilities were just 14 per cent of total capital and the company had 6.9 billion[2] SEK in cash and short-term investments (22.5 per cent of total assets) at the end of 1995. This liquidity allowed Sandvik to make selective acquisitions to develop and strengthen selected business areas. And, the company had been active in this way.

---

[2] As of early 1996 one SEK was equal to approximately US$0.15.

CHART 2   **Sandvik AB: Financial Performance**

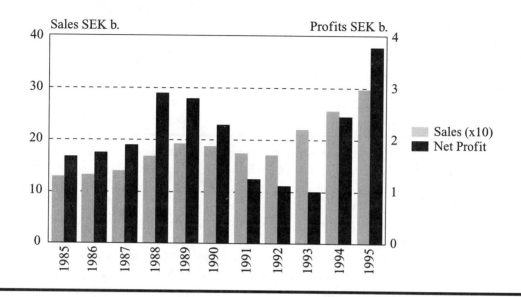

Sales SEK b.   Profits SEK b.

Legend: Sales (x10) | Net Profit

SAWS AND TOOLS GROUP: PERFORMANCE TOOLS—ALWAYS AVAILABLE

Sandvik Saws and Tools with invoiced sales of 2 674 MSEK accounted for nine per cent of Sandvik AB's turnover. Historical information on sales and profit for this business area are presented below.

millions of SEK	*1991*	*1992*	*1993*	*1994*	*1995*
Sales	1 437	2 049	2 363	2 583	2 674
Profit before financial items	(16)	(82)	(3)	185	184
# of Employees	3 676	3 275	3 060	3 050	2 998

Saws and Tools had 40 sales units around the world and 16 production units in 8 countries. Saws and Tools made and marketed a wide range of hand tools including: pliers, wrenches, ratchets, screwdrivers, hammers, chisels, scrapers; files; hand saws, bow saws, hacksaws and blades; as well as gardening/agricultural hand tools (pruners, loppers and secateurs). It also manufactured and sold forestry products (chain saw bar and chain) and industrial band saw blades. Sales for 1995 by major product centre were:

Product Centre	% of 1995 sales
Gardening	10%
Hand Tools (carpentry)	16%
Mechanics Hand Tools (forged)	27%
Files and Handles	6%
Metal Cutting Saws (excl. bandsaws)	<u>19%</u>
Hand Tools and associated products	<u>78%</u>
Bandsaws	13%
Forestry Products	9%
Total	2 674 MSEK

Saws and Tools' hand tool product range included more than 8 000 items.[3] Over the last five years product offerings had been globally rationalized. All products were the same in all markets and available on a global basis. With its wide range of products customers could meet their needs in hand tools and machine-saw accessories from a single source, almost anywhere in the world.

Manufacturing was globally rationalized. Most products were made at one facility, and for those products made in more than one place the assortment was usually rationalized between the facilities. Exhibit 2 provides the location of major manufacturing facilities. Direct labour costs per hour differed by country. Germany had the highest cost followed closely by Sweden. Costs at facilities in the southern U.S. and England were about 60 per cent of those in Sweden. Portugal and Argentina were even lower labour cost areas. Overall labour costs, including production staff and administration, accounted for 30 to 60 per cent of total manufacturing costs, with the average being 50 per cent.

The business unit's products were designed to appeal to professional users in many different markets. The following statement made this focus clear.

> More than 80 per cent of everything we sell is bought by professionals. Professionals will be our most important customers for a long time, even though nonprofessional use is expanding. If our products are accepted by the professionals and discerning users who often buy their tools privately, then we don't have to worry about the non-professionals. Our reputation will induce them to buy our tools.[4]

Of course quality and performance were very important to professional users. Saws and Tools management felt their "do it ourselves" approach was important to delivering value to their customers.

> A main reason why we manage to maintain a high standard of quality is that we control the entire cycle from basic research, through product development and manufacturing to distribution. The Sandvik Group is a world leader in materials technology. We regularly introduce innovations that put us ahead of competitors: Ergonomic design, hard pointing of hand saws, bimetal hacksaws and roll-top guide bars are just a few examples.[5]

Distribution

Sandvik was organized with sales units in each major country responsible for local sales and distribution. Global product centres (PCs) were responsible for manufacturing of the product, and with input from the sales units, for marketing and pricing. Product profit responsibility was with the product centres. The management for most hand tool PCs were located in Sweden.

---

[3] This included all SKUs. It was estimated that only about 400 SKUs were amenable to Ergo design.

[4] We're determined..., May 1994, page 16. (Internal publication by company.)

[5] We're determined..., May 1994, page 24.

Whenever possible Saws and Tools sold through resellers into each local market. However, its own distribution was increasingly centralized. There were only two distribution points for all of Europe. A new state-of-the-art distribution centre in the Netherlands serviced the EU. Nordic countries were served from Sandviken. This approach was a dramatic change from a few years earlier when each country's Sales Unit held its own inventory and ran its own distribution system. With the new system, delivery was promised anywhere within Europe in 72 hours, and to major cities within 48 hours. Many resellers were linked by EDI to Sandvik's computers. North American distribution was not yet as rationalized. But it had never been as fragmented. Currently it was done from facilities in Scranton, PA and Mississauga, Ontario. Other regions of the world tended to have local, country-based distribution.

Distribution of hand tools was through a number of channels. Consumers, non-professional users, generally bought their tools through hardware stores or mass merchandisers. Most hardware stores were members of large buying groups. Professional users either bought their tools personally, or had them supplied by their employers. In either case they tended to buy from industrial or agricultural supply companies. Distributors tended to work on a regional basis and often carried competing products from different manufacturers.

In most of Europe Saws and Tools had strong distribution for its hand tools. In North America the distribution system had been built around bandsaw blades. The general mill supply distributors carried an assortment of products including bandsaw blades and hand tools. But in almost all instances these distributors already carried the product assortment of one of the major U.S.-based competitors, such as Cooper and Stanley products.

A sales force of 22 Sandvik people (16 in the U.S. and 6 in Canada) and 9 manufacturers representatives[6] serviced industrial distributors. Other channels, like electrical and plumbing supply houses, retail "big box" stores and hardware chains, were served by agencies and manufacturers' representatives. All together they had about 40 field sales people. Saws and Tools had one manager coordinating this channel.

Saws and Tools did not sell hand tools directly to the end user. They had a policy of not bypassing resellers. Sales people would, however, often do joint sales calls on industrial customers with the reseller's representative. Saws and Tools participated in all the major trade shows.

Sandvik Brand: The Fish-and-Hook

The Sandvik brand, represented by the fish-and-hook symbol, was well recognized by many professional users within Europe. It did not have the same degree of recognition in North America, or the Asia-Pacific. As one manager explained:

> In Europe we have strong brand recognition among industrial distributors (the trade) and professional end users. However, our brand recognition does vary between countries and product lines. The trade knows us everywhere (in Europe); the end users primarily in Scandinavia, UK, Switzerland and Holland; less in Germany and very little in France and southern Europe. Overall we have strong brand recognition for hand saws, adjustable wrenches and electronic pliers. In the USA, our brand recognition with the end user is weak, or even non-existent except for bandsaw blades and electronic pliers. In Latin America Sandvik has very strong brand recognition in Argentina; in the remaining parts we are mainly known for Sandflex™ hand hacksaw blades. In Asia we are recognized for hacksaw blades and to some extent for adjustable wrenches.

Amongst casual users Sandvik was widely known in Scandinavia and the Netherlands for handsaws and adjustable wrenches, in the U.K. for handsaws, in Switzerland for chisels and handsaws and in France for pruning tools and handsaws. In the Americas and Asia Sandvik was not known to casual users.

---

[6] Manufacturers representatives were not employees of the company. They worked on commission and usually represented several non-competing manufacturers.

These differences in brand recognition were reflected in different market shares by region. As shown below Saws and Tools had larger shares in Europe.

	USA			*Europe*	
Category	**Market MUSD 1994**	**Sandvik Share**	**Category**	**Market MUSD 1994**	**Sandvik Share**
Screwdrivers	218	~0	Screwdrivers	~200	3
Adjustable & pipe wrenches	116	~0	Adjustable wrenches	~50	~15
Pliers	140	~0	Pliers	250	4
Handsaws	150	10	Handsaws (carpenter)	100	25
Hacksaw blades	17	5	Hacksaws & Blades	100	20
Mechanics' Tools	~1200	~0	Mechanics' Tools	2000	6
Other	1000	3	Other	2000	6

In the U.S., Saws and Tools did have a more substantial presence in forestry (chain saws bars and chain) and industrial band saw blades. But these products were not amenable to ergonomic design.

Sandvik endeavoured to have the customer associate Sandvik with "performance tools, always available". High performance had always been a Sandvik hallmark. With the new distribution strategy availability was improving.

Sandvik's pricing policy was related to its business strategy. Its prices were based upon the market leader for that (professional) product line in that region. The policy stated, "Our price should stay within a range of 90 to 105 per cent of the market leader. We never undercut the leader by more than 10 per cent."[7] Saws and Tools also tried to keep prices consistent between countries in a region (although not necessarily between regions).

STRUCTURE OF THE HAND TOOL MARKETS

In general, the hand tool industry had been fragmented, with many small, local companies making one or two types of tools. (For example, fifty companies make screwdrivers.) Sandvik was the only European-based manufacturer with a wide range of products for professional users. In Europe the 50 largest companies accounted for 50 per cent of the market. However, the industry was less fragmented in the U.S., where five firms accounted for 50 per cent of the industry.[8] Larger players like Cooper Industries and Stanley produced and sold a range of branded tools. But retailers, like Sears with their Craftsman™ tool line, also had a strong position particularly in the consumer market.

Both Craftsman and Stanley brands were more oriented to the home market, less towards the professional user. Stanley claimed to be the "largest manufacturer of consumer hand tools in the world."[9] Stanley also had a line of products oriented to the professional user. Stanley's tool business included consumer, industrial and engineered segments. The first two segments were most directly competitive with Sandvik. Consumer tools included hand tools such as measuring instruments, planes, hammers, knives and blades,

---

[7] We're determined..., May 1994, page 49.

[8] We're determined..., May 1994, page 6.

[9] Stanley Works, 10-K, 1995.

wrenches, sockets, screwdrivers, saws, chisels, boring tools, masonry, tile and drywall tools, paint preparation and paint application tools. Industrial tools included industrial and mechanics' hand tools, and high-density industrial storage and retrieval systems. The consumer segment had 1995 sales of $739 million (US); industrial sales of $552 million. Seventy-two per cent of Stanley total sales were in the U.S.; 16 per cent in Europe. The U.S. accounted for 79 per cent of operating profits.

Professionally oriented products were generally produced by specialized, single product line firms of limited geographic scope: single product, single market companies. Of course Sandvik with a broad product line and wide geographic scope was an exception to this rule, as was Cooper Industries in the U.S. Cooper had 1995 tools and hardware sales of $962 million (US). It competed directly with Sandvik in pliers, conventional and adjustable wrenches, files, saws, hammers and screwdrivers. Cooper also had other products within its tools and hardware segment including: drapery hardware, power tools, chain, soldering equipment torches and cutting products. Cooper had many identifiable brands, e.g., Crescent™ in adjustable wrenches and Kirsch™ in drapery hardware. However, Cooper itself was a holding company with no strong brand identity. Sales outside the U.S. were 37 per cent of total sales, up from 31 per cent two years earlier.

Cooper and Stanley, like Sandvik, produced a range of tools supplying a variety of markets. Snap-on Tools had a very different strategy. It focused exclusively on automotive service technicians and serviced them through 5 400 franchised dealers. These dealers drove large vans stocked with the popular products and visited the customers at their repair shops at least once per week. Snap-on had sales of $1.3 billion (US), 40 per cent in hand tools; 80 per cent in North America, 15 per cent in Europe.

Distribution of hand tools was changing. An interesting North American phenomenon was the emergence of big-box specialty retailers, companies like Home Depot and Builder's Square. With their large stores and wide product assortment these outlets targeted both the professional and the do-it-yourself market.

Acquisitions

Many of Saws and Tools' markets were highly fragmented, but restructuring was occurring. This was a situation the company recognized:

> The hand-tool industry in Europe is ripe for restructuring. Sandvik Saws and Tools has taken the initiative in this process... We've acquired competent tool manufacturers and added strong brands. We've gained economies of scale in production, marketing and distribution. We've improved customer service and will continue to do so.[10]

During the last few years Saws and Tools had acquired Bahco (spanners and pliers), Belzer (screwdrivers and ratchets), Lindstrom (electronic pliers) and Milford (industrial band saw blades).

THE ERGO STRATEGY

The awareness of ergonomics is growing and it is going to continue to grow. The cost of NOT addressing ergonomics is also going to continue to grow.

Professor Thomas Armstrong
Center for Ergonomics, The University of Michigan

Saws and Tools had an ongoing interest in ergonomic design. This interest was enhanced when in early 1992 Sandvik acquired the Bahco Tool Group, headquartered in Enköping, Sweden. Bahco, working with an

---

[10] We're determined..., May 1994, page 6.

industrial design firm, Ergonomi Design Gruppen, had developed a methodology for designing ergonomic tools. (See Exhibit 3.) Prior to the Sandvik acquisition Bahco had used this process to develop ergonomic screwdrivers (1983), adjustable wrenches (1984), wood chisels (1985), slipjoint pliers (1986), side cutters (1989), combination pliers (1991) and a combination adjustable wrench (1991).

The ergonomic approach to hand tool design fit well with Sandvik's basic strategy and appealed to Saws and Tools management. The 11-point Ergo process became the standard for the Saws and Tools group and the formal Ergo strategy came into being in mid-1993 when the Ergo Project Committee was formed.

The Ergo Project Committee was asked to build, direct and co-ordinate the Ergo Concept across the group, specifically to:

- Ensure that all products designated as Ergo had followed the 11-point process.
- Identify products to add to the Ergo range.
- Establish guidelines for pricing Ergo products.
- Produce documentation and promotional materials.

The committee had eight members; six from different Saws and Tools units and two from EDG. It was chaired by Connie Jansson, R&D manager for Sandvik Bahco.

One of the first tasks of the committee was to identify those products most amenable to the Ergo concept and establish priorities for conversion to the Ergo standard. Major considerations were volume, existing and potential, and the prospects for global sales, as well as recognizable benefits and the potential to enhance Sandvik's market position. Exhibit 4 provides a list of Ergo products done to date or immediately pending. Each Ergo product had undergone the 11-point process and was done in collaboration with Ergonomi Design Gruppen.

Ergonomi Design Gruppen (EDG)

EDG was an industrial design firm located in an old converted church on the outskirts of Stockholm. Sweden was asserted to have a comparative advantage in design, and EDG was one of the best mid-sized independent industrial design firms in Sweden. EDG assumed a major role in the initial Ergo design process. Olle Bobjer was the senior ergonomist at EDG and Hans Himberg was the principal of the firm. Both played an active role with the Sandvik account. The firm employed 16 professionals, mostly industrial designers.

Sandvik's relationship with EDG was very close. EDG did work on a wide range of products for many different companies but had agreed to do hand tool design only for Sandvik. And, as a portion of their fees was tied to the sales volume of the finished product Sandvik felt the relationship gave them the benefits of an in-house design group, but with a much higher level of expertise.

EDG managed the 11-point development and certification process. Ergonomics was an applied science. The process was based upon feedback from sophisticated professional users of the tool under development. The process began with studies of how end-users worked. Work sites were visited, people interviewed and videos of the tools in use were made. Multiple prototypes were built, tested and assessed by end users. (See Exhibit 5.)

If sufficiently unique, aspects of an Ergo product could be patented by Sandvik. But this type of protection was unusual. Most often design patents were applicable when Ergo tools differed from traditional tools in appearance. Saws and Tools used both types of protection whenever possible. Several competitors had been stopped from copying Sandvik products.

The combined capabilities of EDG and Sandvik provided Saws and Tools with an area of distinctive competence. They felt no competitor could match their ability to design, develop and manufacture ergonomic hand tools. But from the beginning the Ergo Committee had recognized that, "a product can successfully combine all the right things but stumble in the marketplace because of failure to communicate effectively about the product to potential purchasers."[11]

Ergo Benefits

Designing and manufacturing ergonomic hand tools was one thing; selling them was another. Hand tools had been used for centuries. Many of these tools had incorporated local norms and evolved into effective instruments; others remained largely unchanged since the industrial revolution. A better understanding of how the human body functioned in relation to work, the science of ergonomy, and the ongoing development of new materials presented opportunities for significant improvements in most hand tools.

The specific benefits of ergonomic design varied by tool (see Exhibit 6). But generally there were two principal benefits of ergonomic hand tools that were in fact both related to reduced physical stress on the worker:

- reduction in work-related physical disorders, and
- increases in productivity.

Work related disorders, more properly called Cumulative Trauma Disorders (CTD) or Repetitive Motion Injuries (RMI) were recognized as the number one occupational hazard of the 1990s by experts. Carpal Tunnel Syndrome was one such work-related injury. Nerves and tendons to the hand pass through the carpal tunnel, inside the wrist. Repetitive, stressful hand motions can cause the tendons to become inflamed, putting pressure on the nerves in this area, resulting in pain and numbness.

The highest risks for CTD was encountered when a job or tool required a combination of force and precision used repeatedly, without sufficient rest time for the body to recover. For example, a vineyard worker pruning grape vines and making up to 10 000 cuts per day would be at high risk.

Properly designed ergonomic tools reduced musculo-skeletal stresses and strains and provided sensory feedback to the user for accuracy and optimum control. They were proportioned to the dimensions of the user and were efficient in the use of human energy. While good styling and ergonomic design often went hand-in-hand there was a difference. Styling looks at the superficial aesthetics of the object. Ergonomics goes deeper. Shapes, materials and textures are selected for their functionality.

Ergonomics had also caught the attention of governmental health and safety agencies. Legislation had been proposed in the U.S. that would make employers liable for damages if they were not using ergonomic best practice. This proposed legislation had been shelved and was not under active consideration.

There were sound economic reasons for a company to use ergonomic tools. These included: fewer on-the-job accidents and worker sick days; reduction in injuries that sometimes result in disability claims, law suits and higher insurance costs. They could also improve worker morale and job satisfaction.

Naturally workers using well-designed tools could be more productive. While this benefit was recognized within Saws and Tools, it was not explicitly mentioned in any of the marketing materials. Groups related to worker health and safety, like unions, were seen as key opinion leaders in getting the Ergo concept accepted. Generally, they were more concerned with the health benefits than the possible productivity improvements.

It was recognized from the outset that, "there is a latent demand within the professional hand tool users for ergonomic products. Many people need them, but few ask or know anything about them."[12] The original report went on to say, "it is our job to educate the users/dealers about real ergonomic tools. This will be difficult as many competitors claim to have ergonomic tools."

---

[11] *A Research Approach to Ergonomic Hand Tools*, April 1994, page 3.

[12] *A Research Approach to Ergonomic Hand Tools*, April 20, 1994, page 23.

Indeed, although the user may prefer one type of tool, it was difficult to conclusively demonstrate the ergonomic benefits of one tool over another. Because most CTD were caused by repetitive motions it took weeks, if not months to emerge. Comparative testing, a technique used to demonstrate the value of many other Sandvik products, was difficult under these circumstances. Thus while Sandvik believed its Ergo tools were better than competitors', they could not easily prove this claim. Instead the initial marketing program relied on Sandvik's reputation for quality and explained the 11-point development program for Ergo tools.

Introduction of Ergo Tools

When Sandvik acquired Bahco their product line included a number of Ergo tools. With Sandvik's resources distribution of these tools was broadened and the application of the Ergo concept to other products accelerated.

When first introduced, Ergo products were additions to the top-end of Sandvik's product range. They did not immediately replace an existing product. As a consequence a product range, like screwdrivers, included both Ergo and non-Ergo product. However, the adjustable wrench category had evolved to the point that it included only Ergo product (1st and 2nd generation). Ergo products were positioned as the premium product within the Sandvik assortment and priced to reflect this positioning.

After Sandvik launched the Ergo strategy, the initial marketing/communication program targeted opinion leaders who could influence the tool purchase decision: ergonomists, health and safety engineers, safety (union) representatives, human resource managers, etc. Sales unit staff were trained in the benefits of ergonomic hand tools and provided with aids: brochures, videos, etc. to help them communicate the concept.

Sandvik had not had significant hand tools sales in the U.S. prior to Ergo. Using the Ergo products it was hoped Saws and Tools could expand its position in the U.S. hand tools market. Because of the investment required and the lack of warehouse space only about 2 000 handtool SKUs were currently available in the U.S. (compared to 8 000 in Europe). Because of this limited assortment Sandvik could not offer to replace a distributor's other hand tool suppliers. They positioned themselves as an innovative product specialist targeted on niche markets. Ergo was introduced into the U.S. during the spring of 1995. As part of the introduction Dr. Thomas Armstrong, a well-known U.S. ergonomist, along with Sandvik personnel explained the Ergo concept to interested health and safety professionals, mostly from large automotive and aerospace manufacturers.

Cost of Ergo Tools

The incremental costs of the Ergo strategy were difficult to ascertain precisely. Sandvik periodically redesigned its hand tools and the added cost of employing the Ergo methodology was hard to calculate. Upfront design costs paid to EDG for an Ergo tool and associated with the 11-point program ranged from 200 000 to 1 500 000 SEK depending on the complexity of the project. A typical project would be about 600 000 SEK. In addition to this amount EDG also received a royalty. For a successful product EDG design costs would account for one to two per cent of sales[13] during its first 10 years.

Any design change, ergonomic or otherwise, required the retooling of the manufacturing process. The Ergo strategy had accelerated the number of design changes but it was not necessarily much more expensive. These costs differed. The new Ergo screwdrivers had cost about a million dollars (US), the Ergo ratchet about $200 000. The Ergo loper saw had required a new injection mold for the handle at $100 000 and a new grinding technique for the blade that required an investment of $400 000 in equipment.

---

[13] Internal transfer price from the product centre to the sales unit.

Generally retooling costs ranged from $500 000 to $1 000 000 (US), assuming the equipment for producing the same type of non-ergo tool was available.

Ergo products were sometimes more difficult and costly to manufacture. Most often this was the result of a more complex shape and/or a special gripping surface being incorporated into the product. As one manager observed:

> Any increase in costs has to be seen in light of the previous state of the tool. Ergo tools incorporate a higher level of end user input and preference… The cost change, from our experience, and as a rule of thumb is 5 to 10 per cent.

While some of the manufacturing processes were more challenging, none were proprietary. Smaller companies might have difficulty replicating some Ergo products, but larger manufacturers willing to expend the effort would be able to do so.

Price Premium

Sandvik tried to adhere to its normal pricing policy with Ergo products. Because of the unique Ergo design it was often difficult to find a comparable product. But in most instances there was a somewhat similar competitive offering to serve as a benchmark. This product was most likely a niche product and not the market leader, at least in terms of volume. Ergo products were priced at a zero to 20 per cent premium over competitive products. The amount of the premium took into account the cost of the product, the additional value it offered the user and the pricing of competitor products. The price premium over low-end, non-professional products could be much greater. The latest generation of Ergo adjustable wrench was five times the (retail) price of the cheapest product available in the Scandinavian marketplace. In North America the premiums tended to be even greater.

GOING GLOBAL

The Ergo strategy also reinforced Sandvik's global approach to the hand-tool business.

> In the past the hand-tool business was local. Customer preferences varied widely even within one country. Patterns of tool choice and use were passed on from one generation of craftsmen to the next. Local manufacturers and small-town businesses, which were often family-owned, served local customers.

> Now...the hand-tool business has gone from local to regional to global. The industry still leans toward tradition. There are still local preferences and idiosyncrasies that we will have to deal with for some time to come... The market as a whole is moving toward universal acceptance of tool types and ranges. It's increasingly feasible to sell the same product design in many countries.[14]

Of course Ergo tools were designed for optimal function with the human hand. Something that did not differ between countries, or cultures. (When required Ergo products came in a range of sizes to accommodate different sized hands.)

Tariffs were not judged to be a significant factor. On hand tools shipped between the EU to the U.S. tariffs ranged from five to nine per cent; from the U.S. to the EU tariffs tended to be slightly lower, from three to four per cent. Adjustable wrenches were an extreme case with tariffs from the EU to the U.S. of nine per cent and from the U.S. to the EU of three per cent.

SITUATION IN EARLY 1996

By 1995, there were seven categories of Ergo products with variations within each category. (See Exhibit 7.) As shown in Chart 3 sales were 224 million SEK, or 8.4 per cent of the groups overall sales and about 10.7 per cent of hand tool sales.

---

[14] We're determined…, May 1994, page 8.

CHART 3 **ERGO Branded Products**

1995 External Invoicing

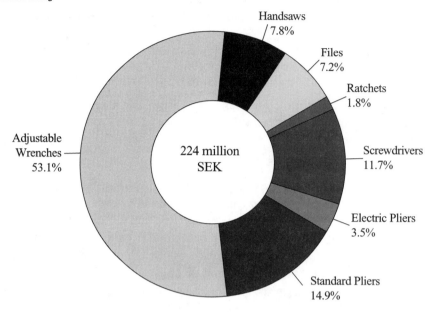

But these sales were not evenly distributed. As shown below Europe accounted for most of the Ergo sales.

Unit Sales (000) of Ergo Product	Europe	North America	Rest of World
Adjustable Wrenches	1 300	8	200
Standard Pliers	300	4	60
Screwdrivers	996	25	16
Handsaws f/c 1996	177	9	28
Files, handles	587	15	38
Electronic Pliers	-	20	-
f/c 1996	10	30	-
Ratchet Wrenches	16	1.1	0.1
f/c 1996	22	0.1	0.4

Of course the Ergo hand tools had just been introduced in a limited range to North America during 1995. It was difficult to assess the precise impact of the Ergo strategy. As Per Tornell, the Nordic Sale Unit manager, explained:

> We dominate certain product categories in the Nordic countries. In adjustable wrenches we have 50 to 60 per cent share of the unit volume and 90 per cent of the value for professional users. And, we've (Bahco) had this position for a long time. Ergo has helped us to maintain our strong position. But in ratchets we are one of ten competitors with about a 20 per cent share. I feel that the new Ergo ratchet will help us to improve our position but it is too early to tell. It takes years for this type of thing to have a noticeable impact.

Screwdrivers are a good example. Over ten years ago Bahco introduced the Ergo screwdriver. At that time it was a radical redesign; very different from the traditional product. The difference in the product was obvious to the user. We are now the market leader in Sweden and Finland. But it took ten years.

In North America the situation was different. Sandvik Saws and Tools was known in the U.S. for its forestry products, and industrial band saws. The only hand tool for which it had even limited recognition were hand saws and electronic pliers. In the U.S. Ergo had been launched in February 1995. The concept had been well-received by health and safety professionals. But their endorsements had not yet materialized as significant orders. Saws and Tools was targeting large industrial users like Ford and GM. It was hoped these users could appreciate the benefits of the Ergo product and pull it through the distribution channels.

As one U.S. manager observed:

Distributors will not really push a product. They stock what their customers ask for. Since we have a limited assortment and not much brand recognition and our prices are at, or above the top end it's a difficult sell. The availability of our hand tool products through distributors is not as extensive as we would like. We would like to use Ergo to develop, expand and strengthen our channels.

Another manager went further:

The health and safety people have not been able to convince the purchasing people to specify our product. They'll look at our product but it usually comes back to an issue of price. Most hand tools are only used occasionally and repetitive motion injuries are not considered to be a major factor. Naturally we try to sell the advantage—the prevention of one lost-time accident will more than pay for the tool. And, where RMI is a factor, like in trimming electronic circuit boards with snippers, we have done well. For the same reason we expect our Ergo metal shears, when they are developed, will be well accepted. But again this is a niche where the benefit is clear.

Meanwhile the ergonomic idea seemed to be gaining popularity with other competitors. Stanley had recently distributed marketing literature stating that their products were ergonomically tested by an independent testing firm. However, there was no evidence that Stanley employed a rigorous process for incorporating ergonomics into the design of their hand tools. It was also known that Cooper had formed an ergonomic working group, including customers and ergonomists, as well as company personnel. Nothing had yet emerged from this group.

CONCLUSION

Göran Gezelius observed:

Interest and recognition in Ergo from our own sales people, as well as distributors has been excellent. We have not succeeded yet in turning this recognition into big sales figures in markets where we were not previously known with our hand tools. In markets where we are known—Scandinavia, UK, Netherlands—it appears as if Ergo helps us to increase our market share. However, if we are to become a truly global, professional hand tool company, we need to improve our position where we are less well-known, especially North America. It is not clear whether Ergo will help us in a significant way to accomplish this objective; or what more needs to be done.

EXHIBIT 1 AB SANDVIK Results by Business Area 1995

Business Area	Sales SEK m.	%	Operating Profits[15] SEK m.	%	Return on Sales (%)
Tooling	9 576	32	2 436	47	25.4%
Rock Tools	2 015	7	219	4	10.9%
Hard Materials	1 224	4	185	4	15.1%
Steel	9 807	33	1 623	31	16.5%
Saws and Tools	2 674	9	184	4	6.9%
Process Systems	1 810	6	101	2	5.6%
Seco Tools[16]	2 555	9	542	10	21.2%
Intra Group	39	/	(96)	/	
Group Total	29 700	100	5 194	100	17.5%

Description of Business Areas

Business Area (# of employees)	Description
Tooling (11010)	Sandvik Coromat was the global leader in cemented carbide inserts used for the machining of metal. Inserts were the cutting edge in machine tools, like lathes. CTT Tools produced principally high-speed steel tools like drills, threading tools and reamers.
Rock Tools (1877)	This business was a leading supplier of cemented-carbide-tipped rockdrilling tools (and tool systems) used in mining, civil engineering and water-well drilling.
Hard Materials (1447)	This business manufactures and markets unmachined carbide blanks, as well as customized wear parts (e.g., seal rings). Sandvik was the largest competitor in this business, and the only one with global scope.
Steel (7257)	Steel manufactures tube, strip, wire and bar for demanding applications. Products are produced in stainless and high alloy steels and in titanium, nickel and zirconium alloys.
Saws and Tools (2998)	Used mainly by professionals, S&T products included: hand saws and saw blades; wrenches, spanners, pliers, files, pruning tools, as well as guide bars and saw chains.
Process Systems (888)	Manufactures the steel belts and engineers the complete systems used in automated sorting and chemical and food-processing.

[15] After depreciation, before financial charges.

[16] A separately listed public company. Sandvik owned 61 per cent.

E X H I B I T 2   Location of Saws and Tools Manufacturing Facilities

Location	Product Centre	# of Employees
Edsbyn, Sweden	Forestry Tools	147
Bollnäs, Sweden	Hand Tools (handsaws)	160
Sveg, Sweden	Hand Tools (bowsaws)	40
Enköping, Sweden	Pliers (pliers & adjustables)	336
Lidköping, Sweden	Metal Saws (hack)	242
	Bandsaws	23
Hasborn, Germany	Wrenches	90
Wuppertal, Germany	Wrenches	80
Maltby, England	Metal Saws	37
	Bandsaws	23
Vila do Conde, Portugal	Files	243
Branford, CT, USA	Bandsaws	140
Milan, TN, USA	Forestry (chain saw bars)	51
Dyer, TN, USA	Forestry (saw chain)	97
Santo Tome, Argentina	Wrenches	312

E X H I B I T 3   Development of Ergonomically Designed Hand Tools

11 Points, in Chronological Order

1. Specification of demands
2. Analysis of competitors—tools and markets
3. Background material
4. Production of functioning model
5. User tests I
6. Evaluation and modification of models
7. User tests II
8. Design proposal
9. Product specification
10. User test III and preparation before launching
11. Follow up on statistics

Approved by: The Scientific Committee on Musculoskeletal Disorders of the International Commission on Occupational Health (ICOH).

EXHIBIT 4 ERGO Tools Since 1992

Type of Tool (by Product Centre)	Launch Date
Sandvik Bahco	
Combination Adjustable	Cologne[17]-93 (2nd generation)
Gripping Pliers	1994
Electronic Pliers	1995
Pipe Wrenches	pending
Sandvik Belzer	
Screwdrivers	pending (2nd generation)
Ratchet Wrench	1994
Sandvik Gardening	
Secateurs	pending
Plate Shears	pending
Sandvik Hand Tools	
Paint Scrapers	pending
Hand Saw(2600)	1995
Sandvik Files	
File Handles	1995
Metal Saws	
Hack Saw Frame	pending

[17] A major trade fair held in Cologne, Germany each year in May.

EXHIBIT 5   Prototypes of Electronic Nippers

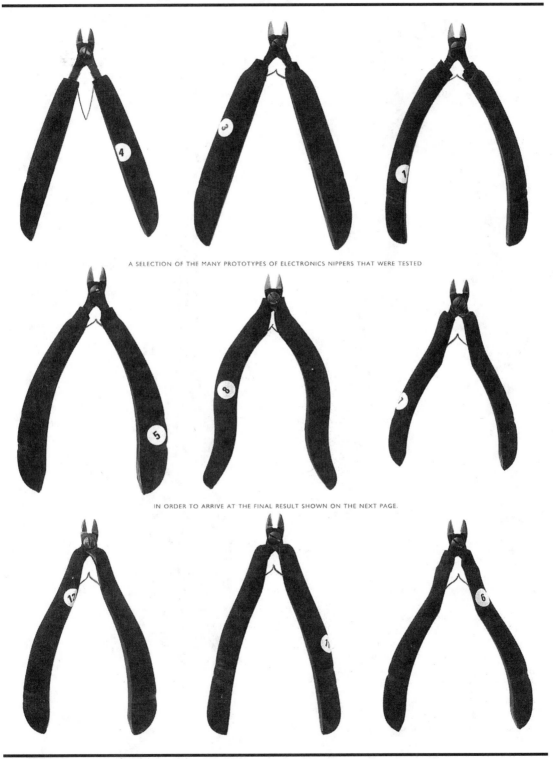

A SELECTION OF THE MANY PROTOTYPES OF ELECTRONICS NIPPERS THAT WERE TESTED

IN ORDER TO ARRIVE AT THE FINAL RESULT SHOWN ON THE NEXT PAGE.

EXHIBIT 6 **Typical Benefits of Ergo Hand Tool**

1. Hexagonal nut, so you can use a wrench if you need to pull hard.

2. Small diameter lets you tighten or loosen the screw quickly.

3. Plenty of room for precision control with thumb and index finger.

4. Completely rounded handle, so you avoid pressure points on your hand.

5. Fits your hand well – the right diameter provides maximum power. Ridged surface increases friction even when the handle is oily.

6. The handle is designed for both power and precision.

7. Large, rounded end minimizes pressure in your hand.

1. Long, narrow jaws make it easy to reach the places you need to.

2. Jaws grip tightly in three places, so you don't have to squeeze the handles so hard.

3. Larger jaw opening than other slip joint pliers. Can be adjusted with parallel jaws in 11 different positions.

4. Unique thumb grip lets you adjust jaw opening without letting go or losing control of the pliers.

5. Long, softly rounded grip that doesn't end in the middle of your hand.

6. The handles can't close, so your hand won't get caught between them.

EXHIBIT 7 ERGO Product Categories—1996

Sandvik ERGO Products

Accompanying this brochure you will find literature on many of the products that Sandvik is proud to include in their Ergo range. The tools are one important part of the work process which can be improved by the application of ergonomics. Other important factors are the work-stations, posture and rest.

The durability, strength, availability and diversity of the Sandvik tool range is an established fact, as are the fast delivery and service we offer. Ergonomic design adds a whole new dimension of cost-saving through health awareness to our tools. Since the potential benefits to our customers are clear, Sandvik is looking positively and "ergonomically" at the future.

How about you?

An expanding range
A selection from the increasing range of Sandvik "Ergo" hand tools. All of these tools meet the exacting criteria of the Sandvik 11 Point Ergo Program.

CONTINENTAL REALTY

case

13

R a n d y   A .   P e p p e r
a n d   J o s e p h   N .   F r y

"This company has been immensely successful," said John Morrison, president of Continental Realty Ltd., as he looked west from his Vancouver office window, "and we intend to continue that way." His view of the skyline was punctuated by construction cranes rising above the foundations of new office towers. The west was booming and the company was growing apace. "The challenge," he said, "will be in finding the best people and keeping them with us."

IVEY

Randy A. Pepper prepared this case under the supervision of Professor Joseph N. Fry solely to provide material for class discussion. The authors do not intend to illustrate either effective or ineffective handling of a managerial situation. The authors may have disguised certain names and other identifying information to protect confidentiality.

BACKGROUND

Continental Realty was among the largest commercial and industrial real estate agencies in Canada. In its most recent fiscal year the company had acted in lease and sales transactions totalling more than $200 million. The first office and present headquarters of the company was in Vancouver. Branches operated in Calgary, Edmonton, Toronto, Houston and Phoenix. Continental currently employed over 40 agents; but its early days were very much the story of one man, Gordon Nelson, owner and chairman.

Nelson grew up in small-town Alberta, where he caught a sense of the coming promise of the west. He went east to obtain an Honours Business Administration degree from the University of Western Ontario, and then spent a year travelling and studying in Europe. On his return, he entered the real estate business. In three years he moved from Toronto to Winnipeg to Vancouver.

Nelson derived his approach to operating a real estate agency from his experience during these early years. His employers and colleagues were secretive—unwilling or unprepared to teach him the business. Information, even technical and background data, was treated as a resource to be rationed. Nelson persisted and eventually met a senior industry executive who was prepared to share his knowledge and who helped Nelson develop the technical expertise needed to move ahead in the business.

Nelson sold over $7 million worth of property in his first year with J.B. Hobbs & Co. in Vancouver. Shortly after, with two partners, he bought out the Hobbs agency and changed its name to Continental Realty.

Continental prospered, but the deal that established Nelson's reputation was Burrard Square. While examining an aerial photograph of Vancouver, Nelson became intrigued with a spread of property between the railway mainline and Burrard Inlet immediately west of the city's downtown core. The property, owned by Construction Aggregates Ltd., was the first fully assembled yet undeveloped parcel in the area. Through his investment contacts, Nelson determined that a British-financial firm, Tate Development Corp., was seeking attractive investment opportunities in North America. He evaluated Construction Aggregates' willingness to sell, convinced Tate of the property's investment potential, and the concept of Burrard Square was born. The steps from concept to reality were protracted, and marked by continuous negotiation as designs, approvals, financing and tenants were brought together. But five years later, in what was then a landmark deal for Vancouver, arrangements were completed and construction started on the multi-million dollar integrated apartment, commercial and retail complex.

After Burrard Square, Continental grew in volume and geographic coverage, and Nelson crystallized a strategy and set of operating policies that made the company unique in the industry.

THE BUSINESS

Continental confined its operations to the commercial and industrial realty markets, where it aimed to operate as one of the few true "agency" businesses, as compared to the hundreds of "brokerage" operations across the country. According to Bob McLaren, Continental's general manager, the distinction lay in the degree of professionalism in the operator's methods.

To draw a clear contrast, McLaren compared residential selling to Continental's approach. He explained, in his usual hyperbolic style:

> The residential business is largely a clearing-house operation. That's what the Multiple Listing Service (MLS) is all about. All the houses for sale are in a big pot with an index card and they are picked out of a hat and fed to the prospects. The residential realtor aims at completing a sales transaction. He derives his commission not from counselling his client but from moving the property.

It was not surprising, according to another industry source, that the popular image of a real estate broker was "a guy with a bright yellow jacket who leads housewives through endless kitchens and comments on the abundance of closet space."

Commercial and industrial negotiators, particularly Continental's, operated in a different world, with business clients and high-value properties. But the broker approach was also prevalent here. One of Canada's largest firms, a competitor of Continental, advertised a national computerized system that could quickly supply a list of potential properties to fit a client's space, location and cost requirements. To Continental, this shotgun approach served a client's interests poorly.

Continental negotiators operated on an exclusive basis, as the only agent attempting to sell or lease a client's property. Like a lawyer, a Continental negotiator would act for only one party in a transaction, the client, and in this relationship acted as much as an advisor as a salesperson. For example, he or she might advise a client not to accept an offer to purchase or lease if the agent established that it was not to the client's advantage. In this way, Continental sought to position itself as a true agency, more consistent with European than North American practice, under a single basic policy: "Treat the property as if it were your own."

If the cornerstone of Continental's agency concept was the exclusive concentration on client interest, the building blocks were formed from the creative pursuit of realty opportunities. The Burrard Square deal demonstrated this: through imagination, knowledge and contacts, Nelson was well-positioned to conceive a project. Continental aimed to do more than represent other people's ideas or projects for clients, and in so doing add value to its agency role and, for that matter, to the economy as a whole.

In developing this approach, Continental pioneered a transformation in procedures for selling commercial and industrial real estate. For generations, the realty industry had been an old man's game, where commercial transactions took place among well-acquainted, senior colleagues. In such an environment, the building of social links was paramount in the operation of a successful realty business. Continental outflanked these industry norms by emphasizing technical and analytical skills. Gradually, the industry became a young person's field, where business relationships based on trust and skill became the basis of successful client-negotiator interaction.

Creating and negotiating a deal was the essence of the agency business. The following examples illustrate the frequently circuitous, sometimes protracted, and often frustrating aspects of a transaction.

A Land Assembly

A Canadian chartered bank approached Continental and R.E. Lang and Co., a significant Continental competitor, asking them to work together to assemble a major site in Edmonton's downtown core. Continental refused to collaborate, suggesting as an alternative that each agent propose six potential properties that the bank could then review. The bank agreed.

A senior Continental negotiator, through whom the initial contact had been made, took responsibility for the project. His activities included identifying potential rentable sites; judging the willingness of the site owners to sell and estimating prices; consulting with architects and planning consultants on the suitability of each site; checking out the necessary approvals and establishing a time frame for the regulatory process. He had to do all this discreetly and confidentially. Continental was first to propose sites to the bank and ultimately the bank chose a property on Continental's list.

The site selected was owned by an international utility company that had a policy of never selling its investment properties. The first step was to determine what amount to offer the company—an amount that would at least induce the utility to counter with an asking price. The situation was complicated by the bank's unwillingness to disclose its identity. This made the utility company even more nervous. It was not interested in selling to a speculator and giving that person the opportunity to flip the property at a later date.

After lengthy talks the utility sold, but on the condition that development would begin on the site within 18 months. The transaction had taken countless meetings over approximately six months. The Continental negotiator walked away with a handsome commission, however, and a good chance of becoming the leasing agent of the future bank tower.

Developing an Office Tower

Hugh Thorburn, a veteran Continental negotiator, first saw this potential opportunity while trying to lease space in a new office tower. Thorburn had attended a board meeting of the subsidiary of a large American mining firm to propose that an above-ground walkway be built between its building and an adjoining tower that he was trying to lease. At this meeting he learned that a committee was looking into the expansion of office space.

Conscious of its U.S. headquarters' attitudes, the subsidiary wanted to be very thorough in its examination of relocation space. It sent out an extremely detailed call for tender to 18 different office buildings in Vancouver. Meanwhile, Continental's general manager, Bob McLaren, who had been briefed by Thorburn on the mining company's search for space and who was the agent for a medium-sized Vancouver developer, decided that his client had the most suitable site for the mining company. The site was essentially raw land—a group of derelict buildings—but advantageously located for the mining firm. McLaren did not submit a proposal, but sent Thorburn a letter with a copy to the mining company outlining his client's plan to build on the site. The developer, inexperienced in the commercial market, was unwilling to begin construction unless the mining company was secured as lead tenant. Within two months McLaren obtained a letter of commitment from the mining subsidiary.

The mechanics of the process were as follows. As with most major development projects, McLaren's client had formed a team composed of an architect, a space planner, a contractor and a realty agent, to study the project's feasibility. Public relations and advertising people later helped to put presentations together. Proposal costs were shared between Continental Realty and the negotiator. In a deal such as this, McLaren was the "lister" of the property. His responsibilities included searching the property's title, preparing and distributing promotional material, advising the landowner on the project's marketability and negotiating with major tenants.

The amount of client/developer involvement usually depended on the client's size and experience in the negotiation process. In this deal, McLaren's nervous developer was constantly trying to involve himself in direct negotiations despite his inexperience in commercial dealing. It therefore became important for McLaren, a hard-nosed, number-oriented salesperson, to maintain firm control over his client. Meanwhile, the more affable Thorburn was continually assuring the mining company of the project's wisdom. As Thorburn observed, the different personalities of the two negotiators were very well suited to the job requirements.

"In a major leasing agreement," explained Thorburn, "the resolution of several common negotiating points determines the deal's success." Rent was not in dispute in this deal; however, the prospective tenant wanted to alter the building's design. The mining subsidiary was also determined to extend the lease period from 10 to 20 years, and to obtain a guaranteed lease rate should it require more space on additional floors. After all these points had been satisfactorily resolved, the mining company's Los Angeles head office decided that it wanted either 50% or 100% ownership of the building. McLaren's client agreed to a 50% equity participation by the mining firm. A further catch arose here, for Continental assessed the building's replacement value at $29.4 million, but the mining company's head office had authorized a capital expenditure of only $13 million. After several trips to the U.S. and hard negotiation, much of it aimed at avoiding having to resubmit a capital expenditure proposal and risk a turndown by the U.S. parent, the deal was concluded.

THE CONTINENTAL FORMULA

Providing genuine agency services had helped Continental grow, and charge full commission rates in the process. (The specific rates varied by the size, nature and location of the project, but were generally in the range of 3–5% of the dollar value of a transaction.) Gordon Nelson's ability to impose discipline on the activities of the high-flying, performance-oriented individuals who made up his negotiator team was a crucial ingredient in Continental's success. His company was known throughout the industry for its rigorous operating policies.

To remain with the firm, Continental negotiators (after a period of training) were required to generate a minimum of $90 000 in commissions annually. The average production in the past year for negotiators with greater than one year's experience was $234 000. Negotiator compensation was based on a sliding scale starting at 20% of commission generated, to 60% for commission earned over $100 000. The $15 000 salary was tied to the sliding scale, so that when a negotiator achieved the $90 000 minimum his total income would be $45 000. Negotiators were required to pay their own expenses, and they were not paid their share of commissions billed until Continental was in full receipt of the invoiced amounts.

Continental encouraged an open flow of information concerning client activity. Negotiators were required to submit a weekly applicant report, which identified their clients and outlined the probability of success of current deals. If clients were not so listed, they were regarded as fair game for other negotiators. This report allowed the branch manager to monitor negotiator progress (and discourage over-registration, if necessary) and informed other negotiators of development activities in various sectors of the city. "There is no fear of being scooped," as one negotiator put it. In contrast, negotiators with most Canadian brokerage houses tended to be secretive with details of their potential deals.

There were no sales territories, but most deals were transacted within the negotiator's city base. Management encouraged negotiators to focus their activities, to limit their client list, and to concentrate on big deals. Continental, in Nelson's words, was "not after all the business available, but all the big business." Deals completed by a negotiator outside of this branch were credited to the negotiator as usual, but for credit to the branch territory in which the deal occurred.

Continental procedures required all offices to hold sales meetings commencing no later than 8 a.m. on Monday, Wednesday and Friday of each week. These meetings were the primary forum for announcements of new development activities, for the collection of information on prospective buyers or sellers, and for discussion of proposed or current projects' sale or lease potential. The first item on the agenda of a Calgary meeting attended by the casewriter, for example, was a presentation by branch manager Steve Jannock. It began with a discussion of the marketing feasibility of a new condominium office building and whether or not the concept would sell in south-west Calgary. One negotiator noted that a rival developer was planning a similar project at the opposite end of the block. The discussion then moved to potential customers and a price estimate for such a project. Jannock pointed out that the proposal was complicated by the developer's desire for a short-term investor before proceeding. An architect's layout was then examined and suggestions were offered regarding the amount of glass space, the number and speed of elevators, and other improvements to increase the project's salability. Finally, the total credibility of the project was examined; two points of concern were that it was the developer's first effort in the condominium market, and that the architect was from out of town.

An important part of Continental's application of the agency concept was a strict investment policy. All Continental personnel were forbidden to purchase speculative real estate in Canada or any state in the U.S. in which the company maintained an active office. Infringement of the rule was grounds for immediate dismissal. McLaren explained that the logic of the policy was easy to understand: the time spent investing and developing one's own real estate holdings should be spent representing one's clients. Moreover, sophisticated clients came to respect their negotiator's advice because the latter was not plucking out the good properties for himself. Continental was one of very few real estate agencies in Canada operating with such a policy.

Continental maintained a high level of internal competition. Each negotiator's performance was charted on a graph, which was reviewed monthly before a panel of his or her peers. At the annual meeting of all Continental personnel, each negotiator's graphs were projected on a screen, and his or her performance was reviewed. Another meeting, held in the late summer or early fall, is further illustration of Continental's approach: with the chairman, president, general manager, and all branch managers present, negotiators who had not yet reached $50 000 in annual production had to account for their performance, and were offered advice for improvement by this executive team. A past Xerox salesperson who had risen quickly within Continental saw these practices as straightforward and reasonable: "One has to play on these guys' egos. It's the only way to motivate such achievement-oriented people."

Working trips were another ingredient in the Continental recipe for success. These trips were described in the company procedure manual as an incentive program to encourage negotiators to broaden their concept of commercial real estate. The manual noted that a good negotiator was expected to make many trips on his or her own, but the company would help to defray the cost of specific trips. During a negotiator's first year, western negotiators were to fly to eastern Canada and the U.S., while eastern negotiators were to fly west. In the third year, the destination was Europe; in the fourth, it was southeast Asia; and in the fifth year, the negotiator was to visit the Caribbean or Hawaii. In the course of these trips, while the negotiators were acquainting themselves with the dynamics of a new market, they were also required to update and expand the company's Buyer's Book. This book was a listing of international investors who had expressed interest in North American real estate. It included details on the clients' buying behaviour, investment criteria and history.

CORPORATE AND BRANCH MANAGEMENT

Continental operated with a lean management structure (Exhibit 1). Senior managers, including the president, general manager and branch managers, all acted as negotiators as well as administrators, and had their production charted. It was argued that few services were necessary for the effective operation of the company. The primary organizational function was the supply to negotiators of current information—applicant listings, sales data, office-space surveys, Buyer's Book—and each branch was responsible for its own surveys and record updating.

In recent years, Gordon Nelson had removed himself from management of Continental's day-to-day activities in order to spend more time as a property developer. As chairman, he remained involved in policy matters and in quite close touch with the business, informally and through quarterly board meetings.

Nelson's first replacement as president was Larry Newman, at the time branch manager in Calgary. Newman remained in Calgary after taking on his new responsibilities. He grew restless in his dual role, however, and left Continental after two years to start his own agency firm. Nelson filled the gap for a time, and then asked John Morrison to join the firm as president.

John Morrison was senior vice-president of a large insurance company at the time. He had received his B.A. from the University of Western Ontario, M.B.A. from Harvard Business School, and was a Chartered Life Underwriter. He had known Nelson for some time because of his insurance company's participation in several financing deals. Morrison was attracted by Continental's prospects, and moved to Vancouver to become president.

A few months after John Morrison's appointment, Stan Jameson, the general manager, left Continental. Jameson had been an exception in the Continental ranks. His background was as a developer rather than an agent, and he did not himself get involved in transactions. Rather, most of his time was spent travelling from branch to branch reviewing progress with individual negotiators and offering counsel and advice. He was, several negotiators mentioned, very respected in this role, and his branch visits were welcomed.

Bob McLaren, Jameson's successor, was cut from different cloth, not unlike that of his mentor, Gordon Nelson. McLaren had joined Continental after completing his M.B.A. at the University of Western Ontario. He had recently been promoted from Vancouver branch manager to executive vice-president.

McLaren was an aggressive and knowledgeable negotiator whose advice was highly valued by fellow negotiators. He continued his selling activities and was a consistently high producer, travelling about 160 000 km a year and working 70–75 hours a week. Administratively, McLaren saw his prime function as that of recruiting and training branch managers, although he could not avoid involvement in many spot problems, ranging from difficulties with deals to personnel issues. McLaren turned the monthly performance-review task over to the branch managers. On the demands of his job, McLaren commented:

> You don't enjoy success without paying the price. And you don't do it unless you want do. You have to enjoy it. You can't dedicate such physical and mental energy and sacrifice unless you get a lot of enjoyment out of what you are doing. A person who says he doesn't is a person who's not going to be successful at it.

Morrison and McLaren both felt that sales involvement and a proven sales record were important for a leadership position in Continental. The rationale was basically that of credibility, plus a latent feeling that perhaps the worst thing that could happen to Continental would be the building of "non-productive" overheads and becoming "over-administered." In this context, Morrison and McLaren had assumed a largely implicit division of management tasks. Morrison dealt with the general tasks of corporate administration and representation, McLaren with the more immediate problems of branch supervision and production.

Planning and budgeting in Continental were relatively simple procedures. Revenue by branch was estimated annually on the basis of branch input and forecasts of market activity. By far the largest cost item was negotiator commission expense and it was directly variable with revenue. Branch-office and head-office expense budgets were also prepared, and these tended to reflect a no-frills approach to operations. Only a limited amount of savings could be squeezed out of the administrative process, however, since the costs were already pared to the bone.

THE BIG BRANCHES

Vancouver

Continental's lead market, Vancouver, was beginning to emerge from a slump in office development. With 25 million square feet of existing space, compared to Calgary's 14 million square feet, Vancouver was often viewed by developers as more stable than the overheated Calgary market. Continental's Vancouver branch had maintained a relatively stable production level with a fluctuating rate of sales to leasing. The branch employed ten negotiators whose average age was 37 years.

The Vancouver branch manager, Per Ek, had less than two years with Continental when he succeeded McLaren as branch manager. Born in Sweden, Ek was raised in Switzerland and had obtained a Ph.D. in Economics from the University of Geneva. After work with a major Swiss bank, Ek moved to Montreal where he assembled properties for a consortium of European banks. Ek was brought into Continental as a European representative to supplement Gordon Nelson, who had reduced his global travelling. Ek did not see himself as a high-powered salesperson, but as a professional who specialized in large sales projects. His production graph, which bounded upward in large steps, attested to his ability. Ek believed that it was important to lead by example and, though he had hired an administrator to handle office affairs, he still found only Sunday afternoons free. With his three hats—branch manager, agent and international representative—Ek was unable to devote much time to work with individual agents.

Edmonton

The Edmonton branch consisted of eight agents, and represented an increasing proportion of Continental's total production. A year before, a group of four senior agents had left the branch, led by the previous manager, John Thompson. Those left were young (average age 32), and were managed by Cliff Baetz, who maintained a relatively relaxed atmosphere. In spite of the defections, production was only 10% below the levels of the year before, an accomplishment that was cause for a great deal of pride among the Edmonton negotiators.

At 36, Cliff Baetz was the old man of the Edmonton office. C.B., as his fellow negotiators called him, held a B. Comm. from the University of Alberta and had joined Continental in Edmonton as an assistant to the branch manager. Baetz's responsibilities included making the branch productive and setting the office's pace, but he maintained a casual, sociable atmosphere. As a point of comparison, negotiators in Edmonton sometimes wandered into the 8:00 a.m. sales meeting ten minutes late; in Vancouver, the door was locked at 8:00 a.m. Baetz noted that Edmonton's productivity per negotiator was higher than that of any other Continental office.

The Edmonton manager's laid-back nature was deceptive. His typical day began at 7:00 a.m. and stretched to 6:30 p.m.; on the two days that the casewriter was present, his lunch was two hot dogs swallowed while dialing the phone. Baetz was currently Continental's top producer. He described his job as "a pressure cooker," but he enjoyed the autonomy of his work. He liked to give his negotiators similar freedom. While Baetz admitted that he had little motivation to train his employees, he believed that few negotiators required or would tolerate direct supervision.

Calgary

The Calgary commercial-development business was in the midst of unprecedented growth and Continental had just enjoyed a superb year. Production was substantially improved over the relatively poor record of two years earlier when several key personnel had left the Calgary office, some to expand the company into Houston, others to strike out on their own. Production had dropped by over 50%. The branch had rebuilt, however, from nine negotiators to 17, with an average age of 38.

The Calgary branch manager, Steve Jannock, had ten years of experience with Continental. A former Xerox salesman, Jannock, 44, believed that more effort had to be put into retaining Continental's leading producers. "Calgary was seriously injured by Newman's departure, and Edmonton may still feel the effects of Thompson's exit," he cautioned. Talking with the commitment of a man who understood the high producers' predicament, Jannock explained, "When the investment policy removes a successful negotiator's most obvious tax shelter and participation is not offered, at some point it is no longer economical for an individual to remain in the company." The investment policy was too important a selling tool to sacrifice, according to Jannock, but something had to be done to retain Continental's "shooters." Another veteran negotiator quipped, "Gordon Nelson created a monster; he produces wealthy prima donnas that the tax system forces out of the company!"

NEGOTIATOR MANAGEMENT

Recruiting, training and retaining negotiators were the acknowledged keys to Continental's future growth.

Recruiting

Continental recruited from the universities and from the ranks of experienced salespeople. In recent years, university recruiting had been confined to the Universities of British Columbia, Reading (near London, England) and Western Ontario. British Columbia and Reading had courses specifically related to the real estate field, and Reading offered a Master's degree in urban land appraisal.

Recently, Xerox and IBM sales managers had been recruited into the company as junior negotiators. As well-trained, professional salespeople, these recruits brought a new style to the negotiation task. Their concentration on selling technique, combined with Continental's traditional stress on product knowledge, had produced some very satisfactory results. Negotiators with a Xerox background thought that individual negotiator productivity could be substantially improved at Continental. They identified in particular a need for instruction in more effective selling methods. As one successful, ex-Xerox negotiator put it, "Everybody here works hard, but only a handful work smart."

There was no shortage of potential recruits to Continental. As Steve Jannock noted, "I have more people phoning me for jobs than I know what to do with." The question was one of quality, of being able to succeed in the Continental milieu.

Training

An assistantship program was Continental's primary training vehicle. With the permission of the company, a negotiator could hire an assistant if he had achieved $100 000 production for two consecutive years. A second assistant could be hired if the negotiator had achieved $200 000 production over the past two years, or if he had obtained a new major office or industrial listing (over 150 000 square feet). A new assistant was paid $700 per month for the first six months, $750 per month after six months, and could be eligible for a salary of $800 per month if he or she had experience. No production bonus was allowed during the assistant's first year. One recent Western M.B.A. recruit described his initial reluctance to join Continental at $700 per month: "Hell, that was less than I was making during my summers at school!"

An assistant was hired by a single negotiator who became responsible for the assistant's training. The quality of training provided by the negotiator varied, and this factor contributed, at times, to assistant turnover. In the Calgary branch, for example, approximately five assistants had moved in and out of the office in the past two years.

For most trainees, the apprenticeship period lasted 12 months. At the end of that time, the negotiator in charge and the assistant determined a future course. On occasion, the assistants would stay on in a trainee capacity, with increased responsibilities and a cut into the bonus system. Otherwise they became full negotiators subject to the performance requirements.

Some prospective recruits were unwilling or financially unable to accept the reduction in earnings involved in an assistant position. In particular cases, if past sales experience justified it, certain recruits were permitted to enter the negotiation field directly. Their training period was typically three months, after which they became regular negotiators with $15 000 salary and a more lucrative commission rate. The junior negotiators were usually "blinkered"—assigned to a specific project or area to improve their understanding of a particular aspect of real estate development.

Apart from the assistantship program, Continental had no formal training procedures or materials. However, one senior negotiator, Brad Connelly, was assembling an extensive and detailed manual of procedures and techniques. Connelly planned to enter the consulting field eventually, providing advice on realty matters to major developers, and the manual tied in with these plans. Negotiators and branch managers alike felt that Connelly's efforts would substantially fill the present training gap in the company. One branch manager, who felt that training was critical to the company's continued success, praised Connelly's activities; he was relieved to have the responsibility off his desk.

Retaining

High turnover was characteristic of Continental's operation. Two-thirds of Continental's present negotiator group had been with the company in that capacity for less than two years. Over past years, there was an 84% probability that a negotiator would leave before his or her fifth year with the company. Part of the turnover, of course, was due to recruits who found they did not fit, or who could not produce the required $90 000 in annual commissions. Another part of the turnover, more consequential for the firm, was made up of successful negotiators who, for reasons varying from economics to personal autonomy, chose to leave.

Whether it was possible or desirable to lengthen the stay of negotiators was somewhat of a moot point at Continental. The company had implemented incentive programs aimed at stimulating continuity (Exhibit 2) and had developed a pension plan that would allow a negotiator to collect $60 000 per year on retirement and vested in ten years. These did not, however, seem to have had a major tangible impact. McLaren took a pretty hard-nosed view of the situation: "After a person has made $200 000 to $300 000 for three or four years, you can't expect him to stay." Shortly after having said this, McLaren met the casewriter at another Continental office; he had just received a message that the Toronto branch manager had resigned.

FUTURE GROWTH

There were, in the view of senior Continental personnel, two broad avenues of future growth. The first was through opening additional branches, and the second through expansion of branch volume by entry into new product areas.

Branching

New branches were generally seen as the prime growth vehicle, although it was by no means clear, on the record, that the Continental approach could be easily transferred out of the Vancouver-Calgary-Edmonton triangle. The performance of the Toronto branch had been erratic, and was attributed variously to market conditions, well-established competition, and poor management and recruiting. In spite of the difficulties, there was a general opinion in the west that an effective and energetic manager could put the operation on its feet. In the U.S., the two branches in Houston and Phoenix had been open for only a short time. Houston was, nevertheless, regarded as somewhat of a disappointment, due perhaps to the timing (relatively late in Houston's development boom) and narrow initial contact base (Continental had entered the market to work with one Canadian developer who was also entering the market). There was greater enthusiasm for the Phoenix office, which had just been opened by an aggressive negotiator. The Phoenix market was growing rapidly and had become an attractive expansion point for Canadian developers moving south.

In Bob McLaren's view, Continental should have offices established in 15 key cities within seven to ten years. The major constraints, he explained, were the availability of suitable people and his own time.

> It will take from four to seven years to build a base in a new city. By the time the lead producer peaks out in a new area, the base for effective dealing has been established. My job is to identify when a young negotiator has ripened sufficiently, place him in the new market, and help him get going. We must do this with our own people. Bringing in negotiators from outside the firm or acquiring an existing firm would bring us the worst of both worlds.

On this program, branch growth was limited by McLaren's capacity to train and supervise new managers, which amounted, in his view, to having no more than two junior branches at any one time.

New Products

An area of immediate growth potential lay in the further expansion of Continental's activities in the industrial and property-management markets.

In both Calgary and Edmonton, industrial opportunities were being pursued, but no particular priority had been given to them. Development and decision-making in the industrial market were different, Continental personnel pointed out, involving different customers and different criteria. "They are an earthy lot," one negotiator explained, "but I get along better with the tire-kickers than the oil executives." Most of the negotiators concentrating on the Calgary industrial market had not selected their placements; they had been assigned to the market. Another industrial negotiator explained, "The deals are small, you work twice as hard and make half as much." Edmonton had always had its finger in the industrial area, but, historically, only one negotiator in that office specialized in such deals.

Continental's property-management operations were headquartered in Vancouver under Ted Foster, a public accountant who had joined the company in its early years. The essential function provided was coverage of the ongoing tasks of operating an office; property-tenant relations, physical maintenance, insurance, security, etc. The major competitor was the owner himself, who was always tempted to perform the management function. Management contracts were sought by negotiators and turned over to Foster when a deal was made. In the coming year the property-management operation was expected to gross about $1 million, with Vancouver contributing about 50%, Calgary 25% and the balance from Edmonton and Toronto. The business was profitable and was growing at about 15% per year.

Another, quite different, view of growth objectives and methods was presented by a veteran representative, Dick Thorson, reflecting in some degree the thoughts of some other senior agents. His concern was that dynamic growth might cause the company to trade off quality for quantity and slip toward becoming a "brokerage" house. Using Calgary as an example, Thorson suggested that there should be only five to seven negotiators, rather than the current 17. Only these negotiators would attend the morning meetings, ensuring a free flow of information and counsel. Each negotiator, however, would have two executive assistants and would be held accountable for the production and profit of his three-person group. To retain the senior negotiators, Thorson proposed a change in the investment policy: negotiators would still be prohibited from dealing in city-core or raw land, but a sector of land would be opened for investment. All Continental clients would be informed of the nature and extent of the investment area. Finally, Thorson would limit branch expansion to the high-growth markets in western Canada and to a few dynamic American cities. Thorson's proposal thus preserved the firm's strategy, but recommended a fundamental change in operating method. Few negotiators were so presumptuous. Most felt that Gordon Nelson had developed a wondrous formula for success that should not be tampered with. Asked why others had not been able to duplicate Continental's methods, one negotiator replied, "Nobody else has copied the formula because nobody else has the spunk."

EXHIBIT 1   **Continental's Organization Chart**

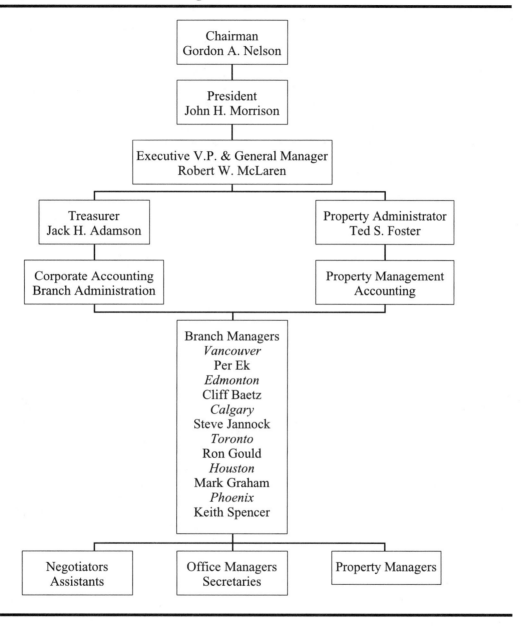

EXHIBIT 2 Continental's Incentive Program

Old System	Present Schedule	Prize
$100 000	2.5 x minimum production	Gold watch
$ 300 000	5 x minimum production	Colour television
$ 750 000	10 x minimum production	Lincoln Continental automobile
$1 000 000	20 x minimum production	University education for salesperson's children
Proposed 30 x minimum production		Option to purchase 5% interest in $5 million property
Proposed 40 x minimum production		Entitled to exercise option

ATLANTIC PAPER COMPANY

case

14

J. Peter Killing

In January 1991, Jack Vickers was appointed President of the Atlantic Paper Company, Australia's largest producer of linerboard and brown paper. Atlantic was a wholly owned subsidiary of Cumberland Industries, and provided almost 50% of Cumberland's total sales volume, but its recent financial performance had not been encouraging. In spite of its historically dominant position in its businesses, the company had been losing market share to two smaller competitors since the early 1980s, and had also seen its markets shrink through the introduction of plastic products such as shrink wrap and plastic checkout bags used in supermarkets. Vicker's predecessor Marcel Ruban had taken early retirement at age 55, having spent his last years in office struggling with unions and local governments in a successful but exhausting battle to close the company's smaller and less efficient paper mills.

Jack Vickers, age 40, had become a part of the Cumberland organization in 1988 when Cumberland acquired the Australian transport company of which he was majority owner and president. Vickers had founded the company in 1979, after completing his MBA in the United States. A series of well-executed

INTERNATIONAL

acquisitions in the early 1980s not only tripled the size of the trucking company, but earned Vickers the reputation of being a very shrewd financial operator whose eye was firmly fixed on the bottom line.

After the 1988 takeover, Vickers continued to manage what was now the transport division of Cumberland Industries, and joined the company's board of directors. The board included, among others, Cumberland's president and chief financial officer, and the presidents of its Atlantic Paper and Diamond Cement subsidiaries. Vickers was widely seen as an "up and comer" in the organization, but as time passed, it became clear that if he were to have a chance of becoming president of Cumberland, he would first have to successfully manage one or the other of Cumberland's two major subsidiaries. In late 1990, when Marcel Ruban's retirement was announced, Vickers was taken aside by the president of Cumberland and asked if he would take over Atlantic and "get the company back on track."

THE COMPANY

In 1988, Atlantic's head office staff moved out of Cumberland's downtown office tower to much more modest offices in Acton, a suburb 20 kilometres away. The instigators of the move were Jim Smythe and John Collins, two of Atlantic's vice-presidents. Jim Smythe explained:

> The distance between Cumberland's head office and ours is not far, but psychologically it's an important gap. Their head office is full of mahogany and plush carpets. Our relatively austere offices in Acton are much more appropriate for a company that has been closing mills and laying people off for the past three years.
>
> Another advantage of the move is that we have gained a little independence from Cumberland's president and financial people, most of whom used to work for Atlantic. They still like to tell us how to run the company. Also, we took the opportunity presented by the move to eliminate about 30 technical staff, who were necessary in our expansion stage, but aren't now.

As shown in Exhibit 1, Atlantic was a functionally organized company, with five vice-presidents reporting to the president. There were currently approximately 65 employees in the Acton head office, 60 in regional sales offices, and 2 500 spread across the company's four remaining mill sites. Within the past 18 months, employment had been reduced by approximately 800 people through mill and machine closings and head office cutbacks. Two hundred of these cuts had come in the last six months.

Each of the company's mill sites is described below.

The Northern Mill

The Northern Mill was Atlantic's largest. Built on a rural site in a timber growing area approximately 200 kilometres from Acton, the Northern Mill housed three pulp mills and three paper machines. Two of the pulp mills were relatively old and small, but the third was new and very large, and due to come on-stream in late 1991. With the new mill in place the company's pulp capacity would more than triple. The new pulp mill was being financed "off balance sheet," which meant that Atlantic would make lease payments of approximately $15 million per year to the (related) company that would own the pulp mill. These fixed annual payments, beginning in 1991–92, would not vary with the mill's output.

Atlantic's paper machines were highly specialized, efficient at producing only a specific type of product. Two of the paper machines on the Northern site, N1 and N2, used virgin pulp and recycled wasted paper to produce brown paper, which was sold to paper bag makers. The third machine, N3, was the largest and most efficient machine the company owned. It was used to make linerboard, which was sold to manufacturers of corrugated boxes. The efficient operation of N3 was of such importance to the company that Chris Reid, the senior vice-president to whom the mills reported, was aware of its production on a daily basis, and even Marcel Ruban usually knew if there were any problems on N3.

Because of the complex interrelationships between the pulp mills and the paper machines, and the fact that these pulp mills supplied all of Atlantic's other mill sites, the Northern site was very difficult to run well. There would be, in fact, few sites as complex in the world, once the new pulp mill was operational.

Jim Smythe, who had successfully managed the Northern Mill in the 1980s when N3 was installed, was concerned that with the addition of the new pulp mill the job of managing the Northern Mill would be beyond the capabilities of any of Atlantic's managers. The successful operation of the new pulp mill was a high priority both because of its economic importance, and the fact that the decision to build it had been made by Hector Day, currently the president of Cumberland Industries. Smythe commented, "It was difficult enough managing that site in my day, now I wonder if we have anyone who can do it." Smythe himself was reported to have been one of the two most effective Northern Mill managers in Atlantic's history.

The Senator Mill

The Senator Mill was located about 20 kilometres from Acton on the edge of the city. It was a very old mill with two active paper machines, one of which produced linerboard, and the other brown paper. The Senator Mill was plagued by hostile labour relations, and had been the site of many industrial disputes. The mill seemed to be caught in a vicious circle: its poor industrial relations record had led to even more aggressive union behaviour. Few aspiring managers in Atlantic were eager to run the Senator Mill, and it was widely believed that the current manager had now proved beyond doubt that he could not handle the unions and would soon have to be replaced. Whether a new mill manager would prove any more successful was an open question.

The Lautrec Mill

The Lautrec Mill was furthest from Atlantic's head office, about 800 kilometres, and to some within the company that was sufficient explanation of why it was so well managed. The Lautrec Mill contained one paper machine, Atlantic's only machine that could produce white papers. However, the machine was very old, and was being run constantly at speeds well above its designed capacity levels. As a result, quality was suffering in a market in which quality was becoming ever more important. Ken Mauger, the mill manager, claimed that he was "hanging on by the skin of his teeth." He explained:

> White papers is one of Atlantic's few markets that shows any growth at all. But the growth is in higher quality paper than we can make. Even for the low quality end of the market our product is marginal. We are very vulnerable. We clearly need a new paper machine. The cost will be high (about $80 million) but this company has to build a future for itself.

The Johansson Mill

In 1991 the Johansson Mill was also a single machine mill, although as recently as 1989 it had housed three machines. Located in a major urban centre, the mill specialized in the conversion of recycled waste paper (plus a little pulp) into low-grade linerboards. Formerly the site of many industrial relations problems, the mill now appeared to be stable and running without major problems.

VICKERS' FIRST WEEKS

Jack Vickers' first two weeks at Acton were devoted to meeting his senior management team, and reviewing the company's past and projected financial performance. One of the first documents he read was the company's five-year plan, dated October 1990, excerpts of which follow. He was not surprised to learn that Atlantic had met Cumberland's target of a 17.5% return on funds employed only once in the past five years, or that the most recent financial year, ended June 30, 1990, had come in at 6.7% (Exhibit 2). He was, however, startled to discover that Atlantic's plan showed that the 17.5% target would not be met in the foreseeable future.

Vickers discovered that the prime author of the five-year plan was Jim Smythe, and that much of its content was the result of a three-man task force that Smythe had headed up over a recent six-month period. Alarmed at the company's apparently bleak future, Smythe had formed the group on his own initiative, involving the market services manager and a senior accountant. The three-man group met widely with customers, suppliers, personnel in Atlantic's mills, and gathered what data they could about the competition. Jim Smythe described the results to Jack Vickers as follows:

> Our conclusion was that there was no reason to be optimistic about the future of this company. Our five-year plan may not look too good to you Jack, as an outsider, but believe me if we sit here and do nothing our future is going to be a lot worse than this. Even meeting these projections is going to be a big job.
>
> Let me give you one example of the kinds of problems we face. Fibrebox Ltd. is our largest single customer. It's a well run, aggressive, growing company. They have just bought a new paper machine which will allow them to recycle their own waste. They don't need pulp to make low quality linerboard, and their box plants are now big enough that their own waste, combined with some purchased scrap paper are sufficient to supply a 40 000 ton per year machine. One of the things our task force did was to calculate Fibrebox's return on investment on that new machine. It's about 45%! There is nothing we can do in terms of pricing or anything else to make that into a bad investment for them. So we're going to lose 35 000–40 000 tons next year.
>
> We have two other big linerboard customers. Are they going to just sit and watch? So far they have done nothing, but how soon will they act?

Excerpts from Atlantic's Five-Year Plan

> We have set ourselves a profitability objective of 17.5% earnings before interest and tax on total assets.
>
> This is high compared to earlier achievements. Over the past 11 years our return before interest and taxes on total assets has ranged from 4.4% in 1982 to 18.5% in 1987. Achievement of our aim is made more difficult because of our recent $67 million investment in forest lands that currently does not yield any significant return. Our total forest assets comprise $156 million of the total funds employed in 1990–91 of $541 million, rising to $178 million out of a total of $550 million in 1995.
>
> A 17.5% return is higher than the average return achieved by each of the various industry sectors in this country and would put us in the top 75 performers of all listed companies. This may be ambitious but we consider it an appropriate aim which will highlight the question of idle assets.

The financial projections in the five-year plan (summarized) were as follows:

Earnings Forecast, Years Ending June 30

(millions of dollars)

	1991	*1992*	*1993*	*1994*	*1995*
Sales	420	425	470	514	585
Profits before interest and tax	55	48[1]	70	73	89
Net profit	38	27	37	40	48
Total assets[2]	539	541	546	545	550
PBIT as a percentage of funds employed	10.2%	8.7	12.8	13.4	16.2
Deliveries forecast (thousands of tons)					
Base forecast	587	576	577	572	578
Backward integration of Fibrebox Ltd.	—	(39)	(50)	(50)	(50)
"Super Pulp" project	—	(38)	(38)	(38)	(38)
New white paper products	—	—	9	22	41
Exports	45	50	50	50	50
Total	632	549	548	556	581

[1] Profit decline due to start up of a new pulp mill.
[2] Major asset changes were the projected white paper investment and a mill closure due to the super pulp project.

This conversation triggered a series of meetings to discuss the five-year plan which lasted most of Vickers third week in the company. These meetings included Bill Leroy, Vice-President of Finance, and John Collins, Vice-President of Marketing, in addition to Vickers and Smythe. Although invited to the meetings, Chris Reid put in only a minimal appearance, explaining that he had urgent issues that had to be dealt with at the Northern Mill. The meetings touched on a wide variety of topics, and it was clear to Vickers by the end of the week that three major initiatives were being proposed to him, none of which had yet been presented to Cumberland management. These were the white papers project, the super pulp project, and the reorganization of the company. All appeared to have had their origins in Jim Smythe's task force.

THE WHITE PAPERS PROJECT

Jim Smythe explained the origin and rationale of the white papers project:

> Ken Mauger, the manager of the Lautrec Mill, had been telling us for a couple of years that we're missing out on a growth market in copier and computer paper because we can't produce the right qualities of white paper. We haven't paid too much attention because the capital required to produce the necessary quality seemed to be prohibitive.
>
> Several things have prompted us to reconsider. One is that this company can no longer afford to overlook any growing markets in related business. Another is that it looks like we're going to have to reinvest $20 million or so to upgrade Ken's existing machine, just to let him hang on to the market he's got. Maybe we should spend an extra $60 million to increase his capacity and let him produce these other grades.
>
> The task force commissioned a market research study on the white papers market which concluded that there is a market worth going after, and we think we can get 90 000 tons of new business in this area within four or five years of arriving on the market, if we get serious about it. In our geographic area Benson Industries is the only major company in the business, and its customers tell us that they would welcome a second reputable supplier.

Vickers learned that the white papers project had not yet reached the official proposal stage. No one, for instance, had contacted equipment suppliers to get exact prices, developed an in-depth marketing plan or worked out the financial implications of the proposal in other than a fairly rough fashion. Some back of the envelope calculations suggested that the financial return on the project might be in the range of 25–30%

before tax. Smythe indicated that he was reluctant to talk to equipment suppliers until Cumberland's board indicated that it was willing to change its long standing policy of not competing directly with Benson Industries. Benson and Atlantic were approximately of equal size. Benson was dominant in white paper markets, and Atlantic in linerboard and brown paper.

THE "SUPER PULP" PROJECT

The super pulp idea was created about eight months before Vickers' arrival by the members of Smythe's task force. The idea, which was to use much more pulp and much less recycled waste paper in the company's linerboards, had been debated by the senior management group ever since. Technical trials carried out in the interim indicated that making super pulp linerboard would not be a problem. The company could do it. The question was whether or not it should.

The attraction of the super pulp project was that it might solve three problems at once.

First, by increasing the company's need for pulp, the project would mean that Atlantic's new pulp mill would be run at capacity. Without the project it would run at 75% of capacity, primarily because the demand projections put together when the mill was planned had been too optimistic. Selling excess pulp to other companies was not a viable option as the market was poor and Atlantic's pulp was wet, which meant it was expensive to transport. Running the pulp mill below capacity would reduce its efficiency, and would mean that the large lease payment might not be offset by increased earnings.

Secondly, if the firm were to switch to super pulp linerboards, it would produce fewer tons of linerboard per year even while producing the same area. This was because the new linerboards would be thinner and lighter than existing ones of the same strength. Thus even though a square metre of linerboard would cost more to produce (as the variable cost of pulp was about 20% higher than that of recycled paper), total costs could be reduced because less machine time would be required to produce the linerboard. In practice this meant that if Atlantic switched to super pulp linerboards the Senator Mill could be closed. The net saving would be approximately $6 million per year, and the continual headaches associated with the mill would be ended.

Finally, the introduction of the super pulp linerboard might slow down the inroads which Atlantic's two smaller competitors had been making into the linerboard market. (Atlantic's market share had fallen from approximately 70% to 50% over the past seven or eight years.) Neither of these companies had access to pulp, and there was no way that either of them could produce a super pulp linerboard in the foreseeable future. If super pulp linerboard became the norm for all but the lowest grades of linerboard, these two firms would be restricted to the bottom end of the market, which was where plastic products such as shrink wrap were making inroads and margins were the lowest.

John Collins told Vickers that he was not particularly impressed by these arguments. He commented:

> This is a production and finance driven initiative. Our customers, the boxmakers, aren't asking for it. Neither are their customers, the end users. Not much of the market really cares about box performance in a major way. Most of the time it's just a question of price. We're talking now about introducing super pulp liners at a 3% cheaper price per square metre than normal linerboard. That's a joke, because as soon as we do our competitors will put their prices 3% below ours, just as they always have.
>
> What this product could do is create a lot of confusion in the market, and we could be the big losers. We're better off to stay away from it.

Bill Leroy countered Collins' final argument by stating that the paper machines of both of Atlantic's linerboard competitors were currently at capacity, and that it would be impossible for them to take advantage of any confusion in the market. He also liked the fact that no capital investment would be required. Leroy supported the initiative, and thought its timing was ideal.

Another argument that Vickers heard concerning the super pulp project was that, by withdrawing from the wastepaper market, Atlantic would lower prices of industrial waste paper and thus help out their competitors, who placed heavy reliance on such waste. On the domestic waste collection side, some managers argued that the large wastepaper collection trucks with "Atlantic" written on the side were a significant source of goodwill for the company, necessary to offset their image in environmental circles as a company primarily interested in cutting down trees, raping the forests, and so on.

REORGANIZATION

Jim Smythe had sent an eight-page handwritten memo to Marcel Ruban shortly before he retired, suggesting that Atlantic be reorganized into four product divisions. Because of Ruban's impending retirement, of which Smythe was unaware, no action had been taken. Smythe explained the proposal to John Vickers.

> One of the conclusions that I came to as a result of our task force investigation was that Atlantic would perform much better if separate groups of people focused on each of our three product areas, and a fourth group concentrated on making pulp. Right now we all spend a lot of time worrying about linerboard because it has the largest sales volume, but a lot of important issues in the other businesses slip by unnoticed.
>
> The marketing group, for instance, spends all its time thinking about Fibrebox and our other two big linerboard customers, but we know very little, as the market research study revealed, about white papers. I am certain that this is also true of brown papers. Also, we have always used the same salesforce to sell all three product lines, but we could do much better with one for each product.
>
> The biggest improvement, I have no doubt, would come from having a general manager looking after each business. Maybe we could eventually pay bonuses based on product group performance. Right now everyone here is on straight salary.

Smythe's memo contained the proposed organization charts which are shown in Exhibits 3 and 4. It also listed some further advantages and some disadvantages of his proposed reorganization.

Other Advantages

- Each product group would get more individual attention, which in turn should give faster reactions, better digestion of market intelligence, more thought to product performance and profitability, and less complex product development.

- Bringing marketing and manufacturing closer together may reduce some of the present counter productive activity.

- Promising staff members can be more readily exposed to broader business concerns, and be offered general management experience earlier in their careers.

- Reorganization may change the market's view of Atlantic as a slow moving monolith.

- Current head office staff (engineering, technical, industrial relations) can be moved to the Northern Mill where their involvement in mill operations will be useful. Other mills needing technical assistance can seek it from Northern.

- Reorganization will reduce numbers at head office by rationalization and reduction of one level of management.

Disadvantages

- More flexible attitudes will be required at the Northern Mill, Senator Mill, regional sales offices, and head office.

- This is a radical change to the traditional marketing and operations organizations. Change will be neither easy nor pleasant.

- Mill managers at Northern and Senator Mills will become site managers, responsible for managing the site, but not the product mix or output.

- The four groups are not of even size.

- Some additional marketing/sales staff may be required.

After reading Smythe's memo, Vickers asked him to elaborate on the probable reaction of Atlantic's senior employees to such an organizational change. Smythe replied:

> Neither the senior marketing nor the senior operations people will support this move because it means breaking up their big functional groups. The mill managers, for instance, have long been the "kings" in this organization. With this plan, machine managers would report directly to their own product group. On multi-machine sites like Northern and Senator the machine managers would also have a dotted line relationship to the site manager, who would be responsible for insuring that the site was properly run.
>
> Managers without an organizational axe to grind, like Bill Leroy, believe that this is an excellent idea. (Vickers later confirmed that this was indeed the case.)

THE FOURTH WEEK

On the Monday of his fourth week in Acton, Vickers received the financial report for the six months ending December 31, 1990 (Exhibit 5). It did not make good reading. In spite of the fact that sales were as budgeted (which meant that the company had made an 8% price increase stick, its first in several years), profit before tax was only 68% of budget. Even with what looked like some creative tax accounting, earnings after tax would show less than a 10% return on shareholders equity.

In discussing this report with Chris Reid, Vickers learned that the fundamental problem was that N3, the big linerboard machine, had not been operating efficiently. Reid had made some personnel changes, but to no avail. He now wanted to bring in a very experienced "hands-on" American papermaker for two years to get the machine operating well and to raise the skill level of the machine crews. He had found such a man—but he was asking more in salary than any of Atlantic's vice-presidents were earning. This was a result of the fact, Vickers discovered, that when the man's current employer learned he was talking to Atlantic, they gave him an immediate 30% raise. Vickers told Chris Reid he would "think it over and get back to him."

Reid's request, on which he wanted a quick answer, pushed Vickers to the conclusion that it was time to decide what changes he wanted to make at Atlantic, and how he should go about them. He did not want to start making ad hoc decisions on single issues which, when added together, would make little sense.

The problem was where to start and how fast to move. In considering Jim Smythe's reorganization plan, for example, Vickers could not see how he could find four general managers in an organization that had no one with general management experience. After living with Atlantic's senior managers for a month, he felt he could bet on Jim Smythe and Bill Leroy as good potential general managers, but as for the rest, he wasn't sure.

EXHIBIT 1   **Atlantic Paper Company, Organization Chart**

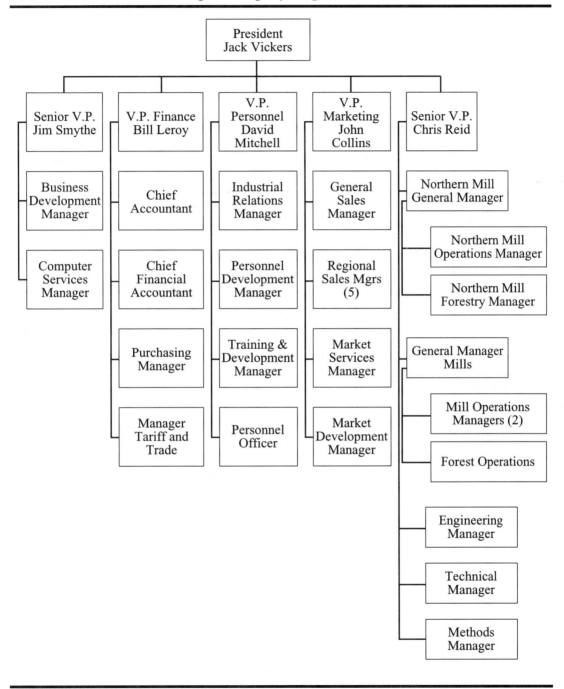

EXHIBIT 2 **Atlantic Paper Company Summary Statements**

12 months ending June 30

	1990		1989
	Budget	*Actual*	*Actual*
Earnings ($000)			
Net sales	$ 445 420	$ 397 630	$ 420 058
Gross earnings before depreciation	94 470	68 840	92 391
Less: Depreciation	22 000	21 550	20 789
Overheads	11 670	10 960	10 514
Earnings before interest and tax	60 800	36 330	61 088
Less: Interest	11 600	7 790	10 304
Earnings before tax	49 200	28 540	50 784
Less: Income tax charge	13 400	7 030	20 759
Net earnings after tax	$ 35 800	$ 21 510	$ 30 025
Other Information			
Earnings before interest and tax as a percentage of funds employed	11.2%	6.7%	12.9%
Gross margins (based on earnings before depreciation and overheads)	21.2%	17.3%	22.0%
Deliveries (tons)	685 000	640 296	715 476
Average selling price ($ per ton)	650.2	621.0	587.1
Average cost ($ per ton)	560.9	564.2	501.7

E X H I B I T 3   **Atlantic Paper Company, Jim Smythe's Proposed Organization Chart**

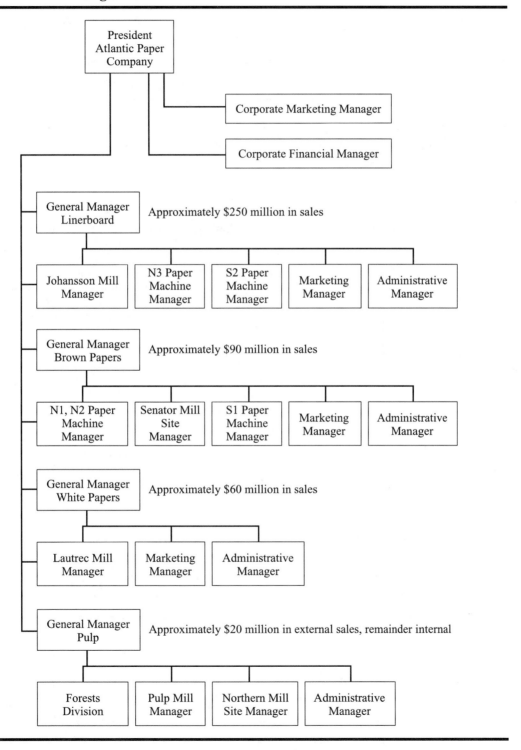

E X H I B I T 4 **Atlantic Paper Company, Jim Smythe's Proposed Corporate Marketing Organization**

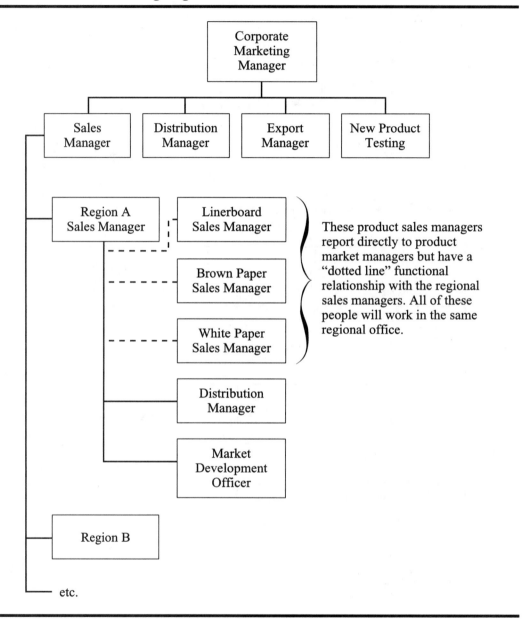

These product sales managers report directly to product market managers but have a "dotted line" functional relationship with the regional sales managers. All of these people will work in the same regional office.

EXHIBIT 5   **Atlantic Paper Company Six-Month Financial Results**

6 months ending December 31

| | 1990 | | 1989 |
	Budget	Actual	Actual
Earnings ($000)			
Net sales	$ 211 550	$ 217 600	$ 214 210
Gross earnings before depreciation	51 120	40 860	39 380
Less: Depreciation	12 950	11 830	11 660
Overheads	5 950	6 190	6 130
Earnings before interest and tax	32 220	22 840	21 590
Less: Interest	4 690	4 090	3 780
Earnings before tax	27 530	18 750	17 810
Less: Income tax charge	4 920	10	3 690
Net earnings after tax	$ 22 610	$ 18 740	$ 14 120
Other Information			
Annualized earnings before interest and tax as a percentage of funds employed	11.9%	8.4%	7.9%
Gross margins (based on earnings before depreciation and overheads)	24.2%	18.8%	18.4%
Deliveries (tons)	323 000	326 240	346 680
Average selling price ($ per ton)	654.9	666.9	617.8
Average cost ($ per ton)	555.2	596.9	555.6

TWILL ENTERPRISES LIMITED

William R. Killeen and
Joseph N. Fry

Ken Shelstad leaned forward in his chair, flashed a great smile and said, "Look, I love what I'm doing! I'm at it 70 hours a week—but that's the limit, after that I feel fuzzy and I can't concentrate. I enjoy every minute! Hell, I own half this company and we're making money. Lots of it! Profits, I love 'em!"

Shelstad, 51, was President of Twill Enterprises Limited, a growing and prosperous company in the printing and packaging industry. He was clearly in his element, but he expressed some misgivings about

IVEY

William R. Killeen prepared this case under the supervision of Professor Joseph N. Fry solely to provide material for class discussion. The authors do not intend to illustrate either effective or ineffective handling of a managerial situation. The authors may have disguised certain names and other identifying information to protect confidentiality.

the future as he pushed the company into one of its most aggressive expansion projects. The issues, he thought, were not so much in the market opportunity as in his and his peoples' ability to handle the anticipated growth. "What concerns me," he said, "is that the company may be outgrowing me. I used to know exactly what was going on in every department. Lately, I feel like I've lost some of that control. The consultants have been telling me for years that I should change the way I run things. Maybe they are finally right."

COMPANY BACKGROUND

In 1945, Barry Shelstad, Ken's father, purchased a small Toronto-based producer of business forms and labels, and started Twill Enterprises. Over the next 20 years, Barry Shelstad built the business by internal growth, and by the careful acquisition of similar small companies in Canada and the United States. With time Barry Shelstad brought his sons John and Ken into the business. By 1965 John, the eldest, was the president, and in 1974 he became chairman. Ken began in the company as a salesman, moved up through the ranks to become vice-president of manufacturing, and in 1974 became president. When Barry Shelstad passed away in 1975, he left the ownership of the company in equal shares to the two brothers.

By 1988, Twill revenues were over $150 million, and the company's product range encompassed blister and flexible packaging, labels and business forms. The company operated seven packaging, ten business form and seven label plants at various locations in North America. In recent years, Twill's growth had been somewhat higher than the 5–7% rates experienced by the industry, and profitability had been consistently higher than the 2–3% after tax return on sales and the 4–7% return on average assets of comparable firms.

Twill's new venture was in the rigid plastic container business. Ken Shelstad had acquired the rights to European technology, which promised greater design flexibility and lower cost production in some lines of jars and bottles than was currently in place in North America. His projections showed the new lines would add over $40 million to Twill's revenues within three years of start-up. The capital investment implications of the venture were sizeable, however, and for the first time ever Shelstad had run into difficulty working out financial arrangements with Twill's long-time bank. "They wanted to know who the project manager was going to be," said Shelstad, "and when I told them, first, that it was none of their business, and, second, that it was going to be me, they wanted to have a consultant hired to monitor the operation. Well, there was no way I was going to operate with some jerk looking over my shoulder, so we got financing elsewhere." At the time of this case, Twill had made commitments for land in Toronto, and for the purchase of the major items of equipment.

INDUSTRY CHARACTERISTICS

The markets in which Twill operated were fiercely competitive. Typically, a few large competitors would account for about 70% of the sales in a region, and the balance would be filled by literally hundreds of small companies. Most products were made to customer specifications so operations took on job-shop characteristics. Profitability was a reflection of efficient manufacturing operations and local pricing, customer and product mix decisions. Raw materials usually represented over 60% of direct product costs.

Price, delivery, quality and service tended to become equated among local producers. Often a competitive edge was decided by the reputation of the producer for especially good service, and the personal relations between the supplier firm personnel and their customers. The larger suppliers had somewhat more of an advantage with larger accounts because the scope of their operations allowed them to meet the national requirements of their customers.

Twill was fortunate to have focused its operations in Toronto, one of the two largest centres for printing concentration in North America (Chicago being the other). On the downside, this created a fiercely competitive environment, in which suppliers had to offer a high degree of sophistication, technical capability and a range of production options. The challenge was to make more complicated products with faster response times and lower costs.

The outlook for industry demand in Twill's market areas was generally positive. Demand tended to follow the fortunes of the economy as a whole, and in recent years had been outpacing this indicator. Existing competitors had reacted by expanding their capacity, and new entrants had been attracted to the industry. Competition would continue to be intense and there was some concern that an economic downturn would leave suppliers in a state of serious overcapacity.

TWILL'S STRATEGY

Goals

The Shelstad's goals for Twill were for it to continue to operate as a large, successful, growing, family firm. Twill had been owned and run by the Shelstad family for nearly 45 years. Ken had three sons working for the firm, and while they were still in their early 20s, he hoped they would provide for family succession.

The Shelstads were known as prudent, successful businessmen. They had built Twill with a conservative growth strategy. Typically, whether acquisition or internal expansion was involved, Twill started new projects and followed them to completion before progressing to a new venture. Twill's recent plastic container expansion represented a more aggressive step than had been typical for the company.

Product Market Strategy

Twill had always chosen to expand into markets in which it could be profitable by exploiting its competitive strengths—in particular, high-service levels, low-cost production and in-house capabilities. When a market opportunity was uncovered (usually in the form of a neglected niche with high prices and low customer satisfaction), Twill was quick to respond. Table 1 provides a general review of Twill's market position.

TABLE 1 Twill Market Position

	Blister and Flexible Packaging	Labels	Business Forms
Expect overall market growth[1]	4–6%	1–3%	3–4%
Industry key	Product development	Personal relationships	
Success factors	Range of technical capabilities	Service reputation	
	Quality and service	Cost control	
	Cost control		
Twill share of served market[2]	12%	19%	10%
% Twill revenues	Over 50%	About 15%	About 35%
Plants[3]	7	7	10

[1] Management estimate.
[2] Twill did not compete in all product formats or geographic regions in North America. The market share estimates are based on Twill's sales in its served markets.
[3] Some of Twill's plants occupied the same site and even the same building. They had distinct plant managers, however.

In recent years, Twill had experimented with a variety of plastic container products. Their strategy had been to "test the waters" with product entries based on sub-contracted production. Over time, the company had developed its understanding of the market. In 1989, Twill planned to start up its own production facilities in Toronto. The new facility represented a major step by Twill into a highly competitive market. The Shelstads were confident, however, that their current competitive advantages would transfer readily into the new market.

Competitive Strategy

Twill aimed to be competitive in price and distinctive in service. The company had always endeavoured to ensure that customers got the product they wanted, when they wanted it. To this end, Twill offered their own in-house design and typesetting service, and employed a large direct-sales organization and delivery fleet.

The Shelstads ran a no-nonsense, low-cost operation. Money was spent where it was necessary—on equipment modernization and maintenance. Otherwise, there were few frills at a Twill plant. Parking lots were not paved, and offices were not carpeted. The salesforce shared spartan office space, which kept costs to a minimum and "forced" them to stay on the road. Expediting and cost control were inbred habits throughout the organization.

Recently Twill had been attempting to supplement its low-cost emphasis with a greater concern for quality. The aim was to eliminate situations in which substandard but usable products would be sent to customers. Under the current program, such a client could be informed of quality problems, given a sample, and asked for their approval prior to shipment.

TWILL'S ORGANIZATION

The practice of management at Twill had remained relatively unchanged for 20 years. Growth had added to the complexity of the business, but to this point had not forced any significant change in basic management structures or systems and style. There were, however, continuing questions about how best to handle the inherently and increasingly complicated operations of the company, as will be illustrated in the following description of the way in which the organization worked.

Management Structure

Twill was managed through a functional structure as outlined in the partial organization chart in Exhibit 1. The senior managers in the structure—John and Ken Shelstad, Larry Dixon, Vice-President of Sales and Marketing, and Doug Burgess, Vice-President of Production—had been in their positions since 1974. Each senior manager, based on long experience, would step outside of their strict functional responsibilities to handle specific projects, and often, day-to-day activities. Together they nurtured an intense, "hands-on" style of management.

Top-level coordination was handled through a management committee. The committee consisted of six members—the Shelstads, Doug Burgess, Larry Dixon, Tim O'Dowda, and Jeff Bak. The group attempted to meet weekly (schedules limited this number to about 30 meetings annually) for two to four hours. John Shelstad set an agenda but new topics could be informally introduced. No minutes were taken. The group's role was to develop strategy; day-to-day operations were not discussed. Final decisions rested with the Shelstads, but no decisions were made without the assistance and input of the committee.

John and Ken Shelstad's roles in the management structure were vastly different. The older brother, John, had a number of outside interests and limited his involvement to strategic issues. Ken, on the other hand, was highly involved in all of the company's activities—from the management committee to daily decision making. As one manager observed: "Twill gets its pulse from Ken. He commands respect and he gets it. He's very dynamic. He drives this company. But there is a problem—I think people are losing contact with him."

Another added an ominous note: "Ken is going to kill himself. He pushes himself too hard. He recently delegated the monthly cheque signing. Umpteen hundred a month and he used to sign—and check—every one. That's 15 hours minimum right there."

From time to time, Twill had attempted to modify its structure and decentralize its operations through the use of general management positions. These attempts had been unsuccessful, however, for a variety of reasons that ranged from incapable personnel to corporate culture to head office interference. Twill's experience with its Denver plant was a prime example.

Twill had purchased a profitable business in Denver, and had put a "general manager" in charge. Within one year, however, the revenues and profits of the Denver operation had declined to the point where consideration was being given to shutting it down. The cause of the problem was not clear. The manager may not have been competent, head office might have stifled him—or whatever; head office did take over, the manager was fired, and another notch was marked against a general manager concept.

Management Systems

Twill's job-shop operations were inherently complex, and worked under the pressure of tight delivery schedules and cost containment. The following description of order processing gives some idea of the manner in which the operating problems were handled by the company.

ORDER PROCESSING
In 1971 Twill had implemented an on-line electronic data interchange (EDI) system. Orders were either brought, phoned, or mailed in, and then keyed into a terminal at the order department. By 1987, three separate systems were in use, reflecting the differing information needs of the major product lines—packaging, labels and business forms.

An EDI file was created for each client. After entering an order, a delivery slip was created and sent to shipping. Stock items were shipped immediately. Made-to-order product delivery dates were confirmed by the order department representative, who acted as an interface between manufacturing and the salesman or client.

Each salesperson at Twill (over 100 in all) had a corresponding representative in the order department. The order department people served as the vital link between sales and production, and helped to maintain the excellent relations between these two departments. This was a significant accomplishment since the processing of a job was very complex.

When a new product order was received, it passed through some or all of the order, graphics, art, typesetting, scheduling, plant and shipping departments. There was no set pattern within these departments because of the iterative steps required to process each order. The graphics people, for example, could theoretically handle one order dozens of times.

Each department at this level of the organization had its own hierarchy. The order and art departments reported to the sales vice-president, while graphics, typesetting, and scheduling reported to the production vice-president. Budget authority did not necessarily follow these lines: the graphics budget, for example, was set by sales, yet that manager reported to production personnel.

The complex nature of Twill's structure was also apparent in the sales organization. It was separated as two distinct entities, but in fact operated as a single salesforce. The salesforce for the packaging division was arranged geographically, while the labels and forms salesforce was arranged along product lines. In both cases, large single accounts were handled by a few national salespeople. In spite of these formal differences, each salesperson tended to be a generalist, selling all products to their individual customers.

CONTROL Budgets and standards were the way of life at Twill. In production, for example, standard objectives included waste, productivity, safety and cost. These standards were set by discussion with everyone right down to the machine operators who were paid piecework rates related to the standards. Meeting standards was both a corporate goal and an individual goal at Twill. The value system created by the Shelstads dictated that meeting standards would result in a reward and security.

In larger scope, Twill's planning and accounting system was based on 18 separate profit centres, representing individual products, product ranges, or plant/product combinations. Monthly reports were prepared that identified the contribution of each product at each profit centre. Ken Shelstad and Doug Burgess followed these monthly reports very carefully, and were quick to pick up on any problems that they observed.

But the pursuit of control at Twill went much deeper than this. Both Ken and Doug personally reviewed the monthly general ledger, in which every transaction of the company was entered and allocated to the profit centres. By combining this with the ledger overview, they could examine activities down to the level, for example, of specific orders, customers or purchases. It was a common occurrence for either Ken or Doug to question a plant manager, for example, about costs that were only slightly off standard or about a specific purchase transaction.

Ken explained the ledger reviews as a type of policing: "You can cross-check the allocations and make sure costs are being charged against the right profit centre and you can identify potential problems right at the start. Just the other day I picked off a cheque for $300 that had been issued to one of our competitors—I had to go down and ask why the hell we were doing business with them." Doug Burgess was proud of the fact that, as he put it: "We ask more questions and discover more horror stories than any other company. That is what has led to our success." Despite his claims, Burgess, at the time of the interview, had been unable to review his ledger, which was literally hundreds of pages deep, for two months. Time was a problem.

Staffing

Twill had always strived to take care of its employees through internal promotion, job security and profit sharing. Twill encouraged employees to move up through the ranks. In addition, as Doug Burgess explained: "No one has ever been laid off. Jobs have been eliminated but we've always been able to shift people around." Pay was above industry averages, and a pension plan was currently under consideration. Every six months all staff, above and including the supervisory level, received a bonus based on company profits. This system was highly reliant on the Shelstads' credibility since actual profit figures were not revealed.

In 1986, Twill had initiated a Management Assistant Program. "We've got to increase our management team," said Larry Dixon, "our recent management assistant hirees are a step in this direction." In 1987, two young men were hired to assume various roles in the organization, with the goal of assuming management (and ultimately, executive) positions within a few years. Slow development from within was essential. Twill's culture dictated that managers ask questions, be nitpickers, work long hours, and get involved in everything. Only by having moved up through the ranks could one develop the essential experience and attitudes. Initiative was the trait most often looked for in personnel, and the trait that most often led to promotions.

KEY MANAGER VIEWS

The casewriter interviewed ten key Twill employees to secure their views about the issues facing Twill. These managers were cooperative and candid in their remarks.

It is worth noting that these interviews were frequently interrupted. The diversity of roles and the informal nature of management meant that senior people were inextricably involved in the problems of the day. For example, during an interview with Larry Dixon, Ken Shelstad and Jeff Bak dropped into the office, unannounced, seeking pricing information for Denver. Three hours later, Ken interrupted a meeting with Doug Burgess, this time to discuss a firewall at one of the new plants under construction. Within 30 minutes, Ken was back for an answer to a shipping problem—no space was available for a loaded truck in the yard.

Doug Burgess

Doug Burgess had been vice-president of production since 1969. He was an extremely hard worker, a detail-man, and a man with a lot of authority.

I'm very cognizant of my authority, and sure, I like power. I really enjoy it when Ken is away. Don't misunderstand me, because I respect Ken a lot. I think he is Twill's biggest asset. He's also our biggest drawback.

I don't like detail! It's the culture of the company though. Things have to get done and I'm the one who does it. What I like is solving problems and developing people.

I usually work 8 to 8, with a little weekend work. It ends up being a 70-hour week and it's been steady like this for the last ten years. I'm definitely at my limit and I've been actively trying to cut back by delegating a fair bit. I'm tied to my desk too much right now. I get bored with the paperwork.

I see a couple of things occurring within ten years. Personally, I believe that I'll be managing more generalities, rather than specifics. We must manage towards growth. This may require us to also move towards general managers, with much more sales involvement. I realize that our strength has been in production but there has been a shift in recent years towards sales.

Twill has had difficulties with general managers. A real general manager wants autonomy and we haven't provided it. At Excelon, our Canadian poster plant, we tried a general manager and he delegated too much. He basically abdicated his office. I fired him. The new guy starts next week—with much less authority. In our plastic container start-ups, one guy was given a general manager title but he never grabbed all the reins. He still has the title but he certainly doesn't run the area.

It's been difficult to change things because the people have been here for too long. We were here when you could check on everything. Now we can't. Another justification for our structure is our results. Both our space utilization and inventory turnover are excellent. We're making money in areas other companies are not.

I acknowledge that we've done little to develop managers here but we're now at a junction in our history where something has to be done. I believe we'll have to develop from within. Jeff Bak is an exception because he's such a nitpicker that he fit right into the Twill culture.

Larry Dixon

Larry Dixon was vice-president of sales and marketing, and nominally had profit and loss responsibilities for 17 (of 18) profit centres. He worked 60-hour weeks, with the majority of his time spent in meetings. When he started at Twill in 1959, he worked 80- to 90-hour weeks.

I enjoy what I'm doing so I don't mind the long hours. I get my kicks from the diversity—of the job and the organization. The success of the company has also been an incentive. Many people work hard and don't get the rewards. To use a cliché, at Twill we've seen our hard work bear fruit.

In the early sixties I was general manager of business forms but over the years I've grown from a generalist to a specialist. We all have. Twenty years ago the four of us did everything. We can't anymore. The day-to-day work is diminishing because it has to diminish. Likewise, we've got to increase our management team. The recent management assistant hirees are an admission of this.

Managing is getting things done through people. We're getting more people to get more done. Perhaps general managers will be that way in the future, but we have not been successful with this concept. The main reason is that we're all "hands-on" managers and we can't let go. After thirty years of experience, I've seen situations that allow me to understand things better than others. So I get involved to make things happen right.

We've also discussed creating the positions of senior V.P.'s for sales and production and bringing in more V.P.'s (or some other title). I don't know what will happen. We do recognize that we must pass on authority and give people responsibilities for areas.

Each year the six of us (on the Committee) go down to a management retreat in Florida for four days in September. This year we are each assuming another's role and providing recommendations to achieve given goals. I want to do a bang-up job on my production role, so I'm putting in 40 hours on the task. I'm sure the others will do the same. Sure it's a challenge but it's supposed to give each of us a better base of knowledge at Twill.

Jeff Bak

Jeff Bak, the vice-president of finance, was responsible for all accounting functions including payables, cost accounting, payroll, and credit.

I've only been here for four and a half years. I guess that makes me the new kid on the block. I've had to adjust somewhat to fit in with these guys but it hasn't been difficult.

My role here is mainly administrative. The finance title is really a misnomer. When I arrived here the payables were screwed up so I spent half my time fixing them. Last year, half my time was spent in Denver. I still spend one day a week there. Ken thought this was too much time away but it had to be done. We had purchased this plant and the operations were not in good shape. Doug Burgess was already on another plant project so I was given this one.

I like getting responsibilities for these projects. I get a kick out of finding something that's not right, making it right, and then backing off. Denver is a prime example. It's at a point now where production is all set—all we need are sales. I'm a hired hand here. They gave me Denver, so I turned it around.

Another role of mine at Twill is to sit on the management committee. Ken and John are very good at getting the opinions of other people, so that is the ultimate purpose of the meetings. They end up deciding things, because we can't have decision by committee. After all, it is their company!

John and Ken have proven they are knowledgeable businessmen. Twill has been successful and I don't foresee any problems with the new plastic container expansion. This is what keeps things exciting around here—growth. I don't want to get bored and as long as we keep growing I won't get bored.

As for general managers, well, it seems that all of our attempts with them have been mistakes. I don't foresee a change in our organizational structure for just that reason. I also believe that a reorganization is generally done to wake people up. We don't need to be woken up at Twill.

Tim O'Dowda

Tim O'Dowda, the packaging sales manager, has been with Twill for 16 years. He oversees the sales of packaging products, one of Twill's core product lines, representing one-half of the company's annual sales. Eighty percent of his time is spent in his office, and seven sales managers report directly to him.

Twill has always been a strong manufacturing company. It's been dominated by four individuals for 20 years—John and Ken Shelstad, Larry Dixon and Doug Burgess. I think the major strength of this company is the dominance of these four individuals. I also think it's our major weakness.

Inside the management committee, Ken and Doug are the two major players and they haven't got a sales bone in their bodies! Ken is the autocratic king at Twill in my opinion, but he's on overload now. He's the best internal auditor I've ever seen. He's always reading. It's amazing, I thought he was at his limit ten years ago but he keeps on going. He really isn't a good delegator, either of tasks or authority. If someone makes a decision he'll end up questioning it.

Doug Burgess. I've never met anyone who works harder than Doug. His detail is incredible. He's on overload too. He's got no social life. He's also a real taskmaster—I sure wouldn't want to work for him. This has led to quite a turnover in production. In sales, I've lost one person in ten years, so I know that they don't have the depth of quality that we have.

Twill is unique because of the domination of these two men. They're always involved in new plants and construction. Ken really gets his jollies there. They get involved in all the materials purchasing—and I mean all. They are tough buyers. I couldn't sell to them.

We've had growing pains. An example right now is a salary problem we're having with our sales-force. Hay Associates have been in here to try and fix things up. Some of the salespeople are pulling in a lot more than their managers. One 24-year-old made $48 000 last year. That's obscene and he knows it. This is one control system that I've got to get a hold on.

One thing we've done in the last year is install Crosby's QYS culture at Twill. The management committee took Crosby's three-day course in Florida. Doug Burgess actually took it first and got hooked. If someone else had brought it back, say, Larry, I'm sure it wouldn't have caught on. Anyways, it's certainly helped. Errors in the sales department alone have been reduced 75%. We're at the "confrontation stage" as Crosby describes it. We're policing everybody and some people don't like it. This will only last another three months though.

Twill has to expand. There are too many opportunities out there. I want to double my sales force. I also believe that we'll have to go divisional and "general-managerized" within ten years. But we're too people-poor now. There's also a low level of trust. General managers have only stepped on the toes of the vice-presidents, especially Doug's and Larry's, so it's been difficult to change the organizational chart. I started in production and I would love the opportunity to be general manager of packaging and oversee everything in that area. We'll see. I think that Ken's kids are going to end up running the company eventually so they'll probably be the ones forced to change the structure around here.

Bruce Roberts

In 1987, Twill began a new hiring program to enhance their managerial staff. The new so-called management assistants were to complete a rotation with each member of the management committee during their first two years with Twill. Bruce Roberts, 27, was the first of two assistants hired.

I remember going through the interview process last year. There I was, sitting in this boardroom with eight guys that run Twill. That's the way things work around here. Everyone seems to get involved in everything. "Hands-on" is a very appropriate term here, especially when applied to Ken and Doug.

We were hired with the impression that John and Ken Shelstad were looking for people to step into the upper management at Twill within ten years. They're not going to last forever and they're trying to develop people that can assume their roles. Seeing firsthand how hard these guys work makes me question whether that's where I want to end up.

It has been quite a learning experience thus far. At times it gets frustrating though. I'm currently trying to solve a problem we have with our branch dealers. Twill bought them years ago and they represent about $20 million in annual sales. But they are losing money, very little, mind you, but at Twill any loss is a shock. I've been on this now for six months but my project boss, Tim O'Dowda, had been on it for two years. I can't find a solution. It's really a no-win proposition. I've suggested two alternatives, sell or franchise, and boy, was I shot down by Ken! "No way," he said, "find an answer that I want to hear." Ever since he's been checking on me weekly. He's interested but he's really provided no help.

CROSSROADS

Ken Shelstad was quite aware of the pressures and cross-currents in Twill. In fact, some flipcharts in his office summarized his position. One sheet identified the "Corporate Success Factors" as: (1) low-cost production; (2) maintaining account relationships; and (3) broad service. However, in small print at the bottom of the sheet, the following words jumped out: "Get competent people at all levels."

A second sheet, entitled "Power Thinking," provided a laundry list of the major personal concerns facing Ken Shelstad. These included questions about himself, his brother, his family, and the business. These sheets had been on Shelstad's wall for over a year, and he acknowledged their importance. He, and the others, had to give considerable thought to all of these issues. Management could tire, and they would find themselves short of suitable replacements. People could limit the growth. And an economic downturn could severely impact the performance of both the new and existing products. Ken Shelstad and Twill faced an interesting future.

"I know what you are thinking," said Shelstad, smiling again, "I've had smart guys tell me to change our management structure before. And in general I agree—we must free up our time. Why, general managers would allow this simply by taking the phone calls we currently get! But it's not that simple. Our plant and distribution setup makes the general management concept difficult. We have a tough time finding good people—the general management pool is small, and most of the prospects don't even know how to spell profit. And we are smarter than they will ever be. I do have an answer though, when people get pushy. I say, 'Look, let's compare tax returns.'"

EXHIBIT 1 Twill's Simplified Organization Chart

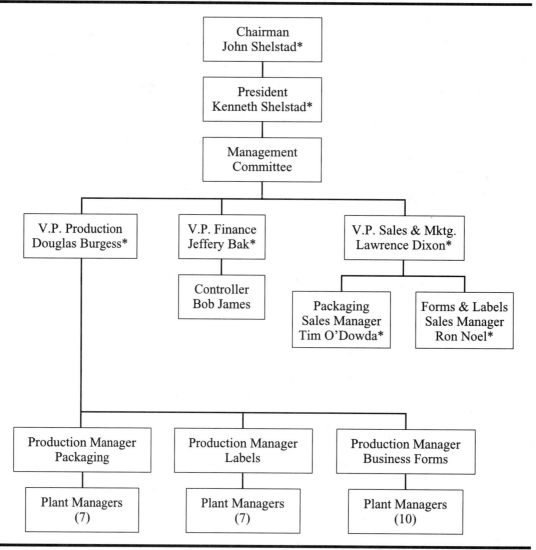

* Member, Management Committee.

LEO ELECTRON MICROSCOPY LTD. A ZEISS-LEICA COOPERATION

J. Peter Killing

In the spring of 1996, the leadership team of LEO, a 50-50 joint venture owned by Leica AG of Switzerland and Carl Zeiss of Germany, was discussing the proposed production site of the LEO P1, the high end scanning electron microscope (SEM) they were developing. The P1 would be the first product developed by the LEO research and development group, and it would combine the electronics know-how of the former Carl Zeiss technologists with the software expertise of the Cambridge-based scientists who had formerly worked for Leica.

The original plan had been to produce all SEMs, including the P1, in Cambridge, but several developments had led the management team to reconsider. Jan Ludwig, the head of LEO's German operations, and a former employee of Carl Zeiss, explained:

> The assembly and test of electron microscopes is not something that you can just hire someone off the street to do. Our workers in Oberkochen have what we refer to as "golden hands." It takes years

to learn the skills. If we were to assemble the P1 in England, we would have to add unskilled workers to the Cambridge workforce and train them. In Germany, we have the capacity. We should do this work in Germany.

Dick Manley, who was in charge of Human Resources for LEO on an interim basis (until a German-speaking HR manager could be hired) added:

> Morale in our Oberkochen plant is not high. It might be the result of cross cultural issues and communication problems, but it could be just plain insecurity about the future. If we assemble the P1 here in Cambridge, we will probably have to lay off German workers, which would only make matters worse. On the other hand, giving the work to them will be a clear vote of confidence, a real morale booster.

JOINT VENTURE BACKGROUND

The Market

After continuous growth between 1970 and 1989, the world market for electron microscopes declined between 1989 and 1994, dropping by about 20% in unit volume. By 1994, the market appeared to have stabilized at about $145 million and 320 units per year for Transmission Electron Microscopes (TEMs) and $300 million and 1650 units for SEMs[1]. However, approximately 45% of the SEM market consisted of microscopes used in the manufacture of semiconductors, an application demanding extremely sophisticated equipment that neither Carl Zeiss nor Leica manufactured. Both SEM and TEM markets were dominated by the Japanese companies Hitachi and Japan Electron Optical Ltd (JEOL).

Leica and Carl Zeiss, who had a combined market share of approximately 14% of the SEM market and 11% of the TEM market, were not achieving satisfactory financial results. Carl Zeiss had reportedly been losing money in its electron microscope business for many years, and Leica was earning a small amount, primarily because of its after sales service activities.

Further market information is provided in Exhibit 1.

The Rationale

The impetus for the creation of the LEO joint venture had come from Dr. Peter Grassmann, a Siemens executive who had been brought in to turn around the faltering Zeiss organization in late 1994. Originally formed by Carl Zeiss in 1846 in Jena (later part of East Germany), the Carl Zeiss organization (a German trust) comprised approximately 15 800 employees in the mid-1990s. Plans to reduce this number to 12 000 had led to worker demonstrations on the Oberkochen site immediately prior to Peter Grassmann's arrival. Grassmann's publicly declared objective was to create a "more professional, cost-aware, performance-oriented and customer-oriented company." At the time of LEO's formation, Dr. Grassmann commented that it would be at least two years before the joint venture was operating at a profit.

Eugen Wild, a former Carl Zeiss manager, now LEO's vice president of marketing, commented on the decision to form LEO:

> It was difficult for us in Zeiss to accept the need to create LEO, as we have some truly unique technology—in fact technology which Leica unsuccessfully tried to duplicate. But if the alternatives were to sell the business or shut it down, then a joint venture looked okay.
>
> It was my idea that we consider Leica as a partner. They were small enough that they would not dominate us. It was vital that the venture be 50-50 in its management as well as its ownership. We would never have achieved that with someone like Philips as a partner.

---

[1] SEMs were used for examining the surface of the specimen under study, whereas TEMs were used to look inside the specimen.

Leica's electron microscope business was based in Cambridge, England, and had originally been part of Cambridge Instruments, a company that had been merged with Wild Leitz of Switzerland in 1990 to form Leica. Markus Rauh, the CEO of Leica, was interested in Grassmann's proposal to improve the performance of both company's electron microscope businesses by forming a joint venture, although his preference would have been to create a venture in which Leica had a share greater than 50%.

The new company was expected to begin life with annual revenues of more than DM100 million, and its products would be sold exclusively under the LEO name. Approximately 35% of revenues would come from Germany, 30% from North America, 15% from France, between 5 and 10% from Asia Pacific and less than 5% from the U.K.

The original venture plan called for a manager from neither parent to be hired as Chief Executive Officer. However, as he saw the plans taking shape, Karl Kalbag, a British citizen who had worked for Cambridge Instruments prior to the 1990 merger and was now the Chief Financial Officer of Leica in Switzerland. liked what he saw. He commented:

> From the outset, I thought that the venture was a good idea. At one point, one of the Zeiss managers said, "why not you as CEO?" Why not? I thought it over and discussed it with Markus Rauh—he was reluctant to lose me, but he said that he could see it in my eyes. And I could feel it in my heart. This was what I wanted to do! I later met with Peter Grassmann and he said that he was comfortable, and we went from there.

In May 1995, Karl prepared a set of financial projections for the new company which indicated that he expected to grow the company's sales volume by about 20% over a three year period, primarily through increasing the average price per unit sold. In addition, he expected to improve the bottom line by reducing costs—particularly in research and development and sales and marketing. Karl also presented his personal view of how the venture should be managed.

1. There would be one single management team—no "castles" or "forts".
2. There would be a business process orientation. There would be no functions, only activities, and each activity would be included only if its value added to the business exceeded its cost.
3. There would be three key processes between customer and shareholder: Value management, innovation and strategy. Karl's "ideal" organization chart is shown in Exhibit 2.
4. Ideally, all senior management would be based in Cambridge.

The board of directors would contain an equal number of directors from each parent, with Peter Grassmann as Chairman for the first two years. It was also established that neither parent could sell their shares for the venture for at least two years. Karl's contract was for three years, but he could be replaced after two years if it was judged that his actions in the job were biased toward Leica.

The New Company

LEO was formed on October 2, 1995 with 350 employees. Forty were in R&D, 120 were in the assembly and test area, 80 were service engineers, 33 were in sales, and 25 in logistics. No employee had an automatic right to return to his or her parent company, but in the words of Karl Kalbag, "no one would be fired for economic reasons, only for poor performance". The official language of the company was English. The company was given enough initial funding (the initial share capital was reported to be £5 million) that it was not expected to have to return to its parents for further funds, and it was agreed that Karl was to operate the company as he saw fit.

LEO's organization chart is shown in Exhibit 3. This chart reflected Karl's belief that processes, not functions, were key. He wanted to do away with the usual hierarchical organization and build a company based on horizontal team work. Dick Manley commented:

Karl has a strongly held view that participative management is the key to success. In Cambridge, this philosophy fits very well, because this is an organization full of very competent, technically oriented people who are used to working across functions. You might say that Karl is preaching to the converted. However, in Oberkochen hierarchy is an established way of life—and to add new management philosophies to the turmoil that our people there are already going through...well I don't think that they really understand what Karl is on about.

Prior to the creation of LEO, both parent companies manufactured many of the components needed to make electron microscopes, as well as performing the final assembly and test of the finished products. When LEO was created, the component manufacturing activities were retained by the parent companies. As a result, LEO sourced components from parents (approximately 70% of the cost of goods sold was brought in from the outside—most of it from the parents), and less than 10% of LEO's total costs were its own direct assembly and test labour.

One of the advantages of forming LEO, according to Karl Kalbag, was the degree of focus that it put on the electron microscope business, not least in the areas of sales and marketing. Prior to the creation of LEO in the United States, for example, the salesforce of each company had sold a portfolio of products, including both optical and electron microscopes. Most sales people were instinctively more comfortable with one product than the other, however, and many preferred to focus on optical microscopes as the sales cycle was not as lengthy, which meant that commission cheques were more frequent. With the creation of the joint venture, LEO was able to build a focused sales force of people highly interested in electron microscopes, and used to the long sales cycle.

LEO sold its products throughout the world via 50 dealers, who were serviced by the 80 sales engineers referred to earlier. These people also had "golden hands" and were frequently called on to disassemble and reassemble operating units in the field. In any given period, one quarter to one third of LEO's revenues came from service work.

INTEGRATION

One of Karl's early priorities was to meld the two organizations into one smoothly functioning unit. He wanted to establish strong horizontal links that cut across geographical boundaries. However, his objective of locating the senior management team in Cambridge was proving difficult, as Eugen Wild explained:

It might be more efficient if Jan and I were located in Cambridge, but it is very important to our workforce in Germany that we are located there. Many foreign companies have made acquisitions in Germany and then closed plants. We want to make sure that it does not happen to us. Our Oberkochen workforce already feels somewhat abandoned by the Carl Zeiss "family"—we cannot abandon them further by moving to England. I know that Jan feels the same.

The area in which British-German coordination was most advanced was Research and Development. There were approximately 20 researchers in Oberkochen and 20 in Cambridge. Henry Watts, LEO's Cambridge-based Vice President of R&D, commented:

There has not been a week go by that we have not had German research people here or Cambridge people in Oberkochen. Their strength is electronics, ours is software development. It's a good match. The English language skills of the German research people are excellent.

The biggest challenge that we face is in the TEM business, which in Europe is dominated by Philips. When we started LEO, we had five TEM products, all produced in Oberkochen. We have discontinued two old machines, and a third is not competitive. We have no new TEM products in the pipeline.

Four of my people in Germany are not doing very much—and cannot do very much—until we decide how to move forward in the TEM business. We have to make up our minds quickly, because in this business the performance of the equipment keeps going up, while prices come down. You cannot stand still. But we do not know enough about what is going on in the TEM market.

On the subject of the TEM business, Karl Kalbag added:

> One of the major reasons for Leica to enter this joint venture was to get into the TEM business. It is the high end part of the microscopy business, and we can see that eventually the semi-conductor manufacturers might move to TEMs. Carl Zeiss has some unique technology in this area.

Close coordination in the assembly and test areas was proving more difficult to achieve. The assembly and test employees in Germany did not speak English, and Nick Brady, LEO's Cambridge-based vice president of manufacturing, had a difficult time impacting the work practices in the Oberkochen plant. He explained:

> Costs in both plants are too high—but the problem is particularly acute in Germany, where cost levels are 60% above those in the U.K. In the U.K. we have created six measures [refer to Exhibit 4] which we are tracking as a way to improve our performance. I have translated these into German and been trying for months to get Oberkochen to adopt them. But they will not. There is always some excuse or other. I travel there once or twice a month for two or three days, but it is very frustrating as I have to do everything through an interpreter (the local financial manager).
>
> When I ask questions from Cambridge, I get the clear impression that there is a discussion up and down the German hierarchy before they decide what answer to give me. I am starting to give up. It makes more sense to expend my energy here in Cambridge, where I can make a difference. No one in Germany is listening.

Jan Ludwig was LEO's vice president for business process re-engineering and responsible for the German plant. He commented:

> We face a totally different set of issues in Germany than they do in England. In Cambridge, the microscope business was already a separate business unit, but in Germany we were an integrated part of a much larger operation, which means that we have to disentangle ourselves from the Carl Zeiss organization. We are moving into our own building, which will help. We need to set up our own systems, get our own Human Resource manager, and so on. At the moment, our information is buried in the Zeiss system and it's hard to get anything usable. We are not ready to give Nick the kind of measures that he wants. My priorities are to get the Zeiss organization to start treating us like a customer, and to build our people in Oberkochen into a team. There are 127 of us, and everyone is feeling a little insecure.
>
> Karl and I disagree about the horizontal process-based organization he wants to create. I agree that integrating R&D and sales and marketing makes sense—which means having one boss in each area—but in assembly and test, we should build a centre of competence in TEM in Germany, and SEM in Cambridge. I will manage the German operation and have responsibility for the whole TEM business, which needs a lot of attention. It makes no sense to have Nick try and be responsible for German assembly and test from Cambridge. We can't build teams of German and British workers when they don't speak the same language. But we can build a strong team here in Oberkochen.

David Gates, the Vice President of Dealer Support, completely supported Nick Brady's assessment that LEO's costs were too high. David commented:

> Three years ago, Philips went through a major cost reduction exercise, and they now have supply sources in the Czech Republic which give them very low costs. As a result, they are pricing low when they have to, and they are growing, particularly in the TEM business. In our first three months of operation, we did not get a single order in France, because Philips underpriced us in every case. There is no doubt that they are trying to put us out of the TEM business. However, they seem to have realized that we are here to stay, as we recently did win a couple of orders in France.

Although 85% of our sales force is located in our traditional markets of Europe and USA, there is no growth there. The market of the future is Asia Pacific, but we are weak there. Our company-owned dealers, for example, are in Europe and the United States.

THE WAY FORWARD

LEO's leadership team offered a variety of views on the best way for the young company to move forward.

Jan Ludwig:

> If we decide to give the P1 project to Oberkochen, we will have made a great step forward in the building of this company. With this decision behind us, we can turn our attention to the opportunities in the TEM business.

Henry Watts:

> The P1 project is important, because it is creating momentum and energy in the company, and will show our competitors that we are alive. But the product is not going to earn us a lot of money, because it is going to be expensive to produce. The German researchers are designing us a gold-plated product. They just do not have much concept of cost and its relation to price. If I insisted that they get the cost out, however, it would take another year to develop. As it is, I have a British team developing a less expensive version of the product that will appear at a later date as a different model. The German team is well aware of this.

Eugen Wild:

> I have the responsibility for sorting out what we do about the TEM business. We need to collect all our sales prospects and sort them out, develop a strategy for this product line, and possibly improve our dealers in this area. Henry also has to develop us a new product.
>
> In general, I would say that we are being too conservative. We have to grow to survive. Let's compete with Philips on price when we have to; we need to generate cash, not percentage gross margins. The good news about Karl is that he has clearly demonstrated that he is no slave to Leica's interests; he clearly cares about LEO first and foremost. Also, he is soon going to start taking German lessons. The bad news is that he wants to produce good financial results too soon, and he controls pricing too closely. Let's spend on R&D so that we can develop high-end microscopes for the semiconductor fabrication business. The P1 will not do this for us. Sure it's a risk, but that's where the growth is.

Karl Kalbag:

> We recently had a series of meetings to think through our strategy. One question was "what do we want to be best at?" We discussed innovation, cost leadership and customer intimacy. We decided that we would be the best company in our business in the area of customer intimacy. This makes a lot of sense for us, as about 180 of our 350 employees talk to customers on a daily basis. At that same meeting, we identified 12 internal constraints to success. The top three were cost, communication and lack of market knowledge. We set up three teams to work on these issues.
>
> Jan and I disagree about how the company should be run. He wants his own operation in Germany, but that will not happen. To him, geography and nationality are very important. I want to get rid of them.
>
> Financially, my focus is on managing cash. We are doing fine; in fact, we are ahead of budget, even though our first year losses are going to be slightly greater than planned. We are on track.

Excerpts from Karl's diary in early 1996 are represented in Exhibit 5.

EXHIBIT 1A   Electron Microscopy—Market Share 1995

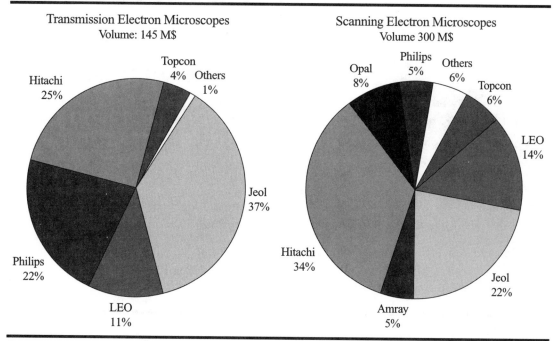

Transmission Electron Microscopes
Volume: 145 M$

Scanning Electron Microscopes
Volume 300 M$

Source: Frost & Sullivan, Dataquest, Info Science.

EXHIBIT 1B   Electron Microscopy—Market Segmentation 1995

Transmission Electron Microscopes
Volume: 145 M$

Life Sciences: 54%   Materials Science: 46%

Scanning Electron Microscopes
Volume 300 M$

Materials Science: 42%   Semiconductors: 45%

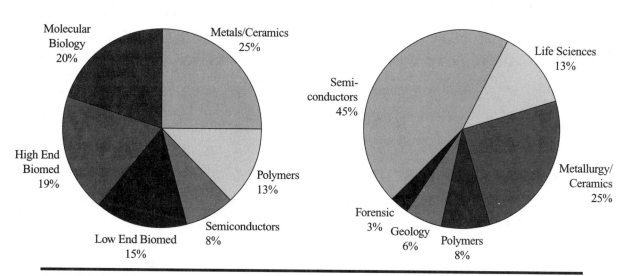

Source: Dataquest, Various.

EXHIBIT 1C   **Electron Microscopy—Regional Market Segments 1995**

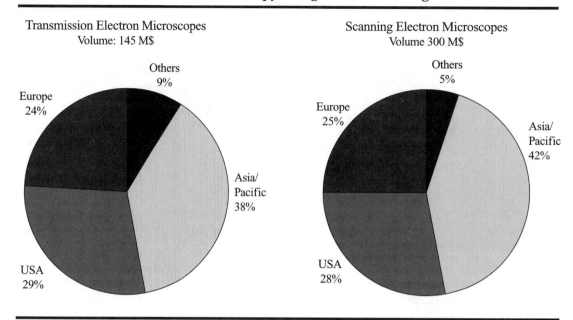

Transmission Electron Microscopes
Volume: 145 M$

Others
9%

Europe
24%

Asia/
Pacific
38%

USA
29%

Scanning Electron Microscopes
Volume 300 M$

Others
5%

Europe
25%

Asia/
Pacific
42%

USA
28%

Source: Info Science, Frost & Sullivan.

EXHIBIT 2   LEO Electron Microscopy Ltd. "Ideal" Organization Chart

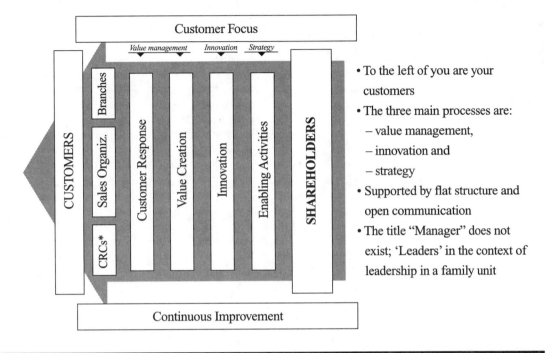

- To the left of you are your customers
- The three main processes are:
  - value management,
  - innovation and
  - strategy
- Supported by flat structure and open communication
- The title "Manager" does not exist; 'Leaders' in the context of leadership in a family unit

*CRCs = Customer Response Centres.

EXHIBIT 3 **LEO Organization Chart**

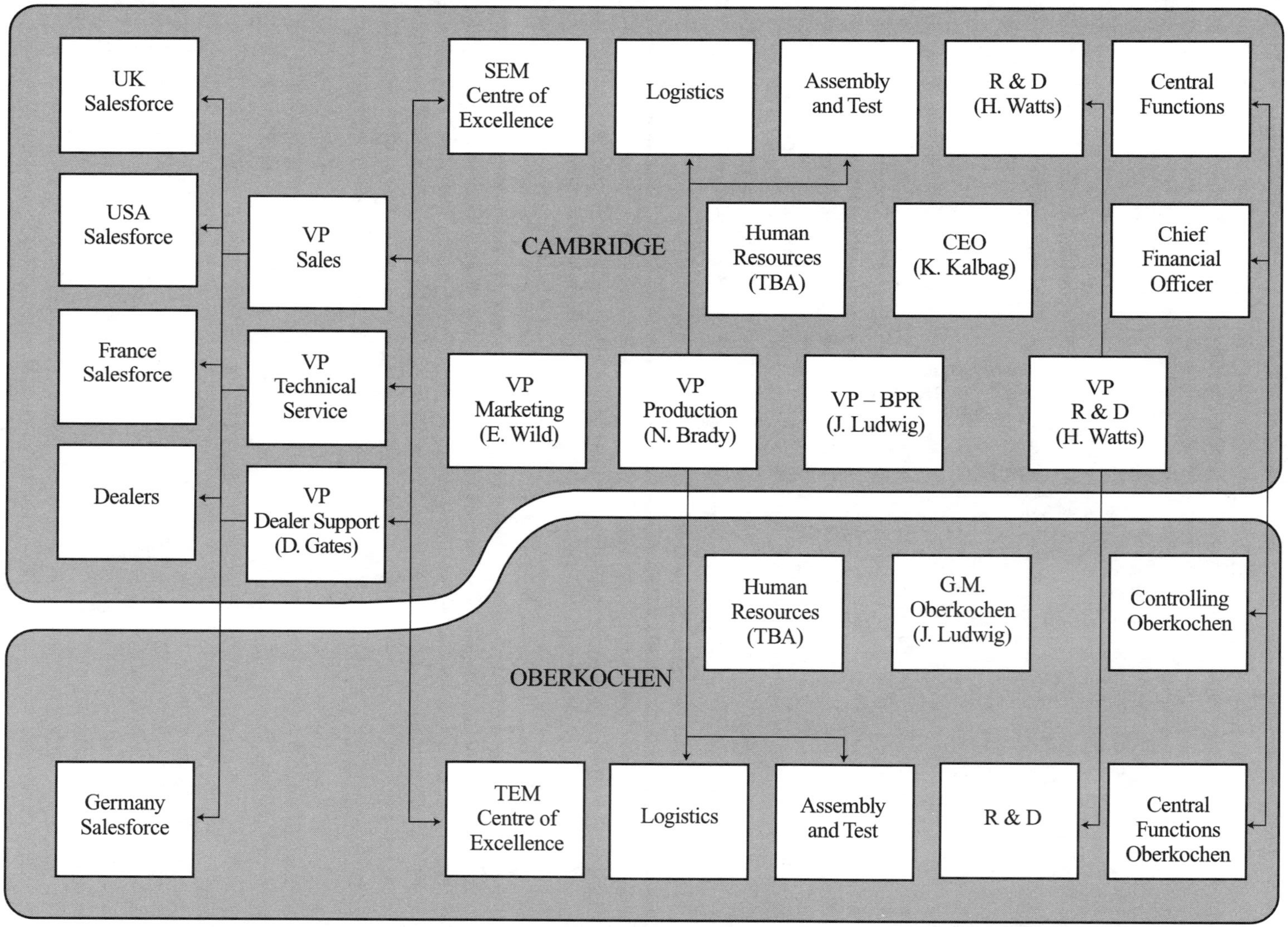

EXHIBIT 4 Leo Manufacturing Measures

The following were agreed in Oberkochen on the 27 September 1995. Initially there are six; however, these will be added to during October 1995.

Manufacturing Measures

M1. CUSTOMER DELIVER PERFORMANCE (CDP)

Measures the percentage of orders delivered on or before the customers order acknowledgment delivery date, by line item. Target is 99% clean installations.

M2. CUSTOMER CLEAN INSTALLATION (CCI)

Measures the percentage of customer orders installed first time without problems. Target is 99% on-time delivery.

Logistics Measures

L1. ORDER RECEIPT TO ACKNOWLEDGMENT PERFORMANCE (ORAP)

Measures the elapsed time between receipt and acknowledgment of a customer order. Target is 99% of orders acknowledged in less than 72 hours.

L.2. LINE ITEM SHORTAGES AT KITTING (LISK)

Measures the percentage of line items short in all kits at the point of kitting. Target is 99% of all kits are clean (i.e., 99% of all kits have no shortages).

Assembly & Test Measures

A1. PRODUCTION PROCESS DEVIATIONS (PPD)

Measures the deviations (variances from standard time in the areas of job cost, scrap, rework, modifications and loss). Target is zero deviations (variances).

A2. VALUE CREATION LEAD-TIME PERFORMANCE (VCLP)

Measures the Assembly and Test lead-time by customer order from commencement of build to delivery. Target is to establish current lead-times by product and reduce by 25% in first year.

Nick Brady
4 October 1995

EXHIBIT 5 Annotated Excerpts from Karl Kalbag's Diary

Week of January 8 1996

Tuesday and Wednesday—First ever review meetings. These will be monthly in Cambridge. One with sales people, one with manufacturing people, one with R&D[2]. These turned out to be training sessions (by me) for the managers involved on how to set objectives for such meetings, how to set up the agenda, and so on.

Wednesday—meeting with Japanese dealers with respect to three pending sales in Japan on which price expectations varied greatly between us and them. I explained that there would be no special deals—we would not reduce our margin, regardless of the expectations of their major customers.

Thursday and Friday—TEM Product Strategy Meeting. This meeting of 28 people from all parts of the LEO world (who were in Cambridge for the Management Development weekend) was run by Henry Watt. It was a no-holds-barred brainstorming session at which we focused on development priorities for the TEM business. We came out with three main conclusions. We should consider the development of a low end TEM machine, to be manufactured in Eastern Europe. We need to find a way to focus more attention on TEM sales. These machines are expensive, and the customers' decision-making period may be two or three years. Salesmen, thinking of immediate commissions, are likely to focus on SEMs, which are easier to sell. We should develop an all-new TEM product.

Friday noon to Sunday noon—Management Development Weekend. There will be a weekend like this every seven months or so, with a group of approximately 35 LEO people from all over the world. This one focused on marketing, as we need to develop our marketing strengths. We brought in outside lecturers to talk to us about pricing, the development of marketing strategies, and so on.
It was as result of this weekend that we decided to focus on customer intimacy.

Week of January 15

Monday—Meeting of our people in charge of dealer relations who were here for the management development weekend. Brought in dealer from Italy who is highly successful, asked him to explain to all of us how he runs his business so well. This was extremely valuable.
Friday—Off-site confidential lunch—potential strategic alliance.

Week of January 22

Monday—Travel to Germany—seal the three Japanese deals (referred to earlier) with Japanese representative who was visiting Oberkochen.
Tuesday—Meet with South American dealer (in Germany) to sort out difficulties between local dealers in that region.
Wednesday—Brief the Oberkochen personnel (perhaps 100 people) on recent events. Doing this through an interpreter but must take German lessons so can do it myself. I will do these presentations monthly, and the same on the Cambridge site.

Week of January 29

Spent week in Germany, mainly listening.

---

[2] These labels were created by the casewriter. Inside the company these teams were known as "Value Creating," "Value Delivery" and Innovation.

EXHIBIT 5   (continued)

Week of February 5

In Cambridge.

Monday—Cambridge briefing meeting.

Rest of Week—Second round of management meetings with manufacturing, sales, research and development.

Week of February 12

In USA—Went to three sites: East Coast, mid-West and West Coast to meet with sales and service people. First time that many of them had met—as some were former Leica, others former Carl Zeiss. Ten or eleven people in each group. Included customers in some of these meetings to tell us what they expect from us. Extremely valuable. My major purpose was to get their buy-in to the focus on customer intimacy.

Week of February 19

In France, Germany and U.K. Reviewed business and budgets for fiscal year 1997.

THE LOEWEN GROUP

*Ariff Kachra
and Mary M. Crossan*

On September 17, 1996, Ray Loewen, Chairman and CEO of the Loewen Group, North America's second largest funeral home consolidator, was seeking approval from his Board for the purchase of the largest cemetery in the U.S., Rose Hills Memorial Park in California. As he was speaking about the $240 million [1] acquisition, one of the investment bankers at the meeting responded to a '911' on his beeper display. He returned with a news wire bulletin announcing the launch of a hostile takeover bid by SCI (Service

---

[1] All dollar values in this case are in U.S. dollars unless otherwise noted.

IVEY

Ariff Kachra prepared this case under the supervision of Professor Mary Crossan solely to provide material for class discussion. The authors do not intend to illustrate either effective or ineffective handling of a managerial situation. The authors may have disguised certain names and other identifying information to protect confidentiality.

Corporation International), the world's largest funeral consolidator. What began as a meeting seeking approvals for acquisitions had turned into a war council. The entire Board turned to Mr. Loewen for his reaction. Should Loewen Group fight the takeover, or should it accept SCI's offer? (See Exhibit 1 for a copy of the letter sent by William Heiligbrodt to Ray Loewen, outlining the parameters of the proposed bid.)

THE FUNERAL SERVICE INDUSTRY

Typically, when a person passed away and had not made provisions for a pre-planned funeral, the process began with a phone call to book a meeting with the funeral director at a home. The funeral director used this meeting to grasp initial perceptions and thoughts of the bereaved family. The family had many choices including anything from a simple disposition to a traditional, full visitation service. With the help of the funeral director, the family made decisions on the elements of the funeral service, such as embalming, visitation, music, chapel, etc. As required by law, the funeral director reviewed the fee schedule with the family. The family then purchased merchandise such as caskets and urns. The family was then referred to a local cemetery, where they purchased a burial plot and any other related merchandise like vaults, markers, and headstones. After obtaining the family's legal authorization, the funeral director proceeded with the arrangements. Typically, a few weeks after the service, the funeral home made an after-care call to determine if the family needed additional support or had any bereavement-related concerns.

The following chart maps out the industry players that made up the funeral industry's business system:

Suppliers	Funeral Homes	Combination Facilities	Cemeteries
Caskets	Traditional Funeral Service		Burial plots
Embalming	Simple Services		Cremation niches
Related Items	Cremations		Perform cremations
	Pre-need Insurance		Pre-need plots

Funeral Homes

Funeral homes did everything from selling pre-need insurance[2] to arranging a cremation, a simple burial and, more often than not, a traditional funeral service. Sources of revenue for a funeral home included professional services, facility and automotive rentals, and casket and urn sales. Expenses were made up of personnel, automotive equipment, promotion, business services, supplies, after-sale expenses and sundry items (see Exhibit 2). The funeral home was usually the customer's first point of contact. Whether the customer wanted a simple burial or a traditional funeral, the funeral home had the first opportunity to sell all related services and supplies.

Suppliers

Funeral home consolidators had consistently put a great deal of pressure on suppliers to reduce prices. This had a negative impact on the profitability of suppliers because they were very dependent on funeral homes. The potential threat to the casket producers and embalming suppliers was that as the funeral industry gave way to more and more consolidation, they would become increasingly dependent on a few large customers. With this dependence would come decreased margins and potential consolidation in the supply side of the industry.

---

[2] The consumer who wished to pre-plan and pre-pay for his/her funeral purchased pre-need insurance.

Cemeteries

The sources of revenue for cemeteries included the sales of at-need[3] and pre-need burial plots, cremation niches,[4] burial stones and plaques and professional services related to cremation and burial. Expenses consisted of personnel, maintenance of facilities, and sales and promotion (see Exhibit 3). Historically in Canada and the U.S., the vast majority of cemeteries had been privately owned. At the beginning of 1996, in Canada alone, there were over 10 000 private cemeteries. There were two key benefits of purchasing a cemetery. The first was that cemeteries offered a secure revenue stream for about 30 to 50 years. This revenue stream slowly began increasing as cemeteries concentrated on merchandising. The second was that cemeteries accrued pre-need revenues upon receipt, and used the money for investment purposes. This was a legal use of the funds, as long as 10 to 15 per cent of the revenues were invested in a perpetual care fund.[5] This represented a marked advantage over funeral homes, whose pre-need sales revenues had to be placed in trust until the time when the beneficiary passed away.

Combination Facilities

A recent development in the industry was the concept of combination facilities. Combination facilities afforded consumers the very attractive option of one-stop shopping, i.e., both the funeral home and the cemetery were located in one facility. The growth opportunities were vast in terms of combinations because industry statistics indicated that: "within six to eight years of opening, the average funeral home operating within a cemetery should perform the number of funerals approximately equivalent to 80 per cent of the number of interments at that cemetery." (*The Death Care Industry*, July 16, 1996, Darren Martin, TD Securities Inc.)

IMPORTANT INDUSTRY TRENDS

Consolidation

The North American funeral industry was very large and fragmented (see Exhibit 4 for industry structure). This made it ripe for consolidation. Consolidators felt that there were many opportunities for growth and profitability. With an increasing death rate (see Exhibit 7) and more funeral homes being typically family-run businesses, there was great potential for increased revenue generation and cost cutting.

One industry characteristic that directly affected consolidation was the succession crisis. Independent funeral homes needed to deal with the issue of succession, since the average age of a funeral home owner was older than 50. Most independently owned funeral homes were family businesses. As with many family businesses, there was often no one who was interested in taking on the succession responsibility. Generally, only 30 per cent of family businesses made it to the second generation, and 10 per cent to the third generation.

Consolidators were typically the only buyers who had access to enough capital to make a market price offer to purchase a funeral home. Obtaining a fair price was crucial to funeral home owners because the equity in their business was often their only form of savings.

---

[3] Sales of at need burial plots referred to sales that occurred when someone had died.

[4] When a body was cremated, the remains were usually stored in an urn. If the family chose not to scatter the ashes, the urn could be placed in the family home, buried in a cemetery or stored in a cremation niche. Usually cremation niches were structures in cemeteries that allowed families to store the cremation remains of loved ones. Niches afforded family members an alternative to burying cremation remains while retaining the benefit of having a place where they could visit and remember the departed.

[5] A perpetual care fund was a perpetual annuity that ensured that cemeteries would always have funds for up-keep of the cemetery.

With issues like a succession crisis, and an increasing death rate, it would seem that there would be a number of new funeral facilities in the market. This was not the case because there were many barriers to entry associated with establishing new facilities. These included elements such as high fixed costs, lack of history in the local community, zoning regulations, and "not-in-my-backyard" protests.

Increasing Consumer Price Sensitivity

There were indications in the market that consumers were looking for lower priced products and services. In response to this demand, there was an increase in "no frills" funeral homes. "No frills" referred to companies who specialized in simple funerals, grave-side services, limited or no visitation and frequently no embalming. Another reaction to the demand for lower priced products and services, was the casket shop. Most major cities had casket shops that exclusively sold caskets at prices much lower than those offered by the funeral home. These shops, although in their infancy, had the potential of decreasing casket sales revenues for funeral homes.

Pre-Need Funerals

Pre-need planning was gaining in popularity with consumers. This was because it afforded individuals peace of mind that, upon their death, their loved ones would not be faced with the often-difficult task of making funeral arrangements. In addition to emotional security, pre-need planning also offered financial security. It allowed individuals to determine which types of products and services they were willing to pay for when it came time for them to pass on. It also allowed them to lock into present-day prices.

Pre-need plans were usually financed through trust funds or the purchase of pre-need insurance. Money placed in trust was usually invested in bonds, stocks and other investments; these decisions were very strongly regulated. Money placed in insurance was typically placed with a third-party insurance provider who guaranteed a fixed rate of return, typically 4 to 6 per cent. The very conservative approach to investing pre-need dollars did not afford the seller any real opportunities for revenue generation. In fact, with every pre-need contract sold, there was a threat that when the contract came due, on average after 10 to 12 years, the amount of money available would not cover the at-need price of the service. Despite all of these risks, consolidators were very actively selling pre-need contracts.

Cremations

According to the CANA (Cremation Association of North America), cremation rates in the year 2000 would be 35.72 per cent and in the year 2010, they would be 41.80 per cent. The increasing rate of cremations could be attributed to the increasing income and education levels, immigration rates, environmental concerns and the perception of cost savings.

There were significant differences in the way that funeral homes treated cremations relative to traditional funeral services. A traditional service involved a casket, visitation, and a burial ceremony. Traditional cremations had typically been marketed with no visitation, an extremely simple casket, and an urn (see Exhibit 5).

Combination Facilities

Cemeteries had traditionally been considered as suppliers to funeral homes. They supplied burial plots, stones, plaques, etc. With an increase in cremations and combination facilities, cemeteries were very well poised to take a larger role than that of a simple supplier. This represented a threat to the traditional funeral home on many levels. First, the cemetery culture was a sales-oriented culture, i.e., they had been actively selling pre-need plots for decades and, therefore, had access to an extensive list of sales leads, if they decided to sell full pre-need funeral services. Second, with an increase in cremations, items such as crematory niches and cremation viewing facilities (a necessary part of many cultures) represented opportunities for potentially high margins. It was plausible that with increased combination facilities, cremations could become a solely cemetery phenomena. This would steal market share away from the funeral homes and then pose a barrier to entry for new funeral homes. In addition to all of this, combination facilities were able to offer real one-stop-shopping, a definite advantage to the consumer.

Cost Control

Consolidators maintained a cost advantage over independent funeral homes because they were able to take advantage of economies of scale. By using "clustered locations", consolidators were able to significantly reduce their operational costs. Clustering involved centralizing vehicle fleets, embalming operations and corporate management, in addition to buying supplies in bulk and sharing staff.

Competitors

Consolidators in the funeral service industry could be classified by size. The first group consisted of large public companies such as Service Corporation International (SCI), The Loewen Group (Loewen) and Stewart Enterprises (Stewart), whose current equity market capitalization and public float by company exceeded $1 billion. The second group consisted of small companies such as Arbor Memorial Services, Equity Corporation International and Carriage Services, whose current equity market capitalization and public float by company did not exceed $1 billion.

SERVICE CORPORATION INTERNATIONAL

SCI, located in Houston, Texas, was the largest funeral service provider in the world with 2 795 funeral homes and 324 cemeteries. In 1996, SCI was expected to have an equity market capitalization of $6.04 billion and revenues of $2.4 billion. Establishments that it owned performed 9, 29, 14 and 24 per cent of the funeral services in North America, France, the U.K. and Australia, respectively. SCI was also active in the funeral service industries of Malaysia and Singapore. Finally, it was becoming active in the funeral industries of six European countries in addition to France and the U.K.

SCI had initiatives in response to all the major industry trends. For example:

- SCI had the second largest backlog (1.5 years) of pre-need funeral services.[6] It also consistently tried to increase its pre-need revenue base. In 1995, 22 per cent of all funerals performed by SCI were pre-arranged. This was the highest percentage in the industry.

- SCI was increasing its presence in the area of combination facilities.

- In response to the potential threat of a more price-sensitive consumer, SCI started its own chain of discount operators called Family Funeral Care.

SCI was successful at leveraging its size through its aggressive use of clustering. At SCI, clustering drove the decisions on where to locate new homes and where to purchase existing ones. SCI was so committed to the concept of clustering that it had developed maps showing death rate projections by zip code and by the company's market share in different areas. Analysts believed that clustering was one of the key drivers of SCI's profitability. Although costs were an important element of operational management,

---

[6] A backlog of 1.5 years in pre-need funeral services was interpreted as follows: If all the company's pre-need funerals came due, the company would be able to run at full capacity for 1.5 years without performing any at-need services.

sometimes equally as important, for a consolidator, was the facility with which it integrated new acquisitions. Of all of the large capital companies, SCI seemed to be the most aggressive in terms of integrating its existing acquisitions. This was clearly seen in the following comments made by Robert Waltrip, Chairman of the SCI Board of Directors:

> What many in this industry don't seem to understand or want to believe is that when we make a purchase, we have to introduce our way of doing business. You can't spend $100 million to buy a business of that size and just go on doing business the old way.[7]

SCI's approach to integration was aggressive and detail oriented. Previous owners and managers were often asked to step aside. Owners who were retained, worked solely in public relations on a part-time basis. This allowed SCI to benefit from the owners' community presence and network. SCI used a decentralized approach to manage its network of homes. SCI had recently changed its organizational structure from 8 regions to 17 regions. This was done to allow regional managers to be more in touch with their areas and to be able to make decisions in more proximity to their respective homes.

In terms of acquisitions, SCI tended to concentrate on urban homes. It prided itself on owning quality institutions. Like most industry players it retained the original names of its acquisitions to benefit from the goodwill. However, SCI claimed that goodwill was not the only factor that kept its customers coming back. Excellent service levels and quality personnel also played a key role in customer retention. SCI acquired many of its homes based on referrals from Provident. Provident was SCI's financial subsidiary. It lent money to independent funeral home operators. Provident played an important role in allowing SCI to keep its fingers on the pulse of the industry.

MR. LOEWEN AND THE LOEWEN GROUP

Ray Loewen

In 1961, Ray Loewen graduated from Briercrest Theological College before joining his father in the family funeral home in Steinbach, Manitoba. He left the family firm to purchase, along with his wife, Anne, their own funeral home in Fort Frances, Ontario, and subsequently another home in the Lower Mainland of B.C. Times were good and by 1975, Loewen owned a number of different funeral homes. He turned to politics to serve one term as the Social Credit MLA for Burnaby-Edmonds in the B.C. legislature. In 1979, he returned to his business career. More and more, the owners of funeral homes whose children were either unable or unwilling to take over the family business were searching for an answer to the question of their own succession. This represented an excellent opportunity for the Loewen Group. Loewen knew that by raising money on the stock exchange and using it to acquire these homes, while enabling local owner families to remain as active in the business as they would like, he could make Loewen Group a national presence. In 1987, fuelled by Loewen Group's first public offering, Ray Loewen acquired $24 million in funeral establishments and acquired its first U.S. property.

Mr. and Mrs. Loewen owned 15 per cent of the company's voting shares and, in his capacity as CEO and Chairman of the Board of Directors, Ray Loewen played an active role in guiding senior management. He took a real interest in the operations of the company and had a grass roots understanding of the business, given his background. This meant he was sensitive to the needs of funeral directors.

Mr. Loewen looked on his growing complement of employees as part of a family and felt they should all be able to participate in the company. This led to the introduction of "Sharing The Vision," an employee

---

[7] "Robert Waltrip Takes on His Critics," *Mortuary Management*, May 1993.

stock plan with employees receiving five free shares and being offered a stock purchase program. This reflected Mr. Loewen's vision of having a company in which every employee was a shareholder. When he described his management philosophy, he liked to use the analogy of an eagle's flight: one wing was the care-giving at the heart of funeral service, the other, fiscal responsibility. The eagle needed both wings to soar. Mr. Loewen was passionate about the Loewen Group and he counted on his management and employees for their full support.

Acquisitions Group

Since 1992, the acquisition growth rates for Loewen, SCI and Stewart had all been greater than 50 per cent (see Exhibit 6). Loewen attributed its position to four key competitive advantages. First and foremost, it had an acquisition group that was very skilled and very dedicated to identifying and closing the sale. Second, Loewen's Regional Partnership Program had often accounted for more than 50 per cent of its yearly acquisitions. This program allowed Loewen to capitalize on the skills and network contacts acquired through its acquisitions by partnering up with the previous owners. These owners helped Loewen initiate new acquisitions in return for a 10 per cent ownership stake in every successful referral. Loewen participated in about 20 of these types of partnerships. Third, Loewen had built a reputation for doing its utmost to satisfy the needs of sellers. Fourth, with its acquisition of Osiris Holdings, a large and successful cemetery management company, Loewen was building its in-house expertise in cemetery management.

Competition around acquisitions was not entirely price-based, since all major industry consolidators were amply capable of matching each other's price offers. Instead, competition was based on the more intangible nature of acquisitions. Loewen claimed it had one of the most customer-focused approaches and a genuine concern for sellers' needs. In every single acquisition, Loewen maintained the funeral home's name. It also strove to increase the brand equity of this name by offering excellent service, being involved in the community, and improving the facilities. When Loewen purchased a home, it tended to keep all employees in place. This allowed seamless service during the acquisition process and was in line with preserving the home's heritage and community appeal. Also, the salaries and benefits it introduced were usually an improvement over what had previously been offered. Owners and their families could remain active in the management of the business. In terms of capital gains and other financial issues, Loewen was extremely flexible. It did anything from paying a large cash portion up front, usually 75 per cent, to a share for share stock issue. In some cases it had even agreed to lease a home, although this was not common practice.

Given Loewen's penchant for smaller homes, it has a reputation as the "country bumpkin" of funeral home acquirers. This was a misnomer because like its competitors, Loewen also acquired large, urban funeral homes in the $10 million to $50 million range. However, given that these opportunities were not commonplace, Loewen had developed an infrastructure that allowed it to identify and purchase smaller, yet very profitable, homes in more rural areas.

As the number of acquisitions grew, Loewen became increasingly strategic in its expansion planning. This was explained by Mr. J. P. Gabille, Loewen's Vice President of Corporate Development: "We use many different criteria to evaluate a home. For example, we prefer larger operations, reputable operations, profitability, good staff, etc. Until about two or three years ago we just bought funeral homes that met our criteria. Now we are much more strategic, i.e., trying to build hubs, consolidating existing properties to create new, more high quality properties, building new homes to fill the gaps. We currently have 20 to 25 new homes in progress."

Loewen believed that its reputation as "the preferred acquirer" was a significant advantage in attracting high quality acquisitions. Loewen endeavoured to develop this image by paying competitive prices for homes and cemeteries, being very flexible in the integration of these establishments, and going the extra mile to satisfy the needs and concerns of sellers. Many independent funeral establishments indicated that they would prefer selling to the Loewen Group rather than to other consolidators, a position that saw many holding on until Loewen's 1995 Mississippi court case problems were resolved in early 1996. The company planned to sign or close a record number of acquisitions that year. Although the percentage fluctuated from year to year, incremental annual revenue represented 82 per cent of the dollar value of the acquisition. Historically, for every dollar spent acquiring a company, Loewen generated annual revenues of 82 cents.

Operations Management

Mr. Harry Rath, VP of Eastern Canada, described how Loewen integrated its acquisitions: "Loewen does not have homogeneous operating guidelines for the various homes we own. We understand the importance of local culture and allow our homes a great deal of leeway in operations. We make one very important change, i.e., we impose the utilization of budgets[8] that can be agreed upon together, and we insist on regular accountability and encourage accountability. Our expectations are clear. We are also very interested in helping funeral homes achieve their goals, i.e., you don't only see us during budget time. For example, as VP Operations of Eastern Canada, I oversee 62 funeral homes, with the help of some regional managers. All my homes know me personally. I am available to them for guidance and assistance."

One of the challenges faced by Loewen was the balancing act between operational profitability and commitment to its corporate culture. Loewen paid close attention to cost control and efficiency improvement. However, with the pressures for continual growth and with the various events in the life of the company, Loewen found the balancing act more and more difficult to manage.

Marketing Orientation

In terms of pre-need, Loewen's unfulfilled prearranged funeral contracts amounted to $750 million. This equated to a backlog of just under 1.5 years of services. Loewen realized the importance of increasing its pre-need sales and hoped to be more aggressive in the future. At present, 16 per cent of all funeral services performed by the Loewen Group were pre-arranged. It was hoped that by 1997, Loewen would increase its pre-need funeral revenues by 5 to 10 per cent.

In terms of cremations, Loewen expected that by the year 2000, its cremation rate would jump from 26 per cent, in 1995, to 28.21 per cent. To deal with the industry's gradual shift towards cremations, Loewen had increased its acquisition of cemeteries and had developed a "Celebration of Life" program. This program allowed Loewen to sell cremations in such a way that they were almost as profitable and often more profitable than the traditional funeral service. Traditionally, cremations were treated in the same way as dispositions. No effort was made to provide families with visitation, a memorial service, a reception, etc. This was because funeral homes did not understand their cremation customers. When a customer chose cremation, he/she was not choosing a less dignified funeral service; he/she was only choosing not to be buried. Loewen's Celebration of Life program trained its funeral directors to sell cremations just like traditional funerals. Brian Falvey, Loewen's Celebration of Life program coordinator for Cape Cod, explained:

> The family had never had a cremation before...but they wanted to respect the mother's wishes...They also wanted to have some type of religious service and a final chance to say good-bye to her.[9]

By explaining the Celebration of Life philosophy, Brian assured the couple that together they could tailor arrangements to include a private family viewing at the funeral home, followed by a religious service conducted by a local minister. Furthermore, he would personally supervise the burial of the cremated remains at an out-of-state family plot.

---

[8] Once a home had been acquired, the use of Loewen's legal counsel and insurance provider was non-negotiable.

[9] *VISION Magazine*, November/December 1996, The Loewen Group Inc.

They were surprised that all this could take place. Like many people, they didn't realize that these arrangements could be made in conjunction with a cremation.[10]

Organizational Culture

> Stock at funeral home-owner Loewen Group has risen nearly $5, to a recent 35¼, since a recent promotion that carried the message: Exercise, Eat Well, Stay Healthy—We Can Wait.[11]

Loewen's organizational culture was truly captured in the above few lines. The key tenet of the Loewen culture was that employees believed that the company was doing something good, something beyond just making money. The Loewen Group insisted that they were not solely a funeral consolidator or a funeral service operator, they were both. This belief provided a strong sense of purpose to employees.

Shareholder Relations

From 1990 to 1994, when Loewen was experiencing high growth levels and good profitability, there was never a need for formal shareholder relations. However, with the loss of a major legal battle[12] causing share prices to fall from $41 to $18, shareholder relations became crucial. After this immense drop in share price, Loewen's financial people became very active and for two months they never stopped talking to investors. Their goal was to communicate the key message that Loewen's stock was undervalued and, with a little time, would be trading at its previously high multiples. These trips were very successful, as the market saw some active purchasing of Loewen stock and an increase in stock prices. Other methods by which shareholders were kept abreast of Loewen's activities included: a detailed annual report, Loewen's *VISION Magazine*[13] and conference calls between Mr. Loewen and the company's major shareholders. However, despite all of these tactics, the most important link to shareholders was that, notwithstanding any crises, Loewen maintained its acquisition pace and operational profitability.

Finance

Every year since 1990, Loewen had successfully raised funds from the public. Loewen had a very innovative financial group that regularly developed new types of issues that allowed increased fund raising and increased returns for potential buyers. For example, even after coming close to bankruptcy after the Mississippi trial, Loewen's financial people, with the assistance of Nesbitt Burns and RBC Dominion Securities, designed a convertible preferred security with a seven-year term to raise funds for increased acquisitions. Funds were placed in trust to ensure that they would be used for acquisitions and not legal obligations. This financing tool helped Loewen raise $200 million US.

Another innovative tactic used by Loewen was a partnership with Blackstone Capital Partners II Merchant Banking Fund LP. This partnership allowed Loewen to make strategic acquisitions off the balance sheet. The first was Prime Succession Inc., a consolidator that had 16 cemeteries and 146 funeral homes in the U.S. Prime Succession was purchased for $295 million. Loewen paid $72 million and held 20 per cent of the shares, with an option to buy the remaining 80 per cent after four years. Until that time, the 80 per cent would be held by Blackstone. Loewen's holdings were primarily preferred shares and

---

[10] *VISION Magazine*, November/December 1996, The Loewen Group Inc.

[11] *Forbes*, July 3, 1995.

[12] The major legal battle in question was the Mississippi Case. Details of the Mississippi case are provided later on.

[13] *VISION Magazine* was a publication that Loewen sent to all its funeral establishments, industry analysts, shareholders and other industry stakeholders. It allowed Loewen to explain what was going on in the company, from the perspective of an individual funeral home right up to major issues like the Mississippi case.

Blackstone's holdings were common shares. Its partnership with Blackstone allowed Loewen to make strategic deals, while leaving enough capital free to continue to make other acquisitions.

Competitive Rivalry

The two largest competitors in the North American Market were Loewen and SCI. Nationally, they competed with each other in terms of acquisitions and regionally for market share. Increasing acquisitions and ensuring their successful integration were fundamental to the success of both companies. However, both Loewen and SCI approached acquisition and integration in different ways.

Business Activity	SCI	Loewen
Personnel	Almost all of the homes purchased by SCI were part of a clustering strategy. Clustering allowed the company to decrease operational costs by pooling and sharing resources among regionally proximate homes. Clustering saved personnel costs because it allowed homes to operate with a skeletal staff while being able to call upon floater employees for assistance.	It was part of Loewen's integration strategy not to make significant changes to the staffing levels of a newly acquired funeral home. The preservation of a funeral establishment's brand equity was very important to Loewen and it viewed personnel as a key component.
Facilities	Clustering allowed SCI to centralize functions such as embalming and preparing the body.	Loewen did not centralize its embalming or preparation facilities.
Automotive Equipment	Typically at SCI, every cluster shared one fleet of cars.	Loewen did not actively centralize its use of automobiles. However, some homes often shared automobiles.
Management	SCI offered a great deal of training and had a large number of managers available to assist homes with specific problems. From an organizational perspective, a home was about four management tiers away from the head office.	Training was an important component of Loewen's integration process. Funeral home managers worked closely with the Regional Vice Presidents to develop budgets together. Budgeting was done on an individual home level, taking into account factors in each home's micro-environment. All Regional Vice Presidents reported directly to the Head Office.
Locations of Acquisitions	The driver behind SCI's growth strategy was clustering. Rarely were homes purchased that did not fit into one cluster or the other.	Loewen tended to acquire profitable homes that showed the potential for sustainable and/or increasing future profits and growth. It focused on smaller "mom & pop" operations with larger returns on investment. Loewen developed greater regional market share in some areas via strategic (large, urban) acquisitions.
Purchasing	SCI used a centralized purchasing program, both at the regional and national levels. Purchases of vehicles, caskets, cremation urns and grave markers were centralized at the national level.	Loewen often allowed funeral establishments to keep their suppliers intact, especially if relationships were profitable. However, Loewen had established large volume contracts for most of its supply needs.
Legal Counsel/ Insurance	Centralized	Centralized

These different approaches were very important to potential funeral home sellers. Funeral home sellers were not only interested in selling to the highest bidder, but typically had a number of criteria that had to be met before a sales deal could be signed. For example, funeral home owners were very concerned with:

- preservation of the funeral home's name and heritage
- job security of their managers and non-management staff
- fair staff remuneration
- maintenance of the home's community involvement
- the maintenance of a service to the community image as opposed to a corporate business image

Of these owners, those who were selling larger establishments involving stock trades were also concerned with issues related to:

- the company's acquisition growth rate
- historical and future growth in the stock price
- meeting industry trends head on
- company cost structures and profitability

See Exhibit 10 for a comparison of SCI and Loewen along some key financial indicators.

Strategy

Loewen's strategic direction had not significantly changed in the last few years. It was clearly and simply stated in its 1995 annual report as follows:

> The company capitalizes on these attractive industry fundamentals through a growth strategy that emphasizes three principal components: (i) acquiring a significant number of small, family-owned funeral homes and cemeteries; (ii) acquiring strategic operations consisting predominantly of large, multi-location urban properties that generally serve as platforms for acquiring small, family-owned businesses in surrounding regions; and (iii) improving the revenue and profitability of newly-acquired and established locations. The first element of the Company's growth strategy is the acquisition of small, family-owned funeral homes and cemeteries. Management believes the Company has a competitive advantage in this market due to its culture and its well-known and understood reputation for honoring existing owners and staff. The final element of the Company's growth strategy is its focus on enhancing the revenue and profitability of newly-acquired and established locations.

Cemeteries were going to play a major role in Loewen's strategy over the next few years. Loewen executives forecasted that from 1997 onwards, 30 to 40 per cent of all revenues would come from cemeteries.

THE FAMOUS MISSISSIPPI CASE

In 1990, Loewen made two major purchases in Mississippi. The first was an insurance company and funeral homes from the Riemann Family of Gulfport, Mississippi and the second was a Jackson-based funeral home from Wright & Ferguson funeral directors. A large funeral home operator in the Gulfport area was Jerry O'Keefe, who owned Gulf National Life Insurance Company and some funeral homes and cemeteries. Prior to Loewen's acquisition of the Wright & Ferguson funeral homes, Gulf National had an exclusive contract with Wright & Ferguson, to exclusively sell its "burial insurance" as this product was defined in Mississippi. Gulf National also had an unexclusive representation contract with Wright & Ferguson, to sell "pre-need" insurance (a different product than burial insurance) on behalf of Wright & Ferguson. O'Keefe commenced a court action, following Loewen's acquisition of Wright & Ferguson, claiming that since the Loewen acquisition, Wright & Ferguson had not been honoring the exclusivity agreement with respect to burial insurance. O'Keefe sued Loewen for breach of contract. In reply, Loewen's position was that it had at all times scrupulously honored the exclusivity contract with burial insurance; however, burial insurance had become out of date, and most funeral insurance being sold was of the pre-need variety, and Gulf National had no exclusivity provision with respect to pre-need insurance.

The parties subsequently entered into a settlement agreement settling the litigation, whereby Loewen agreed to sell to Gulf National its insurance company (purchased from Riemann) and O'Keefe would sell to Loewen, two of its funeral homes. The settlement agreement was clearly made subject to subsequent agreement on the valuation of the funeral homes; the valuation of the insurance company; mutually satisfactory design of a new insurance product; and mutually satisfactory agreement on a new agency representation agreement. A number of these "subject to" provisions were never satisfied, and the settlement agreement therefore did not complete. O'Keefe then amended his lawsuit to claim that Loewen breached the settlement agreement and acted in bad faith.

The litigation took place in Jackson, Mississippi, before judge and jury. With respect to the settlement agreement, the total value of the assets involved (the insurance company and two funeral homes) was approximately $6 million. Close to trial, O'Keefe hired Willie Gary, a renowned Plaintiff's contingency-fee lawyer in the United States. Many people felt that, as a result, the case was not based on facts in law but rather on an emotional, "theatre of mind" approach to the jury.

The jury's verdict was in favour of O'Keefe for an amount of US$500 million, which amounted to 20 times the damages stated by the Plaintiff in pre-trial motions. Loewen wished to appeal the result, but under Mississippi court rules, a pre-condition of the appeal was that Loewen post a full-cash bond in the amount of $625 million (U.S.). Accordingly, Loewen's lawyers began making preparations to voluntarily file for Chapter 11, since a filing in Chapter 11 would permit the appeal to go forward without the necessity of filing the $625 million bond.

In the result, the Company was able to settle with O'Keefe on an after-tax basis to the Company of $85 million (U.S.), consisting of a combination of cash, shares and a promissory note.

The initial result of the bizarre jury award was to send Loewen's share price spiralling down from $41.00 (CDN) to $18.00 (CDN) per share. The process of dealing with the aftermath of the Mississippi jury award, and the consequent need to refinance the Company left management tired after a challenge that lasted many months. About six months after the settlement of the case, SCI announced its hostile takeover bid.

Options Facing the Loewen Group

As Mr. Loewen heard the letter, sent by SCI's President William Heiligbrodt, several thoughts ran through his head:

- Was the price being offered for Loewen shares a fair value?
- Was selling the Loewen Group in the best interest of shareholders and other stakeholders?
- Could the Loewen Group guarantee that dollar for dollar it would be able to generate a better return than SCI?

EXHIBIT 1

L. William Heiligbrodt
President
September 17, 1996

Mr. Raymond L. Loewen
Chairman of the Board and Chief Executive Officer
The Loewen Group Inc.
4126 Norland Avenue
Burnaby, British Columbia, Canada

Dear Mr. Loewen:

As you know, I have tried to reach you several times since September 11. While your office has assured me that you received my messages, my calls have not been returned. In view of that, and in view of the importance of this matter, I am sending this letter.

I would like to discuss with you a combination of our two companies. The combination would involve a stock-for-stock exchange accounted for as a pooling which values Loewen Group at US$43 per share. We believe that this transaction can be structured in a manner that is tax-free to both companies and (except for a relatively nominal amount in the case of U.S. stockholders) to the U.S. and Canadian stockholders of Loewen Group.

I think you and your Board and stockholders would agree that our proposal is a generous one, resulting in the following premiums for Loewen Group stockholders:

- 48.9% above the price at which Loewen Group stock traded 30 days ago;
- 39.3% above the price at which Loewen Group stock traded one week ago; and
- 27.4% above the price at which Loewen Group stock is currently trading.

This represents an opportunity for your stockholders to realize excellent value, by any measure, for their shares. In addition, and importantly, since your stockholders would be receiving stock, they would continue to participate in Loewen Group's business as well as share in the upside of our business.

Thus, in essence, your stockholders would:

- continue their investment in our industry;
- get an immediate, and very significant, increase in the market value of their investment;
- get that immediate and substantial increase on an essentially tax free basis; and
- diversify their risk by participating in a much larger number of properties.

This is a "win-win" situation for you and your stockholders.

Finally, with respect to consideration, I would note also that our proposal is based on public information. After a due diligence review, we may be in a position to increase the consideration that your stockholders would receive.

We, of course, recognize that our businesses overlap in various locations. We have carefully reviewed this matter and are convinced that competition issues can be cured by selecting divestitures without impairment of the values that a combination would achieve for the stockholders of our two companies.

I would very much like to discuss any and all aspects of our proposal with you and your Board of Directors. We believe you and they will recognize the tremendous benefit to your stockholders of our proposal. Our proposal is conditioned upon approval of our Board and upon negotiation of mutually satisfactory agreements providing for a combination on a pooling basis.

We hope that after you meet with us, you will similarly determine that the transaction should be pursued. We look forward to hearing from you.

In view of the importance of this matter, we are simultaneously releasing this letter to the press.

Sincerely,

William Heiligbrodt
President

EXHIBIT 2   Typical Income Statement of an Independent Funeral Home ($)

	1986	1991	1992	1993	1996
Average "Regular Adult Funeral"					
Services & Casket	2 766.26	3 507.19	3 663.49	3 819.17	4 287.14
Operation Cost per Adult Funeral	2 015.75	2 597.69	2 717.2	2 823.03	3 160.33
Percentage of Operating Cost to Selling Price	72.87%	74.07%	74.17%	73.92%	73.72%
Casket Cost	469.99	606.04	627.7	652.18	729.68
Percentage of Casket Cost to Selling Price	16.99%	17.28%	17.13%	17.08%	17.02%
Profit Before Federal Income Tax	280.52	303.46	318.59	343.96	397.13
Percentage of Profit to Selling Price	10.14%	8.65%	8.70%	9.01%	9.26%

Breakdown of Operational Expenses for a Typical Independent Funeral Home ($)

	1986	% of Rev.	1991	% of Rev.	1992	% of Rev.	1993	% of Rev.	1996	% of Rev.
Personnel	913.33	33.02	1 209.51	34.49	1 266.75	34.58	1 347.55	35.28	1 507.2	35.16
Cost of Facilities	602.78	21.79	789.55	22.51	811.81	22.16	830.13	21.74	919.32	21.44
Automotive Equipment	207.43	7.50	213.11	6.08	222.42	6.07	223.2	5.84	256.5	5.98
Promotion	118.48	4.28	146.72	4.18	157.1	4.29	159.12	4.17	173.06	4.04
Business Service	65.06	2.35	86.49	2.47	90.12	2.46	93.52	2.45	107.46	2.51
Supplies	59.51	2.15	74.69	2.13	79.35	2.17	83.08	2.18	92.32	2.15
After Sale Expenses	41.05	1.48	66.9	1.91	78.5	2.14	75.49	1.98	93.57	2.18
Sundry	8.11	0.29	10.72	0.31	11.15	0.30	10.94	0.29	10.9	0.25
Total Operating Expenses	2 015.75		2 597.69		2 717.2		2 823.03		3 160.33	

Using data from Federated Funeral Directors of America.

EXHIBIT 3 Typical Income Statement of a Cemetery

	$	%
Revenues		
Pre-Need Sales	$1 173 000	65.9%**
At-Need Sales	213 000	11.9%**
Other	395 000	22.2%**
	1 781 000	100.0%**
Cost & Expenses		
Cost of Sales	313 000	22.6%*
Selling	446 000	32.1%*
Cemetery Maintenance	259 000	14.5%**
G & A	215 000	12.1%**
	1 233 000	69.2%**
Cemetery Gross Margin	$ 548 000	30.8%**

* Percentage of P/N + A/N Sales
** Percentage of Total Revenues

EXHIBIT 4 Ownership Distribution in the Industry

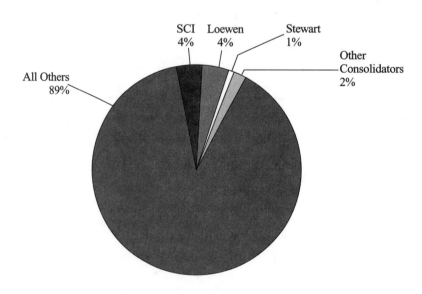

Funeral Homes

SCI 4% Loewen 4% Stewart 1% Other Consolidators 2% All Others 89%

EXHIBIT 4   (continued)

Cemeteries

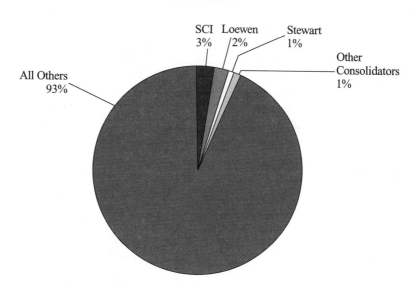

Breakdown of Death Care Industry Revenue by Company in the United States and Canada

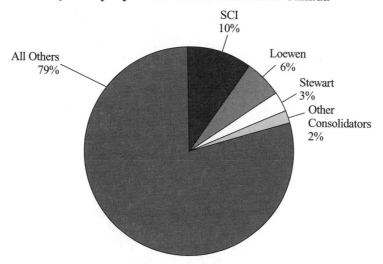

From "The Death Care Industry," TD Securities, 1996, Darren Martin.

EXHIBIT 5 **Typical Charges for a Funeral Service ($)**

Itemized Charges	Home 1 Traditional Service	Home 2 Traditional Service	Home 3 Traditional Service	Average Traditional Service	Average Simple Cremation
Professional Services					
Basic Service	730	255	1 070	685	NA
Visitation	370	365	0	245	NA
Day of Service	300	275	0	192	NA
Documentation	130	155	145	143	NA
Embalming	60	150	285	165	NA
Other Preparation	50	0	0	17	NA
Facilities and Equipment					
Basic Facility	450	275	625	450	NA
Visitation	130	300	0	143	NA
Day of Service	200	0	0	67	NA
Preparation Room	90	110	150	117	NA
Retaining Room	140	0	0	47	NA
Motor Vehicles					
Initial Transfer	260	120	195	192	NA
General Purpose Vehicle	100	85	125	103	NA
Funeral Coach	205	195	195	198	NA
Total Charges	3 215	2 285	2 790	2 763	827
Casket	3 500	2 500	2 700	2 900	288
Urn					567
Total	**6 715**	**4 785**	**5 490**	**5 663**	**1 682**

Using Data from Consumer Funeral Home Information Packages, July 1996.

EXHIBIT 6   **Dollar Value of Acquisitions as estimated by Loewen**

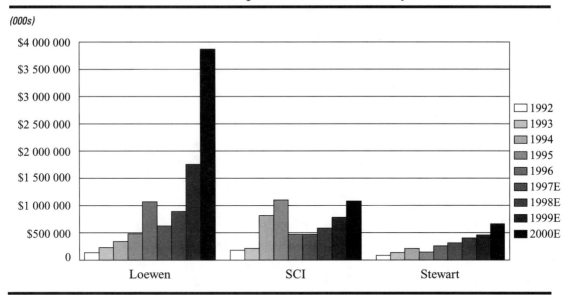

EXHIBIT 7   **Projected Death Rate**

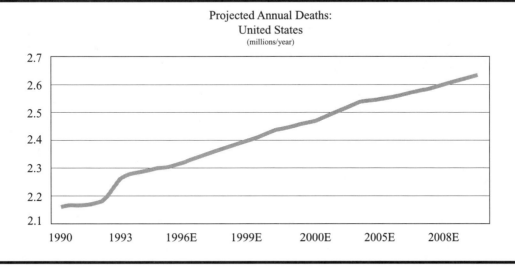

From "The Death Care Industry," TD Securities, 1996, Darren Martin.

EXHIBIT 8 Income Statement

(US$ 000s)

	1995	1994	1993	1992	1991	1990	1989	1988
Revenue								
Funeral	441 352	353 904	275 106	202 748	150 943	92 391	52 856	35 566
Cemetery	143 577	63 424	27 905	16 159	11 662	8 565	4 427	1 987
Insurance	13 564	0	0	0	0	0	0	0
Total Revenues	598 493	417 328	303 011	218 907	162 605	100 956	57 283	37 553
Costs and Expenses								
Funeral	258 872	210 471	166 782	123 044	90 861	55 237	29 759	20 557
Cemetery	103 726	48 003	21 111	12 155	8 657	5 152	3 152	1 240
Insurance	10 533	0	0	0	0	0	0	0
Cost of Goods Sold	373 131	258 474	187 893	135 199	99 518	60 389	32 911	21 797
Revenues—Costs of Goods Sold	225 362	158 854	115 118	83 708	63 087	40 567	24 372	15 756
Expenses								
General and administrative expenses	67 652	34 751	28 225	17 086	12 981	7 495	4 278	2 101
Depreciation and amortization	40 103	28 990	21 196	16 059	11 053	5 876	3 254	2 166
Total Expenses	107 755	63 741	49 421	33 145	24 034	13 371	7 532	4 267
Earnings from Operations	117 607	95 113	65 697	50 563	39 053	27 196	16 840	11 489
Interest on long-term debt	50 913	34 203	21 801	19 083	14 913	10 914	7 177	4 916
Legal Settlements	184 914	0	0	0				
Earnings (loss) before undernoted items	–118 220	60 910	43 896	31 480	24 140	16 282	9 663	6 573
Dividends on preferred securities of subsidiary	7 088	2 678	0	0				
Earnings (loss) before income taxes and undernoted items	–125 308	58 232	43 896	31 480	24 140	16 282	9 663	6 573
Total Income Taxes	–47 178	19 738	15 714	11 714	9 715	6 549	4 215	3 152
Net Income not including equity & earnings from assoc. companies	–78 130	38 494	28 182	19 766	14 425	9 733	5 448	3 421
Equity and other earnings of associated companies	1 446	0	0					
Net Earnings (loss) for the year	–76 684	38 494	28 182	19 766	14 425	9 733	5 448	3 421
Basic Earnings (loss) per common share	–1.69	0.97	0.77	0.59	0.46	0.39	0.31	0.23
Dividend per Common Share	0.050	0.070	0.045	0.032	0.017	0.000	0.000	0.000
Dividend per Preferred Share	0.000	0.000	0.000	0.000	0.000	0.288	0.586	0.327
Number of common shares at year-end (in thousands)	48 168	41 015	38 647	35 534	32 754	28 391	19 977	12 849
Common share price at year-end ($Cdn.)	34.38	36.75	33.25	19.63	15.63	12.50	9.31	5.31
Common share price at year-end ($U.S.)	25.31	26.50	25.38	15.50	13.38	10.63	n/a	n/a

EXHIBIT 9 Balance Sheet Loewen Group

(US$ 000s)

	1995	1994	1993	1992	1991	1990	1989	1988
Current Assets								
Cash and term deposits	39 454	15 349	18 167	12 176	16 035	9 706	17 940	3 180
Receivables, net of allowances	115 953	70 547	51 684	37 211	27 451	25 063	10 574	5 882
Inventories	27 489	19 673	15 952	12 323	8 165	6 381	2 919	1 805
Prepaid expenses	8 185	4 299	4 941	3 974	2 248	785	956	645
Total Current Assets	191 081	109 868	90 744	65 684	53 899	41 935	32 389	11 512
Prearranged funeral services	245 854	178 982	175 216	146 109	127 086	104 413	49 524	33 343
Long-term receivables net of allowances	167 367	67 895	30 059	11 460	5 725	2 319		
Investments	86 815	78 269	3 749	1 338	915	921		
Insurance invested assets	97 024							
Cemetery property at cost	369 022	114 861	48 158	24 135	15 939	15 230	3 160	2 859
Property and equipment	551 965	426 038	346 244	284 654	216 851	159 438	79 417	52 442
Names and reputations	424 944	314 599	199 514	126 156	87 547	72 982	25 363	17 910
Deferred income taxes	61 959							
Other assets	66 949	35 763	19 977	15 575	10 530	6 881	2 845	4 091
Total Assets	2 262 980	1 326 275	913 661	675 111	518 492	404 119	192 698	122 157
Liabilities and Shareholders' Equity								
Current Liabilities								
Current indebtedness	38 546	3 700	4 435	3 558		5 404		
Accrued settlements	53 000							
Accounts payable and accrued liabilities	80 058	48 436	37 952	22 715	13 601	14 013	6 504	4 188
Income taxes payable				446	730		589	1 582
Long-term debt, current position	69 671	45 529	6 572	7 553	6 073	6 088	4 431	2 990
Total Current Liabilities	241 275	97 665	48 959	34 272	20 404	25 505	11 524	8 760
Long-term debt	864 838	471 125	335 405	239 162	187 780	141 072	61 280	44 613
Subordinated debentures						8 956	8 571	8 240
Other Liabilities	136 433	83 678	22 327	16 439	9 415	5 956	375	458
Insurance policy liabilities	84 898							
Deferred income taxes		8 686	5 864	2 812	1 413	385	1 364	1 485
Deferred prearranged funeral services revenue	245 854	178 982	175 216	146 109	127 086	104 413	49 524	33 343
Preferred securities of subsidiary	75 000	75 000						
Total Non-Current Liabilities	1 407 023	817 471	538 812	404 522	325 694	260 782	121 114	88 139
Shareholders' Equity								
Common shares	490 055	282 560	227 968	172 133	139 151	98 031	42 418	11 828
Common shares issuable under legal settlements	72 000							
Preferred shares							7 566	7 566
Retained earnings	36 439	115 492	79 867	53 382	34 651	20 720	11 275	6 414
Foreign exchange adjustment	16 188	13 087	18 055	10 802	−1 408	−919	−1 199	−550
Total Shareholders' Equity	614 682	411 139	325 890	236 317	172 394	117 832	60 060	25 258
Total Liabilities and Shareholders' Equity	2 262 980	1 326 275	913 661	675 111	518 492	404 119	192 698	122 157
Number of funeral homes	815	640	533	451	365	268	131	98
Number of cemeteries	179	116	70	38	23	21	7	5
Number of funeral services	114 000	94 000	7 900	64 000	52 000	34 000	22 000	18 000
Number of employees	10 000	7 000	5 000	4 000	3 000	2 000	1 000	1 000
Business acquisitions in millions	487.9	265.6	148.0	83.2	68.5	140.2	31.5	30.8

EXHIBIT 10 Key Financial Indicators

	1995	1994	1993	1992	1991	1990	1989	1988
Gross Profit Margins on Funeral Homes for Loewen	41.4%	40.5%	39.4%	39.3%	39.8%	40.2%	43.7%	42.2%
Gross Profit Margins on Cemeteries for Loewen	27.8%	24.3%	24.4%	24.8%	25.8%	39.9%	28.8%	37.6%
Gross Profit Margins on Funeral Homes for SCI	25.3%	29.5%	29.4%	28.8%	28.7%	29.4%	28.2%	29.5%
Gross Profit Margins on Cemeteries for SCI	34.6%	32.1%	28.4%	24.4%	22.9%	20.0%	18.8%	19.7%
EPS for Loewen (US$)	-1.69	0.97	0.76	0.58	0.46			
EPS for SCI (US$)	1.70	1.43	1.17	1.07	1.00			
Growth per Year in EPS at Loewen	-274.2%	27.6%	31.0%	26.0%				
Growth per Year in EPS at SCI	18.9%	22.2%	9.4%	7.0%				
Share Price at Loewen (US$)	25.31	26.50	25.38	15.50	13.38			
Share Price at SCI (US$)	33.17	25.56	22.00	17.38	16.09			
Growth per Year in Share Price at Loewen	-4.5%	4.4%	63.7%	15.8%				
Growth per Year in Share Price at SCI	29.8%	16.2%	26.6%	8.0%				
Return on Sales for Loewen	-12.8%	9.2%	9.3%	9.0%	8.9%	9.6%	9.5%	
Return on Sales for SCI	11.1%	11.7%	11.5%	11.2%	11.4%	10.7%	9.0%	
Return on Total Asset for SCI	2.4%	2.5%	2.8%	3.3%	3.5%	3.6%	2.9%	
Return on Total Asset for Loewen	-3.4%	2.9%	3.1%	2.9%	2.8%	2.4%	2.8%	
Return on Equity for Loewen	-12.4%	9.4%	8.7%	8.4%	8.4%	8.7%	9.1%	
Return on Equity for SCI	9.3%	11.0%	11.7%	12.7%	11.9%	13.9%	8.4%	

From the Annual Reports of the Loewen Group and Service Corporation International.

DESIGNER CLASSICS CARPET MANUFACTURING LTD.

c a s e

18

R o d e r i c k   E .   W h i t e

Jim Dunlop, a self-admitted entrepreneur and the principal owner of Designer Classics Carpet (DCC), had just received the financial results for 1986. Dunlop, age 39, had gotten into the custom wool carpet business four years earlier by acquiring the assets of Conestoga Carpet, a failed company located in Waterloo, Ontario. Using over $300 000 of his own capital, he had modernized and added some production equipment, moved the plant to a nearby location, added new products, and perhaps most importantly, expanded the firm's market scope greatly through his own efforts.

IVEY

In mid-January 1987, as Dunlop reflected on the four-year financial summary (Exhibit 1), he was proud of the large increases in sales. However, this growth had resulted in scheduling problems and bottlenecks in the plant. Additional sales from the Waterloo plant would require alleviating these problems. Dunlop, always on the lookout for opportunities to expand and strengthen the business, had recently acquired a wool yarn-spinning mill in Waterford, about 75 kilometres from Waterloo. This purchase would allow DCC to set specific standards for its yarn and secure a source of supply for this major raw material. Several other growth opportunities could be pursued. Preliminary negotiations were underway for the acquisition of Elite Carpet, a woven carpet manufacturer in Quebec with $5.1 million in sales and significant unused capacity. Dunlop was also considering the establishment of an importing/distribution company in Seattle, Washington, to bring in custom wool carpets from Thailand. In addition, one of DCC's major dealers in the U.S. had expressed an interest in selling a minority interest to DCC.

Picking up on new initiatives would have to be done by Jim Dunlop. There was no one else available. Since he also had to deal with many of the day-to-day demands of the business, establishing priorities and timing were critical.

THE BUSINESS

All of DCC's current products were custom ordered for residential and commercial buyers. Each was unique in size, colour, pattern and texture. Sales were made through sales agents and dealers, with only a very few direct transactions with customers. In 1986, residential customers accounted for about 20 per cent of annual sales. Of the remaining 80 per cent for commercial applications, half were used as carpet murals for subdividing passenger aircraft, and the remainder were sold as floor covering in offices and hotels.

Products and Markets

Costing between $50 per square metre for broadloom and up to $500 per square metre for a hand tufted product, custom carpets appealed to small, specialized segments of the carpet market. The custom wool carpet market in North America was estimated to be approximately $300 million and growing at 15 per cent annually (Table 1). In all except the aircraft segment, DCC's share was not large. Currently, commercial sales outside North America were small, less than 10 per cent of the total; Canada accounted for about 20 per cent of DCC's sales; and the U.S., about 70 per cent.

T A B L E 1   North American Custom Wool Carpet Market

Market Segment	Size	DCC's Share	Sales
Residential	18%	2.0%	20%
Commercial:			40%
Hotel	50%	1.5%	
Office	30%	2.0%	
Aircraft	2%	60%	40%
	$ 300m		

Source: Estimates by Jim Dunlop and selected carpet dealers.

Residential Segment

Custom wool carpet appealed to upscale home-owners. The home-owner would either deal directly with a dealer having in-house design expertise, or through an interior decorator/designer who would ultimately source through a dealer. Many dealers served both the residential and commercial market. Some dealers competed with manufacturers for part of the value added by doing not only the design work but also their own in-house "cutting and pasting" of the carpet. However, this was the exception and most dealers preferred to have the carpet completed by the manufacturer. No really close substitutes existed for wool carpets. High-end synthetics did not have the same "feel" or snob appeal. Oriental rugs could be viewed as an alternative to the customer, but generally had somewhat different applications, and appealed to different customer tastes than custom wool area carpets.

Quality was important in all DCC's markets, as was on-time delivery performance. Order lead times for the residential segment were typically three to five months; rapid response to orders was not usually critical, since customers generally ordered well in advance. Customers did not tend to comparison shop for price. This segment was believed to be growing at 10–15 per cent annually.

Commercial Segment

This segment was composed of two different customer groups: office and hotel. Office applications were limited to lobbies, board rooms and executive suites. Recently the U.S. office market appeared to be growing, but the Canadian market was in decline. The other group, luxury hotels, used this product in high visibility areas like lobbies. Woven wool carpets were typically used in rooms. Luxury hotels were increasing their penetration of the North American market.

Delivery time was important, especially for most office applications, as was price. Some hotel chains had in-house designers, but many hotels and most office customers used an outside design house or carpet consultant to develop specifications and aid in product selection. Roughly 80 per cent of the business was tendered directly to carpet manufacturers, and the remainder was placed through dealers.

Aircraft Segment

Carpet murals were used for decorative purposes on bulkhead walls in some commercial passenger and corporate aircraft. Currently carpet murals were not used by air carriers outside North America. Approximately 50 per cent of the North American fleet had these murals. However, recent proposed changes in FAA regulations governing material content of aircraft cabin interiors had put this market in jeopardy. Although Dunlop believed the likelihood of a permanent ban on wool bulkhead murals was unlikely, sales could be disrupted during negotiations between the FAA and aircraft manufacturers.

Customers in this segment were somewhat price sensitive, but tended to buy on reputation for quality. Airlines working with a design house and/or the firm finishing the aircraft's interior would develop carpet specifications. Orders were placed by the finisher, either the aircraft manufacturer (e.g., Boeing) or a specialized interior finisher (e.g., Innotech Aviation), with an aircraft supply house or directly with the manufacturer. In the U.S., one supply house handled a large part of the aircraft interiors market, including floor and wall coverings, seats, etc., as well as bulkhead murals. DCC was this firm's exclusive supplier of carpet murals. Eighty-five per cent of sales in this segment were made in the U.S.; and 15 per cent in Canada primarily to Canadian Pacific Airlines.

DCC's Position

DCC faced three major competitors (Table 2). The remaining competition was fragmented, although some were significant in small niches (e.g., Carter and Carousel).

TABLE 2 Competitive Position

	Market Share— Excluding Aircraft	Market Share— Aircraft
Hong Kong Carpet	65%	—
Edward Fields	5	10%
V'Soske	4	9
Designer Classics	2	60
Carousel	0.5	14
Carter	0.5	8
Other	24	

Source: Industry estimates.

Hong Kong Carpet (HKC) was a large, apparently well-financed corporation with manufacturing facilities scattered around the Far East. It produced under several different labels. HKC was believed to be the low-cost producer and typically offered the lowest price, but also had a reputation for somewhat lower quality and had 12- to 24-week delivery times. HKC had extensive dealer representation in North America and advertised exclusively to dealers.

Fields and V'Soske were similar in many respects. Both were high-priced and high-quality with long delivery times: about 21 weeks for Fields and, partly because of its Puerto Rican production facilities, 23 weeks for V'Soske. V'Soske utilized exclusive dealers and had strong representatives in most markets. Fields, headquartered in New York City, had company showrooms in major metropolitan centres. Like V'Soske, Fields branded its product and had high awareness.

DCC, by way of comparison, was medium to high quality and price. DCC had the ability to deliver a small sample of the desired colour, pattern and texture within ten days to two weeks; compared to four weeks for most of the competition. The finished order would follow in about six weeks. According to Dunlop, DCC was able to offer faster sample turnaround because of their proximity to major customers and the capabilities of the sample making department. To the extent economically feasible, sample making had separate facilities. However, some equipment, tufting and dying, was shared with regular manufacturing and inevitable conflicts arose. While still good compared to other manufacturers, this turnaround time, because of capacity constraints and labour turnover, had been increasing. DCC did not have a strong brand identity, and in certain markets, the prior association with Conestoga was a hindrance. All four major manufacturers, including DCC, had in-house dye facilities.

THE COMPANY

DCC's product range was all wool and made to order. It included completely hand tufted carpets and murals, machine tufted and overtufted carpets (machine tufted but finished by hand), both for broadloom (wall-to-wall) and area applications. As shown in Table 3, gross profit margins differed amongst product categories.

TABLE 3 DCC Cost and Gross Profit by Major Custom Tufted Product Group

(per cent of selling price)

	Hand Tufted	Hand + Machine			Machine Tufted	
	Area	Broadloom	Area	Aircraft	Broadloom	Area
Materials	34%	44%	30%	20%	49%	29%
Labour	52	34	43	31	22	37
Gross Profit	14	22	27	49	29	34

Source: Sales records August through October 1986.

Marketing and Distribution

In total, DCC had about 200 customers. However, the top ten accounted for 61 per cent of sales during 1986, and the top two for 53 per cent. One of these was an aircraft supply house representing DCC's carpet murals, and the other was a residential and commercial dealer in the southwestern U.S. The old Conestoga Carpet had focused almost exclusively on the Toronto residential and commercial market. Over the last four years, Jim Dunlop, with his real flair for sales and marketing, had expanded distribution and sales into the U.S. market, and the airline carpet mural business in particular.

Designer Classics had two salespersons covering the U.S. They serviced the dealer network as well as direct sales to major hotel customers. The company had one European sales representative with responsibility for direct sales to hotel clients, and an agent network in six countries that sold to local dealers. Two sales agents, one in Europe and the other in the U.S., covered the aircraft market. The company's general sales manager, with an in-house staff of three, handled Canadian sales, both through the dealer network and direct to hotels and aircraft finishers. Jim Dunlop maintained contact with key customers, and was involved in developing most new dealer or agent relationships. His salesmanship and interpersonal abilities were important strengths in this area.

Once access to the customer was established, the selling task involved producing a suitable sample. The ability to match the colour, texture and pattern needs of the customer with this sample was critical to making the sale. Delivery of a finished product consistent with the sample was important to a firm's reputation. Accomplishing this required close coordination with the production department. The importance of delivery and price varied by segment.

Manufacturing

The production process was a custom job shop. Basic steps for a tufted carpet are outlined in Exhibit 2. The mix of skills varied; dyeing was a complicated operation—part art, part science, requiring a high level of skill and experience. Finishing was semi-skilled; an operator could be trained in one to two months. However, because this step was the last in the chain, mistakes were costly. Tufting skill requirements varied with the complexity of the pattern.

DCC had trouble retaining production employees. The Kitchener-Waterloo area was in the midst of an economic boom. Unemployment was 4 per cent, and an Employment Canada official reported that unskilled labourers were changing jobs for as little as 10¢ to 15¢ per hour wage differentials. DCC currently paid $6.20 for unskilled labour (after a three-month probationary period). The factory workforce of 101 people, many of them recent immigrants to Canada, turned over by 34 per cent in 1986.

The labour situation was further complicated by the company's recent unionization. The union and the company were negotiating their second contract, and management's goal was to achieve a "no wage increase" settlement. Historically, DCC had not laid off plant workers, even when sales volumes were low. Dunlop had taken the unionization as a personal affront, and was determined not to lend legitimacy by conceding a wage increase in the upcoming contract negotiations. He felt most employees did not want a union, and he was anxious to return his firm to non-union status.

Union problems aside, labour availability was limiting output in certain areas. In hand tufting, it was difficult to get reliable, low-cost labour. In addition to the availability of labour, variability in skill requirements on a job-by-job, pattern-by-pattern basis complicated breaking this bottleneck. Capital requirements for expanding hand tufting capacity were small. However, bottlenecks existed in other areas. There were quality and capacity problems in the dye shop. Waterloo had very hard water, which required softening before use in dyeing operations. The addition of storage tanks for softened water, an investment of about $12 000, would hopefully solve this problem, reducing delays and rework. The quality of wool yarn had also been affecting the dyeing process, causing delays and rework. It was hoped the acquisition of Waterford Spinning Mills would alleviate this problem.

In order to meet demand, DCC's key manufacturing operations were operating three shifts of eight hours each on weekdays, and two 12-hour shifts on weekends. The business was somewhat seasonal, increasing during the last quarter of the year. During the October to December 1986 period, over 70 per cent of orders were late, averaging 15 days; 90 per cent were labelled RUSH. In addition, quality as measured by remakes had been deteriorating (Exhibit 3). Adding more capacity would be expensive and, Dunlop suspected, unnecessary. He felt the real problem lay with manufacturing management:

> The growth in sales has overtaxed our current manufacturing management. We have gone from 14 to 130 employees over the last four years. The ability to manage a schedule in a complex job shop is now very important. It has been complicated by quality and availability problems for wool yarn.
>
> We need someone with experience managing a complicated job shop. The specifics of the carpet business can be picked up quickly.

And while Jim Dunlop understood the importance of manufacturing to his business, he had stated:

> Manufacturing frustrates me, it's not something I'm personally really interested in or good at. I'm a marketer rather than an administrator.

Two months earlier Dunlop had created and staffed the position of manufacturing manager. This person was to help sort out the problems at the Waterloo plant and assume overall responsibilities for all of DCC's manufacturing plants, Waterford Spinning Mills, and the Elite plant, if purchased. The individual hired for this position had recently, by way of letter and without explanation, informed Dunlop of his immediate resignation. The position remained unfilled.

Suppliers

In addition to labour, the other key input into the product was wool yarn. Raw wool from Great Britain and New Zealand was most suitable for high-quality carpets. There were numerous suppliers of raw wool. DCC used a broker who bought their wool at auction; and while a "commodity," it varied dramatically in quality and required considerable buying expertise. Spinners were then contracted to process the wool into yarn. In North America, there were seven wool carpet yarn producers. The recently purchased Waterford Spinning Mills, with some equipment modifications and additions, could supply about 95 per cent of DCC's wool yarn requirements and still have considerable additional capacity. The remaining 5 per cent of DCC's requirements were yarn types Waterford could not make.

Waterford Spinning Mills (WSM) had been purchased because of quality and delivery problems with two yarn suppliers. The plant became available when Sunbeam, which had been spinning yarn for its electric blankets, decided to exit this part of the business. Sunbeam had another larger facility in the area, and in order to avoid any bad feelings from a plant closure, was prepared to "give the spinning equipment to DCC." Dunlop Holdings had purchased the old building and equipment for $110 000. However, conversion to spinning wool for carpets required purchasing some additional (used) equipment and building improvements at a cost of $65 000. The deal closed in July 1986, and the plant was producing (at a low level) by August. By year end things were running relatively smoothly, and capacity exceeded demand.

Dunlop knew of no other custom carpet manufacturer with their own spinning mill. WSM was already providing more consistent quality and delivery of this major raw material. This facilitated operations at Waterloo. Failure of an earlier supplier to meet delivery promises had resulted in disruptions to the manufacturing process, and on one occasion a plant shut-down. DCC had been partially coping with this supply problem by holding large yarn inventories. When the WSM operation was coordinated with DCC's Waterloo plant, much of the inventory could be held as raw fleece at WSM. Other materials, like poly backing, were easily available. Production equipment, while specialized, could be obtained from several suppliers.

Financial Capacity

DCC had substantial leverage (Exhibit 1). However, working capital could be financed by customer deposits, normally 50 per cent of sales and government assisted financing for export sales.

After the sale of an earlier venture in the production of turkey breeding stock, Jim Dunlop had emerged with considerable personal wealth. He commented on his willingness to infuse additional capital into the business:

> We've been the rounds with venture capitalists. They have a real get-rich-quick mentality and I do not foresee us using them.
>
> Our financial policy is to leverage these operations as much as possible through the use of debt. However, if the right opportunity should come along, Dunlop Holdings[1] would be willing to back it financially. I do attempt to limit our exposure. I have not given personal guarantees for DCC's obligation. In addition, DCC only holds the operating assets. Real estate assets are held by a separate company owned by my wife, and DCC makes lease payments.

Management and Organization

Jim Dunlop and the four key managers described below made up the management group:

Name	Position	Time with DCC	Background
Jim Dunlop	Owner	4 years	International marketing
Larry Weiss	V.P. Finance	2 years	Chartered accountant
Chris Spence	Controller	3 years	Accounting at Electrohome
Wayne Pauli	Sales Manager	1 year	Large-scale manufacturing
—	Manufacturing Mgr		
Rick Hennige	Plant Manager	4 years	Conestoga Carpets

In the pursuit of opportunities, Dunlop spent almost half his time away from the office. As a result, the firm did not have a full-time, resident general manager. Jim Dunlop did most of the missionary marketing, but also felt it was important for him to be involved in key operational decisions. Even when he was away, Dunlop maintained daily contact with the office. However, problems between functions often remained unresolved and decisions unmade during his absence.

---

[1] A family holding company that held DCC and several other ventures.

Employees received annual bonuses as part of their regular pay cheques. They were set at Jim Dunlop's discretion. All supervisors were required to make an annual performance appraisal of their subordinates. Personally, Dunlop had some aggressive goals for the company:

> Dunlop Holdings, of which DCC is a part, will continue to have rapid growth and some diversification. We plan to stay within architectural and design materials and services, but might add fabric, other kinds of flooring, like hardwood, things like that. Of course any decision will be made when the opportunity knocks.
>
> I would like us, in the foreseeable future, to grow to $100 million in sales. We will probably, at some point, have to go public to finance this growth. You might say I want to build a little empire, a significant Canadian, even international, entity in this field.
>
> Of course my role has to change as we grow. I've been very active in the business, heavily involved in marketing. I'll have to get more involved in general management.

STRATEGIC INITIATIVES

Dunlop and DCC were confronting several important decisions. Perhaps the most significant was the acquisition of Elite Carpet in Quebec.

Elite was the only manufacturer of woven wool carpets remaining in Canada. The woven product was more equipment, less labour intensive, and more long-run oriented than custom tufted carpets. Woven carpets could have intricate but necessarily repetitive patterns. Unique patterning, overtufting, sculpting and custom borders were only possible with a custom tufted product.

Elite's product was currently sold only in Canada, primarily to hotels. Woven carpets tended to be used in corridors, restaurants and rooms, whereas tufted custom carpets were used in lobbies and suites. Elite's reputation and good sales representation in the Canadian market and the overlap in customer group with DCC, and the potential in the U.S. for Elite's product was what initially had attracted Dunlop's interest.

Dunlop had visited their facility in Ste. Therese, Quebec, in 1984 to explore the possibility of the two companies collaborating on contracts requiring both tufted and woven carpets, but nothing had come of this initial contact. In early 1986 Dunlop had again approached Elite, this time to suggest they manufacture a woven line for DCC to brand and distribute. The proposal had been rejected. However, when they learned of the WSM acquisition, Elite had enquired about sourcing yarn. Dunlop had invited the president of Elite to Waterloo in October. At this time Dunlop had proposed the purchase of an equity interest in Elite. Unexpectedly, Elite's president had asked if Dunlop would like to buy all of Elite.

Jim Dunlop was surprised by the proposal for an outright purchase, and visited Elite in late December 1986. Elite's management had not been prepared to provide detailed financial statements at this time. However, Dunlop had learned that since the firm had been sold by its original Scottish owners to the employees in 1978, Elite had declining sales and losses in six of the subsequent years and small profits in only two. For the 11-month fiscal year ended in October, Elite had sales of $5.1 million, gross profits of $1.1 million, and an operating loss of $138 000 with an estimated tax loss carried forward of $750 000. Total current assets were about $1.7 million; total current liabilities, $1.8 million. Fixed assets including the land and building were $1.1 million. Long-term debt was about $500 000 and equity about $600 000 (but this latter amount included a $1.12 million government "loan"). The current assets were made up of about $1 million in good quality accounts receivable and $700 000 in inventory.

Dunlop judged the inventory level was too high, but based on a quick walk-through inspection, it appeared to be current. The building and production equipment appeared well maintained. Dunlop also learned that Elite was under pressure from their banker to secure additional financing and turn around their sales and profit performance. Dunlop foresaw several areas for improvement. Elite currently purchased yarn from England and paid a 12 per cent duty. There was no duty on fleece. WSM could provide yarn at less than the price Elite was paying their English supplier before duty and transportation costs. Yarn costs were about 35 per cent of sales. Furthermore, WSM had more than sufficient yarn capacity to supply Elite's needs. By combining product lines, sales effort and expanding the sale of Elite's products beyond Canada, Dunlop felt sales could be increased considerably. The plant had estimated capacity to support over $25 million in sales. Some savings could also be realized by centralizing administration and bookkeeping.

While net book value for the company was negative, Dunlop felt he would have to offer something for its equity. He was informed that about 100 of the employees had each invested $3 000 when they had purchased the company in 1978. In addition, the bank would expect an equity infusion.

On another front, Dunlop had been having discussions with his major U.S. wholesaler/agent about an exchange of ownership. Dunlop explained:

> My major wholesaler in the U.S. accounts for about 35–40 per cent of our sales. Because they're so important to DCC, we've been talking about an exchange of shares. Although we haven't gotten to specifics, they have very few hard assets, basically an office, a few sales people and a phone, we would probably give 4 per cent of DCC for 25 per cent of their operation. It's a small business and the owner takes a large salary, but I'm more interested in cementing the relationship than making a big return on my investment.

Dunlop also wanted to set up an importing company, probably in Seattle, Washington, in order to bring in hand-tufted carpets from Thailand. DCC already did a small amount of importing of hand-tufted carpets. Rather than lose a sale to a price-sensitive customer who was willing to accept longer delivery terms, DCC sales representatives would offer the import option. The order would be placed through Dunco International, another company owned by Dunlop Holdings, with a supplier in Thailand.

Geographic growth was also being pursued. DCC had two European agents, and had just hired a full time representative based in England. Much of this offshore business was for major commercial development projects. For example, through a European dealer DCC had just been asked to bid on a major hotel/commercial complex in the Middle East. DCC's international competitiveness was influenced by strong local competition, the 14 per cent tariff and currency fluctuations. This latter factor was currently in DCC's favour.

EXHIBIT 1 DCC Financial Summary

($000s)

	Designer Classics Carpet				WSM
	1983	*1984*	*1985*	*1986*	*1986*
Gross Sales	1 140	2 430	3 721	5 200	
Less deductions**		380	595	810	
Net Sales		2 050	3 126	4 390	
Cost of Goods Sold					
Labour	160	435	530	700	
Material	610	677	792	1 142	
Overhead —variable	206	331	507	680	
— fixed		219	408	500	
Gross Margin	164	388	889	1 368	
Selling Expense**	226	150	285	580	
Unusual item				75*	
Administrative Expense	159	346	497	650	
Income Before Tax	(209)	(108)	108	63	
Excluding unusual item				138	
Assets					
Accounts receivable			769	1 036	51
Inventories			412	707	18
Prepaid expenses			86	117	4
Total Current Assets			1 268	1 862	73
Machinery & Equipment (net)			349	363	183†
Trademarks				10	
Total Assets	591	1 380	1 617	2 234	256
Liabilities & Equity					
Bank loans			139	298	39
Accounts payable††			688	801	67
Payable to affiliates				49	
ODC export loans			157	423	
Shareholder loan			11	10	
l-t principal due			51	68	
Total Current Liabilities			1 046	1 648	106
Long-term Debt			310	235	139††
Equity & Retained Earnings			261	352	10
Total	591	1 380	1 617	2 234	256
Number of Employees	45	60	85	130	

* Unusual item: upfront payment to U.S. sales representative who delivered no sales.
** Commissions to agents, duties, freight, etc. included as selling expense in 1983 deducted from sales 1984 onward.
† Includes land (25), buildings (103) and equipment (58) less depreciation (3).
†† Includes Small Business Loan and loan from parent company (48).

EXHIBIT 2 DCC Tufted Carpet: Production Steps

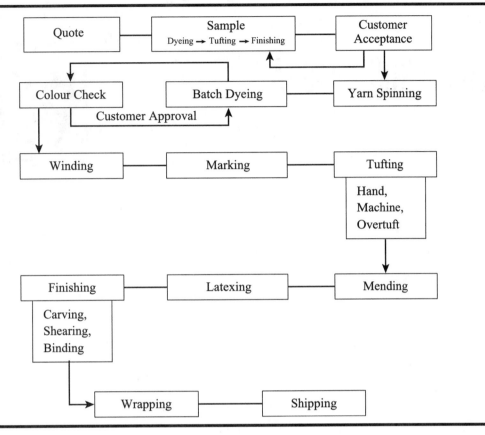

EXHIBIT 3 DCC Remake Charges as a Percentage of Sales

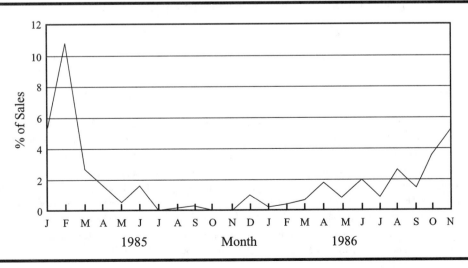

AER LINGUS—ATS (A)

J. P e t e r K i l l i n g

On July 15, 1985, Denis Hanrahan was flying from Dublin to Toronto, as he had many times over the past 11 months, to meet with Klaus Woerner, the owner and president of Automation Tooling Systems (ATS), a robotics firm based in Kitchener, Ontario. Mr. Hanrahan's job was to expand the "non-airline" activities of Aer Lingus, and ATS was a company in which he wanted to acquire an equity position.

IVEY

J. Peter Killing prepared this case solely to provide material for class discussion. The author does not intend to illustrate either effective or ineffective handling of a managerial situation. The author may have disguised certain names and other identifying information to protect confidentiality.

The negotiations between Denis and Klaus had been friendly but protracted, and it appeared that they were finally nearing an end. The deal, which both sides had agreed to verbally, was that Aer Lingus would purchase 75 per cent of the shares of ATS, and that Klaus would stay on and manage the company. The price that he would receive for his shares would depend on the earnings of ATS in the years ending September 30, 1985, and 1986. If ATS met the profit forecast that Klaus had prepared for it, he would receive a total of $4.6 million in cash, and retain a 25 per cent interest in the company.

AER LINGUS

Aer Lingus was the Irish international airline, wholly owned by the Irish government. Like many airlines, Aer Lingus had difficulty producing a consistent high level of earnings (Table 1). The early 1980s in particular were not good years for the airline (nor for any other), and only the consistent profitability of the group's hotels, airline-related businesses (maintenance and overhaul of the other firm's aircraft, training of flight crews and so on), and financial and commercial businesses kept the company's overall losses in check.

T A B L E 1   Aer Lingus Financial Results[1] Years Ending March 31

(millions of Irish pounds)[2]

| | 1985 | | 1984 | | 1983 | | 1982 | | 1981 | |
	Revenue	Profit	Revenue	Profit	Revenue	Profit	Revenue	Profit	Revenue	Profit
Air Transport	281	.5	270	1.4	244	(2.7)	218	(11.2)	164	(15.9)
Ancillary Operations										
Airline Related	110	12.7	82	11.1	66	9.0	62	8.6	47	7.5
Hotel & Leisure	79	11.7	82	7.7	82	6.0	71	7.8	54	7.7
Financial & Commercial	33	5.4	24	4.5	11	3.6	8	2.0	6	1.3
Net Profit After Head Office Expenses, Interest, Tax[3]	11.6		4.9		(2.5)		(9.2)		(13.6)	

[1] In 1985 the group total assets stood at £285 million. A breakdown of assets employed in each business area was not publicly reported.
[2] Canadian dollars per Irish pound: 1981—1.90; 1982—1.75; 1983—1.54; 1984—1.41; 1985—1.44
[3] The company earned a positive net profit in each of the four years preceding 1981.

A small group of managers under the leadership of Gerry Dempsey were responsible for managing and expanding Aer Lingus's non-airline activities. Denis Hanrahan, second in command, commented:

> We all recognize that the airline business is a cyclical one, and our goal is to create a stable base of earnings which will see the airline safely through the bottom of the cycles. We have been successful so far so we don't know if the government would bail us out if we did make continued heavy losses, and we don't want to have to find out! The mission of our "ancillary activities" is to increase the Group's reported earnings and to strengthen its balance sheet.

The "financial and commercial" results in Table 1 include a data processing firm, an insurance company, a helicopter company, a hospital management firm, a land development company, and a 25 per cent interest in GPA, formerly Guiness Peat Aviation. Many of these firms, with the exception of the hotels, were founded by former Aer Lingus employees. Although most of the companies were performing well, the undoubted star was GPA. A manager explained:

> In 1975 or so, Tony Ryan, our New York station manager, was transferred back to Ireland and asked to lease out a 747 which we did not need for the winter. In looking at the leasing market, he thought he saw a very good business opportunity, and he convinced us and a related British company to

each put up 45 per cent of the capital required to start an aircraft leasing company. He kept the remaining 10 per cent. As things have developed, he was certainly right about the opportunity. In the ten intervening years, we have received almost 20 million Irish pounds from that business, and our initial investment was only 2.2 million! We still own 25 per cent of the company, and now have firms like Air Canada and the General Electric Credit Corporation as partners. GPA is one of the Irish success stories of the past decade.

THE MOVE INTO ROBOTICS

In 1983, Denis Hanrahan began an informal search for a new area of investment that could provide healthy financial returns to Aer Lingus for at least the next decade. By January 1984, he had concluded that robotics was an extremely interesting field. Robots had been used in Japan since the 1960s but were not adopted in Europe and the U.S. until the late 1970s. Many analysts expected a robotics boom, with growth rates as high as 30 per cent per annum, as Western firms strove to catch up.

Although robot manufacturing appeared to Denis to be an overcrowded field, he was excited about the possibility of becoming a developer of the ancillary technology and components that were required by firms wanting to install robot-based flexible manufacturing assembly lines. His figures suggested that the market value of ancillary systems was at least equal to the value of the robots themselves. Although the volume of business being done in this new area was impossible to quantify with any degree of precision, it appeared to be growing quickly and offer high margins. There were as yet no major companies in the business. Denis described Aer Lingus's initial entry into the field:

> The first company we looked at was in the UK. We quickly decided that it was too big, too sexy, and considering its size, depended too heavily on a single supplier of robots. One thing you have to watch out for in this business is guys in very classy suits who know more about doing deals and driving for the initial public offering which is going to make them rich than they do about robotics. It turned out that we were right about that company, as it went bankrupt afterwards.

> The company we did buy was Airstead Industrial Systems of the UK. This is a very small company, much smaller than ATS, but it has the rights to distribute Seiko robots in England. Seiko, in addition to producing products such as watches and Epson computer printers, is a prominent robot manufacturer and doing very well in some fast growing niches.

After the acquisition of Airstead, Aer Lingus dispatched an analyst to North America to examine six companies that Seiko had identified as the most promising North American robotics systems firms. On August 15, Denis received a telex containing a thumbnail sketch of ATS, indicating that it was the best of the three firms the analyst had seen to date, and was worth a closer look. On August 28, Denis was in Kitchener for his first meeting with Klaus Woerner.

KLAUS WOERNER AND ATS

Born in Germany in 1940, Klaus Woerner emigrated to Canada at age 20 after serving an apprenticeship in the tool and die business. He subsequently worked for a variety of manufacturing firms in Canada but, tired of the "hierarchies and rigidities of large corporations," founded ATS in 1978. The new company was not successful, however, until Klaus turned it away from manufacturing and into systems work. The move into robotics was made in late 1981.

By the summer of 1984 ATS had grown to employ 44 people, including 26 tool makers, 15 hardware and software designers, and 3 in sales and administration. Denis was encouraged to see that Klaus was a technically oriented hands-on manager whose elegant and creative solutions to systems problems played a major role in the company's success. Klaus, Denis observed, was more at home on the shop floor than talking to accountants, bankers or lawyers. In his summary of their first meeting, Denis made the following points:

1. Woerner was an easy individual to get along with, though I would anticipate that he is used to getting his own way. He is the key decision-maker in the company, although he does solicit the opinions of his senior colleagues.

2. The company currently turns over approximately $3.5 million per year, and expects to double its sales this year on last year, after a number of years of relatively slow growth. Woerner reports a current backlog of $3 million.

3. The major financial problem with the business is that there is a significant working capital requirement. I have heard a rule of thumb that suggests 40 per cent of turnover is required in this business, but Klaus thought that was far too high. The practical problem is that the final payment of 30 per cent of systems costs tends to be delayed for several months after completion of the work while fine tuning is being performed.

4. Woerner recently came very close to selling ATS to Berton Industries,[1] a major Canadian corporation in the automotive components business. One hundred percent of ATS was to be acquired and, depending on results, it would have been valued at $3–4 million. Woerner got very concerned, however, at what he perceived to be the inordinate length of time being taken in detailed negotiations, and at the aggressive attitude of the other party's attorneys. In addition, Berton would not give him any assurances about future investment in ATS, and apparently Woerner learned that plans had been made to move ATS to another location without any consultation with him. When the president of Berton then ignored Woerner's request that a number of written commitments be made within one week, the deal was off.

5. Woerner's proposal was that Aer Lingus would take 50 per cent of the company for an undetermined amount, 50 per cent of which would be left in the company, and that he would take 50 per cent out. I indicated to him that 50 per cent would probably be the minimum share that we would require, and it could be that we would want considerably more. However, any deal that we would do would be structured in such a way that he and his key people would be committed to staying with the company. He had no difficulty with this point, and conceded that he was not wedded to the 50–50 formula, which was clearly an ideal going-in position from his point of view.

6. On balance, I found ATS to be very impressive. Though operating in cramped facilities, it does appear to have a real technical depth, and undoubtedly has an established customer base. The company appears to be an appropriate size to take over since it is neither so small as to be extraordinarily risky nor so big as to be extraordinarily expensive.

The meeting ended with the two men agreeing to continue discussions, and to try to reach a gentlemen's agreement reasonably quickly rather than getting bogged down in protracted technical or legal discussions. Woerner promised to send some financial information as soon as he could get it together, although he warned that his business plan should not be taken too literally as "these things are more exercises than necessarily forecasts of reality."

SUBSEQUENT MEETINGS

Over the next six months, Denis Hanrahan held a number of meetings with Klaus Woerner, bringing with him on occasion Gerry Dempsey and Larry Stanley, two of Aer Lingus's ancillary business managers. Both men subsequently supported Denis's view that ATS would be a good acquisition. This positive feedback was also strengthened by comments from Seiko's North American sales manager, who stated that in ten years ATS would be "one of the top three robot systems integrator firms in North America" if it grew to

---

[1] Disguised name.

its potential. The meetings with Klaus also yielded more information about his expectations and the operations of ATS. The following excerpts are taken from Denis Hanrahan's notes and comments on various meetings, all of which were held in either Kitchener or Toronto.

Meeting of November 6

Present: G.P. Dempsey, Denis Hanrahan, Klaus Woerner, and Peter Jones,[2] who was Klaus Woerner's personal financial advisor and company accountant.

1. Woerner outlined his expectations for growth of the automation and robotics industry and for ATS. It seems clear that they have not done very much forward planning. Woerner quoted Laura Conigliaro of Prudential-Bache as suggesting growth from $250 million in 1984 to $1 billion by 1987, but these figures were not very convincing since they related to the total industry rather than to the sub-segment in which ATS is involved.

2. Woerner stated that he expected ATS revenues to total $4 million for the year ending September 1984, $6 million for 1985 (rather than the $5 million he had earlier been projecting), and to reach $10 million in three years' time. He believed that growth to $10 million could be financed through a combination of retained earnings and bank debt.

3. Northern Telecom, a major Canadian multinational firm, apparently accounts for approximately 40 per cent of ATS revenues. Woerner indicated that this proportion would fall to one-third in 1985 due to the growth of ATS. He stated strongly that in spite of the company's high dependence on Northern Telecom he could, if necessary, survive a total loss of Northern's business by falling back on traditional non flexible production line work ("hard" automation). However, he expressed the view that Northern Telecom could not break the relationship with him since they were dependent on ATS for maintenance and software updates.

4. There was an extensive discussion on the subject of control. Woerner's recent negotiations with Berton have left him very uneasy about the behaviour of large corporations, and he again expressed his strong preference for a 50–50 partnership. Dempsey responded that our whole approach to subsidiaries was to work in partnership with the management of them, and that this approach was not altered whether the shareholding was 2 per cent, 50 per cent, or 99 per cent. Woerner appeared to implicitly accept that we might go to 75 per cent or higher of the equity as long as we were concerned only with issues such as overall earnings and growth rather than the detailed operating practices involved. Dempsey suggested that Woerner should write to us in simple, non-legal terms outlining those issues upon which he believed he would require assurance from us. Woerner accepted this suggestion.

5. Woerner also expressed concern that his was a small company in danger of being "trampled on" by Aer Lingus. While he was happy enough with the people he currently knew in Aer Lingus, he felt that these individuals could change and he could thus find himself exposed to changes of policy or personality. Dempsey responded that we could not fully reassure him on this issue. We had now had a wide range of relationships with subsidiaries over a long period of time; this had not occurred historically, and he saw no reason why it should happen in the future.

6. There were no specific discussions on the matter of price. Dempsey stated on a number of occasions that it was purposeless to discuss price until the financials were available and had been reviewed. Woerner concurred.

7. The meeting ended on a positive and progressive note. It was agreed that we would appoint Peat Marwick to review the affairs of ATS, and they would contact Jones as necessary. Also Jones would shortly produce a three-year forecast for ATS.

---

[2] Disguised name.

Meeting of January 10

The next meeting between Klaus and Denis included Bill Harcourt[3] of Peat Marwick Mitchell. During this meeting the ATS financial statements and projections (Exhibits 1 and 2) were given to Denis. These were to have been sent to Ireland several weeks earlier.

Denis learned during this meeting that Klaus had not written the promised letter concerning his specific issues of concern because he preferred to discuss them face to face. Further discussion ensued during which Klaus reiterated his general unease at the prospect of being controlled, and repeated his desire for a 50–50 deal. While still not raising any specific concerns, Klaus repeatedly referred to the Berton deal and how lucky he was to have avoided it. Denis commented after the meeting:

> All of this was territory that we had covered several times previously with him, and we essentially just covered it again. It was clear that, as the discussion progressed, Klaus began to get more comfortable, and his fears began to recede. I have no doubt that after I depart from Canada he begins to get uneasy again at the unknown. He reiterated that he was quite comfortable working with Mr. Dempsey or myself, but that he could naturally have no assurance that we would be around forever.
>
> In the earlier part of the meeting when Klaus was appearing very reluctant, Bill Harcourt asked him directly if he, in fact, wanted to sell ATS. Klaus replied that he didn't really want to—he had devoted all of his time in the last few years in building up the company, and wished to continue to do so in the future—but because ATS would not be producing large amounts of cash in the short term he had no choice. He believes that ATS can and must grow very rapidly to forestall the competition—the opportunities are there, and if ATS does not take advantage of them, someone else will. In this vein he mentioned that he had just revised his estimate of the current year's sales from $6 million to $9 million.
>
> The other reason that Klaus feels that he has to sell ATS is that important customers like Northern Telecom are nervous of becoming too dependent on him, as long as he does not have a major corporate backer. Klaus told us in the meeting that Northern had in fact deliberately cut back their orders to him for this reason, and we independently checked that this was indeed the case.

The meeting ended on a very friendly note with Denis again encouraging Klaus to make up a list of his specific concerns so that they could be addressed, and Klaus inviting Bill Harcourt to visit the ATS plant before the next meeting so that he could develop a better understanding of what they were doing.

Meetings of January 24 and February 20

The meetings of January 24 and February 20 were devoted to discussions of a deal whereby Aer Lingus would acquire 75 per cent of ATS' stock, with Klaus Woerner holding the remaining 25 per cent. At the January 24 meeting, Klaus appeared to accept the idea that he would sell the 75 per cent of the company, but apparently as a result of his earlier negotiations with Berton, was adamant that ATS was worth at least $6 million. In the February 20th meeting, Denis finally agreed that ATS could be worth $6 million if the company met Klaus's new projections for it, but at that moment it was not. As a consequence, Denis proposed that the amount paid to Klaus should depend on the company's performance in 1985 and 1986. The details, spelled out in a letter from Denis to Klaus following the February meeting, were as follows:

1. We propose that a valuation be established for ATS as of September 30, 1986. This valuation will be calculated by taking 3.5 times the pretax income for the fiscal year ended September 30, 1985, and adding to it 3.5 times the incremental pretax income earned in the fiscal year ending September, 1986. By incremental income here, I mean the excess of pretax income in fiscal 1986 over that earned in fiscal 1985.
2. In determining pretax income, research and development costs shall be charged at the rate contained in your financial projections or at a higher rate if so incurred. Profit sharing to employees shall be

---

[3] Disguised name.

charged at 10 per cent of pretax income before profit sharing or such higher rate as may be incurred. In addition, we would require the company to maintain a key-man insurance policy on yourself in the amount of $5 000 000, and the cost of such coverage would be borne as a charge before striking pretax income.

3. On the basis of the pretax income figures outlined above, the company would have a total value of $6 835 000 as of September 30, 1986.

4. Under the above formula, the maximum value that we would be prepared to put on ATS would be $7 000 000, even if the results are better than projected.

5. It is our view that the company is in need of significant additional funds to allow it to develop to the sales and income levels in your projections. Accordingly, we are willing to inject $2 000 000 into ATS for agreed working capital and investment use in the form of a secured debt with a 10 per cent interest rate. It would be our intention to make available $750 000 at time of closing, $750 000 at time of completion of the 1985 audit, and the remaining $500 000 as needed by the company on an agreed basis during 1986.

6. It would be our intention that this loan would be used to purchase treasury stock from ATS at the end of 1986, using the valuation for the company as established by the formula outlined above. In other words, if the company was valued at $6 835 000, the $2 000 000 loan would convert to give us 22.6 per cent of the enlarged equity in the company. The attraction of this arrangement from your point of view is that it provides you with the money now to grow, but that the shares are ultimately purchased in ATS at the valuation achieved in 1986 rather than at a current valuation. Depending upon the ultimate valuation of the company, the percentage of its enlarged equity that would be bought by the $2 000 000 referred to above would vary. It would then be our intention to purchase directly from you existing shares held by you in ATS such as would give us 75 per cent of the then-enlarged equity of the company. In the example quoted above, we would need to purchase 67 per cent of your shareholding to give us a total of 75 per cent of the enlarged equity. Using the value above, this would cost $4 600 000. In other words, what you would receive would be $4 600 000 in cash plus 25 per cent interest in the $2 000 000 injected by us: for a total of $5 100 000, which is 75 per cent of $6 835 000.

7. We propose that you would be paid for these shares as follows: on closing, $500 000; in March 1986 and March 1987, further payments of $500 000; in March 1988 and March 1989, further payments of $1 000 000 each; the balance, payable on March 1990. To the degree that the final value of the company is larger or smaller than the $6 835 000 figure, the above payments would be prorated.

MOVING FORWARD

On March 16, Bill Harcourt phoned Denis to report that he had met with Klaus, subsequent to the February 22 meeting. Denis recalled the discussion:

Apparently Klaus was initially very unhappy with the limit of $7 million that we put on the company, although he is now willing to live with it, and in fact has become very positive about doing a deal with Aer Lingus. He appears to have overcome his hesitance and concern at another party becoming the majority shareholder of ATS. This may be due to the fact that he has taken advice from a friend named Bob Tivey, who is a retired president of Monarch Canada.[4] Some minor improvements are required, however.

One of these is that Klaus wants us to increase the $500 000 coming to him on closing so that he can pay employee bonuses—these will come out of his own pocket—and have more for himself. He also wants us to pay interest on the portion of the purchase price which remains unpaid until the earn-out is completed. Finally, he would like a personal contract which will last five years, and include a good salary, plus a bonus that is 2 per cent of pretax earnings, and a car.

Other news included the fact that Klaus is in the process of hiring a financial person, and is considering a second-year registered industrial accountancy student. Bill suggested that he discuss this matter in

---

[4] Disguised name.

some detail with us, as it might be advisable to opt for a more high-powered person. Bill also told me that Klaus was facing an immediate decision with respect to new premises for ATS—the major question being whether the company should rent or buy. Purchase cost will be close to $1 million.

Shortly after his phone call, Denis received a letter from Klaus, which began, "I wish to advise you that I am prepared to accept the proposal as outlined...subject to the following changes." As expected, the most important of the requested changes were an increased initial payment, the payment of interest on the unpaid portion of the purchase price, and a five-year employment contract.

After some negotiation, Aer Lingus agreed to increase its initial payment to allow Klaus to pay employee bonuses, and to increase the initial funds going to his own pocket by approximately 50 per cent, which was less than he had requested, but was deemed satisfactory.

In early April, Klaus travelled to Ireland for a meeting with the Chief Executive of Aer Lingus, and later that month the Aer Lingus board approved the purchase of a 75 per cent shareholding of ATS on the terms which had been agreed with Klaus.

At the end of April, Denis was once again in Kitchener, where he and Klaus held a most amicable meeting. Denis learned that Klaus and Bob Tivey had prepared a new business plan that they had used to obtain an increase in the ATS credit line. Also, Klaus had decided to proceed with the acquisition, his only objection being that eight board meetings a year was too many. Denis concluded his notes on the meeting with the following:

> We discussed at length the need for ATS management to develop credibility with me, and for me to develop credibility on ATS subjects in Dublin, which he seemed to accept. All in all, the discussions were satisfactory and straightforward, and have put to rest a significant number of my fears concerning Mr. Woerner's independence and his unwillingness to accommodate the requirements of a major corporate shareholder. In my view, he will accept direction, provided that the direction is fast-paced and is seen by him as being responsive to ATS's needs.

Due to some apparent foot-dragging on the part of Klaus's lawyers and intervening vacations, it was July before Denis arrived in Kitchener to review the drafts of the sale contracts, and bring the deal to a conclusion.

THE MEETING OF JULY 16

Klaus attended this meeting with Ron Jutras, his new financial controller, who had been hired without consultation with Aer Lingus, and Bob Tivey, who was acting as a consultant to Klaus. Denis recalled the meeting as follows:

> They opened the meeting by tabling a number of requirements which they said were critical to the deal going ahead. These were:

1. A reluctance to hand over control to us before the valuation date of September 1986.
2. A five-year guaranteed contract for Klaus, with a ten-year period before we can force him out of share ownership.
3. A degree of protection against the possibility that one-off costs may depress 1986 earnings—specifically a minimum buyout price of $6 million!

> I was very distressed to find such a total about-face on something that we had agreed three months earlier, and when faced with this, Klaus acknowledged that he was changing his mind, but said that he could not afford the possibility of one bad year depressing his buyout price. As for the contract length, Klaus was very emotional when the possibility of anything shorter than a five-year contract was raised.
>
> The question facing me as I sat in that meeting was how to react. Was it time to give up on this long and apparently fruitless process, or should I continue—and if so, how?

E X H I B I T 1   ATS Financial Statements

(C$000)

	1980	*1981*	*1982*	*1983*	*1984*
Sales	332	765	1 210	1 753	4 168
Cost of Sales	187	491	902	1 450	3 197
Gross Margin	145	274	308	303	971
Overheads	58	127	188	243	451
Operating Profit	87	147	120	60	520
Interest	2	10	20	26	71
Tax	11	22	4	0	18
Net Profit	74	115	96	34	431
Balance Sheets					
Fixed Assets	106	211	308	390	517
Current Assets	113	282	384	457	1 300
Current Liabilities	(35)	(129)	(209)	(252)	(390)
Working Capital	78	153	175	205	910
	184	364	483	595	1 427
Funded by					
Share Capital	1	6	5	3	3
Revenue Reserves	79	114	177	(160)	164
Shareholders' Funds	80	120	182	(157)	167
Loan Capital	104	244	301	752	1 260
	184	364	483	595	1 427

EXHIBIT 2   Projected ATS Financial Statements*

(C$000)

	1985	1986	1987	1988
Sales	8 000	11 000	14 000	17 000
Cost of Sales	5 920	8 360	10 920	13 260
Gross Margin	2 080	2 640	3 080	3 740
Overheads	1 040	1 430	1 750	2 210
Operating Profit	1 040	1 210	1 330	1 530
Interest	70	120	200	300
Tax	427	480	497	541
Net Profit	543	610	633	689
Dividends (Projected)	0	0	250	300

Projected Balance Sheets	1984	1985	1986	1987	1988
Fixed Assets	517	680	1 030	1 310	1 860
Development				1 000	1 000
Current Assets	1 300	2 417	4 904	5 740	6 580
Current Liabilities	(390)	(760)	(1 720)	(1 886)	(2 260)
Working Capital	910	1 657	3 184	3 854	4 320
	1 427	2 337	4 214	6 164	7 180

Funded by					
Share Capital	3	750	2 000	2 300	2 700
Revenue Reserves	164	707	1 317	1 701	2 090
Shareholders' Funds	167	1 457	3 317	4 001	3 790
Loan Capital	1 260	880	897	2 163	3 390
	1 427	2 337	4 214	6 164	7 180

* These projections were prepared by Klaus Woerner and Peter Jones.

EXHIBIT 3   Revised ATS Income Projections*

(C$000)

	1985	1986	1987	1988
Sales	8 000	14 000	20 000	30 000
Gross Margin	2 080	3 360	4 400	6 000
	(26%)	(24%)	(22%)	(20%)
General & Admin.	862	1 190	1 578	2 159
Income	1 218	2 170	2 822	3 841
Profit Sharing	120	217	282	384
Pretax Income	1 098	1 953	2 540	3 457
Tax at 45%	494	879	1 143	1 556
After Tax Income	604	1 074	1 397	1 901

* These revisions were dated February 20, 1985. They were prepared by Klaus Woerner, working with Bill Harcourt.

VISIONING AT XEROX CANADA

case
20

Nick Bontis
and Mary M. Crossan

On June 15, 1994, Diane McGarry, Chairman, CEO and President of Xerox Canada, asked Bryan Smith, a consultant working for the company, if he would join her outside the conference room for a brief tête-à-tête. They had been meeting with her leadership team[1] since 8:00 a.m. to craft the organization's new vision statement.

It was now past 11:30 a.m. and the "visioning" session was scheduled to end at noon. During the previous three and a half hours, some progress had been made, but Smith felt that more time would be needed

---

[1] Consisting of 23 senior managers (many of which were McGarry's direct reports).

IVEY

Nick Bontis prepared this case under the supervision of Professor Mary M. Crossan solely to provide material for class discussion. The authors do not intend to illustrate either effective or ineffective handling of a managerial situation. The authors may have disguised certain names and other identifying information to protect confidentiality.

to give the decision its due process. Smith suggested that they extend the allotted time into the afternoon or postpone the session. However, McGarry was hesitant to delay the final selection of the vision statement because it was very important to her. As they both returned to the conference room, McGarry contemplated her next move.

XEROX CORP.

Xerox Corp. was a global player in the document processing market. Its activities encompassed the designing, manufacturing and servicing of a complete range of document processing products. Xerox copiers, duplicators, electronic printers, optical scanners, facsimile machines, networks, multifunction publishing machines and related software and supplies were marketed in more than 130 countries.

Xerox Corp. had won many accolades in the United States, Australia, Belgium, Brazil, Canada, Colombia, France, Hong Kong, India, Ireland, Japan, Mexico, the Netherlands and the United Kingdom, reflecting its prestigious standing in the business world. In 1980, Fuji Xerox won the Deming Prize, Japan's highest quality award. The major U.S. award was the Malcolm Baldrige National Quality Award, which Xerox Business Products and Systems won in 1989. Then in 1992, Rank Xerox won the first European Quality Award. The pursuit of these awards often incited organizations to participate in the visioning process. Vision statements were a critical element in the evaluation process.

XEROX CANADA

Although Xerox Corp. controlled its Canadian subsidiary from a regulatory perspective, it often allowed the smaller organization enough latitude to pursue its own initiatives (this included developing its own vision statement). The parent considered its Canadian subsidiary as a laboratory for strategic experiments. With this unofficial mandate, the Canadian operation had developed a solid reputation for the implementation of various employee-inspired programs. Xerox Canada was also known for its publicly displayed corporate ideals. A senior manager described the company's situation this way:

> Our company is very well known and respected in the business community for integrating its various "corporate concepts."[2] In fact, CEOs of other large multinational enterprises often marvel at the way we are able to harmonize our numerous strategic initiatives into a coordinated effort. They often sit in our boardroom and just admire the programs we proudly display on our walls. Many of these strategic initiatives are sponsored by our parent company in Stamford, Connecticut, while others are independently developed by our own employees here in Canada.

One of the main themes in Xerox Canada's philosophy deals with "satisfied customers." To further improve service to its customers, Xerox Canada announced an organizational restructuring that would create special customer business units in order to maintain closer ties with the marketplace. This restructuring was McGarry's responsibility.

McGarry's Arrival in Canada

McGarry was promoted to the top position in Canada in October 1993 because she was recognized as a team player who prided herself on open communication. Her leadership skills and risk-taking attitude were exactly what Xerox Canada needed during this restructuring period. In the first 60 days in her new position, she visited 14 cities across Canada and talked to thousands of employees, customers, and suppliers in order to "get to know Canada." She came back from this trip with a better understanding of the company,

---

[2] Including Xerox's signature, philosophy, priorities, cultural dimensions (see Exhibit 1).

the domestic market, Canada's economy and its government. McGarry's most important mandate since her arrival in late 1993 was to bring this restructured design to life and make it work in Canada.

While the restructuring took place, Xerox Canada employees continued to develop and support innovative strategic initiatives. Many of these programs, including the new employee evaluation system, went on to become worldwide initiatives that eventually helped shape the culture and the values of the whole organization.

Employee-Inspired Initiatives

A commitment to community involvement was basic to the company's business philosophy. Xerox Canada contributed $1.3 million in 1994 to charities and nonprofit organizations across Canada. About 65% of the contributions were focused on projects which support Information Technology Literacy, which includes the Xerox Aboriginal Scholarships program for aboriginal students studying programs that could lead to a career in information technology. The remaining funds were focused on community programs such as the United Way, matching employee gifts to post-secondary institutions, and the Xerox Community Involvement Program (XCIP). The XCIP offered financial support to community organizations in which employees volunteer on a regular basis.

In addition to its sense of community involvement, Xerox Canada shared the public's concern about the environment and integrated that concern into its business activities. The company was dedicated to protecting the environment as a responsible corporate citizen. In its marketing materials, Xerox described itself as setting standards for its products that went beyond many government requirements for health, safety and environmental protection in the countries in which it operated. The company was proud to communicate its commitment to the philosophy of sustainable development, which meant meeting the needs of the present without compromising the needs of future generations.

Another very successful program that symbolized the progressive culture of the organization was a new collaborative, performance-feedback process: COMIT (Communication of Objectives and Measurements and ensuring our success through Inspection and Teamwork). COMIT's objective was to extend beyond Xerox Canada's standard business results by incorporating its five key priorities with eight new cultural dimensions (see Exhibit 1 for details). Senior management hoped the union of these 13 elements would allow the COMIT process to affect the behaviours of the employees and to create a more empowered and dynamic organizational culture. Although Xerox Canada could be criticized for its overzealous pursuit of these and other programs, which went above and beyond its operational duties, the company never ignored its pledge of boundless service to its customers. In the 1994 Annual Report, Diane McGarry stated:

> We focus on what will make a difference for our customers—anticipating their needs, satisfying and exceeding all their expectations, and creating relationships that will serve them into the next century.

During the restructuring period, McGarry also familiarized herself with the most recently developed employee-inspired initiatives to get a better sense of what important issues interested the employees of Xerox Canada. The following describes three more employee-inspired programs developed at Xerox Canada:

> *Xerox chez moi*—in this work-from-home or work-from-anywhere program, nearly 750 staff "telecommuted" as part of a work-at-home experiment that began company-wide in March 1994. Reaction so far was favourable. Employees claimed that they got double and triple the work done without normal office interruptions.

> *Keeping customers forever*—the objective of this program was to get customers and keep them forever. The advent of CBUs provided for a system that allowed service employees to build loyal and long-term relationships in which customers felt satisfied.

Xerox flexplace—ninety per cent of surveyed employees said that being able to balance the needs of both family life and the needs of the business was a key factor in the satisfaction of an employee. This program offered a wide range of flexible work arrangements, including the opportunity for men to nurture new babies while on a parental leave.

As the restructuring continued and new initiatives were launched, the parent company watched over McGarry closely. This prompted her to re-examine not only her contribution to the organization, but the contribution of every other employee as well. The genesis of the visioning process had emerged. Senior management felt that a new vision statement would convey the ideals of the corporation, encompass present attitudes, and continue to align employees in their operational activities and in their innovative efforts.

THE VISIONING PROCESS

By mid-1994, Diane McGarry's leadership transition into Xerox Canada was running smoothly. Business performance was favourable (see Exhibit 2) and customers and employees alike were supporting new developments in the organization. Furthermore, corporate insiders predicted that Xerox Canada was slowly becoming the jewel of the Xerox Corp. empire worldwide.

As Xerox Canada moved comfortably into the latter half of the 1990s, McGarry believed that a vision statement for the company should be developed to help integrate all of the company's diverse activities. Previous vision statements for Xerox Canada were not widely known throughout the organization and had been practically forgotten by most employees since McGarry's arrival in Canada. Although McGarry recognized that Xerox Canada already had several important "corporate concepts" such as the signature (The Document Company), the philosophy, five priorities and eight cultural dimensions (see Exhibit 1), she believed that it was imperative to synthesize a vision statement for the company that would coordinate all of the concepts, initiatives and activities of the organization. This was considered a critical exercise early in her tenure and one she felt would prove to be highly insightful.

McGarry invited her leadership team to Niagara-on-the-Lake for a two-day corporate retreat. The first scheduled item on the program was a four-hour session to create the new vision statement. McGarry also brought in a management consultant, Bryan Smith, who had prior experience with visioning with several other large corporate clients.[3] Smith had also done some prior consulting with Xerox Canada and was, therefore, somewhat familiar with the company's history.

Several weeks prior to the meeting, McGarry asked each team member to review the company's earlier vision statements. Approximately 90% of the team members had been through a visioning process at least once in their careers. The last time any of the participants had been through this process was during David McCamus' tenure in the early 1990s. Bryan Smith also played a significant role during McCamus' tenure and had earned a solid reputation for himself amongst the senior managers by running several successful workshops and joint projects. Current members of Xerox Canada's leadership team were already familiar with Smith's work and respected his contributions. McCamus' team had developed the following vision statement during the early 1990s:

> Our raison d'être is to create a dynamic growth oriented business by providing superior customer satisfaction through quality products and innovative services supported by an inspired team of skilled individuals.

When Richard Barton took over the leadership position from McCamus in 1991, he personally developed a vision statement that was subsequently confirmed by his management team at a meeting in August 1991. This statement was printed on the 1992 COMIT documents for all employees:

---

[3] In fact, he had published an article on the topic: Bryan Smith, "Vision: A Time to Take Stock," *Business Quarterly* (Autumn 1989), pp. 80–84.

We will know we have reached the desired state of Xerox when The Document Company is the leader in providing Document services that enhance business productivity.

Now that McGarry was in charge, she felt that it was necessary not only to create a new vision statement, but to seek input from her direct reports and their subordinates. She wanted this to be a team effort. The first task she had her team accomplish was to seek feedback from Xerox Canada's largest customers on what their needs were. The following describes some of the comments received from customers:

- we want someone with skill, expertise, resources and the creativity that is needed to take cost out of operations, and add speed and quality;
- we want someone to identify what our needs are, recommend solutions, and work every step of the way to ensure success;
- we need software that will allow us to access information and respond far more quickly than we could in a paper-based environment.

As the visioning session approached, McGarry's team reflected on the organization's recent accomplishments and carefully considered the values that motivated the employees to work each and every day. At the start of the visioning session, the team members collectively selected the criteria that they would use to help guide the process. The three chosen criteria ensured that the statement would be: (1) clear; (2) motivating; and (3) inspiring. The brainstorming session commenced once the criteria were set. Each participant was asked to write down three words on a flip chart to help spark the brainstorming process. At this point, the tone of the session was very positive and there was a tremendous amount of energy and excitement in the conference room. Soon after, the participants were asked to create and write down one vision statement that included their three key words.

Eventually, twenty-four individual statements (one from each member of the leadership team plus McGarry) were posted around the room on flip charts. Participants were asked to read out their own statements twice while emphasizing the key words. The whole group cheered after each participant was finished. Smith then facilitated the session by grouping the statements together and removing duplication.

JUNE 15, 1994, 11:32 A.M.

McGarry had allotted four hours for the whole visioning process. Each of the participants had brainstormed ideas all morning and it was becoming increasingly difficult to select the "one statement." After three and a half hours, they had only narrowed it down to about half a dozen possibilities (see Exhibit 3 for the final statements). Many participants became discouraged as time elapsed and the tone of the session turned 180 degrees as their energy drained away. Although the morning had started off with a bang, now there were concerns that the rest of the two-day retreat would be consumed by this visioning process. Other planned activities risked being cancelled.

By 11:32 a.m., McGarry was becoming concerned with the team's progress. She asked Smith to join her outside the conference room for a brief private meeting. She told Smith that she was hesitant to extend the session past noon because she realized that continued discussion of the vision statement would preclude work on other scheduled initiatives. However, she recognized that the visioning process deserved a dedicated commitment by the whole group and a concerted amount of time and effort. Furthermore, Smith suggested that it was going to be very difficult to assimilate all the agreed-upon suggestions thus far into one coherent statement within the next half hour. On the other hand, Smith also knew that time pressure could facilitate the creative process. McGarry returned to the conference room with Smith and spoke to her team.

EXHIBIT 1   Xerox Canada's Priorities, Philosophy and Cultural Dimensions

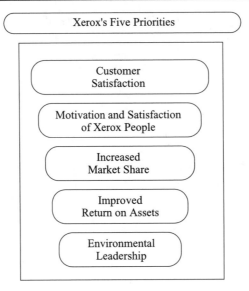

Xerox's Five Priorities

- Customer Satisfaction
- Motivation and Satisfaction of Xerox People
- Increased Market Share
- Improved Return on Assets
- Environmental Leadership

XEROX'S PHILOSOPHY IS STATED AS: "We succeed through satisfied customers. We aspire to deliver quality and excellence in all we do. We require premium return on assets. We use technology to develop product leadership. We value our employees. We behave responsibly as a corporate citizen."

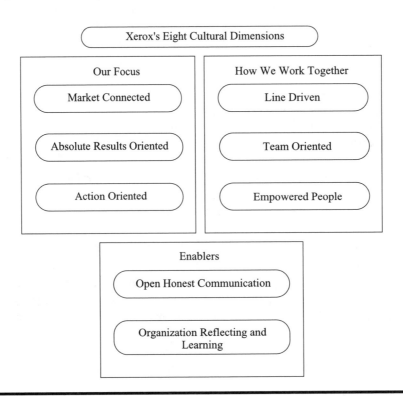

Xerox's Eight Cultural Dimensions

Our Focus
- Market Connected
- Absolute Results Oriented
- Action Oriented

How We Work Together
- Line Driven
- Team Oriented
- Empowered People

Enablers
- Open Honest Communication
- Organization Reflecting and Learning

EXHIBIT 2   **Historical Business Performance**

($ millions)

Operational Highlights	1994	1993	1992	1991	1990
Revenues: Sales	767.1	722.3	656.7	651.1	641.9
Revenues: Service and Rental	302.9	310.3	307.1	281.2	274.3
Revenues: Finance	101.7	112.1	115.5	119.0	122.8
Total Revenues	1 171.7	1 144.7	1 079.3	1 051.3	1 039.0
Net Earnings	88.8	25.8	61.1	39.5	35.7
Total Assets	1 601.3	1 706.8	1 717.5	1 686.9	1 904.8
Shareholders' Equity	670.7	676.3	610.9	578.0	569.3
Cash Flow from Operations	182.3	95.1	35.4	317.4	139.1
Number of Employees	4 315	4 775	4 802	5 017	5 059
Return on Equity	13.4%	3.9%	10.4%	6.8%	6.4%

Source: Company reports.

Xerox Canada Monthly Stock Close

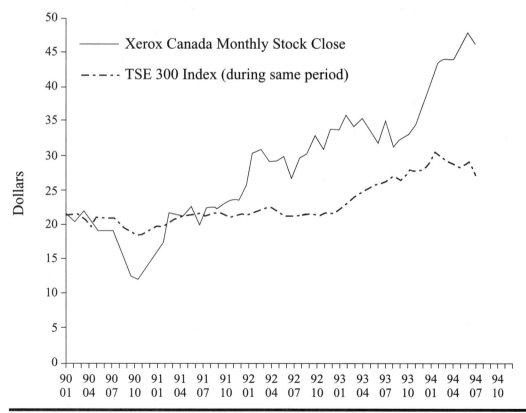

Note: Monthly close stock prices of XXC.B on the TSE.

Source: Casewriter's illustration (data taken from Bloomberg).

EXHIBIT 3   **Final Remaining Vision Statements**

Fast, focused and fun.

Providing personal and professional development while exceeding our customers' expectations.

To provide our customers with innovative products and services that fully satisfy their needs.

To boldly go where no company has gone before .

To maintain 15% growth and 20% return on equity.

Employee energy and quality work keeps customers for life.

Xerox, a market-driven, customer-focused company.

ARCHIMAX SYSTEMS LTD.

case

21

Stephen Jack
and Joseph N. Fry

Early in June 1994, Charles Douglas, a recently graduated MBA, and an equally recent employee of Archimax Systems Ltd., met with R.J. Bates, the president of Archimax, to review plans for the company's exhibition booth at SIGGRAPH 94. Douglas was standing in for his boss, Gary Hopkins, who had just left for an extended holiday sailing in the Greek Islands, confident that the plans for the booth were set, and that Douglas would carry through with the implementation.

IVEY

But Bates was not satisfied with the plans. He was concerned that the exhibit was not impressive enough and didn't fully reflect Archimax's accomplishments and technology. He instructed Douglas to make a number of significant changes in the content and mechanics of the presentation.

Douglas left the meeting with more than a few concerns. SIGGRAPH opened in just six weeks. He wasn't at all sure that the changes could be completed by then. Further, he had been cautioned in earlier conversations with Max Emery, the company controller, that cash was tight, and that holding the line on costs was important. Most recently, as Hopkins was preparing to leave on his holidays, Emery had warned, "no changes without agreement from Hopkins." But a quick guess indicated that the new requirements might add nearly $500 000 to the original estimates of slightly over $1 million for the exhibit. Finally, Douglas felt that he had been put in a situation in which his boss's boss had hijacked the project. The changes that Bates had in mind were in significant conflict with the approach Hopkins had been taking to the exhibit. What was he to make of this?

THE VIRTUAL REALITY INDUSTRY

The Technology

Archimax was a fledgling company in the emerging virtual reality industry. Virtual reality was the term given to the effects made possible by the convergence of two technologies, three-dimensional (3-D) computer imaging and robotics. By ingeniously merging the technologies, subjects in a virtual reality experience were given the illusion of an alternate reality, a world in which manufactured images and sensations were perceived as if they were reality itself. This effect was achieved by immersing the subject in an environment of created objects that looked and acted like real objects; (for example, a subject would feel a bump on visually "walking" into a wall image), and by adding other sensory input such as sound, temperature and smell. Flight training simulators were an early application of the possibilities of the concept of virtual reality. In current development projects, however, the ambitions of virtual reality were reaching well beyond the limited repertoires of simulators, to encompass a much wider range of user input and experience.

The creation of a virtual reality experience required the integration of a system of supporting equipment and related database, as illustrated in Exhibit 1. The main elements of hardware in a generic virtual reality system were: 1) an image generator, 2) a host computer, 3) an input device, and 4) an output device. The image generator processed input and database information to produce images—objects, colour, texture, motion, background, etc. Image generator manufacturers sold their product in units of capability called "channels," which were currently priced at $150 000–$200 000 per channel. Image generators usually represented at least half of the cost of a virtual reality installation and were the key to the quality of the experience. Like most electronic equipment, image generator prices were falling, even as they increased in performance.

The host computer housed the custom database and software for the experience and operated to control the system by bringing together the stored data and input device feed to drive the image generator and associated output devices. The required host computer capabilities were on the order of a competent engineering workstation.

Input and output devices were directly dependent on the type of experience being created. The input devices for a car racing experience, for example, would include a gas pedal, brake, steering wheel and gear shift. The output devices for the same experience would include a head mounted or projection display system and a motion platform that would react to events as they occurred.

The database software was the raw material from which the virtual reality system produced the user's virtual world. The larger the database, the larger and the more detailed the world in which someone could participate—but also the more powerful and expensive the image generator and host computer/software would have to be. The minimum cost to create a database of usable size was about $175 000. Databases could be used in a number of sites and/or experiences if the targeted end results were similar.

THE VIRTUAL REALITY MARKET

The market for virtual reality applications was in its infancy and thus difficult to categorize and quantify. In general, virtual reality applications were positioned as an integral part of a broader, $6 billion, 3-D imaging market. Elements of virtual reality were found, for example, in such major 3-D imaging sub-markets as flight simulation, entertainment, computer assisted design, and Medical/Catscan. Among the 3-D sub-markets, however, the entertainment segment was widely regarded as the most attractive for the short-term development of virtual reality applications; with these applications leading industry observers had forecast sales for virtual reality systems of about $1 billion in 1996.

The major prospective customer groups or channels in the entertainment business were: 1) mall developers and owners, 2) theme and amusement parks, 3) location-based entertainment centres such as casinos and retail stores, 4) edu-tainment centres such as museums and science centres, and 5) cross promotion prospects, such as beer and athletic shoe marketers. The appeal of virtual reality in these markets ranged from offering a quantum improvement over arcade games in malls and amusement parks, to providing a powerful custom-designed package in the case of museums and product promoters, to the possibility of a proprietary range of experiences in a theme park. To this point, however, most customers had had minimal experience with virtual reality and were for the most part testing a promising, but unfamiliar and relatively expensive product. In many cases, and particularly with independent customers such as small amusement parks, prospective customers were seeking manufacturer support for their entry into virtual reality.

THE SUPPLY STRUCTURE

The supply structure of the virtual reality-entertainment market was split between specialized producers on the one hand and system integrators on the other. Within each of these categories there was a handful of sizeable companies and a multitude of smaller players. The specialized producers concentrated on one element of the system described in Exhibit 1, such as image generators, or database software. Among these specialized producers, Silicon Graphics Inc. (SGI) was by far the largest and best known company. SGI had been a pioneer in 3-D imaging and was best known for its engineering workstations for computer assisted design. SGI was a major supplier of image generators to companies assembling virtual reality entertainment experiences and was known to be working closely on product development with the video games giant, Sega. Other competent companies, such as Evans and Sutherland and Martin Marietta, sold image generators, and a wide and changing range of suppliers, most of which were small enterprises, worked on other systems and components such as database software development and robotics.

System integrators designed and assembled a total virtual reality product. The degree of vertical integration among the integrators was quite low, although some, such as Disney Imagineering, encompassed design and software, and others such as Evans and Sutherland, built their own image generators into their products. But even the large firms such as Sega relied heavily on the efforts of a range of independent suppliers.

Among the integrators, the larger firms such as Disney and Sega tended to concentrate on total experiences such as a full game park. Smaller integrators, such as Magic Edge and W Industries, focused on the development and sale of specific experiences. Some integrators had begun to develop the concept of indoor theme parks, called Location Based Entertainment Centres (LBEs). This new concept was a step forward in the value chain for the integrators as the LBEs would be stocked with the integrators' equipment. Some integrators planned to operate the locations and others planned to franchise. There were also independents seeking to design and operate/franchise LBEs. These companies had the theme and location but neither the equipment nor the software.

In spite of its promise, the market for virtual reality products had proven to be a difficult one. As one industry observer put it, "So far the only people who have made money in virtual reality are those who write about it—and SGI who sells to those who try." The shortage of proven products and markets meant that long-term financing was difficult to come by. The larger companies, of course, could rely on cash-flows from other product/markets, but many of the smaller companies were forced to operate on a shoestring and to devote a significant proportion of their energy to financial survival.

ARCHIMAX

Archimax was incorporated by R.J. Bates and Greg Raidler in Richmond, British Columbia, in 1989. Bates had just moved west after a successful marketing career which included experience in high tech and entertainment companies and in the operation of his own advertising and PR firm. From this experience he had become convinced that technical developments would make it possible to open new markets in entertainment, but he had been unable to persuade his employers of the potential of his vision. He had met Greg Raidler, an accomplished electronics engineer, at an industry association meeting and after a number of conversations the two decided to pursue a start-up from a new base.

For almost three years Bates worked from his home trying to raise money for a major development project and Raidler did contract work for various companies to keep the company afloat. The dream was to build a unique computer system, dubbed the C21, which would serve as an image generator and control system specifically for virtual reality applications in entertainment. Several small grants from the B.C. and federal governments had helped to keep the project alive, but the prospects of survival were pretty grim when Bates was introduced to Evan Lee.

Lee was a well-known personality in the West Coast technical and financial communities. Earlier in his career he had built a very successful disk-drive company, only to see it crash as a result of over expansion and industry squeeze. Lee vowed at the time never to expand a project until the money was in the bank, and true to his word, he had used conservative strategies to rescue and rebuild two other computer industry start-ups. He was impressed by Bates and Raidler and ultimately a deal was struck under which he became a shareholder, and chairman, part time, of Archimax.

Lee's early moves were to raise some private funding for Archimax, and to arrange a public stock listing by way of a reverse takeover under which Archimax was acquired by a shell Vancouver Stock Exchange company. Most recently he had been instrumental in Archimax's acquisition of PS Technologies, an Austin, Texas, based developer of image generators.

THE ARCHIMAX STRATEGY

The focal point for Archimax's efforts remained with the development of virtual reality experiences for the entertainment market. A key element in this approach was the completion of the C21, which would give Archimax an industry-leading position in low cost, high quality graphics. The C21 would be available for sale to equipment integrators but Archimax also intended to supplement the C21 through alliances to provide a complete product, for example, by working with design firms and software houses to provide a turnkey product and merchandising service to the theme parks and shopping malls.

C21 was an ambitious project. It was based on new technologies and design concepts, which promised superior results and economies. As of June 1994, however, the C21 development program was behind schedule and over budget. Raidler was unperturbed by this, saying only that in a development project as complex as this, delays and unforeseen costs were bound to occur. He was confident that a working prototype would be completed by the end of 1994, with systems available for sale by mid 1995.

As a result of the delays with C21, the original Archimax was still very much a development company. Operations statements and balance sheets for the period ending April 30, 1994, and just prior to the PS Technologies acquisition, are presented in Exhibits 2 and 3. A rough statement of planned uses and sources of financing, including the PS Technologies acquisition, is outlined in Exhibit 4. Beyond this, Archimax's financial aims were to be self-financing from operations in two years.

The PS Technologies Acquisition

In Lee's view, the acquisition of PS Technologies fit into the overall Archimax strategy by providing some immediate credibility in image generation, a cash flow bridge, and a faster accumulation of the business base needed to secure a NASDAQ listing.

PS was an organization of about 40 people that operated as a division of Larson Electronics, a very large avionics and general electronics manufacturer based in Austin. PS had been losing money and had been through two years of uncertainty as its parent went through a process of refocusing on its core avionics products and customers. An assessment team from Archimax concluded that PS still had a nucleus of good technical people and some attractive projects underway, but that its sales force had been badly mauled in the ups and downs of the divestment process. Notably, PS had a fully developed product on the market, the PS 100 image generator and a $4 million agreement in principle to develop a custom product for Petco, a Taiwanese video game manufacturer. These products nicely fit into a capabilities/price range below the C21.

Lee was particularly intrigued by PS's inventory of fully and partly assembled PS100s, worth an estimated $2.8 million, albeit in a rapidly changing market. In late May of 1994 he made a deal for PS for $900 000 cash, Archimax shares valued at $1.8 million, and an assumption of $1.4 million of PS's liabilities. An immediate aim following this transaction was to generate cash as quickly as possible by selling off the PS100 inventory.

THE ARCHIMAX ORGANIZATION

The Archimax organization in Richmond consisted of fewer than 15 people and operated on a very informal basis. It was Douglas' view that management, from Bates on down, was stretched thin and was under tremendous pressure to balance their time between long-term needs and critical short-term demands.

At the time of the case Archimax was in the process of setting up PS Technologies to operate as an autonomous profit centre. It was thought that the freedom to operate, which had not been the Larson Electronics style, and the spur of tangible business goals would energize PS to work off its inventory and finalize a contract on the Petco development project. To Douglas, this was making a virtue of necessity— Archimax had minimal resources to commit to supervising and assisting PS management.

THE SIGGRAPH EXHIBIT

SIGGRAPH was the acronym for an industry association called the Special Interest Group on Graphics. To achieve its objectives of providing education and information on computer graphics, SIGGRAPH organized an annual convention that was the showcase for everything that was new to the graphics industry. The convention was known as an image show, where exhibitors demonstrated their best ideas, rather than a sales show aimed at specific product sale. Attendance had grown in the 15 years of SIGGRAPH's life to over 30 000 for the three-day show.

Early in the year, Lee and Bates had decided that Archimax needed exposure and that attendance at SIGGRAPH was an essential step. The task of carrying this through fell primarily to Gary Hopkins, vice-president for marketing and product development, and next to Bates and Raidler, the longest-term member of the management team. In preliminary meetings it was decided that Archimax would commit to a 50' x 60' booth, which would rank it among the largest exhibits at the show. The prime concerns centred around the look of the booth and what the main focus would be. The problem was that the C21 was still in development and the PS100 was nothing new. Bates and Hopkins were concerned that too great a focus on a development project would create the impression of promoting "vapourware"—a term used in the industry for products that were announced even though they didn't exist. It was decided that Archimax would present a full virtual reality experience that demonstrated its design and integration capabilities, although, of necessity, outside suppliers would have to be used for the system components.

There was a further aim in developing the SIGGRAPH exhibit. The IAAPA (International Association of Amusement Parks of America) convention was scheduled three months after SIGGRAPH. IAPPA was a key sales show in the industry and would attract a very different audience of buyers and owners from amusement and theme parks. Archimax could use this same booth with some relatively inexpensive changes.

Work started on the design of the exhibit and sourcing of components. This was a major job that involved people from across the organization in very significant tasks. Hopkins worked full time and then some to get the concept and technical components agreed and to coordinate the effort of various internal and external participants. One major accomplishment was recruiting Apex Images, an emerging "hot" software developer, to collaborate in creating the exhibit database.

It was clear from the start that the exhibit would be an expensive proposition, but no specific numbers were available until Douglas put together a formal budget as one of his first tasks on joining Archimax. This budget, dated June 1 and calling for expenditures of $1 050 000, is outlined in Exhibit 5. Then, with the concepts, budget, and most arrangements seemingly settled, and Douglas working into the picture, a very tired Hopkins felt he could leave on a long-planned vacation. There had not been an opportunity in Bate's schedule for a final presentation and agreement, but Douglas could handle that within a week.

CONCLUSION

Following his meeting with Bates, Douglas sat back in his office and reviewed his situation. He recognized that he had been shaken by the events of the morning. He felt that his next actions would be critical to whatever role he was going to carve out for himself at Archimax. But what was that role? What would be the best course for himself and Archimax? And beneath this lay an even more fundamental concern. Did Archimax have a future in this emerging industry, or was it an illusion itself? He reflected on some advice given to him by a professor at the business school—that his challenge in this kind of company would be deciding on "how native you go."

E X H I B I T 1   Virtual Reality Industry System

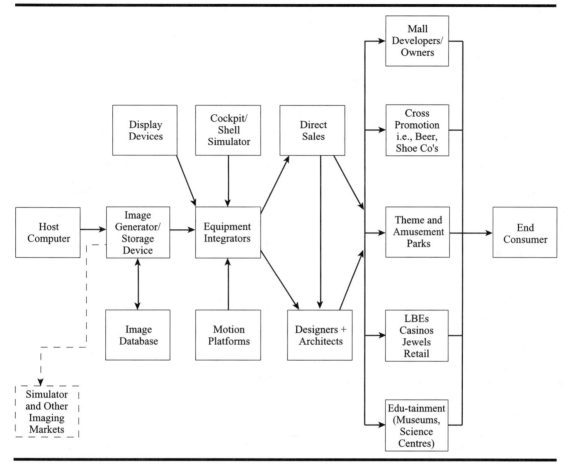

EXHIBIT 2   **Consolidated Balance Sheet April 30, 1994**

(C$)

	April 30, 1994	January 31, 1994
Assets		
Current Assets		
Short-term Deposits	$ 523 900	$ 0
Grants Receivable	58 700	133 200
Subscription Receivable	0	882 000
Advances and Prepaid Expenses	37 300	31 300
Total Current Assets	$ 619 900	$ 1 046 500
Furniture and Equipment	92 600	52 700
Deferred Financing Costs	66 200	66 000
Total Assets	$ 778 700	$ 1 165 200
Liabilities and Shareholders' Equity		
Current Liabilities		
Bank Indebtedness	$ 94 900	$ 22 500
Accounts Payable	66 200	131 300
Total Current Liabilities	$ 161 100	$ 153 800
Debentures Payable	750 000	750 000
Shareholders' Equity		
Capital Stock Issues and Outstanding:		
100 000 Class A Non-voting Preference Shares	100 000	100 000
4 750 000 Common Shares	1 286 100	396 600
Share Subscriptions	0	882 000
Deficit	(1 518 500)	(1 117 200)
Total Shareholders' Equity	($ 132 400)	$ 261 400
Total Liabilities and Shareholders' Equity	$ 778 700	$ 1 165 200

EXHIBIT 3   **Consolidated Statement of Operations Three Months Ended April 30, 1994**

(C$)

Expenses	
General and Administrative	$ 105 700
Legal and Consulting	157 300
Research and Development	125 800
Research and Development	
—Government Assistance	(25 200)
Selling	10 200
Interest, Net	18 100
Depreciation and Amortization	9 400
Loss for the Period	($401 300)

EXHIBIT 4 **Planned Sources and Uses of Cash**

Item	
Monthly Cash Use by Archimax, Richmond	$ 60 000
Monthly Cash Use by Archimax-PS	375 000
SIGGRAPH Budget	1 050 000
IAAPA Budget	200 000
Debenture Payout (October)	750 000
PS Purchase	900 000
Total Uses	**$ 3 335 000**
Arranged Sources	
Private Investor (Late June)	$ 750 000
New York Bridge Financing [1]	4 000 000
Public Offering of $15mm (November) [2]	15 000 000
Petco Development Money [3]	4 000 000
Total Sources	**$23 750 000**

[1] Conditional on applying for NASDAQ listing, which is dependent on an asset level that the PS purchase provided, stock trading at $2.50 per share. Money to be drawn down $2 million in August, $1 million in September, $1 million in October.

[2] Conditional on full NASDAQ listing. A full listing is dependent on a minimum of US$4 million in assets, US$2 million in net worth and a minimum of 300 shareholders.

[3] Part of PS purchase. Timing on funds was $1 million in June, the rest contingent on achieving development targets. The expected timing was $1 million in September, $1 million in November and $1 million in January.

EXHIBIT 5 **Summary of SIGGRAPH Budget June 1, 1994**

Asset Purchase and Display Total	
Exhibition Booth	
Formula One Cars	
Software	
Projection Booth and Installation	
Projection Equipment	
Contingency—10%	
Sub-total—Asset Purchases	$ 875 000
Marketing Direct Cost	
SIGGRAPH Fee	
Promotional (Brochures, etc.)	
Total Direct Marketing Cost	130 000
Travel and Attendance	
19 people from Archimax, PS, and Apec	45 000
Grand Total	$ 1 050 000

case

22

HYDRO-QUEBEC AND THE GREAT WHALE PROJECT

Allen J. Morrison and Detlev Nitsch

In February 1992, managers at Hydro-Quebec were concerned about the possible cancellation of a major contract to export electricity to the New York Power Authority (NYPA). The agreement, which was set to run for 21 years and was worth $17 billion in revenue, formed the backbone of a massive effort by Hydro-Quebec to further expand electrical generation in the north of the province. While a contract had been signed more than two years earlier, it was still subject to confirmation by both parties. At the request of

IVEY

NYPA, the original ratification deadline of November 30, 1991, had already been extended by one year. Now, political pressures from environmental groups in the United States, along with reduced demand forecasts for Northeast U.S. power needs, were causing New York State officials to consider terminating the deal.

For Hydro-Quebec, cancellation of the contract would have a severe impact on the economics of the project named after the Great Whale River, a major waterway in northern Quebec. Managers at Hydro-Quebec realized that a decision to halt development of the government-owned utility could also have far-reaching effects on Quebec's economy, as well as an adverse influence on the province's economic leverage in ongoing Canadian constitutional talks. A decision to proceed would carry its own economic risks; namely, whether the massive amounts of electricity generated could be sold at a price that would cover both fixed and variable costs. In addressing the tradeoffs, managers at Hydro-Quebec realized that fixed costs were influenced in part by the nature and extent of concessions offered to expedite construction. How to proceed was anything but clear.

HYDRO-QUEBEC AND JAMES BAY

Hydro-Quebec was created in 1944 by the Quebec parliament as a government-owned utility. Under its charter of incorporation, Hydro-Quebec's mandate was to provide energy to industrial and commercial enterprises, as well as to Quebec citizens through municipal distributors. With the backing of the province, Hydro-Quebec took control over essentially all electrical generation in the province thereby streamlining production, eliminating redundancies and encouraging the development of new sources of power generation.

In the late 1960s, Hydro-Quebec officials became increasingly convinced of the huge potential of the province's northern regions for hydroelectric power generation. Shaped by ice-age glaciers, northern Quebec was covered with thousands of lakes and fast running rivers. Advocates of commercializing the hydroelectric potential of the region argued that every day millions of potential kilowatt-hours of electrical energy flowed out to sea. The energy potential from the James Bay region of the province was regarded as particularly high. If the James Bay region were fully developed, estimates of its power generation topped 30 000 megawatts (MW) at peak production.

Set against this generating potential was the growing demand for electricity in Quebec and the Northeast United States. Throughout the 1970s, Quebec and Northeast U.S. electrical energy demand was predicted to rise at an average annual rate of over 7 per cent. The forecast growth for the 1984 to 1993 period was considerably less, at 2.7 per cent for the U.S. and 3.1 per cent for Canada. However, even this more modest rate of growth would require huge increases in generating capacity over the next decade. The cost and pollution associated with coal and oil-fired generators, together with the growing opposition to nuclear power, convinced Hydro-Quebec officials that demand for cost-effective and clean hydro-electrical power would remain buoyant for the foreseeable future.

On July 14, 1971, the James Bay Development Corporation (JBDC) was organized by the Government of Quebec. JBDC's initial capitalization of $100 million was underwritten by the Province of Quebec. Hydro-Quebec held 51 per cent of JBDC's shares and was given authority to begin development work on a 150 000 square mile region east of James Bay. On December 21, 1972, James Bay Energy Corporation (JBEC) was established to complement JBDC. This new organization was capitalized with CDN$ 1 billion, 70 per cent of which was underwritten by Hydro-Quebec. With large sums of capital at their disposal, engineers planned to dam a number of major rivers, flooding much of the 150 000 square mile project area.

The region affected was enormous—equivalent in size to the entire Northeast United States, including New York, New Jersey, Pennsylvania, and all of New England. The area lay to the east of James Bay, at the south end of Hudson Bay, extending almost to Labrador. The southern boundary of the project was the 49th parallel—approximately the latitude of Paris, France, and just north of Seattle, Washington. The 55th parallel marked the project's northern border—the latitude of Copenhagen, Denmark, or the tip of the Alaska Peninsula. The annual temperature in this rugged region averaged slightly below freezing. Because the only means of access to most of the region was by chartered float planes, the area remained isolated from population centers hundreds of miles further south. Only a handful of non-aboriginal Canadians had ever lived in or even visited the region. Exhibit 1 presents a general overview of the geography of the region.

OPPOSITION FROM NATIVE GROUPS

The announcement of extensive development plans for the James Bay region caught many Aboriginal people by surprise. Approximately 10 000 native Cree Indians and 5 000 Inuit inhabited the area. To these groups, the extensive flooding that would result from the project spelled the destruction of the habitat for wildlife such as moose, caribou, beaver, owls, geese, and a variety of fish, including salmon and Arctic char. The majority of Aboriginal people earned at least part of their livelihoods from hunting and fishing and, not surprisingly, worried that the James Bay project represented a serious threat to their way of life.

Both the Inuit and Cree had been in the James Bay region long before European explorers first arrived in the 16th century. Since first interacting with settlers, the Aboriginal people's relationship with them had always been strained. Despite assurances from generations of first European and later North American governments that their culture would be protected, the economic potential of resource-rich northern Quebec led to increasing industrialization of the region. By the early 1970s, mines, pulp mills, and other resource-intensive industries established operations in what had been Native hunting areas in northern Quebec. This was often done, especially in the early days, with little or no regard for the fate of either the natural environment or the lives of Aboriginal people.

While the Cree and Inuit had different base languages and generally lived apart, they shared many similarities in their lifestyles and cultures. Both groups shared a reverence for the land and a value system centered around the family unit, with no real central authority. Individually, both the Cree and Inuit were often described as non-assertive and reluctant to become involved in others' affairs. Most Native beliefs were alien to the predominant North American culture, which emphasized self-aggrandizement and material consumption. Aboriginal people felt a reverence for nature's gifts and believed that animals and other elements of their natural environment should be treated with respect and dignity. While the Cree and Inuit acknowledged the abstract principle of land ownership, hunters used land belonging to someone else as frequently as their own, with boundaries between areas typically loosely defined. To most Native hunters it was not so much geographic boundaries but animal movements that determined where one should place trap lines or catch fish.

When forced to live under transplanted European laws and customs, many Aboriginal people underwent changes to their lifestyles that frequently resulted in social problems for their communities. The transaction from being self-sufficient hunters to wage-earners was difficult. Accusations of racial prejudice and exploitation of Native workers were frequent. Native Cree and Inuit often complained that they were the last hired for the worst job and that they would be the first let go in the event of a layoff. The results of these and other social difficulties had contributed to high rates of alcoholism, drug abuse, suicide and crime in native populations.

Citing these problems, Native leaders began in the late 1960s to increasingly reject the notion of cultural assimilation as unworkable and unconscionable. Not surprisingly, Hydro-Quebec's initiatives to develop James Bay led to legal challenges on the grounds that the rights of the Aboriginal people to the land had not been considered. Native leaders sought to put a halt to the entire project on the basis of a 1912 legal statute which, they argued, affirmed their exclusive rights over the entire James Bay region.

Through the ensuing legal process, Cree and Inuit concerns came to be taken seriously by Hydro-Quebec. In November 1975, an agreement was successfully negotiated between both Aboriginal groups and the federal government. The resulting James Bay and Northern Quebec Agreement (JBNQA) provided formal reserves for both groups—2 000 square miles for the Inuit and 3 250 square miles for the Cree—as well as exclusive hunting, fishing and trapping rights over an additional 25 000 and 35 000 square miles respectively. (See Exhibit 2 for a map illustrating these reserves.) In addition, both groups received cash compensation in the amount of $225 million (approximately $18 750 per person) over 20 years, and a voice in future environmental assessment relating to James Bay development. As part of the JNBQA, the government of Quebec also extended to Cree and Inuit groups limited self-government authority related to the administration of social services and education.

THE GROWTH OF HYDRO-QUEBEC

When this agreement had been signed with Native groups, the development of James Bay proceeded at a rapid pace. After having secured additional debt financing primarily through the bond market, Hydro-Quebec began operating the first power plant of James Bay Phase 1 in 1979. Located on the La Grande River, it provided 666 MW of power for transmission to customers in Quebec, New York, and New England. Two more massive stations were completed in 1985, bringing an end to James Bay Phase I. Total generating capacity for Phase I was approximately 10 000 MW. In 1991, Hydro-Quebec's total installed capacity, including both its hydroelectric and thermal generating plants, was approximately 26 800 MW.

By the end of 1991, Hydro-Quebec's assets had grown to $41.85 billion, making it the 12th largest utility company in the world. Of these assets, approximately $9.40 billion was represented by stockholders' equity. It was estimated that heavy borrowing made the utility one of the single largest holders of U.S.-denominated debt in the industrialized world. In the spring of 1992, Standard and Poor rated the utility an AA-credit risk. Despite a relatively heavy debt load, the utility remained highly profitable. In 1991, revenues were $6.28 billion and profits were $760 million, an increase in profits of 88.1 per cent over 1990. Of the 500 largest global service companies ranked by *Fortune*, Hydro-Quebec was rated number 14 in terms of return on revenues. The utility employed 20 000 people directly, with thousands more employed in related construction, investment and support industries. It was estimated that direct and indirect employment related to Hydro-Quebec totalled over 80 000, or about 2 per cent of Quebec's work force. Financial statements for the utility are reported in Exhibit 3.

Critics argued that Hydro-Quebec's high profitability was at least in part a function of lucrative contracts the utility was able to negotiate with power companies in the U.S. Hydro-Quebec's rate structure had recently led to controversy when it was reported through leaks in the Quebec press that the NYPA was paying four times the rate for electricity imports than some magnesium and aluminum smelters in the province were charged and about twice the rate that Quebec consumers were paying. Hydro-Quebec argued that it was simply using competitive pricing to entice businesses into remote and underdeveloped regions of the province, not unlike tax concessions and other inducements offered to companies elsewhere. It also pointed out that contracts signed with heavy power users in the province were often risk-sharing contracts under which the price per kilowatt-hour was pegged to the price of the user's end product (usually on the commodity markets). The utility argued that to criticize the system at a time when commodity prices happened to be very low was misleading and politically motivated.

At the same time, some economists accused Hydro-Quebec of using low domestic electricity rates to artificially inflate demand for electricity in the province, thereby justifying further grandiose expansion plans. Despite these negative points of view, Hydro-Quebec was still a leader in North America in terms of providing competitive rates for residential users, as shown in Table 1.

TABLE 1 Average Costs for Residential Consumers

(1 000 KW-hour consumption per month, sales tax excluded, 1991)

Montréal	$54.81
New York	144.58
Boston	114.73
Toronto	77.55
Vancouver	56.55

Source: Hydro-Quebec 1991, *Annual Report.*

Role of Hydro-Quebec in Quebec Nationalism

Critics of Hydro-Quebec's ambitious expansion plans looked beyond economics to find political motives in the development of James Bay. While legally independent from the provincial government, Hydro-Quebec was often accused of being a tool of the government. The relationship was clearly encouraged by the location of the provincial Premier's Montreal office, which was inside Hydro-Quebec's headquarters building. To the critics of Hydro-Quebec, James Bay served a pivotal role in the broader plans of some Quebecers for greater economic and political independence from the rest of Canada.

Since Canada's creation in 1867, Quebec stood apart from other provinces, not only for the predominant use of the French language, but also for its unique legal system, distinct culture, and separate educational system that focused much more explicitly on language and religious issues. Maintaining Quebec's uniqueness in the face of an ever-shrinking population was the principal concern of a rising group of Quebec nationalists. They saw Quebec's French heritage being increasingly overwhelmed by the predominantly English-speaking majority in Canada. In 1976, the Parti Québecois was elected to govern the province on a platform which many felt was explicitly separatist. Once in power, the new government made substantial changes to provincial legislation governing language and education laws with the objective of promoting the use of French in all facets of life in Quebec. While a referendum in Quebec supporting total independence from English Canada failed, many in Quebec remained suspicious of the other provinces and contemptuous of federal institutions.

Deeply worried about the impact of Quebec nationalism on national unity, the federal government throughout much of the 1970s and 1980s moved to make membership in the Canadian federation as attractive as possible for Quebecers. National policies promoting bilingualism were passed, substantial grants were offered to the people of Quebec as well as the Quebec government, and massive new programs were begun to provide regulatory and monetary support for culturally sensitive industries. While to a degree placating Quebecers, such largesse caused some anglophones in the rest of Canada to view Quebec with disdain.

In the early 1990s, Quebec separatism was again in the forefront in the wake of a failed attempt to bring the province into a revised constitutional framework with the rest of the country. The "Meech Lake Accord", drafted in 1986 by Canadian Prime Minister Brian Mulroney, would have provided official recognition of Quebec's special status within Confederation. However, its ratification in 1990 was blocked by some of the provincial premiers, as well as by Native groups, who worried that a new constitution would result in their disenfranchisement. The failure of Meech Lake once again made secession an attractive option to many Quebecers.

By early 1992, with Quebec now governed by a Liberal government under the leadership of Robert Bourassa, the future status of the province in Canada remained uncertain. However, a healthy Hydro-Quebec was certain to strengthen Bourassa's hand in renewed constitutional discussions, since low-cost electrical energy was a powerful tool in attracting industry, promoting exports and sustaining the economy. A strong, export-oriented economy would add credibility to threats for separation that could translate into concessions from the federal government and other provinces. If accommodation could not be reached and separation resulted, then Hydro-Quebec would play a critical role in the industrial policy of the new country.

JAMES BAY II: THE DEVELOPMENT OF GREAT WHALE

In March 1989, Hydro-Quebec announced plans to begin the second phase of the James Bay hydroelectric development project. At this time, approximately 30 per cent of the total hydroelectrical energy potential of James Bay had been developed. James Bay II was designed to exploit the generating capacity of three river systems in the region: La Grande and the Grande Baleine (Great Whale) rivers, as well as the Nottaway-Broadback-Rupert (NBR) system. The headwaters of these rivers were between 800 and 1 200 feet above sea level and flowed through a system of lakes and minor rivers to the Hudson Bay basin. The plan was to develop these systems sequentially with the first stage harnessing the Great Whale river.

Great Whale's total generating capacity was estimated at 3 168 MW or about 12 per cent of Hydro-Quebec's total capacity in 1991. Plans for the Great Whale complex called for the construction of five dams and 126 dikes, creating four reservoirs used to feed three generating stations. Five rivers were to be diverted, 400 square miles of wilderness flooded, and 4 200 acres of forest removed to make room for 400 miles of roads and two small airstrips. A major independent association of Quebec engineers estimated that approximately 1.5 per cent of the land habitats of the region would be directly affected as a result of Great Whale. Hydro-Quebec engineers estimated that only 0.16 per cent of land habitats would actually be flooded. The total cost for Great Whale was estimated at $13.1 billion. Construction was originally slated to begin in 1991, with completion scheduled for 1999. Supporters of the development argued that by 1998, Quebec would face an energy deficit if no new sources of electricity were developed.

Shortly after announcing plans to begin work on Great Whale, Hydro-Quebec and the NYPA signed a contract worth $17 billion committing 1 000 MW of generating capacity to NYPA for 21 years. Under the terms of the agreement, the contract was to be ratified by November 30, 1991, with exports beginning in 1995. Despite the enormous size of the deal, Hydro-Quebec estimated that growing provincial demand for electricity would account for at least 90 per cent of the utility's total output over the duration of the NYPA contract. Total electricity exports from Quebec had been less than 10 per cent of production over the past several years, with about half that amount going to the U.S., and the rest to neighbouring provinces in Canada. At the end of 1991, Hydro-Quebec had interconnections with neighbouring systems that gave it the capacity to export 2 675 MW to New York, 2 300 MW to New England, and 2 512 MW to the Canadian provinces of Ontario and New Brunswick. Not all of this capacity was used and because of shared transmission installations, Hydro-Quebec's total simultaneous export capacity was limited to 6 337 MW.

By committing the equivalent of 30 per cent of Great Whale's capacity to NYPA, Hydro-Quebec would not only add to its U.S.-denominated revenue, but would see its profitability potentially rise. By the year 2000, it was estimated that Hydro-Quebec's total export commitments including NYPA would represent 7.5 per cent of revenues and 28 per cent of profits. Cash flow and the security associated with a NYPA contract would enable Hydro-Quebec to service much of the massive debt it would have to secure to finance construction. By locking in these revenues, Hydro-Quebec would also enhance investor confidence in its other bond issues, keeping interest and underwriting expenses at a minimum.

Concerns of the Aboriginal People

Already uncomfortable with the disruptions brought about by James Bay I, the Aboriginal people in the region worried that massive additional changes to the landscape would irreversibly affect the complex interrelationships of flora and fauna in the area. A related concern was that the flooding of areas not currently under water would release bacteria that would transform the abundant but innocuous mercury in the rocks into deadly methyl mercury, a known toxin that caused disease and death in humans. Among other ecological effects, caribou calving grounds would be shifted, James Bay's beluga whale populations threatened, and the habitats of many other species altered in unpredictable ways. There was also a possibility that the climate of the region might be changed because of the much increased surface area of the proposed reservoir systems. Evidence from Russia—where efforts to divert water from the Aral Sea had produced an ecological disaster—showed that environmental engineering could go terribly wrong.

The Campaign to Beach Great Whale

When Hydro-Quebec announced its intention to pursue the Great Whale project, the utility argued that the JBNQA gave it authority to proceed without the consent of Aboriginal groups. The Inuit, believing that the project was thus inevitable, argued for additional concessions from the utility. As part of these concessions, the Inuit demanded financial compensation from the Quebec government, as well as concurrent talks on Native self-government. It was hoped that money generated from a new James Bay II settlement would provide a greater degree of independence for the Inuit, making full autonomy an attractive option.

The actions of Hydro-Quebec provoked a much angrier reaction from the Cree, who vowed to fight the Great Whale project on all fronts. Many Cree leaders wondered how they could ever benefit from Great Whale, arguing that they would lose their hunting and fishing grounds so "that Americans can plug in their blowdryers". Matthew Coon-Come, leader of the Grand Council of the Cree, asserted that the Cree might resort to civil disobedience by lying down in front of earth moving equipment to stop the project. In May 1989, a lawsuit was launched by the Cree challenging Quebec's right to exclude the federal government from an environmental review of the project. By bringing the federal government into the equation, the Cree hoped Great Whale would get bogged down in endless delays as the national and provincial governments fought it out over issues of jurisdiction and sovereignty.

At the same time, the Cree, with the encouragement of the Inuit, mounted a major public relations campaign designed to raise public awareness about Great Whale's (and James Bay as a whole) environmental impact. Their often-emotional message focused on the negative effects of the project, while claiming that its economic viability was, at best, questionable. In support of this effort, they retained the world's largest public-relations firm, Hill & Knowlton Inc. For fees reported to have exceeded $230 000, Hill & Knowlton helped gather public opinion data, produce videos and provide media training for Cree leaders.

The efforts of the Cree first made headlines when they organized a voyage in a traditional canoe/kayak called Odeyak. This trip, begun in March 1990, culminated with a handful of Native leaders paddling into New York City's harbour on Earth Day, April 22. The Cree were subsequently invited to make speeches at Cornell, Columbia and New York Universities. Immediate grass-roots support for the cause came from environmental groups in the U.S., as well as student activists on campuses throughout the northeast region. The press appeared overwhelmingly sympathetic to the Native viewpoint. Negative articles appeared in a wide variety of publications including *Time*, the *Boston Globe Magazine*, and *Penthouse*. Government officials in Quebec denounced the articles, saying they contained exaggerations, inaccuracies and errors. It was felt that complete disregard for the positive aspects of the Great Whale project presented a distorted and unfair view.

In New York City, two highly organized groups calling themselves the "James Bay Defense Coalition" and "PROTECT" were created to encourage New Yorkers to begin letter-writing campaigns to elected municipal officials. Other groups were formed including "No Thank Q Hydro-Quebec", which claimed to have been instrumental in blocking an additional $4.1 billion power sale to Maine. Another group called the "New England Coalition for Energy Efficiency and Environment" became highly critical of Vermont for taking the easy way out by also agreeing to buy Quebec's power.

In August 1991, NYPA asked for and was granted a one-year extension on the no-penalty escape clause in its contract. According to Richard Flynn, NYPA's chairman, the agency was already re-evaluating its anticipated power needs, in light of revised demand forecasts. As a result of the ongoing recession and improved conservation measures, NYPA had reduced its annual growth rate estimates from 1.5 per cent in the mid-1980s to 0.6 per cent in 1991. In arguing for the extension, Chairman Flynn also cautioned that Hydro-Quebec should not use the NYPA contract to create a false sense of urgency about the Great Whale project and that it could not justify taking short cuts in assessing the environmental impact of the project. Within days, Quebec Environment Minister Pierre Paradis reversed his previous decision and announced that a global environmental assessment would be conducted. Such an assessment could take up to two years to complete.

In September 1991, a Canadian federal judge ruled in favour of the Cree in their outstanding lawsuit against the government of Quebec. The judge argued that the JBNQA fell under the jurisdiction of both the federal and provincial governments and that both levels of government were required by law to provide environmental assessments of the project. Plans were immediately announced by the federal government to establish an environmental review committee that guaranteed prominent positions for Cree and Inuit representatives. Quebec announced that it would appeal the judge's ruling and hinted that it might ignore a federal assessment in determining whether or not to go ahead.

The delay in ratifying the contract did not put a stop to the public relations campaign. Three "Ban the Dam Jam for James Bay" rock concerts were held during the week of October 7, 1991, featuring well-known musicians such as Bruce Cockburn, Dan Fogelberg, Roseanne Cash, Jackson Browne and James Taylor. These concerts raised close to $300 000 in support of the Native peoples' cause. Two cyclist groups also toured Vermont and New York to spread word of the project's negative aspects to villagers in those states. At Hampshire College, students from Boston, Hartford, New York City and Newark watched a performance incorporating a slide show, songs and speeches about ecology. A new protest group called "Dam No" was created at the end of the evening.

On October 21, 1991, the crusade reached its climax with a Greenpeace-sponsored, full-page advertisement in the *New York Times*. Environmental groups including the Friends of the Earth, the Humane Society of the United States, the Sierra Club and the National Audubon Society, as well as Native-rights groups signed the ad, identifying themselves collectively as "The James Bay Coalition." In paying for the ad, Greenpeace vowed to make Great Whale a major campaign issue if New York Governor Mario Cuomo were ever to run for president. In response to mounting political pressure, Governor Cuomo asserted that he would not let himself be manipulated by special interest environmental groups. Similar statements of defense were offered by Vermont Governor Howard Deans.

Despite these assertions, it was becoming increasingly apparent that the negative campaigning was having a major impact. In testimony before a committee of the New York State Legislature on November

15, 1991, Assemblyman William Hoyt argued that the state's review process must take into account the environmental impact on the Great Whale region, not just New York, to ensure that "...we are not participating in the creation of a major environmental disaster." New York Mayor David Dinkins, while visiting Montreal for an international mayors' conference, offered his official support to the Cree and Inuit, arguing that "environment rights and human rights go together". In Vermont, State Senator Elisabeth Ready and Burlington Mayor Peter Clavell began to actively campaign against importing energy from Quebec.

Some observers argued that the inflammatory and sensational tone of the public relations campaign would eventually hurt the credibility of the environmentalists. Denunciations were provided by the Quebec government, as well as several smaller environmental groups. The Greenpeace ad in particular was criticized for impeding a serious and credible evaluation of Quebec's energy policies in general and the Great Whale project in particular. Even the Audubon Society's chief scientist, Dr. Jan Beyea, while remaining firm in his opposition to Great Whale, admitted that the project's opponents had made "embarrassingly misleading" statements about it.

Throughout most of the campaign to discredit the Great Whale project, Hydro-Quebec's policy had been to avoid debating the issues in public. While some observers interpreted this silence as arrogance, many managers at Hydro-Quebec thought that the utility's financial track record, its importance to Quebec's economic future, and the commercial merits of Great Whale would ultimately act to overwhelm the accumulation of negative popular opinion. This strategy did not appear to be working, however, and three days after the Greenpeace ad, Hydro-Quebec placed its own full-page ad in the *New York Times* rebutting the arguments made by the environmentalists. The major points made by Hydro-Quebec included:

- that hydroelectric power was inherently cleaner and safer than the alternatives of nuclear or fossil-fuelled generators;
- that over $500 million in cash compensation had been paid out to Aboriginal people (as of November 1991) under the JBNQA and other agreements;
- that as a result of James Bay I, the Cree population was growing at a rate faster than the Quebec population as a whole—the infant mortality rate had been cut in half; and life expectancy had been increased by 50 per cent—clearly the net effect of James Bay I on Native health was positive;
- that as a result of its reforestation efforts, and the apparent health of the ecosystem, the James Bay caribou population had tripled since the early 1970s, and fish and bird populations had stabilized;
- that these were the same activists who had supported anti-fur campaigns who were now insisting on the Aboriginal peoples' rights to pursue their traditional way of life, which depended, in part, on the fur trade.

FEBRUARY 1992

By February 1992, the public relations campaign had slowed and management at Hydro-Quebec had more time to reflect on whether to proceed with Great Whale. There was a growing recognition that Hydro-Quebec had been too slow in reacting to the environmentalists south of the border. Many had felt that a pro-development campaign would only stir up the rhetoric and end up being counter-productive. The situation evoked memories of European and U.S. activists' opposition to the Canadian seal hunt in the 1960s and 1970s, all but shutting down that industry. Managers at Hydro-Quebec wondered about the appropriate limits to national sovereignty, as well as the rights of special interest groups and governments to determine the outcome of these matters in a free market economy.

In reviewing its alternatives, Hydro-Quebec faced several different courses of action. Some argued that Hydro-Quebec should simply go it alone and begin work on Great Whale at the earliest possible moment. Under this scenario, the utility would have to approach the provincial government to underwrite potential losses should NYPA cancel the contract. The utility could argue that NYPA represented less than three per cent of Hydro-Quebec's electricity production and that even if this business were lost, NYPA would be back just as soon as the controversy had died down and demand for energy began to rise. And if they never came back, the province would need the energy itself by the time Great Whale was on stream. Any energy not exported could be used to attract foreign businesses to the province at subsidized rates.

By February 1992, there had been no ruling on Quebec's appeal of the verdict requiring the involvement of both the provincial and federal governments in an environmental assessment of Great Whale. Quebec had publicly supported an environmental review and could not back away now. It could, however, carry out its own independent review and ensure that it was completed well in advance of any federal assessment. Once a favourable provincial review had been prepared, construction would commence, thus pre-empting the federal government from taking any action. The federal government had backed off similar confrontations in the past and might not want to risk national unity over this issue. Indeed, Canadian Prime Minister Brian Mulroney had come to the defense of the Great Whale project in a confrontation with a member of the European Parliament during a Francophone Summit in November 1991. In an emotional presentation, Mulroney had argued that the European Community had no right to meddle in the internal economic affairs of Canada. How could Mulroney, himself a native Quebecer, now move to stop Great Whale?

Despite the appeal to go it alone, a number of top managers at Hydro-Quebec thought that a combination of patience and good management would eventually win over both the environmentalists and the NYPA. It was too much of a financial gamble to act unilaterally. Hydro-Quebec was one of the world's largest U.S. dollar borrowers. Of its total $29.7 billion debt, $8.4 billion was in U.S. currency, and a large proportion of the contemplated $9.5 billion debt to finance Great Whale would also be in U.S. dollars. (See Exhibit 4 for a breakdown of debt by currency.) Some observers argued that the negative publicity generated from an orchestrated "go it alone" strategy would ensure that NYPA would never sign a contract. A decision by NYPA to pull out would also make it much more difficult for Hydro-Quebec to service its existing debt. Bond rating agencies already had the utility on credit watches, and if its rating were downgraded, the resulting higher interest rates and tougher underwriting terms for new issues would reduce the possibility of profitability from planned expansion projects. In addition, the lack of U.S. dollar revenue would significantly increase Hydro-Quebec's exposure to the risks of exchange rate fluctuations. Its U.S. debt was not hedged because of expected offsets in revenue of the same currency; without this revenue, it would be at the mercy of foreign exchange markets.

It was becoming increasingly clear that without the full backing of the provincial government, Great Whale could seriously undermine the financial integrity of Hydro-Quebec. Taxes in Quebec were already among the highest in North America, thus limiting the government's ability to act as a guarantor. A move to load the province with debt for a money-losing mega-project risked being interpreted as a blatantly political act that would jeopardize both the credibility of the government in power, as well as the ability of the province to raise funds for other purposes.

It seemed that no matter which direction management turned, it faced significant opposition. And yet time was running out. In just nine months—and perhaps less—NYPA would commit to a course of action that would dramatically impact on Hydro-Quebec's future. With it enormous size, many wondered how Hydro-Quebec had lost so much control over its own future. Perhaps there was still time to act.

EXHIBIT 1   Area Affected by the Great Whale Project

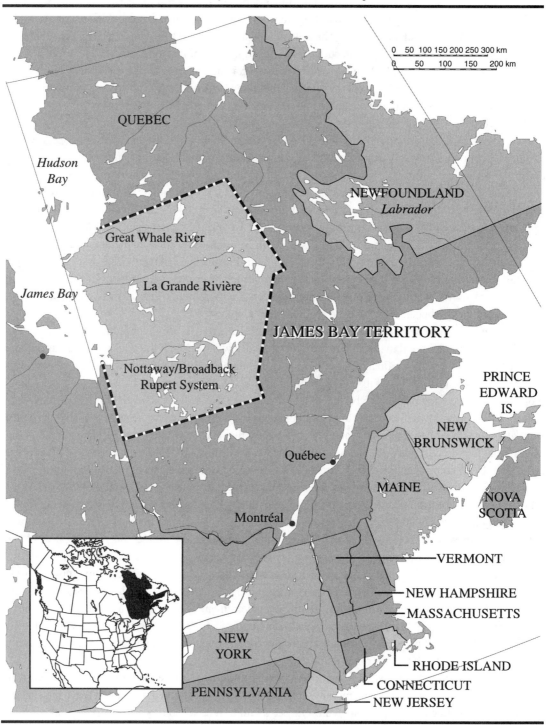

EXHIBIT 2 Cree and Inuit Reserves

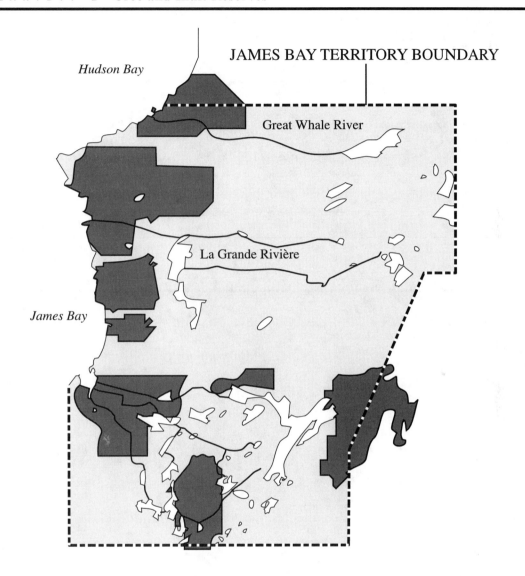

Reserves created by James Bay and Northern Québec Agreement (1975)

EXHIBIT 3 Financial Results: Hydro-Quebec

(in millions of Canadian dollars)

Income Statement

	1989	1990	1991	1992*
Total Revenue	$5 559	$5 885	$6 284	$6 916
Expenditures	2 759	3 047	3 183	3 702
Income Before Interest and Exchange Loss	2 800	2 838	3 101	3 214
Interest and Exchange Loss	2 235	2 434	2 341	2 514
Net Income	$ 565	$ 404	$ 760	$ 700

Balance Sheet

	1989	1990	1991
Total Assets	$33 873	$36 684	$41 851
Long-Term Debt	21 957	24 072	28 111
Shareholders' Equity	8 233	8 637	9 397

* Projected

Source: Company Annual Reports.

EXHIBIT 4   **Breakdown of Debt by Currency**

■ Other currencies

□ U.S. dollars

□ Swaps

■ Proportion in Canadian dollars before swaps

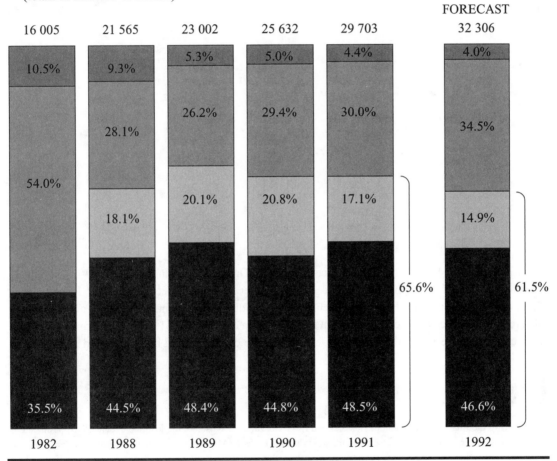

(totals in millions of dollars)

					FORECAST
16 005	21 565	23 002	25 632	29 703	32 306

Source: Company document "Hydro-Quebec: A Sound Investment," Financing and Treasury Branch, 1992.

DAMARK PACKAGING INC.: WRAPPING UP MEXICO

c a s e

23

David   Ager,
Luvy   Gonzalez   de   Wilson   and
Mary   M.   Crossan

In early June, 1994, William (Bill) Steel, vice-president of Damark Packaging Inc. (Damark) of Markham, Canada, reflected on the implications of accepting the order he had just received from Dr. Roberto Silva Nieto, whose company, SINIE, held the exclusive Mexico distribution rights for Damark's products. Dr. Silva reported that he had received an urgent request from a client for US$1 million in shrink wrap packaging equipment. He was calling Bill to offer Damark the order, but said he would need a quick reply

IVEY

David Ager of the Richard Ivey School of Business and Luvy Gonzalez de Wilson of the Instituto Technológico des Estudios Superiores de Monterrey prepared this case under the supervision of Professor Mary M. Crossan solely to provide material for class discussion. The authors do not intend to illustrate either effective or ineffective handling of a managerial situation. The authors may have disguised certain names and other identifying information to protect confidentiality.

because he would have to get back to his client within the week, and that he would need time to pursue other suppliers if Damark was not prepared to handle the order. For Damark, the order would represent a fundamental shift in the primary source of the company's sales, such that over 50% of total corporate revenues would originate from Mexico. Although the order satisfied Damark management's objective to expand through foreign markets, Bill was uncertain about the future viability of the Mexican market and he was worried that Damark was foregoing opportunities that were sustainable in the long run. Specifically, Bill wondered whether Damark's long-term survival would be better ensured by focusing on more stable markets such as those in Europe or by increasing the company's efforts in the United States.

Although almost 25% of Damark's sales currently originated in Mexico, Bill had always looked upon Mexico as an experiment. Clearly, he could no longer do so, and he would need to decide if and how Mexico fit into the company's long-term plans.

THE SHRINK WRAP PACKAGING INDUSTRY

Shrink wrapping is a packaging process whereby a product or a bundle of products is surrounded by a loose-fitting sheet of plastic film[1] and fed along a conveyor belt through a heated chamber where the plastic film, activated by the heat, shrinks so that it forms a tight skin around the product or bundle. It was discovered that shrink film offered several advantages: it provided good protection from water, dust and bugs; it allowed the merchandise to be clearly displayed; and it offered, depending on the quality of plastic film that was used, rigidity so that the group of products could be held together for easier transportation.

Shrink wrapping also provided a versatile form of packaging. It was used for food products such as frozen and canned goods, printed materials, toys and games, and industrial products such as oil filters and jugs of windshield wiper fluid. Exhibit 1 presents a number of products that have been packaged using the shrink wrapping process.

Packaging: Industry Overview

Packaging was a multi-billion-dollar industry in North America. Sales trends for the industry reflected trends in the unit sales of goods, particularly foods, beverages and personal products, although pharmaceuticals and industrial products were also important. The most recent development was a move away from expensive, elaborate, fancy packaging toward lower cost packaging that used less material. End customers in the industry insisted on innovation in packaging design, help with planning their filling and packaging production lines, and prompt service. Competition in the industry was described as fierce, with several different packaging materials vying for a position in the market.

Shrink Wrap Packaging: Industry Overview

As a sub-sector of the packaging industry, shrink wrapping competed against alternative packaging such as glass, metal, paperboard, Styrofoam and other formats of plastic packaging.

Shrink wrap packaging had been introduced in the late 1960s, although almost a decade had passed before it became popular as a viable alternative to traditional packaging formats. Three phenomena have been credited with increasing the awareness and popularity of shrink wrap packaging.

The first phenomenon was the Tylenol scare that had erupted in 1978 when Johnson & Johnson found that someone had laced a shipment of Tylenol tablets with cyanide. Pharmaceutical companies responded to the crisis by quickly developing a tamper-evident package. Shrink wrapping provided an easy, cost effective solution to their problem. Bill described the situation in the industry in 1978:

---

[1] Plastic film used in shrink wrapping was a thin sheet of plastic that resembled cellophane wrap, but possessed unique physical properties.

Pharmaceutical companies went crazy for six months after the incident buying shrink wrap packaging equipment. If someone had wanted to give the shrink wrap packaging industry a kick in the rear end to get it started, he couldn't have come up with a better plan.

The second phenomenon occurred in the mid- to late-1980s. Traditionally, plastics had been considered the "bad boys" in the packaging industry. However, by the late 1980s plastic had become a more desirable substance in terms of disposal than cardboard. First of all, because of its compressibility, it consumed much less space. In addition, it burned fairly easily. And finally, it was a stable substance which, when buried, did not fall apart like paper or cardboard and leech many unpleasant chemicals into the water table. These findings had led consumers to put pressure on retailers to replace corrugated cardboard with an alternative packaging medium.

The third phenomenon was the emergence of warehouse clubs such as Price Club and COSTCO. Almost 90% of all the merchandise sold in these stores was shrink wrapped. The strategy behind these organizations was to sell bundles of products, rather than one product, and therefore offer the consumer better prices. Shrink wrapping allowed these stores to bundle several products (e.g., 12 cans of peas) together securely and at the same time clearly display the product to the consumer. Because most companies spent large amounts of money on labels, it was important that they not be hidden inside boxes where they would have little opportunity to influence the customer's buying decision. The warehouse clubs spawned an entirely new industry that specialized in supplying custom packaged merchandise. Most often, these new companies used shrink wrapping equipment to bundle products together.

Shrink Wrap Packaging: Industry Structure

The industry consisted of shrink wrap film manufacturers, shrink wrap equipment manufacturers, distributors and end-users (consumer goods manufacturers, custom packaging companies and retail operations).

The industry mechanism was simple. Independent[2] distributors purchased plastic film and shrink wrap packaging equipment from manufacturers and sold it to end customers. Distributors preferred to carry films manufactured by DuPont and WR Grace (operated under the name Cryovac in Canada) because end customers, who had come to associate films manufactured by these two companies with quality and reliability, were prepared to pay a premium for them. In addition, both companies were very active in research and development and were responsible for most of the innovations in the industry both in terms of applications and films. Other plastic film manufacturers, which didn't enjoy the same position as DuPont and WR Grace, were forced to compete on the basis of price in order to convince distributors to carry their products. These second-tier film manufacturers were known to sell their films at prices 20 to 45% less than those charged for DuPont and WR Grace films.

Shrink wrap packaging equipment manufacturers competed on the basis of price. The two largest manufacturers were Shanklin and Weldotron, each of which enjoyed annual sales in excess of US$20 million. These two companies were the exception. Most equipment manufacturers had sales of less than US$2 million.

The manufacturers were divided into two groups: those which manufactured machines capable of process speeds of 60 products per minute or greater, and those whose machines operated at speeds of less than 60 products per minute. Very few manufacturers did both. Damark manufactured machines that fell in the latter category. As a result Bill did not consider Shanklin and Weldotron to be competitors. He explained:

> We tend not to think of them (Shanklin and Weldotron) as competitors because in excess of 95% of their market are machines that we don't make. They might do the same thing—they might make a form-fill-seal machine—but it operates at a much higher level. It's one that will do 150 packages a minute.

---

[2] While some film and equipment manufacturers maintained their own sales forces, most sold their product through distributors.

Shanklin and Weldotron could probably serve the "60 products per minute or less" segment of the market but it would require a complete re-organization of their manufacturing operation to focus on slower, non-custom machines. The profits are so lucrative in the upper segment of the market that I don't believe they have much interest in the lower segment. In 1994, annual sales in North America of shrink wrap packaging equipment were estimated to be the following:

Country	Number of Manufacturers	Sales of Machines that Operate at Speeds of Less Than 60 Products per Minute (C$)	Sales of Machines that Operate at Speeds of Greater Than 60 Products per Minute (C$)	Total Industry Sales (C$)
Canada	43	$2 000 000	$1 000 000	$3 000 000
United States	172	$16 500 000	$45 500 000	$62 000 000
Mexico	?	?	?	?

Distributors

Distributors sold both plastic film and shrink wrap packaging equipment, although they earned their primary income through the sale of plastic film. As one distributor explained:

I can almost afford to give the machines away as long as the customer buys the film.

Distributors played a critical role in the industry. Many sold the equipment of several different manufacturers and the end customer often left the decision of what equipment best suited their needs to the distributor. Many manufacturers agreed that given the choice between the best machine in the market or the best distributor in the market, without a doubt, the best distributor was the obvious choice because as the leader in the industry, end customers gravitated to this person regardless of the equipment he or she sold. As well, the leaders almost always sold the leading films in the industry and as such were closely involved in new film and new applications research. Information on future trends in the industry was extremely important to manufacturers for both new product development and market forecasting.

Distributors expected manufacturers to promote the equipment in trade magazines and to attend trade shows. They also expected manufacturers to provide a high level of sales support before, during and after a sale was made. The sales support requirement was particularly important in the case of larger, more expensive machines, which often required a significant amount of custom design work.

THE MEXICAN SHRINK WRAPPING EQUIPMENT MARKET

Dr. Silva described the Mexican shrink wrapping equipment market:

In the eighties, the market for shrink wrapping equipment in Mexico was characterized by slow, steady annual growth of about 5%. Industries such as the egg industry were end-users, but there was no real force pushing growth as corrugated paper dominated the packaging industry and the companies that did use plastic, such as Cerveceria Cuauhtémoc-Moctezuma (brewery), required machines that handled 75 to 120 packages per minute.

By mid-1991, there were rumours that U.S. discount retailers were planning to enter the Mexican market. In June, 1991, Comercial Mexicana, a large Mexican retailer, formed a strategic alliance with Price Club. Two weeks later, CIFRA, the largest Mexican retail conglomerate, announced a joint-venture with U.S. retail giant Wal-Mart to open a version of Sam's Club stores called Club Aurrera in Mexico. One year later, the first Club Aurrera opened in Mexico City and became the second largest store, in terms of sales, in the Wal-Mart empire. These retailing successes led CIFRA and Wal-Mart to expand rapidly, with several new store openings planned in the coming years. These new U.S. retailers offered Mexican consumers, many of whom had previously travelled to the U.S. to purchase foreign manufactured products, the opportunity of acquiring this merchandise without the expense of a trip. The potential for growth of discount retailers in Mexico was expected to drive the demand for shrink packaging equipment in Mexico. By 1992, the annual growth in the shrink packaging industry was projected at 20%.

According to Dr. Silva, the packaging industry in Mexico relied on trade shows as its primary means of promotion, followed by trade magazines and direct selling. Promotion, although necessary in Mexico, was not as critical because the market was far from being saturated.

A practice that frustrated Dr. Silva was that of Mexican equipment manufacturers who would bypass their distributors and sell direct to the client, a client that very often had been obtained through the distributor. This occurred because most people who bought shrink wrapping equipment were looking for only one thing, the lowest price. Although the contractional monetary policies of the government that had fuelled this attitude were expected to continue, Dr. Silva believed that in the future, companies would pay more for packaging equipment in response to the North American Free Trade Agreement (NAFTA), which had forced Mexican companies to manufacture globally competitive products. Dr. Silva believed that the only way Mexican manufactured goods could meet international standards was through the adoption of world class technology and machinery.

DAMARK PACKAGING

Damark Packaging Inc. was founded in 1980 in Toronto, Canada, by William Steel and Derek Camden. The company was established to design and manufacture automated sleeve wrap packaging equipment, which was suitable for packaging a broad range of items including industrial, consumer and pharmaceutical products. Prior to founding Damark, both men had worked for a Canadian company that was one of only three in the world that designed and manufactured automated shrink wrap packaging machines.

By 1983, sales of the shrink wrap packaging equipment had led the company to grow to five employees and had resulted in annual revenues of approximately C$600 000–C$700 000. It was at this time that Allied Automation of Dallas, Texas, made a bid to purchase Damark from Bill and Derek. Shortly thereafter, Damark became the research and development department for Allied Automation. Bill and Derek were retained by Allied to continue to manage the Canadian subsidiary.

By 1990, Allied Automation had undergone several changes that led Bill and Derek to make a bid to repurchase Damark from its U.S. parent. As William Steel described the situation:

> The recession hit them and they (Allied) went into a tailspin. The last thing they needed was a foreign-based subsidiary.

In the sales agreement, Allied agreed to turn all Canadian assets[3] over to Bill and Derek. Allied also agreed to continue to act as a distributor for Damark's product in the U.S. When Damark was repurchased in June 1991, annual sales were approximately C$1.8 million and the company had grown to 20 employees.

Upon repurchasing the company Bill and Derek, motivated by a strategy to increase the size of the company in terms of sales and profits, relocated Damark from Toronto to Markham, and redesigned the Damark product line. Most U.S. manufacturers were trying to build the sleeve wrap packaging equipment more cheaply, often by removing features from the machines or by replacing better quality components with cheaper components of poorer quality; however, Damark management chose to use the best quality materials and components in their machines and to incorporate more features into each. They reasoned that because of the forthcoming North American Free Trade Agreement (NAFTA) between Canada,

---

[3] The Canadian assets consisted primarily of manufacturing equipment, raw materials, work-in-process, and finished goods inventory.

the U.S. and Mexico, and the 15% difference in production costs between Canadian shrink wrap packaging manufacturers and their U.S. counterparts, there was no way that Damark would be able to compete on the basis of price. Instead, the company would compete on the basis of quality equipment. Bill and Derek decided that any promotional material would emphasize the fact the Damark's equipment was made of superior components and offered many more features than the machines of most of its competitors. To reinforce the quality concept, Damark offered 10-year warranties on most of its equipment.

Bill and Derek had also realized that, if Damark expected to experience sales growth and increased profitability, the company could not depend on the stable Canadian market. Instead Damark would need to expand into foreign markets. By 1994 Damark had focused its efforts on selling equipment in the United States and Mexico. While Damark had also sold equipment in Greece, Saudi Arabia, Nicaragua and Panama, these sales were unsolicited, and had come as a result of an advertisement in a trade magazine or someone having seen Damark's booth at a trade show. Both Bill and Derek considered such sales to be bonuses. Initially, the company's expansion strategy appeared to be effective and by November 1994, Bill estimated that sales for fiscal year 1995 would reach C$2.6 million. Damark's Income Statement and Balance Sheet for 1992, 1993 and 1994, and year-to-date figures for fiscal 1995 appear in Exhibit 2.

Internal Organization and Operations

Damark was run by William Steel and Derek Camden and their spouses. Phyllis Steel, who worked as a Chartered Accountant at a firm in Toronto, served as the company's accountant, and Lorraine Camden managed the company's human resource function. Exhibit 3 presents the company's organization chart. While Derek was designated as the company's president, Bill explained that this was purely for psychological reasons:

> If you are in sales and marketing and your card says President, you have no excuse for hesitating on a deal. If on the other hand your card says Vice President you always have the option of telling the client that you must check with the President first.

Managing the company required an enormous amount of time, and left both Bill and Derek with little time to think about strategic issues or the development of formal management systems. When they had sold Damark to Allied Automation in the early 1980s, part of what had motivated them to sell the company had been their belief that they would acquire management systems. Much to their disappointment this had not occurred. As Bill described it:

> Apart from our accounting system, most information travels through the company informally by word of mouth. As a result, it is very difficult to develop an idea about costs or the actual time it takes to put an order through the plant.

In early 1994, in response to the company's increased activity, Bill hired a person to be responsible for shipping and receiving and the collection of accounts receivable.

Manufacture of Packaging Machines

Damark's manufacturing process was not complex. Raw steel was fabricated in-house according to order specifications, or in some cases the stamped pieces were received from a local company. These pieces were then painted and were shipped to one of three assembly areas where the equipment was built.

Bill organized the company's products, as detailed in Exhibit 4, into three broad categories:

- Smaller semi-automatic systems
- Larger semi-automatic systems
- Automatic systems

The smaller semi-automatic systems required little or no custom work and were manufactured at the rate of 28 to 33 per month. Because these machines sold so quickly and with such consistency, they were manufactured without prior orders. On the other hand, the larger semi-automatic systems and the automatic systems often required a significant amount of custom work and their manufacture was begun once an order had been received. However, production of the latter two categories was usually backlogged because of the more complicated engineering required for their construction, and because of the unpredictability of orders. Unfortunately, hiring more plant workers would not alleviate this problem, as it originated in the design rather than the manufacturing department. Damark had once tried to find a solution by hiring a recent engineering graduate to design two in-feed mechanisms; however, when the product he developed had been impossible to manufacture, management had been forced to terminate his contract.

Damark had also considered hiring an experienced design engineer at C$80 000 a year, a price that Bill believed Damark could not afford. Another option had been to hire experienced design engineers on a contractual basis. Although this would be less expensive, it would require time (on the part of Derek and Peter Ellis, the Mechanical Design Manager) spent training this person to ensure that he or she understood how the equipment worked and appreciated the company's manufacturing capabilities, in order to avoid an experience similar to that which had occurred with the recently graduated design engineer.

Sales and Promotion

Damark sold its equipment almost exclusively through distributors because the volume of equipment the company sold was insufficient to sustain a sales force. This practice was typical of the industry. As Bill explained:

> The salespeople would starve to death if they relied exclusively on selling our equipment to make a living.

The company provided support to its distributors by advertising in trade magazines, participating in trade shows, working closely with customers on custom orders, and responding quickly to customer requests for assistance.

Damark management had found that it could service its clients quite well from its head office in Markham. Often a client required the greatest level of support when the system was being designed and installed. After the machine was operational, most repairs and routine maintenance could be performed by an in-house technician. Specialized repair technicians were not necessary because of the simplicity of the design.

The equipment was very well known and was highly regarded in the "less than 60 units per minute" segment of the Canadian shrink wrap packaging equipment market. Bill believed that Damark controlled in excess of 60% of this segment of the market. As a result, Damark had little trouble finding Canadian distributors to carry its product, and it was able to work closely with the larger plastic film manufacturers in Canada to develop new applications for shrink wrap packaging films and machines. Unfortunately, the company had not experienced the same reception in the United States.

DAMARK IN THE UNITED STATES

In 1991, shortly after their repurchase of the company, Damark's management team realized that any future growth would have to come from the U.S. Anxious to proceed, Bill and Derek located four film and equipment distributors spread throughout the U.S. and arranged for these companies to sell Damark products to U.S. clients. Bill described the results of this strategy as marginal and explained the company's performance:

We met with limited success (few repeat customers) and we were very disappointed, especially when it was clear that, despite the fact that the benefits of our products far exceeded those of our U.S. competitors, their products continued to be selected over ours. Between Derek and me, we were spending about 10% of our time concentrating on the U.S. market. This was clearly insufficient. Further exacerbating the situation was our lack of a physical presence in the U.S. that resulted in our being perceived as foreign.

The shrink wrapping equipment business in the U.S., especially at the low end, required that you constantly be at the doorstep of the customer. It didn't matter how good your prices and products were, if you weren't there you were forgotten and if you weren't American, you were immediately at a disadvantage.

We concluded that in order to expand we needed to spend more time there, as having a physical presence in the U.S. was essential.

In late 1992, Bill and Derek decided that Damark would establish a presence by founding a new company called Damark U.S. They would hire a manager for this project who would work with U.S. distributors to convince them to sell Damark's machines.

In June 1993, Damark U.S. opened its doors. Bill and Derek had hired John Salamone, a colleague of theirs from Allied Automation who had recently left that company. By November 1994, the new company was supplying machines to over 16 U.S. distributors. Bill, who estimated that 20% of Damark's sales and 10% of Damark's profits came from the U.S. operation, explained, "Damark U.S. was profitable, and it seemed to have turned the corner."

DAMARK IN MEXICO[4]

The Monterrey Trade Show

In early 1992, Damark was invited by Industry Canada to participate in the Canadian Government Trade Show at Cintermex in Monterrey, Nuevo León, Mexico. Bill described his initial reaction:

> Prior to receiving the invitation to participate in the trade show, Mexico wasn't even on the list of countries that Damark was considering in its expansion plans. My and my partner's perception of Mexico was of a country where labour rates were low, people didn't speak English and manufacturing equipment and systems were antiquated. I knew that shrink wrap packaging equipment was being manufactured in Mexico and that this equipment was much less expensive than our own. Apart from the above, neither I nor my partner knew much about Mexico.

Despite their lack of knowledge about the Mexican market, Bill and Derek decided to participate in the trade show. Bill explained their decision:

> We had committed ourselves to growing the company through expansion into foreign markets. The Mexico trade show represented an opportunity to see what was in Mexico with a minimum drain on corporate resources.

In February 1992, Bill arrived at the Monterrey trade show armed with a small shrink wrap packaging machine and some brochures that described Damark and its products. Bill described what ensued:

> The first day at the trade show exceeded my wildest expectations. All my brochures were gone, I had received offers from four companies to distribute Damark products in Mexico and I had sold the shrink wrap packaging machine and had been paid in U.S. dollars.
>
> It had become obvious to me that there was a lot more potential in Mexico than I had originally imagined. In addition, the people I had talked to were telling me that despite the fact that Damark machines were more expensive, the reasons for the higher price were obvious and they were prepared to pay more for a better quality product.

---

[4] Exhibit 5 presents some leading economic indicators for Mexico, and Exhibit 6 presents a discussion of the history of the country's economy.

While in Monterrey Bill was invited to visit a number of manufacturing operations in which he had observed the following:

> These people were using equipment that looked as if it had been made out of Meccano. It was no wonder that they were anxious to put our equipment in their plant.

The people Bill met with all conveyed the same message:

> If we are going to be a part of NAFTA, like we believe that we are, we are going to have to start producing products of a higher quality than we are producing right now. It's pretty hard to ship consumer products in Mexico. As barriers drop and we are required to compete against foreign imports and as we try to expand by moving outward, we are going to have to go for higher quality product ourselves. One of the ways we are going to do that is in improving the packaging. In order to improve our packaging we are going to need something (equipment) of a high quality to move us to that level.

Although there was some less expensive U.S. shrink wrapping equipment of similar quality in Mexico, Bill thought that his Canadian company would have an advantage in future sales. He sensed that Mexicans, in general, preferred to do business with Canadians over Americans because Canadians shared their dislike of high pressure U.S. sales tactics. Bill concluded that:

> Canada is in the same boat as Mexico vis-à-vis the United States and I believe that Mexicans find comfort in that.

After the trade show, Bill appointed two of the four Mexican distributors that had approached him at the trade show to represent Damark products in Mexico.

In May 1992, Bill attended a second Mexican trade show, this time in Mexico City. Although he had been optimistic about prospects in Mexico after the Monterrey trade show, three months had passed and Bill had not yet received an order. During the Mexico City trade show, Dr. Roberto Silva Nieto, president and owner of SINIE, a packaging machinery and plastic film company, approached Bill regarding the distribution of Damark products in Mexico. Dr. Silva had approached Bill at the Monterrey show, but Bill had decided against appointing SINIE to represent Damark in Mexico because SINIE represented Allied Automation (Damark's former parent) in Mexico. Despite his previous reluctance to do so, and in response to the dismal performance of the first two Mexican distributors, Bill appointed SINIE Damark's exclusive distributor in Mexico.

Up to 1988, SINIE had exclusively handled national brands of equipment and material. As the Mexican economy had opened and doing business with foreigners had become easier, Dr. Silva decided to start importing machinery in a move that proved to be an excellent growth strategy for the company because foreign partners tended to honour their distribution contracts, a practice which was less common in Mexico.[5] By 1992, SINIE was handling several U.S. brand name products including Afisamatic, Allied Automation, APV Rockford, Clamco, and Shanklin and had offices in the three largest industrial centres in Mexico: Monterrey, Mexico City and Guadalajara. Combined these three centres accounted for over 80% of all the industrial activity in the country.

Appointing SINIE appeared to be the break that Damark needed. After only six months in Mexico Damark had sold over C$250 000 worth of shrink wrap packaging equipment. By June 1994, Bill estimated that over 25% of Damark's sales originated in Mexico, and this most recent request from Dr. Silva could push that figure to well over 50%. Specifically, the most recent order was broken down as follows:

---

[5] In order to guarantee a sale, some Mexican equipment manufacturers and film manufacturers would by-pass their distributor and sell direct to the end user in order to be able to offer the end user a more competitive price on the product. In most cases the end user was a client that the distributor located and with whom the distributor had established a relationship.

- Category 1 Packaging Machines—20 units
- Category 2 Packaging Machines—10 units
- Category 3 Packaging Machines—45 units
- Category 4 Packaging Machines—17 units

Through his association with SINIE and the various sales of shrink wrap packaging equipment that had been made to Mexico, Bill had learned a great deal about doing business in Mexico, but most importantly he had come to understand how Mexicans used the word mañana. Literally translated mañana meant tomorrow. Very often, when used in a business context by Mexicans, the word meant "sometime in the future." Often Bill had received telephone calls from Dr. Silva who was calling to say that "mañana" he would receive an order for equipment. In the majority of cases it wasn't until three weeks later that the client actually placed the order.

FUTURE GROWTH

Bill commented that both he and his partner were particularly interested in seeing Damark's future growth coming in part from Europe, in particular the United Kingdom. As former Britons, both men knew the culture and the market, and because of the heavy concentration of people in areas they were confident that Damark's prospects looked favourable. As well, such an operation would give them an excuse to travel to Europe at least once or twice a year.

The two partners were also excited about what was happening in Europe in the shrink wrapping industry. As Bill explained:

> Europe tends to be a couple of years ahead, not in technology but in the application of technology. This could definitely help us in our North American operation. As well, it's almost as if people over in Europe get together and fix the price and then go away and build the machines, because prices appear to be incredibly high.

On several occasions, Damark had made attempts to penetrate the European market; yet, despite the favourable aspects, the company had not succeeded. The phenomenon seemed very strange, because both men were perceived as British, although clearly some factor was working against them. Bill commented:

> All we knew was that we if we were to seriously pursue the European market, we would have to devote a considerable amount of time and energy to understanding "how" the market over there worked. Time right now is non-existent.

Most of the time the partners felt stretched and wondered whether they might not be better off by selling the company. They had talked about the flexibility and freedom they would have "to do other things" if they were to sell the company. And yet, they had put so much energy and time into building Damark that they desired passing it along to their children. In fact, both men's daughters, aged 14 and 15, had indicated an interest to take over the business in the future.

In spite of their desire for growth, whether it be Canada, the United States, Mexico or Europe, Bill and Derek considered other options:

> Damark almost needs to take six months where we don't manufacture anything and instead, think about where the company is headed in the future.
> Perhaps we should bring someone in from outside to help us to put better systems in place. Maybe then we could better understand our costs and keep better control of our inventory.

THE DECISION

In order to deal with the situation temporarily, Bill had considered accepting part of the Mexican order, but was informed by Dr. Silva that the end client insisted on dealing with only one supplier. Bill was certain that Dr. Silva would find a U.S. company which was prepared to fill the entire order, if Damark refused it, and in the process Damark would lose its status as a preferred supplier. Bill had long known that the distributor was the key to succeeding in any market, and SINIE had proven to be an exceptional distributor. He did not know how he could continue in Mexico without SINIE.

As Bill reflected on Dr. Silva's request and on the opportunity this presented for Damark, two employees from the plant came to the door with a "problem" that needed to be resolved immediately. As he left his office, he wondered whether Mexico was the right place for Damark. Perhaps the company would be better off focusing on the U.S. Then again, Mexico had provided much greater returns for the effort than had the U.S. Why would Damark abandon such a lucrative market? Then there was always Europe, and after all, because he and his partner had always sought some sort of venture in the UK, perhaps by abandoning Mexico, they could realize their dream. More confused than ever, Bill left his office for the plant.

EXHIBIT 1 Products Packaged Using Shrink Wrap

EXHIBIT 2   Year End Balance Sheet 1992–1995

	1992[6] (9 mths)	1993	1994	1995[7] (3 mths)
Current Assets				
Cash	(77 972.70)	(11 719.27)	36 684.76	(9 775.98)
Accounts receivable	323 424.02	276 374.87	301 720.82	417 563.76
Allowance for doubtful accounts	(10 000.00)	(10 000.00)	(10 000.00)	(10 000.00)
Inventory	207 663.47	113 712.87	104 271.83	120 890.84
Prepaid expenses	13 377.93	9 789.82	18 216.32	23 097.70
Total current assets	456 492.72	378 158.29	450 893.73	541 776.32
Fixed assets net	32 607.53	24 064.63	19 989.51	28 185.06
Other assets	(7 523.14)	(7 523.14)	(7 523.14)	(7 523.14)
Total assets	481 577.11	394 699.78	463 360.10	562 438.24
Current Liabilities				
Bank loan	91 000.00	110 000.05	140 000.07	110 000.07
Accounts payable	126 151.87	155 793.94	123 572.56	157 666.83
Deposits on hand[8]	17 335.00	27 519.57	54 829.55	95 829.55
Accrued liabilities	4 799.15	1 327.36	13 689.65	19 568.51
Taxes payable	0.00	0.00	0.00	(1 448.00)
Total current liabilities	239 286.02	294 640.92	332 091.83	381 616.96
Long-Term Liabilities				
O.D.C.[9] Grant	47 138.98	40 320.57	34 487.62	31 961.35
Note payable Allied	40 033.54	0.00	0.00	0.00
Due shareholders	8 572.79	19 972.79	0.00	0.00
Total long-term liabilities	95 745.31	60 293.36	34 487.62	31 961.35
Shareholders' Equity				
Equity	49 254.41	49 254.41	29 254.41	49 254.41
Retained earnings	97 291.37	(9 488.91)	67 526.24	99 605.52
Total liabilities and Shareholders' Equity	481 577.11	394 699.78	463 360.10	562 438.24

[6] 1992 figures are for the period June 1991 (when the company was repatriated) to February 1992 (the company's year end).

[7] 1995 figures are estimates of year to date figures taken at May 31, 1994.

[8] Customers will advance Damark a certain percentage of the contract price on custom orders.

[9] O.D.C.–Ontario Development Corporation.

EXHIBIT 2 (continued) Income Statement Year End 1992–1995

	1992[10] (9 mths)	1993	1994	1995[11] (3 mths)
Sales:				
Manufactured products	1 743 547.60	1 601 970.84	1 901 816.94	597 956.23
Imported prod. U.S.	17 827.50	10 567.50	622.50	0.00
Imported prod. other	0.00	0.00	0.00	0.00
Parts & service	137 318.44	123 921.14	159 188.62	53 190.73
Less discounts taken	(3 909.88)	(4 262.32)	(6 669.87)	(2 170.93)
Total revenue	1 894 783.66	1 732 197.16	2 054 958.19	648 976.03
Cost of Goods Sold[12]	766 822.98	756 414.87	839 562.84	268 227.17
Gross profit	1 127 960.68	975 782.29	1 215 395.35	380 748.86
Operating expenses				
Manufacturing	585 773.16	544 882.16	697 190.38	207 970.25
Engineering	139 748.62	122 641.94	133 365.24	40 801.18
Sales	90 539.45	110 661.70	107 981.92	21 788.97
Administration	205 162.74	208 406.71	218 741.49	61 318.66
Total expenses	1 021 223.97	986 592.51	1 157 279.03	331 879.06\
Earnings (loss)				
from operations	106 736.71	(10 810.22)	58 116.32	48 869.80
Net Interest	(13 354.63)	(15 573.09)	(1 084.93)	(3 071.05)
U.S. exchange gain (loss)	433.41	1 617.45	11 875.00	(1 884.67)
Net earnings (loss)	93 815.49	(24 765.86)	56 906.39	43 914.08

[10] 1992 figures are for the period June 1991 (when the company was repatriated) to February 1992 (the company's year end).

[11] 1995 figures are estimates of year to date figures as May 31, 1994.

[12] Includes materials costs only. Assembly and fabrication wages are included in the Manufacturing line item under OPERATING EXPENSES.

337

EXHIBIT 3   Company Organization

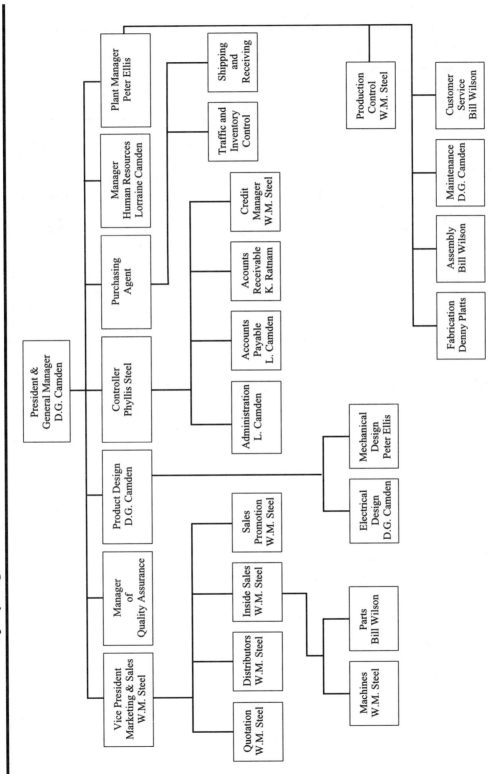

EXHIBIT 4   **Product Information**

Categories of Packaging Machines

Smaller semi-automatic systems

Category	Net Distributor Price (C$)	Margin (%)	Quantity Manufactured (per month)	Manufacturing Time Required
1	3 500	10 – 15	16 – 18	26 hours
2	7 500	15 – 20	12 – 15	40–50 hours

Larger semi-automatic systems

Category	Net Distributor Price (C$)	Margin (%)	Quantity Manufactured (per month)	Manufacturing Time Required
3	12 000 – 15 000	20	3 – 4	Depends on level of customization

Automatic systems

Category	Net Distributor Price (C$)	Margin (%)	Quantity Manufactured (per month)	Manufacturing Time Required
4	35 000 – 40 000	25	2	Depends on level of customization

Note: Margins were estimated by Bill Steel after consideration of materials and manufacturing costs.

EXHIBIT 4   (continued) **Product Information**

Sales and profit breakdown by country

	Canada	United States	Mexico	Other[13]
Sales (%)	45	20	25	10
Profit (%)	40	10	30	20

Product mix by country (in percent)

Category	Canada	United States	Mexico
1	26.8	25.1	7.3
2	23.3	21.9	
3	27.4	24.7	92.7
4	22.5	28.3	

Order turn around times — November 1994

Category	Turn Around Times Considered to be Acceptable	Damark Turn Around Times
1	2 – 3 weeks	4 weeks
2	2 – 4 weeks	5 – 6 weeks
3	4 – 6 weeks	8 – 10 weeks
4	12 weeks	16 + weeks

[13] There is no distributor involvement in "other" sales.

EXHIBIT 5 Economic Structure—Mexico

Economic Indicators	1980	1981	1982	1983	1984	1985	1986	1987	1988	1989	1990	1991	1992	1993
GDP Billions of New Pesos	4.5	6.1	9.8	17.9	29.5	47.4	79.2	193.3	390.5	507.6	686.4	865.1	1019.2	1025.3
Real GDP growth %	8.3	7.9	−0.6	−4.2	3.6	2.6	−3.8	1.9	1.2	3.3	4.5	3.6	2.6	0.6
Consumer price inflation %	26.4	27.9	58.9	101.8	65.5	57.7	86.2	131.8	114.2	20.0	26.7	22.7	15.5	9.7
Population millions	69.66	71.35	73.02	74.67	76.31	77.94	79.57	81.20	82.84	84.49	86.15	87.84	89.54	91.21
Exports U.S.$ billions	15.570	19.646	21.214	21.819	24.407	22.112	16.347	20.887	20.765	23.048	27.131	27.318	27.618	30.190
Imports U.S.$ billions	19.460	24.068	15.128	8.023	11.788	13.993	11.997	12.731	19.591	24.438	29.969	38.124	48.160	49.627
Current account U.S.$ billions	−10.750	−16.061	−6.307	5.403	4.194	1.130	−1.673	3.968	−2.443	−3.958	−7.117	−14.896	−24.806	−23.393
Trade balance U.S.$ billions	−3.385	−3.846	6.795	13.762	12.941	8.451	4.599	8.433	1.668	−0.645	−4.433	−11.329	−20.667	−18.891
Treasury Bill Rates % [a]	22.46	30.77	45.75	59.07	49.32	63.20	88.01	103.07	69.15	44.99	34.76	19.28	15.62	14.9
Exchange rate New Pesos: U.S.$ [b]	n/a	n/a	n/a	0.1503	0.1852	0.3102	0.6374	1.3782	2.2731	2.4615	2.8126	3.0184	3.0949	3.1156

[a] Period averages in percent per annum.
[b] Average for the year.

Source: International Financial Statistics, International Monetary Fund.

EXHIBIT 6 **Mexico's Economy—Historical Perspective**

Before it joined the General Agreement on Tariffs and Trade (GATT) in 1986, Mexico was a closed economy. The protection of domestic industry was the main principle underlying all government economic policy. If a product could be manufactured in Mexico, it was, even if it was more expensive and of lower quality than similar products available internationally. The Mexican government implemented several economic policy tools to ensure the achievement of this goal. High tariffs (often over 100%), restrictions on foreign ownership and investment, import permits, and export requirements succeeded in dampening foreign interest in Mexico.

From 1958 to 1970, Mexico thrived. The country's gross domestic product (GDP) grew at an average annual rate of approximately 6.8%, with GDP per capita growth of 3.2% annually. Consumer price inflation over the same period averaged only 2.9% per year. The ratios of public-sector deficits and public external debt to GDP were low and stable, and real interest rates were positive. During this period neither the current-account deficit nor the balance of payments exceeded 3% of GDP.

According to the statistics, all should have been well in Mexico. Unfortunately, this was not the case. Wealth in the country was very unevenly distributed with 30% of the population controlling over 65% of the country's annual income. To correct this inequity and to reduce the widespread poverty in Mexico, President Echeverría (1970–76) and his successor President López Portillo (1976–82) attempted to increase the country's economic growth by pursuing a policy of higher government expenditure. In theory, such a policy would permit a more plentiful 'trickle down' to those on the lowest incomes; higher public expenditure, and, in particular, higher welfare spending and transfer payments, would soften the rigours of an inegalitarian system.[14]

Increased government spending throughout the 1970s and early 1980s was financed through foreign borrowing. The discovery of the large Capecha oil fields in the State of Chiapas in the late 1970s allowed the government to intensify its expenditures by borrowing more furiously from foreign banks that were ready and anxious to lend money to Mexico because they anticipated rising oil revenues for the country.

When oil prices began to fall in the early 1980s, the Mexican economy was destabilized with large increases in inflation and the current account deficit. Under pressure from the international financial community, the Mexican government responded with severe import restrictions and high domestic interest rates.

In 1982, investors, anticipating a devaluation of the currency, moved out of pesos into more stable currencies. This put strains on the government as it used foreign currency reserves to maintain the country's fixed exchange rates. Oil prices softened further, the global recession peaked, interest rates increased, and private capital in international markets disappeared. On August 15, 1982, the Mexican government announced that it was no longer able to meet its interest obligations on its US$88 billion foreign debt. The government signed an agreement with the International Monetary Fund (IMF) that rescued the country, but forced it to introduce a program of economic reforms. Public expenditures were reduced, taxes were increased and some small public service enterprises were closed. Exchange controls were abolished, and the currency was devalued by over 100%. Prices for public services and administered prices (for foodstuffs) were brought into line with production costs or international prices. The group who suffered most was Mexico's middle class. Real wages fell and savings were all but wiped out. Unlike

---

[14] The Economist Intelligence Unit, *Mexico: Country Profile* (New York: Business International Limited, 1992), p. 10.

EXHIBIT 6 (continued)

Mexico's elite class, this group did not have the luxury of investing abroad in order to insulate their savings from currency devaluations.

The debt crisis of 1982 forced Mexico to abandon its inward-looking policies of protection and state regulation in favour of new policies that stressed a more outward-focused development strategy that would be led by the private sector.

The results from 1983–85 showed a resumption in real growth and a decrease in inflation from over 90% in 1982–83 to approximately 60% in the following two years. The public sector deficit as a share of GDP was halved. The fall in the real exchange rate stimulated export growth and reduced the level of imports from US$25 billion in 1981 to US$9 billion 1983. From 1985–87 real GDP fell to 3% and inflation accelerated to over 130%. Oil prices softened and Mexico neared crisis once again. A new debt repayment plan was introduced by the IMF that tied Mexico's debt repayment schedule to the health of the country's economy.

Upon assuming office December 1, 1988, President Carlos Salinas de Gortari introduced the first of what was to become a series of pacts among government, labour and employers' organizations. The intention of these pacts was to reduce inflation without causing a recession. These pacts used publicly-controlled prices, minimum wages and the nominal exchange rate as the tools to eliminate the economic distortions that had led to inflation in the past. Fiscal and credit policies were tightened and a more equitable tax system was introduced. Tariffs were reduced, as was the number of products subject to import licenses. Another significant element of the government's strategy to curb inflation was a reduction in the money supply growth rate. In 1982, when foreign capital disappeared, the Mexican government borrowed from domestic banks. After 1988, government borrowing was done predominantly through bonds.

In 1989, the Salinas government introduced its National Development Plan (1989–94), which committed the government to the liberalization of foreign trade and investment policies. These changes were intended to force Mexican enterprises to introduce stricter efficiency standards and new technologies in an effort to render Mexican products more competitive on domestic and world markets. The government sought foreign investment as a means of complementing domestic capital in this plant modernization process. It introduced a new tax policy that protected the lowest income groups without adversely affecting public finances. Finally, it introduced subsidy policies that were intended to increase the purchasing power of the needy.

The Salinas government appeared to have ushered in a new era of improved performance of the Mexican economy. Inflation fell from 52% in 1988 to approximately 7% in the first seven months of 1994. Most of the fall was attributed to the government's wage and price restraints and its trade liberalization policies that had culminated in the North American Free Trade Agreement (NAFTA), effective January 1, 1994. The public sector deficit was reduced from 12.5% of GDP in 1988 to a surplus of 0.1% of GDP in 1993. A reduction in interest rates through the liberalization of markets and lifting of interest controls and cash reserves had also had a positive influence on the economy.

The country's 1993 current account deficit, fueled by growth in imports, led to a merchandise trade deficit (1993 US$13 billion, 1994 estimated at US$18 billion) that was expected to be US$27.8 billion or 8% of GDP in 1994. While foreign capital inflows had acted to cover the shortfall, the bulk of these inward flows had been in the form of portfolio investment, money going to both the stock market and to government securities such as Treasury Certificates (CETES), both of which were intrinsically volatile and were required to offer high rates of return in order to continue to attract capital inflows and avoid capital outflows.

Finally, in August of 1994, the country elected Ernesto Zedillo of the PRI party to replace outgoing President Carlos Salinas. President-elect Zedillo had committed to political reform and to continuing the economic programs that had been begun by his predecessor, although he planned to place more emphasis on job creation and addressing the problem of poverty. The new president would also need to resolve the conflict that had erupted in the southern Mexican state of Chiapas where rebel leaders had attracted world attention through their demands for democratic reforms within the state.

LABATT—FEMSA: AMIGOS FOR GROWTH?

*David   Ager
and   Joseph   N.   Fry*

In May 1994, George Taylor, president and chief executive officer of John Labatt Limited (Labatt), was reviewing the preliminary terms of a proposal under which Labatt would enter into a partnership with Cerveceria Cuauhtémoc Moctezuma (FEMSA Cerveza) of Monterrey, Mexico. A successful agreement with FEMSA Cerveza, in the face of contending overtures from Philip Morris/Miller Brewing of the U.S., would represent a major recommitment of Labatt to its brewing roots and a significant improvement of its position in the North American brewing industry. Appendix A presents a brief description of Philip Morris/Miller Brewing.

IVEY

David Ager prepared this case under the supervision of Professor Joseph N. Fry solely to provide material for class discussion. The authors do not intend to illustrate either effective or ineffective handling of a managerial situation. The authors may have disguised certain names and other identifying information to protect confidentiality.

JOHN LABATT LIMITED

Founded in 1847 in London, Ontario, by John Kinder Labatt, Labatt was one of Canada's oldest companies and largest brewing concerns. For over a century the company had focused, with significant success, on developing its brewing operations in Canada. In the early 1960s, however, the decision was taken to diversify the company and seek growth in other areas as well. This was marked in 1964–65 by a company reorganization under which Labatt became a holding company for four main subsidiaries: Labatt Breweries of Canada; General Brewing Corporation (U.S. brewing operations); Labatt International (international property operations); and Labatt Industries (bio-technical interests). This was the first of several corporate re-organizations that the company would undergo over the next 25 years as it pursued an aggressive acquisition and development strategy in Canada and the U.S. In addition to beer assets, Labatt acquired subsidiaries involved in the processed foods, dairy, and packaging industries, as well as the Toronto Blue Jays baseball club, the Toronto Argonauts football club, a stake in the Skydome stadium, sports networks, and a company that specialized in rock concert promotion.

By 1989 Labatt reported consolidated revenues of C$4.8 billion and net profits of C$141 million on an asset base of C$2.8 billion and described itself as a broadly based North American food and beverage company. Consolidated financial statements for 1988–1994 are presented in Exhibit 1, and segmented financial results for the same period are presented in Exhibit 2.

Then, in 1990, Labatt changed direction. The company, which was having difficulty supporting and achieving acceptable returns in its agriculture and food-related businesses, decided to dispose of them and concentrate on its brewing, and broadcast and entertainment businesses. The 1990 annual report put it this way:

> With the increasing globalization of its core businesses, John Labatt's long-term objective is to concentrate on fewer, larger businesses and to grow internationally.

By 1994 the divestiture program had for the most part been completed, and consolidated results showed revenues down to C$2.3 billion while earnings had increased slightly to C$155 million. The business comprised two segments: brewing, and sports and entertainment. Brewing accounted for about 74 per cent of the company's revenues and 80 per cent of its profits.

Labatt's Brewing Business

Labatt was a national brewer in Canada and had significant operations in the United States, the United Kingdom and Italy. Segmented financial information for these operations is presented in Table 1. Context for these numbers is provided in the following review of trends in the North American brewing industry and of Labatt's current position in each of its geographic markets.

TABLE 1   Segmented Financial Data from Labatt's Brewing Division

(Millions of C$)

	Net Sales		EBIT		Net Assets Employed	
	1994	*1993*	*1994*	*1993*	*1994*	*1993*
Labatt Canada	$1 245	$1 241	$ 283	$ 239	$ 495	$ 534
Labatt's USA	$ 228	$ 180	$ 4	$ 5	$ 74	$ 67
Tariff	—	—	$ (4)	$ (8)	—	—
Birra Moretti	$ 134	$ 130	$ (1)	$ (3)	$ 203	$ 180
Labatt UK	$ 74	$ 42	$ (2)	$ (8)	$ 110	$ 75

Source: John Labatt Limited 1994 *Annual Report.*

THE EVOLUTION OF THE NORTH AMERICAN BREWING INDUSTRY (POST 1980)

In the late 1970s, brewing in North America was a regional business, with international borders creating three separate national markets. Nine independent national brewers dominated the markets:

In Canada: Labatt Breweries (a subsidiary of John Labatt Limited), Molson Breweries (a wholly owned subsidiary of Molson Group of Companies), Carling O'Keefe Breweries of Canada Limited (a wholly owned subsidiary of Foster's Brewing Group Limited—a division of Elders IXL Limited of Australia).

In the United States: Anheuser-Busch, Miller Brewing Company (a subsidiary of Philip Morris Companies Inc.), Adolph Coors Company.

In Mexico: Cerveceria Cuauhtémoc (a wholly owned subsidiary of Fomento Económico Mexicano, S.A. de C.V. a division of Valores Industriales S.A.), Cerveceria Moctezuma, Cerveceria Modelo S.A. de C.V.

By 1994 the structure of the industry had changed significantly through mergers that consolidated competition in Canada and Mexico, and by alliances and ownership arrangements that crossed the national borders. The resulting relationships among the major breweries, as of 1994, are summarized in Exhibit 3. The major events in this evolution were as follows:

1980

Labatt enters a licensing agreement with Anheuser-Busch to brew and market Budweiser, Busch's prime U.S. brand, in the Canadian market. In 1983 Carling-O'Keefe enters into a similar agreement with Miller for Miller's key brands and in 1985, Molson follows suit with an agreement with Adolph Coors.

1985

In Mexico, Valores Industriales S.A. acquires Cerveceria Moctezuma, and in 1990 combines this property with Cerveceria Cuauhtémoc to form FEMSA Cerveza, a division of its Fomento Económico Mexicano, S.A. de C.V. (FEMSA) group.

1988

Molson enters a distribution joint venture which, among other things, imports and distributes Cerveceria Modelo beers in Canada.

1990

Molson Breweries and Carling O'Keefe merge to form Molson Breweries with the Molson Group of Companies and Foster's each carrying a 50 per cent ownership.

1992

Philip Morris Companies acquires a 7.9 per cent interest in FEMSA, the parent of FEMSA Cerveza, from Citicorp.

1993

Anheuser-Busch acquires a 17.7 per cent stake in Grupo Modelo, for an estimated US$447 million, and carries an option to increase its stake to as much as 50 per cent.

Miller acquires a 20 per cent interest in Molson Breweries for US$273 million or about 6.9 times earnings before interest, taxes, depreciation and amortization (EBITDA). As part of the transaction Miller acquires exclusive marketing rights to Molson brands in the U.S. Molson retains the right to brew and sell Miller brands in Canada.

The introduction of "ice" beers touches off a storm of legal battles. Labatt claims ownership of a fundamental ice brewing technology and insists that terms such as "ice beer" can be used only for beers brewed using this technology. This claim is widely ignored by other brewers, including Anheuser-Busch. Labatt sues Busch, Molson and Miller for trademark infringement. Busch countersues.

1994

Coors signs an agreement with Labatt for the ice brewing technology. Coors also goes to court to seek early termination of its license agreement with Molson's, which technically requires a ten year notice of termination. Coors also launches an antitrust suit against Miller, claiming Miller's 20 per cent stake in Molson will substantially lessen competition in the U.S. beer market.

LABATT IN CANADA

The Canadian market was of critical importance to Labatt. About 75 per cent of its brewing revenues and virtually all of its earnings were delivered by the Canadian business. This was of some concern to the company since demand in Canada was flat, competition for market share was intense, and the role of government in regulating the industry and buffering it from foreign competition was increasingly uncertain. Labatt was well aware of the view of some international investors that the profitability of the company's brewing operations was the product of a contrived, unsustainable, Canadian brewing environment, made all the more uncertain by separatist political developments in Quebec.

Demand

The aggregate demand for beer in Canada had been relatively stable at around 21 million hectolitres (hL) for several years. Little, if any growth was anticipated for reasons including demographic changes, taste shifts away from alcoholic beverages, high prices due in large part to very heavy taxes, and regulatory constraints on marketing and distribution. Key aspects of the Canadian brewing industry are summarized in Exhibit 4.

Competition

In 1994, the Canadian market was dominated by two companies: Labatt, with a 44.2 per cent share and Molson, with a 48.9 per cent share. In recent years, a number of local and micro brewing businesses had emerged to serve regional and specialty tastes but these together amounted to less than five per cent of the market.

Competitive activities among the breweries were constrained by government regulation of pricing and distribution and, to a lesser extent, by advertising and promotional practices. In this context competition focused on product and brand differentiation. New product introductions such as "Ice Beer" and "Dry Beer" were common, and although they gave some advantage to the first mover, they were usually quickly copied. In the same way, heavy spending on brand advertising and clever new advertising approaches often cancelled out, yielding no significant and sustainable change in market share. The relative share positions of the two majors had been stable although Labatt had slowly gained market share at the expense of Molson. Since 1990, the year that Molson acquired Carling O'Keefe, its market share had fallen from 52.2 per cent to its current level of 48.9 per cent, while Labatt had increased its market share from 42.0 per cent to 44.2 per cent.

The Canadian breweries operated at a substantial cost disadvantage relative to their U.S. counterparts. As a result largely of geography and provincial regulation, the Canadian brewing industry consisted of a series of small- and medium-sized production plants across the country. The average brewery size in Canada was estimated at 1.24-million hL, much smaller than the average size of a U.S. brewer that was estimated at 3.0-million hL. Supplies such as malting barley were purchased in the U.S. on the open market, whereas Canadian brewers had to purchase at a (premium) price set by the Canadian Wheat Board. As a consequence, Canadian breweries operated under the continuing threat of U.S. entry, which to this point, had been limited in two ways: (1) by tariffs and by provincial non-tariff measures such as packaging requirements and minimum pricing requirements, and (2) by the alliances between the major Canadian and U.S. breweries under which "Can-Am" brands were produced in Canada with license fees going to the U.S. brand owners. But this still left second-tier U.S. brewers with a thirst for the Canadian market.

Government

Government involvement in the brewing industry, and particularly at the provincial level, was a traditional "given" of life in Canada. This grew from the desires of various governments to achieve several, not necessarily consistent objectives such as controlling the sale of an alcoholic beverage, maximizing tax revenues and ensuring local employment.

In recent years, however, international developments and consumer pressures had started to modify traditional policies. For decades, brewers had been required to brew beer within a province in order to list it for sale there. This requirement was eliminated as a result of several complaints launched by U.S. brewers and adjudications by the General Agreement on Tariffs and Trade (GATT) panel, which ruled that inter-provincial trading policies in Canada were inconsistent with international trading policies. As a result of this change, Labatt breweries closed three of its 12 breweries between 1992 and 1994, although it maintained its domestic sales volume at approximately 8.3 million hL.

Further, under the Canada–U.S. Free Trade Agreement, tariffs on brewing products shipped between the two countries were to be reduced to zero per cent by 1998. This agreement had been reached despite repeated protests on the part of the industry and a one-day strike by brewery workers who were convinced that without pre-1988 tariff protection the Canadian industry would cease to exist.

The government, however, still held some good cards. The traditional method of distribution of beer in Canada was through government owned or regulated outlets. The exceptions were Quebec and Newfoundland, which allowed sales through corner stores as well. Control of distribution provided some degree of control over supply and suppliers. Complaints had been made, for example, by some prospective U.S. exporters about the difficulty of gaining distribution access and meeting distribution requirements. In time, this leverage on the industry might diminish with popular demand for wider distribution and government policies of privatization. Alberta, for example was in the process of privatizing its retail system for alcoholic beverages. But other provinces such as Ontario, which had also considered the idea, did not seem to be rushing in this direction.

Another area of government control was pricing, in which it was common to have regulations requiring minimum prices and distribution mark-ups and uniform prices across a jurisdiction. While serving domestic political purposes, these policies also had the effect of constraining low price competition from the U.S. Naturally, these policies were under attack by elements of the U.S. industry and their maintenance was subject to substantial political uncertainty.

LABATT IN THE USA

While Labatt had actively exported its portfolio of brands to the U.S. since the early 1960s, it was not until 1987 with the acquisition of the Latrobe Company (Latrobe) that it established a brewing presence in the U.S. Latrobe brewed the premium brand Rolling Rock which had, since Labatt's purchase, steadily grown from a regional beer to a niche premium brand distributed throughout the U.S.

Beer Demand in the U.S.

The U.S. beer market, estimated at 237 million hL in 1994, represented the largest single beer market in the world. Overall demand was static but significant opportunities were emerging as consumers traded up to premium beers that offered something different, something that was not mass-produced and was more full-bodied in taste. These emerging demands were being met by a plethora of specialty beers and imports. Key aspects of the U.S. brewing industry are summarized in Exhibit 4.

Competition

The maturation of the U.S. mass market for beer had turned the industry into a gruelling battleground for market share. Three brewers accounted for nearly 80 per cent of the market: Anheuser-Busch (46 per cent), Miller (23 per cent) and Coors (11 per cent). While there were several smaller brewers operating throughout the U.S., they operated on a regional basis because they lacked both the production capacity (minimum 26 million hL) and the financial resources (Anheuser-Busch spent in excess of US$300 million in 1993) to support a national brand.

Imports accounted for 4.4 per cent of beer sales in the U.S. Heineken of the Netherlands was in the top position, accounting for 29.4 per cent of imports. Canada was second at 25.8 per cent, followed by Mexico at 18.4 per cent. The top three imported brands in the U.S. were Heineken (2.7 million hL), Corona Extra (1.2 million hL), and Molson Golden (0.62 million hL). The import segment was expected to experience volume growth of 5.5 per cent in 1994.

The microbrew segment of the U.S. brewing industry, which had at one time been considered insignificant, was expected to experience a 50 per cent growth in volume in 1994. Although this segment accounted for less than two per cent of the entire U.S. industry, with overall beer sales showing little growth the four largest U.S. brewers had begun to aggressively enter the micro segment through the purchase of significant stakes in microbrewers and through the development of "micro-style" brands.

Labatt and FEMSA Cerveza's combined sales volumes in the U.S. for all their brands represented approximately 2.7 million hL[1] in 1994.

Supply and Distribution

In the U.S., the brewing infrastructure of plant locations and distribution systems was a function of market size, geography and transportation costs, not of state legislation. Breweries could ship product across state lines. The average new brewery built in the United States was in the 8 to 10 million hL size.

---

[1] *A Winning North American Brewing Partnership*, John Labatt Limited, July 1994.

Government

Unlike in Canada, governments in the U.S. influenced prices only to the extent that excise and sales taxes were levied on beer. Wholesale and retail prices were set by the members of the distribution and retail network in response to market conditions and supply. While beer could be shipped across state lines, 27 states had packaging and labelling requirements that favoured U.S. producers and discriminated against imported products.

LABATT IN THE UNITED KINGDOM

The six largest brewers in the United Kingdom (U.K.) controlled over 75 per cent of the domestic market. Brewers had vertically integrated to include not only beer production but also wholesale and retail outlets for beer distribution. This arrangement allowed brewers to control the products that were for sale and their prices. The result was that independent suppliers faced difficulties in distributing and selling their products.

Labatt first entered the U.K. in 1988 when it began marketing its Canadian draught products through Greenall Whitley pubs. By 1993, Labatt U.K. held interests in partnerships and joint ventures owning approximately 300 pubs. In all, Labatt brands were marketed through approximately 12 000 pubs, in addition to sales through outlets for off-premise consumption. However, the trading environment in the U.K. was difficult and was expected to remain so; total industry volume in the U.K., for example, had declined one per cent in 1993. Labatt's strategy was to continue to focus its activities on augmenting its strong brand franchises and building a solid pub estate. Labatt had yet to earn an operating profit from its U.K. activities, recording losses of C$2 million and C$8 million in 1994 and 1993 respectively, although the company was confident that the coming year would reflect improvements.

LABATT IN ITALY

Labatt International, a division of Labatt Breweries, began operating in Italy in 1989 when it acquired a 77.5 per cent interest in a joint venture with Birra Moretti S.p.A. of Italy. Birra Moretti, in turn, acquired Prinz Brau S.p.A., another Italian brewery, which was integrated to form the fourth largest brewing group in Italy. In 1992, Labatt acquired the 22.5 per cent minority interest in Birra Moretti to achieve full ownership.

Despite poor industry growth, nationwide discounting by competitors, deepening recession, and successive upsets in Italy's political, economic and industrial environments, Labatt had continued to make sales volume gains in Italy, although earnings had been negative in 1994 and 1993. Its main strategy was to establish a premium position for its brands rather than compete on price simply to gain volume. The company believed that this strategy, which was driven by creative advertising and promotional programs, was proving to be successful, and expected its first operating profit from its activities in Italy in the coming year.

FOMENTO ECONÓMICO MEXICANO, S.A. DE C.V. (FEMSA)[2]

FEMSA was a sub-entity of Valores Industriales, S.A., more commonly known as VISA. VISA, Mexico's fifth-largest publicly traded company, was founded in 1890 as Cerveceria Cuauhtémoc. Through the years the brewery expanded into other industries, and in 1936, VISA was created as a holding company to

---

[2] Information for this section is taken from: *Annual Report* 1993, Fomento Económico Mexicano, S.A. de C.V.; *A Winning North American Brewing Partnership*, John Labatt Limited, July 1994 (this public document was provided to all Labatt's shareholders and was reported widely in Canada's press); Laboy, Carlos, *Special Report: The Mexican Beer Industry*, Bear Stearns & Co Inc, New York: February 16, 1994; and *Siempre Los Mejores*, Edición Especial, Diciembre 1993.

manage the portfolio of enterprises. FEMSA was the result of a consolidation of VISA's food-related activities and was organized into four divisions: Beer, Retail, Coca-Cola FEMSA and Packaging.

The brewing division of FEMSA was a consolidation of two Mexican brewers: Cerveceria Cuauhtémoc and Cerveceria Moctezuma. FEMSA management had proved itself in the mid-1980s when, in the midst of a general economic collapse in Mexico, it had acquired Cerveceria Moctezuma, a Mexican brewer that was experiencing significant financial and operational difficulties. At the same time, however, Grupo Modelo S.A. de C.V. (Modelo), known internationally for its Corona brand, began to compete aggressively on the basis of price. Although FEMSA lost market share to Modelo, by the end of the 1980s both Modelo and FEMSA emerged as the key competitors in the Mexican beer market. FEMSA's accomplishment, and its ability to absorb Moctezuma, led some analysts to suggest that FEMSA's management's experience might be a hidden corporate asset.

Recent Financial Developments

In October 1991, FEMSA's parent Grupo VISA, acquired Bancomer, one of Mexico's largest financial services companies, from the Mexican government for an estimated US$2.8 billion.[3] FEMSA was called upon to increase debt significantly to help fund this move. Proceeds from the sale of 49 per cent[4] of Coca-Cola FEMSA, S.A. de C.V. and the sale of 60 per cent of Aguas Minerales, the company's mineral water division, had been used to help pay down the debt. In addition FEMSA issued US$300 million worth of five-year Eurobonds at 9.5 per cent. At the end of fiscal 1993 the company's long-term debt totalled N$2 345 million or US$752.7 million. Of this amount N$1 844 million or 78.6 per cent was denominated in U.S. dollars and German marks.[5]

By 1994, the company remained very heavily indebted and was believed to be talking to prospective foreign partners over arrangements, similar to that with its Coca-Cola division, for its packaging and beer subsidiaries. Philip Morris, holder of eight per cent of FEMSA stock, and its subsidiary Miller Brewing, were known to be interested in the beer business.

The chairman of the board of FEMSA, in the 1993 annual report, stated that the company would:

> Continue to pursue our objective of identifying and carrying out strategic joint ventures that will improve our position in the industries and markets where we operated and will open new opportunities for growth.

Exhibit 5 presents financial data for FEMSA for fiscal 1992 and 1993 and segmented financial information for the period 1991 to 1993.

FEMSA CERVEZA AND THE MEXICAN BREWING INDUSTRY

Demand

The Mexican beer market, which was estimated to be 41 million hL in size in 1994, was almost twice as large as Canada's. Unlike the Canadian and U.S. brewing industries, the Mexican beer market had grown in excess of six per cent per annum through the 1980s and early 1990s and was expected to continue to grow at the same rate in the foreseeable future. Improving economic conditions, a young population and lower

---

[3] Poole, Claire, "The Resurrection of Don Eugenio," *Forbes*, February 17, 1992, p. 106.

[4] Thirty per cent was resold to Coca Cola International and 19 per cent was distributed in a public offering.

[5] *Annual Report* 1993, Fomento Económico Mexicano, S.A. de C.V., p. 65.

per capita consumption rates were all factors in this expectation. Key aspects of the Mexican brewing industry are summarized in Exhibit 4.

Competition

The Mexican beer market was essentially a duopoly shared by FEMSA Cerveza (49 per cent) and Grupo Modelo, S.A. de C.V. (Modelo) (51 per cent)[6]. FEMSA had enjoyed a dominant position in the northern and southern regions of the market, while Modelo (known internationally for the Corona brand) had led in the central and Metropolitan Mexico City markets.

Although FEMSA was considered to be more aggressive than Modelo in expanding its brand portfolio and in the growing non-returnable segment of the market, these moves had yet to improve aggregate market share. Table 2 presents Mexican domestic beer shipments and Mexican beer exports by company.

T A B L E 2 Mexican Domestic Beer Shipments

(millions of hL)

	1993	1992	1991	1990	1989	1988
FEMSA	19.1	19.1	18.9	18.7	18.3	15.9
Modelo	20.7	20.0	20.0	18.4	18.1	15.1
TOTAL	39.8	39.1	38.9	37.1	36.4	31.0

Mexican Beer Exports

(millions of hL)

	1993	1992	1991	1990	1989	1988
FEMSA	0.65	0.60	0.68	0.69	0.61	0.70
Modelo	1.85	1.75	1.37	1.41	1.46	1.90
TOTAL	2.50	2.35	2.05	2.10	2.07	2.60

Source: ANAFACER.

Over 95 per cent of FEMSA's exports, primarily under the Tecate and Dos Equis brand names, were destined for the U.S. Wisdom Import Sales Co. was acquired by FEMSA in 1986 and was the company's exclusive importer in the U.S. Wisdom distributed FEMSA products throughout the country, although its strength lay in the U.S. south and southwest. FEMSA Cerveza's sales from exports totalled US$56.8 million in 1993, up six per cent from 1992. Export earnings were of particular importance to FEMSA as a hard currency offset to import requirements.

Production and Distribution[7]

FEMSA and Modelo operated production facilities spread throughout the country. FEMSA's production facilities ranged in size from 0.36 million hL to 6.0 million hL, whereas Modelo's ranged in size from 0.5 million hL to its plant in Mexico City that had a production capacity of 11.1 million hL. Between

---

[6] Laboy, Carlos, *Special Report: The Mexican Beer Industry*, Bear Stearns & Co. Inc., New York: February 16, 1994, p. 1.

[7] This section is taken from: Laboy, Carlos, *Special Report: The Mexican Beer Industry*, Bear, Stearns & Co. Inc, New York: February 16, 1994, p. 22–24.

1988 and 1993, FEMSA had invested US$950 million as part of a capital expenditure program designed to modernize its manufacturing and distribution facilities.[8]

The most significant barrier to entry in the Mexican beer market was its distribution system. The nature of the retail system and the prevalence of returnable presentations required far-reaching distribution capabilities. FEMSA and Modelo distributed their product to over 348 000 retailers in Mexico, many of whom (in excess of 80 per cent) had exclusive arrangements with one producer or the other. Each company also operated its own chain of retail outlets (FEMSA's chain of 700 outlets operated under the name of OXXO). Supermarkets accounted for less than five per cent of total industry sales.

FEMSA's distribution network consisted of 274 wholly owned distribution centres that operated a fleet of 3 100 trucks and moved 73 per cent of the brewery's volume. In addition, the company's product was also delivered to retailers through 122 franchised third-party distribution outlets which operated 1 500 trucks. Modelo operated in much the same way as FEMSA, with 88 per cent of its product being distributed through 82 majority-owned distributors and the remainder through third-party distributors. In total, Modelo claimed to operate a fleet of 6 379 trucks and service vehicles.

The preceding distribution characteristics made it unlikely that domestic or foreign competitors would be able to independently penetrate the market in a meaningful way in the near future.

Government

The primary influence of the Mexican government on the brewing industry was in the form of pricing controls. Price wars between the two brewers throughout the 1980s and then the inclusion of beer as food in the Pacto de Solidaridad Económica (Pacto)[9] introduced in December, 1987, had resulted in real producer beer prices being fixed at levels about 35 per cent below pre-price-war levels. Most recently there had been a modest improvement in the real price of beer.

The number of retail outlets authorized to sell beer was regulated by the Mexican government through licenses which were granted to beer producers which, in turn, authorized specific dealers to carry their products under their permits. This practice further reinforced the closed nature of the Mexican beer distribution system.

CONSIDERATIONS IN A LABATT-FEMSA PARTNERSHIP

In a series of discussions with FEMSA management Labatt management had formulated a provisional approach to link the two companies. It called for Labatt to purchase a 22 per cent interest in FEMSA Cerveza for C$720 million (US$510 million), with an option to acquire an additional eight per cent position within three years. Further, it called for a cooperative approach in exchanging skills and experience and jointly exploiting the U.S. market. The parameters of this approach had been set by a valuation[10] that Labatt thought was reasonable, a share position that was meaningful and within the capacity of Labatt to finance, and the need to establish a relationship with FEMSA Cerveza managers that would be of value to all parties in the future. Labatt understood that Philip Morris/Miller and perhaps other suitors were also interested in FEMSA Cerveza, but were of the view that Labatt's cooperative approach and provisions for partnering in operations were of significant interest to the FEMSA executives.[10]

---

[8] *Annual Report* 1993, Fomento Económico Mexicano, S.A. de C.V., p. 6.

[9] The Pacto was an agreement among government, industry and labour which froze wages, prices and the exchange rate. It was designed to fight against inflation.

[10] This valuation was reported to be consistent with valuations derived from trading and initial public offering (IPO) multiples of Latin American brewers and consumer products companies believed to form FEMSA-Cerveza's "peer" group and it was believed to be consistent with the price paid by Anheuser-Busch for its 17.7 per cent stake in Grupo Modelo.

The corporate structure envisaged in the approach is presented in Exhibit 6. Under this structure:

- FEMSA would continue to hold 51 per cent of FEMSA Cerveza, and 19 per cent of the division's equity would be earmarked for sale at an appropriate time in the Mexican and international equity markets.
- FEMSA would appoint the chairman and Labatt the vice-chairman of FEMSA Cerveza; the board would comprise 11 FEMSA nominees, 5 Labatt nominees and 2 public members. The current FEMSA Cerveza chief executive officer would retain his position, although he would now be advised by a six person management committee consisting of three FEMSA and three Labatt members.
- In Mexico, the partners would jointly select the best portfolio of U.S. and imported brands for market development. All of Labatt's Canadian, U.S. and European brands and brewing technology would be made available to FEMSA Cerveza. Labatt would also bring its brand management skills to Mexico, where Labatt executives believed the company's experience in "pull" marketing in diverse cultural markets would produce significant results.
- In the U.S., Labatt USA and Wisdom (FEMSA's U.S. import company) would be merged into a U.S. specialty beer company. Labatt would hold a 51 per cent position in this entity, FEMSA would hold 30 per cent, and the remaining 19 per cent would go to additional partners when appropriate.

  The merged entity would be managed jointly by both companies and would give each company access to the other's wholesaler and distribution networks (Labatt had traditionally been strong in the U.S. northeast, and FEMSA in the U.S. south and southwest). Both partners would work together to seek and develop additional quality, specialty brands that would complement their own brands in order to achieve faster growth in the U.S.
- In Canada, Labatt would position a portfolio of FEMSA Cerveza's brands throughout the country, aiming to become the leading Canadian importer of Mexican beer.

If the partnership proposal was successful, plans were to finance it through cash on hand of C$300 million, drawdown of a bank loan facility by C$300 million, and issuance of commercial paper of C$100 million. The bank loan facility would be new and involve a revolving extendable facility at floating rates with a minimum term of three years, and could be drawn in U.S. or Canadian dollars.

Labatt management thought that one of the important considerations in the investment was the currency risk of both the Canadian dollar and the Mexican peso. Historically, Mexico had been subject to significant inflation and currency devaluation. For this reason, in putting together its proposal, Labatt assumed that inflation in Mexico would be 5 per cent higher per annum than U.S. inflation and that the peso would devalue by 5 per cent per annum.

POLITICAL DEVELOPMENTS IN MEXICO

On January 1, 1994, the day that the North American Free Trade Agreement (NAFTA) took effect, Indian peasants in the southern state of Chiapas had risen in armed rebellion. Led by the Zapatista National Liberation Army (EZLN), the Indians claimed that they had been cheated of their land, denied basic services and had had their culture eroded. Many people claimed that the roots of the rebellion lay in poverty, racial discrimination and the failure of regional and social policy. Others claimed that Guatemalan guerillas were behind the situation and were using it to destabilize Mexico.

On March 23, shortly after the uprising in the state of Chiapas appeared to have been brought under control, Luis Donaldo Colosio, the presidential candidate for the PRI party, was shot at a rally in Tijuana.

In the days that followed, many stories emerged in the press suggesting that the assassination might have been conceived by ultra-conservatives within the PRI party who were allegedly opposed to the economic and political reforms that Colosio was promising to continue if he were elected.[11]

On March 28, Ernesto Zedillo, Mexico's former education minister, accepted the presidential candidacy for the PRI. Many people in the country questioned the political skills and abilities of Zedillo because of the previous bureaucratic positions he had held and the limited time available for him to prepare for the position of president. This widespread concern gave rise to speculation that one of Mexico's two other national political parties might be elected to power, although neither had any experience in running the country. Presidential elections were scheduled for August, 1994.

Many investors were concerned with events in Mexico: Chiapas, bombings in Mexico City, kidnappings, and the assassination of the presidential candidate. By April 1994, the peso had been devalued to 8 per cent below its January level and interest rates had been raised to 18 per cent, double the figure of two months before.

Appendix B contains economic data on Mexico and a brief discussion of the country's political and economic history.

CONCLUSION

As he worked through the various aspects of the proposal to partner with FEMSA, George Taylor continued to ask himself the same question: Was it or was it not a sound move in furthering Labatt's future as a global brewer?

---

[11] "Mexico's whodunit," *The Economist*, New York: October 15, 1994, p. 53.

Appendix A   Philip Morris/Miller Brewing—Description

Philip Morris Companies Inc. was the world's largest consumer packaged goods company. Tobacco products, which accounted for 43 per cent of Philip Morris' operating revenues in 1993 and 1992, food products, beer, and financial services and real estate represented the company's significant segments. Philip Morris owned Kraft Foods, the second largest food business in the U.S. after ConAgra, and Miller Brewing, the world's third largest beer producer after Anheuser-Busch and Heineken.

A summary of Philip Morris' segmented results for the most recent three years is presented below:

Consolidated Operating Results (US$ millions)

(Year Ended December 31)

	Operating Revenues			Identifiable Assets [12]		
	1993	*1992*	*1991*	*1993*	*1992*	*1991*
Tobacco	25 973	25 677	23 840	9 523	9 479	8 648
Food	30 372	29 048	28 178	33 253	32 672	31 622
Beer	4 1543	976	4 056	1 706	1 545	1 608
Financial Services and Real Estate	402430	384	5 659	5 297	4 538	
Other			1 064	1 021	968	
TOTAL	60 901	59 131	56 458	51 205	50 014	47 384

Operating Profit (US$ millions)

	1993	*1992*	*1991*
Tobacco	4 910	7 193	6 463
Food	2 608	2 769	2 016
Beer	215	258	299
Financial Services and Real Estate	249	219	178
Less: Unallocated Corporate Expenses	395	380	334
OPERATING PROFIT	9 449	7 587	10 059

Miller Brewing was the second-largest brewer in the U.S. The brewer's primary brands were: Miller Lite, which was the largest selling reduced calories beer and second largest selling beer in the United States in 1993; Miller High Life; and Miller Genuine Draft which was one of the fastest growing premium beers in the U.S. Based on the company's estimates of beer shipments in the U.S., and the industry's sales of beer and brewed non-alcoholic beverages, Miller reported that its share of the industry had remained relatively stable since 1991, as per the following:

	1994[13]	*1993*	*1992*	*1991*
Miller's Share of the Industry	22.7%	22.2%	21.4%	22.2%

Source: Philip Morris Companies Inc. *Annual Report* 1993.

---

[12] Identifiable assets are those assets applicable to the respective industry segments.

[13] Estimate based on year-to-date figures.

Appendix B   Mexico's Economy—Historical Perspective

Before it joined the General Agreement on Tariffs and Trade (GATT) in 1986, Mexico was an inward-looking country. The protection of domestic industry was the main principle underlying all government economic policy. If a product could be manufactured in Mexico, it was, even if it was more expensive and of lower quality than similar products available internationally. The Mexican government implemented several economic policy tools to ensure the achievement of this goal. High tariffs (often over 100 per cent), restrictions on foreign ownership and investment, import permits and export requirements succeeded in dampening foreign interest in Mexico.

From 1958 to 1970, Mexico thrived. The country's gross domestic product (GDP) grew at an average annual rate of approximately 6.8 per cent, with GDP per capita growth of 3.2 per cent annually. Consumer price inflation over the same period averaged only 2.9 per cent per year. The ratios of public-sector deficits and public external debt to GDP were low and stable, and real interest rates were positive. During this period neither the current-account deficit nor the balance of payments exceeded three per cent of GDP.

According to the statistics, all should have been well in Mexico. Unfortunately, this was not the case. Wealth in the country was very unevenly distributed. To correct this inequity and to reduce the widespread poverty in Mexico, President Echeverría (1970–76) and his successor, President López Portillo (1976–82) attempted to increase the country's economic growth by pursuing a policy of higher government expenditure. In theory, such a policy would:

> Permit a more plentiful "trickle down" to those on the lowest incomes; higher public expenditure, and, in particular, higher welfare spending and transfer payments, would soften the rigours of an inegalitarian system.[14]

Increased government spending throughout the 1970s and early 1980s was financed through foreign borrowing. The discovery of the large Capecha oil fields in the State of Chiapas in the late 1970s allowed the government to intensify its expenditures by borrowing more furiously from foreign banks that were ready and anxious to lend money to Mexico because they anticipated rising oil revenues for the country.

When oil prices began to fall in the early 1980s, the Mexican economy was destabilized with large increases in inflation and the current account deficit. Under pressure from the international financial community, the Mexican government responded with severe import restrictions and high domestic interest rates.

In 1982, investors, anticipating a devaluation of the currency, moved out of pesos into more stable currencies. This put strains on the government as it used foreign currency reserves to maintain the country's fixed exchange rates. Oil prices softened further, the global recession peaked, interest rates increased and private capital in international markets disappeared. On August 15, 1982, the Mexican government announced that it was no longer able to meet its interest obligations on its US$88 billion foreign debt. The government signed an agreement with the International Monetary Fund (IMF) that rescued the country, but forced it to introduce a program of economic reforms. Public expenditures were reduced, taxes were increased and some small public service enterprises were closed. Exchange controls were abolished, and the currency was devalued by over 100 per cent. Prices for public services and administered prices (for foodstuffs) were brought into line with production costs or international prices. The group who suffered most was Mexico's middle class. Real wages fell and savings were all but wiped out. Unlike Mexico's elite class, this group did not have the luxury of investing abroad in order to insulate their savings from currency devaluations.

---

[14] The Economist Intelligence Unit, *Mexico: Country Profile* (New York: Business International Limited, 1992), p. 10.

Appendix B   (continued)

The debt crisis of 1982 forced Mexico to abandon its inward-looking policies of protection and state regulation in favour of new policies that stressed a more outward-focused development strategy that would be led by the private sector.

The results from 1983–85 showed a resumption in real growth and a decrease in inflation from over 90 per cent in 1982–83 to approximately 60 per cent in the following two years. The public sector deficit as a share of GDP was halved. The fall in the real exchange rate stimulated export growth and reduced the level of imports from US$25 billion in 1981 to US$9 billion 1983. From 1985–87, real GDP fell to 3 per cent and inflation accelerated to over 130 per cent. Oil prices softened and Mexico neared crisis once again. A new debt repayment plan was introduced by the IMF that tied Mexico's debt repayment schedule to the health of the country's economy.

Upon assuming office on December 1, 1988, President Carlos Salinas de Gortari introduced the first of what was to become a series of pacts among government, labour and employers' organizations. The intention of these pacts was to reduce inflation without causing a recession. These pacts used publicly controlled prices, minimum wages and the nominal exchange rate as the tools to eliminate the economic distortions that had led to inflation in the past. Fiscal and credit policies were tightened and a more equitable tax system was introduced. Tariffs were reduced, as was the number of products subject to import licenses. Another significant element of the government's strategy to curb inflation was a reduction in the money supply growth rate. In 1982, when foreign capital disappeared, the Mexican government borrowed from domestic banks. After 1988, government borrowing was done predominantly through bonds.

In 1989, the Salinas government introduced its National Development Plan (1989–94), which committed the government to the liberalization of foreign trade and investment policies. These changes were intended to force Mexican enterprises to introduce stricter efficiency standards and new technologies in an effort to render Mexican products more competitive in domestic and world markets. The government sought foreign investment as a means of complementing domestic capital in this plant modernization process. It introduced a new tax policy that protected the lowest income groups without adversely affecting public finances. Finally, it introduced subsidy policies that were intended to increase the purchasing power of the needy.

The Salinas government appeared to have ushered in a new era of improved performance of the Mexican economy. Inflation fell from 52 per cent in 1988 to approximately 7 per cent in the first seven months of 1994. Most of the fall was attributed to the government's wage and price restraints and its trade liberalization policies that culminated in the North American Free Trade Agreement (NAFTA) which came into effect on January 1, 1994. The public sector deficit was reduced from 12.5 per cent of GDP in 1988 to a surplus of 0.1 per cent of GDP in 1993. A reduction in interest rates through the liberalization of markets and lifting of interest controls and cash reserves had also had a positive influence on the economy.

The country's current account deficit, fuelled by growth in imports which led to a merchandise trade deficit (1993 US$13 billion, 1994 estimated at US$18 billion) was expected to be US$27.8 billion or 8 per cent of GDP in 1994. While foreign capital inflows had acted to cover the shortfall, the bulk of these inward flows had been in the form of portfolio investment, money going to both the stock market and to government securities such as Treasury Certificates (CETES), both of which were intrinsically volatile and were required to offer high rates of return in order to continue to attract capital inflows and avoid capital outflows.

Appendix B   (continued)

Purchasing Power Parity Estimates of GNP

Country	PPP estimates of GNP per capita United States = 100		Current International dollars[15]
	1987	*1992*	*1992*
Mexico	31.6	32.4	7 490
Canada	91.0	85.3	19 720
United States	100	100	23 120

Source: World Development Report 1994: Infrastructure for Development, The World Bank.

---

[15] The "international dollar" has the same purchasing power over total GNP as the U.S. dollar in a given year.

EXHIBIT 1 John Labatt Limited Consolidated Statement of Earnings[16]

(Millions of Canadian dollars)

Year Ended April 30	1994	1993	1992	1991	1990	1989	1988
Net sales	2 321	2 135	3 837	4 760	4 681	4 857	4 611
Operating costs	2 085	1 896	3 562	4 602	4 450	4 661	4 390
Earnings before interest, income taxes, and restructuring charges	292	274	301	199	264	263	295
Income taxes	85	64	37	50	72	57	85
Earnings before share in partly owned business	151	130	93	108	159	129	142
Net earnings	155	(70)[17]	101	109	169	135	141

John Labatt Limited Consolidated Balance Sheet[18]

(Millions of Canadian Dollars)

Assets

Year Ended April 30	1994	1993	1992	1991	1990	1989	1988
Current assets	1 102	1 187	1 634	1 234	1 184	1 227	964
Fixed assets less depreciation	813	784	1 027	1 257	1 181	1 002	992
Other assets	621	597	520	647	581	528	582
TOTAL ASSETS	2 536	3 020	3 320	3 138	2 946	2 757	2 538

Liabilities

Year Ended April 30	1994	1993	1992	1991	1990	1989	1988
Current liabilities	721	932	836	913	628	683	736
Non-convertible long-term debt	610	630	646	416	544	533	482
Deferred income taxes	86	141	90	133	130	143	162
Convertible debentures and shareholders' equity	1 119	1 317	1 748	1 676	1 644	1 398	1 158
TOTAL LIABILITIES	2 536	3 020	3 320	3 138	2 946	2 757	2 538

Source: John Labatt Limited, *Annual Reports* 1988–1994.

---

[16] Over the period 1988 to 1993, John Labatt divested itself of several of its businesses. This explains the significant drop in net sales over the period.

[17] In 1993, John Labatt incurred a loss from discontinued operations of C$ 203 million as a result of provisions for estimated future liabilities from businesses sold in prior years, and a provision to write down the assets of its U.S. dairy business.

[18] Over the period 1988 to 1993, John Labatt divested itself of several of its businesses. This explains the significant drop in net sales over the period.

EXHIBIT 2   John Labatt Limited Segmented Financial Results

(Millions of C$)

	1994	1993	1992	1991	1990	1989	1988
Net Sales							
Brewing	1 769	1 672	1 564	2 043	1 920	1 818	1 633
BS&E[19]	630	—	—	—	—	—	—
Entertainment	—	546	374	—	—	—	—
Dairy	—	—	2 110	—	—	—	—
Food	—	—	—	3 327	3 354	3 606	—
Agri Products	—	—	—	—	—	—	2 450
Packaged Food	—	—	—	—	—	—	1 024
Earnings Before Interest, Restructuring Charges and Income Taxes							
Brewing	260	218	181	109	174	157	140
BS&E	32	—	—	—	—	—	—
Entertainment	—	56	58	—	—	—	—
Dairy	—	—	62	—	—	—	—
Food	—	—	—	90	90	106	—
Agri Products	—	—	—	—	—	—	91
Packaged Food	—	—	—	—	—	—	64
Capital Expenditures							
Brewing	103	191	122	104	98	78	77
BS&E	20	—	—	—	—	—	—
Entertainment	—	12	5	—	—	—	—
Dairy	—	—	45	—	—	—	—
Food	—	—	—	87	108	160	—
Agri Products	—	—	—	—	—	—	71
Packaged Food	—	—	—	—	—	—	61
Net Assets Employed							
Brewing	960	1 146	799	727	717	516	527
BS&E	308	—	—	—	—	—	—
Entertainment	—	283	140	—	—	—	—
Dairy	—	—	629	—	—	—	—
Food	—	—	—	1 319	1 233	1 110	—
Agri Products	—	—	—	—	—	—	657
Packaged Food	—	—	—	—	—	—	651

Stock Price (1985–1994)

	1994	1993	1992	1991	1990	1989	1988
High	26.25	30.38	27.88	26.00	27.50	24.38	29.75
Low	20.50	24.25	22.25	18.38	20.50	20.63	20.13
Dividend Record (C$ per share)	0.82	3.82	0.795	0.77	0.73	0.685	0.62
Dividend Record (millions of C$)	88	344[20]	83	84	73	50.6	45.5
Dividend as % of Net Profits	56.8	NA	82.2	77.1	43.2	37.5	32.4

Source: John Labatt Limited, *Annual Reports* 1988–1994.

---

[19] BS&E is an abbreviation for the Broadcast, Sports and Entertainment division.

[20] Large dividend payout to shareholders as a result of the sale of Labatt's food-related assets.

E X H I B I T 3   North American Brewing Alliances 1994

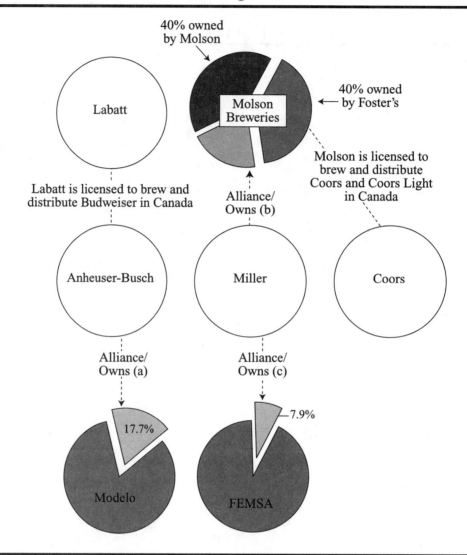

(a) Has the option to increase ownership to 35 per cent, which may be exercised between mid-1995 and end of 1997.

(b) Pursuant to this alliance, Miller acquired the U.S. distribution business of Molson Breweries. Molson Breweries will also continue to brew and sell Miller brands in Canada.

(c) Miller parent Philip Morris owns the 7.9 per cent interest in FEMSA, the parent company of FEMSA Cerveza.

Source: John Labatt Limited.

EXHIBIT 4 Key Aspects of the North American Brewing Industry

	Canada	United States	Mexico
Demand			
Market size (millions hl)	21	237	41
Market growth (forecast)	flat	flat	+6.0%
Per capita consumption (litres)	78.3	87.4	44.2
Competition			
Market structure	Duopoly	Mass market	Duopoly
Market share (major brewers)	Labatt Breweries (44.2%)	Anheuser-Busch (46%)	FEMSA Cerveza (49%)
	Molson Breweries (48.9%)	Miller Brewing (23%)	Modelo Cerveza (51%)
		Coors Brewing (11%)	
Market share (imports)	2.9%	4.4%	Less than 1%
National vs. Regional brands	both	focus on national	both
Avg. brewery size (millions hl)	1.24	3.0	3.90
Market strategy	Advertising and marketing limited price competition. Some new product introductions	Price competition Some niche-targeted products	Price competition Controlled distribution system Some market segmentation and limited attempts to use marketing to develop brand awareness
Distribution			
Characteristics	Beer was sold through government owned stores or regulated retail outlets except in Québec (grocery stores were permitted to sell beer) and Newfoundland (corner stores and privately owned liquor stores were permitted to sell beer).	In most states beer was distributed through a free enterprise system based on wholesalers and distributors, with supermarkets as the main retail outlet.	Beer was sold through government authorized retail outlets. Distribution was the most significant barrier to entry in the Mexican brewing industry. FEMSA and Modelo distributed their products to over 348 000 retail outlets throughout Mexico of which over 80 per cent had exclusive arrangements with one of the two brewers. FEMSA and Modelo operated distribution fleets of 3 100 and 6 400 vehicles respectively.
Bottle/can ratio	80:20	30:70	78:22
Government			
Tax (per cent of retail price)	53	18	22 to 25
Involvement in the industry	Provincial governments regulated where beer could be sold and imposed constraints on pricing such as minimum price mark-ups, minimum allowable prices and uniform pricing throughout a province. Provincial governments regulated the sale of beer.	Packaging and labeling requirements in some states that favoured U.S. producers.	Pricing controls through PACTO, an agreement between business, labour and government that limited wage and price increases. The government also regulated the number of retail outlets permitted to sell beer through licenses that it granted to beer producers who, in turn, authorized specific dealers to carry their products.

EXHIBIT 5 **Financial Statements Fomento Económico Mexicano, S.A. de C.V. and Subsidiaries**

(Amounts in Millions of New Pesos (N$) and Millions of U.S. dollars)

Consolidated Income Statement

For the years ended December 31

	1993		1992	
	N$	*US$*	*N$*	*US$*
Sales	7 571	2 430	7 090	2 275
Gross profit	3 515	1 128	3 122	1 002
Operating expenses:	2 718	872	2 382	764
Income from operations	777	249	710	227
Income tax, tax on assets and employee profit sharing	348	111	359	115
Income before extraordinary items	243	78	289	93
Net income for the year	684[21]	219	552	177

Consolidated Statement of Financial Position

For the years ended December 31

	1993		1992	
Assets	*N$*	*US$*	*N$*	*US$*
Current assets	1 895	608	1 832	588
Investments and other assets	21	6	42	13
Property, plant and equipment	7 981	2 561	7 711	2 474
Other	226	72	139	44
TOTAL ASSETS	10 123	3 247	9 724	3 119

	1993		1992	
Liabilities and Stockholders' Equity	*N$*	*US$*	*N$*	*US$*
Current liabilities:	1 226	394	1 718	551
Long-term liabilities	2 345	753	2 679	860
Other liabilities	437	139	453	146
Stockholders' equity	6 115	1 963	4 874	1 564
TOTAL LIABILITIES AND STOCKHOLDERS' EQUITY	10 123	3 249	9 724	3 121

Note: Mexican peso figures for 1992 and 1993 have been restated in U.S. dollars using 1993 average annual exchange rate, because 1992 figures were restated in terms of the purchasing power of the Mexican peso as of 1993 year-end. This practice was commonly referred to as "Accounting for Changing Price Levels."

Source: *Annual Report* 1993, Fomento Económico Mexicano, S.A. de C.V.

---

[21] In 1993 the sale of Coca-Cola FEMSA shares resulted in a N$353 million gain that was recorded as an extraordinary item.

EXHIBIT 5   **(continued) Segmented Financial Information Fomento Económico Mexicano, S.A. de C.V.**

(Millions of Average New Pesos and Millions of US$)

Sales	1993		1992		1991	
	N$	*US$*	*N$*	*US$*	*N$*	*US$*
Brewing	4 089	1 312	4 072	1 306	4 077	1 308
Retail	1 061	340	872	279	737	236
Coca-Cola FEMSA	1 838	589	1 601	513	1 468	471
Packaging	1 214	389	1 104	354	1 056	339

Operating Profit	1993		1992		1991	
	N$	*US$*	*N$*	*US$*	*N$*	*US$*
Brewing	449	144	443	142	438	140
Retail	20	6	31	10	25	8
Coca-Cola FEMSA	277	88	247	79	230	73
Packaging	187	60	156	50	142	45

Cash Flow from Operations	1993		1992		1991	
	N$	*US$*	*N$*	*US$*	*N$*	*US$*
Brewing	379	121	504	161	459	147
Retail	14	4	30	9	25	8
Coca-Cola FEMSA	245	78	181	58	199	63
Packaging	194	62	175	56	171	54

Total Assets	1993		1992		1991	
	N$	*US$*	*N$*	*US$*	*N$*	*US$*
Brewing	6 542	2 099	6 196	1 988	5 950	1 909
Retail	396	127	366	177	230	73
Coca-Cola FEMSA	1 384	444	1 172	376	1 024	328
Packaging	1 440	462	1 327	425	1 268	407

Note: Mexican peso figures for 1991, 1992 and 1993 have been restated in U.S. dollars using 1993 average annual exchange rate, because 1991 and 1992 figures were restated in terms of the purchasing power of the Mexican peso as of 1993 year-end. This practice was commonly known as "Accounting for Changing Price Levels."

Source: *Annual Report* 1993, Fomento Económico Mexicano, S.A. de C.V.

EXHIBIT 6   Envisaged Labatt/FEMSA Partnership Structure

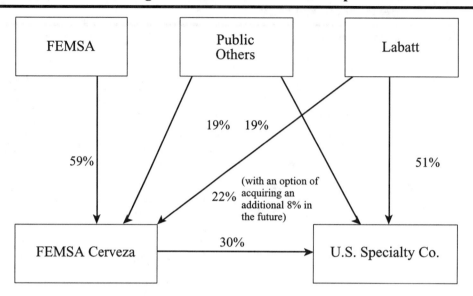

- FEMSA Chairman

- Labatt Vice Chairman

- 11 FEMSA directors, 5 Labatt directors, 2 public directors

- Current FEMSA Cerveza CEO, retains leadership role

- CEO advised by 6 member management committee (3 FEMSA, 3 Labatt)

- Labatt-FEMSA management interchange program

- Shared FEMSA-Labatt management

- Manage Labatt & FEMSA brands in the U.S.

- Utilize Labatt USA and Wisdom existing management & distribution network

- Utilize Labatt USA's and Wisdom's national wholesaler and distribution presence

- Jointly seek other brands for portfolio

Source: *A Winning North American Brewing Partnership*, John Labatt Limited, July 1994.

MR. JAX FASHION INC.

case

25

C. Patrick Woodcock
and Michael Geringer

It was 6:30 a.m., Monday, January 16, 1989. Dawn had not yet broken on the Vancouver skyline, and Louis Eisman, President of Mr. Jax Fashion Inc., was sitting at his desk pondering opportunities for future growth. Growth had been an important objective for Eisman and the other principle shareholder, Joseph Segal. Initially the company had focused on the professional/career women's dresses, suits and coordinates market, but by 1986 it had virtually saturated its ability to grow within this market segment

IVEY

C. Patrick Woodcock and J. Michael Geringer prepared this case solely to provide material for class discussion. The authors do not intend to illustrate either effective or ineffective handling of a managerial situation. The authors may have disguised certain names and other identifying information to protect confidentiality.

in Canada. Growth was then sought through the acquisition of four companies: a woolen textile mill and three apparel-manufacturing companies. The result of this decade-long expansion was a company that had become the sixth largest apparel manufacturer in Canada.

In the future, Eisman felt continued growth would require a different approach. A good option appeared to be expansion into the U.S. market. Strong growth was forecast in the women's professional/career market, Mr. Jax's principal market segment, and the recently ratified Free Trade Agreement (FTA) provided an excellent low tariff environment for expansion into the U.S. Yet, Eisman wanted to ensure the appropriate growth strategy was selected. He was confident that, if the right approach was taken, Mr. Jax could become a major international apparel company by the end of the next decade.

THE INDUSTRY

The apparel industry was divided into a variety of market segments based upon gender, type of garment and price points. Based on price points, the women's segments ranged from low-priced unexceptional to runway fashion segments. Low-priced segments competed on a low-cost manufacturing capability, while the higher quality segments tended to compete on design and marketing capabilities. Companies in the higher priced segments often subcontracted out manufacturing.

The professional/career women's segment ranged from the medium to medium-high price points. During the late 1970s and early 1980s, this segment had experienced strong growth due to the demographic growth in career-oriented, professional women. In the U.S., it had grown by 50% annually during the first half of the 1980s, but had slowed to about 20% in 1988. Experts predicted that by the mid-1990s, growth would drop to the rate of GNP growth. The U.S. professional/career women's segment was estimated to be $2 billion in 1988. The Canadian market was estimated to be one-tenth this size and growth was expected to emulate the U.S. market. Yet, the exact timing of the slowing of growth was difficult to predict because of extreme cyclicality in the fashion industry. During difficult economic times, women tended to delay purchases, particularly in the mid-priced, fashionable market-sectors. Then during times of economic prosperity, women who would not otherwise be able to afford fashionable items tended to have more resources to devote to these items.

Competition

Some of the more prominent Canada-based companies competing in the professional/career women's segment included the following.

JONES NEW YORK OF CANADA Jones New York of Canada, a marketing subsidiary of a U.S.-based fashion company, was thought to share the leadership position with Mr. Jax in the Canadian professional/career women's market. The company focused exclusively on marketing clothes to this market segment. Manufacturing was contracted out to Asian companies.

THE MONACO GROUP The Monaco Group had become a major Canadian designer and retailer of men's and women's fashions during the 1980s. By 1988, the company had sales of $21 million and a rate of return on capital of over 20 per cent. The company designed their own fashion lines, which were merchandised through their own retail outlets as well as major department stores. Manufacturing was contracted out to Asian companies. Recently, the company had been purchased by Dylex Inc., a large Canada-based retail conglomerate with 2 000 retail apparel stores located in both Canada and the U.S.

NYGARD INTERNATIONAL LTD. Nygard International Ltd., with revenues of over $200 million, was Canada's largest apparel manufacturer. Approximately one-third of their sales and production were located in the U.S. This company had historically focused on lower priced clothing, but they had hired away Mr. Jax's former designer to create the Peter Nygard Signature Collection, a fashion line aimed at the professional/career women's market. This new line had been out for only six months, and sales were rumoured to be moderate.

Additional competition in this Canadian segment included a wide variety of U.S. and European imports. These companies generally manufactured garments in Asia and marketed them in Canada through independent Canadian sales agents. Historically, most had concentrated their marketing resources on the rapidly growing U.S. market, yet many had captured a significant share of the Canadian market based upon strong international brand recognition. Prominent U.S.-based competition included the following companies.

LIZ CLAIBORNE Liz Claiborne, as the originator of the professional/career women's fashion look, had utilized their first-mover advantage to build a dominant position in this segment. This company, started in 1976, grew tremendously during the late 1970s and early 1980s, and by 1988 they had sales in excess of US$1.2 billion, or nearly two-thirds of the market. Claiborne generally competed on price and brand recognition, a strategy copied by many of the larger companies that had begun to compete in this segment. To keep prices low, Claiborne contracted out manufacturing to low-cost manufacturers, 85 per cent of which were Asian. The company's large size allowed them to wield considerable influence over these manufacturing relationships. Recently, the company had diversified into retailing.

J.H. COLLECTIBLES J.H. Collectibles, a Milwaukee-based company with sales of US$200 million, had one of the more unique strategies in this segment. They produced slightly upscale products that emphasized an English country-sporting look. Using facilities in Wisconsin and Missouri, they were the only company to both manufacture all of their products in-house and to produce all of them in the U.S. In addition to providing stronger quality control, this strategy enabled J.H. Collectibles to provide very fast delivery service in the U.S. Limiting distribution of their product to strong market regions and retailers also enabled them to maintain production at levels estimated to be at or near their plants' capacities.

JONES OF NEW YORK Jones of New York, the parent company of Jones New York of Canada, was a major competitor in the U.S. market. In fact, the majority of their US$200 million in sales was derived from this market.

EVAN-PICONE Evan-Picone was a U.S.-based apparel designer and marketer which had become very successful in the slightly older professional/career women's market. This company also contracted out their manufacturing function, and had annual sales in excess of US$200 million.

In addition, there were myriads of other apparel designers, marketers and manufacturers competing in this segment. They included such companies as Christian Dior, Kasper, Pendleton, Carole Little, Susan Bristol, J.G. Hooke, Ellen Tracy, Anne Klein II, Perry Ellis, Adrienne Vittadini, Tahari, Harve Bernard, Norma Kamali, Philippe Adec, Gianni Sport, Regina Porter, and Herman Geist.

Profitability in this segment had been excellent. According to data from annual reports and financial analyst reports, Liz Claiborne led profitability in the apparel industry with a five-year average return on equity of 56 per cent and a 12-month return of 45 per cent, and J.H. Collectibles had averaged over 40 per cent return on equity during the last five years. This compared to an average return on equity in the overall apparel industry of 12.5 per cent in the U.S., and 16 per cent in Canada during the past five years.

Distribution

The selection and maintenance of retail distribution channels had become a very important consideration for apparel manufacturers in the 1980s. The retail industry had gone through a particularly bad year in 1988, although the professional/career women's segment had been relatively profitable. Overall demand had declined, and retail analysts were predicting revenue increases of only 1–2 per cent in 1989, which paled beside the 6–7 per cent growth experienced in the mid-1980s. The consensus was that high interest rates and inflation, as well as somewhat stagnant demand levels, were suppressing overall profitability.

Although initially considered a mild downturn, recent market indicators suggested that this downward trend was relatively stable and long lasting. Industry analysts had begun to suspect that permanent market changes might be occurring. With baby boomers reaching their childbearing years, further constraints on disposable income might result as this group's consumption patterns reflected increasing emphasis on purchases of homes, or the decision by many women to permanently or temporarily leave the workforce to raise their children. In addition, the effects of rampant growth in the number of retail outlets during the 1980s were beginning to take their toll. Vicious competition had been eroding margins at the retailer level, and the industry appeared to be moving into a period of consolidation. As a result of these developments, a shift in power from the designers to the retailers appeared to be underway.

To counter the retailers' increasing power, some apparel designers had been vertically integrating into retailing. The attractiveness of this option was based on controlling the downstream distribution channel activities, and thus enabling an apparel company to aggressively pursue increased market share. The principal components for success in the retail apparel industry were location, brand awareness and superior purchasing skills. The apparel companies that had integrated successfully into retailing were the more market-oriented firms such as Benetton and Esprit.

The Free Trade Agreement

Historically, developed nations had protected their textile and clothing industries through the imposition of relatively high tariffs and import quotas. Tariffs for apparel imported into Canada averaged 24.5 per cent, and 22.5 per cent into the U.S. Tariffs for worsted woolen fabrics, one of the principal ingredients for Mr. Jax's products, were 40 per cent into Canada, and 22.5 per cent into the U.S. Import quotas were used to further limit the ability of developing country manufacturers to import into either country. Despite these obstacles, Canadian apparel imports had grown from 20 per cent to 30 per cent of total shipments during the 1980s; most of which came from developing countries. Shipments into Canada from the U.S. represented an estimated $200 million in 1988, while Canadian manufacturers exported approximately $70 million to the U.S.

The FTA would alter trade restrictions in North America considerably. Over the next ten years, all clothing and textile tariffs between the two countries would be eliminated, but stringent "rules of origin" would apply. To qualify, goods not only had to be manufactured in North America, but they also had to utilize raw materials (i.e., yarn, in the case of textiles, and fabric, in the case of apparel) manufactured in North America. Unfortunately, these "rules of origin" favoured U.S. apparel manufacturers as 85 per cent of the textiles they used were sourced in the U.S., while Canadian manufacturers utilized mostly imported textiles. To ameliorate this disadvantage, a clause was appended to the agreement that allowed Canadians to export $500 million worth of apparel annually into the U.S. that was exempt from the "rules of origin" but would have a 50 per cent Canadian value-added content. There was much speculation as to how this exemption would be allocated when, in approximately five years, exports were projected to exceed the exemption limit. Experts expected the companies successfully demonstrating their ability to export into the U.S. would have first rights to these exceptions.

Many industry experts had contemplated the consequences of the FTA. There was some agreement that in the short-term, the FTA would most severely impact the lower-priced apparel segments in Canada because of the economies of scale that existed in the U.S. market (i.e., the average U.S. apparel manufacturer was ten times larger than its Canadian counterpart). Yet, long-term prospects for all segments were restrained because the industry was slowly being pressured by the Canadian government to become internationally competitive. The question was when international negotiations would eliminate more of the protection afforded to the industry. It was with this concern in mind that Eisman had been continuously pushing the company to become a major international fashion designer and manufacturer.

Overall, Eisman considered the FTA a mixed blessing. Competition in Canada would increase moderately over time, but he felt that the lower tariff rates and the company's high-quality, in-house woolen mill presented a wonderful opportunity for potential expansion into the U.S. market.

MR. JAX FASHIONS

In 1979, a venture capital company owned by Joseph Segal acquired a sleepy Vancouver-based apparel manufacturer having $3 million in sales, 70 per cent of which was in men's wear. Segal immediately recruited Louis Eisman, a well-known women's fashion executive, who proceeded to drop the men's clothing line and aggressively refocus the company on the career/professional women's market segment.

Eisman appreciated the importance of fashion, and for the first three years he designed all of the new lines. In 1982, he recruited an up-and-coming young Canadian fashion designer, yet he continued to influence the direction of designs considerably. He travelled to Europe for approximately two months annually to review European trends and procure quality fabrics appropriate for the upcoming season. He personally reviewed all designs. The combined women's fashion knowledge and designing abilities provided Mr. Jax with a high-quality, classically designed product which differentiated it from most other Canadian competition. In 1989, the designer resigned, and Eisman recruited a New York-based fashion designer, Ron Leal. Leal had excellent experience in several large U.S. design houses and, unlike the previous designer, he brought considerable U.S. market experience and presence.

Eisman's energy and drive were also critical in establishing the merchandising and distribution network. He personally developed relationships with many of the major retailers. He hired and developed sales agents, in-house sales staff, and in 1983, recruited Jackie Clabon who subsequently became Vice-President of Marketing and Sales. The sales staff were considered to be some of the best in the industry. Clabon's extensive Canadian sales and merchandising experience, combined with Eisman's design and marketing strength, provided Mr. Jax with considerable ability in these critical activities.

Initially, acceptance by Eastern fashion buyers was cool. The fashion "establishment" was highly skeptical of this new Vancouver-based apparel designer and manufacturer. Thus, Eisman focused on smaller independent retail stores, which were more easily swayed in their purchasing decisions. As Mr. Jax gained a reputation for high quality, classical design and excellent service, larger retail chains started to place orders. By 1988, Mr. Jax's products were sold in over 400 department and specialty stores across Canada. Major customers included The Bay, Eaton's, Holt Renfrew and Simpson's, and, although initial marketing efforts had been aimed at the smaller retailer, the majority of Mr. Jax's sales were now to the larger retail chains. The apparel lines were sold through a combination of sales agents and in-house salespersons. Ontario and

Quebec accounted for 72 per cent of sales. In addition, two retail stores had recently been established in Vancouver and Seattle; the Vancouver store was very profitable, but the Seattle store was very unprofitable. Industry observers had suggested a number of factors to explain the two stores' performance differences. These factors included increased competition in U.S. metropolitan areas due to increased market density, lower levels of regulation and other entry barriers, greater product selection, and more timely fashion trend shifts compared to the Canadian market, which often exhibited lags in fashion developments of six months or more. Mr. Jax also had a local presence in Vancouver, which was believed to have helped their store by way of reputation, ancillary promotions and easier access to skilled resources.

Many industry experts felt that Mr. Jax's product line success could be attributed directly to Eisman. He was known for his energy and brashness, as well as his creativity and knowledge of the women's fashion market. In his prior merchandising and marketing experience, he had developed an intuitive skill for the capricious women's apparel market. This industry was often considered to be one of instinct rather than rationality. Eisman was particularly good at design, merchandising and marketing (Exhibit 1). He worked very closely with these departments, often getting involved in the smallest details. As Eisman said, "It is the details that make the difference in our business." Although Eisman concentrated a great deal of his effort and time on these functions, he also attempted to provide guidance to production. The production function had been important in providing the service advantage, particularly in terms of delivery time, which Mr. Jax held over imports. By 1988, Mr. Jax's professional/career women's fashion lines accounted for $25 million in revenues and $3 million in net income (Exhibit 2).

Diversification through Acquisitions

In 1986, Segal and Eisman took Mr. Jax public, raising in excess of $17 million although they both retained one-third of equity ownership. The newly raised capital was used to diversify growth through the acquisition of four semi-related companies.

SURREY CLASSICS MANUFACTURING LTD. Surrey Classics Manufacturing Ltd., a family-owned, Vancouver-based firm, was purchased for $2 million in 1986. This company was principally a manufacturer of lower priced women's apparel and coats. The acquisition was initially made with the objective of keeping the company an autonomous unit. However, the previous owner and his management team adapted poorly to their position within the Mr. Jax organization, and, upon expiration of their noncompetition clauses, they resigned and started a competing company. Unfortunately, sales began to decline rapidly because of this new competition and the absence of managerial talent. To stem the losses, a variety of designers were hired under contract. However, Surrey's poor cash flow could not support the required promotional campaigns and the new fashion lines faired poorly, resulting in mounting operating losses.

In late 1988, Eisman reassigned Mr. Jax's Vice-President of Finance as interim manager of Surrey Classics. As Eisman stated, "The company needed a manager who knew the financial priorities in the industry and could maximize the effectiveness of the company's productive capacity." Several administrative functions were transferred to Mr. Jax, including design, pattern making, sizing and scaling operations. Marketing and production continued to be independent operations housed in a leased facility just outside of Vancouver. Surrey Classics now produced a diversified product line which included Highland Queen, a licensed older women's line of woolen apparel, and Jaki Petite, a Mr. Jax fashion line patterned for smaller women. During this turnaround, Eisman himself provided the required industry-specific management skills, which demanded a considerable amount of his time and attention. Eisman kept in daily contact and was involved in most major decisions. During this time Surrey's revenues had declined from $12 million in 1986 to $10.8 million in 1988, and net income had dropped from $100 000 in 1986 to a loss of approximately $2 million in 1988. Eisman felt that in the next two years Surrey's operations would have to be further rationalized into Mr. Jax's to save on overhead costs.

WEST COAST WOOLEN MILLS LTD. West Coast Woolen Mills Ltd. was a 40-year-old family-owned, Vancouver-based worsted woolen mill. Mr. Jax acquired the company for $2.2 million in 1987. Eisman was able to retain most of the previous management, all of whom had skills quite unique to the industry. West Coast marketed fabric to customers across Canada. In 1986, its sales were $5 million, profits were nil, and its estimated capacity was $10 million annually. The company was the smallest of three worsted woolen mills in Canada, and in the U.S. there were about 18 worsted woolen manufacturers, several being divisions of the world's largest textile manufacturing companies.

Both Mr. Jax and West Coast had mutually benefited from this acquisition. The affiliation allowed Mr. Jax to obtain control of fabric production scheduling, design and quality. In particular, Mr. Jax had been able to significantly reduce order lead times for fabric produced at this subsidiary, although the effects of this on West Coast had not been studied. West Coast benefited from increased capital funding, which allowed it to invest in new equipment and technology, both important attributes in such a capital intensive industry. These investments supported the company's long-term strategic objective of becoming the highest quality, most design-conscious worsted woolen mill in North America. This objective had already been reached in Canada.

Mr. Jax was presently fulfilling 30 per cent to 40 per cent of its textile demands through West Coast. The remainder was being sourced in Europe. By 1988, West Coast's revenues were $6.5 million and profitability was at the break-even point.

OLYMPIC PANT AND SPORTSWEAR CO. LTD. AND CANADIAN SPORTSWEAR CO. LTD. Mr. Jax acquired Olympic Pant and Sportswear Co. Ltd. and Canadian Sportswear Co. Ltd., both privately owned companies, in 1987 for $18.3 million. The former management, excluding owners, was retained in both of these Winnipeg-based companies.

Olympic manufactured lower priced men's and boys' pants and outerwear as well as some women's sportswear. Canadian Sportswear manufactured low-priced women's and girls' outerwear and coats. Canadian Sportswear was also a certified apparel supplier to the Canadian Armed Forces, and, although these types of sales made up a minority of their revenue base, such a certification provided the company with a small but protected market niche. The disparity in target markets and locations between these companies and Mr. Jax dictated that they operate largely independently. The expected synergies were limited to a few corporate administrative functions such as finance and systems management.

Combined revenues for these companies had declined from $35 million in 1986 to $30 million in 1988. Both of these companies had remained profitable during this period, although profits had declined. In 1988, combined net income was $1.2 million. Management blamed declining revenues on increased competition and a shortage of management because of the previous owners' retirement.

The Corporation's Present Situation

Diversification had provided the company with excellent growth, but it had also created problems. The most serious was the lack of management control over the now diversified structure (Exhibit 3). By 1988, it had become quite clear that without the entrepreneurial control and drive of the previous owners, the companies were not as successful as they had been prior to their acquisition. Therefore in late 1988, Eisman recruited a new CFO, Judith Madill, to coordinate a corporate control consolidation program. Madill had extensive accounting and corporate reorganization experience, but had limited operating experience in an entrepreneurial environment such as the fashion industry. Madill suggested that corporate personnel, financial and systems management departments be established to integrate and aid in the management of the subsidiaries. Eisman was not completely convinced this was the right approach. He had always maintained that one of Mr. Jax's competitive strengths was its flexibility and rapid response time. He thought increased administrative overhead would restrict this entrepreneurial ability, and that extra costs would severely restrict future expansion opportunities. Thus, he had limited the administrative expansion to two industrial accountants for the next year.

Consolidation was also occurring in the existing organization. Eisman was trying to recruit a vice-president of production. Mr. Jax had never officially had such a position, and, unfortunately, recruiting a suitable candidate was proving to be difficult. There were relatively few experienced apparel manufacturing executives in North America. Furthermore, Vancouver was not an attractive place for fashion executives because it, not being a fashion centre, would isolate him or her from future employment opportunities. Higher salaries as well as lower taxes tended to keep qualified individuals in the U.S. Yet, a manager of production was badly needed to coordinate the internal production consolidation program.

Originally, production had been located in an old 22 000-square-foot facility. By 1986, it had grown to 48 000 square feet located in four buildings throughout Vancouver. Production flow encompassed the typical apparel industry operational tasks (Exhibit 4). However, the division of tasks between buildings made production planning and scheduling very difficult. Production problems slowly accumulated between 1986 and 1988. The problems not only restricted capacity, but also caused customer service to deteriorate from an excellent shipment rate of approximately 95 per cent of orders to recently being sometimes below the industry average of 75 per cent. Mr. Jax's ability to ship had been key to their growth strategy in Canada. Normally, apparel manufacturers met between 70 per cent and 80 per cent of their orders, but Mr. Jax had built a reputation for shipping more than 90 per cent of orders.

Consolidation had begun in the latter part of 1987. An old building in downtown Vancouver was acquired and renovated. The facility incorporated some of the most modern production equipment available. In total, the company had spent approximately $3.5 million on upgrading production technology. Equipment in the new facility included a $220 000 Gerber automatic cloth cutting machine to improve efficiency and reduce waste; $300 000 of modern sewing equipment to improve productivity and production capacity; a $200 000 Gerber production moving system to automatically move work to appropriate work stations as required; and a computerized design assistance system to integrate the above equipment (i.e., tracking in-process inventory, scheduling, planning and arranging and sizing cloth patterns for cutting). The objectives of these investments were to lower labour content, improve production capacity, and reduce the time required to produce a garment.

In the last quarter of 1988, Mr. Jax had moved into this new head office facility. The building, which was renovated by one of Italy's leading architects, represented a design marvel with its skylights and soaring atriums. The production department had just recently settled into its expansive space. However, the move had not gone without incident. The equipment operators had difficulties adapting to the new machines. Most of the workers had become accustomed to the repetitive tasks required of the old technology. The new equipment was forcing them to retrain themselves and required additional effort; something that was not appreciated by many of the workers. In addition, the largely Asian work force had difficulty understanding retraining instructions because English was their second language.

To further facilitate the implementation of the consolidation program, an apparel production consultant had been hired. The consultant was using time-motion studies to reorganize and improve task efficiency and effectiveness. An example of a problem that had resulted from the move was the need for integration between overall production planning, task assignment, worker remuneration and the new Gerber production moving system. If these elements were not integrated, the new system would in fact slow production. Unfortunately, this integration had not been considered until after the move, and the machine subsequently had to be removed until adjustments were made. The adjustments required converting workers from a salary base to a piece rate pay scale. The consultants were training all the workers to convert to piece rate work, and to operate the necessary equipment in the most efficient manner. Three workers were being trained per week. The conversion was expected to take two years.

Despite these ongoing problems, production appeared to be improving, and operational activities were now organized and coordinated with some degree of efficiency. Eisman was hopeful that production would gain the upper hand in the fight to remedy scheduling problems within the next six months.

Opportunities for Future Growth

Despite problems such as those detailed above, Mr. Jax's revenues and profits had grown by 1 500 per cent and 500 per cent respectively over the past eight years. Furthermore, Eisman was extremely positive about further growth opportunities in the U.S. market. During the past two years, Eisman had tested the Dallas and New York markets. Local sales agents had carried the Mr. Jax fashion line, and 1988 revenues had grown to US$1 million, the majority of which had come from Dallas. Follow-up research revealed that retail purchasers liked the "classical European styling combined with the North American flair."

This initial success had been inspiring, but it had also exposed Eisman to the difficulties of entering the highly competitive U.S. market. In particular, attaining good sales representation and excellent service, both of which were demanded by U.S. retailers, would be difficult. Securing first-class sales representation required having either a strong market presence or a promising promotional program. In addition, Mr. Jax had found U.S. retailers to be extremely onerous in their service demands. These demands were generally a result of the more competitive retail environment. Demands were particularly stringent for smaller apparel suppliers because of their nominal selling power. These demands ranged from very low wholesale prices to extremely fast order-filling and restocking requirements. Eisman recognized that Mr. Jax would have to establish a focused, coordinated and aggressive marketing campaign to achieve its desired objectives in this market.

Eisman had studied two alternate approaches to entering the U.S. market. One approach involved establishing a retailing chain, while the other involved starting a U.S.-based wholesale distribution subsidiary responsible for managing the aggressive promotional and sales campaign required.

Establishing a retail chain would require both new capital and skills. Capital costs, including leasehold improvements and inventory, would be initially very high, and an administrative infrastructure as well as a distribution and product inventorying system would have to be developed. Yet, starting a retail chain did have benefits. The retail approach would provide controllability, visibility and rapid market penetration. It was the approach taken by many of the aggressive apparel companies in the women's professional/career market segment, such as Liz Claiborne, Benetton and Esprit. Furthermore, Mr. Jax's marketing strength fit well with this approach. It was estimated that the initial capital required would be about $10 million to open the first 30 stores, and then cost $300 000 per outlet thereafter. Sales revenues would grow to between $300 000 and $750 000 per outlet, depending upon the location, after two to five years. Operating margins on apparel stores averaged slightly less than 10 per cent. Experts felt that within five years the company could possibly open 45 outlets; five the first year, and ten each year thereafter. In summary, this option would entail the greatest financial risk, but it would also have the greatest potential return.

The alternative approach was to establish a U.S. distribution subsidiary. This alternative would require capital and more of the same skills the company had developed in Canada. In general, the company would have to set up one or more showrooms throughout the U.S. The location of the showrooms would be critical to the approach eventually implemented. Exhibit 5 illustrates regional apparel buying patterns in North America.

A wholesale distribution approach could be carried out in one of two ways: either on a regional or national basis. A regional approach would involve focusing on the smaller regional retail stores. These stores tended to attract less competitive attention because of the higher sales expense-to-revenue ratio inherent in servicing these accounts. The approach required the new distributor to provide good-quality fashion lines, and service the accounts in a better manner than established suppliers. An advantage to this approach was that regional retailers demanded fewer and smaller price concessions compared to the larger national chains. The obstacles to this approach included the large sales force required and the superior service capability. Even though Mr. Jax had utilized this strategy successfully in Canada, success was not assured in the U.S. because of the very competitive environment. These factors made this approach both difficult to implement and slow relative to other approaches. Experts estimated fixed costs to average $1 million annually per region, of which 75 per cent would be advertising and 25 per cent other promotional costs. Additional operating costs would consist of sales commissions (7 per cent of sales) and administrative overhead costs (see below). Revenues would be dependent upon many factors, but an initial annual growth rate of $1 million annually within each region was considered attainable over the next five years. In summary, this approach would minimize Mr. Jax's risk exposure, but it would also minimize the short term opportunities.

The national approach was also a viable option. The greatest challenge in a national strategy would be the difficulty in penetrating well-established buyer/seller relationships. Floor space was expensive, and national chains and department stores tended to buy conservatively, sticking with the more reputable suppliers who they knew could produce a saleable product and service large orders. They also tended to demand low prices and rapid reorder terms. In summary, the national approach provided significant entry barriers, but it also provided the greatest potential for market share growth. Clearly, if economies of scale and competitive advantage in the larger North American context were the desired goals, this had to be the eventual strategy.

The principal costs of this approach would be the advertising and promotional expenses. National apparel companies had advertising expenditures of many millions of dollars. In discussions with Eisman, industry advertising executives had recommended an advertising expenditure of between $3 and $5 million annually in the first three years and then, if successful, increasing it by $1 million annually in the next two successive years. Additional operating costs would be required for sales commissions (7 per cent of sales) and administrative overhead. The results of this approach were very uncertain and two outcomes were possible. If the approach was successful, Eisman expected that one or two accounts grossing $1 to $2 million annually could be captured in the first two years. Eisman then felt the sales would expand to about $5 million in the third year, and increase by $5 million annually for the next two successive years. However, if the expected quality, design or service requirements were not sustained, sales would probably decline in the third year to that of the first year and then virtually disappear thereafter.

Both the national and regional approaches would require an infrastructure. Depending upon the approach taken, the head office could be located in a number of places. If a national approach was taken, Mr. Jax would have to locate in one of the major U.S. apparel centres (e.g., New York or California). Eisman estimated that the national approach would require a full-time Director of U.S. Operations immediately, while the regional approach could delay this hiring until required. Such a managing director would require extensive previous experience in the industry, and be both capable and compatible with Mr. Jax's marketing, operating and strategic approach. To ensure top-quality candidates, Eisman felt that a signing bonus of at least $100 000 would have to be offered. The remuneration would be tied to sales growth and volume, but a continued minimum salary guarantee might be necessary until the sales reached some minimum volume. In addition, a full-time sales manager would be required. Eisman estimated that the subsidiary's administrative overhead expense would be $500 000 if a regional approach was taken, versus $1 million for a national approach in both cases. These overhead costs would then escalate by approximately $0.5 million annually for the first five years.

Eisman had now studied the U.S. growth options for over six months. He felt a decision had to be made very soon, otherwise the company would forgo the window of opportunity that existed. The new FTA environment and the growth in the professional/career women's market segment were strong incentives, and delaying a decision would only increase the costs as well as the possibility of failure. Eisman realized the decision was critical to the company's evolution toward its ultimate goal of becoming a major international fashion company. The challenge was deciding which approach to take, as well as the sequencing and timing of the subsequent actions.

E X H I B I T 1   **Mr. Jax Fashion's President Helping in a Promotional Photo Session**

EXHIBIT 2 Mr. Jax Fashion Inc. Financial Statements

(000s)

Income Statement

	1981	1982	1983	1984	1985	1986	1987 9 months	1988
Sales	4 592	4 315	5 472	7 666	13 018	24 705	53 391	72 027
Cost of sales	2 875	2 803	3 404	4 797	7 885	14 667	38 165	49 558
Gross profit	1 717	1 512	2 068	2 869	5 133	10 038	15 226	22 469
Selling & gen. admin.	1 172	1 117	1 458	1 898	2 434	4 530	9 071	18 175
Income from operations	545	395	610	971	2 699	5 508	6 155	4 294
Other income	22	25	25	10	16	564	418	117
Loss from discontinued operation								(554)
Income before taxes	567	420	635	981	2 715	6 072	6 573	3 857
Income taxes–								
Current	150	194	285	432	1 251	2 874	2 746	1 825
Deferred	47	2	(5)	28	24	57	245	(195)
Net income	370	224	355	521	1 440	3 141	3 582	2 227
Share price						$7.5–	$8–	$7.5–
						$11	$18	$14

Note: In 1987, the accounting year end was changed from February 1988 to November 1987. This made the 1987 accounting year nine months in duration.

(000s)

Balance Sheet

	1981	1982	1983	1984	1985	1986	1987	1988
Assets								
Current Assets								
Short-term investments	—	—	—	—	—	5 027	1 794	495
Accounts receivable	709	874	961	1 697	2 974	6 430	16 133	14 923
Inventories	464	474	684	736	1 431	3 026	15 431	16 914
Prepaid expenses	11	15	20	22	201	398	404	293
Income taxes recoverable	—	—	—	—	—	—	—	1 074
Prop., Plant & Equip.	318	349	424	572	795	4 042	7 789	13 645
Other Assets	—	—	—	—	—	273	526	513
Total Assets	1 502	1 712	2 089	3 027	5 401	22 196	42 077	47 857
Liabilities								
Current liabilities								
Bank indebtedness	129	356	114	351	579	575	1 788	4 729
Accounts payable	490	435	678	963	1 494	3 100	4 893	6 934
Income taxes payable	126	58	86	153	809	1 047	546	
Deferred Taxes	84	86	81	109	133	217	462	267
Shareholder Equity								
Share equity	127	7	13	5	4	12 252	26 577	26 577
Retained earnings	546	770	1 125	1 446	2 347	5 005	7 811	9 350
Total Liabilities	1 502	1 712	2 097	3 027	5 401	22 196	42 077	47 857

Note: Years 1981–84 were estimated from change in financial position statements.

EXHIBIT 3   Mr. Jax Fashion's Organization Chart

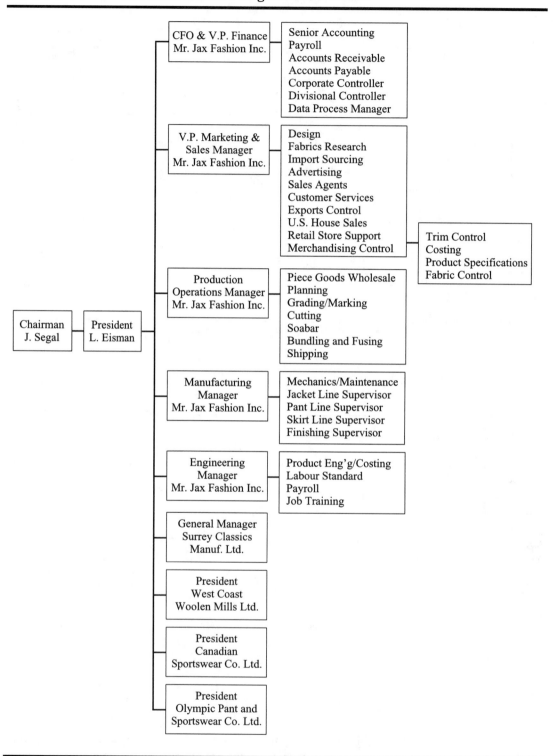

Chairman J. Segal — President L. Eisman

CFO & V.P. Finance Mr. Jax Fashion Inc.
- Senior Accounting
- Payroll
- Accounts Receivable
- Accounts Payable
- Corporate Controller
- Divisional Controller
- Data Process Manager

V.P. Marketing & Sales Manager Mr. Jax Fashion Inc.
- Design
- Fabrics Research
- Import Sourcing
- Advertising
- Sales Agents
- Customer Services
- Exports Control
- U.S. House Sales
- Retail Store Support
- Merchandising Control
  - Trim Control
  - Costing
  - Product Specifications
  - Fabric Control

Production Operations Manager Mr. Jax Fashion Inc.
- Piece Goods Wholesale
- Planning
- Grading/Marking
- Cutting
- Soabar
- Bundling and Fusing
- Shipping

Manufacturing Manager Mr. Jax Fashion Inc.
- Mechanics/Maintenance
- Jacket Line Supervisor
- Pant Line Supervisor
- Skirt Line Supervisor
- Finishing Supervisor

Engineering Manager Mr. Jax Fashion Inc.
- Product Eng'g/Costing
- Labour Standard
- Payroll
- Job Training

General Manager Surrey Classics Manuf. Ltd.

President West Coast Woolen Mills Ltd.

President Canadian Sportswear Co. Ltd.

President Olympic Pant and Sportswear Co. Ltd.

EXHIBIT 4   Mr. Jax Fashion's Production Flow Chart

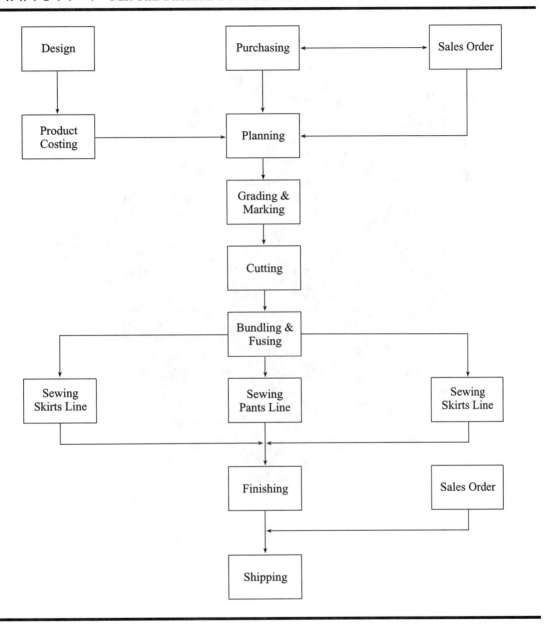

EXHIBIT 5   North American Apparel Consumption by Region

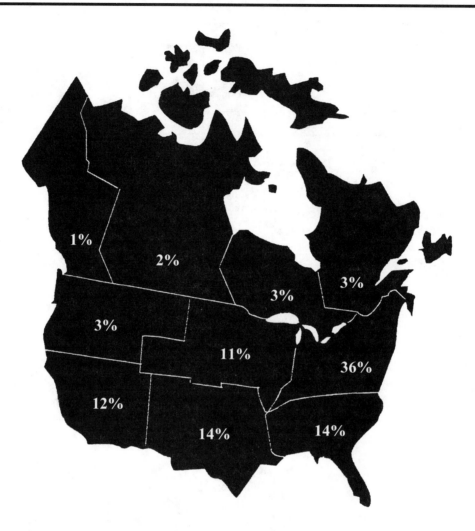

Source: U.S. and Canadian governments.

KENNY ROGERS ROASTERS IN CHINA (A)

Allen J. Morrison,
J. Steward Black,
Tanya Spyridakis
and Jan Visser

It was mid-October 1995 and Tony Wang, President of Franchise Investment Corporation of Asia (FICA), had just returned to Hong Kong from a one week visit to Beijing. FICA had earlier in the year been granted the franchise rights for Kenny Rogers Roasters (KRR), a rotisserie chicken restaurant concept, for both Beijing and Shanghai. While Wang was eager to move forward, serious concerns had emerged over the challenges of doing business in China. Just as most foreign companies had looked to local partners to help ameliorate some of these concerns, Wang had begun joint venture discussions with three companies. Although each potential partner appeared eager to work with FICA, Wang was wondering whether the time was right to proceed and if so, with which company.

THUNDERBIRD
THE AMERICAN GRADUATE SCHOOL
OF INTERNATIONAL MANAGEMENT

This case was prepared by Professor Allen J. Morrison in collaboration with Professor J. Steward Black and Tanya Spyridakis. Additional assistance was provided by Jan Visser. this case study is not intended to illustrate either effective or ineffective handling of a managerial situation. copyright © 1996, Thunderbird—The American Graduate School of International Management.

KRR OVERVIEW

The driving force behind KRR was John Y. Brown, an entrepreneur with a long history in the food service industry. In 1964, Brown, who at the time was a 29-year-old Kentucky lawyer, and his partner, 60-year-old Jack Massey, purchased Kentucky Fried Chicken from 74-year-old Harland Sanders for US$2 million. Over the next five years the partners added 1 000 new stores and grew sales by an average of 96 per cent per year. Observers attributed this growth to two main factors: (1) the company's reliance on less costly franchise expansion over company-owned stores, and (2) Brown's ability to select hard charging and entrepreneurial franchisees. KFC was sold to Heublen Inc. in 1971 for US$275 million, making both partners wealthy men.

During the 1970s Brown went on to become Governor of the State of Kentucky and owner of three professional basketball teams including the Boston Celtics. In 1979 he married 1971 Miss America, Phyllis George. During the early 1980s Brown helped launch Miami Subs and Roadhouse Grill franchises and bankrolled his wife's Chicken by George line of prepared chicken sold in grocery stores.

By the late 1980s, Brown was becoming increasingly convinced of the enormous market potential for roasted chicken. The health craze that swept the U.S. in the 1980s significantly increased the demand for lighter, non-fried food options. This affected many segments of the food industry, and the poultry industry was no exception. Many restaurant owners began investing in rotisserie ovens and introducing more healthy menus.

In looking for a new way to grab the customer's attention, Brown thought it a natural to team with longtime friend Kenny Rogers. Kenny Rogers, once described as "the most popular singer in America," had a career that spanned more than three decades, half of which as a solo artist. Rogers's popularity manifested itself in the many awards and honours that he had received over the years: 3 Grammies, 11 People's Choice Awards, 18 American Music Awards, 5 Country Music Association Awards, 8 Academy of Country Music Awards, 4 platinum albums, 5 multi-platinum, 1 platinum single, and numerous gold albums and singles. Rogers also dabbled in several businesses including a partnership in Silver Dollar City, considered country music's capital, in Branson, Missouri. When Brown came up with the concept of a rotisserie chicken restaurant chain, Rogers was very enthusiastic.

> When I saw this concept, I thought it was so outstanding I was willing to put my reputation on the line, not just as an endorser, but as an owner and partner. I believe non-fried chicken is the wave of the 90s, and working with folks who made fried chicken a billion-dollar business gives me the confidence we are doing it right.

Kenny Rogers Roasters (KRR) began operations on January 17, 1991, in Louisville, Kentucky and opened its first restaurant in August of that year in Coral Gables, Florida. The menu: citrus-and-herb-marinated wood roasted chicken and about a dozen side dishes such as mashed potatoes and gravy, corn-on-the-cob, baked beans, and pasta salad. Growth was rapid. From an original group of five people, the company grew to include a corporate staff of more than 100. By late 1995, the company had moved headquarters to Ft. Lauderdale, Florida and had over 310 stores. KRR operated in approximately 35 U.S. states, had more than a dozen stores in Canada and had at least one store in Greece, Cyprus, Israel, Malaysia, Korea, the Philippines, Japan, Jordan and Singapore. Company plans called for the addition of almost 1 200 new stores in the U.S. and 240 stores internationally by 2002.

The Rotisserie Chicken Business

The market's switch to rotisserie chicken did not escape the competition. In 1993, KFC spent $100 million to roll out its Colonel's Rotisserie Gold in all 5 100 of its stores in the United States. Rotisserie chicken constituted about 25 per cent of KFC sales in company-owned stores by the end of 1995. In all,

KFC enjoyed a 58 per cent share of the retail chicken industry, and gross sales of over $3.5 billion. Other fast-food restaurants, noting the trend, also attempted to expand into the non-fried market. For example, Popeye's Famous Chicken entered the non-fried market despite its lack of capital; it featured a roasted chicken that could be cooked in the same ovens as its biscuits. Boston Market (formerly known as Boston Chicken) was another up-and-coming competitor in the rotisserie chicken segment. Opening its first store in 1985, by 1993 the company had 166 stores in approximately 25 states, and sales of $154 million (more than triple its 1992 sales). By the end of 1995, Boston Market had become a public company with over 825 stores operating (none outside the U.S.) and was opening a new store each business day.

While sales of rotisserie chicken were still considerably smaller ($700 million versus $6 billion for fried chicken in 1993), advocates of non-fried chicken firmly believed that the gap would close within ten years. Statistics confirmed the growing popularity of non-fried chicken in the U.S.: sales of fried chicken consumed outside the home grew an average of 3.5 per cent from 1989 to 1995, while sales of non-fried chicken grew an average of 10.75 per cent in the same period. Annual growth in per capita chicken consumption between 1984 and 1994 was 38.5 per cent.

Despite its rapid growth, rotisserie chicken had several drawbacks. Uncooked rotisserie chicken had a shorter shelf life than fried chicken. Rotisserie chicken took 75 to 90 minutes to cook compared to 30 minutes for fried chicken. Additionally, a cooked rotisserie chicken needed moisture and would spoil if kept under a heat lamp for too long; this, however, posed no problem for fried chicken. Finally, customer demand would often be greater than supply in peak hours, which was difficult for rotisserie chicken vendors due to the longer cooking times.

Kenny Rogers Roasters

By 1995 KRR was still a privately held company, with no immediate plans to go public. The equity breakdown was approximately John Y. Brown, Jr., 28 per cent; Kenny Rogers, 14.5 per cent; and a group of Malaysian investors, 35 per cent; various friends of Brown and Rogers held the remaining 22.5 per cent. Brown served as the company's CEO and Chairman of the Board. Rogers sat on the board of directors and, though he was not directly involved in running the company, attended many meetings and assisted in promoting the company. In building his management team, Brown recruited several people with whom he had worked in his days at KFC. Other management talent was recruited from fast-food chains such as Wendy's, Burger King, Pizza Hut, Arby's and McDonald's.

In the U.S., KRR's restaurants averaged 2 800 square feet in size, with seating capacity for 80 to 100 people. The stores had a country-western motif and were decorated with memorabilia from Rogers's career. Television monitors were also located throughout the restaurant showing customized music videos featuring performances by Rogers and other country and western entertainers. Advertising and promotional messages were interspersed with the music videos. A signature wood-fire rotisserie with surrounding wood piles were placed in full view of the customer. The serving counter was buffet-like in style, with a wide range of side dishes kept warm in a glass display case. Servers on the other side of the counter put together plates for customers based on their choice of entree and side dishes.

All menu items at KRR restaurants were prepared on-site. The chicken was marinated overnight and roasted the next day over a hardwood fire to an internal temperature of about 180°. Most side dishes were made from scratch, though a few items were prepared from mixes developed at the company's training and development centre near the corporate headquarters. The labour-intense nature of KRR was not without its downside; labour costs averaged between 26 and 27 per cent of sales, food costs ran just under 30 per cent.

A free-standing Kenny Rogers restaurant with a drive-through window generally went through 1 800 chickens a week and generated approximately $1 million in annual sales. By 1995, take-out orders comprised about 45 to 50 per cent of sales; the company's goal was to increase this to around 60. Total KRR revenues in 1995 were estimated at $321 million, up from $68.7 million in 1993 and $150 million in 1994.

KRR Franchises

From the very beginning, franchising played a big part of the company's expansion. By 1995, franchise stores accounted for about 85 per cent of KRR's 310 stores. All of KRR's international stores were owned by franchisees. Though the company had solicited a few of its franchisees, most franchisees had approached KRR. The company carefully screened all franchisees for previous restaurant experience, especially multi-unit operations experience, references, credit rating and net worth. KRR wanted franchisees who knew and liked the restaurant business, who were or had been in it, and who appreciated the difference the company was trying to make with customer service and product quality.

KRR set up *franchise* and *development* contracts. Both typically had a duration of twenty years. A franchise agreement was for a single store; a development agreement was for a specified number of restaurants, within a set time frame, in a designated area. When signing development agreements, KRR typically awarded territories in small clusters of 5 to 50 restaurants. The boundaries of the territory varied depending on the size and experience of the group or individual involved, as well as availability within the region requested.[1]

The costs involved in a franchise agreement included the initial franchise payment of $29 500; a royalty fee of 4.5 per cent of gross sales; and contributions to the company advertising production fund, the national advertising fund, as well as a local or regional advertising fund of 0.75 per cent, 2 per cent, and (a minimum of) 3 per cent of gross sales, respectively. The initial franchise fee was due upon signing the franchise agreement; all other fees were due monthly once the store was in operation. Fees related to a development agreement were similar to those of a franchise agreement. In addition to normal franchise fees, a developer was typically required to pay a development fee of $10 000 for each restaurant covered under the agreement. This fee was non-refundable and was due (along with the full $29 500 for the first store to be built) upon signing the development agreement. The development fee was to be applied in equal portions as a credit against the initial franchise fee for each restaurant to be developed under the development agreement. The balance of each additional store's (within a development area) franchise fee was due as each store went into construction, according to the development schedule.

Company research showed that the average costs to build a new restaurant in the U.S. ranged from $560 000 to $672 000; the costs to convert an existing site ranged from $405 000 to $545 000. These costs included such expenses as property rental or payments, architectural and engineering fees, insurance, business licenses, equipment, furniture, signs, office supplies, opening inventory, and so forth.

Training and Development

KRR put great emphasis on training and provided franchisees and operators with three training courses. These courses took place at the company's training and development centre located near corporate headquarters in Ft. Lauderdale, Florida. All expenses (travel, living, etc.) incurred in the training process were the responsibility of the franchisee. The first course was an optional three-day executive orientation program for all first-time franchisees and partners. The remaining two courses were not optional. All franchisees were required to certify and maintain a minimum of two managers for each store. The company's level one

---

[1] The franchising scheme of KRR's principle rival, Boston Market, differed considerably. Boston Market sold whole regions and provided up to 75 per cent of its franchisees' financing. Boston Market did have an unusual caveat that accompanied the financing plan: After two years, Boston Market had the right to convert the unpaid debt into an ownership share in the franchise.

course for all managers was an intense four-week program held four to six weeks prior to the store's opening. Dubbed as KRR's version of boot camp, management-trainees essentially lived with their trainer, learning all aspects of daily operations. Once a developer had opened a substantial number of stores within the designated territory, it was possible to apply for accreditation, that is, to set up its own level-one management training program. The second level of management training was required for any manager before being promoted to a general store manager. Held either before or after a store opening, this six day program focused not so much on operational procedures, but rather on how to deal with the more sensitive issues of management, i.e. how to deal with staff members and customers, especially when there were problems.

In addition, for each new store opening, franchisees were provided an opening team to assist in the initial training of hourly employees. The size of the team and the duration of its stay depended on the number of stores the franchisee already had in operation. The opening team would be sent once KRR had received a "Certificate of Occupancy" and a completed "Pre-Opening Checklist" from the franchisee. The franchisee was responsible for making sure that the store was ready for pre-opening training, though the opening date of the store could be pushed back if the store was not ready.

In the U.S., typically 60 to 65 hourly employees were hired for each new store. Of those initially hired, approximately 60 per cent would quit within the first few months. KRR's training and development centre designed a twelve-part video training program, which demonstrated proper operating procedures for equipment and preparation of food items. These videos were used to train new employees in all stores, both domestic and international.

Control Issues

Menu adjustments were a particular concern for international stores. Some side dishes did not go over well in various parts of the world. For example, baked beans with bacon was not served in Jordan and other Muslim countries. Franchisees were encouraged to offer alternative side dishes that would be better received in their country or region of the world, while still meeting the company's quality standards. Sometimes recipes of existing dishes had to be altered for regional tastes. Most notably sugar content had to be reduced for dishes served in the Asia-Pacific region where people had less of a "sweet tooth" than Americans. All new menu items or variations in recipes had to be pre-approved by corporate headquarters.

In addition to approving menus, KRR developed standards and specifications for most of its food products and equipment. To ensure consistency, KRR approved suppliers of chickens, breads, spices, mixes, marinades, plastic products, packaging and so forth in each territory or country where the company operated. Generally, finding approved local suppliers for chickens and other major food products was not a problem. However, many overseas franchisees ordered such specialized products as marinades and packaging materials from KRR's contracted U.S. distributor.

In order to maintain constant communication between KRR's corporate office and any given store, franchisees were required to install computer systems in each store. This system allowed KRR to instantly receive information concerning sales of each restaurant, and, in turn, to provide franchisees with information necessary to prepare financial statements and better manage the restaurant. Also, the company had standard forms for use in such areas as inventory control, profit-and-loss control, and monitoring daily and weekly sales.

TONY WANG AND KRR IN CHINA

KRR's efforts in China were spearheaded by Ta-Tung (Tony) Wang, a former KFC executive with considerable experience in the Far East. Wang was born in Sichuan province in the People's Republic of China in 1944 and raised in Taiwan. In the late 1960s he moved to the United States to complete graduate work. Upon graduation he took a management position with KFC in Louisville, Kentucky. A series of promotions culminated with Wang's appointment as KFC Vice President for Southeast Asia in 1986. The position, based in Singapore, charged Wang with aggressively expanding KFC throughout the Asia-Pacific region. Wang focused his efforts primarily on China, a country of 1.2 billion people with an undeveloped food service industry. In 1987, he gained considerable international notoriety by opening the first Western style fast food restaurant in China. The store was KFC's largest in the world and was located just opposite Mao's mausoleum off Tiananmen Square.

Wang credited the careful selection of joint venture partners as key in securing the store's prime location and in expediting the opening of the store. Three Chinese partners were selected and each played a different role in the start-up and on-going operation of the store: Beijing Animal Production Bureau (which owned 10 per cent of the joint venture) accessed locally grown chickens; Beijing Tourist Bureau (which had a 14 per cent ownership position) helped with site selection, permits, lease issues and hiring; and the Bank of China (which had a 25 per cent ownership position) assisted in converting soft currency renminbi profits to hard currency. Despite high chicken prices (KFC-approved chicken in China cost over $1 per pound, well over twice U.S. levels), the operation was a major success. In reflecting back on that time Wang noted: "We were the first Western quick service restaurant in any communist country. It was very exciting. There were crowds lining up outside the store in the morning even before we opened. It was not unusual for us to have to call the police to control the crowds."

After opening additional restaurants in China, in September, 1989, Tony Wang left KFC to become president of CP Food Services Co., a subsidiary of the Charoen Pokphand Group, the largest agri-business company in Asia. In September 1991, Wang moved back to the United States to become president of Grace Food Services, a subsidiary of W.R. Grace & Co. A year later Tony Wang left Grace to become president of Foodmaker International, the $1.2 billion parent company of Jack-in-the-Box and Chi-Chi's restaurants. Wang had a mandate to open 800 new restaurants over an 8-year period, primarily in the Pacific Rim. In January 1993, catastrophe struck when contaminated hamburgers were served at a Seattle Jack-in-the Box restaurant. Although the tainted hamburger was traced to a California-based supplier, Foodmaker was hit with a series of costly lawsuits and devastating publicity. Sales nose-dived and, in order to conserve finances, the company's international expansion plan was shelved.

Wang sensed an important win-win opportunity for all and offered to continue the company's expansion using his own money. An agreement was struck whereby Wang's own company, QSR (Quick Service Restaurant), became a Jack-in-the-Box Master Licensee with franchise and development rights for 20 countries in the Middle East and Asia (including China but not Japan). The agreement with Foodmaker, which came into effect on January 1, 1994 and lasted 10 years, gave QSR complete control over the selection and development of all franchises within these 20 countries. QSR had the right to select stand-alone franchisees, establish joint ventures with franchisees, or set itself up as a franchisee within any or all of the designated countries. Under the Master License agreement, Foodmaker and QSR split all franchise fees for Jack-in-the-Box restaurants. In assessing Foodmaker's rationale in setting up the Master License agreement, Wang commented: "this is a mutually beneficial concept for both parties. If they have the know-how but not the money, what have they got? They have a great concept but are not able to implement it internationally."

FICA (Franchise Investment Corporation of Asia)

Once Wang left Foodmaker, he began to explore other franchise investment opportunities in Asia. For assistance, Wang turned to American International Group, Inc. (AIG), one of the largest U.S.-based insurance companies.[2] Wang had been discussing franchise investment concepts with several senior AIG (Asia)

---

[2] In 1994, AIG had net profits in excess of $4 billion on revenues in excess of $24 billion and assets of approximately $130 billion.

managers since the late 1980s. In 1990, AIG (Asia) formed FICA as a subsidiary company designed to pursue multiple franchise options and invited Wang to serve as its first president. Wang declined, saying that he thought it was premature at the time. Consequently, FICA was put on hold.

In early 1994, Wang reopened discussions with AIG and in January 1995 joined FICA as its president and co-owner. FICA's ownership was split between AIG (60 per cent) and QSR (40 per cent). Wang served as president and primary decision maker in an office that was established by FICA in Hong Kong. Wang commented on the ownership structure: "as president of FICA, I am also an employee of FICA. I am president because of my skills and contacts. But my 40 per cent ownership is based on financial contribution."

FICA had a three-fold mandate: (1) to develop and invest in franchise concepts in Asia, (2) to act as a consultant to franchisees in the region, and (3) to establish food processing and other franchise support/commissary functions. Primary emphasis focused on investing in established franchise concepts. The philosophy was explained by Wang:

> Every franchiser has a very strict non-compete clause for products in the same category. Our strategic plan was for FICA to become a multi-concept regional franchise investment and development company. We began to look at categories of products that did not compete.

After considerable effort, FICA signed far-reaching franchise agreements with Circle-K for both the Philippines and Thailand and with Carrel Ice Cream for China. By the fall of 1995, the company was continuing negotiations with these companies for additional franchise territories within Asia-Pacific. In 1994, FICA also began investigating KRR in the context of a broader China strategy. (Economic and social trends for China are shown in Exhibit 1.) Wang explained why KRR seemed natural for China:

> We identified various franchise categories and one of those was chicken. I knew a lot of people at KRR who used to work for KFC. I knew John Brown and Loy Weston [former General Manager of KFC in Japan and for 18 months President of KRR Pacific]. Some of the best people who worked for KFC now work for KRR. I also knew Lenny Abelman, [KRR's newly appointed Vice-President in Charge of International Development] who I had used as a consultant while I was at Foodmaker. But beyond having a lot of contacts, KRR made good business sense for China. It represents American lifestyle. It is not fast food like KFC or McDonald's. It is an entirely new category. Also, young people in China really like Kenny Rogers as a singer.

Wang's negotiations focused on gaining the franchise rights for KRR for both Shanghai and Beijing.

> I didn't need the rights to the whole country. Beijing and Shanghai are on the leading edge of China. I am sure that KRR will not partner with anyone else until they see what happens in Beijing and Shanghai. If they can get someone else to do it better, fine. But if I do a good job, why would John Brown want someone else to do it? In any case, Beijing and Shanghai are both huge.

In the spring of 1995, FICA was granted the KRR rights for both Beijing and Shanghai. While FICA did not pay a fee for the KRR rights to these two cities, it did agree to pay an up-front franchise fee for each store based on opening 15 stores in total. According to Wang, the up-front franchise fees "were consistent with U.S. per store fees discounted by an allowance for new market development." FICA's 1995 structure is presented in Exhibit 2.

Beyond franchise fees, Wang recognized that considerable money would be required to build the first KRR store. Costs were not directly comparable with U.S. levels. The location of the store, terms and conditions of the lease and size of the store all affected costs. To Wang, "I didn't even ask what a U.S. store cost. I knew it would be irrelevant. U.S. stores are 90 per cent free standing. They also involve a lot of real estate. None in China are or will be free standing. Also you can't buy real estate in China."

In deciding on a Beijing or Shanghai location for the first store, Wang commented:

> I didn't make the decision of predetermining where the first store would be located. I looked at the opportunities and at supporting functions.
>
> The first concern was where we could get good employees and managers. We settled on Beijing.

Finding a Partner

Once the decision had been made to focus on Beijing, Wang began the process of finding an appropriate local partner. Despite years of open door economic policies, Chinese investment regulations remained complex and cumbersome. There were also legal issues to be considered. Wang explained:

> The law in China is both clear and uncertain in the area of ownership. The regulations state that you cannot have 100 per cent foreign ownership in food services. Beyond that it is not clear. So we had to think about a partner or several partners... I wanted to find a partner who could bring me some skills and organizational strength. The organizational strength might be an understanding of retailing in Beijing or an understanding of real estate or something else valuable.

Wang initially thought of contacting his old KFC partners. However, this was ruled out because of strict non-compete agreements that Wang had forced upon each partner when the original KFC joint venture was established in 1987. Wang then turned to East City Food Services and Distribution Co., a firm with which he had some familiarity. East City was a city-government-owned enterprise with 30 different Chinese style sit-down restaurants and over 100 retail food outlets in the greater Beijing area. Preliminary discussions with East City's management indicated considerable excitement at partnering with KRR. East City promised access to its extensive labour pool that could either be transferred to KRR or hired through the company's normal channels. East City also had extensive local market knowledge and could be useful in marketing efforts and pricing issues. Finally, through their up-stream contacts, the company promised to assist in accessing chickens and various food ingredients that would be essential in the smooth running of KRR restaurants. In assessing their potential contributions, Wang commented:

> We would save some starting legwork by partnering with them. They could represent a smart option given my other FICA commitments. I think they are seriously worth considering. One drawback, however, is that they couldn't provide much in the way of finances.

A second option Wang was considering was the Beijing Branch of the China Great Wall Trading Co., a major investor-owned international trading company. China Great Wall had extensive international contacts and was very familiar with Western business practices. They were also very entrepreneurial and were seeking new investment opportunities with multinational corporations in Beijing. Wang sized up this option:

> China Great Wall has a lot of appeal because it can provide a bridge between the Chinese and American ways of doing business. Mr. Lu Hong Jun, the General Manager, was someone I have known for some time. He seems quite easy to work with. I admire his entrepreneurial spirit. China Great Wall also seems to have plenty of money, including access to hard currency.

As a third option, Wang considered D&D Realty Co. D&D was a Hong Kong-based real estate development and leasing company with revenues in excess of US$1.8 billion. In 1993 it began a major push in to China and in 1994 opened its first office in Beijing. In early 1995 it signed a contract as leasing agent for a new 14-story office complex being built by Hong Kong investors in a commercial area in central Beijing. It was interested in filling ground floor space with a signature store and in September 1995 approached FICA with an offer to form a partnership with KRR. D&D communicated its plans for aggressive expansion in Beijing and promised Wang that as a partner it could provide relatively easy access to prime retail space within the city. Wang was clearly intrigued by the potential. "It is a very interesting concept. My worry is that they are still new and don't have mature contacts. Still, they deserve careful consideration."

FUTURE DIRECTION

Wang was clearly committed to moving KRR forward in Beijing in as expeditious a manner as possible. While he clearly had other responsibilities as President of FICA, Wang realized KRR's approach to the Beijing market would set a clear precedent for the expansion of other FICA retailing concepts in China. He was also aware that the competition was not standing still. By the fall of 1995, McDonald's had 17 restaurants running in Beijing; KFC was operating 10. Other restaurant companies including Hard Rock Cafe, Pizza Hut, and TGI Friday's, had either established operations or had broken ground for new stores in the Beijing area.

Despite the obvious popularity of Western food and the enormous potential of the Chinese market, the Chinese food service industry remained poorly developed and at risk. McDonald's and KFC were both involved in difficult lease negotiations. In February 1995, McDonald's managers were informed that its flagship restaurant in Beijing (and McDonald's largest in the world) would be razed to accommodate the construction of an enormous shopping, office, and residential complex being developed by Hong Kong billionaire Li Ka-Shing. McDonald's refused to vacate its building arguing that it had a valid long-term lease. Demolition of the surrounding area continued and by October 1995 the restaurant was still operating, but in what appeared to be a war zone. A spokesperson for the developer asserted that McDonald's never had a clean lease on the property. Rumours that McDonald's had cut a special deal with Li Ka-Shing's group were circulating among Western business people in Beijing. One other rumour circulating was that KFC would not renew its 10-year lease on its flagship Tiananmen Square store because of soaring rent costs.

The problems of doing business in China did not stop with leasing issues. Wang learned that import duties for equipment and materials would average 50 to 100 per cent. It was estimated that each KRR store would require a minimum of US$150 000 in imported equipment (not including lease-hold improvements). While import permits were relatively straightforward, Wang lacked the staff to manage the development of 15 new stores in a short period of time. Another concern was hiring and training the new workers. With 15 restaurants, over 1 000 new employees would be required over the next few years. Who would interview them, hire them and train them? No one in KRR's training group spoke Mandarin nor were Chinese language training materials available.

Wang also learned that wage rates had climbed substantially over the past decade. Multinational companies were paying from a low 1 500 RMB per month for office clerks who spoke some English to as high as 10 000 RMB per month for senior managers who spoke fluent English.[3] Over 95 per cent of employees in Beijing worked for state-owned enterprises where salaries averaged between 500 to 700 RMB per month. In Beijing, anyone—including those who worked for multinational companies—making less than 2 000 RMB per month was entitled to subsidized housing. Government subsidies reduced rent costs to less than 80 RMB per month. The cheapest unsubsidized apartments started at over 1 000 RMB per month and increased sharply according to location, size and quality.

Wang was also acutely aware that by October 1995 none of the local food suppliers had been either identified or approved by KRR's head office. Related to this was a real concern over the menu. KRR's menu had never been tested in Beijing. While chicken was commonly eaten in China, would the Chinese be attracted to a premium product that was promoted in the U.S. as a healthy alternative to fried chicken? Furthermore, should KRR develop new menu items for China and if so, who would actually develop the

---

[3] In October 1995, the Chinese renminbi (RMB) had an exchange rate of 1 $U.S.=8.11 RMB.

concepts? Even if tasty new concepts could be developed, how long would they take to get corporate approval and could they be produced economically without costly new equipment?

These were all questions that were weighing heavily on Wang's mind. One thing that was clear was that whoever was selected as FICA's local partner would have a major impact on the success or failure of KRR in China. With so many unresolved issues, Wang was wondering whether the time was right to formalize a partnership.

EXHIBIT 1 Economic and Social Trends in China

Economic Indicators	1989	1990	1991	1992	1993	1994	1995*	1996*	1997*	1998*	1999*
GNP at current market prices ($ bn)	424.8	369.9	380.1	435.9	544.6	477.2	525.9	569.6	616.7	670.4	730.2
Real GNP growth (%)	4.4	4.1	8.2	13.0	13.4	11.8	9.8	8.6	8.3	8.4	8.5
GNP, per capita ($)	380.0	324.0	330.0	374.0	462.0	399.0	434.0	463.0	494.0	530.0	569.0
Consumer price inflation (%)	17.5	1.6	3.0	5.4	13.0	25.0	18.0	12.0	11.5	11.5	11.0
Exchange rate (av.) Rmb:$ (official rate)	3.89	4.8	5.3	5.5	5.8	8.6	8.6	9.5	10.0	10.5	11.0
Av. growth rate in wages; urban workers (%)[a]	10.8	10.5	9.4	15.8	19.6	18.0	15.0	13.0	12.5	13.0	12.5

Demographics	1989	1990	1991	1992	1993	1994[b]
Urban population (billion)	295.4	301.9	305.4	323.7	333.5	
Rural population (billion)	831.6	841.4	852.8	848.0	851.7	
Total population (billion)	1 127.0	1 143.3	1 158.2	1 171.7	1 185.2	

Demographic and Social Trends	1991	1996*	2001*	Annual average % change 1991–2001*
Total population (billion)	1.15	1.13	1.31	1.3
Population growth rate (% per year)				1.3
Age profile (% of population)				
0–14	27.5	26.9	26.4	0.9
15–64	66.5	66.9	67.2	1.4
65+	6.2	6.4	6.4	2.0
Life expectancy (years)				
Male	66	67	68	N/A
Female	69			N/A
Literacy rate (% of population) 10 years and over	80	82	84	N/A
Labour force (million)	584	645	712	2.0

* EIU estimates.

Source: These tables were compiled from *China: Country Report* and *Country Forecast. Economist Intelligence Unit*, 1995.

---

[a] State enterprises only.
[b] Data not yet available.

E X H I B I T 2   **FICA (Franchise Investment Corporation of Asia), 1995**

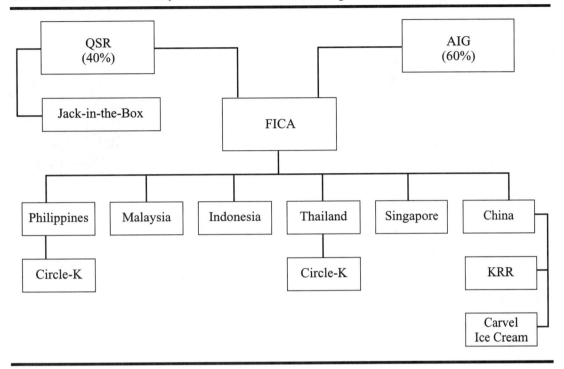

CAE ELECTRONICS

*Mary M. Crossan
and Barbara Pierce*

In August 1993, after having spent one year and $500 000 on a bid for three power plant simulators for the Korean Electric Power Corporation (KEPCO), valued at over $50 million, Allan Abramovitch, Manager for Power Plant Simulators at Canadian Aviation Electronics (CAE Electronics), was reconsidering how aggressively his firm should continue to pursue the contract. Allan's recommendation would be considered by CAE management, who would ultimately make the final decision. CAE's initial approach had been to go after KEPCO's business aggressively. Each new request for information, however, provided an opportunity to re-evaluate the bidding strategy, and there had been many. As well, it was evident that

IVEY

Mary M. Crossan and Barbara Pierce prepared this case solely to provide material for class discussion. The authors do not intend to illustrate either effective or ineffective handling of a managerial situation. The authors may have disguised certain names and other identifying information to protect confidentiality.

Ivey Management Services prohibits any form of reproduction, storage or transmittal of this material without its written permission. This material is not covered under authorization from CanCopy or any other reproduction rights organization. To order copies or request permission to reproduce materials, contact Ivey Publishing, Ivey Management Services c/o Richard Ivey School of Business, The University of Western Ontario, London, Ontario, Canada, N6A 3K7; phone (519) 661-3208; fax (519) 661-3882; e-mail cases@ivey.uwo.ca

KEPCO might start the bidding all over, as it appeared that none of the proposals would meet their new budget. This was an opportune time to revisit the bidding strategy. Abramovitch was growing increasingly uncomfortable with the nature of this project and was beginning to worry about the potential implications, even if CAE did win the contract.

CANADIAN AVIATION ELECTRONICS

Since its founding in 1947, Canadian Aviation Electronics (CAE Inc.) had become a diversified high-tech company with sales in excess of $1 billion (Exhibit 1). Its portfolio of international companies, eight in all, was divided into two product groups: Aerospace and Electronics, and Industrial Products. CAE Electronics, based in Montreal, came under the Aerospace and Electronics group. Although it designed and manufactured shipboard machinery control systems, supervisory control and data acquisition systems (primarily for utility companies), and airborne magnetic anomaly detection systems for anti-submarine warfare forces, these products represented less than 10 per cent of CAE Inc.'s total sales. The major products designed and manufactured by CAE Electronics were training simulators (65 per cent civil aviation simulators, 13 per cent military aviation simulators and 13 per cent power plant simulators). Simulators were an important training tool in settings where mistakes made by inexperienced trainees could have dangerous or costly consequences. Simulation provided a safe, cost-efficient and effective supplement to live training for pilots, cabin crews, air traffic controllers or power plant operators. Examples of CAE Electronics' products are provided in Exhibits 2 and 3.

By 1993, CAE Electronics was the world leader in flight simulators with 65 per cent of the total market share. It was known as the innovator in the industry, reinvesting 20 per cent of its sales on research and development activities each year. It had ISO 9001 QA Certification for Avionics, Naval, Nuclear and Space. Over half of its 3 400 employees were scientific and technical personnel. Of the remainder, 1 125 worked in manufacturing and 450 in management and administration. CAE's customers included international and regional airlines, defense forces, power utilities, government agencies, research establishments and space agencies. In total, there was a 70/30 split between sales for commercial and military applications. Eighty-five per cent (85 per cent) of its products were exported to 43 countries: 49 per cent sold in the Americas, 30 per cent in Europe and 21 per cent in Africa, Asia and the Pacific.

Nuclear Power Plant Simulators

CAE had carved out a niche in the design and construction of simulators for the CANDU nuclear power plant. Simulators for nuclear power plants were constructed using the control panels and equipment of the actual power plant. Manipulating the controls, however, activated sophisticated computer programs rather than a nuclear reactor. These programs could be adjusted to mimic actual operations and appeared to the operators exactly the same as real installations.

In 1970, CAE developed its first power plant simulator for the Pickering, Ontario nuclear plant using CANDU technology. Supplying training simulators to Ontario Hydro for subsequent plants became an attractive, although relatively small, component of its business. In 1983, CAE entered the U.S. market. Although the first few programs were difficult, requiring some upfront entry investment on the part of CAE, the company subsequently developed strong management and technological capability in the area of power plant simulators.

As indicated in Exhibit 4, from a peak of $38.8 million in 1987, CAE had experienced a slump in new orders for power plant simulators. This decline was primarily due to a decline in the number of nuclear plants being constructed. CAE had considered getting out of the business, but was persuaded that changes in the regulatory environment would generate substantial demand for power plant simulators. Furthermore, since changes in the airline industry were having an adverse effect on the demand for CAE's other product lines, CAE felt it was important to keep a diversified portfolio of products.

INDUSTRY TRENDS

While CAE Electronics had experienced steady sales and profit growth in flight simulators, there were two disturbing trends that it felt might influence future sales growth. First, there was the major worldwide slump in the airline industry resulting in a major decline in the sale of flight simulators. In an attempt to attract passengers to fill empty seats, airlines had been slashing fares. As a result, profits in the industry had quickly eroded. Those companies that had managed to survive were slashing costs and deferring major capital expenditures, hoping to ride out the downturn and wait until better times returned. In spite of the lack of profitability in the industry, the future did not look entirely bleak. Passenger volume was expected to grow 5 per cent a year throughout the 1990s. As well, it was expected that 4 000 new long-range wide-bodied aircraft would be required by the year 2010 to meet the increasing demand for business travel in world markets.

Second, military spending was being cut, particularly in the U.S. With cold war tensions removed and major national economies in recession, governments saw military budgets as a potential source of spending restraint. It was difficult to determine if this trend would result in permanent reductions to military spending, but, in the near term, it was definitely a factor to consider. On the other hand, the U.S. Department of Defense had identified simulation as one of its seven major technological thrusts in order to reduce its expenditures; simulator training costs averaged US$600 per hour, while training on a military aircraft could cost US$10 000 per hour. The U.S. National Training and Simulation Association had forecast a doubling of the U.S. Army's simulation budget by 1994.

Although CAE Electronics was still in the process of filling orders made in previous years, the order book for the next five years was beginning to show the effects of these trends. CAE's perspective on this industry upheaval was captured in its annual report:

> (In)... the commercial airline industry, there will be no quick fixes to the problems of overcapacity and tight financing. The industry's turnaround will take at least another two years. But air travel itself will continue to grow. And once the airline industry undergoes its unprecedented change, it will be a stronger, healthier, and more profitable industry.
>
> And as for the defense forces, potential conflict between two rival superpowers no longer threatens. Unfortunately, however, the promise of peace has also dimmed. Rising nationalism is fostering greater regional hostilities. New nations are stillborn amid bloody ethnic conflicts. Greater instability endangers the Middle East, Africa, regions of Asia, Eastern Europe, and former republics of the Soviet Union. The new world has precious little order. In fact, the challenge for defense forces throughout the world has grown in complexity, rather than diminished.

CAE was advised that new regulations being planned in the U.S. would require simulators for every nuclear plant, potentially creating a large number of new orders. In addition, CAE felt there would be continuing demand for fossil fuel power plant simulators and existing installations would always require updating and modification. Exhibit 5 provides Ontario Hydro's estimates for nuclear and fossil training simulator demand for the 1990s. Other market studies indicated that there were 30 active nuclear power plants in the U.S. that would be required to have operator training simulators in the near future.

REPUBLIC OF KOREA (ROK)

The Republic of Korea (ROK) or South Korea was located on the southern portion of the Korean peninsula, adjacent to the Democratic People's Republic of Korea (North Korea). Despite continued tensions and mutual suspicion resulting from years of disputes and confrontations between the two countries, there were hopes of renewed political harmony, if not eventual reunification. However, having seen the price West Germany had paid in its reunification with East Germany, the South Koreans had become more cautious and concerned about reunification with the Northern communist population of 21 million, with an expected price tag of hundreds of billions of dollars.

One of the most densely populated countries in the world, South Korea's population of over 43 million covered a geographic area equal in size to Portugal, the state of Indiana, or twice the size of the province of Nova Scotia. Over one quarter of the population lived in the capital city of Seoul located near the North/South border.

At the end of the Korean war in 1953, South Korea (hereafter Korea) was one of the poorest countries in the world with GNP per capita of less than US$100. With its capital city, Seoul, levelled, Korea literally began rebuilding from the ground up. In what has been termed an "economic miracle," Korea transformed itself from an agrarian to an industrially based economy with economic growth averaging 10 per cent through 1990. Korea achieved NIC (Newly Industrialized Country) status by 1970, and was expected to achieve advanced country status by the late 1990s.

Technology Transfer

One key to Korea's phenomenal growth was its aggressive accumulation of technology from higher-income countries. When Korea entered the race to industrialize, like other developing countries, it suffered from a significant deficit in industrial technology. Korea could never have hoped to become competitive through its own R&D or basic research activities alone. It had neither the time nor the capability. It was forced instead to borrow, license and imitate technology to compensate for its initial position.

At first, borrowing, licensing and imitation were sufficient. Low wage levels and government subsidization allowed Korean products to compete on a global basis. Koreans became extremely proficient in acquiring technology from other countries and using it to manufacture products for export. These products were often priced lower than the same product manufactured in the country where the technology originated.

Eventually, as productivity and economic benefits increased, so did worker demands for a greater share of the gains. Mounting wage pressure began to erode the competitive position of labour-intensive Korean products prompting Korean companies to explore product and process innovation for increases in productivity and competitiveness. This emphasis on product and process innovation signalled a significant change in industrialization policy. Not only did technology need to be transferred, but after transfer, it needed to be improved upon to enhance productivity. While it was not uncommon for the first plant in an industry to be built on a turnkey basis with little Korean involvement, the development of subsequent plants relied heavily on the involvement of local engineers and technicians who assumed an expanding role. This growing capability eventually reduced reliance on the initial foreign investor. The "apprentices" graduated to assume full journeyman status. Koreans had added the ability to develop and enhance technology to their existing ability to acquire it.

As Korea became more successful, its wage advantage deteriorated further and, by the late 1980s, it began to emphasize the development of technology-intensive industries. Koreans expected significant changes in the near future given the new emphasis in economic development, and the change in political leadership. In particular, the development of technology was high on the agenda of the Korean government. A recent survey by the Korea Industrial Technology Association (KITA) showed that in spite of Korea's impressive improvements in technology over the previous two decades, it still lagged far behind the United States and Japan. As a result, foreign companies were required to have a high level of "localization" in manufactured products, i.e., finished products could not be imported to Korea but instead a significant proportion of the product had to be manufactured and preferably sourced in Korea. As well, foreign companies wishing to do business in Korea were required to submit a detailed plan to the government on how they planned to transfer technology to Korean companies. The government hoped that the transfer of technological knowledge to Korea would fuel economic growth through productivity increases and new product introduction. This technology-based strategy was considered critical to Korea's long-term economic success since it increasingly felt the effects of being sandwiched between the lower-labour-cost economies of China and Taiwan, and the high-value-added economies of Japan and the United States. Korea's aspirations were to match the technological development of the G7 group.

Government's Role in the Economy

Korea's economic success had been attributed to a number of factors: "strong leadership, creative policies tailored to concrete situations, a deep understanding of international opportunities, sound utilization of domestic resources and, most important, sacrifice and hard work on the part of the Korean People."[1] The government exercised significant controls on business activities to achieve planned economic results. In 1962, Korea began a series of five-year economic plans that initially focused the country's efforts on the development of heavy industry and labour-intensive manufacturing with a strong export orientation. The "export first" principle was strongly enforced by the government. For example, sales of domestic colour television sets were prohibited until 1980, forcing manufacturers to focus on overseas markets. The strong export orientation was coupled with a high level of restrictions on imports. For example, there was a ban on 258 Japanese import products ranging from cars to appliances. In recent years, the government had been willing to ease import restrictions somewhat but only permitted imports and foreign investments which it felt would contribute to Korean economic development, improve its balance-of-payments position or bring in advanced technology.

Most companies in Korea were small and closely held by family groups. However, during the early stages of economic reform, certain economic sectors, such as the auto industry, received preferential treatment from the government in terms of better access to capital, lower interest rates, R&D support and tax incentives. Given the limited capital available, these industries developed into highly leveraged, very large diversified multinational conglomerates known as *chaebols* (pronounced chi-bols) (Exhibit 6, Exhibit 7). Most notable among the chaebols were Hyundai, Daewoo, Lucky-Goldstar and Samsung. These octopus-like conglomerates, which were predominantly family-owned, were an indispensable part of the Korean economy, which they clearly dominated. For example, Samsung's revenues of US$17 billion in 1986 ranked it 35th in the world and represented 14 per cent of Korea's GNP. The taxes paid by Samsung represented 5 per cent of the government's total tax revenue.

The Korean government invested heavily in the development of human resources. At over 10 per cent of GNP, Korea's investment in education was second only to the United States. Children in the United States attended school for a net 158 days per year while Korean students attended for 250 days. Much of this investment was directed at acquiring scientific and technical knowledge. Between 1960 and 1980, employment of general managers only doubled while the employment of engineers increased tenfold.

The new President, Kim Young-Sam was expected to have a significant impact on the country. President Roh Tae-Woo, a former general, had stepped down after completing his maximum five-year term in office. Although the Roh administration had already made inroads into political reform, it was

---

[1] Richard Ibghy, Taieb Hafsi, *South Korea's National Strategies 1962 to 1988*; Monographs on International Business and Economics; National Library of Canada.

felt that there was a long way to go. It was only in 1980 that 200 students were killed and 1 000 injured in the Kwangju uprising. It was a wave of similar demonstrations in 1987 that brought down Roh's predecessor, Chun Doo-Hwan. Roh himself had faced three weeks of demonstrations throughout the nation in response to the fatal beating of a university student by riot policemen.

The recent election was the first since the Second World War, in which none of the Presidential candidates had a military background. President Kim Young-Sam promised sweeping changes to clean up the corruption that was considered rampant in the country. The situation had been ripe for perks and kick-backs given the heavy involvement by the government in developing the economy, coupled with weak measures on the financial side to track investments. The head of one of Korea's major companies stated that "we pay as much in extortion—legal, semi-legal and illegal extortion—as we do in legitimate taxes."[2]

Korea was Canada's fifth-largest trading partner with trade between the two countries projected to reach $12 billion by the end of the decade. By 1991, two-way trade had reached $4 billion and Canada was third on the list of foreign investors in Korea. Many countries viewed Korea as a gateway to other Asian countries, particularly China. Although history had shown that both Japan and China had been Korea's aggressors, there were much closer geographic, ethnic and linguistic ties between Korea and China. While there still remained a great deal of animosity between Korea and Japan, China viewed Korea much like a "little brother," a role that Korea was anxious to grow out of. Korea's fear of dependence on Japan was evidenced by the ban on Japanese cars that persisted three years after the ban on other foreign cars had been lifted.

CAE'S KOREAN OPERATIONS

CAE had been very successful in penetrating the Korean market for flight simulators. Korean Air Lines (KAL), part of the Hanjin chaebol, had been very pleased with CAE's products and service. CAE representatives had developed long-term relationships with KAL personnel in what one CAE employee referred to as the need to build "off-shore friendships." Despite the 12-hour time difference, the team of CAE employees in Canada who supported the KAL simulators made themselves available 24 hours a day to discuss any concerns. CAE also placed a Korean-speaking employee on the team to facilitate communication between the two companies. Although the CAE team observed that the Koreans were very conscious of hierarchy and titles, they often spoke directly to the Korean-speaking CAE employee in spite of his lower status in the company.

CAE's experience in Korea with power plant simulators was more limited. It had acted as a contractor through Atomic Energy of Canada Limited (AECL) to supply a CANDU digital control system to KEPCO when it had purchased a CANDU power plant a few years previously. This was very much an arm's-length transaction, in which CAE had little contact with its Korean counterparts, although the equipment had worked well and KEPCO was pleased with the installation.

KEPCO POWER PLANT SIMULATOR BID

In early 1991, KEPCO initiated a bid process for three power plant simulators. The process began with a high degree of information exchange between the parties involved. An informal request for information was issued asking potential bidders for generic technical specifications and an approximate price. Based on its submission, CAE was asked to make a presentation to KEPCO in Korea. The CAE contingent arrived

---

[2] "Corruption: The Cost of Politics," *Far Eastern Economic Review*, March 30, 1991.

jetlagged to what appeared to be an "executive triathalon." On the Friday they arrived, they were handed plant drawings, and asked to develop a fully functional set of plant-specific models on the workstation they had brought with them. They were then asked to demonstrate their customized model on Saturday. In one day, they did the best they could on a task that would normally take two months, and came up with the demo as requested.

Based on the information received during the presentation round, KEPCO sent out an unofficial request for proposals (RFP). This RFP was developed by combining the best technical specifications from each of the original informal submissions. The CAE bid team found this approach interesting, since in many cases it appeared as if KEPCO had not fully understood the nature of the components they were requiring; when in doubt, they had indicated a company's proprietary name for a particular component. As the informal process moved toward a more formal request, the stakes were getting higher; technical requirements were escalating, the acceptable price was dropping and there seemed to be no limit to the amount of technology transfer demanded.

When the formal request for quotation (RFQ) came, it allowed for only one week to respond, as KEPCO needed to meet some internal deadlines. The procedure was that proposals would first be screened on the basis of their technical strength, and those meeting the first test would then be evaluated on price.

KEPCO required foreign companies to partner with a Korean "prime" contractor. Most of CAE's competitors had chosen to partner with one of the chaebols; Hyundai was partnering with ABB-CE (U.S.), Lucky-Goldstar with Westinghouse (U.S.), Samsung with S3 Technologies (U.S.), Daeyong with General Physics International (GPI) (U.S.) and Daewoo with Thomson CSF (France). As was the custom, CAE had engaged a consultant in Korea. The consultant used his knowledge of the market and competition plus his influence through a network of contacts to bridge geographic and cultural differences. The consultant had recommended that CAE partner with Iljin Electronics, which was a much smaller company than the Korean conglomerates, yet was comparable in size to the divisions of the other companies Iljin would be competing against. As well, given that Iljin was much smaller than CAE, CAE would not be overshadowed by its Korean counterpart. The consultant also assured CAE that Iljin had solid contacts within KEPCO.

The playing field had shifted throughout the bidding process. All potential partnering relationships had to be approved by the Korean government to ensure that the government's policies for localization and technology transfer were being met. The Daewoo-Thomson partnership did not receive approval, because Thomson, one of CAE's biggest competitors in flight simulators, was unwilling to meet the requirements for technology transfer. As well, since GPI could not come to an agreement with Daeyong, it decided to partner with Hyundai. Hyundai was released from its initial agreement with ABB-CE (U.S.) when ABB-CE decided not to participate in this competitive procurement.

Iljin Electronics

Iljin Electronics was a division of Iljin Electrics and Machinery, which was founded in 1967 as a non-ferrous metal manufacturer. Iljin had grown into a diversified company with sales of over $250 million. While still maintaining a strong position in non-ferrous metals, it was also involved in manufacturing industrial machinery and electrical equipment, construction, and electronics and communications. Iljin Electronics was established in 1983 to focus on electronics and communications, including computer networking, factory automation, computers and facsimile. With sales of $35.7 million and assets of $21.7 million, it employed 170 people.

From a somewhat difficult beginning, CAE's relationship with Iljin had developed over time. The partnership experienced some turbulence early on when Iljin "strongly recommended" that CAE bid on a smaller deal with Korean Gas. Iljin advised CAE that it was not likely to win the bid, but that CAE needed to bid to establish credibility in the Korean market. However, CAE won the bid, then ended up losing money on the project. What started out as a ten-month project ran six months over schedule, creating a great deal of frustration between the project managers at Iljin and CAE.

With respect to the KEPCO proposal, it was apparent to CAE that all of the Korean prime contractors, not just Iljin, were moving into a new area of expertise. Therefore, while Iljin was very responsive to CAE's input, there were some questions about how the project would be implemented should CAE and Iljin win the bid.

Localization

The project was divided almost equally between hardware and software. CAE was bidding solely on the software, which represented approximately $25 million of the $50 million project. For the software portion, KEPCO required localization of 50 per cent on each of the first two simulators and 80 per cent on the third. The percentages pertained to cash flow but inferred technical performance. Each new power plant required a software package to replicate the plant. As a result, each power plant required the development of new software. However, CAE was continually developing tools and modelling techniques to support the software development process. The localization requirement referred to software development. It was not apparent at this point how CAE would fulfill not only its obligations for quality, cost and delivery, but also meet the localization requirement.

Technology Transfer

The requirements for technology transfer had escalated with each iteration of the process. Originally, the transfer of technology was such that it would enable KEPCO to do its own maintenance on the simulator, which quickly evolved into maintenance of simulators for all similar power plant simulators. The requirements seemed to escalate incrementally, with the most recent request being a complete transfer of technology including the basic software source code for the tools and modelling techniques, which KEPCO could then use to develop software for any simulator.

Opinion at CAE was mixed concerning the potential threat from the transfer of technology. Views ranged from truly significant to nonexistent or manageable. Those who felt the threat was significant pointed to how quickly the Koreans had been able to pick things up during the process of putting the request for information and request for proposal together. They suggested that others were underestimating the Koreans in the same way that many North Americans had underestimated the Japanese in their early years of technological development. With respect to power plant technology, the example was given of the Romanians who bought their first and second plants, and produced the last three themselves.

Others felt that the risk was negligible, suggesting that the Korean partner was really not capable of assimilating the technology. One person stated that "intellectual transfer of technology would be extremely difficult. It took 15 years to develop at CAE; they can't possibly learn it in two to three years, especially not in English." Another person suggested that "even after the extensive in-house training that CAE was required to offer, if an engineer could get a working knowledge of the technology, he was likely to get promoted into a position that did not utilize the knowledge." Finally, several people suggested there was little threat given CAE's rate of innovation; "if CAE could stay one step ahead of its direct competitors, surely it could stay ahead of a new entry into the field."

In general, risk to intellectual property in Korea was considered to be high. The laws regulating monopolies and enforcing fair trade had only been enacted in 1980. However, it was widely recognized that legislation guarding against inappropriate transfer of technology was not enforced. The Canadian Embassy, who had often interceded on behalf of a Canadian company registering a violation, indicated it had not won any of the cases that had been put forth. Infractions were most notable in consumer products where watches, audio and video cassettes, garments and electronics products were often copies of more expensive branded products.

CAE had previous experience in the Korean market with its KAL flight simulators and their contribution to the CANDU reactor project with AECL. In these deals, however, there had been no requirement for offset or any local work requirements. CAE had worked closely with its Korean customers in the past but partnering with a Korean company and engaging in this level of technology transfer presented new territory for CAE.

Although S3 Technologies was a strong competitor in the area of power plant simulators, CAE was confident it was well positioned to be competitive on the bid with respect to both technology and pricing given that it had won the last two contracts awarded worldwide. In addition to its success in recent contracts, CAE's experience in Korea with the sale of flight simulators had been quite positive. Finally, it had a great deal of confidence in its consultant who was well connected with KEPCO.

CAE was concerned about the potential competitive repercussions of losing the bid, since the nuclear simulator would provide one of its competitors with a potential advantage in bidding for a follow-on contract with KEPCO to supply a simulator for its CANDU nuclear plant. Since CAE had built all the simulators for the CANDU plant project, it was confident of winning the Korean Wolsong II CANDU simulator.

The project had been costed out, and it was clear that margins were shrinking with each round in the bidding process. At this stage, it was evident that from a financial standpoint, the returns would be low. Abramovitch had to weigh the project's associated risks against the financial and non-financial returns to assess how aggressively CAE should continue pursuing the project.

To complicate matters, KEPCO had received budget approval of only US$13.7 million. CAE, Iljin and the Korean consultant believed that KEPCO would either have to lower its technical specifications, reduce the number of plants, or seek a higher budget. At this stage, all that was clear was that the process would be delayed.

E X H I B I T   1   CAE Revenues and Earnings

	1992	*1991*	*1990*
Consolidated			
Total Revenue	1 045 812	1 097 728	1 119 546
Operating Earnings	73 287	69 754	61 370
Aerospace and Electronics			
Total Revenue	966 293	1 021 296	1 028 554
Operating Earnings	63 092	62 410	48 460
Industrial Products			
Total Revenue	79 519	76 432	90 992
Operating Earnings	10 195	7 344	12 910

EXHIBIT 2   **CAE's Simulator Products**

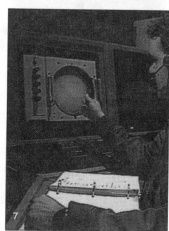

CAE Electronics
C.P. 1800 Saint-Laurent,
Québec, Canada H4L 4X4
Tel (514) 341-6780
Tlx 05 824856
Fax (514) 341-7699

Where new frontiers become reality

1. Helicopter Simulators
2. Energy Management and Control Systems
3. Magnetic Anomaly Submarine Detection Systems
4. Helicopter Research & Development Facilities
5. Civil Flight Simulators
6. Tactical Aircraft Systems Support
7. Air Defense Anti-Tank System Trainers
8. Power Plant Control Systems and Simulators
9. Telerobotics
10. Flight Training Devices
11. C-5B Galaxy Weapon System Trainers
12. Naval Integrated Platform Management Systems
13. Air Traffic Control Systems

EXHIBIT 3 CAE's Power Plant Simulator Products

EXHIBIT 4   CAE Electronics Orders Received

	Nuclear Simulator Order ($ millions)	Total CAE Orders ($ millions)	Percentage
1984	22.6	131	17%
1985	35.4	206	17%
1986	10.0	196	5%
1987	38.8	297	13%
1988	0	315	0%
1989	11.4	367	3%
1990	3.7	363	1%
1991	7.8	335	2%
Overall	129.7	2 210	5.9%

EXHIBIT 5   Potential Training Simulator Market

	Canada	U.S.	Other
Nuclear Training Simulator	2	0	25
Nuclear Simulator Updates	7	75	?
Fossil Training Simulator	8	12	50

EXHIBIT 6   **Korean *Chaebols*—The Top 15**

Group	Core Firms	Family Ownership	Debt Ratio
Samsung	Samsung Shipbuilding*	98.3	544.2
	Samsung Electronics	30.7	398.1
	Samsung Petrochemical*	83.0	474.3
Hanjin	KAL	28.4	644.3
	Hanjin Shipping	91.2	C.I.
	Hanil Development	24.1	354.1
Daewoo	Daewoo Corp.	14.9	290.8
	Daewoo Electronics	7.1	251.5
	Daewoo Shipyard*	83.9	296.3
Hyundai	Hyundai Motors	29.9	453.0
	Hyundai Electronics*	100.0	568.9
	Hyundai Petrochemical*	100.0	171.8
Lucky	Lucky Ltd.	10.8	176.2
	Goldstar	15.3	344.6
	Goldstar Electron*	100.0	991.9
Ssangyong	Ssangyong Cement	20.7	170.8
	Ssangyong Oil Refinery	44.7	186.4
	Ssangyong Motor	17.3	282.2
Sunkyong	Yukong Ltd.	26.3	398.0
	SKI	30.4	412.6
	SKC*	84.1	881.3
Hanil	Hanil Synthetic Fiber	47.7	235.7
	Kyungnam Woolen Textile	40.8	207.3
	Kukje Corp.	43.2	C.I.
Kia	Asia Motors	36.8	303.5
	Kla Machine Tool	89.6	889.1
	Kla Steel	66.7	456.1
Daelim	Daelim Motor*	100.0	C.I.
	Daelim Ceramic*	100.0	154.8
	Daelim Concrete*	66.3	171.6
Kumho	Kumho	19.8	309.6
	Kumho Petrochemical	23.4	78.5
	Asiana*	57.5	C.I.
Hyosung	Hyosung Corp.	17.2	374.3
	Hyosung Heavy Ind*	62.5	624.7
	Tongyang Nylon	26.8	262.1
Doosan	Oriental Brewery	36.3	470.8
	Doosan Machinery	58.8	262.4
	Doosan Glass	38.2	354.0
Explosives	Korea Explosives	31.5	178.3
	Hanyang Chemical	29.3	187.1
	Kyongin Energy	44.3	442.6
Dongkuk Steel	Dongkuk Steel	42.2	95.4
	Korea Iron & Steel	63.7	120.5
	Dongkuk Ind.*	83.6	546.4

* C.I. means Capital Impairment.
* Those in asterisks are unlisted affiliates (OBSE).
* The figures are based on the end of 1990.
* Family ownership encompasses family members, and affiliates, excluding shares held by executives of those groups.

Source: Office of Bank Supervision and Examination, *Far Eastern Economic Review*, May 30, 1991, p. 52.

E X H I B I T   7   **Korean *Chaebols* Major Statistics of the Samsung Group**

(billion won)

	1976	1980	1986
Employment (000s)	25.8	75.0	147.2
Sales	455.3	2 385.5	14 615.8
Domestic sales	237.6	1 136.8	7 241.1
Exports	217.7	1 248.7	7 374.7
Capital	50.9	392.3	1 101.9
Fixed assets	110.3	697.1	2 948.4
Long-term liabilities	72.8	782.0	5 168.4
Net profit after tax	10 370	10 850	161 150
Tax	68.1	254.5	717.1
R&D Expenditure	1.9	9.8	163.1
Training expenses			10.9
Exchange rate (WON/US$)	484	659.9	861.4

Source: The Office of the Secretary to the Chairman, Samsung Conglomerate, *Samsung Osipynyonsa* (A 50-Year History of Samsung), Seoul, Samsung Group, 1988.

WESTMILLS CARPETS LIMITED (CONDENSED)

case

28

J o s e p h   N .   F r y

"**W**e are in quite a pickle with Westmills, and in dire need of a rescue program," said Derek Mather, Senior Vice-President of Canadian Enterprise Development Corporation Ltd. (CED), a venture capital company with a major equity position in the Calgary-based carpet manufacturer.

> Our losses are continuing and the prospects for early relief are poor since the market is soft and our operations disorganized. The banks are very nervous. Garry Morrison, whom we groomed for a year, has just resigned after two months as president. Harry Higson, his predecessor, is filling in on a stop-gap basis, but neither Harry, the board, nor the banks want this to continue for more than a few weeks. The balance of the management team look promising but are as yet untested.

IVEY

Joseph N. Fry prepared this case solely to provide material for class discussion. The author does not intend to illustrate either effective or ineffective handling of a managerial situation. The author may have disguised certain names and other identifying information to protect confidentiality.

As shareholders, we (CED) have to sort out our options and position on this investment, but the matter, for me, is a personal one as well. I've just been asked to step in as president, at least until we are in position to hire a new man. I'd appreciate your views on where to go from here.

THE CANADIAN CARPET INDUSTRY

The carpet industry in Canada, as it is presently known, had its beginnings in the late 1950s with the introduction of carpet tufting technology from the United States. Tufting was a low cost, flexible process for producing carpets of various qualities and styles. The new production capability coincided with expanding affluence in the Canadian marketplace and a prolonged boom in residential construction. Carpet sales grew dramatically in the 1960s and early 1970s, reaching a volume of 74 million square metres in 1975.

The growth of the Canadian market slowed in 1976 and 1977 with total sales of 76.5 million and 78.6 million square metres respectively. Nevertheless, Canadian consumption of 3.4 metres per capita was approaching that of the United States.

Between 85 per cent and 90 per cent of Canadian sales were domestically produced. Imports were limited to the less price-sensitive segments of the market by a tariff of 20 per cent plus $.375 per square metre.

Carpet Manufacture

A tufted carpet was made in three principal sequential production steps: the tufting itself, dyeing and finishing. Equipment and process flexibilities were such that in each step there were a number of design options (Figure 1). By pursuing combinations of these options, carpet mills, within the constraints of their particular equipment configuration, could produce a variety of carpet lines. A major mill might produce over 25 different products and each of these would be produced in 10 to 15 different colours. This capacity for diversity had the effect of complicating both manufacturing operations and the nature of competition in the industry.

As noted in Figure 1, there was a variety of construction possibilities open for the design of carpets for particular functional and/or aesthetic purposes. A level loop pile design made with relatively coarse nylon yarn might be developed for a heavy-traffic commercial application, for example, or a plush, cut pile design of fine yarn might be produced for a high fashion location. Different carpet designs implied different materials costs and processing efficiency. The actual design decision was thus a mixture of craft, science and economics, as aim was taken at a particular target product market and a balance was struck between fashion, function and production costs.

The value added in carpet manufacture was relatively low in relation to the total value of the finished product. Purchased materials typically amounted to 75 per cent or more of total costs, plant labour 5 per cent and general overhead 20 per cent. Production scheduling was a critical function in carpet mills— the challenge was to maintain customer service on the one hand and avoid excessive inventories, with their built-in working-capital demands and fashion risks, on the other hand.

FIGURE 1 Main Steps in Tufted Carpet Manufacture

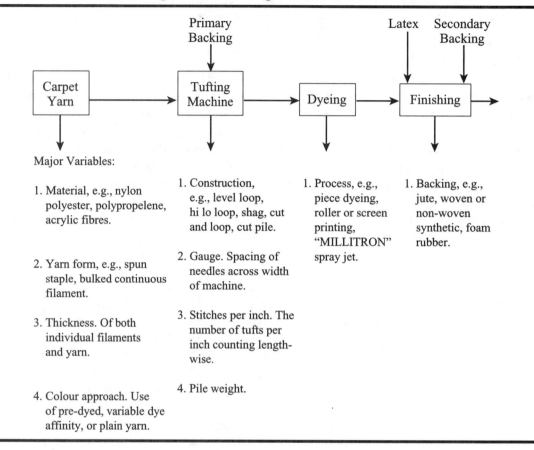

Major Variables:

1. Material, e.g., nylon polyester, polypropelene, acrylic fibres.

2. Yarn form, e.g., spun staple, bulked continuous filament.

3. Thickness. Of both individual filaments and yarn.

4. Colour approach. Use of pre-dyed, variable dye affinity, or plain yarn.

1. Construction, e.g., level loop, hi lo loop, shag, cut and loop, cut pile.

2. Gauge. Spacing of needles across width of machine.

3. Stitches per inch. The number of tufts per inch counting lengthwise.

4. Pile weight.

1. Process, e.g., piece dyeing, roller or screen printing, "MILLITRON" spray jet.

1. Backing, e.g., jute, woven or non-woven synthetic, foam rubber.

Carpet Marketing

The Canadian carpet market was comprised of three major segments: retail, residential contract and commercial contract. An approximate division of the market into these categories is given in Table 1.

TABLE 1 The Canadian and Western Canadian Carpet Markets by Segment, 1977

(estimated volume in million square metres)

	Retail	*Residential Contract*	*Commercial Contract*	*Total*
Canadian market	51.0 (65%)	14.0 (17.8%)	13.4 (17.2%)	78.5
Western Canadian	8.8 (40.2%)	7.6 (34.7%)	5.5 (25.1%)	21.9

Source: Canadian Carpet Institute, casewriter's estimates.

Retail Market

The typical retail customer was a homeowner purchasing a relatively small amount of carpet for first-time or replacement installation. The rough order of importance of purchase criteria in the retail market was generally cited as colour, style (texture), price, dealer service and guarantees. There was a very low awareness of brand names in the market, with perhaps only Harding (a carpet manufacturer) and DuPont (fibre supplier) having any significant recognition. Similarly, consumers had very little knowledge of the technical characteristics of carpets and the variables that would influence wear and care.

The retail market was serviced by a wide variety of outlets, including department stores, specialty floorcovering dealers, promotional carpet warehouses, furniture stores and home decoration centres. These outlets, depending upon their volume, their proximity to the mill and the manufacturer's distribution strategy, were in turn supplied directly from the mill, by mill-owned distributors or by independent distributors. The approximate proportions of the retail market serviced by mill-direct, mill-owned distributor and independent distributor were for Canada 35 per cent, 45 per cent and 20 per cent respectively, and for western Canada 25 per cent, 40 per cent and 35 per cent. The trend in the previous decade had been for the mills to seek greater control of their distribution by implementing mill-direct or mill-owned distribution programs.

RESIDENTIAL CONTRACT This market consisted of home/apartment/condominium builders and mobile home manufacturers. It was serviced directly or through contract dealer/installers. Builder preferences tended toward basic carpet styles at price points below those popular in the retail and commercial markets. Order sizes were quite large and price competition was severe, with orders switching on differentials as low as 5 to 10 cents a metre. Assuming price and style competitiveness, service elements—and particularly the dependability of delivery—were important in maintaining mill/account relationships (Table 2).

T A B L E 2   Ranking of Channel Service Aspects by Segment

Service Item*	Retail	Residential Contract	Commercial Contract
Speed of delivery	2	4	
Delivery when promised	1	1	1
Update of samples	4		3
Complaint handling	3	2	
Notification of price changes			4
Regular representative contact		3	2

* Original lists contained many additional items such as mill warranties, co-op advertising, salesperson personality, etc.

Source: Westmills research files.

COMMERCIAL CONTRACT The commercial market consisted of new or replacement installations in offices, hotels, retail outlets, schools, etc. The majority of commercial business was controlled by specialty installation firms that purchased directly from the mills. Unlike residential contract sales, the product was usually specified for particular projects by architects and interior designers on the basis of information from many sources (building owner, project manager, architect, etc.). The most popular styles were patterned multi-colour carpets with specific wear characteristics for the intended use.

Competitive Structure

There were 28 firms engaged in the manufacture of tufted carpet in Canada in 1977. These firms could be divided into three categories on the basis of their scale, scope of activities and degree of integration in marketing and manufacturing.

GROUP 1 This group consisted of firms with sales of $20 million or more, wide product lines and, in most cases, yarn spinning and substantial captive distribution operations. Operating results for the five firms in this group are summarized in Table 3. Together these firms accounted for somewhat less than 50 per cent of the carpet market.

TABLE 3 Summary Performance of Major Carpet Firms

($000 000s)		*1977*	*1976*	*1975*
Harding Carpets	Sales	$73.0	$74.5	$58.7
(as of Oct. 31)	Profit before tax	(.2)	3.0	2.1
Celanese Canada Carpet Division	Sales	37.6	39.0	47.7
(as of Dec. 31)	Profit before tax	(5.5)	(4.1)	.9
Peerless Rug	Sales	40.0	37.8	32.4
(as of Feb. 28)	Profit before tax	.6	.9	(.7)
Peeters Carpets	Sales	22.0 (E)	22.0 (E)	20.0
Westmills	Sales	21.7	23.1	21.7
(as of Aug. 31)	Profit before tax	(1.5)	(2.4)	(.7)

Source: Corporate financial reports.

GROUP 2 This group consisted of approximately eight firms with sales ranging from $10 to $20 million. They were generally somewhat more specialized than the Group 1 firms in product line or geographic market coverage. Most were private firms or divisions of U.S. manufacturers, with the result that specific financial data are not available.

GROUP 3 The balance of the industry consisted of small firms specializing in particular product, channel or geographic markets. Firms with sales as low as $2 million were apparently viable operations. Such firms might use pre-dyed yarns exclusively in order to limit operations to tufting and minimal finishing.

As the total market grew in the 1960s and early 1970s, entry had been relatively easy. By 1977 there was substantially more capacity in the Canadian industry than was justified by current demand. Excess capacity, coupled with a fragmented industry structure and the dynamics of style obsolescence, had led to fierce competition, price cutting and a deterioration of industry profitability.

Style competition was a major aspect of rivalry in the industry, stemming from a heterogeneous and fashion-conscious market on the one side and flexible manufacturing on the other. The benefits of design innovations were frequently short-lived, however, as other manufacturers "knocked-off" the popular styles. The time lag before a new innovation could be imitated by competitors was as short as six to nine months. With lasting product advantages difficult to achieve, success in specific markets often turned on price and a mill's ability to deliver high quality and excellent service.

WESTMILLS' BACKGROUND

Westmills Carpets Limited was incorporated in February 1966 in Kelowna, British Columbia. The company was (and remained through 1977) the only carpet manufacturer in the west. The intention was to capitalize on the fast-growing mass housing markets in British Columbia and Alberta through the manufacture of a relatively narrow range of tufted carpet products. Westmills commenced production in September of 1966 and by 1969 had sales of $2.4 million.

Early Growth

After some start-up difficulties, Westmills capitalized on the emerging popularity of shag carpet to fully establish its operations. Growth accelerated and facilities were expanded. In 1970, a distribution centre was opened in Winnipeg. In 1971, the Kelowna distribution facility was enlarged and sales were commenced in Ontario. In 1972, the capacity of the Kelowna plant was almost doubled.

The pace of activity increased even further in 1973 as the company moved to become a national manufacturer and distributor. "We felt we were an awfully clever carpet company," Derek Mather recalled, "and that we might as well be clever on a national scale."

In January 1973, Westmills acquired Globe Mills of Meaford, Ontario, in a move to reduce its dependence on outside yarn suppliers. In February, Westmills was converted to a public company. "This provided additional equity money for the company and an opportunity for the original investors to realize a profit," Mather explained. Financial statements for Westmills from 1973 onward are given in Exhibits 1 and 2.

Later in 1973, Westmills acquired the assets of Centennial Carpets in Trenton, Ontario. Further, to expand the company's marketing base, major exclusive distributors were appointed in Quebec and Ontario. By the end of 1973, Westmills had manufacturing plants in Kelowna, Meaford and Trenton and distribution facilities in Vancouver, Calgary, Winnipeg and Trenton.

"In retrospect it was overconfidence, but we felt awfully good about ourselves at that time," said Mather. Markets remained buoyant in early 1974. In Kelowna, however, the company was becoming entangled in changing political jurisdictions with different views and rules affecting plant effluent. Since this posed uncertainties and constraints on operation and expansion, a decision was made to move all dyeing operations to Calgary. This transfer to a purchased 13 000-square-foot plant was initiated during the year. Distribution in Calgary continued to be handled through a separate 8 000-square-foot facility. The fiscal year (to August 31, 1974) closed strong, with the company booking record sales and profits.

Decline

In the last quarter of 1974, the carpet market across Canada turned soft and Westmills' fortunes started to sag. For the first time, the company faced significant price and style competition and found itself overextended.

In 1975, the Kelowna plant was completely closed and all manufacturing equipment was moved to Calgary for installation on an ongoing basis in 1975 and early 1976. The Trenton manufacturing facility and distribution centre were also closed. Sales volumes were maintained near $22 million but gross margins slipped from 23.4 per cent in 1974 to 16.5 per cent in 1975 and a before-tax loss of $715 000 was incurred (Exhibit 1).

Markets remained soft in 1976 and Westmills further consolidated facilities and attempted to reduce costs. The Winnipeg distribution centre was closed; now all carpet manufacturing and distribution was handled out of Calgary. Cost reductions were hampered by the need to re-establish production with an untrained labour force earning in most cases $1.50 more per hour than workers in eastern mills; quality declined, deliveries became erratic, inventory grew and market credibility slipped. In fiscal year 1976, the company experienced a before-tax loss of $2.4 million.

Mather explained:

> Through this period we (the board) were slow to realize that there was something fundamentally wrong with the company and the way it was being run. The market problem, withdrawing from carpet manufacture in the east, and the plant relocation from Kelowna to Calgary, all confused our perception of the real situation.

Management Changes

As poor operation results continued, the Westmills board moved to strengthen management. Mather commented:

> Harry's [Harry Higson, the president] difficulty was in building a team; he couldn't develop strong men around him. As a result, he was working under tremendous pressure and his health was beginning to suffer. The scale of operation wasn't for him and he realized it. But improving management meant going outside. There was no one in a functional job that was near strong enough to step up.

Mr. Garry W. Morrison was hired as executive vice-president in late 1976. Morrison, aged 32, was an American citizen and now a Canadian landed immigrant. He held a B.Sc. in Textile Technology, an M.B.A. and had had seven years of management experience with U.S.-based Riegel Textile Corporation. At Riegel, Morrison had moved quickly through management ranks. Just prior to moving to Westmills, he had been a significant figure in the turnaround of a Canadian division of Riegel. His initial job at Westmills was to back up Harry Higson, but it was generally assumed he would become president in the not too distant future.

Morrison set out to learn the business, address some of the more pressing issues and recruit a second echelon of management.

OPERATING CHANGES From January through August 1977, steps were taken to improve Westmills' financial condition, to cut operating costs and to bolster the product line. The vacant Trenton and Kelowna plants were sold; the former for $915 000 cash and the latter for $200 000 cash plus mortgage receivable for $1 million. The cash proceeds were used to reduce Westmills' long-term indebtedness to its banks and the mortgage was assigned to the banks as additional security. Inventories were reduced by fiscal year-end to about $4.3 million in an attempt to reduce the pressure on interest costs and working-capital levels. Salaried and hourly personnel were cut and more stringent guidelines were introduced for administrative, travel and other expenses. Five new high-end commercial carpet lines and six new residential lines were designed and prepared for introduction in the fall selling season. This brought the total Westmills product range to 34 lines.

MANAGEMENT ADDITIONS In August 1977, Mr. J. William Ford joined Westmills as secretary-treasurer and chief financial officer. Ford, aged 33, was an American citizen and a Canadian landed immigrant. He was also married to a Canadian. He had known and worked with Garry Morrison at Riegel's Canadian subsidiary. Bill Ford's background included undergraduate and graduate studies in management at Virginia Polytechnic and Clemson University; service with the U.S. Army including combat experience and decoration in Vietnam; and experience in senior financial positions in two Canadian-based textile companies. Ford explained his move to Westmills: "Garry didn't pull any punches in describing the situation, but we'd been through a difficult turnaround before and I knew I could work with him. It seemed like a great challenge and opportunity."

At the time, Higson and Morrison were also engaged in negotiations with David Hirst, which would lead to Hirst joining Westmills as vice president of manufacturing in January 1978. Hirst, aged 54, was born in Yorkshire and educated in the U.K. at Batley Technical College (Textile Engineering) and Bradford Technical College (Cloth Manufacture). He had moved to Canada in 1957 and worked in a variety of carpet-mill plant supervisory and general management positions. Hirst was well known in technical circles in the industry and highly regarded for his capability in carpet design and particularly for designing around equipment constraints. Prior to committing to Westmills, David Hirst had visited Calgary to review the operation and recalled, "It was clear to me that there were also significant opportunities to improve productivity and quality. I welcomed the challenge."

A third senior manager was also hired by Westmills in this period to assume the top marketing position. By the time of the case, however, it was apparent that this appointment was not working out and that the marketing/sales function would have to be covered by James W. Hamilton, the current general sales manager. Hamilton, aged 36, had 18 years' experience in sales and sales management in the floorcovering business. He had started with Westmills in 1971 as a contract sales representative in Vancouver and shortly thereafter had been moved to Toronto to "open up" the east for Westmills. This he had done very successfully and after a short sales management stint with another company had been persuaded by Harry Higson to come back to Calgary and address the now apparent sales problems in the west. He had been general sales manager since mid-1976. Jim Hamilton knew the grassroots workings of the carpet business and had a reputation as a top-flight sales rep and sales manager.

For fiscal year 1977, however, there were no miracle cures. The year closed with another significant loss having to be booked—this time about $1.5 million pretax. Working capital was at a perilous level and the banks were becoming increasingly uneasy about their position. Now the financial as well as operating foundations of the business were deteriorating and the very survival of the firm was coming into question.

THE RECOVERY PLAN

Through the latter part of the 1976–77 fiscal year, Westmills had been working on a recovery plan, which took form at the beginning of the 1977–78 period. The essence of the plan was to reduce the company's product/market base somewhat, but maintain or improve volume by achieving greater penetration in the commercial and retail markets in western Canada. At the same time, steps would be taken to relieve financial pressure through the sale and lease-back of the Calgary plant. Projections for the 1978 fiscal year, which management regarded as conservative, are given in Exhibits 3 and 4. Significant parts of the new plan follow.

Marketing

In late 1977, Westmills distributed carpets through nearly 3 000 accounts across Canada, but primarily in the west. Geographic, customer type and product type segments, and Westmills' share therein, are given in Table 4.

TABLE 4 Westmills' Position in the Canadian Carpet Market, 1976

(volumes in millions of square metres)

| | | Western Market | | Eastern Market | |
	Retail	Residential Contract	Commercial Contract	All Segments	Total
All Product					
Volume	8.80	7.60	5.50	56.60	78.5
Westmills'					
Volume	0.51	1.76	0.25	0.80	3.32
Share (%)	5.80	23.10	4.60	1.40	4.20
Solid Colour					
Volume	4.40	4.60	1.80	n/a	
Westmills'					
Volume	0.40	1.41	0.20	n/a	
Share (%)	9.10	30.60	11.10	n/a	

Source: Company and casewriter's estimates.

Under the plan for 1977–78, sales in the west were to be emphasized. Representation would be maintained in Quebec, but at a minimum level. There was some anticipation of better results in Ontario through a new sales agency arranged by Garry Morrison. This latter activity had been debated in the company as not fully consistent with the western focus, but Morrison had prevailed, arguing that the incremental volume was essential.

SEGMENT AND PRODUCT EMPHASIS Westmills' traditional market in the west had been residential contracts. The new carpet lines mentioned previously had been developed as part of a program to increase Westmills' retail and commercial market penetration. Most were multi-coloured lines developed from pre-dyed acrylic-nylon blends. The reasons for emphasis on pre-dyed yarns in the new products were market preferences and the limitations of Westmills' post-tufting colouring capabilities. It should be noted that many dealers in the west serviced more than one and perhaps all three segments, although most had a particular emphasis in their trade. It was also true that certain carpet styles could suitably be used by purchasers in one or more of the segments. The ultimate market mix of a mill could thus be only roughly estimated.

As a complement to the new product lines, Westmills was readying a foam backing application process in the Calgary plant. Foam-backed carpet accounted for about 20 per cent of carpet sales by volume, and was particularly popular in lower-priced print and multicolour styles. Since foam-backed carpet was easier and less expensive to install than jute-backed carpet, it had a specific advantage in the "do-it-yourself" market and in certain residential contract applications. Westmills intended, at least initially, to put foam backing on selected current solid-colour lines to build volume at minimum incremental investment.

PROMOTION Westmills' sales force numbered 23 representatives, each covering a specified geographic territory or, in the major cities, a specific account list. The sales reps were paid a guaranteed minimum of $16 000, plus a commission which varied from 1 per cent to 3 per cent of sales, depending on the carpet line.

Each sales rep had a $200 per month car allowance and a travel and entertainment budget. The average gross earnings of the sales force were about $30 000. No changes were anticipated in the size or nature of the sales organization, although certain specific personnel adjustments were foreseen.

A major promotional expense was the cost of samples, sample kits, "waterfalls," etc., for use by the sales reps, in trade showrooms and in retail stores. While as much of the sample cost as possible was recovered from the trade, the net cost of sampling a new line was in the order of $50 000. Overall, sampling expense in 1976–77 was about $420 000. Only incidental amounts were spent on media advertising.

DELIVERY AND CUSTOMER SERVICE
Westmills' 8 000-square-foot Calgary distribution centre housed the majority of the finished goods inventory as well as the customer service and shipping departments. This facility had never operated to management's satisfaction and was believed to be the weak link responsible for mounting customer complaints about late or mistaken delivery. There were plans for 1977–78 to reduce the space used by half, to relocate personnel to the plant (making changes and reductions in the process) and to ship more goods directly from the plant. One objective of the move was to reduce finished goods inventory by $1 million.

Manufacturing

Westmills' manufacturing costs had recovered somewhat from the effects of relocation and the coincident plateauing of sales. Efficiency had improved through 1976–77, but costs were still about 20 per cent higher than those incurred by similar mills in the U.S. (after adjustments for differences in input costs).

A consultant hired by Westmills noted that the high costs in the plant were due to production scheduling problems, low equipment utilization (in dyeing) and inappropriate equipment utilization (in finishing). The production process, in short, was not as yet running in a smooth and balanced fashion. Regarding quality, the consultant commented:

> Off quality in manufacturing is approximately double what one would expect... Part of this may be due to operational reasons... some must be attributed to attempts to utilize substandard fibres and blends in the carpet yarns (creating problems at Globe as well as Calgary)... some is due to the high personnel turnover in Calgary.

While identifying these problems, Wilson noted that if Westmills could achieve the "U.S. level" costs it would be competitive with any mill in Canada and could dominate the west in the demand segments which fit its yarn and carpet production capabilities. The 1977–78 plan anticipated the following changes.

1. Reducing plant direct labour.
2. Shifting the product line to achieve greater utilization of Globe Mills' spinning capacity, and having Globe seek external contracts.
3. Implementing more stringent quality control, with the goal of reducing "second" yardage from 7 per cent to 4.5 per cent.
4. Changing certain dye and chemical formulations to cheaper equivalently effective materials.
5. Eliminating a 4 000-square-foot warehouse currently housing raw materials and off-quality or slow-selling goods.

The aggregate savings were forecast to be slightly more than $1 million on a volume base equivalent to 1976–77. Morrison wrote, "We are performing major surgery on our operations to reduce their size to conform with sales volumes dictated by the marketplace." Westmills would still retain the capacity, however, to produce about 4.6 million metres of carpet, provided there were no unusual product-mix demands.

Finance

As part of the recovery plan, Westmills was pursuing financial arrangements that would "reduce long-term debt, improve working capital and generally put us in a better situation financially." The main elements of this plan were the sale and lease-back of the Calgary plant and the discounting and sale of the Kelowna mortgage.

Discussions with potential purchasers of the Calgary plant indicated that a $3 million price might be acceptable, with a lease-back based on an 8–10 per cent capitalization rate. It was probable that one year's lease cost in advance would have to be maintained in a trust account. Negotiations were underway, with an anticipated closing in January or February 1978. Other discussions regarding the mortgage on the Kelowna property indicated that the mortgage might be sold for something in the order of $900 000 cash. It was anticipated that this, too, would close early in the new year.

THE CRUNCH

As Westmills moved through January and February of 1978, it became increasingly apparent that events were not unfolding as anticipated. Sales were substantially below forecast and losses were accumulating at a distressing rate (Exhibits 3 and 4). Garry Morrison had left the company to be replaced on an interim basis by Harry Higson. The company's plight became well known in the industry and it was losing credibility as a continuing supplier. Management was working, as Jim Hamilton put it, somewhere between desperation and chaos.

Westmills, seen from outside, was on the verge of collapse. Within the company the difficulties were recognized, but there was a resilience in management's attitude that offered at least the possibility of continuity and survival. The question they were asking was not whether, but how. An assessment by various managers of their areas of operation follows.

Marketing—Jim Hamilton

The problems Jim Hamilton was facing in the marketplace were, in simple form, credibility, both in the product and in reliability in quality and delivery "Right now," he said, "we have a terrible image in the market."

Credibility

Hamilton commented:

> Most of our accounts have been real good and have tried to support us; but they have heard rumours of us folding and they are really very concerned about the availability of goods. Some have come to us saying they just have to protect themselves by adding other suppliers. Others just won't do business with us; they say we are too shaky. Naturally our competitors are taking as much as they can and have kept prices real keen.

PRODUCT The new product programs had not met expectations. The foam-backed solid-colour carpets had encountered market and salesperson resistance and took an inordinate time to run in the plant. The new multi-colour retail lines had been based on yarn imported from the United States; the depreciation of the dollar had sharply increased materials costs, forcing Westmills into a noncompetitive situation. No Canadian supplier had the capacity to supply on a reliable basis. Further, there was resistance at the retail level to purchasing samples and inventories, at least in part because of Westmills' uncertain position. It was too early to evaluate the contract lines, as the selling cycle in this market was considerably longer.

In spite of these difficulties, as Hamilton notes, "We have a good basic line in solid-colour goods, particularly for residential contract. We make a good solid-colour fabric. What we don't have are reasonable upgrades to cover the higher price points."

QUALITY/DELIVERY RELIABILITY

Good intentions to the contrary, Westmills was not living up to its promises to customers. The "mechanics" of order processing, commitment, scheduling, production and shipping were, in Hamilton's words, the "worst ever." He commented, "We are missing delivery dates and we are having quality problems; we have had to issue a pile of credit notes for problems we have created. I have a 4 000-square-foot warehouse full of seconds to dispose of. How do I do this without upsetting the market?"

As a result of the foregoing, Hamilton was having trouble with sales-force morale. "There has been a tendency in this company to treat salesmen as a necessary evil anyway," he noted, "and now we aren't giving them product and service. How am I supposed to keep good men?"

Manufacturing—David Hirst

In the plant, Hirst was confronted with problems of morale, production scheduling and control, and product quality. His first test was immediate: on the very day he arrived in Calgary for work (having moved his family across the country), Garry Morrison had announced his resignation as president, to the surprise of all.

MORALE

There was a bad morale problem in the plant, David Hirst noted, stemming from inadequate direction and control of work and further instability rising from concerns that there was "every possibility... (we)... may not be there tomorrow."

In his first weeks at the plant, Hirst had had a chance to assess his supervisory staff and was quite pleased, with the exception of one or two areas where he anticipated making changes. But overall he felt he could build on the strengths and experience of these people and that the problems being experienced were more the result of the context they had been working in than of particular personal shortcomings. In light of this assessment, Hirst felt his first priority was to earn the respect of the plant personnel, establish that one person was in control and from this foundation isolate and address the operating problems.

PRODUCTION SCHEDULING

The production scheduling of Westmills had fallen into progressive disarray as market pressures, new-product development, quality problems and financing difficulties had accumulated, driving operations into a vicious circle of deterioration. Hirst commented, "We are dealing in chaos...the tufters are being scheduled on the spot by telephone calls, slips of paper that people walk in with...there is no way we can operate efficiently like this...sales and customer service just don't see the costs...how can they make the promises they do?" Such were the difficulties of coordination between sales, customer service, manufacturing and delivery that one sales rep had recently verified that an order he had placed for 2 500 square metres of carpet had, quite simply, been lost.

The key to manufacturing efficiency in a carpet plant, Hirst pointed out, was proper scheduling and integration of equipment loads through the entire production process. This was quite impossible in the current circumstances and it was essential, as he put it, "to reduce the interference factors."

QUALITY

The sources of product quality problems were not all known but there appeared to be three principal contributing factors: the quality of the incoming yarns from Globe Mills, certain product designs, and deficiencies in training and experience in Calgary.

The limitations of Globe Mills had not been fully appreciated or considered in some product designs, with the result that it was stretching its capabilities to make certain yarns. Hirst, among others, agreed that Globe did a good job on yarns within its range and that the core problem was one of not balancing capabilities and efficiency in Globe and Calgary when designing fabrics.

Certain product designs, as well, were ill-fitted to the Calgary plant. An internal memo commented that one of the new multi-colour lines "makes our inadequacy in the multi-coloured area only too evident."

On training and experience, Hirst noted that "Calgary is not exactly a textile centre and there is little access to trained workers." Westmills was thus forced to hire in a booming, resource-based economy with the attendant high wage-rates and worker mobility. Substantial progress had been made in developing a stable work force, but it was clear from the kind of problems arising from the plant floor that a great deal of training and experience were yet necessary.

Hirst weighed the circumstances:

> Sure we have problems. We have limitations in our equipment in Meaford and Calgary. But, with the exception of multi-colour, we can produce volume and quality and make carpets that sell. We can do more than has been done with what we have now. I guess, coming from Yorkshire, if that's all you have, use it well. The job can be done...I have no reservations.

Control and Finance—Bill Ford

In early 1978, Bill Ford was working to improve the quality and use of the company's information systems and at the same time doing battle day-to-day for cash to meet immediate obligations.

INFORMATION SYSTEMS On arriving at Westmills, Ford had reviewed the control and financial systems and found that "a lot of good things had been started, but they were still in a half-finished state." The computer facility had been applied to the financial side of the business for such tasks as payroll and receivables accounting and financial reporting. These areas, he felt, were in pretty good shape.

The problems lay more in the lack of development and use of operating and cost accounting systems. Here there were shortcomings in most areas, from order entry through manufacturing cost control to inventory control. The general frame-work for a workable system was in place but the actual work being done was not up to a reasonable standard in either effectiveness or efficiency. The matter was further complicated by a lack of understanding and communication between accounting and the line managers and supervision. "There was a problem of attitude and capabilities both inside and outside the accounting department," Ford noted, "and it has been necessary to change some personnel and segment the general and management accounting functions." Work was proceeding to improve the control system, but in the prevailing circumstances progress had been fairly slow.

CASH FLOW Westmills' cash position in early 1978 was so tight that Bill Ford was personally monitoring all receipts and approving all disbursements. The noose was drawing tighter every day.

On the receipts side, sales were down and collections were becoming more difficult. To prop up sales, credit had been granted in questionable circumstances. Difficulties with deliveries and quality claims had led to a flurry of credit notes being granted in the field, which meant a very complicated reconciliation of accounts. Some accounts were deferring payment until such matters were clarified; others, sensing weakness, were simply being very slow to pay. On the payables side, suppliers were getting tougher about terms and some had put Westmills on COD for orders incremental to existing balances.

Ford described the situation: "I'm in daily discussions with the banks. They are very skeptical and very close to pulling the plug. If they did now, my guess is that they might end up 10–15 per cent out of pocket. They have asked for a meeting within the next few days."

Derek Mather and CED

Derek Mather, aged 45, had started his business career as an investment analyst for Sun Life Assurance Co. In 1962 he had joined CED as an investment officer and was currently senior vice-president. In his time at CED, Mather had been involved in recruiting and screening new corporate ventures and the monitoring of venture investments. He had been a member of Westmills' board of directors since 1967. These jobs, he pointed out, had not brought him into direct operating management.

> I see my own involvement as a dubious solution...a solution with many flaws. Although I've been on the board for many years, I don't know the industry from a technical standpoint, nor do I know the market particularly well. I don't have the high level of skills in the business which I think financial people, considering an investment, would demand.

The countervailing problem at the moment was the expected difficulty of finding an experienced and credible presidential candidate. Mather commented, "I don't think we've got a hope of finding a guy like that in this present environment. I think whatever solution we are able to work out at this time...and by that I mean the next few days...will be a patchwork solution...if we were to go out and try to hire a new man we'd just be wasting our time." He continued, "It may be, from a banker's point of view, that if CED is prepared to supply additional equity capital and personnel, then that degree of shareholder commitment would be impressive."

CED was currently Westmills' major shareholder, holding approximately 40 per cent of the 1 100 984 common shares issued and $402 000 worth of the $1.144 million in unsecured convertible debentures (convertible to common shares at $2.50). Westmills common stock was currently trading on the Toronto Stock Exchange at from $.70 to $.90.

On CED's future involvement, Mather and Gerald Sutton, CED's president, were of one mind: within reason, CED must stick with the investment and do what was necessary to revive the company. Sutton explained, "We took Westmills public and in so doing reduced our holdings, recaptured our initial investment and made a profit. Under the circumstances we can't just withdraw from this situation; we have a moral responsibility to the public." Mather added, "The business community in the west knows we started this company...we can't have them say we walked away when times got tough."

E X H I B I T 1 Westmills' Consolidated Operating Results for Fiscal Years Ending August 31

($000s)

	1977	1976	1975	1974	1973
Net sales	$21 678	$23 056	$21 725	$22 823	$14 407
Cost of sales	17 886	19 594	17 506	17 098	10 622
Depreciation	712	660	638	347	188
Total	18 598	20 254	18 144	17 445	10 810
Gross margin	3 080	2 802	3 581	5 378	3 597
%	14.2%	12.1%	16.5%	23.4%	25.0%
Marketing expenses	2 625	2 478	2 141	3 063	1 933
Administration	876	900	610	—	—
Financing:					
Long-term	756	681	597	309	133
Short-term	308	514	333	156	37
Extraordinary costs	—	635	615	—	—
Total	4 565	5 208	4 296	3 528	2 103
Net income before tax	(1 485)	(2 406)	(715)	1 849	1 494
Income tax	(305)	(361)	(309)	798	651
Net income	(1 180)	(2 045)	(405)	1 051	842
Extraordinary items	314	—	96	96	—
Net profit	(866)	(2 045)	(309)	1 147	842

Source: Company documents.

EXHIBIT 2   Westmills' Consolidated Balance Sheets for Fiscal Years Ending August 31

($000s)

	1977	1976	1975	1974	1973
Current Assets					
Cash	$	$	$	$ 77	$ 169
Accounts receivable	3 880	3 874	4 506	3 480	2 337
Inventories	4 584	6 198	5 316	6 033	3 857
Prepaid expenses	253	227	169	168	173
Income taxes recoverable	—	—	354	—	—
	8 717	10 296	10 345	9 757	6 536
Current Liabilities					
Short-term borrowings	4 497	4 230	2 576	2 463	421
Accounts payable, accrued liabilities	2 458	2 796	3 421	3 279	2 164
Income and other taxes	195	255	236	231	519
Current portion, LT debt	470	402	397	653	442
	7 620	7 683	6 630	6 626	3 546
Working capital	1 097	2 613	3 715	3 131	2 990
Net fixed assets	6 644[1]	7 811	8 075	7 841	3 887
	$ 7 741	$10 424	$11 790	$10 972	$ 6 877
Long-term debt[2]	4 989	6 500	5 461	4 459	4 873
Deferred income taxes	408	713	1 074	948	586
Shareholders' equity:					
Common stock	3 362	3 362	3 362	3 362	3 362
Retained earnings	(1 018)	(151)	1 893	2 203	1 056
	$ 7 741	$10 424	$11 790	$10 972	$ 6 877

[1] Includes mortgage receivable of $1 000 000 on sale of Kelowna plant.
[2] The structure of the long-term debt as of August 31, 1977 was as follows:

9.5% First mortgage on land and buildings; payments $9 000 per month, including interest	$1 017 950
Term bank loans at 1.5% over prime; payments $30 000 per month plus interest. Secured by assignment of mortgage receivable plus a charge on land, buildings and equipment	$1 556 000
12% Series A debentures, due 1980; payments $22 000 per month including interest. Secured by charge on land, buildings and equipment ranking with bank term loan	$1 444 775
12% Convertible, redeemable unsecured debentures. Series A and B Semi-annual interest	$1 441 000
	$5 459 725
Less current portion of long-term debt	$ 470 705
	$4 989 020

Source: Company documents.

E X H I B I T 3 Westmills' Forecast Profit and Actual Experience, 1977–78

($000s)

	Recovery Plan Pds 1–6	Forecast FY 1978	Estimated Actual Pds. 1–6
Square metres (000s)	1 550	3 340	1 230
Net sales	$10 217	$ 22 138	$ 7 966
Cost of sales	8 712	18 611	6 888
Gross margin	1 505	3 527	1 078
Percent net sales	14.7%	15.9%	13.6%
Marketing	968	2 029	893
Administration	412	871	432
Finance-interest	415	777	461
Total	1 795	3 677	1 786
Operating income (loss)	(290)	(150)	(708)
Taxes recoverable	(96)	(201)	(106)
Income (loss before extraordinary items)	(194)	51	(602)
Extraordinary Items:			
Sale of mortgage (net)	(48)	(48)	—
Sale of plant (net)	92	892	—
Income tax recovery	356	356	—
Net profit (loss)	$ 1 006	$ 1 251	$ (602)

EXHIBIT 4   Westmills' Balance Sheet Forecasts and Actual Experience, 1977–78

($000s)

	Recovery Plan Forecast		Estimated Actual
	End Period 6	*End 1978 FY*	*End Period 6*
Current Assets			
Accounts receivable	$4 750	$4 500	$4 191
Trust account	300	300	—
Inventories:			
Raw material	1 600	1 600	1 355
Work in process	650	650	1 087
Finished goods	1 425	1 176	1 947
Total inventory	3 675	3 426	4 389
Prepaid expenses	225	316	156
Total current assets	8 950	8 632	8 736
Mortgage	—	—	1 000
Net fixed assets	3 691	3 495	5 427
Total	$12 641	$12 127	$15 163
Liabilities & Shareholders' Equity			
Bank indebtedness	5 501	4 507	5 701
Accounts payable	1 847	2 198	1 943
Taxes payable	225	214	220
Current portion:			
Long-term debt	—	—	470
Current liabilities	7 573	6 919	8 334
Long-term debt	1 441	1 441	4 785
Deferred taxes	278	173	302
Shareholders' Equity:			
Common shares	3 362	3 362	3 362
Retained earnings	(13)	232	(1 620)
Total	$12 641	$12 127	$15 163

HIRAM WALKER-GOODERHAM & WORTS (A)

Joseph N. Fry

In 1985, Hiram Walker-Gooderham & Worts (Hiram Walker) was one of the world's largest and most profitable producers of distilled spirits. Hiram Walker's five key brands—Canadian Club Canadian whisky, Ballantine's Scotch whisky, Courvoisier cognac, and Kahlua and Tia Maria coffee liqueurs—were sold internationally and held strong positions in their individual categories. Revenues were steady at about $1.5 billion, yielding consistent after tax returns of between 15 per cent and 16 per cent on invested capital. Hiram Walker's recently appointed President and Chief Executive Officer, H. Clifford Hatch Jr.,

IVEY

Joseph N. Fry prepared this case solely to provide material for class discussion. The author does not intend to illustrate either effective or ineffective handling of a managerial situation. The author may have disguised certain names and other identifying information to protect confidentiality.

Ivey Management Services prohibits any form of reproduction, storage or transmittal of this material without its written permission. This material is not covered under authorization from CanCopy or any other reproduction rights organization. To order copies or request permission to reproduce materials, contact Ivey Publishing, Ivey Management Services c/o Richard Ivey School of Business, The University of Western Ontario, London, Ontario, Canada, N6A 3K7; phone (519) 661-3208; fax (519) 661-3882; e-mail cases@ivey.uwo.ca was pleased with the company's performance and impatient to build on its prosperity: "We have done a great job with profitability...but we want to grow, and we have yet to show results in this area...we have to work this out, how are we going to grow?"

THE WORLD DISTILLED SPIRITS BUSINESS

Achieving growth would not be easy. World consumption of distilled spirits had peaked in recent years, and was now in slow decline. Shifting consumer tastes and aggressive competitive activity were threatening traditional product and brand positions. Market share had become a major source of growth and power, triggering a consolidation of producer and distributor structures. Observers expected these trends to continue, and to create unprecedented opportunities and risks for industry participants.

Demand

From a global perspective, the demand for spirit products and brands was highly fragmented. Product preferences varied widely by country market in relation to local traditions, tastes and pricing. And within markets these same factors often led to a broad distribution of brand preferences across local brands and global brands, which may or may not be locally produced (e.g., Smirnoff vodka, Bacardi rum), and global brands with unique national sources (e.g., Scotch whisky, cognac). Statistics for selected spirits product categories and country markets are presented in Exhibit 1.

In most country markets, domestic demand was served largely by local production. The reasons for this, which varied in importance by market, included unique national tastes, production and distribution economics, and government protection. The residual import volumes, which amounted to about 15 per cent of world demand, were still significant, however, and crucial to the exporters of unique source products.

The United States was widely regarded as the most attractive of the world's spirits markets. The U.S. market accounted for about 22 per cent of total world spirits demand and about 46 per cent of world imports, and it was relatively open to competitive innovation. Thereafter the opportunities represented by specific markets dropped rapidly in magnitude, and became dependent on a wide variety of specific local conditions.

Competition

In spite of on-going consolidation, competitive concentration in the spirits industry was still quite low. In the U.S., for example, 30 brands sold over 1 000 000 cases per year, and the top 60 brands, sold by 24 different firms, held only 60 per cent of the market. There were very large firms in the industry, of course. Table 1 lists the sales, profits and growth rates of the top 18 companies. In spite of their scale, however, these firms probably accounted for less than 40 per cent of world spirit sales. The balance of business was done by virtually dozens of smaller competitors.

The emergence of intense competition had been an unsettling development for many participants in the spirits business. They were used to dealing in what was historically known as a gentleman's trade. Now they were engaged in an all-out battle, in which the major weapons were aggressive new product and brand marketing, forward integration to control distribution, and acquisitions to balance and expand product portfolios.

TABLE 1 Top 18 International Spirits Firms,[1] 1985

(US$000 000s)

	Sales	Operating Income	Sales Growth (%)	
Distillers Co. (UK)	$1 600	$293	5.2	(81–85)
Seagram (Canada, U.S.)	2 821	246	0.4	(81–85)
Hiram Walker (Canada)	1 102	213	0.9	(81–85)
Grand Metropolitan (UK)	1 319	181	18.7	(80–84)
Brown-Forman (U.S.)	905	167	4.1	(81–85)
Heublein (U.S.)	N/A	152	N/A	
Bacardi (Bahamas)	950	150	8.0	(80–84)
Moet-Hennessy (France)	597	120	25.2	(80–84)
Allied-Lyons (UK)	1 334[2]	85	7.1	(81–85)
Pernod-Ricard (France)	581	78	–2.1	(80–84)
Schenley (U.S.)	416	48	–11.7	(80–84)
Arthur Bell (UK)	305	48	5.0	(80–84)
Martell (France)	236	38	18.0	(80–84)
Whitbread (UK)	672	34	N/A	
National (U.S.)	648	28	–2.8	(81–83)
Wm. Grant (UK)	101	19	7.9	(81–83)
Remy Martin (France)	110	16	11.4	(80–84)
Suntory (Japan)	2 191	N/A	–7.4	(83–85)

[1] Estimates for spirits and wine divisions where possible.
[2] Includes wines, spirits and soft drinks.

Source: Hiram Walker records.

Marketing

The great strength of the multinational firms was in their ability to build and support global brands. Their established premium brands provided very attractive returns and were protected from attack to some degree by traditional tastes and habits, and, in most countries, government regulations that limited advertising, sampling, price promotion and so on. Even when a traditional brand was affected by new developments, its decline was more a matter of erosion than critical failure. There was another side to this, of course. It was very difficult to grow in these mature, competitive markets. New product launches were expensive, time-consuming and risky. Similarly, campaigns to capture market share by the further penetration of current markets or geographic expansion required long-term thinking and a willingness to make risky investments.

Competitive innovation in the industry was focused on three fronts. The first was the introduction, often by local producers or distributors, of low-priced brands into traditional categories. The second was the search and exploitation of niches as demand in the mature categories fragmented—such as in the promotion of single-malt Scotch whiskies. The third was in the pursuit of "new" categories, like those in the liqueurs business in the U.S., where there was a constant parade of new formulas and flavours—from peach, to kiwi, to root beer. Collectively these efforts created considerable turmoil in the industry, and chipped away at the traditional brand leaders.

Forward Integration

There were two basic channels of distribution for distilled spirits. In the monopoly markets, which included 18 American states, Canada and the northern European countries, spirits products were sold by a producer or import agency directly to government distribution organizations.

In the open markets, which accounted for the majority of industry revenue, two- and three-tier channel structures were common—involving producer sales companies and/or import agencies, distributors, and retailers.

In the open markets the proportion of sales through retail chain organizations was increasing. This had stimulated the development of fewer and larger distributors. Producers were facing increasing demands for marketing support, price concessions and private brands, and were finding it more difficult to keep channel attention on marginal brands.

One of the producer responses to increasing channel power was forward integration through the purchase of channel units. There was by no means a consensus in the industry that this was a wise move. It was expensive, took distillers beyond their traditional expertise, and could result in channel conflict. Nevertheless, many of the major firms were moving in this direction.

Horizontal Diversification

A number of major firms were pursuing acquisitions to diversify and to achieve greater market power. These included steps to diversify (1) outside the alcoholic beverage industry, such as with Seagram's purchase of a major position in DuPont; (2) across the major product classes within the alcoholic beverage industry, such as with Guinness' (a brewer) acquisition of Bell's (whisky) and takeover bid for Distillers (mainly spirits); and (3) across product categories within distilled spirits, such as with Hiram Walker's acquisition of Tia Maria. There was agreement throughout the industry that acquisition activity would accelerate in the coming years.

HIRAM WALKER'S BACKGROUND

In 1856, Hiram Walker crossed the Detroit river from Michigan, and built a distillery in the raw timberland on the Canadian side. The company grew, and a small community called Walkerville developed around the distillery. In the 1870s, Walker was the first to brand a Canadian whisky, calling his premium product Canadian Club.

Hiram Walker died in 1899, and his family managed the firm for the next quarter century. In 1926, Harry C. Hatch organized the purchase of Hiram Walker from the family, and merged its operations with those of the Toronto-based Gooderham & Worts distillery. The new company was in an ideal position to benefit from the prohibition laws in force at the time in the U.S. Spirits could not legally be produced or sold in America, but if products made and sold in Canada found their way south, well, so be it.

By the end of prohibition in 1934, Canadian whisky in the U.S. market had become a preferred drink beyond all previous measure. Canadian distillers such as Hiram Walker and Seagram moved quickly to consolidate their gains, and to establish new and now legal distribution and sales organizations.

Over time Hiram Walker added to its key brand portfolio, and broadened its geographic sales coverage. The major brand acquisitions were Ballantine's (1935), Tia Maria (49 per cent in 1954, increased to 100 per cent in 1984), Courvoisier (1964), and Kahlua (1964). Under Harry Hatch's son, H. Clifford Hatch, who became president in 1964, Hiram Walker developed the potential of these brands, grew profitably, and became a truly multinational operation.

Hiram Walker Resources

In response to the threat of a takeover, Hiram Walker was merged in 1980 with Consumers Gas and its subsidiary Home Oil to form what was ultimately known as Hiram Walker Resources (HWR). The new company encountered some early and serious difficulties with a major resource investment, but by 1985 it had recovered and was regarded as a healthy management company with holdings, as outlined in Table 2.

T A B L E 2 Hiram Walker Resources Holdings, 1985

($000 000s)

	Identifiable Assets	Revenue	Operating Earnings
Distilled spirits	$ 1 511	$ 1 516	$ 282
Natural resources	2 052	482	167
Gas utility	1 634	1 767	216
Other investment	551		
Total	$ 5 748	$ 3 765	$ 665

Source: Hiram Walker Resources Ltd. *Annual Report*, 1985.

T A B L E 3 Hiram Walker Five-Year Performance Summary

(C$000 000s)

Fiscal Year Ending August 31	1985	1984	1983	1982	1981
Sales:					
Cases (000s)	20 780	20 616	20 575	21 899	22 975
Revenue	$ 1 504.8	$ 1 437.4	$ 1 394.5	$ 1 435.8	$ 1 435.9
Gross Margin	695.6	659.2	623.6	623.7	624.1
%	46.2	45.9	44.7	43.4	43.5
Operating income	291.2	294.5	290.3	320.8	294.0
Net (after tax) operating income	176.4	169.1	175.1	189.6	N/A
Invested capital*	1 171.5	1 089.1	1 059.4	1 199.2	N/A
Return on average invested capital (%)	15.6	15.7	15.5	15.6	N/A

* Invested capital was comprised of current, net fixed and other assets less non-bank current obligations and deferred income taxes. This is a different concept than "identifiable assets" as used in Table 2. Other smaller accounting differences explain the discrepancies in revenues and income numbers between Tables 2 and 3.

Source: Company records.

Hiram Walker's Role in HWR

Hiram Walker was a significant contributor to HWR earnings. Hiram Walker's revenue and profit trends were essentially flat, however, as shown in Table 3. Up to very recently the company had not been encouraged to grow by acquisition. A new and provisional role statement had opened the acquisition avenue, although Cliff Hatch Jr. noted that there was no particular pressure from HWR's board to pursue it because "they are more interested in the energy business." HWR's position was that:

> Hiram Walker is responsible for all HWR's distilled spirits and wine business. Requiring only small capital expenditures, Hiram Walker provides HWR with high levels of cash flow that can be used for additional investment. Hiram Walker is expected to maintain its relative industry strength with high steady return on invested capital of 16–18 per cent from its current brands and assets. In addition, Hiram Walker is expected to capitalize on industry rationalization and propose profitable beverage alcohol acquisitions of at least $250 million within the next five years.

HIRAM WALKER'S STRATEGIC POSITION

In 1985, Hiram Walker operations encompassed production plants, marketing units and investments throughout the world. The company's key brands accounted for over 60 per cent of Hiram Walker's revenues, and over 70 per cent of profit contribution after direct selling expenses. Geographically, the U.S. accounted for about 60 per cent of corporate revenues. The strategic positions of the key brands are outlined below. A summary of sales trends is presented in Exhibit 2.

Canadian Club

Canadian Club was Hiram Walker's historic flagship brand. It was produced and bottled in Canada for domestic and international sale. The brand's primary market was in the U.S. There, for years, Canadian Club and its archrival, Seagram's V.O., had dominated the Canadian whisky business. Of late, however, both brands had been losing ground to lower-priced entries, such as Canadian Mist and Windsor Supreme, which were imported in bulk from Canada. The loss of nearly a million cases of volume each over the past five years had left Hiram Walker and Seagram with significant problems of balancing current production levels and maturing stock inventories. Seagram had to some extent buffered its V.O. sales decline by the successful promotion of its super premium Crown Royal brand. Until 1985, however, there was no Hiram Walker entry in this category.

The strength of Canadian Club was with older, traditional whisky drinkers who, unfortunately, represented a declining market base. To revitalize the brand, Hiram Walker was shifting its marketing focus toward younger, upscale adults. The total advertising approach was being changed, and spending levels were being increased somewhat. Furthermore, a super premium brand, Canadian Club Classic, was being introduced to support and extend the brand range.

Ballantine's

Ballantine's was the world's fourth largest selling brand of Scotch whisky, after Johnny Walker, J&B and Bell's. Ballantine's was strong in continental Europe and selected markets throughout the world. It was weak, however, in the U.K. and U.S., which together represented about 50 per cent of the world's Scotch whisky consumption.

Hiram Walker expected Ballantine's to show volume increases of a little less than 2 per cent per year through 1990. To this point Hiram Walker had not attacked the U.K. because of a very competitive and relatively low-profit market environment there. Further, in the U.S., Hiram Walker was unhappy with its current distribution arrangements. These were in the hands of an independent distributor who had been under contract since 1938. The company had yet to find a satisfactory resolution for this situation.

Courvoisier

Courvoisier's share of the cognac market had varied over time from a low of 12 per cent in 1965 to a high of 21 per cent in 1975, at which point it was the leading brand in the industry. Courvoisier's position had fallen more recently to 15.3 per cent, placing it third behind Hennessy and Martell. Geographically, Courvoisier was strong in the U.K. and U.S., but relatively weak in continental Europe and the Far East.

The drop in Courvoisier's share was attributed to product development and marketing spending problems. Courvoisier had been late with new super premium qualities and package formats. This problem was now being addressed. There was a continuing issue, however, with respect to the unprecedentedly high marketing spending of Hennessy and Martell, which Courvoisier, to this point, had been reluctant to match. Striking a trade-off between profit and market share was a key strategic issue for the brand.

Kahlua

Kahlua was Hiram Walker's most profitable brand. It was a premium priced coffee liqueur produced in Mexico and sold primarily in the U.S. and Canada.

Hiram Walker's Los Angeles-based Maidstone Wine & Spirits organization had capitalized on Kahlua's versatility to build a strong position in the liqueur market. Kahlua was marketed variously as a traditional liqueur, as a spirit to be used in a mixed drink (e.g., with milk in the "Brown Cow" or vodka in the "Black Russian"), or as a flavouring in a host of cooking applications. Kahlua's position was now being challenged directly by low-price imitators, and indirectly by the emergence of rapidly changing taste fads for liqueurs and liqueur-based drinks.

In Hiram Walker's view, the major growth opportunities for Kahlua were outside the U.S. and Canada. Here there were two as yet unresolved positioning issues: whether Kahlua would be sold as a traditional liqueur or as a multiple-use product, and how the potential positioning and distribution overlap with Tia Maria should be handled.

Tia Maria

Tia Maria was a coffee-based liqueur produced in Jamaica. Tia Maria's traditional positioning was as an upscale, imported, classic liqueur product. Its prime market's were the U.S., Canada and the U.K. The brand was faltering in all of these markets, however, as a result, it was thought, of inadequate focus and effort, shifts in liqueur market tastes, and the ambiguity (in the U.S. and Canada) of positioning and emphasis relative to Kahlua.

The strategic issues facing Tia Maria were those of revitalizing the brand in its key markets, and developing distribution in other markets, particularly in western Europe. The latter efforts would be particularly complicated since Tia Maria, by itself, was in a relatively weak bargaining position in seeking distribution. It needed to be allied with other brands, but such natural allies as Ballantine's might not be available if, for example, Ballantine's and Kahlua were combined together in another distribution portfolio.

HIRAM WALKER'S ORGANIZATION

Hiram Walker was run through a functional management structure of production, marketing, financial and administrative units (Exhibit 3). This structure reflected a long-standing management philosophy of engaging top management in critical strategic and operating issues. Decisions involving brand strategy, price, image, packaging and labelling, distributor representation, trade practices production levels, quality assurance, and so on, were made at Walkerville.

The top management group at Hiram Walker's consisted of Cliff Hatch Jr., Jim Ferguson, Jim Ford, John Giffen, Steve McCann and Ian Wilson-Smith. Short biographies of each are given in Table 4. Ferguson, Giffen and Wilson-Smith each headed up functional units as outlined in Exhibit 3. At the time of the case there was no corporate level marketing head. This role was being covered by Cliff Hatch Jr. Ford and McCann, both company veterans, were responsible, respectively, for the Courvoisier and Ballantine's supplier companies.

T A B L E 4 Hiram Walker's Senior Management

H. Clifford Hatch Jr., 44, was a native of Windsor, Ontario, and a graduate of McGill University and the Harvard Business School. He joined Hiram Walker in 1970, and in 1976 was appointed CEO of Corby Distilleries Ltd. (a Canadian firm in which Hiram Walker held a majority interest). In 1979, he became corporate vice-president for marketing of Hiram Walker, and became president and CEO in 1983.

James P. Ferguson, 49, was born in Landis, Saskatchewan, and earned a degree from McGill University. He worked for several years with the accountancy firm of Price Waterhouse, and joined Hiram Walker in 1974. He was currently corporate vice-president for finance and treasurer of the company.

James D.N. Ford, 49, was raised in Glasgow, Scotland, and was a graduate of the University of Glasgow and a chartered accountant. He joined Courvoisier in 1965, and moved to Canada in 1968 as controller of Hiram Walker and later vice-president. He returned to Courvoisier in 1980, and presently was head of French operations.

John A. Giffen, 47, came from Ingersoll, Ontario, and held B.Sc. (Engineering) and M.B.A. degrees from the University of Windsor. He became Hiram Walker's corporate vice-president for production in 1980.

W. Steve McCann, 64, was a native of Edinburgh, Scotland, where he received his education and became a chartered accountant. He joined Hiram Walker in the Ballantine's organization, and became managing director of the Scottish operations in 1971.

Ian M. Wilson-Smith, 52, was born in Middlesex, England, and was a graduate of Cambridge University. His early experience was in production with Harveys of Bristol England, and later in production and general management positions with other firms in the beverage alcohol business in England and Canada. He joined Hiram Walker in 1980, and was currently corporate vice-president for administration.

The Marketing Units

Hiram Walker International and the American and Canadian sales companies were the primary marketing units. They were responsible, within their territories and for assigned brands, for proposing marketing strategies and budgets, building distributor relationships and achieving sales targets. Special marketing services for legal, packaging, research and other needs were provided by Walkerville staff groups. Revenues and direct marketing expenses were directly attributable to each of the line marketing units, and further analysis of profitability was possible after allocating product and other costs.

The Supply Units

The supplier units, such as Courvoisier, were responsible for product availability, quality and cost and, depending on the situation, performed local accounting and administrative functions. The supply unit heads in North America, with the exception of wine operations, reported to John Giffen. Those in Europe reported directly to Cliff Hatch Jr., although the European units drew on technical assistance from John Giffen's groups. Wine operations, which were relatively small by Hiram Walker standards, reported to Ian Wilson-Smith, who had a special interest and expertise in this area. The supplier units were essentially cost centres, although profitability could be assessed by the attribution of revenues and marketing costs.

Formal Integration

The annual budgeting process was the primary vehicle for tying the marketing and supply units together. Budgets were initiated by the marketing units, reviewed and extended by the supplier units, and approved at the corporate level. In practice this was a complicated process. Hiram Walker International, for example, had to deal with forecasts and marketing budgets for a number of brands across a range of countries, distributors and currencies. Further, as the planning process progressed, Hiram Walker International had to strike agreements with the supplier units, whose interests—in brand progress, capacity utilization, operational stability, and so on—were not always consistent with the marketing view. Finally all of this had to be assembled by marketing units across suppliers, and by supplier units across sales entities for corporate review.

Over the years the budget process had become increasingly complicated and time-consuming. This was the result of more complex operations and the tendencies of senior managers to micro-manage the operating units. John Harcarufka, head of W.A. Taylor in the U.S., would note, for example, that he had more autonomy in pricing and promoting Drambuie, an agency brand, than he did for Courvoisier. With the latter, he had to negotiate detailed approvals two ways, as he put it, with both Courvoisier in France and corporate marketing in Walkerville. There was also a strong feeling within the operating units that "Walkerville's" requests for information were too frequent, too detailed, occasionally unrealistic, and often unnecessary.

At the corporate level, the primary formal groups for coordinating the functional units were the management and strategic planning committees. The management committee consisted of Hatch, Giffen, Ferguson and Wilson-Smith; it met formally on a regular basis to consider corporate issues, and to review the proposals and performance of the marketing and supply units.

Informal Integration

A great deal of the burden of coordinating Hiram Walker activities was accomplished informally, by old hands working together. Hiram Walker took pride in the long service of its people, and in their development and advancement. The company promoted from within whenever possible; most of the top and middle management positions were filled by individuals who had worked their way up from entry-level positions.

The management committee members worked together very closely. Their working relationships were strengthened by their long experience in the industry, the traditions of the company, and even by the relatively small size and isolation of corporate headquarters. Formal systems and meetings aside, it was perhaps more important for the running of the company that these managers met casually and frequently in the course of the day, in their offices, at lunch in the executive dining room, and in business and social entertaining.

The members of the management committee comprised the first circle of internal influence on corporate affairs. The second level included Jim Ford and Steve McCann who, in spite of distance, maintained a fairly high level of interaction with the Walkerville group through membership on the strategic planning committee, phone, correspondence and travel. The second circle might also have included David Evans, head of Hiram Walker International, except that he had only recently (1981) joined the company from Nestlé, and had not had the same opportunity to work with the Walkerville executives. The third circle of influence consisted of perhaps eight to ten executives, most of whom were marketing unit heads in North America and Europe.

Strategic Planning

Formal strategic planning at Hiram Walker was coordinated by a strategic planning committee consisting of the members of the management committee plus Ford and McCann. This committee met annually for two or three days to consider issues of corporate direction and priority, and to review progress in specific project areas such as acquisitions. On an informal basis, it served as a sounding board for most corporate initiatives.

For years Hiram Walker had based its forward planning on five-year rolling forecasts submitted by the operating units. These were discussed with Walkerville, adjusted where necessary, and used as the based for corporate financial and production forecasts. This forecast system was still in use, although top management was concerned that it placed too much reliance on a projection of the status quo. The February 1985, corporate forecast submitted to HWR projected 1989 revenues from continuing operations of $1 925 million and operating income of $350 million.

To remedy the limitations of existing procedures, the strategic planning committee started in 1982 to introduce a new strategic planning process. The aim was to push strategic thinking as far down the organization as possible—corporate management would be responsible for developing strategic guidelines and conducting reviews, while the unit managers would be responsible for proposing and implementing strategy for their operations. The process was tied to the existing organizational units, but strategy reviews were separated from forecast/budget activities.

The new process was slow to take hold. In spite of adjustments to provide headquarters coordination for new products and "brand champions" to coordinate information on existing brands, the system was not generating clear-cut priorities, commitment and action. Many of the business possibilities that had been identified remained just that. The terminology that came into use was that "more bite" was needed in the planning process, meaning more definitive guidelines and choices, more resources to back approved programs, and more delegation of authority and responsibility to get ideas implemented.

THE BIG ISSUES

As fiscal 1985 closed, very profitably but still without tangible progress on growth, Cliff Hatch Jr. was growing increasingly concerned. He had recently asked Ian Wilson-Smith to survey 35 to 40 unit managers to seek their ideas about what the company could do to become more aggressive in the market. Virtually all of the managers polled had responded in writing, often after consulting their colleagues and subordinates, and cumulatively they had offered literally dozens of suggestions. There was a focus, however, on three broad issues: (1) acquisitions, (2) new product development and (3) organizational refinement. A summary of the views together with comments by members of the top management group follows.

Acquisitions

It was generally agreed that acquisitions were necessary to improve Hiram Walker's growth and competitive position. The sheer volume of suggestions from the management ranks on potential acquisitions and new ventures outnumbered the rest by a wide margin. The major themes were the need to think big rather than small, the desirability of acquiring a few significant "white goods" brands (vodka, gin, etc.), the need to increase Walker's involvement in the wine industry, and a strong interest in beer (especially high-image imports), soft drinks and mineral waters. The general opinion would have squared with John

Giffen's remark that "the pluses and minuses of the existing brand areas add up to really slow growth...our only avenue for real progress is through acquisition."

The problem in acquisitions, as expressed by several managers, was that Hiram Walker was simply not moving aggressively enough. Jim Ferguson put it bluntly: "Our strategic planning hasn't accomplished very much...we haven't done anything yet!" While this was not strictly true—since the company had made three small acquisitions—it captured the prevailing view that significant action was needed.

Although the formal position of the strategic planning committee was to focus on acquisitions within the spirits industry, there was informal disagreement about this focus within the group. The arguments were classic. Several managers felt that acquisitions should be limited to the business Hiram Walker knew, and within this were concerned about availability, cost, synergy and returns. Other managers cast a wider net, suggesting the spirits industry was in decline, and that diversification was necessary, at least into allied fields of prestige products such as perfumes and cosmetics.

There was some feeling that the procedures for screening and pursuing acquisitions were delaying the acquisition process. Currently, various members of the strategic planning committee were asked to follow up on possibilities under the general coordination of Cliff Hatch Jr. and Ian Wilson-Smith. A count of the assigned projects indicated that most managers on the committee had upwards of five leads to pursue. The formation of a dedicated headquarters unit to screen and analyze acquisitions had been discussed by the committee, but no action had been taken on this matter.

New Product Development

There was an ongoing controversy in the company over what were perceived to be unnecessary delays in bringing new product initiatives—including types, flavours, packaging, labels, etc.—to market. On the one hand, some managers, primarily from marketing positions, argued that more resources and more discretion were necessary to speed up the pace of development. They saw a newly formed product development committee as a dubious solution, as just another corporate hurdle of which there were already too many. Gerry Gianni, who had joined Hiram Walker in 1981 from a large spirits import house and now ran Hiram Walker Incorporated in the U.S., commented on the four years that it had taken to bring Canadian Club Classic to market: "A disaster...the project was mandated from the top, but after that nothing seemed to happen...the very first thing you should not do is appoint a committee, nor set up a coordinator that will not be around to see the project through...politics and bureaucracy set in and the coordinator was forced into a referee's position deciding who should win instead of thinking about benefits for the consumer...we are still trying to come to grips with packaging."

Other executives argued that checks and balances were necessary to avoid expensive product proliferation, to provide for the orderly development of production facilities, and to ensure that new initiatives were consistent with corporate policy. As one production executive pointed out, "Some of the marketing units seem to change their priorities with the weather...one moment it's miniatures in plastic for the airlines, the next it's 1.75 litre bottles...they don't seem to appreciate the supply, inventory and equipment complications." Furthermore, at the corporate level, the traditional position was reiterated: "We rely on just a few brands and we operate in markets where brand and corporate reputations are crucial factors...we can't afford to have someone going off half-cocked and creating a quality or public relations problem."

The Organization

Organizational suggestions were abundant in the managers' responses. The recurring themes were the need to decentralize decision-making, adopt a profit centre approach, and set up separate and properly staffed units to handle acquisitions and new products. These comments were echoed by Jim Ford and Ian

Wilson-Smith. Ford noted that "Hiram Walker's highly centralized functional management structure is inappropriate for an increasingly competitive environment...it creates confusion and conflict between the functions and between field and geographical management...further, under the present structure, I cannot see us developing the well rounded businessmen we will need in the future...we will always have to go outside in the crunch."

Ian Wilson-Smith was of a similar mind: "We have no adequate framework for the integrated management of our key brands on a worldwide basis or, indeed, of our key markets on a geographical basis; we have succeeded in getting the worst of both worlds and the end result is a further reinforcement of the centralized decision-making process...we need major structural changes to combine production and marketing activities into manageable business units, integrate the responsibility for our key brands on a worldwide basis and redefine the role of corporate headquarters."

Other top managers disagreed. They admitted that the organization was not working as well as it should but argued that the current structure was essentially sound. All that was needed were refinements in staffing, policy and procedures. Jim Ferguson's position was, as he put it, "You have to understand that our big problem is not in operations... we have strong brands and we are doing well...it is that we haven't gotten on with acquisitions...(Insofar as current operations are concerned)...what we need to do is get a marketing vice-president into place and get Cliff out of that role...and then use our budgeting and accounting procedures to hold the sales companies more clearly responsible for results...we haven't pushed hard enough."

Steve McCann spoke of international operations, "I was involved (in 1965) in the initial conception of HWI and my position then was that the brand-owning companies (e.g., Hiram Walker Scotland) should be complete entities entirely responsible for success and failure...this view was not accepted and HWI was made responsible to Walkerville. While I continue to prefer my original position in principle, I cannot see how HWI can now be unscrambled (whether by returning its functions to the brandowner—in whole or part—or in some other way) without great disruption. And the likely benefits are insufficient to compensate for the disruption...HWI should be allowed to get on with its job without interference from Walkerville, which, in my view, should confine itself to decisions on...(elements of brand, strategy, operating policy)...the approval of the annual budget and rigorous ex post facto examination of HWI's performance." Another top manager put the point bluntly in an informal conversation: "There is *no* way that we are going to reorganize this company."

ACTION CONSIDERATIONS

Cliff Hatch Jr. was quite prepared to act, subject to two broad conditions. First, he ruled out major strategic or organizational gambles. As he noted: "I have no mandate to wreck this company." Change could and should proceed, but the steps would have to be carefully developed. He was particularly concerned that the disagreements among managers demonstrated that the obstacles to growth were not well understood. As a result, he had tried to this point to keep the options for change open, and to avoid the endorsement of specific "solutions." One of the reasons for postponing the appointment of a corporate vice-president of marketing, for example, was that this would tend to reinforce past structure and practices.

Second, change would have to respect the corporate values that had helped to build Hiram Walker. "As a company," Hatch said, "we have tried to take the long-term view, to build lasting relationships, and to respect individuals and individual contributions. We have tried to avoid short-term and temporary solutions. I believe these principles will serve us as well in the future as they have in the past."

EXHIBIT 1 Demand for Alcoholic Beverages in Selected Categories and Countries, 1984

(9-litre case equivalents, 000s)

	Canadian Whisky	Scotch Whisky	Bourbon	Cognac	Brandy	Gin	Vodka	Rum	Cordials Liqueurs	Other Popular Cordials Liqueurs	TOTAL Spirits	TOTAL Wine	TOTAL Beer
United States	23 800	19 200	36 700[1]	1 800	5 200	14 300	31 200	12 200	16 300		179 400	232 900	2 385 300
Growth rate (80/84)	-0.5	-5.7	-4.3	10.0	-1.0	-2.0	.0	1.9	4.7		-1.3	4.1	0.7
Canada	6 700	1 200	LV	300	700	1 600	2 500	3 100	2 000		18 800	25 200	212 000
Growth rate (80/84)	-6.2	-3.9		3.5	-1.4	-7.6	-1.0	-2.9	1.7		-3.8	4.0	-1.4
United Kingdom	LV	12 000	LV	1 000	1 000	3 400	3 700	2 100	1 700		25 500	68 700	691 200
Growth rate (79/84)	-3.8	-5.3	3.4	-3.0	1.5	-5.3	3.6	-2.9	4.6		-1.8		
West Germany	LV	1 900	500	900	10 600	400	900	5 800	4 000	9 500[4]	44 000	178 000	985 700
Growth rate (79/84)		-3.7	-7.7	-1.8	-0.8	-2.0	1.8	-3.5	-7.5	.0	-3.7	0.7	-0.1
France	LV	5 300	200	800	1 000	300	300	2 100	N/A	12 700[2]	30 000	522 000	250 000
Growth rate (79/84)		6.2	6.8	-8.0	-4.6	14.8	9.9	-7.4		-1.4	-0.6	-1.9	-1.6
Italy	LV	3 100	100	200	6 900	300	200	100	3 400		24 800	525 400	119 700
Growth rate (80/84)		2.4	20.0	-1.7	-3.5	15.0	-8.3	-13.0	-3.0	-1.4	-3.6	-1.9	2.7
Spain	LV	2 000	LV	LV	11 200	6 700	500	2 400	5 200	1 600[3]	332 800	200 800	251 000
Growth rate (80/84)		1.9			-3.9	1.0	3.4	0.4	-0.3	10.4	-1.2	-2.4	2.9
Japan	LV	2 200	LV	500	2 000	200	N/A	300	LV	31 700[6]	50 800[5]	10 300	516 200
Growth rate (79/84)		-4.1		10.7	10.6	-2.7		4.8		-0.3	4.0	6.5	0.7
Australia	LV	1 900	LV	LV	800	200	300	800	400		4 900	35 000	204 700
Growth rate (79/84)		3.7			1.5	-2.0	1.3	3.4	-0.5		2.9	5.9	-0.8
World consumption (1982)		65 000		8 900	43 000	59 400	51 800						

[1] Includes straight bourbon and blends
[2] Anis, ougo
[3] Spanish whisky
[4] Korn, aquavit
[5] Totals include sake consumption of 186 million cases
[6] Japanese whisky

Note: LV—Low volumes.

EXHIBIT 2 Sales of Selected Hiram Walker Brands in Selected Areas[1]

(9-litre case equivalents, 000s)

	Canadian Club	Ballantine's	Kahlua	Courvoisier	Tia Maria
United States, 1984 case sales (000)	2 900	380	1 570	540	130
Market share, point change (84/80)	12.1, –4.9	2.0, 0.3	26.1, –7.4	29.8, –3.3	2.1, –2.7
Canada, 1984 case sales (000)	650	130	210	60	130
Market share, point change (84/80)	9.7, –2.3	10.5, –0.2	18.6, –1.6	21.6,–5.0	11.5, –10.4
United Kingdom, 1983 case sales	LV	90	LV	320	120
Market share, point change (83/79)			1.0, N/A	30.0, 2.2	6.8, –3.2
Selected European,[2] 1983 case sales	LV	1 401	LV	160	LV
Market share, point change (83/79)			13.5, –1.1	8.2, 1.0	
Japan and Hong Kong	LV	130	LV	100	LV
Market share		10.0, N/A			
Company shipments, 1985 fiscal year	3 300	3 500	2 200	1 350	683
% Change (85/84)	–5.6	–10.3	3.0	1.8	N/A

[1] Individual brand/market data based on commercial estimates of wholesalers depletions known to somewhat overstate actual volumes. Market share based on category totals, e.g., Canadian Club share of Canadian Whisky sales.

[2] France, Italy, West Germany. Excludes duty free sales.

Note: LV—Low volumes.

E X H I B I T   3   **Hiram Walker-Gooderham & Worts (A) Simplified Organization Structure**

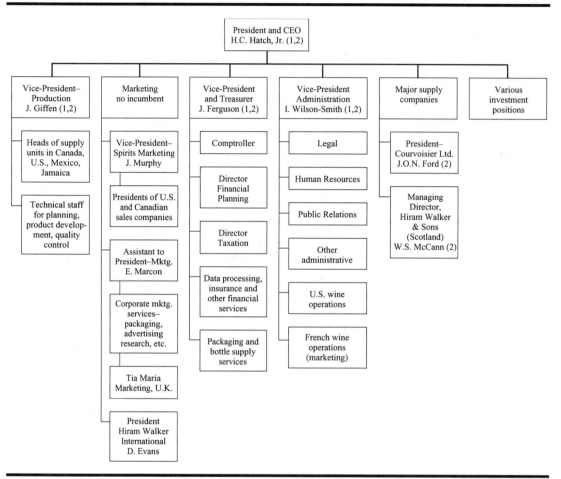

Source: Derived from company documents.

THE LONDON FREE PRESS (A): STRATEGIC CHANGE

Detlev Nitsch
and Mary M. Crossan

c a s e

30

Phil McLeod had been appointed as the new editor of the *London Free Press* (LFP) in November 1987, with a mandate to make changes. Like most other North American daily newspapers, the LFP had been gradually losing readership, and its share of advertising revenues in the community was shrinking. Despite its ability to remain profitable, McLeod thought that it was not living up to its potential, especially since it was the only daily newspaper in London. He feared that there were ominous signs of a continuing decline in market share, which could only mean still lower profits in the future.

IVEY

Detlev Nitsch prepared this case under the supervision of Professor Mary M. Crossan solely to provide material for class discussion. The authors do not intend to illustrate either effective or ineffective handling of a managerial situation. The authors may have disguised certain names and other identifying information to protect confidentiality.

McLeod had been hired from the *Toronto Star* and put in charge of LFP's newsroom and editorial department to do whatever was necessary to reverse this trend. Now, in 1991, he wondered if it would be possible to stop the slow decline of the newspaper or if its shrinkage was an inevitable consequence of broader trends in the information industry and Canadian society.

THE NEWSPAPER INDUSTRY

Newspapers obtained revenues from two sources: from readers, who paid for papers through regular subscriptions or on a single-copy basis, and from advertising clients, who hoped to expose their messages to as many members of a community as possible. Conceptually newspapers could be seen as a medium that attracted readers with its editorial content, and in turn delivered those readers to advertisers as potential purchasers.

Advertising sales accounted for about three-quarters of a typical paper's total revenues, but these amounts were closely linked to the paid circulation of the paper. Advertisers' willingness to pay a given rate depended on the size of the audience they could expect to reach with their messages. The price advertisers paid for space in a newspaper was usually based on a combination of (1) total circulation and (2) penetration, expressed in terms of the percentage of total households reached.

McLeod saw newspapers as having two basic functions: gathering information, and packaging it for resale. Information came in two varieties: public "news;" and private, or advertising information. The news information-gathering function could be further broken down by source:

1. A paper's own reporters gathering local news.
2. Staff reporters responsible for news from distant locales. Many larger newspapers had "bureaux" staffed by their own people in important cities around Canada and the rest of the world, so they could have proprietary access to any information these reporters uncovered.
3. Exchange arrangements through the corporate umbrella—for example, LFP had a contractual link with Southam News that enabled it, for a fee, to tap into this large organization's worldwide network of news sources. This also allowed papers access to news developed initially for other media.
4. Wire services. Canadian Press (CP), American Press (AP) and Reuters were examples of news agencies that existed solely to provide news on a fee basis to anyone who was willing to pay for it. In some cases (CP for example), the agency was a cooperative owned by newspapers.

The LFP was fairly typical of daily newspapers in that approximately 60 per cent of its space was allocated to advertising (paid messages), with the "newshole," or editorial content, occupying the rest. Of the 40 per cent of the available space dedicated to the newshole, 60 per cent was purchased from wire services or other sources. McLeod estimated that approximately 30 per cent of his $10 million editorial budget was spent on purchased news; one-third of the balance was devoted to reworking or repackaging these stories for publication, and the rest was spent on maintaining the LFP's in-house news-gathering apparatus.

As advertisers became more sophisticated, they were no longer merely interested in a newspaper's raw circulation figures, but rather in its ability to reach those most likely to purchase their products. Electronic media in particular were often able to target very narrow market segments with a high degree of precision. Television programming was being geared to ever-smaller segments of the population, as cable and satellite proliferation expanded the choices available to consumers. With sophisticated demographic market research data, programmers could produce and schedule shows designed to appeal to specific groups, and have relatively high confidence that their target would be reached. This was attractive to advertisers because they could spend their advertising budgets more efficiently, avoiding messages sent to members of the community who were not potential customers. In contrast, daily newspapers were seen as a rather blunt instrument, with potentially broad mass-market coverage but little ability to ensure that a given message had reached its target segment.

Past Performance, Future Outlook

Newspaper companies had enjoyed a very profitable history in North America: at the beginning of the 1980s they boasted a median 9.6 per cent profit margin, compared to a median of less than 5 per cent for Fortune 500 Industrials. Even though, depending on commodity prices, newsprint accounted for anywhere from 20–25 per cent of total costs, newspapers' return on sales ranged from 14–18 per cent, while industrials averaged 6 per cent. In 1992, U.S. newspaper companies enjoyed a resurgence in the stock market, outperforming index averages by a large margin (Exhibit 1). This followed several years of sluggish performance during which consolidation and downsizing were the norm in the industry.

Despite this evidence of good performance potential, there were several signs that indicated a long-run trend to declining circulation, reduced revenues and smaller profit margins. Exhibit 2 shows the decline in profitability of a typical North American newspaper company.

Newspapers' level of penetration, or market share as a percentage of households reached, was dropping for newspapers all across North America. In the U.S., 124 copies of daily newspapers were sold for every 100 households during the 1950s. By the 1970s, the comparable figure was 77, with the drop attributable in part to a decline in the number of two-newspaper households. The Canada-wide circulation growth rate, at 1.7 per cent, was also well below the growth rates of the adult population (2.1 per cent) and of households (3.0 per cent) during the 1970s, even though it still outpaced the growth of total population (1.0 per cent). Similar trends seemed to apply to London, where McLeod had noted that the LFP was losing about a percentage point per year in penetration, down to below 60 per cent in the early 1990s.

While the total circulation of daily newspapers was still increasing, other indicators such as average daily circulation and penetration levels suggested that newspapers were losing readers, and were thus becoming less attractive as an advertising medium. As recently as 1973, daily newspapers had attracted 30.5 per cent of total Canadian advertising expenditures, compared to television in that year with 13.4 per cent. In fact, until 1977, daily newspapers held a larger share of ad revenues than radio, television and weekly newspapers combined. But the long-run trend since 1972 showed a gradual decline in the newspapers' share, while television and other media continued to gather strength. Daily newspapers still had the largest share of total advertising revenues, but this share was gradually shrinking (Table 1).

TABLE 1   Canadian Advertising Expenditures Percent Share of Total, by Medium

Medium	1973	1989 (Estimates)
Daily Newspapers	30.5	22.8
Catalogues, Direct Mail	20.6	21.9
Television	13.4	15.6
Radio	10.8	8.3
Weekly Newspapers	5.1	6.9
Magazines	2.4	3.1
Other	17.2	21.4

Source: Maclean Hunter Research Bureau.

Breaking total advertising revenues down into national and local categories yielded further insights into the differing strengths of the competing media. For example, in 1973–1974 daily newspapers received 19.8 per cent of their advertising revenues from national accounts. The corresponding figure for television was 73.9 per cent, which shifted upward to 75.3 per cent by 1980, while the dailies' proportion fell to 18.7 per cent. This suggested that newspapers' heavy reliance on local retail and classified advertising was, if anything, increasing.

Demographics of Readership: Long-Run Implications

A 1986 study of newspaper readers showed that most readers were in the over-35 age category, and that 75 per cent of people in their 20s did not regularly read the paper. In the past, there had been some support for the notion that newspaper reading habits grew as individuals aged. Cross-sectional studies had turned up much the same data decade after decade, as young non-readers in an early study evolved into 50-year-old newspaper aficionados 30 years later.

But McLeod feared that times had changed, and that these non-readers would be difficult to turn into loyal newspaper customers in the future. The current crop of young adults were the first who had been raised in an age in which television was accepted as a legitimate news source. Unlike previous generations, these people believed and trusted what they saw on the small screen, and did not feel the need to see it in print. The public's familiarity and comfort level with television had grown over time, aided by the medium's presence on the scene of historic events such as the 1963 assassination of U.S. President Kennedy, and the first moon landing in 1969. Also, McLeod admitted that television had proved competent in areas where newspapers were once thought to have a competitive advantage: background and analysis. Network news and news-only cable TV channels were increasingly supplying high-quality, in-depth coverage of important events, with a timeliness and sense of immediacy that newspapers could not match.

Television's new-found strengths might make it impossible for newspapers to attract the current group of younger people. This meant that the expected shift in preference, from television to newspapers as people aged, might not take place this time. Thus the old assumption that readership would stay more or less constant over time appeared to rely on a "no change" scenario which did not fit reality.

Some evidence suggested that, by 1991, newspaper readership was recovering from its precipitous decline. Gross circulation was actually up by 32 per cent from 15 years before, while population had only risen 16 per cent. Also, the proportion of Canadian adults reading newspapers had increased from 63 per cent to 68.5 per cent. However, McLeod thought that these numbers were misleading because they focused on overall total circulation instead of daily averages, and they ignored the fact that new newspaper formats had begun to penetrate the market. The gross circulation statistic compared present total readership with comparable figures before the "tabloid era" in many major Canadian centres. Tabloids were new and very different newspapers, adding 700 000 new readers who were, arguably, in a different category than traditional ones. Also, 14 new Sunday editions had been started in the past seven years, contributing another 1.5 million new readers to the circulation total, but not raising the daily average circulation. Thus, while total circulation was up, daily average circulation per newspaper was still in decline across the country (Table 2).

TABLE 2   **Daily Circulation Averages**

(For 12 Months Ended March 1991, Change from Previous 12 Months)

Vancouver Sun	Down 5.5%
Montreal Gazette	Down 5.2%
Ottawa Citizen	Down 4.0%
Kitchener Record	Down 3.7%
Kingston Whig-Standard	Down 3.7%
London Free Press	Down 3.6%
Calgary Herald	Down 3.4%
Calgary Sun	Down 2.5%
Toronto Sun	Down 2.4%
Hamilton Spectator	Down 2.4%
Toronto Star	Down 2.2%
Edmonton Sun	Down 1.3%
Edmonton Journal	Down 0.6%
Windsor Star	Even
Vancouver Province	Up 2.6%

Source: LFP internal documents.

On this basis, circulation was being outpaced by population growth in virtually every market in Canada. Among other things, this had also placed increasing pressure on the sales function. The *London Free Press* in 1990 had to sell 81 364 new subscription orders to maintain its average daily home delivery at 85 646 in the city of London. In the previous year, the home delivery average had been slightly higher but only 63 000 new orders had to be sold. A recent study conducted in the United States and Canada had suggested three main reasons why readers were abandoning newspapers:

1. No time:
   - your paper is hard to read
   - I really don't have any time
   - you don't make it clear why I should make time
2. No news:
   - I saw it all on TV; you gave me nothing new
   - insufficient insight, understanding, depth
3. No interest:
   - nothing for me in the paper
   - I don't share your idea of what is new or important
   - you don't care about what I care about—in fact you often belittle the things my friends and I enjoy

The same study had reconfirmed that one of the causes of newspapers' decline in importance to readers was the fact that other media, principally television, had made news more easily consumable by the public. Comparing statistics over time exposed a trend away from newspapers on virtually every dimension (Table 3).

TABLE 3 Comparison of Television and Newspapers

(percentage of respondents who responded positively to each question)

	1986	1991
Main source of international news:		
Television	63%	73%
Newspapers	21%	16%
Main source of national news:		
Television	69%	75%
Newspapers	19%	16%
Main source of local news:		
Television	41%	43%
Newspapers	34%	35%
Most believable:		
Television	no data	30%
Newspapers	no data	24%
Most accurate:		
Television	no data	33%
Newspapers	no data	19%
Most likely to be fair:		
Television	no data	33%
Newspapers	no data	19%

Source: Environics, reproduced in LFP internal documents.

Industry Consolidation Trend

The competitive dynamic among newspapers in Canada had changed gradually over the years. In the past, newspapers had competed as a collection of geographically dispersed individual markets. While there had been virtually no competition between cities, there had often been intense rivalry among papers within cities. But by the 1980s, cities with two or more dailies had become a rarity (Table 4). Even in the few locations that still had more than one daily, the papers tended to be positioned in fairly well-defined niches, such as Toronto's *Globe and Mail*, *Sun*, and *Star*. Through consolidation and attrition, the industry had evolved into a series of local newspaper monopolies.

Consolidation had also led to domination of the Canadian industry by a few national or regional chains. Advantages to group ownership were (1) shared resources, including pooled information services from abroad; and (2) the owner's deep pockets, which enabled a chain newspaper to weather temporary downturns in its financial performance, and gave it access to capital for major investments in technology.

The two largest chains, Southam and Thomson, together controlled 58 per cent of the English-language circulation in Canada. Southam, with 17 of the total 95 Canadian English dailies, had 33.5 per cent of overall circulation, while Thomson, with 36 papers, had 24.5 per cent. These percentages did not, in themselves, suggest that the newspaper market had taken on the characteristics of a monopoly. But by avoiding head-to-head competition among papers in individual cities, the chains' newspapers had managed to enjoy local monopolies and high profits.

T A B L E 4   Major Newspapers and Circulations (1993)

City	Newspaper	Daily Average Circulation
Calgary	Herald	125 000
	Sun	76 000
Winnipeg	Free Press	154 000
Regina	Leader-Post	68 000
Hamilton	Spectator	135 000
Edmonton	Journal	137 000
	Sun	69 000
Vancouver	Province	185 000
	Sun	221 000
Victoria	Times-Colonist	77 000
Winnipeg	Free Press	154 000
Halifax	Chronicle Herald	97 000
Waterloo	K-W Record	75 000
London	Free Press	115 000
Ottawa	Citizen	178 000
Toronto	Star	544 000
	Globe and Mail	311 000
	Sun	272 000
Windsor	Star	86 000
Montreal	Gazette	163 000
	Journal de Montreal	293 000
	La Presse	205 000
Quebec City	Journal de Quebec	102 000
	Le Soleil	99 000

Source: Canadian Advertising Rates and Data, March 1994.

Threat to the Public Interest?

Critics of industry consolidation favoured some form of government intervention to help support financially troubled newspapers and to preserve competitive rivalry. Arguing out of concern for the public interest, they cautioned that in single-paper monopolies, readers' opinions would be manipulated by selective reporting and by opinion masquerading as objective journalism. Further, since advertisers would have no alternative outlets for their print messages, they would be at the mercy of greedy newspaper owners, and would become the victims of price-gouging and other undesirable tactics.

Those who saw no problem with the demise of direct competition maintained that newspapers in monopoly markets were able and willing to sustain a high level of journalistic quality, because their resources were not eroded through needless duplication and price competition with rivals. A section of the 1981 Royal Commission on Newspapers suggested that there was no evidence of declining quality or journalistic integrity as a result of industry consolidation. Publishers in single-newspaper towns were characterized as being able to "afford excellence," while still having to compete with other media for advertisers' dollars.

Neither was the trend to group ownership of newspapers seen, by these observers, as a threat to editorial independence. Publishers of chain newspapers frequently made mention of their freedom from interference by their corporate bosses. In support of this contention they cited the fact that some of Canada's most respected papers were being run at a loss by large chains (for example, Thomson's *Globe and Mail*), implying that high quality standards were not being eroded in pursuit of corporate profitability.

Even the Supreme Court of Canada had indirectly supported the position that the public interest was not threatened by industry consolidation. In ruling on a 1977 case brought under anti-combines legislation, the court held that "the Crown was unable to prove, as the law requires, that a single owner of the [only] five dailies in New Brunswick would be detrimental to the public." In reaching this conclusion, the Court noted the Irving chain's success in increasing the circulation of all five papers, the fact that capital investment had been made in them, and that money-losing papers had been subsidized to enable them to continue operating.

Social Role of Newspapers

In Western society, the press had long been viewed as an expression of the right of free speech, and as one of the pillars of democracy. Independence from government and other interference was held to be absolutely essential if editorial quality and integrity were to be preserved. The press was seen as the "watchdog" charged with informing the public about the activities of the state.

There was a sense that the press had a larger role in society than that of other commercial enterprises. Some observers and industry insiders had concluded that newspapers have higher ideals than just making money, and responsibilities beyond simply keeping shareholders happy. While admitting that, at some level at least, financial viability was important, many people nevertheless felt that newspapers had an altruistic mission to present the complete truth, and that the naked pursuit of larger profits would put their editorial objectivity at risk. Newspapers were thus seen to be driven by both a service ethic and a market ethic.

Partly as a result of this extra-commercial role, a mystique had arisen about journalism which led to the belief, among many reporters, that journalists alone were competent to judge what stories the public should see in print, and in what form they should be presented. Among many traditionalists, journalistic quality (as defined by them) should be emphasized over the pursuit of mere profit. Papers which "sold out" in order to target a larger audience were seen to be pandering to the whims of an unsophisticated public whose members often did not know what was good for them.

McLeod saw the notion of newspapers' "altruistic mission" as a self-serving rationalization. He felt it was invoked to support the idea that maintaining the existing editorial process was more important than the consumption of the product, thus providing a rationale for preservation of the status quo. The result, he thought, was that newspapers had lost touch with their communities. By refusing to respond to readers' needs, under the pretext of preserving journalistic integrity, papers were becoming increasingly irrelevant to many potential readers. Print journalism's insular mentality, bred of a grandiose view of its role in society, its professional arrogance, and its past success, had isolated it from those on whom it depended for its survival.

Evidence about the relative profitability of different editorial approaches was equivocal, in any event. Observers could point to successful and unsuccessful examples at both ends of the "quality" continuum. For example, the *Globe and Mail*, widely perceived as a high-quality paper, was operating at a loss, while other quality papers such as the *Washington Post* and the *New York Times* were earning money. At the tabloid end of the spectrum, the *Toronto Sun* was a financial success, while *USA Today* was still struggling to break even. It seemed that, for all the criticism levelled at papers that tried to boost circulation by appealing to a larger and, arguably, less-discriminating mass market, this "sell-out" tactic was no guarantee of profits. There seemed to be profitable market niches for newspapers following either strategy.

THE LONDON FREE PRESS

The *London Free Press* was the only daily newspaper in London, Ontario, a southwestern Ontario city of approximately 300 000. It was part of the Blackburn Group Inc. (BGI), which was made up of businesses in the communication and information fields. Begun in 1849, The London Free Press had been owned and operated for five generations by the Blackburn family of London, and maintained a strong tradition of community service.

As communications technology evolved, so did the organization's activities in various media. An AM radio station was started in 1922, and in 1953 television was added to the Blackburn empire.[1] An FM radio station completed the growing conglomerate's coverage of the available "instant media."

In addition to these holdings, BGI had also launched Netmar Inc. in 1974, and purchased Compusearch in 1984. Netmar published and distributed weekly newspapers, shopping guides, and advertising flyers in Ontario and Alberta. Compusearch, based in Toronto, was a North American leader in market information and analysis.

In 1991, BGI established Blackburn Marketing Services Inc. (BMSI), an investment and management company formed to develop a portfolio of businesses in the direct marketing area. BMSI had made inroads into the U.S. market through acquisitions and mergers with American market research organizations.

BGI and its operating subsidiaries were private companies, and had been run under Blackburn family control since their founding. The LFP had the longest history, and was the most "legitimate" in terms of traditional journalistic values. Blackburn's senior management were proud that they had been able to maintain both the financial health of the paper and its high journalistic quality while creating a work environment that was described as caring and paternalistic.

The LFP had up-to-date production facilities, and its distribution system was described by McLeod as leading-edge, given the current state of technological development. Minimizing printing and distribution costs was an ongoing effort at the LFP, but any gains made in this area would be incremental. For true strategic impact, McLeod thought he had to focus on the revenue-generating side of the profit equation. This placed the onus for change on the editorial department.

Organization

The LFP, like most newspapers, was organized along functional lines. The principal departments were advertising, production, administrative and editorial. The editorial department of approximately 130 employees was headed by McLeod, and divided into sections that corresponded to the principal sections of the newspaper. Staff were assigned to sports, entertainment, business, political, or local/regional sections on a more or less permanent basis, under the leadership of a senior editor who was in charge of that part of the paper.

Exhibit 3 presents a chart showing the organization of editorial staff within sections of the paper. In operation, it worked as follows: For a typical local news event, a reporter was sent into the field by a senior editor to gather the facts, and to write the story. The piece was then turned over to a copy editor, who would check spelling and grammar, alter its length, or make other changes. After this step, the graphics people took over, adding pictures, diagrams, or maps as required, and physically reworking the story to fit into the page layout that was being planned for that edition. Again, the original story could be changed to meet space restrictions.

---

[1] The TV station was sold in 1993 because the Blackburn Group felt it no longer fit the news focus of its other holdings, and because it needed substantial new investment to stay competitive in the entertainment field.

McLeod saw several weaknesses in this system. For example, a typical reporter might be assigned to cover local news, and be routinely sent to cover regular meetings of some special-interest group. This reporter might return with a story about a particularly colourful and lively meeting, at which members expressed various forms of outrage and stated their political positions for the record. The story would run in the newspaper, suitably headlined with attention-getting phrases, and the responsible section editor would feel that the job of covering local news had been accomplished. However, the only "outrage" felt might be on the part of the 20 people attending the meeting, and the significance of the event for the greater community could be nonexistent. Without probing more deeply into the reasons behind the meeting, and investigating the possible consequences on a level that went beyond the narrow interests of a particular group, the LFP might not be reporting anything meaningful to readers. Many reporters' roles had been created in response to a specific need in the past, but were maintained today, McLeod had decided, more out of habit than for the intrinsic "newsworthiness" of the material that was ultimately written. When making decisions about how to deploy limited reporting resources to the best possible effect, the test of community relevance was often not applied.

Another problem was that, throughout the traditional process, there was little or no communication between the various production stages. Because the printing schedule of the LFP dictated that the presses start rolling at midnight, the latter steps in the process were often not done until evening, while the original story may have been written that morning. By the time the editors and graphics people first saw the story, its original author could be home in bed, with no opportunity for input or influence over how it would finally appear in the paper.

The lack of a perceived connection with the community was symbolized by the LFP's physical premises as well. With only one access door, the building itself was not easy for the public to enter. Once inside, they faced a forbidding security checkpoint, a symbolic barrier between the public and the reporters who chronicled their lives. At the same time, McLeod remarked on the fact that none of the editorial staff had a view of the outside from their work area. The lack of a visual link to the city of London reinforced the inward-directed focus of those who purported to be writing about issues and events that were important to the community.

The organization structure also isolated departments within the newspaper from one another. Each section was conceptually and editorially an independent entity, and there was little communication or sharing of information among them. McLeod thought that this arrangement had led, on occasion, to stories falling through the cracks because they did not fit neatly into one of the pre-defined categories. An example of this occurred when a major World Wrestling Federation (WWF) event was scheduled to be held in London. The match was to be held at the London Gardens, which was the biggest arena in the city, and frequently the venue for major music concerts and sports events. *The London Free Press* often reported on these activities in the next day's edition, and it had been informed by the WWF's sophisticated publicity department about the major wrestling stars who would be making a rare appearance in London. The most popular and biggest money-making wrestlers were more accustomed to appearing in places such as New York's Madison Square Garden or the Fabulous Western Forum in Los Angeles than in a relative backwater such as the 8 000 seat London Gardens.

As it happened however, the sports section of the LFP declined to cover the WWF event because they felt that professional wrestling was not a true "sport," but more a form of staged entertainment. The entertainment editor meanwhile assumed that, since wrestling billed itself as a sport, and its participants were "athletes," the sports section would be reporting on it. The lack of communication between sections, and the fact that professional wrestling could not be neatly pigeonholed as either "sport" or "entertainment," led to neither section covering what was, for many London residents, a major news item.

Strategic Response

To halt further declines in readership, a major makeover of the LFP was undertaken in 1989, to give it a different look and make it more contemporary, "breezy," and attractive to readers. In what was seen in the trade as a major departure from tradition, the front page was redesigned. The number of stories it contained was reduced in favour of making it more of a road map for the contents of the inside pages. More colour was used, in conjunction with other cosmetic changes designed to make the paper look more user-friendly and less boring.

These changes, while hardly revolutionary to the eye of an average reader, were perceived by some members of the editorial staff as an abandonment of its tradition of editorial excellence. They interpreted the emphasis on readability and graphic attractiveness as an effort to lure readers with pretty pictures and colourful presentation. In the detractors' opinions, an emphasis on the quality of writing was being supplanted by less meaningful priorities.

The increased use of graphics meant that, for the first time, charts, maps and graphs were incorporated into stories right from the outset, as opposed to being added as an afterthought on a "space available" basis. One group that felt threatened as a result was the staff photographers, who saw their work competing for space with that of the graphics designers. Another unhappy group was the reporters. They felt their pre-eminent position in the LFP newsroom being eroded, since now much of what they wrote might be captured in a chart or graph. While this had always been the case to a certain extent, graphics and pictorial summaries of key story points were now intended to be an integral part of the creation of an article, to be included in the process right from the start. Reporters thought that their influence over how a story would be presented would now have to be shared with others, who often might have little training in journalism.

Results

Reader response to the changes was mixed. Evidence favouring and criticizing the changes was gathered from focus groups, and was revealed in letters to the editor. From these sources, it became clear that some readers were upset with the new look of the paper and found it disconcerting that items they were interested in were relocated to unfamiliar sections. On the other hand, some reported that they liked the new format, and saw it as a step toward making the paper more readable. While it was difficult to draw quantitative conclusions from this, McLeod estimated that the split "for" and "against" the redesign was about 50–50.

Circulation for 1990, the first full year of operation with the new format, was down 3 per cent from the year before. However, London was just beginning to feel the effects of a recession at that time, and this made it difficult to disentangle the effect of the change from broader economic trends. The question of how much circulation would have dropped without a change remained impossible to answer.

At the same time as changes in the appearance of the LFP were being implemented, a drive to unionize the newsroom was successfully completed. Though professing considerable philosophical discomfort with their decision, supporters of the unionization effort had decided that this was the only way they could combat what they saw as unilateral and wrong-headed action by the paper's management. In what many saw as a result of the unhappiness of editorial staff about the new direction the LFP appeared to be taking, they voted to go on strike in early 1990. The strike was settled after a few weeks, during which the paper was put together by managerial staff, but unresolved ill feelings remained.

Package versus Content

McLeod had come to believe that, while a newspaper's packaging was closely linked to its content, the two "must become disentangled in our minds" in order for progress to be made. He had changed the package, following the tradition of consumer goods marketers. Now perhaps something a little more substantive was in order.

In order for readers to see the LFP as an important source of information, the content of the paper would need to reflect their wishes more closely. But changing the content would not be easy. As McLeod put it, a newspaper is like a sausage factory:

> You can put as many good ideas as you want into the front end of the machine, but unless that machine has been retooled to think and act in new ways, it will always turn out more or less the same thing. In other words, whatever goes in, sausages come out. Perhaps sausages with better texture or taste, less fat and fewer calories, but sausages nevertheless.

McLeod felt that the changes would require a substantial "rewiring of our heads," and would be risky because they conflicted with traditional attitudes about journalism. More stories needed to be written about topics that readers were actually interested in, and they needed to be covered in greater depth. At the same time, McLeod no longer believed that each piece in the paper had to be written, edited and laid out in the final few minutes before the press deadline. "While I wouldn't know the details of the stories, I can tell you two days in advance what 80 per cent of our paper is going to look like," he said. "If we know, broadly, what the subject matter is going to be, why can't we do a better job of background and analysis on those stories we already know are going to be in the paper?"

Potential Resistance

Opposition to any proposed changes could be high. McLeod was risking criticism for tampering with the natural order of the way newspapers were run, because of the strong entrenched culture that existed in the profession. According to one view, he might be allowing the process of producing a newspaper to be unduly tainted by customer influence.

On a more personal level, the changes might shake many staffers' strongly held beliefs about how newspapers should be produced, and about the role of journalism in a society. Some reporters thought that the atmosphere in the newsroom was already poisoned because of a strong polarization between those in favour of and those opposed to change. Some, who were suspicious of any attempts to solicit their opinion, were guarded about their comments regarding the organizational changes. While these individuals expressed deep concern over the future of the newspaper, they felt alienated, disenfranchised, and devalued because of the changes that had been implemented or proposed. Some had gone for stress counselling to help them deal with the effects.

Opponents also felt that a sacred trust established by the late Walter Blackburn was being violated. The LFP had, until recently, been regarded as a writer's paper because of the consistently high quality of its journalism, as judged by other journalists. There was a strong tradition of editorial freedom, and the reporters had become accustomed to being treated as highly trained and valued professionals. Some feared that, with change, their skills would be devalued in favour of *People* magazine-style writing, which could be executed by relatively unskilled individuals.

One reporter commented:

> Management should be trying to involve people, rather than alienating them. Many of us are deeply concerned about what's going on, but management isn't paying any attention. We've been left behind in this whole thing; nothing coming from us has been listened to. Many people feel disenfranchised, devalued. There's a high level of distrust here, and an adversarial climate. In fact, the environment is so poisoned, I'm worried that what I say to you [that is, the case writer] might be used against me.

There was also resistance to what some saw as the "scourge of MBAs." Market research reports that suggested declining profits and an unsustainable future for the newspaper had been shared with the staff, but they were dismissed by dissidents as mere spreadsheet manipulation. The report authors were characterized as pinstriped automatons bent on forcing higher short-term profits out of a venerable institution by squeezing out its lifeblood. Opponents of change pointed out that none of the blue-suit crowd's forecasts ever came true anyway, and saw the doom and gloom scenarios, with their accompanying recommendations, as a stratagem that allowed the MBAs to increase their own consulting revenue.

Scepticism and mistrust was further fuelled by the fact that McLeod's own managerial style was sometimes less than tactful, especially when he was challenging some of journalism's sacred cows. A typical comment about a proposed story might be: "Who cares?" which was intended to mean: "Do our readers feel strongly about this story, or does the way we've presented it give them a reason to care?" However, some reporters, not accustomed to thinking this way, might misinterpret the remark as a personal criticism or as a lack of confidence in their writing ability.

MCLEOD'S POSITION

Although he felt strongly that change was needed, McLeod was in a quandary about what form it should take, the urgency with which it should be implemented, and what support or resistance the changes might encounter. BGI management had hired McLeod from the *Toronto Star* with the expectation that he would be a change agent. The culture of the *Star*, of which McLeod was a product, was perceived as much less family-like and paternalistic than the LFP. This was partly because it operated in a much more competitive market, but also because of the long tradition of Blackburn family influence on the way the London paper was run. The Blackburn legacy implied that employees would be cared for during difficult periods in their personal and professional lives, and would not be treated as interchangeable chattels or disposable factors of production. McLeod's arrival on the scene, with his outsider's background and perspective, was a signal to some that these traditions might be consigned to history, to be replaced by a much more impersonal bottom-line focus.

Previous editors had also tended to put high-quality journalism at the top of their agenda. As a result, the LFP was widely perceived, both internally and by outsiders, as a "writer's paper." Any change that threatened these priorities would meet with stiff opposition. BGI executives were willing to support any reasonable initiative—Phil McLeod's challenge lay in choosing the right one and avoiding the most serious pitfalls.

EXHIBIT 1   **Year-End Newspaper Results, 1992 Stock Market Performance**

	Gain(**)
A.H. Belo (NYSE—BLC)	30.4%
Dow Jones (NYSE—DJ)	23.7%
Gannett (NYSE—GCI)	11.4%
Knight Ridder (NYSE—KRI)	17.7%
McClatchy (NYSE—MNI)	21.9%
Media General (ASE—MEGA)	17.2%
Multimedia (NASDAQ—MMEDC)	9.8%
New York Times (ASE—NYTA)	68.8%
Times Mirror (NYSE—TMC)	47.5%
Tribune (NYSE—TRB)	37.7%
Washington Post (NYSE—WPO)	23.5%
Average Gain	28.6%
Standard & Poors	
—400 Industrials	6.2%
—500 Composite	10.3%

Source: Company Reports, Alex Brown & Sons estimates.

EXHIBIT 2   **Thomson—North American Newspapers**

(millions of dollars)

	1988	*1989*	*1990*	*1991*	*1992*
Revenues	981	1 081	1 158	1 142	1 160
Operating Profit	306	317	282	228	205
Operating Margin	31.2%	29.3%	24.4%	20.0%	17.7%

Source: Company Reports, Alex Brown & Sons estimates.

EXHIBIT 3   **Partial Organization Chart**

circa 1987

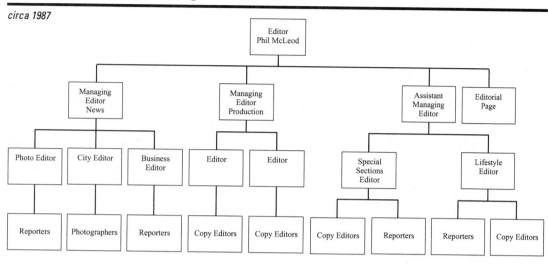

Source: Philip McLeod interview.

ICI COLOURS: FIGHTING FOR THE CUSTOMER

case
31

Joyce Miller
and Terry Deutscher

In January 1989, Patrick Kelly, ICI Colours and Fine Chemicals' (C&FC) U.K. Regional Manager, was urging Mike Parker, C&FC's Commercial Director, to formalize the Customer Charter initiative under the umbrella of "Fighting for the Customer." The intention of the Customer Charter was to hammer out a mutually agreeable service package with key customers and to monitor and report C&FC's performance against their requirements. The program was based on the promise to trace back and forever eliminate service

IVEY

Joyce Miller prepared this case under the supervision of Terry Deutscher solely to provide material for class discussion. The authors do not intend to illustrate either effective or ineffective handling of a managerial situation. The authors may have disguised certain names and other identifying information to protect confidentiality.

deficiencies at their source. Forming partnerships with customers was a powerful idea, but some concern had been expressed within the Colours organization about its ability to deliver.

THE COLOURS INDUSTRY

Colouring was one of the earliest recorded industries. Some 3 000 years ago, the Phoenicians used pigments from ores and minerals to colour fibres and leathers. Pigments were obtained by grinding these strongly coloured insoluble materials into a fine powder so that particles of colour would be dispersed throughout the material. Alternatively, an article could be dyed. In this case, colour was transferred to a piece of cloth, for instance, which was immersed in a liquid in which a soluble colouring agent had been dissolved. Discoveries in the 19th century enabled the manufacture of synthetic colourants. In 1988, 800 000 tonnes of synthetic dyestuffs and pigments were produced. As an example, 150 grams of dye were sufficient to colour six suits, while 50 grams of pigment were enough to paint a small car.

Six European companies dominated the world market for dyes and organic pigments and accounted for more than half of the industry's US$10 billion sales in 1988:

Ciba-Geigy	20%
Sandoz	8%
ICI C&FC (dyes and pigments)	7%
Hoechst	9%
Bayer	5%
BASF	9%

In recent years, "nontraditional" suppliers had begun producing increasing quantities of colourants. These suppliers were mostly agents located in Eastern Europe, Taiwan and China. The Soviet Union also occasionally exported dyestuffs to obtain hard currency when excess production was available. Product quality and delivery were inconsistent as was the case with most non-traditional sources. An industry analyst observed:

> Non-traditional suppliers are biting at the ankles of the six majors, but they mostly compete with each other. They have little overhead and no real structure to get a toehold into the developed markets. The Japanese are really the ones with the ability to make an impact as their chemical industry becomes more developed; their whole mindset is built around total quality and the philosophy is to have one supplier of key materials who never lets you down.

Dyestuffs were used primarily in the textile industry, whereas industrial colours (pigments) were used in the paper, ink, leather, paints and plastics industries. Overall, the market was fairly mature with 2 per cent annual growth, although certain segments like plastics and printing inks were expanding at a faster rate. Demand in most customers' industries tended to follow the business cycle. Consequently, movements in the cycle had direct repercussions on demand levels, prices and margins for dyes and pigments.

On the textile side, the fashion-conscious developed countries of Europe and North America drove the demand for dyestuffs, particularly for colouring knitgoods, denim and polyester blends. The fashion industry experienced continuous change and producers succeeded by rightly anticipating shifts in demand for materials and colours. As a result, dyestuffs buyers were pressuring their suppliers for more information, better response time, and improved delivery reliability. While the turnaround time for industrial colours orders ranged from two days to a week, a textile customer typically wanted delivery within 24–48 hours.

Industrial colours tended to be more price-sensitive than dyes. This was especially the case in the ink industry where pigments represented about 20 per cent of total materials costs. In addition to price, industrial colours buyers valued dependable delivery and consistency from batch to batch. Many were not wholly satisfied with their current suppliers. As one American ink manufacturer said:

> If one of the ingredients for mixing a batch of ink isn't right, we have to adjust the formula, at a high cost in terms of time and production capacity. Furthermore, delivery is critical. If you promise it to me in two weeks, on the 15th, I can schedule around it until then. But get it to me on the 15th, don't dribble it in at the end of the month.
>
> Would I pay 10 per cent more for a perfectly consistent product that was always delivered when promised? Hell, yes! But I'm sceptical that any supplier can actually do it.

ICI COLOURS & FINE CHEMICALS (C&FC)

Located in Blackley, near Manchester, C&FC was a leading global supplier of dyestuffs, industrial colours, and certain chemicals. In 1988, C&FC generated £400 million in revenues through the sale of some 2 000 products to over 14 000 customers worldwide. ICI had national selling organizations in 60 countries and serviced many more through agent or dealer arrangements. Geographically, sales were as follows: 17 per cent in the U.K., 33 per cent in Western Europe, 21 per cent in Asia/Pacific, 20 per cent in the Americas, and 9 per cent in Eastern Europe and Africa. An organization chart is contained in Exhibit 1.

The sale of industrial colours contributed about one quarter of C&FC revenues. Customers were generally major international groups who looked at prices globally and had rigorous standards for pigment consistency. In the case of automotive paint, ten organizations represented 65 per cent of the market worldwide. On the other hand, the textile industry was extremely fragmented and customers ranged dramatically in size. Here, a supplier's success was rooted in quick response time and right-the-first-time product quality. Dyestuffs accounted for over 50 per cent of C&FC sales. The remaining revenue was derived from products used to provide distinguishing effects in agrochemicals, pharmaceuticals and household products such as detergents.

The physical dye or pigment was generally a powder or liquid in a drum. Manufacturing was contracted through ICI's Fine Chemicals Manufacturing Organization (FCMO) which operated as a cost centre serving five ICI businesses. Tony Rodgers, the Principal Executive Officer (PEO) of C&FC, also served as Chairman of the FCMO. C&FC was the FCMO's largest customer and accounted for 73 per cent of its direct expenses. Specialty Chemicals, Agrochemicals, Pharmaceuticals, and Polyurethanes represented the balance of the FCMO's activities. Manufacturing facilities were located primarily in the U.K. and France, although some production was also carried out in Australia, Brazil, India, Korea, Mexico, Pakistan and the United States.

The process to produce dyes and pigments was complex and could take several months to complete, although typically the product was "in the pot" (i.e., directly in process) for only a few weeks of that period. Batches often underwent 10–12 stages in four or five different plants. Equipment breakdowns and batch failures could extend production and distribution lead times. The FCMO's Operations Director, Hugh Donaldson, commented:

> The synthesis of organic chemicals involves multiple stages; it's toxic and sometimes difficult to do. Each reaction requires a minimum of two days which means that the chemistry alone can take three or four weeks. For some products, we needed 18 months' lead time, although the average has gone from nine months down to five through better planning and scheduling and improved plant reliability. The difficulty is that our organization's ability to detect changes in demand falls short of our ability to change manufacturing direction. As a result, the plants are loaded up with stuff we don't want. We not only end up with slow-moving stock, we've also missed opportunities in the market.

Given the complexity of the production process and the inevitable variability in naturally occurring raw materials, it was a real manufacturing challenge to produce a perfectly consistent product. Moreover, because of the nature of the production process, workers were a long way from tangible end products, and they typically had a limited appreciation of customer applications and the range of C&FC's business. For a number of years, the major objective of FCMO had been to minimize the cost of production while maintaining rigid quality standards in the face of very difficult manufacturing conditions.

C&FC'S HISTORY

ICI had been in the business of producing colourants since its formation in 1926. For 50 years, it was a technological leader in expanding markets and had a strong record of growth. The oil shocks of the late 1970s caused a sharp downturn in demand worldwide, throwing the industry into overcapacity and frequent price wars. Like other British producers, C&FC was hit hard by the added effects of high inflation and overvalued currency. This was at a time when C&FC's technology was becoming less unique as competitors picked up products coming off patent.

In hindsight, the situation was exacerbated by the 1982 acquisition of Francolor, a large French textile dye and pigments supplier. This deal was done under a privatization program by the French government. At the time, C&FC was in an expansion phase and believed that Francolor would provide economies of scale as well as an enhanced product line to enlarge its market position. C&FC subsequently discovered, after a £100 million investment, that Francolor was a business "on its last legs." Significant operating costs could not be easily extracted, its products were in very mature market areas, and no new product development was underway. In the 1982–84 period, the attention of C&FC management was increasingly diverted toward managing internal issues and away from the marketplace.

In 1984, C&FC had an 80 per cent working capital-to-sales ratio and experienced a £20 million trading loss and £50 million in extraordinary losses. On-time delivery averaged 57 per cent and there was a chronic deficiency in customer satisfaction. Tony Rodgers was appointed to run the business with a mandate to restore profitability. Some dramatic steps were undertaken. Plants were rationalized and 1 200 people were laid off. The product line was trimmed from 5 000 to 2 000 products, which, in effect, moved C&FC's profile back to where it was prior to the Francolor purchase. This restructuring was keenly felt. An observer noted:

> The Colours business was in bad shape; people were arrogant and unconcerned about their connection to the rest of the company and to their customers, and this was in the middle of a financial downturn. People were used to paternalism and lifetime employment, but the truth finally dawned that, if the business didn't perform, it could get shut down. There's nothing like a wolf at the door to focus the mind. This was a time of great uncertainty and organizational change where everything seemed up for grabs. The challenge was how to get people to believe there even was a future after this.

FIGHTING FOR THE CUSTOMER

Under Rodgers' leadership, a program of "Fighting for the Customer" (FFTC) was launched in 1985 to remotivate C&FC's 5 000 U.K. and 1 000 French staff across a dozen key works and sites. FFTC was to be a symbol that people could rally behind, a symbol of recovery. The FFTC campaign was intended to get people thinking outward, away from internal issues and toward the customer. This was the first major customer service initiative undertaken within ICI. It was distinguished not only by its scale but by its highly visible top leadership. Moreover, it was not just about moving the business back to profitability. FFTC aimed to bring about a cultural change on a grand scale, a change from an internally focused operation to one which was market-focused and customer-oriented. Rodgers explained:

> The intention was to create a new spirit and currency for the organization in which the customer—not the technicalities of chemical products and their manufacture—became the driving force in the culture and strategic approach of the business.

The thinking behind FFTC was that the product itself was no longer the competitive edge. The basic chemistry across competitors was essentially the same; in fact, the last new molecule had been invented in 1956. Although patentable innovations still occurred in the industry, they were not major scientific breakthroughs. Service was one of the few significant ways in which a company could differentiate itself. The critical underlying assumption was that a customer whose product and service expectations were consistently met would buy more and be willing to pay a premium.

Initially, the FFTC message was carried by Tony Rodgers and his executive team through numerous site visits and a video. A three-month "Hollywood Stars" competition, judged by customers, involved the whole work force in submitting ideas for improving customer service. A booklet was distributed which described "how the world had changed" and used cartoon characters to explain what C&FC had to do to succeed in the "new world" (see Exhibit 2). These were unusual, even extraordinary, programs for ICI. Donaldson reflected:

> The "boxing gloves" imagery was right for the time and the organization was ripe for a quality initiative. FFTC was a way to channel the Brits' natural aggression and it was an inspired way to get at quality. It gave the weekly staff something to feel good about.

During this period, the grounds around C&FC's headquarters in Blackley were landscaped to send a symbolic message that senior management was confident of success.

In early 1987, a Fighting for the Customer Steering Group was formed to direct several initiatives taken under the FFTC umbrella (see Exhibit 3). The Commercial Services Group was made responsible for introducing the Business Control Project (BCP), a materials requirement planning system to improve the scheduling and measurement of materials flows. At the same time, the FCMO undertook to register its plants according to British quality standards. Donaldson commented:

> My guys are terror-stricken about losing their registration. This can be a powerful instrument to drive a manufacturing system. We were used to having a high level of work-in-process which insulated us from seeing the problems. But we can't afford to run a fat ship any longer. Moreover, the quality standards audits will uncover any slipping back into the "old ways" of operating. As for materials requirement planning, it was too long in coming. We weren't getting good quality information and we weren't measuring the right things. We had to be able to answer the question "Is the product available?" which means: "Can a customer book it and when can it be delivered?" BCP went quite a distance toward alleviating the rock-throwing mentality that was developing between the FCMO and the businesses. Ultimately, BCP and plant registration are more than just quality initiatives and software systems; they're attempts to put a different culture in place.

On the marketing side, the MARS program (Managed Activities to Realize Strategy) aimed at changing the sales philosophy away from volume and towards profit. As part of this, sales managers throughout the Colours organization worldwide were asked to define key accounts in key segments. In the U.K., 80 key textile customers were identified and 35 were selected on the Industrial Colours side. As a continuation of MARS, the Delta program set out to identify the gaps in knowledge and skills at the sales rep level that would have to be addressed to effectively carry out FFTC initiatives. Exhibit 4 shows C&FC's financial position through to mid-1988.

THE OCTOBER 1988 CRISIS WITH STANDFAST

In the midst of ongoing activities to build the FFTC infrastructure, a crisis was developing in the Sales Office. In early October 1988, Mike Bradbury, C&FC's U.K. Textile Sales Manager, received a letter from Standfast Dyers & Printers that expressed extreme dissatisfaction with the standard of service from the Dyestuffs group and the intention to withdraw its entire business over the next three months and hand it over to a major competitor. Standfast was part of the Courtaulds Group, a British textile and chemicals organization that operated globally. Standfast was a longstanding customer for several C&FC dye specialties and accounted for £750 000 in annual purchases.

C&FC's performance on the Standfast account in terms of both delivery and quality had deteriorated markedly over the past three years. The situation was so severe in 1987 that it was virtually guaranteed that any product Standfast requested would be stocked out or off-quality. Faced with the prospect of losing a major U.K. customer, Bradbury held a meeting with representatives from manufacturing, sales, marketing, quality control, order processing and scheduling. Bradbury recounted:

> The many meetings I'd already had to try and sort out this situation failed miserably. I could fire out the shots but the departmental walls were so high and so thick that they didn't even penetrate. The meeting I convened in early November 1988 started out on an acrimonious note as well. The Manufacturing people said it wasn't their fault—they manufacture based on forecast demand and they can only meet a request if the raw materials are on hand. The Quality Control people said it wasn't their fault—they need two weeks' lead time to test products. Marketing said it wasn't their fault—they give demand forecasts to the Works but the Works goes ahead and makes the products it can, then Marketing has to figure out how to sell them. The Sales people said it wasn't their fault—they're just selling products to customers and they can't sell them if they don't have them. No one would take responsibility.
>
> The Standfast ultimatum made these people realize what poor service they were giving the customer. They finally pulled together. Each department took away action plans. Sales would ask Standfast for offtake information on a rolling basis. Quality Control said they would do same-day testing for Standfast's products. In all this, we discovered a fault in the BCP system that never brought raw materials forward through the Works to produce certain specialty products. We were having stockouts because no one had planned for the next production run.

By January 1989, the Standfast situation was completely turned around. C&FC was able to meet Standfast's next-day delivery requirement with good quality products. Bradbury commented:

> Before, we weren't talking to Standfast about the things that really mattered—production levels, where the demand was. The salesmen talked about football and rugby; this was the way they related with customers. Once we asked, Standfast gave us information about their anticipated demand. All this required was the push of a button. Then it was a matter of scheduling manufacturing so that the right products were on hand when Standfast called. What we really did was look at an individual customer's needs and develop a service package to meet those requirements. The crisis with Standfast actually pushed our hand a bit. The idea of in some way forming partnerships with customers had been kicking around the Sales Department for some time.

Even after the Standfast problem was addressed, however, the question of long-term effects remained. Was this another case of ICI "swarming" a problem and fixing it without really making a fundamental change in the root cause, which related directly to the way the business was being run?

THE CUSTOMER CHARTER PROJECT

In the months preceding the crisis with Standfast, there had been a great deal of discussion over an idea put forward by Patrick Kelly, the U.K. Regional Manager in C&FC's sales organization. He envisioned giving customers something like a "bank statement," which would provide a regular account of transactions to inspire a feeling of confidence in ICI as a supplier. Kelly recounted:

> If we're really prepared to fight for our customers, we should be giving them a statement of service; we need to do better on service than we're doing now and we need to regularly report to customers that we are meeting the promises we make.

Based on the success with Standfast, Kelly saw the potential for adopting something more like a partnership with customers throughout the U.K. He called this the Customer Charter. It would involve identifying problems, tracing them back through the organization, and telling the customer about it. Kelly had recently approached Mike Parker, C&FC's Commercial Director, with the idea of formalizing the initiative as the next logical step in the FFTC campaign.

The cornerstone of the Customer Charter was providing a differentiated level of service to a particular set of customers—key customers. By definition, this would mean comparatively lowering the level of service to some others. Kelly likened this to the way airlines arranged their seating:

> Everyone is on board, but the service package is different. Our key customers are treated like first class passengers. Key prospects are in club class while the cash generators sit in economy. Small customers fly standby. To put it simply, some customers are prepared to pay more for quality service.

Customers chosen for "chartering" would not be selected according to some mathematical formula based strictly on their size or purchasing history. The criteria would be a combination of volume, financial viability, and whether the customer was a leader in its field or operating in segments of interest in the future. Kelly imagined that the Charter document would be hand-delivered by a C&FC account team who would explain the Charter philosophy as well as the mechanics of the performance audit and corrective action plans.

C&FC's performance would be measured against "seven pillars of quality." These represented the most important influences on purchasing according to a U.K. market study, which C&FC had commissioned in 1987. The seven dimensions could be weighted to reflect the supplier attributes a particular customer deemed important (see Exhibit 5). A zero-defect performance resulted in an aggregate score of 200. In a bimonthly audit, C&FC's performance would be rated across the seven pillars. Action plans would be put in place to eliminate the defects that caused performance to fall short of the maximum score. These defects would then be traced back and eliminated at their source.

Kelly believed that the Charter would break down the walls between departments and create a robust, ongoing dialogue about customer needs. Furthermore, the information gained through the auditing process would significantly improve forecast accuracy. Early warning of potential supply problems would mean that corrective actions could be taken in advance of a crisis.

However, some of the people in the Colours organization shared a much different opinion of the Charter. Their sentiments are typified by the remark of a manager in the U.K. regional office in Bolton:

> My first reaction to the Charter was that we're asking for trouble; we're just exposing all our warts to the customer, showing mistakes that customers might have missed or didn't care about, and now they'll know. Some people are not convinced of the strategy; they say there aren't enough people to do it, it's not adding value, and we shouldn't be wasting time with Charter activities. At the end of the day, customers want the right products delivered on time and they won't give a monkey about some Charter document.

Russell Bond, the U.K. Sales Manager for Industrial Colours, added:

> One of the problems is that the Charter will have to compete with other quality initiatives. ICI has a lot of initiatives running concurrently: salary reviews, organizational changes, and then ICI France may have launched some program we don't even know about. We've got too much change all at the

same time. People at my level are caught up in resource issues. Then there's the whole question of whether we can even make the kind of changes the Charter requires. The organization is geared for the efficient running of plant and equipment. Customer awareness stops outside the Sales Department.

IMPLEMENTING THE CHARTER

Over the past three months, the U.K. textile sales team had collected performance data under "dummy charters" that had been set up for several major customers. One market officer in the Bolton sales office elaborated:

> Implementing live Charters seemed like a daunting task after this, and doing the first Charter would be a nightmare. It was taking us up to five days to prepare a single customer audit with the dummy charters. The information had to be manually collected from different files and different systems. The sales office didn't even have a picture of when an order came in and the process it went through. The only indication of how well we performed was if a customer rang up with a problem. And then the complaints were mostly technical: the product was too thick, too weak, the wrong shade. The way the sales office usually worked it out was to throw bricks at anything that got in the way of serving customers.

Clearly, the Charter would require a major systems effort to ensure that the necessary information was collected and available in a usable format. Alan Spall, C&FC's Finance Director, noted "this isn't exciting stuff but it's the stuff that will trip you up if you don't get it right." Exhibit 6 illustrates the range of data that would have to be matched against the Charter's seven pillars. One difficulty was that systems had been installed over the years without too much concern for compatibility in order to meet purely local needs like order processing. These systems simply could not capture the Charter's full dimensions. A package would have to be developed which imbedded local functions within the Charter framework. Ongoing support would be required to ensure that those in the field were not overburdened with the work of collating the Charter data. The first challenge was to agree on terminology, align product definitions, and so on. Mike Bradbury reflected:

> C&FC has been trying for years to get customers in a pecking order, but the Centre and the national selling offices all have different definitions of what a key customer is. We're really not very good at picking key customers; we're good at picking big customers. If the customer has ancient computer systems and the Works are falling down, my guess is it won't be around in the year 2000.

Implementing the Customer Charter would require some dramatic changes. Foremost, was a change in the role of the internal sales support staff. Rather than be troubleshooters interfacing with customers regarding their immediate problems, the sales coordinators would be asked to analyze, anticipate and prevent problems. Bradbury commented:

> At present, the "inside people" correct invoices that are wrong, sort out price queries, get authorization to ship non-standard product, and so on. They also get into a lot of delivery issues because order processing sits within the sales office. These are bright, young people who know the sales organization and can fix anything in it. It's all based on personal contact. They're very successful getting things done in a reactive way, and they get a lot of satisfaction from this. Everyday, they can say "I'm a hero, I've solved problems."
>
> The Charter not only lessens their customer contact, it asks them to be more inward than outward looking, to be more proactive, to prevent problems from happening in the first place through data collection and analysis and lengthy audit preparation. A lot of these people will say "you've killed the job." There will be a lot of dissatisfaction coming from this group. The Charter asks them to solve problems within the bureaucracy, frequently outside the sales office. For some, this would be a deep psychological and cultural change.

Nichola Greening, a sales coordinator in the Bolton Office, continued:

The way I understand it, we would identify non-conformances, trace the defects back through the organization to their source, and put together action plans to try and resolve the problems from our level. The action plans will likely cross functional boundaries, and I'll be interacting with people in Technical Service, Commercial Service, Administration, and so on.

I can see where the Charter will help to identify quality and delivery problems. If we had the product in stock but failed to give it to the customer, I can put an action plan in place. But it gets harder when a product is off-quality or stocked out because these defects would be traced back to a department outside the sales office. These people may understand the Charter concept at an intellectual level, but what if they act the same way as they have in the past. These people have always had a defensive response.

To give an example, we've always had a problem with a yellow vat dye that we have to buy in from Hoechst. The difficulties with delivery, shade, and strength have been highlighted many times, and the sales office has never been able to get a satisfactory response from the centre. With the Charter, I guess I would now raise this non-conformance with the purchasing department and somehow get them to take action.

Bradbury added:

I have trouble seeing how we'll pull this Charter thing off. In the sales office, we're close to the customer every day and we can see the value of the Charter. But some departments might resist the ground forces telling them how they have to act differently, although we might manage to drag a few people along. Implementing the Charter will require a complete change in how we operate, and that's not just in the sales office, it's the whole organization.

As it is, Bolton is only a 20 minute drive from the centre in Blackley, but we barely talk to each other. How are the sales coordinators going to get action on areas when we've never been able to do it before? And will we be able to get marketing on board? The marketing department talks about 20–30 key markets and the sales department talks about key customers. Under the Charter, meeting commitments to key customers ultimately means taking away from other markets within the current system. But there's no mechanism to ensure that product is available for key customers. The way it works now is that if Hong Kong puts in an order for an extra 10 tonnes of Product X, when the U.K. comes along and asks for its scheduled offtake for a key customer, only nonstandard product might be left. The sales coordinator will raise this problem with the marketing department, but the corrective action will be vague. Someone has to say it's our job to sell the right products to the right customers.

Patrick Kelly acknowledged that the Customer Charter was simple to articulate but it would be hard to deliver. It required a complete organization behind it and involved a major change in how C&FC did business. Kelly elaborated:

C&FC has to differentiate itself in ways not easily duplicated by competitors. The Customer Charter creates a mindset that imbeds responsiveness into all of our activities. More importantly, the Charter provides clear evidence of the value of the relationship, and it will make customers think long and hard about what they want to trade off or take out of the relationship. The bottom line is that the Charter is a basis for securing price increases on key accounts. In this business, a 1 per cent increase in price generates almost as much margin as a 2 per cent increase in volume.

Of course we have a long way to go; not all the salespeople are equipped with the skills and confidence to carry it off. There's also the danger that the Charter will be seen as a gimmick, just another "flavour of the month," another head office cost that will have to be met out in the field. There might also be cynicism in the works from those who see the Charter as strictly a sales initiative. The program will have to appear ingrained, sustainable and long term. We've got to demonstrate that "fighting for the customer" is more than just wind. At the same time, we need to build in some slack and be careful to promise only what we can achieve.

Kelly was planning to approach Chilton Brothers in late January 1989 as the first step towards chartering 1 200 key customers worldwide. Privately owned by two brothers, Chiltons was a major British manufacturer of dyed and finished knitted goods and one of C&FC's most important customers.

Mike Parker appreciated Kelly's enthusiasm for the Customer Charter and knew that he was anxious to launch the initiative, but was it the right idea and was it too soon? Had they really thought out what implementation would mean for the organization? And how serious were the obstacles?

E X H I B I T 1 Colours & Fine Chemicals

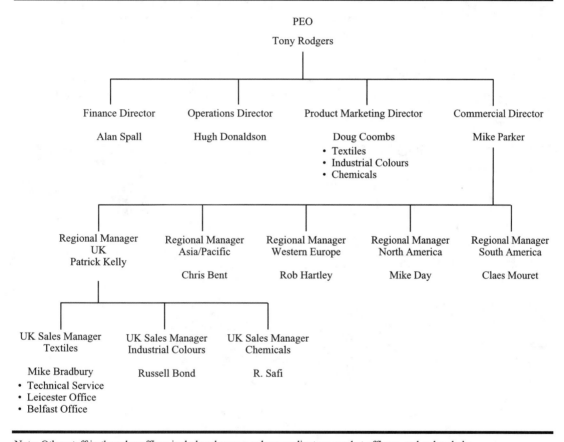

Note: Other staff in the sales offices include sales reps, sales coordinators, market officers, and order clerks.

EXHIBIT 2 **Excerpts**

FIGHTING FOR THE CUSTOMER

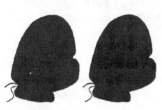

Life is tough in the battle for international markets. It's intensely competitive and it's very fast moving. Only the fittest companies survive, and the fittest are those who never forget that success depends on winning and keeping satisfied customers. This is what FIGHTING FOR THE CUSTOMER is all about.

We've already come a long way in adjusting to the painful changes in world markets over the last few years. We are a lot fitter. We have won new markets. We have the products, the know how and the people to compete internationally. But we could still be a lot smarter.

Fighting for the customer involves us all—in everything we do, everyday. By working together as a team, in FIGHTING for our customers, we can all win.

THE SUCCESS FORMULA TO GUIDE OUR ACTIONS— FOCUS ON CUSTOMER NEEDS

- Focus on the right products and services— Benefit-focused product innovation. Quality on time production. On time distribution. Profit-focused sales.

- Focus on winning customers. Grow with industry winners who need and can pay for the best.

- Deliver what we promise. Good service earns repeat orders and good prices. Good service can make all the difference.

- Look and act as champions— professional, committed, confident.

EXHIBIT 3 **Performance Improvement Initiatives**

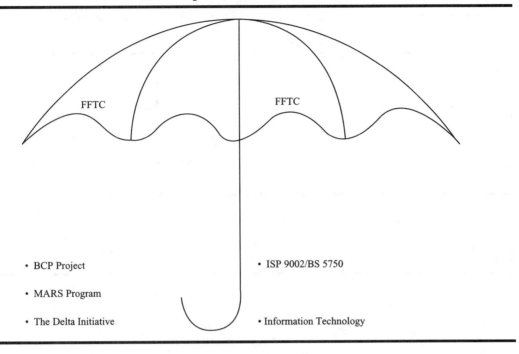

- BCP Project
- MARS Program
- The Delta Initiative

- ISP 9002/BS 5750
- Information Technology

EXHIBIT 4 **C&FC's Profit and Cash Position, 1972–Mid-1988**

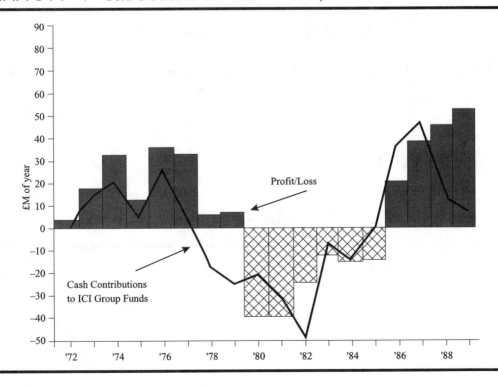

EXHIBIT 5 Customer Charter's Scoring Mechanism

Some variations on weighting the seven pillars of quality. A zero defect performance across all dimensions aggregates to 200.

	Customer 1	Customer 2	Customer 3
Quality of Product	60	40	60
Delivery	40	40	40
Communication	10	20	40
Documentation	20	20	10
Complaint Handling	10	20	10
Visits	30	20	20
Technical Support	30	40	20
	200	200	200

EXHIBIT 6 Data Capture

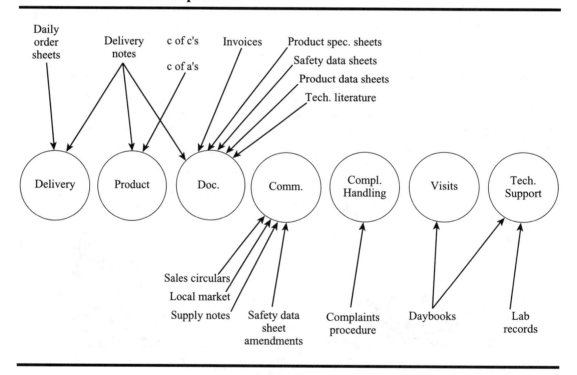

WELLINGTON INSURANCE (A)

case

32

Julian Birkinshaw
and Mary M. Crossan

Murray Wallace, the newly appointed President and Chief Executive Officer (CEO) of Wellington Insurance, realized that he needed to take action swiftly. It was late January 1988, and Wallace had held the post of CEO for less than a month. In that time he had made a comprehensive assessment of Wellington's operations, and had concluded that the company was in a very poor state of health. A consultant's report described Wellington as "a company without hope." It was Wallace's job to prove the consultant wrong.

Wallace had been offered the job of CEO several months earlier by Trilon, the parent company of Wellington. Through his experience as a Wellington board member, and an initial assessment of Wellington's

IVEY

Julian Birkinshaw prepared this case under the supervision of Mary M. Crossan solely to provide material for class discussion. The authors do not intend to illustrate either effective or ineffective handling of a managerial situation. The authors may have disguised certain names and other identifying information to protect confidentiality.

competitive position, he concluded that the best course of action was to sell Wellington. Trilon's board did not take his advice, having committed themselves to maintaining a portfolio of diversified financial services. They asked Wallace to take the job, beginning on January 1, 1988. Despite the need for a sustained long-term change at Wellington, quarterly reporting to Trilon also created a sense of urgency in Wallace's task.

There were multiple problems at Wellington, not least of which was the low morale of the employees. Wallace was aware that a number of change programs had been implemented over the years, with very little apparent success. As a result he realized that any initiatives he came up with would probably be seen as "just another change program." He began to consider what action he could take that would have a positive impact on the attitudes of the employees.

THE GENERAL INSURANCE INDUSTRY

The basic principle of insurance was to share the losses of few among many. It was originally conceived in the shipping industry, through the formation of syndicates of ship-owners who each contributed a "premium" to a common fund that would be used in the event of an accident. The last hundred years, however, had seen a rapid rise in individual prosperity, and in particular the ownership of cars and houses, such that most insurance became directed toward consumers. Commercial ventures made up the minority.

There were two principal types of insurance: Life insurance, which protected the policyholder's health and life; and General insurance, which protected the policyholder's possessions. A critical difference from the insurance companies' point of view was that life insurance usually included a guaranteed payout (on death) while general insurance made payments only to the minority who incurred material loss. Life insurance was the larger industry with 1987 Canadian revenues of $41 billion, compared to $17 billion for general insurance. The combined figures represented 0.6 per cent of the Gross Domestic Product (GDP).

The primary function of the general insurance company was to calculate an appropriate premium for every risk, such as damage to the policyholder's automobile or theft from the home, so that the income received in premiums was larger than the outlay in claims (called underwriting). A secondary role was to invest the policyholders' premiums until claims were made. This provided a relatively predictable return to counterbalance the erratic returns from risk-sharing. A third aspect of the general insurance company's work was loss reduction and prevention: through its experience in dealing with a large number of claims, the insurance company was ideally placed to educate the consumer on how to avoid accidents, deter theft and reduce loss.

Performance measures for general insurance firms were designed to reflect the distinction between underwriting and investment. The key measures are presented in Table 1.

T A B L E 1 Key Financial Ratios in General Insurance

Earned Loss Ratio	The percentage of total premiums paid out as claims. A figure of 70 indicated that for every $1 in policy premiums collected $0.70 was paid out in insurance claims.
Total Expense Ratio	The percentage of total premiums paid out as commissions (to brokers), taxes and general administrative expenses.
Combined Ratio	The earned loss ratio plus the total expense ratio. A figure of less than 100 indicated that the company had made a profit on its underwriting activities.

Investment income was usually quoted as a dollar sum rather than a percentage, and was added to the underwriting profit (loss) to arrive at the total profit. Thus a combined ratio of 108 on total premiums of $1 million represented an underwriting loss of $80 000. If the investment income for the year were $100 000 the company would still make a profit of $20 000.

Business Functions in General Insurance

A general insurance company was typically organized into three main functional areas: underwriting, claims, and marketing and sales.

UNDERWRITING Whenever a new customer required insurance, or its established customers' policies were up for renewal, the underwriters calculated an appropriate premium based on the previous history of the individual, age, sex and so on. For commercial customers (i.e., businesses) premiums were based on industry statistics and an assessment of the business facilities.

CLAIMS Whenever a claim was made, such as an automobile accident or a theft, the claims department worked with the customer and his or her broker to ensure satisfactory payment. Damage would be assessed by an appraiser, either over the telephone or in person. The adjustor would do the rest of the work: ensuring the policy was valid, arranging any legal documentation, and arranging payment.

MARKETING AND SALES This function was responsible for the product: the coverage offered, its price, the commission rate (to brokers), any special features, and the segment of the market it targeted. Marketing employees worked with brokers and with the general public to increase awareness of product features. Every insurance company also had a number of other functions, including capital investment, actuarial work, legal work, and accounting, but these typically involved much smaller numbers of staff.

THE CANADIAN GENERAL INSURANCE INDUSTRY

The Canadian industry had 350 licensed companies in 1988. The top eight held less than 40 per cent of the market, and no single company held more than 7 per cent. In addition there were a number of mutual companies (in which the shareholders were policyholders), and four government-owned auto-insurance companies. Of the $17 billion 1987 revenues, $4 billion were attributable to the government-owned companies. Only 40 per cent of the market was held by Canadian-controlled firms. The rest was held by multinational insurance companies such as Zurich and Royal Insurance. There were no significant multinational Canadian companies.

The industry was heavily regulated to ensure that companies had both the capital reserves and expertise to fulfill their obligations to policyholders. Entry requirements were, however, considered to be straightforward. Foreign acquisitions of Canadian companies were typically not restricted, except in Quebec where foreign ownership was limited to 25 per cent.

Market Segments

The market for general insurance was divided into six sectors. Automobile insurance was by far the largest, accounting for $5.5 billion out of the private-sector total premiums of $11 billion,[1] and was generally the least profitable as well. Property insurance accounted for $3.8 billion of the total, with the re-

---

[1] Note that the private sector revenues of $13 billion (1987) consisted of $11 billion premiums and $2 billion investment income.

mainder being taken up by the various specialty lines: liability, surety and fidelity, boiler and machinery, and marine and aircraft. Most insurance companies and brokers distinguished between "personal lines" and "commercial lines." Personal lines were just written in auto and property; commercial lines were written in all six areas. The major difference between the two was the high level of individual attention needed for commercial assessments. Typically, each business would be assessed through a personal visit by an underwriter, whereas individuals were assessed according to a prescribed formula.

The prevailing wisdom in the industry was to offer a broad range of products across most or all sectors. Automobile insurance, in particular, was offered by nearly all companies because of its predominance, and because there were opportunities to cross-sell into property. A number of companies had opted for a more focused strategy. Cigna specialized in commercial lines only, and Pilot had deliberately restricted its operations to Ontario, with a focus on personal automobile within that. Evidence suggested that a focused strategy could be effective if well executed, but was inherently more risky than the full-line alternative.

Product Characteristics

Most consumers viewed insurance as a commodity. In the automobile and property sectors every insurance company offered similar coverage, and claims were infrequent enough that speed of payment and service were hard to compare. Attempts had been made to differentiate products by branding or by special features, but these were quickly copied. Furthermore, there was no cost to the customer for transferring business to another company, and contracts were renewed annually or biannually. The consequence was that there was little company loyalty, and in periods of price fluctuations many customers changed company. A further concern to the industry was the inelasticity of demand. Insurance purchases were often legislated (e.g., liability insurance) and usually bought grudgingly. A lower price, for property insurance for example, did not encourage customers to buy more insurance. For any individual company, however, volume could be substantially affected by price because it was being achieved at the expense of competitors. A low price strategy, for example, would likely have the effect of increasing sales but with a corresponding drop in quality. Companies did not just want customers: they wanted customers who were unlikely to make claims. The opposing strategies of increasing sales and weeding out the high-risk businesses represented an ongoing dilemma for insurance companies.

There was some potential for differentiation in the niche lines such as surety and fidelity or boiler and machinery because there was a considerable amount of direct contact with the customer. High quality service was rewarded through word-of-mouth referrals so that reputation, rather than price alone, became a source of competitive advantage. These niches were too small to be the focus of the business, but represented a profitable sideline for any company that could secure a position.

Industry Characteristics

While the barriers to entry were moderate, the costs of exiting the insurance industry were substantial. Companies were liable for up to seven years for claims, and often the reserved sums of money were insufficient to pay for future costs. Thus, a company exiting the industry could expect several years of future expenses, with no revenues against which to offset them. The result was an industry with far too many players, all competing on price. Profitability was low, and the consolidation among players, long anticipated in the industry, had not happened. As one analyst commented: "If you can't make a decent return on revenues of $200 million, you think twice about expanding to $400 million." Evidence in the Canadian market suggested that significant economies of scale were attainable up to about $300 million revenues.

Only two players were substantially larger than $300 million and both reputedly had organizational difficulties. However, it was not known whether these difficulties stemmed from the additional complexities of running a larger business, or whether they were attributable to a lack of strategic focus.

Size did, however, confer advantages of a different sort on the multinational insurance companies. By operating in multiple jurisdictions these companies had a certain amount of flexibility in deciding where they would realize profits. A poor performance in Canada, for example, could effectively be smoothed over as long as money was being made elsewhere. This cross-subsidization allowed the multinationals to take a very long-term perspective on their portfolio of operations. The multinationals were also better positioned to pick up the commercial business of multinational customers, such as liability insurance for international trade.

The general insurance industry had typically been very cyclical, with changes in income from year to year as high as 10 per cent of sales. At its peak the industry had excess capital; therefore, insurance companies cut prices or extended coverage to gain market share. This resulted in lower premiums, a reduced capital base and a reduced profit margin. After a number of years of lean profits the major players would push up their prices again to reasonable levels, only to begin price-cutting again. In recent years the upturns had become shorter and the downturns more severe, with the effect that underwriting profits had become something of a rarity. Exhibit 1 shows average industry income for the period 1977–87.

The Broker System

The brokerage industry was highly fragmented with upwards of 3 000 competitors in Canada. They ranged in size from the two-person personal lines broker, with maybe 1 000 customers, up to the big multinational broker interested only in commercial lines for large corporations. A small minority of insurance companies, such as State Farm and Allstate, had tied brokers who were obliged to sell that company's products. All the rest were independent, and saw themselves as agents acting in the best interests of their clients. The depressed state of the insurance industry was hitting the tied broker companies particularly hard, as they were obliged to maintain their brokers regardless of volume. It was rumoured that Allstate's Canadian business was for sale.

Independent brokers typically dealt with several insurance companies and selected policies for their clients according to the client's specific needs. The decision was usually made on the basis of price, but brokers were free to recommend insurance companies with which they had a good relationship, or which provided exceptional service. They were also free to push their worst business (i.e., most risky) towards less-favoured companies. Broker commissions varied from 10 per cent to 25 per cent depending on the segment and on the precise arrangement with the insurance company.

Most independent brokers felt very strongly about retaining their independence. They saw objectivity and freedom of choice as their major services to the customer, and viewed with suspicion or outright rejection any attempt by insurance companies to tie them in to certain products. Nonetheless, insurance companies used a variety of tactics to gain preferential status with their brokers. Some worked on providing swift, efficient claims services; some competed on price or commission; others offered a "contingent profits" scheme whereby the broker received a share in the company's profits over a certain dollar amount. The dividing link between creating a strong relationship with brokers, and encroaching on their independence, was very fine.

The traditional way of doing business in general insurance was to manage the combined ratio, as investment returns were fairly standard across companies. Most companies achieved this through careful underwriting, maintenance of steady relations with brokers, and careful attention to costs in the management and administrative side of the business. One way of ensuring that costs were kept down was to operate with a "centralized" structure, whereby most functions stayed at head office and only those who had frequent contact with customers (e.g., appraisers) positioned themselves in the field. The disadvantage of this approach was that customer responsiveness suffered. Claims could not be assessed quickly, and brokers reported dissatisfaction in dealing with their insurers by phone rather than in person. Some companies had regional sales and marketing offices to alleviate this concern, but most viewed cost control as more important.

The low-cost strategy used by most competitors was responsible for the vicious price-cutting that had damaged the industry's profitability. Some observers thought that opportunities existed for innovative companies to differentiate themselves and break out of the price war, but this had not occurred. Insurance was a very "old fashioned" industry and competitors tended to preserve the status quo.

Trends in the Industry

The underwriting side of general insurance (as measured by the combined ratio figure) was an erratic but persistent money loser in the period 1978–88, and it was only the booming equities market that had sustained the industry. Ten per cent annual increases in premiums had been necessary to counter the increasing number of claims and inflation, but now consumers were pressuring governments to legislate lower increases. Nowhere was this problem more acute than in Ontario, where the Liberal government had recently put a rates freeze on the automobile insurance market. Insurers were already losing money in this sector, and were pressuring the government to consider a "no-fault"[2] insurance package that would stabilize and reduce claims.

The Canadian insurance industry was not expecting to be severely affected by the anticipated Free Trade Agreement with the U.S. Insurance companies in the U.S. were generally much larger than their Canadian counterparts (up to $3 billion in revenues), but this was thought to give them very little advantage: because each state had its own set of regulations, the full scope of insurance activities was duplicated in each one. Furthermore, the Canadian market had been open to foreign competition for years, with American and European companies outnumbering Canadian in the top ranks. The trend in recent years, in fact, had been the exit of a number of American players, who saw the Canadian market as unattractive. They were in a position to use their continuing American revenues to offset the exit costs from Canada.

Further changes in the insurance industry were anticipated if recent policy proposals to break down the traditional barriers among financial institutions went through. The current laws required separate institutions for insurance companies, banks, trust companies and securities firms (the "four financial pillars"). If these laws were relaxed, diversified financial institutions were expected to form. The consequence for the general insurance industry was expected to be a shake-out in which the successful companies were bought up by the major banks, and the less-successful driven out of business. Change at the retail end was also expected, as the broker industry would be duplicating the service of the traditional branch network. Analysts were unsure how this conflict of interests would be resolved. Some saw the insurance broker as a dying breed, unable to compete with the efficient coverage of a retail bank branch network. Others argued that brokers would always retain their competitive advantage over banks. As one broker commented: "You can call me at three in the morning when you've just been burgled, and I'll do my job. Try doing that with a bank."

---

[2] No-fault insurance was intended to reduce the number of questionable damage claims by making each insurance company pay all the costs of its client, regardless of fault. It was expected to lower insurance costs at the expense of the legal profession.

WELLINGTON INSURANCE AND TRILON CORPORATION

Wellington Insurance had been in existence since 1840 under a number of different names. In 1982 it was purchased by Fireman's Fund Insurance Co., an American general insurance company owned by American Express, and became known as "Fireman's Fund Insurance Company of Canada." It wrote property and automobile insurance to individuals (about 300 000) and to small or medium-sized businesses (about 40 000). Operations spanned Canada, but about 50 per cent of the company's business was in Ontario. In 1984 the Company's premium volume was $166 million, or about 2 per cent of the national market, making it the fourteenth largest general insurer in Canada.

In January of 1985, the company was bought by Trilon Corporation for $143 million and renamed Wellington Insurance. Trilon was part of Edward and Peter Bronfman's business empire. It had been set up as a management company to oversee the Bronfman's financial services interests. Trilon already had strong positions in life insurance (London Life), trust service (Royal TrustCo) and Real Estate broking (Royal LePage). The purchase of Fireman's Fund of Canada gave it access to the general insurance industry as well. Trilon's management recognized that these businesses, along with investment banking, were complementary to one another. Trilon expected to generate synergies through cross-selling, integrated broker networks and a consistent approach to customer service. The possibility of future deregulation in the financial services industry was a further rationale for Trilon's acquisition strategy.

The Trilon Business Strategy

Under CEO George Collins (Wallace's predecessor), Wellington's objective had been to reach Trilon's target return on equity of 15 per cent, a significant increase over the 1985 figure of 9.4 per cent. There were two main thrusts to the strategy: overhead reduction, and broker partnerships.

The overhead reduction program was implemented through a massive re-centralization in November of 1985. Staff levels in each branch office were cut by 40–80 per cent. In London, Ontario, for example the numbers were reduced from eight down to four. Those functions that could easily operate over the phone, such as underwriting, were centralized in Toronto, and all other functions began to report back to supervisors based in Toronto rather than spread through the regions.

Staffing costs were significantly reduced through this strategy, but parts of the business started to suffer. The first problem was a backlog in the claims area, as the reduced number of adjustors struggled to keep up with the new claims. This had the immediate effect of damaging customer service and also broker confidence. "There were people out there who never got their car looked at in two or three weeks," commented one employee, "And when they did it was with a different adjustor each time."

A further consequence of the understaffing was in underwriting: "We had such a backlog that there was no underwriting being done. Work was being processed, but we didn't know what we had on the books. There were many high-risk policies that got through." One employee estimated that a backlog of 40 000 pieces of paper had accumulated by 1987.

The second major thrust was a partnership strategy with brokers called "Partnership Pact." The logic was to create partnerships with a select number of brokers so that the interests of both could be better served. Wellington would buy a 25 per cent stake in each broker's business, and the broker would give a minimum of 25 per cent of his or her business to Wellington. Wellington was to receive preferred status in its chosen segments, and in return profits for that business would be split between the broker and Wellington. Long term it was hoped that the brokers would stock other Trilon products such as life insurance and investment plans.

The Partnership Pact strategy never got off the ground. It met with considerable resistance from the Canadian Federation of Insurance Agents and Brokers Associations Agents and Brokers Association

(CFIABA). They valued their independent status, and thought that Wellington's proposal was a departure from "virtually all that Federation sees as being an independent agent."[3] The scheme was quickly dropped, but the relationship with brokers had been soured. Their loss of confidence in Wellington was manifested in a loss of business as Wellington's market share dropped from 2.1 per cent to 1.5 per cent in two years.

The State of the Insurance Industry in 1987

At the same time as Wellington's self-imposed problems, the entire general insurance industry was going through its worst downturn ever. Overcapacity in the industry, in terms of number of competitors, had led to severe price cutting, while claims continued to rise. In 1985 the industry had a combined loss on underwriting of $1.2 billion, a new record. Only strong investment returns prevented a negative return on equity. At the same time, the Ontario Automobile Insurance industry was going through a crisis. All insurers were incurring heavy losses, but the government had frozen rate increases. Steps were being taken to bring in a no-fault scheme, which would lower claims, but for the period since 1985, all auto insurers in Ontario had been badly hit. Wellington was amongst the worst hit, with 40 per cent of its total business in the Ontario Auto segment. For the period 1985–87 it achieved combined ratios of 123.7 per cent, 108.9 per cent and 117.9 per cent respectively. Exhibits 2, 3 and 4 summarize Wellington's performance for the period 1981–87.

THE APPOINTMENT OF MURRAY WALLACE

Toward the end of 1987 Trilon decided that changes were necessary at Wellington Insurance, and appointed Murray Wallace to take over as the new President and CEO on January 1, 1988. Wallace was a senior executive at Royal Trust, a sister company, but had considerable experience in the insurance industry through a period as the president of Saskatchewan's government insurance business. His mandate was to do whatever it took to turn the company around. Trilon had a target return on equity of 15 per cent for all its operating companies. However, Wallace understood that financial targets were really only one measure of a successful turnaround. Equally important was a fundamental change in the way the company operated so that brokers regained their respect for Wellington and staff regained control of internal operations.

Assessment of Internal Operations

The Wellington that Murray Wallace took control of was a very traditional, bureaucratic organization (see Exhibit 5). It had six levels of management, most at the vice-president level. They were distributed through eight centres, but with the vast majority at head office in Toronto. The structure was primarily functional, so that staff belonged to claims, underwriting or sales and rarely communicated with each other. Each manager was responsible for a certain business portfolio, and had strict limits on his or her signing authority. Large claims, for example, had to be referred several steps up the ladder before they could be processed.

The organization was complicated by the fact that each sales group (responsible for a certain region) also had functional staff, such as adjustors or claims managers. These people were accountable both to their region manager and also to the appropriate functional vice-president. They had to ensure that their actions met with the approval of both managers. As a result, processing was often very slow. Furthermore, each region was centralized, so that the few "field" offices such as London, Ontario, still had to refer back to head office for critical functions such as underwriting. London office staff commented that they would spend hours every day discussing claims or premiums by phone with their supervisors in Toronto.

---

[3] Conrad Speirs, President CFIABA, at the 1985 Independent Brokers Association of Ontario convention.

They thought that the dual reporting lines, and the lack of face-to-face contact with managers, were detracting from their ability to serve their customers.

Staff morale was described by John Carpenter, the new Chief Operating Officer (COO), as "deplorable." The backlog in claims, the recent staffing cuts, and the rigid structure had all taken their toll on employee motivation, so that a feeling of demoralization had set in. Carpenter commented: "We had some good people, but they were constrained by the structure. There was no focus on the company." Another employee added that the commitment to the company was missing: "If anybody had got a job elsewhere at that point, he would have gone."

Other aspects of the organization also contributed to the malaise. Promotion was based largely on years in the company rather than on performance; salaries were adjusted on a seniority basis, so that there was no reward for creativity or initiative; and training programs were effectively non-existent. The hierarchical nature of the business was underlined by the physical layout of the building. Each executive had a mahogany-walled suite with a separate dining room, while the rest of the employees were segregated by functional area in an open-plan arrangement. Wallace realized that change at Wellington would hit senior management the hardest. They had the most to lose, and would certainly be expected to resist any move that threatened the security and comfort of their privileged position.

Another critical area of concern was information processing. "The systems to provide timely and reliable information were not in place," observed Carpenter. This had the effect that management did not know which segments or geographical regions were losing money, and also handicapped the claims and underwriting staff in their regular activities.

A final concern became apparent as Wallace began to explore Wellington's financial statements in more detail. In simple terms the company was under-reserved. The previous management had not set aside enough income to cover likely future claims, so that short-term earnings were inflated but long-term earnings damaged. Wallace realized that the shortfall in reserves, estimated at around $15 million, would have to be made up over the following seven-year period.

Wallace's Recommendations

The insurance industry, like much of the financial services sector, had resisted change for a long time. Wallace was convinced that the time was ripe for some new thinking. Product offerings were all very much the same between companies, but he was sure that Wellington could differentiate in one crucial way: customer responsiveness. "There is a real sense of 'this is the way things have always been done' in this industry. Brokers and customers don't know what it means to get good service. They have never dealt with a company that will bend over backwards to help them."

Wallace believed that Wellington could avoid the worst effects of the cyclicity in the industry, and extract a premium price, if an effective customer-oriented operation were put in place. "Brokers should be recommending Wellington because it turns around claims in record time, not because it is the best price," said Wallace. Wallace was also impressed by the focused strategies of companies like Pilot and Lloyd's non-marine. These companies had achieved strong results by specializing in certain product segments and geographical areas. Wellington had traditionally been a full-line competitor, but could feasibly reduce its volume to focus its scope of operations in this way.

A third possible strategic direction that Wallace foresaw was to push for a short-term turnaround, and then sell the company. This would not be easy either, but represented a less drastic shift than the realignment demanded by a differentiation or focus strategy.

One of Wallace's first actions as CEO was to meet with Wellington brokers from across the country. Samples of their comments are listed in Exhibit 6. The process underlined Wallace's belief in a customer service-based strategy, and also drew his attention to the notion of a decentralized organization. Under this structure, all key functions would be grouped together in the field, in close proximity to brokers and customers. Rather than deferring to a central unit for underwriting and claims servicing, each unit would be self-contained and autonomous. Wallace's major concern about a decentralized structure was that no company was using that organizational form. The most successful companies in the industry, in fact, operated with well-managed centralized structures.

The biggest headache for Wallace was the apparent lack of concern for the company's problems among the staff. The company had been through so many changes of ownership that they saw Wallace's appointment as "just another change." Wellington's results were poor, but the company was still turning a small profit. As one manager commented: "Most employees had been doing the same thing for 15 years. They were not interested in any new ideas."

The picture was not all gloom, however. With Trilon as the parent company, Wellington had access to capital, experienced managers and a commitment to long-term profitability. Changes would not have to be compromised for short-term results. In addition, Wallace concluded that the company had some well-respected products, and a lot of good people. In an industry noted for its lack of innovation and dynamism, Wallace predicted that any company, Wellington included, could steal a march on its rivals with some creative management.

Thriving on Chaos

Wallace had developed a clear management philosophy through extensive reading and his own management experiences. His greatest influence was management guru Tom Peters, author of the best-selling *In Search of Excellence* and a number of other books. In particular, Peters' most recent book, *Thriving on Chaos*, detailed a number of strategies for change along the lines of customer responsiveness, empowerment and leadership. Table 2 lists some of the key prescriptions. Wallace found the ideas appealing, and in his previous job at Royal Trust he had begun to put some of them into practice. Wallace wondered if it would be possible to implement the *Thriving on Chaos* prescriptions at Wellington.

TABLE 2 *Thriving on Chaos* Prescriptions

Creating Total Customer Responsiveness	Achieving Flexibility by Empowering People	A New View of Leadership at All Levels
Specialize/create niches	Involve everyone in everything	Develop an inspiring vision
Provide top quality	Use self-managing teams	Manage by example
Provide superior service	Listen/celebrate/recognize	Practice visible management
Achieve extraordinary responsiveness	Spend time lavishly on recruiting	Defer to the front line
Become obsessed with listening	Train and retrain	Delegate
Make sales and service forces into heroes	Provide incentive pay for everyone	Pursue horizontal management
Launch a customer revolution	Simplify/reduce structure	Evaluate everyone on their love of change
	Reconceive the middle manager's role	Create a sense of urgency
	Eliminate bureaucratic rules	

E X H I B I T 1 Canadian General Insurance Industry Aggregate Results 1977–87

Year	Underwriting Income	Investment Income	Net Income	Average Combined Ratio
1977	$ 20m			
1978	69m			
1979	– 163m			
1980	– 513m			
1981	– 890m	$ 937m	$ 160m	111.4%
1982	– 562m	1 054m	456m	108.5
1983	– 328m	1 119m	741m	104.5
1984	– 916m	1 255m	362m	111.7
1985	–1 260m	1 350m	383m	114.0
1986	– 555m	1 509m	1 004m	105.2
1987	– 535m	1 706m	1 165m	104.8

Source: *Canadian Underwriter* 1977–87.

E X H I B I T 2 Wellington's Market Performance 1981–87

Year	Ranking in Canada (market share based)	Market share % (on net premiums earned)
1981	15th	1.68%
1982	12th	2.42%
1983	14th	2.28%
1984	14th	2.13%
1985	18th	1.75%
1986	19th	1.52%
1987	19th	1.55%

Source: *Canadian Underwriter* 1981–87.

E X H I B I T 3 Wellington Key Financial Performance Data 1977–87

Year	Sales (i.e., net premiums)	Costs (i.e., claims)	Earned Loss Ratio	Total Expense Ratio	Combined Ratio	Under-writing Income	Invest-ment Income	Net Income
1977	$123m	$ 73m	59.7%					
1978	124m	79m	63.7					
1979	125m	90m	71.8					
1980	127m	102m	79.0					
1981	131m	104m	79.3	38.9%	118.2%	–$24m	$24m	$ 0
1982	162m	120m	74.0	36.1	110.1	– 16m	27m	11m
1983	168m	126m	74.8	33.3	108.1	– 13m	34m	21m
1984	167m	143m	85.5	33.7	119.2	– 32m	26m	–6m
1985	157m	135m	85.7	38.0	123.7	– 37m	41m	4m
1986	163m	125m	77.0	31.9	108.9	– 15m	53m	38m
1987	172m	145m	84.0	33.8	117.9	– 31m	51m	20m

Source: *Canadian Underwriter* 1977–87.

E X H I B I T 4   Wellington's Business Segmented by Line and Province, 1987

(A): Segmented by product line

Line	Net Prem. Earned ($000)	Net Claims ($000)	Earned Loss Ratio
Property—personal	$ 45 012	$ 27 336	60.7%
Property—commercial	17 573	12 099	68.8
Property—total	62 585	39 435	63.0
Automobile—liability	50 120	59 234	118.2
Automobile—personal acdt.	7 658	5 976	78.0
Automobile—other	47 412	35 688	75.3
Automobile—total	105 190	100 898	95.9
Boiler and Machinery	3	17	566.7
Fidelity	173	−49	−28.3
Liability	3 416	4 078	117.8
Surety	164	168	102.4
Marine	846	523	61.8
Total for 1987	172 422	145 070	84.1

(B): Segmented by province

Province ($000)	Premiums Earned($000)	Province	Premiums Earned
Newfoundland	$ 911	Manitoba	$ 2 451
PEI	1 271	Saskatchewan	59
Nova Scotia	14 128	Alberta	14 278
New Brunswick	1 752	British Columbia	18 790
Quebec	18 496	Yukon & NWT	37
Ontario	100 249	Total	172 422

Source: *Canadian Underwriter*, May 1987.

481

EXHIBIT 5 Simplified Organization Chart, 1987

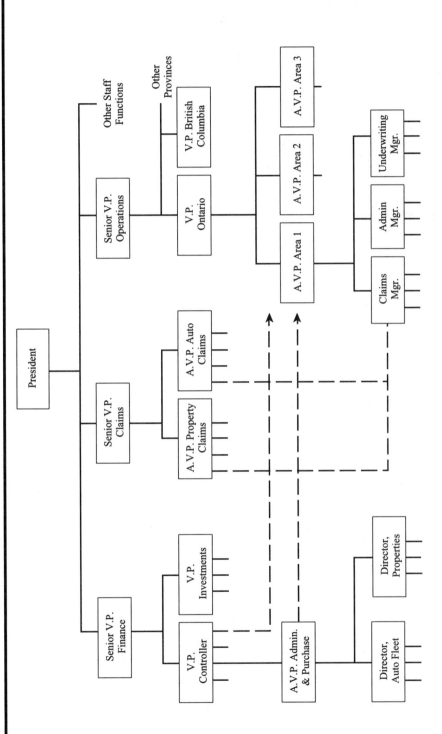

All area-based functional managers report to a Regional V.P. and a Functional Manager/V.P. Profit responsibility is held by both operations managers (for a geographic portfolio) and functional managers (e.g. for all auto claims).

Source: Company interviews.

E X H I B I T 6   Broker Comments

These comments were collected from brokers in January 1988, on a trans-Canada tour by Murray Wallace.

"First class products, good prices, but your service...."

"It sure would be nice to get our policies within a reasonable time."

"I wish you'd get the policy right the first time, most of the time anyway."

"I don't want to talk to a different person every time I call."

"I do expect a return phone call when I leave a message."

"It would be so much easier for me if you had an office right here in town."

"I want to deal with the person who makes decisions."

TACO BELL BACKGROUND NOTE

case

33

Katy Paul-Chowdhury
and Mary M. Crossan

The \$267 billion food service industry in the United States comprised independent establishments and restaurant chains. The market share of the restaurant chains had grown at the expense of independents' market share, accounting for 54 per cent of all U.S. restaurants in 1993, up from 37 per cent in 1986. Chain sales were estimated to grow at 8 per cent in 1993, twice as fast as independent sales.

IVEY

Katy Paul-Chowdhury prepared this case under the supervision of Professor Mary M. Crossan solely to provide material for class discussion. The authors do not intend to illustrate either effective or ineffective handling of a managerial situation. The authors may have disguised certain names and other identifying information to protect confidentiality.

INDUSTRY OVERVIEW[1]

The fragmented, capital-intensive restaurant industry was characterized by low margins and vulnerability to shifts in consumer tastes and spending. For every consumer dollar spent in the typical fast-food restaurant, 30 cents covered the cost of food and packaging, while the remainder paid for advertising, marketing, capital and fixed costs, and labour. Exhibit 1 lists the major fast food chains, their market segments, sales and number of units.

TRENDS

By the early 1990s, the following significant trends were changing the structure of the fast-food[2] restaurant industry: the maturing market, changing customer tastes and the introduction of nontraditional points of distribution.

Maturing Market

After decades of substantial growth, the market for quick service food began to mature during the 1980s. As the market became more saturated, the importance of market share grew. In order to attract customers, quick service restaurants increased the rate of introduction of new products (including low-fat versions of existing menu items as well as new types of food), cut prices on selected menu items and introduced play areas for children.

Although expanded menus resulted in incremental business, they also led to disruptions in the production flow and decreased kitchen efficiency as products were introduced which were incompatible with existing facilities. The rapid introduction of new products contributed to higher costs and slower service in an industry based upon low costs and fast service.

Changing Consumer Tastes

The changing tastes of health-conscious consumers was another factor driving the introduction of new menu items. This shift resulted in growth in chicken, pizza and Mexican food restaurant segments.

The increasing popularity of Mexican food, in particular, could be seen in the upscale restaurant and grocery sectors as well as in quick service. As traditional markets in the Southwestern United States became saturated, Mexican chains pushed eastward into relatively untapped markets.

Nontraditional Points of Distribution (PODs)

Perhaps the most important trend in the quick service restaurant industry was the introduction of nontraditional points of distribution (PODs). These included express stores, kiosks and mobile carts in shopping malls, schools, hospitals, stadiums and airports. With lower capital costs than traditional stores, they were an attractive investment alternative. Traditional quick service restaurants had been labour intensive, taking advantage of pools of inexpensive labour. However, changing demographics and increasing minimum wages dictated a need for the smaller PODs with fewer workers.

With many quick service restaurants currently experimenting with these alternative points of distribution, a fundamental change had taken place in their service objectives. Instead of locating "wherever customers want to purchase the food," they increasingly had to position themselves "wherever customers

---

[1] Articles from *Restaurants & Institutions*; *Restaurant Business*; *Business Week*; *The Wall Street Journal*; *Marketing News*; *Harvard Business School Case*; interviews.

[2] At Taco Bell, it was known as the "quick service restaurant" industry.

want to consume the food." Located in such places as schools and sports complexes, non-traditional PODs also allowed finer segmentation of customer markets.

COMPANY BACKGROUND[3]

A Subsidiary of PepsiCo

Taco Bell was a wholly owned subsidiary of PepsiCo Inc. Originally known as a soft-drink company, the Purchase, N.Y.-based PepsiCo had evolved into a global food giant. PepsiCo's three flagship businesses were: soft drinks under the Pepsi name; restaurants including the Pizza Hut; Kentucky Fried Chicken (KFC) and Taco Bell chains; and snack foods under the Frito-Lay brand. As noted by Chairman and CEO Wayne Calloway, the soft drink division generated more revenue in 1991 than General Mills Inc., the restaurant group was bigger than Campbell Soup Co., and the snack food business was about the size of Kellogg Co. Taco Bell accounted for 30 per cent of the Restaurant Division's 1992 sales and 30 per cent of its operating profits. This represented 11 per cent of PepsiCo's sales and 9 per cent of operating profits.

With market leaders such as Coca-Cola and McDonald's Corp. as its major competitors, PepsiCo was under significant pressure to be cheaper, faster and tastier than the competition. To this end, PepsiCo was building an organization that was capable of supporting continuous change, innovation and risk. For several years, PepsiCo had been removing layers of management, and moving decision-makers closer to the customer. Marketing, operations and research and development were decentralized to push down decision-making and increase market responsiveness.

The company's culture was embedded in a common value system based on integrity and results. Calloway was known for his tough quarterly and annual performance goals. Acting as a check on the performance orientation, however, the concept of integrity went beyond honesty to include showing respect to others and trusting people to do their jobs. The other key element in PepsiCo's culture was the importance of continuous change. The company regularly revamped its marketing, operations and field management in anticipation of the competition rather than in response to it.

THE VALUE STRATEGY

John Martin joined Taco Bell as President and CEO in 1983, inheriting a fringe competitor in the fast food industry. He instituted a series of incremental changes designed to make the organization competitive with the major chains. He clearly defined the company's business and customer, and updated its image, facilities and menu. He also introduced new production techniques, including electronic point-of-sale systems and improved assembly lines. Martin increased training and development for Restaurant Managers (RMs) and Assistant Restaurant Managers (ARMs).

Reflecting on the company's position at the end of the 1980s, however, Martin knew that Taco Bell was a small competitor. He anticipated declining margins in the maturing quick service industry. Instead of competing head-to-head with the major fast food chains, Martin decided to change the basis of competition.

He chose to focus on value. The two components of value were quality and price. Traditionally, the industry had viewed high quality and low price as contradictory goals, with one sacrificed in pursuit of the other. Martin realized, however, that delivering value meant providing both.

---

[3] Articles from *Restaurant Business; The Wall Street Journal; Irvine World News; Financial World; Computer World; Harvard Business School Case;* PepsiCo's *Annual Report.*

FACT

Studies commissioned in 1987 and 1989 revealed that customers wanted FACT: fast-food *Fast*; orders *Accurate*; a *Clean* restaurant; and food at the appropriate *Temperature*. FACT became the company's standard for customer service, and the non-monetary portion of the value strategy. The studies also showed that customers did not place any importance on the preparation of food on the premises.

By 1991, many Taco Bell menu items in the United States were priced at one of three low price points: $0.59, $0.79 and $0.99 (or $0.69, $0.89 and $1.09 in some markets). While the value strategy dramatically increased Taco Bell's sales, the lower prices squeezed already slim margins.

To reduce costs while providing higher levels of service and maintaining its high quality product, Martin redefined Taco Bell's business from "making food" to "feeding people." He knew from the studies that customers wanted value, which was defined as FACT at the lowest possible prices, and recognized that the front line service workers (crew, RMs and ARMs) were in the best position to provide FACT and keep costs down. He began to refocus the organization, eliminating everything that did not support the front line in the provision of value.

K-Minus

Having redefined its business from food manufacturer to food retailer, Taco Bell introduced the K-Minus (kitchen minus) program to invert the space configuration in the restaurants to 30 per cent kitchen and 70 per cent dining room. To achieve this, the preparation of food in the restaurant was minimized and simplified. Virtually all of the food was prepared elsewhere, and arrived at the restaurant ready to be heated or cooled, and used. The kitchen was limited to a heating and assembly space.

In addition to reducing the size of the kitchen, K-Minus allowed the front line workers to spend less time on chopping, cooking and washing up, and to focus more of their efforts on sales and quality of service. It also helped to improve the consistency of the food products. As well, K-Minus increased potential kitchen output, allowing more take-out, drive-through and other out-of-restaurant sales.

SOS

The Speed of Service (SOS) program, introduced in 1990, was designed to reduce the waiting time for customers. It involved reformulating certain recipes, and borrowing the McDonald's system of keeping food in a heated holding area for up to ten minutes. Taco Bell was able to inventory the majority of its most frequently ordered menu items in this way, increasing peak hour transaction capacity by 54 per cent and decreasing customer waiting time by 71 per cent to 30 seconds.

TACO

The Total Automation of Company Operations (TACO) featured the installation in every store of a computer networked to headquarters. TACO provided Restaurant Managers (RMs) with timely information support and communications functions unparalleled in the quick-service industry. Information included cash position, promotional sales, food cost, labour cost, inventory, perishable items and period-to-date costs, all with variances from budget. TACO helped the RMs with labour scheduling and product production planning, while the communications function allowed District and more senior managers to send messages to any combination of their restaurants. This technology let them spend less time in a given restaurant, and manage a larger number of restaurants.

RM paperwork was reduced by up to 16 hours per week. More importantly, TACO provided RMs with the tools necessary to identify and solve problems without involving people any higher in the organization. It supported the empowerment of front line service workers.

In the TACO program, Taco Bell had a comprehensive and evolving system of information and control. As management layers became thinner, however, and supervision less intense, other checks were required to ensure that standards were being maintained. Taco Bell used three mechanisms to monitor restaurant operations: a 1-800 number for customers to call with comments, mystery shoppers and marketing surveys.

Restaurant General Managers (RGMs)

The new organizational focus on value required new behaviours at the RM and Assistant Restaurant Manager (ARM) levels. Supported by TACO and new training, managers were expected to make decisions, manage their restaurants' profits and losses, motivate employees, and generally take ownership of the operations. With this greater responsibility came a significant increase in autonomy. To symbolize the new, self-sufficient role of the restaurant managers, Taco Bell renamed the positions Restaurant General Manager (RGM) and Assistant Restaurant General Manager (ARGM).

Compensation structures were redesigned (see Exhibit 2). Salary ranges and bonus opportunities were increased substantially. The new compensation system continued to reward sales performance and cost management, as well as placing additional emphasis on customer service and teamwork. The increased responsibility dictated that management style move toward management by exception, more coaching and broadening spans of control.

Market Managers (MMs)

The former District Managers (DMs) were renamed Market Managers (MMs) and given responsibility for an increasingly large number of restaurants. Spans of control increased from 6 to 12 to over 20 restaurants in the space of two years. With only 24 hours in the day, it became impossible to continue managing details, so MMs were forced to create organizations where they could manage by exception, and coach instead of police their RGMs. MMs nevertheless seemed to spend much of their time "fighting fires." Many could not make the transition from DM to MM, and either became RGMs or left the organization.

As with the RGMs, compensation structures were redesigned (see Exhibit 2). The maximum salary almost doubled, bonus targets increased over five-fold, and zone performance was included in the new bonus calculation. Bonuses were based on market and zone performance, and progress made toward achieving corporate strategic goals. In the new, flatter organization, creating adequate opportunities for MMs' career advancement was a challenge. Taco Bell had to redefine career success in terms of staying and growing with the job. To support this mindset, the salary range for MMs was very broad, and divided into thirds. MMs progressed through the range on the basis of performance, the complexity of their markets and tenure.

TACO BELL, 1993[4]—ORGANIZATION

With the successful introduction of its Value program, Taco Bell had become a distinctive and formidable competitor in the quick service restaurant industry. It was widely recognized in business and academic communities alike as a leading model for service industry innovation and organization. Worldwide system sales reached $3.9 billion in 1993, having averaged 17.1 per cent annual growth over the preceding five

---

[4] Articles from *Restaurant Business*; Taco Bell internal documents; PepsiCo's *Annual Report*; interviews.

years. Taco Bell had 4 153 restaurants worldwide at the end of 1992, of which 4 078 were located in the United States. It also enjoyed a 70 per cent share of the U.S. Mexican-style restaurant market segment, and a 4 per cent share of the total U.S. quick service restaurant market.

Taco Bell was organized into seven North American Zones, reduced from 13 a year before. Zones were subdivided into between 5 and 23 markets, reporting to zone vice-presidents (ZVPs). Exhibit 3 shows Taco Bell's organization chart.

EXPANSION OBJECTIVES AND STRATEGY

Although Taco Bell's growth had been rapid, its future expansion objectives were explosive. From a 1993 $3 billion in sales, the company planned to achieve sales of $20 billion and 200 000 points of distribution by the year 2000. It viewed its potential market in terms of "share of stomach," or share of calories consumed per day. By redefining its business as "feeding people," Taco Bell increased the size of its market by approximately ten times. Growth so far had been primarily in the U.S. market, with limited expansion into Canada, Mexico, Puerto Rico and the U.K. Taco Bell saw tremendous opportunity for expansion overseas, but continued rapid growth at home consumed much of the available resources and management attention.

To disseminate its bold growth objectives and strategy for achieving them, Taco Bell developed a variety of internal communication materials. Some information was sent out in the form of posters or games. For example, "The New Strategic Intent Game: DOMINATE by becoming the Convenient Food leader and dominating all food occasions!" outlined Taco Bell's mission and strategies as follows:

> Taco Bell's mission is to become the dominant force in an entire new business that we'll create: Convenient Foods. As we did with 'value,' we're not just going to change a few rules, but instead create a whole new way to take our food to anywhere hungry people gather—not only in customary places, but in points of access like stadiums, malls, universities, vending machines, grocery stores—even our own refrigerators.

DOMINATE went on to discuss Taco Bell's four strategies for reaching its goal:

- *Exploding distribution* meant expanding to "tens of thousands of new places... wherever customers want us to be."
- *Leveraging innovation* was a call to "accelerate business transformation" through innovation at every level of the business.
- *Institutionalizing self-sufficiency* was in response to the realization that the only way to achieve such ambitious growth was to "continue giving people bigger, broader jobs and responsibilities... (and) more freedom and empowerment to do their jobs."
- *Building superbrands* referred to the Disney tradition of developing product names which could stretch, in Taco Bell's case, "across many food occasions and points of access."

The Can-Am Zone[5]

Although two of the seven North American Zones encompassed parts of both Canada and the United States, only one MM straddled the two countries. The Can-Am Zone had been created during a restructuring in November 1992, which had increased it from 35 to 110 stores. It was comprised of five distinct markets: Eastern Ontario, Southwestern Ontario, Upstate New York, Boston and New England. Zone vice-president (ZVP) Martin Annese, was based in Mississauga, Ontario. In May 1993, Sanjiv Yajnik, MM for

---

[5] Taco Bell internal documents; interviews.

Southwestern Ontario was also given responsibility for Upstate New York. This increased responsibility was in recognition of the fact that Sanjiv had been very successful in achieving profitability in the previously troubled Southwestern Ontario market. Taco Bell believed that north-south integration facilitated consistency and marketing coordination in neighbouring geographic areas.

Sanjiv Yajink

Sanjiv had graduated from a leading Canadian MBA program in May 1992, and joined Taco Bell as MM for Southwestern Ontario in July of that year. Before starting his MBA, Sanjiv had completed a degree in marine engineering in India, then worked for over 12 years in positions of increasing responsibility as a chartered engineer and chief engineer with Mobil Shipping & Transportation Co. Ltd., in the U.S.

Sanjiv reflected on his management approach at the time he joined Taco Bell as a new MBA:

> Coming out of the MBA program, I had a long-term, big picture focus. My big concerns were driving profit and customer choice. I was most concerned with long-term profitability. I was surprised by the tactical, day-to-day pressures of what seemed to be a simple business, but was really a business growing and changing at a furious pace.

Southwestern Ontario and Upstate New York

There were ten stores in the Southwestern Ontario market when Sanjiv Yajnik joined as MM. Typically, these restaurants were 12–15 years old, and widely spread throughout small towns in the area. Since Taco Bell had traditionally been viewed as less important than Pizza Hut, some of its stores were placed so as to make better use of Pizza Hut land, not strategically located to attract customers. Sales were weak compared to sales in the Toronto area.

The markets and restaurants had been run by a succession of managers in recent years. They were what Zone Manager of Human Resources Christine Maxwell described as "traditional" restaurant managers.

> They were hired from the restaurant industry. They were predominantly low drive, maintenance people. And they were in small communities, so they didn't feel the need to grow....Some of the RGMs needed to learn significantly new behaviours in order to contribute in the new organization, particularly those who were great followers, but not drivers. We've been concentrating on upgrading the talent at the RGM and ARGM levels, both in Southwestern Ontario and Upstate New York.

Sanjiv discussed the markets he inherited in terms of people, operations, facilities, marketing and growth:

> Many of the facilities in Ontario were old, but were in reasonable condition. Some people were not used to being held accountable, and were lax in their jobs. Others were willing, but lacked the skills required to meet their new tasks and responsibilities. All employees had been told that they had to be self-sufficient, that they had to work in teams, etc., but there was no understanding of how to get there. The deficient skills and lack of direction impacted negatively on store operations in the market.
>
> The situation in New York was similar to that in Southwestern Ontario, but the lack of skills and direction was even more pronounced. Overall, the employees were not ready for change: they did not see the need to change, and they did not have the necessary skills. Not surprisingly, the operations were substandard. Some of the facilities were new, but were improperly maintained, and had already fallen into disrepair.
>
> There is minimal market penetration in Southwestern Ontario. As a rule of thumb, we like to have one store for approximately 20 000 people. In London, for example, we have one per 100 000 people. Sales are growing at 15–20 per cent annually.
>
> Sales growth in the New York market has been relatively flat. I see this as a function of market penetration, value perception and competition, the quality of operations and the location of the units.

Higher ingredient and labour costs in Canada resulted in a fundamental difference in focus between the Ontario and New York restaurants. All food purchasing was done in New York. Canadian restaurants needed to add duty, the Goods and Services Tax, transportation and currency translation costs to the price of ingredients. In addition, higher labour costs meant that the number of employees used in Canadian restaurants had to be much lower than in their U.S. counterparts if they were to meet the same target of approximately 28 per cent of sales. Because combined ingredient and labour costs represented a higher portion of the price of a menu item, a smaller portion remained available to cover other costs for any given price point. Therefore, while a 100 per cent productivity level was required to meet target in the U.S. restaurants, the required level in Canadian restaurants was 105 per cent. As a result, the greater focus of the Canadian restaurants was on lowering costs and increasing productivity, while the focus of the U.S. restaurants was on generating sales.

RESTAURANT OPERATIONS[6]

Taco Bell's Highbury Avenue restaurant in London, Ontario, provides an example of restaurant operations. It employed 60 people, including two ARGMs and two shift facilitators. Full-time workers represented most of the day and overnight crew, while part-time employees tended to work afternoons, evenings and weekends. Full-time employees were typically homemakers who had returned to the work force, and high-school graduates, some of whom were working for a few years before going back to school. Although full-time employees were up to 35 years of age, the majority were in the 19–20 year range. Part-time employees were typically high-school or sometimes college students.

The Highbury Avenue store did not have an RGM. Sanjiv explained this phenomenon:

> I need extremely competent people for these positions. But it can be difficult to interest university graduates in managing fast-food restaurants. We call it a "job snob" attitude. Many people don't want to work in this type of service industry, especially in a demanding hands-on job. They are unaware of the opportunities for professional growth and the financial rewards. I refuse to hire someone who is not up to the standard we need. In 18 months or so, I think the ARGMs will have the experience to take on the RGM positions. But I hope we don't have to go that long. Not having RGMs puts additional strain on me and on the ARGMs.

It was the responsibility of the ARGMs to ensure that everything ran smoothly. ARGM Eleni Katsoulas described her position:

> I am responsible for sales, labour costs, overtime, food costs, other controllable costs, speed of service and customer feedback. I am measured on these things and held accountable. Our target for labour costs is around 28 per cent of sales. On sales of $1.5 million annually, even running labour at 32 per cent of sales adds up fast. I check how we are doing every few hours. If we are over 28 per cent, I suggest that someone take a break (for every five hours staff members work, they are required to be given a half-hour unpaid break), or ask if anyone would like to go home.
>
> Food costs should be approximately 42 per cent of sales. Even a per cent or two more puts us well over budget. Overfilling products by an ounce each creates a significant problem over the hundreds of tacos we sell every day. So if it's not prohibitively busy, we weigh every third item. And we try to keep waste at 0.5 per cent. But cooked ground beef only keeps for three hours and chicken and steak for two. And the meat takes half an hour to cook. So planning ahead for peak times is very important.
>
> There are also challenges associated with such a young crew. Remember that they're at a stage in life when everyone is nagging at them and they become very good at blocking it out! So I can't just say,

---

[6] Taco Bell internal documents; interviews.

"Don't overfill." I can't just say, "The customer is always right." I have to explain that the average household spends $10 000 on fast food in a lifetime. And if one dissatisfied customer tells nine friends what's wrong with Taco Bell then that's $100 000 we lose for every dissatisfied customer. So if we want to keep our jobs....

I get frustrated sometimes. I have so many ideas that I want to implement. But I'm always so busy doing what's necessary that I rarely get time to implement them! And the business is changing so fast that often by the time I can get to something, it's no longer as useful as I thought it would be! In any case, we are innovating all the time. And Sanjiv is trying to move toward four shift-facilitators and four crew-trainers in the store, so that will give me time to focus on more external things.

The Market Manager Position[7]

RESPONSIBILITIES In 1993, the average MM managed approximately 30 restaurants, compared to an average of six or seven restaurants for a DM five years earlier. The number of restaurants an MM managed was determined on the basis of quantitative and qualitative performance. Key financial numbers included sales, food costs, labour costs, overhead and profits. Nonfinancial considerations included customer satisfaction and progress in areas such as self-directed work teams. The reward for strong results in existing restaurants was more stores to manage. When Sanjiv had joined Taco Bell in 1992, he had been responsible for ten restaurants, compared to his current portfolio of 27 stores. He described this portfolio as the same size as that of a comparable manager at McDonald's.

The MM was responsible for the development of his or her market through additional points of distribution, as well as for restaurant performance. A job description is shown in Exhibit 4.

John Martin's ideal Taco Bell consisted of the CEO and many restaurants, with nobody in the middle. While the organization was still a long way from that ideal, middle managers at the ZVP and MM levels understood that their ultimate goal was to "coach themselves out of a job." The uncertainty inherent in such a goal was partially offset by the potential for movement within the PepsiCo organization, particularly at the vice-president level.

Ultimately, however, "the only job security was performance," a view echoed by Sanjiv, Eastern Ontario MM Barry Telford, and Zone Human Resources Manager Christine Maxwell. Managers were expected to be forward-looking and to take risks, but were driven primarily by aggressive sales and profit targets.

Barry described the paradigm for evolution in the PepsiCo organization:

> Certain people with certain skills are necessary to bring the organization to a higher level, then new people or new skills are needed to pull the organization to the next level. Not everyone has the same capacity to stretch by themselves....We try to focus on the bottom third performers every year and either develop them, or promote other people, or hire externally.

Throughout the organization, Taco Bell fostered a self-sufficient, "can do" attitude. An internal communication described the seven shared values promoted in daily business practice: focus on the customer, integrity, teamwork, diversity, balance, accountability and commitment to growth. Employees described a feeling of camaraderie, born of teamwork, common values and lofty goals. At every level, they were encouraged to share ideas and innovations with their counterparts elsewhere in the organization.

Performance Measurement

Some markets were much more developed than others. Because of this disparity, performance was measured primarily in relation to that of other MMs in the same zone.

---

[7] Articles from *Restaurants & Institutions;* Taco Bell internal documents; interviews.

Performance was measured according to ambitious quarterly and annual sales and profit targets, as well as specific customer service objectives. In the U.S., zones were held responsible for a certain level of projected sales through existing and new units. A standard formula was applied to projected sales to arrive at optimum cost and profit levels. The zone's sales and profit commitment was then allocated among markets based on current performance and the MM's growth and cost projections. When Sanjiv assumed responsibility for the Upstate New York market, he inherited a budget developed with the input of his predecessor. A series of storms earlier in the year had resulted in significantly lower sales volumes than projected.

The budgeting process in Canada was somewhat different. The Taco Bell head office, through the Senior V.P. International, told the zones what their profit levels would have to be. MMs then worked with their ZVPs to develop plans to meet the required profit level. Despite apparent differences in the level of input MMs had in the U.S. and international budgeting processes, Sanjiv emphasized the fundamental similarity:

> Sales budgets are based to a large extent on our market projections. The cost targets are aggressive, but achievable and fairly standardized throughout the company. Cost targets can vary a bit depending on the market. For example, food costs are higher in Canada than in the U.S. But budgets are really not the result of negotiation at the market manager level. The targets are given to us, based on our input. We have control over all the factors necessary to meet them. My task is always the same: to squeeze costs and inefficiencies out of the system, and to increase profits.
>
> If my sales are above plan, approximately 40 per cent of each additional sales dollar has to flow through to profit, or I am not managing my costs. On higher levels of sales, having profit above plan in absolute terms is not enough!

Targets for individual restaurants were set by the RGM and MM. MM bonuses, with a target of $1 200 per unit supervised, were based on market sales and profit, zone performance, customer service, and specific individual criteria. The unique criteria against which Sanjiv was evaluated included: successfully (defined in terms of sales, costs and customer satisfaction) opening new units; fulfilling responsibilities as the zone's link with the marketing and finance support departments at headquarters; and raising customer satisfaction ratings by a specified amount. Fifty per cent of the bonus was based on market performance, and was only awarded to those MMs who were within 90 per cent of their sales commitment and 95 per cent of optimum profit targets.

It was not enough, however, to focus on short-term objectives. The Taco Bell organization was changing continuously, pushing toward a new product concept, and a much broader, flatter structure with self-directed work teams. While ZVPs assessed restaurant performance quarterly and annually, it was monitored continuously, sometimes in great detail. Sanjiv described the process:

> We have 13 four-week periods when the ZVPs look at performance and follow up. But the TACO system gives them minute-by-minute information every day, and they can call us for an explanation at any time. A lot can happen in a few days. A couple of weeks ago I took four days off to move. When I came back, I had 24 pages of e-mail. That's 200 messages!...Some managers will push you harder for details than others.

However, in a high volume, low margin business such as Taco Bell, the details were of critical importance. Sanjiv explained:

> A $100 mistake each day for 30 days, over 4 000 units becomes a lot of money.

Personal Strategy

MMs had considerable leeway in how they ran their restaurant portfolios. They made the hiring, firing and training decisions. They were free to recommend the closing and relocation of poorly performing restaurants, but needed to work with senior corporate people as well as the real estate department. Sanjiv was reluctant to close a poorly performing store and simply fire everybody without a thorough evaluation of the alternatives. According to him, the key to successfully managing a market was the development of an effective personal strategy:

> I started by thinking, 'Where are we now and where do we want to be?' I want this to be the most competitive market both within Taco Bell and compared to outside competitors. What will success look like and how will it come? We need to focus on revenues, costs, competition and shareholder returns. We can't afford to just do a few things well; we need to do everything well!
>
> Do I hire stars, or develop strong middle-of-the-road people? Which is more sustainable? We will need some good talent and extremely strong leadership. I would prefer to develop people than to replace them. But people are limited by their skill sets and, in a high-growth business such as this one, we need people who already have a strong skill base. Not everyone has the same capacity to develop in ways required by this organization's culture and time frames.
>
> I am convinced that 95 per cent of an organization's problems are due to inadequate management direction. It's like that at any level: 95 per cent of this market's problems are because I haven't provided sufficient direction. I haven't given clear guidelines, or properly thought through the actions necessary to achieve goals. Ninety-five per cent of a restaurant's problems are because the RGM hasn't done those things. It's easy to set goals and hold people accountable. What's not easy is coaching people to reach those goals and making sure that the goals are attainable and supported by organizational processes.
>
> One of the things I need to do is take the company's broad strategic goals and translate them into specific actions. Let's take self-sufficiency. When one of my RGMs phones me with a question, I say: "Did you really need to call me? How did I add value in this situation? Would it have been more efficient if you had made this decision yourself or gone directly to corporate office? Remember that I trust you to make good decisions, and I support the decisions you make." At 10 minutes per call and 27 restaurants, that's 41/2 hours per day of making RGM decisions, which is a big waste of my time. Overlapping responsibilities and supervision are value lost. In a flat organization, there can be no duplication of effort.
>
> I am committed to two things: fairness and performance. These are the principles underlying every decision I make.

Self-Directed Work Teams

John Martin was ever alert to new developments in management practice that might increase efficiency at Taco Bell. He believed that self-directed work teams (SWTs) would be necessary for achieving the flat management structure he envisioned within the company. Although much had been written about the benefits of SWTs, relatively little was known about how best to implement and manage them. Recognizing how difficult it would be to develop a company-wide training program given the high level of uncertainty, Martin pushed the responsibility for learning about these work teams to the front line. Market and restaurant managers were expected to experiment with and eventually implement SWTs in their stores, and were evaluated on their progress in this endeavour.

The development of SWTs was reflected in the MM's performance appraisal under the broader sections on Managing the Business and Leading People. Performance appraisals were then used in the calculation of salary adjustments. They were also used as the primary input into annual meetings between ZVPs and Human Resources to rank MMs, and determine their professional potential and ultimate career paths. Sanjiv explained that not having SWTs would have little effect on his career or compensation in the short term, but that a strategy including SWTs was important in determining an MM's performance and resulting job security in the longer term, relative to his or her peers.

Sanjiv commented on the move toward SWTs:

There's no shared definition of what constitutes a self-directed work team or how an MM should implement one. We each need to find the time to create our own versions. I do know that the first steps toward self-directed work teams must be vision alignment and technical training. This is not really urgent, but it's very important. Maybe later, when we see which models are working, the company will develop a more comprehensive program.

I see some major issues associated with these work teams. The most important one is who's in control? Who is ultimately assuring the safety of the food, the security of the physical premises and customer service? We cannot let these slip, even for a moment. How can we add fail-safe mechanisms to support the teams and avoid major mishaps? And we must remember that this system means a great deal more responsibility for front-line crew. What factors make one person better able to cope with a situation than another?

Another critical issue is how to implement the work teams without either customer service or financial performance being negatively impacted in the short term. If the uncertainty associated with the change causes inattention to some detail, then we could lose a customer. We don't have the luxury of a trial period. In an industry as competitive as this one, an unsatisfied customer simply switches to a competitor.

Because of the low margins in this industry, we must meet profit targets. Every dollar in this organization is accounted for. This is especially important in Canada, because, since Canada is considered to be part of the International Division, our profits are used to fund international growth. So if I want to implement SWTs, then I need to find the money to fund them in my controllable costs and labour costs while still meeting my targets. I estimate that it would cost approximately $200 000 to start moving all my units toward SWTs, and only 50–60 per cent would actually be able to make the conversion. Of the $200 000, approximately $130 000 would be used to train employees. That training would be technical in nature, improving employees' levels of competence in product assembly, customer service and working in groups. That number is as low as I can get it. It provides for a consultant to train the RGMs and ARGMs, and we would do the rest in-house. The remaining $70 000 would be for process re-engineering. And then there are any operational inefficiencies resulting from the change process. I see the gain from SWTs being in the area of competitive advantage, not lower costs.

Introducing SWTs to one unit at a time is not a viable option. It could take eight to 12 months to convert one store, so doing them individually would take a lifetime! Ideally, I would want to introduce SWTs throughout the market over the period of a year. There are efficiencies in training and experience to be gained from making the changes in several units simultaneously. Also, experience in the U.S. has shown that inconsistencies in culture within a market make people feel that they are being treated unfairly.

EXHIBIT 1   Major Fast Food (FF) Chains

Rank '93 ('92)	Company	Segment	'92 Sales in $ millions (% Change)*	'92 Units (% Change)*
1	McDonald's	FF hamburgers	21 855	13 093
(1)			(9.8)	(5.4)
2	KFC **	FF chicken	6 700	8 729
(3)			(8.1)	(2.9)
3	Burger King	FF hamburgers	6 400	6 648
(2)			(3.2)	(4.1)
4	Pizza Hut **	FF pizza	5 700	9 450
(4)			(7.5)	(5.0)
5	Wendy's	FF hamburgers	3 613	3 962
(6)			(12.1)	(4.2)
6	Hardee's	FF hamburgers	3 400	3 365
(5)			(9.7)	(5.2)
7	**Taco Bell **	**FF Mexican**	**3 300**	**4 000**
(8)			**(17.9)**	**(9.0)**
8	ARA Services	Contract mgt.	2 900	2 767
(7)			(2.5)	(1.7)
9	Marriott Mgt.	Contract mgt.	2 620	2 519
(9)	Services		(4.8)	(5.0)
10	Gardner Merchant	Contract mgt.	2 500	4 600
(12)	Food Services		(15.8)	N/A

* Percent change from 1991 level
** Owned by PepsiCo

Source: *Restaurants & Institutions*, July 1993.

EXHIBIT 2   Compensation Structures (US$)

Position	1993	Position	1988
RGM	Salary range: $27 100–40 700 Bonus target: $10 000 Bonus based on: store sales, store profit, store customer service, team sales "kicker"*	RM	Salary range: $22 000–33 100 Bonus target: $4 320 Bonus based on: sales, food costs, direct labour costs, controllable costs
MM	Salary range: $50 000–90 000 Bonus target: $36 000 Bonus based on: market sales, market profit, zone financial performance, individual objectives, customer service "kicker"*	DM	Salary range: $30 600–45 800 Bonus target: $6 240 Bonus based on: district sales, district profit, turnover, individual objectives, customer service "kicker"*

* A "kicker" refers to an amount over and above the bonus target.

Source: Taco Bell Internal Documents.

E X H I B I T 3 **Partial Taco Bell Organization Chart—Company Operations**

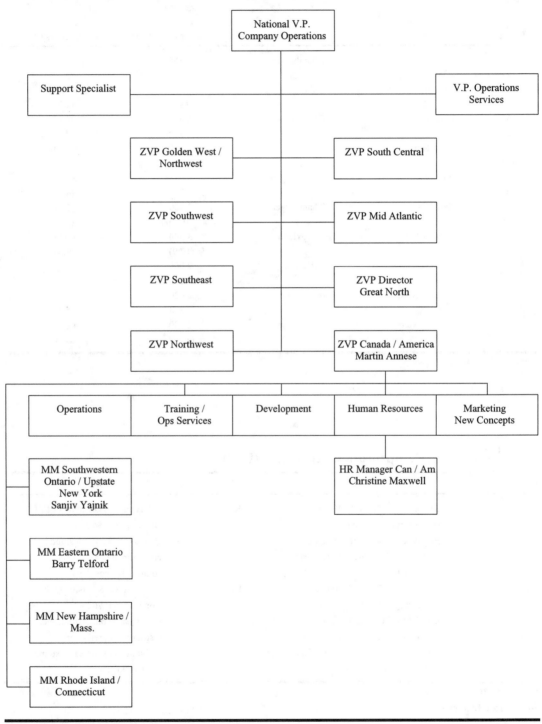

E X H I B I T 4 Market Manager Job Description

Purpose/Objective of the Position

The Market Manager serves as a leader and an expert operations resource to hire, coach, develop and assist 20 to 30 Restaurant General Managers and Team Managed Units Managers in achieving sales and profit plans. These restaurants are typically geographically isolated, requiring the incumbent to demonstrate independence and autonomy in supervision.

Dimensions/Scope

Number of restaurants = 20 to 30
Total sales = $20 to $40 million
Employees = 600 to 1 200

Knowledge/Skills

College degree or equivalent experience required, with a Master's preferred
4–8 years of multi-unit success in Fortune 500 retail, sales, hospitality or customer operations
People leadership/supervision a must
Proven fast track record
Diverse experience a plus
Direct P&L responsibility
Knowledge of restaurants/hospitality not required

Detailed Performance Accountabilities

1. Leading Your People

Proactively builds market toward 100 per cent Restaurant General Manager self-sufficiency.
Promotes teamwork and communications across the market.
Creates alignment between market and company value strategy.
Has an effective staffing plan, which recognizes RGM opportunities within the market and addresses them.
Sets a strong personal example of integrity and commitment to employee development.

2. Serving the Customer

Follows up on customer complaints to ensure action.
Analyzes and acts on customer intercept data to spot trends and corrects them.
Maintains accuracy, hospitality, quality, service and cleanliness (AHQSC) scores at or above the area of dominant influence (ADI) or peer group average.
Demonstrates strong personal commitment to customer satisfaction.
Identifies and removes barriers to maximizing customer value.

3. Representing the Company

Participates in events and public service organizations, which enhance the image of the company.
Knows business influences within the market and works to impact them.
Maintains solid, professional relations with the vendors.

EXHIBIT 4 (continued)

Nature of the Job

Challenge

Maintaining strong HQSC, sales and profits through consultative management and management by request and exception only.

Significant upgrading of manager quality and skill level.
Manage positive interpersonal relationships and motivate with infrequent personal contact.

Source: Taco Bell Internal Documents.

SABENA BELGIAN
WORLD AIRLINES (A)

case

34

Mary M. Crossan
and Barbara Pierce

On July 3, 1990, Carlos Van Rafelghem, Chairman of Sabena Belgian World Airlines, suffered a massive stroke and never recovered consciousness. For months he lay in a coma. When it became obvious that Van Rafelghem would not return to his position, the Belgian government began to search for a suitable replacement. Jean Luc Dehaene, the Belgian Deputy Prime Minister and Minister of Communications, knew that finding a suitable replacement would be a difficult assignment. He described his task as seeking

IVEY

Mary M. Crossan and Barbara Pierce prepared this case solely to provide material for class discussion. The authors do not intend to illustrate either effective or ineffective handling of a managerial situation. The authors may have disguised certain names and other identifying information to protect confidentiality.

Ivey Management Services prohibits any form of reproduction, storage or transmittal of this material without its written permission. This material is not covered under authorization from CanCopy or any other reproduction rights organization. To order copies or request permission to reproduce materials, contact Ivey Publishing, Ivey Management Services c/o Richard Ivey School of Business, The University of Western Ontario, London, Ontario, Canada, N6A 3K7; phone (519) 661-3208; fax (519) 661-3882; e-mail cases@ivey.uwo.ca

Copyright © 1994, Ivey Management Services. One time permission to reproduce granted by Ivey Management Services on September 24, 1998.

out a "rare bird." Given the unfavourable condition of the global airline industry and the difficulties Sabena was experiencing due to months of interim leadership, it seemed obvious that the person hired to replace Van Rafelghem should already have proven himself in the airline industry.

Rumours of potential candidates had been rampant; the Belgian press speculated for months as to possible successors. The much-anticipated announcement of the new Chairman for Sabena Belgian World Airlines caught the entire nation by surprise. On November 9, 1990, the government announced that Pierre Godfroid, Vice-President of European Operations for the U.S. based Campbell Soup Company, would be the new head of the Belgian national air carrier. Dehaene, in making the announcement, explained that the government felt Godfroid's skills in industrial restructuring would more than outweigh his lack of direct involvement in the airline business. It would fall to Godfroid, a man with no experience in managing an airline, but with skills in restructuring, to find a way to ensure the continued survival of Sabena; a clearly troubled airline, in clearly troubled times.

PIERRE GODFROID

Godfroid, born in Antwerp, was a 56-year-old Belgian of Flemish descent. He had been trained as a lawyer but in his early career he worked primarily as an investment banker. In the late 1970s he rescued France's leading catalogue sales company from bankruptcy. By doing so he developed the reputation as a highly competent turnaround manager. In 1981 Godfroid joined Continental Foods, a major European food distribution company and became its President in 1982. While head of Continental, he assumed a leadership role in the European food distribution industry eventually becoming president of the Fédération de l'Industrie Alimentaire, the industry's trade association. In 1984, Continental was acquired by the Campbell Soup Company and after the takeover, Godfroid remained with the company to successfully integrate Continental into Campbell's worldwide operations.

Godfroid accepted the job at Sabena because he felt that the challenge of saving the company was one he simply could not turn down. He knew that the risk of failure was great but the personal rewards of success would be equally significant. If things could be turned around for Sabena, the transformation would establish a model for other state-run businesses trying to make the transition from public to private enterprise. There was potential for the impact he had on Sabena to be felt well beyond the borders of one struggling company.

Godfroid strongly believed that business success was the result of competent leadership and "good people." Leadership set the direction and tone for individual employees to follow but it was their competence, applied within a framework established by the leader, which produced positive results. "I only believe in people—they make the difference." He felt that the right kind of people were those with a simple approach; people who were not pretentious, who saw what needed to be done and went ahead and did it. He stated that, "Success comes to those who are willing to take the greatest risks." He was willing to tolerate mistakes in the belief that the problems they caused would be more than offset by the learning that accompanied failure. Godfroid had little tolerance for bureaucratic ritual or unnecessary paperwork; direct, hands-on control was not of primary importance.

SABENA'S HISTORY

Founded in 1923, Belgium's Sabena Airlines was one of the oldest air carriers in the world. The Belgian people were very proud of the fact that their country had a national airline whose roots could be traced back to the early days of aviation. They believed that a national airline was necessary to ensure Belgium remained connected to the rest of the world. Over the years Sabena had developed air connections throughout Europe and to a lesser extent to North America, but the airline played its most crucial role in the development of Belgium's colonial ties to Africa. The routes that carried wealthy colonists between Africa and Europe linked Belgium to its colonies and at the same time allowed the airline to prosper in spite of Belgium's relatively small domestic market. What was good for the development of the country was good for the development of Sabena.

On a number of occasions, Sabena aircraft had been directed to African trouble spots to air lift Belgian nationals in emergency situations. The airline was seen as a lifeline to the home country and its ability to respond in a crisis increased the perception among Belgians that the airline was an important component of their national sovereignty.

The airline's dependence on African routes, eventually, resulted in long run problems when the ties between Belgium and its African colonies were broken. In 1963, after the colonies achieved independence, the government of Zaire, the former Belgian Congo, ended Sabena's monopoly on routes to Europe. It later expelled the company from domestic air services altogether. The loss of these routes, together with the fact that the company had neglected development of more lucrative routes to North America and Asia while its competition had not, almost resulted in the company's collapse. However, the Belgian government, cognizant of the airline's historical position and its importance as a source of employment (over 12 000 Belgians worked for the airline), continued to support Sabena during the tough times. As long as the company did not lose too much money, there were strong political forces keeping it afloat.

INDUSTRY ENVIRONMENT

In 1990, the European airline industry consisted of over 20 national and private carriers of varying size and profitability. Most of these carriers were wholly owned or significantly supported by their home governments and they enjoyed a strong hold on their national markets (Exhibit 1). Smaller independent regional and charter airlines had emerged and were positioning themselves for smaller niche or under-serviced markets. However these start-up airlines were not perceived to represent significant competition because of their size and the limited nature of their services.

According to the International Civil Aviation Organization, the world's airlines transported over 1.1 billion passengers in 1989; however, there was growing concern that some markets were beginning to mature and growth would slow (Exhibit 2) in future years. In addition, industry profits were extremely variable. While some major airlines were doing extremely well, (Singapore, Delta and AMR) others were on the brink of bankruptcy (Texas Air, Pan Am and TWA). As noted in Exhibit 3, Sabena was the 34th largest airline in the world on the basis of revenues and the 44th on the basis of passenger miles in 1989.

FIXED COSTS

The basic operating economics of an airline hinged upon high fixed costs. Once the airline set its routes, established flight frequencies, and decided on the type of aircraft, most of its costs were in place. Every passenger represented contribution and the airline was under great pressure to fill the planes. Exhibit 4 provides the cost structure for a typical commercial airline. Since fuel costs were about the same for a full plane as an empty one, and the number of flight crew depended on the type of aircraft rather than the number of passengers, the only true variable expenses were services like ticketing and customers' meals. Most airlines used some form of product differentiation to attract customers, preferably high yield customers such as business travellers and first-class passengers.

A UNIFIED EUROPE

In the fall of 1990, a number of changes and potential changes were facing the European airline industry and uncertainty was the most accurate way to describe the state of affairs. A key unknown was the impact of a unified Europe, planned for 1992. No one was sure what impact this new political alignment would have on the airline industry, but companies were beginning to position themselves to take advantage of the anticipated freer borders and the reduced regulatory environment. The European Commission, the regulatory body for European aviation, was seeking greater powers to ensure a competitive environment for post 1992. It was particularly concerned about a potential rise in predatory practices on the part of dominant carriers. For example, such airlines could flood the market with capacity or frequencies, charge fares below a carrier's fully allocated costs, or grant override commissions and other benefits to travel agents and frequent flier programs, which locked in customers to one airline. The Commission was exploring ways in which it could encourage open competition so the consumer would benefit from increased services and lower costs. At the same time it was trying to determine the best way to intervene so that the industry would avoid the pitfalls evident in the post deregulation environment of the United States. European airlines, having had the advantage of watching the U.S. experience, realized that deregulation would inevitably lead to fierce competition and likely result in industry consolidation. There was developing concern among industry officials that, in a deregulated environment, many of the smaller airlines could not survive in their current configuration. There was also uncertainty as to whether the European Commission would be given the appropriate power to intervene to protect the more vulnerable airlines.

ALLIANCES

The potential for industry consolidation seemed even more certain given the emerging trend to privatize national airlines. Many governments were no longer willing, and in many cases, no longer able, to prop up unprofitable operations. With reduced fiscal support and regulatory protection from home governments, airlines were beginning to realize that they could not continue to depend on their governments for preferential treatment. Governments had little to offer in support of their flag carriers. Many of the smaller airlines, seeing the handwriting on the wall, were not waiting to be taken over but were investigating the possibility of joining with competitors in some form of operational alliance. For example, in the spring of 1990, Austrian Airlines joined Finnair, Swissair and SAS in a European alliance created to serve an expanded market in Eastern and Southern Europe, North Africa, the Middle East and India. Sabena had been holding talks with a number of airlines and had recently received a firm proposal to join with British Airways and KLM to develop a European hub in Brussels. However these alliance relationships were new and untested and industry analysts wondered about the long-term stability of such arrangements.

The independent competitors were fighting such alliances, preferring to see the collapse of the smaller carriers. Alliances captured landing rights within existing operations and did not free up slots for expansions or new entrants. The start-up operations were dependent upon access to existing slots because the current European airport infrastructure did not allow for the creation of new and expanded airline operations. Most governments did not have the money to build new airports or even to improve existing facilities. A special report for the International Air Transport Association found that capacity at ten major European airports would be seriously restricted between 1995 and 2000 without major improvements, and a total of 27 major Western European airports would be unable to accommodate traffic demand by the year 2000 without significant enhancements. This meant that airlines with existing slots had a valuable commodity to bargain with, in alliance negotiations.

THE GULF CRISIS

Another major uncertainty facing the airline industry concerned the impact of the Persian Gulf Crisis on airline operations. Since tensions began to mount in the summer of 1990, oil prices had increased significantly resulting in increased airline fuel costs. At the same time, passenger travel declined as people concerned about the unstable conditions delayed or cancelled travel plans. How long would the crisis last and how would it be resolved? How long would the tensions last and would there be any lasting repercussions? Would the oil prices decline when the situation stabilized? The little profitability that remained in the industry was being squeezed out by this unforeseen event.

SABENA BELGIAN WORLD AIRLINES

Sabena had always operated as an instrument of the Belgian government and reflected many of the hallmarks of a government-run bureaucracy. The organization functioned more like a public authority staffed by civil servants than a competitive airline. Under these conditions, the priority was not necessarily what was best for Sabena as a competitive business but rather what was seen as best for the people of Belgium. For example, it was not unusual for purchasing decisions to be made, not on the basis of the least cost alternative, but on the basis of other more politically important criteria.

The government saw the airline as a source of employment and did what it could to maximize the number of people working at Sabena. If this meant that the company lost money, then the government encouraged the airline to protect employment and covered losses until profitability improved. Systems to improve efficiency were given lower priority especially if their implementation resulted in job losses. As a result, the airline was seriously overstaffed and operated with probably the worst efficiency of any airline in Europe. Internal studies had shown that the airline did not have a good image among consumers and was not known for the quality or consistency of its service.

The company had 16 directors, many of whom were appointed because of the need to accommodate Belgium's various political parties, labour unions and linguistic factions. Staffing selections as well were influenced by the need to ensure balanced representation among Belgium's linguistic factions.

The airline operated out of Zaventem Airport, 30 km outside of Brussels and controlled most of the landing rights and runway slots. Access to Zaventem was one of Sabena's most valuable assets since the airport was strategically located near the centre of Western Europe (see Exhibit 5 for map). Many felt that Zaventem would make an ideal hub location if the European airlines decided to replicate the American approach to airline operations.

Management at Sabena

When Godfroid took over many of those in management positions had been appointed to their posts for political reasons and did not necessarily have appropriate work experience or managerial competence. It was not unusual for managers to act in the interests of the people who appointed them rather than the interests of the corporation, which employed them. Skilled individuals who rose through the ranks to attain leadership positions in the company found it difficult to function among less motivated or competent colleagues. Some left in frustration because of the amount of political interference and their inability to function in a true management role. Most of the current senior managers had either an aeronautics or engineering background and saw technical concerns as the focus of their efforts. The planes and equipment were of excellent quality and well maintained, but management had much less appreciation for marketing and customer service requirements.

The management structure at Sabena was multi-layered and hierarchical with management clearly separate from workers. There were no accurate organizational charts or job descriptions. This meant that the organizational units within Sabena developed as separate fiefdoms reflecting the unique relationships developed among managers and workers within the unit. There was little coordination at the management level except in crisis situations and it was not uncommon for open hostility to break out as one set of managers blamed another if problems arose.

There was a similar lack of competence at the supervisory level. Because of rigid compensation rules it was difficult to reward individual performance or to provide increased wages to employees who exceeded maximum levels in specified wage categories. It was common practice, therefore, to create special supervisory positions or to promote individuals to existing supervisory positions to justify a pay raise. This meant that a large number of supervisors were in these positions for administrative reasons rather for their ability to manage people. Such supervisors did not see themselves as management's representatives in their relations with hourly workers. It was not uncommon for them to provide weak leadership on the floor and to provide poor implementation of management direction.

Management did as little as possible to communicate directly with the workers, preferring instead to instruct through written communications and memos. There were those who suggested that management was afraid of the work force and avoided face to face confrontations whenever possible. Management treated the workers as machines, which were not expected, or encouraged, to think for themselves. When an employee had a work-related problem, it was presented to a supervisor for a solution. Employees took no initiative beyond their limited responsibilities. Each worker performed his or her specific job unconcerned about the functioning of the whole. They took little or no pride in the outcome of their work. This attitude, coupled with ineffective supervision, meant that a significant amount of pilfering, work avoidance and shirking took place. Absenteeism was running at 9 per cent per day.

Employer/Union Relations

The unions in Belgium were extremely powerful and dominated every aspect of Belgian life. They were established, not on the basis of job function or industry designation but rather on political affiliation. There were three unions, all of which were represented at Sabena: Socialist (30 per cent of Sabena workers), Christian Democrats (30 per cent) and Liberals (10 per cent). In the past, unions had dominated management at Sabena. Industrial relations were strained and when the unions disagreed with management actions, strikes were a common occurrence. Human Resource (HR) managers at Sabena had not kept up with trends in HR management. They preferred to continue to manage according to the existing status quo, which was unquestionably adversarial. Under this approach both management and unions had clearly defined "roles" and ongoing relations followed well-established rules of the "game." The workers held a trump card, however, in that if they didn't like what they were told by management, their unions would complain to the politicians, who in turn would direct the Chairman to comply with the union demands.

Management was tightly bound by the terms and conditions of collective agreements. Workers were hired and trained to carry out very specific and limited functions. If there was no work available, workers would wait until appropriate work was found. Workers at Sabena were paid well, earning significantly more and working significantly less than workers in private industry. In addition to high wages, the level of employee benefits provided workers in Belgium approached 31 per cent of their salary, significantly more than was required in the countries of competitor firms.

The workers at Sabena knew that they had well paid and secure employment. Wage increases were based on length of service. Pay hikes were automatically awarded for each year of continuous service, for a period of up to 33 years. As long as the worker continued on the payroll, he or she was guaranteed an increase in wages regardless of productivity or performance. It was almost impossible to fire anyone and there was virtually a no lay-off policy. If attempts were made to lay off workers, the union would intervene with the government and the Chairman would be directed to back down.

Corporate Restructuring

Van Rafelghem felt that the lack of management accountability had been a major source of reduced profitability. To resolve this problem he divided the company up into semi-autonomous subsidiaries or divisions. His plan was to hold each division accountable for the management of the assets under its control and to establish clear profit centres to monitor results. There were 12 of these subsidiaries established (airlines, flight school, catering, techniques [airline maintenance and repair], real estate, tourism, finance) each reporting to a holding company referred to as Sabena S.A. Among these subsidiaries, Sabena World Airlines (SWA) was the largest and most important. The Chairman and Vice-Chairman of Sabena S.A. held the same positions in each of the 12 subsidiaries but after that, there was much duplication of administrative functions. This was not perceived as a problem because employment, not efficiency, was the government's key priority. In fact, the restructuring had a positive effect in that it resulted in the creation of a number of new managerial positions.

Although the intent to decentralize and introduce divisional accountability had merit, problems arose because of the lack of complementary integrating mechanisms to focus the subsidiaries on common purposes or goals. Immediately upon establishing the subsidiaries, boundaries were drawn between divisions and coordination became an almost impossible task. Although the change was intended to increase accountability, every time a problem occurred, individual divisions would pass the buck claiming the trouble was the fault of another division. Instead of solving problems, more problems were created. The fragmentation of management effort directed at internal problems diverted the company's attention from the truly important environmental challenges facing it.

Splitting Sabena up into smaller subsidiaries had, unfortunately, taken place before the completion of information systems to track corporate results in line with the new divisions. Although a great deal of effort had been directed at developing information and accounting systems, the company was not capable of sorting out data in meaningful ways to assist in identifying responsibility and the MIS systems were of no help in resolving jurisdictional disputes.

Financial Position

The Belgian state owned 53 per cent of Sabena's shares with the remainder belonging to regional governments or state-run investment funds. In the past, the Belgian government had only asked that the company be marginally profitable. It was willing to absorb small losses from time to time, as long as Sabena provided a maximum number of jobs for the Belgian economy. By 1990, however, the state was beginning to grow concerned about the company's steady stream of losses. Like many countries, Belgium was beginning to feel the effects of deficit financing and the country was experiencing a worsening debt problem. Political pressure was beginning to build to bring the national debt under control. The government was not sure how much longer it could tolerate the continuing drain of Sabena's poor financial results. Sabena expected to post a loss of BFr 3 billion (US$98 million) to BFr 4 billion in 1990, its worst performance in 15 years. In addition it was facing a capital expenditure over the next ten years of BFr 100 billion to pay for new planes on order. It was clear that the poor financial results were showing no signs of reversal. In fact, the losses were escalating at such an alarming rate that the company's equity had all but disappeared (Exhibit 6).

Van Rafelghem had been working on establishing a joint venture with British Airways (BA) and KLM. He was hoping to interest the two carriers into buying into SWA. Both would purchase a 20 per cent equity share leaving Sabena (the Belgian government) with 60 per cent ownership. The intent of the venture would be to establish a European hub at Brussel's Zaventem airport. This would allow these airlines to use the underutilized Zaventem airport to link secondary destinations throughout Europe. Interest in this alliance had cooled, however, because of antitrust concerns among other competitors and Sabena's fears about its loss of autonomy under this arrangement. However, the hub idea had merit in and of itself and there were some who felt that Sabena should consider going it alone or consider interesting other more appropriate airlines in a Brussel's hub arrangement.

After Van Rafelghem's stroke, Sabena's Deputy Chairman Pahault stepped in to take over, but he was in no position to effectively replace Van Rafelghem. The Deputy Chairman position had been established as one of convention to appease Belgium's main linguistic factions. The tradition had been that if the Chairman was of Flemish descent, the Vice Chairman would be French and vice versa. In this case, since Van Rafelghem was Flemish, so Pahault, of French descent, had been appointed as Vice Chairman. Much of the knowledge about the company and how it functioned however, resided only with Van Rafelghem and it was inaccessible as long as he lay in a coma. Some even speculated that establishment of Sabena S.A. had been a masterful feat of financial engineering intended to increase equity through the creation of goodwill. Regardless of Van Rafelghem's intent, it was clear that the situation Pahault inherited was a company very near bankruptcy; immediate action was critical. Recognizing the financial crisis the company faced, Pahault brought in a group of McKinsey consultants to try and straighten out its financial position and to identify cost saving measures to get Sabena's costs under control. In their report, McKinsey suggested that to ensure its survival Sabena either drastically downsize its operations to become a low cost regional carrier or it find the funds to invest in the development of a European hub (estimated to be in the neighbourhood of US$250 million).

GODFROID'S TASK

In offering him the position Dehaene had asked Godfroid to help with the transformation of Sabena from public to private enterprise. The government requested that he prepare a business plan by February 1, 1991, outlining his program for raising new capital and reorganizing the airline. The government was willing to release its control of the company reducing its level of ownership from 53 per cent to 25 per cent, allowing for a much needed infusion of new equity from private sources. To avert bankruptcy, Sabena would need to improve its profitability dramatically and to attract new partners from the private sector. Godfroid had just under two months to come up with a plan to achieve these objectives. What direction should he take the airline and how should he manage this mammoth undertaking? Was Sabena worth saving or would it inevitably be swallowed up by a larger and stronger competitor? Godfroid knew he had to set his direction soon since there was little time to waste.

EXHIBIT 1   **European Airlines**

Airline	Country
Aer Lingus	Ireland
Air France	France
Air Malta	Malta
Alitalia	Italy
Austrian Airlines	Austria
British Airways	Great Britain
CSA Czechoslovakian Airlines	Czechoslovakia
Finnair	Finland
Iberia	Spain
Iceland air	Iceland
JAT Yugoslavian Airlines	Yugoslavia
KLM	Netherlands
Lufthansa	West Germany
Luxair	Luxembourg
Malev Hungarian Airlines	Hungary
Olympic Airlines	Greece
Sabena	Belgium
SAS	Sweden
Swissair	Switzerland
TAP—Air Portugal	Portugal
Turkish Air	Turkey

EXHIBIT 2 Selected RPK Forecasts

(billions)

Domestic Markets			1989 RPK		Forecast Average Annual Growth Rate 1990–2000	
U.S.			505.1		5.1	
WESTERN EUROPE			52.2		6.3	
ASIA-PACIFIC			70.5		6.3	
TOTAL DOMESTIC			627.8		out of total Domestic Market: 981.5	

Between Europe and	1989	1990	1991	1993	1995	2000
Intra-Europe	67.8	72.6	77.7	88.9	100.4	125.7
North America	168.2	178.9	190.0	213.1	237.2	303.3
South America	19.8	21.2	22.7	25.7	28.9	37.8
Africa	34.9	37.0	39.2	43.8	48.8	62.9
Middle East	35.9	37.3	38.8	42.0	45.4	55.2
Asia[1]	33.2	39.4	45.9	58.9	70.9	101.6

[1] Does not include the Indian subcontinent.

Source: Boeing Commercial Airplane Group.

EXHIBIT 3 Top 50 Airline Companies: Rank by Revenues

Rank by Revenues			Country	1989 Revenues		Profit		Traffic	
1989	1988	Airline Company		US$ Millions	% Change from 1988 (U.S.)	$ Millions	Rank	Billions of Passenger kms	Rank
1	2	AMR	U.S.	10 589.5	20.0	454.8	3	118.5	1
2	1	UAL	U.S.	9 914.5	10.0	324.2	6	112.3	2
3	4	Japan Airlines[1]	Japan	8 509.0	17.4	157.3	10	54.4	8
4	5	Delta	U.S.	8 0889.5	17.0	460.9	2	55.9	3
5	7	British Airways[1]	Britain	7 529.1	12.5	309.5	7	90.2	6
6	6	Lufthansa	W. Germany	6 941.2	3.0	56.8	22	57.9	12
7	3	Texas Air	U.S.	6 768.7	(21.0)	(885.6)	47	81.3	4
8	10	NWA	U.S.	6 553.8	16.0	355.2	5	73.7	5
9	9	USAIR Group	U.S.	6 257.3	9.6	(63.2)	41	54.4	9
10	8	Air France	France	6 216.9	4.4	132.0	12	37.0	11
11	11	All Nippon[1]	Japan	4 858.4	9.7	60.2	19	26.0	16
12	12	Scandinavian Airlines	Sweden	4 567.3	3.5	N.A.	—	15.3	26
13	13	Trans World	U.S.	4 507.3	3.4	(298.5)	45	56.4	7
14	15	Hanjin Group	South Korea	4 243.6	13.7	69.6	18	17.9	23
15	14	Pan Am	U.S.	3 794.4	(8.9)	(336.6)	46	46.6	10
16	16	Alitalia	Italy	3 734.2	14.6	(168.1)	44	20.8	21
17	17	Swissair	Switzerland	3 174.5	1.7	103.3	16	15.8	25
18	20	Air Canada	Canada	3 104.3	11.8	125.8	13	26.3	15
19	18	Iberia	Spain	3 015.5	4.9	52.5	25	21.1	20
20	19	KLM[1]	Netherlands	2 938.9	4.1	184.2	8	24.0	17
21	21	Qantas[2]	Australia	2 655.1	18.1	144.3	11	26.6	14

EXHIBIT 3   (continued)

22	22	Singapore[1]	Singapore	2 295.8	15.9	494.7	1	28.9	13
23	24	PWA	Canada	2 252.9	27.7	(47.3)	40	23.7	18
24	23	Cathay Pacific	Hong Kong	2 212.6	14.4	425.2	4	22.1	19
25	25	Saudia	Saudi Arabia	1 910.1	12.5	(140.0)	43	16.3	24
26	26	Varig	Brazil	1 862.1	21.6	10.4	39	13.9	28
27	28	Ansett Transport[2]	Australia	1 743.9	32.7	108.0	15	7.7	42
28	27	Thai International[3]	Thailand	1 683.8	17.9	182.1	9	18.7	22
29	29	Japan Air System[1]	Japan	1 418.3	12.7	12.2	36	7.3	43
30	30	Air Inter	France	1 356.5	9.5	18.3	32	8.5	39
31	34	China	Taiwan	1 246.4	20.3	115.6	14	10.5	33
32	31	Garuda	Indonesia[1]	1 232.6	11.6	N.A.	—	12.9	29
33	33	Hudson Investments[4]	Britain	1,211.6	11.6	11.7	37	6.9	45
34	36	Finnair[1]	Finland	1 160.9	13.5	18.3	33	9.2	35
35	32	Sabena	Belgium	1 146.9	4.9	18.0	34	6.8	46
36	37	Air New Zealand[1]	New Zealand	1 108.7	9.0	46.6	26	10.6	31
37	38	LTU	West Germany	1 094.4	13.6	N.A.	—	9.8	34
38	35	UTA	France	1 058.1	3.2	38.1	28	5.6	48
39	39	Southwest	U.S.	1 031.7	22.6	71.6	17	15	27
40	43	Australian[2]	Australia	1 013.8	27.9	57.4	21	6.1	47
41	45	America West	U.S.	1 004.2	29.5	20.0	31	12.7	30
42	40	Alaska Air Group	U.S.	929.2	14.1	42.9	27	7.1	44
43	49	S. African Airways[1]	S. Africa	912.2	(9.3)	55.9	24	9.0	37
44	44	Aer Lingus	Ireland	899.5	14.5	56.2	23	3.4	49
45	•	Austrian	Austria	850.5	9.7	11.6	38	2.4	50
46	42	Olympic Airways	Greece	*785.0	*(2.2)	*(123.1)	42	8.1	40
47	47	Mexicana	Mexico	764.3	2.0	13.7	35	10.5	32
48	48	Air India[1]	India	745.4	1.2	28.1	29	9.0	36
49	•	El Al	Israel	713.6	7.3	24.2	30	7.7	41
50	•	Malaysian[1]	Malaysia	712.8	14.0	59.0	20	9.0	38

* Estimate.

[1] Figures are for fiscal year ended March 31, 1989.

[2] Figures are for fiscal year ended June 30, 1989.

[3] Figures are for fiscal year ended September 33, 1989.

[4] Figures are for fiscal year ended October 31, 1989.

Note: All figures converted to U.S. dollars using the average official exchange rate during each company's fiscal year.

Source: Kenneth Labich, "America Takes on the World," *Fortune*, September 24, 1990, p. 52. Reprinted from the September 24, 1990 issue of *Fortune* by special permission; copyright 1990, Time Inc.

EXHIBIT 4   Airline Operating Cost Distribution International Civil Aviation Organization Airlines—1988

Direct Costs		Indirect Costs	
Fuel	14.5%	Ticketing and Sales	17.6%
Maintenance	11.6%	User fees, Station expense	14.1%
Flight Operations	11.4%	Passenger Service	10.4%
Depreciation	7.8%	General/Admin.	8.9%
		Landing Fees	3.7%
Total	45.3%	Total	54.7%

Source: Boeing Commercial Airplane Group, *Current Market Outlook*, February 1990.

EXHIBIT 5   **British Airways Plan for a Brussels Hub**

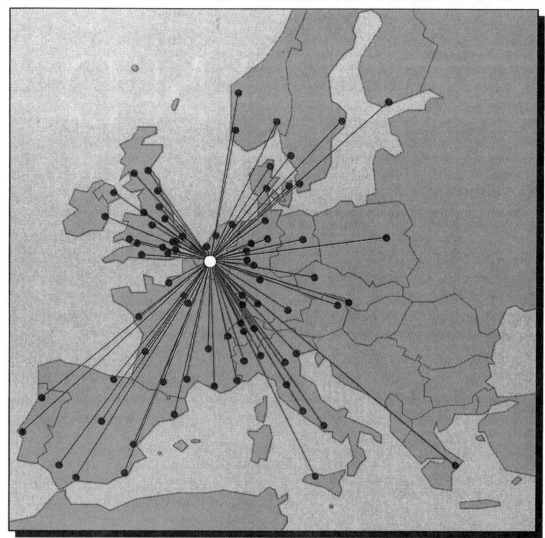

British Airways told the British MMC it plans to link 75 cities in Europe by 1995 through a hub-and-spoke network at Brussels if its proposed 20% stake in Sabena World Airlines is approved.

Source: *Aviation Week and Space Technology*, May 14, 1990.

E X H I B I T   6   **Financial History of Sabena 1984–90**

(billion BFr)

	Debt *	*Equity*
1984	17.0	2.4
1985	19.3	4.8
1986	23.5	10.5
1987	25.4	10.7
1988	25.9	9.0
1989	31.2	7.5
1990	43.4	.1

* Does not include debt owed to the Belgian Government.

DELTA AGROCHEMICALS, INC.

case

35

J. Peter Killing
and Joyce Miller

Based in Denver, Colorado, Consolidated Western Holdings (CWH) was a large Fortune 500 listed industrial company. From its beginnings in the 1940s as an oil and gas venture, CWH had steadily expanded its oil operations and had diversified through acquisition to become a major participant in the chemical industry. The company also owned and managed coal mining operations around the world and had acquired a collection of small, but growing, high technology, energy-related businesses in the United States.

IVEY

CWH's chemical business consisted of four divisions, each run as an autonomous profit centre. The smallest and newest of these was the Western Biotechnology ("Westec") business, managed by John Finlayson. In May 1991, however, Finlayson was considering moving to Delta Agrochemicals, Inc. ("DeltaAg"), a much larger sister division in the agricultural chemicals business. Finlayson knew the senior managers of DeltaAg well, as he had been a member of the division's internal management board since the mid-1980s.

Because of his success in building Westec, Finlayson was widely viewed as a competent manager, and he was sure that if he asked for a transfer to DeltaAg, it would be approved. Although the move would not be a promotion, Finlayson thought that the change would be an interesting one as DeltaAg faced a number of major issues. He added, "I now have someone here who can run Westec with only minor consultation with me, and I am spending so much time working on DeltaAg issues that I think I might as well move over there full time." DeltaAg's head office was about two kilometres from Westec's. Both were located in St. Louis, Missouri.

THE AGROCHEMICALS BUSINESS

Agrochemical companies discovered, developed, registered and sold products for controlling pests (insecticides), plant diseases (fungicides) and weeds (herbicides). Traditionally, it had been a high growth, high margin business, and gross margins in the 60 per cent range were not uncommon. By the 1990s, however, industry profit was eroding as costs skyrocketed and growth flattened. In many countries, the industry was not able to increase its prices sufficiently to offset cost inflation. Moreover, the food supply in the developed world was broadly in surplus, and arable land was being taken out of production. At the same time, mounting public concern about the environmental effects of agrochemicals was delaying registration of new products. Over the long term, no more than 1–2 per cent growth per annum was expected in existing markets.

Some industry observers felt that there was strong market potential in centrally planned and developing countries, but the question was when and where such growth would occur. Hot spots like South East Asia looked very promising, but Eastern European countries were problematic. In terms of crops, it was widely believed that wheat production was likely to decline, while rice and maize, for example, would increase. Eighty per cent of the world agrochemicals market was believed to be found in less than 20 countries.

Overall, the market for agrochemical products was highly fragmented, with more than 40 separate product categories each worth more than $100 million. Herbicides, for example, were sold for approximately 10 different crops, including cotton, rice, maize, soya beans, sugar cane, sugar beets and so on. Within any of these general crop areas were a variety of individual product categories. In the maize segment, for example, there were separate herbicide products available to: (1) kill grass before it emerged; (2) kill grass after it emerged; (3) kill broad-leafed weeds before they emerged; and (4) kill broad-leafed weeds after they emerged. Delta had products in most, but not all, of these product categories.

Expectations were that the fight for market share would continue to intensify. All major companies were spending heavily on research and development. The key to success was to find new "active ingredients" with novel effects for controlling pests, diseases or weeds, and then to get these to the market ahead of the competition. It was, however, a long and expensive process. Gestation periods of 7–10 years were not uncommon as companies took their new products through toxicology tests, metabolism tests, studies of crop residue, environmental impact assessments and so on. Detailed field studies had to be performed before a product could be offered for sale in an individual country and this was both time-consuming and expensive in most major markets. The registration process could cost up to $50 million per product, and of course, it cost the same whether the product turned out to be a world beater or a lacklustre "me too" offering.

A further hurdle facing agricultural chemical producers was the 1988 American legislation that required products, which had been introduced when registration standards were less stringent, to be re-registered, at great cost. The result was that poorly performing old products were taken off the market. For companies like DeltaAg, however, which had a range of successful older products, re-registration was an expensive necessity. Other countries were expected to follow the American lead.

DELTA AGROCHEMICALS, INC.

With almost $2.5 billion in sales in 1990, DeltaAg had a 14 per cent share of the world agrochemical market. The company's product line, which consisted of more than 2 000 individual chemical formulations, was built on 35–40 active ingredients, seven or eight of which accounted for 80 per cent of sales. The company manufactured its active ingredients in a few key plants in North America and Europe, and shipped them to more than 50 formulation plants around the world where final formulation, packaging and labelling took place. DeltaAg's products were sold in more than 100 countries, and the company had its own selling organization in 45 countries. DeltaAg's largest markets were the United States, Canada and France.

In the mid-1960s, shortly after CWH acquired DeltaAg, the company developed a "blockbuster" weed killer, Melinor, which sold well in many markets around the world and fuelled the company's growth for the next ten years. Then in the late 1970s, DeltaAg acquired a mid-sized French company and a British firm, which specialized in insecticides. These acquisitions, combined with strong market growth, brought DeltaAg's sales volume to approximately $1.4 billion by the mid-1980s. In 1988, DeltaAg purchased the agrochemical division of another major American company, which was particularly strong in corn and wheat protection. In addition to growth by acquisition, DeltaAg had been introducing new products at a record rate. George Hill, DeltaAg's research director, commented:

> We spent a decade looking for another blockbuster like Melinor, without success, and then changed our strategy to go for incremental development of existing products. This worked extremely well and by the early 1980s, we were introducing two new products per year, which is remarkable by industry standards. As late as 1979, Melinor accounted for 80 per cent of the company's gross margin—thanks to our new products it is now down around 10–15 per cent.
>
> We are currently spending about $300 million on research and development. The budget is split into three equal parts—one third for invention, one third for the development and registration of new products, and one third for the reformulation and re-registration of existing products.

1988—STRATEGIC AND ORGANIZATIONAL CHANGES

In 1988, DeltaAg underwent a major strategy review. Under the direction of Alan Jemison, who had been the president of DeltaAg for five years, the management team set an objective of becoming "the world's leading agricultural chemical company." Profitability targets were established: the immediate goal was a 16 per cent operating profit to sales ratio (compared with 10 per cent in 1987) and by 1997, the return on assets was to reach 36 per cent, approximately double the 1987 figure. Growth would be at a rate 50 per cent greater than the market. All of these objectives were considered ambitious but achievable—and in the words of the strategy document, they would require "increasingly selective decisions aimed at steering all activities toward the areas of highest reward."

As a first step in implementing the new strategy, countries were divided into six categories, with a different DeltaAg objective established for each. These objectives ranged from "defend dominant position" to "improve market share rapidly." At the same time, three broad product categories were created, namely:

"products of key strategic importance," "high price, high margin specialties," and products with "commercial or technical limitations." Again, different objectives were set for the products in each category.

The 1988 strategy was accompanied by organizational changes. Cost saving reductions were made in the St. Louis head office, particularly in the marketing areas. About 80 of St. Louis' 600 employees were laid off. In addition, a new vice-presidential layer of management was added (see Exhibit 1) in order to free up the senior vice-presidents to concentrate on the long-term future of the business. An employee commented:

> The job cuts created a level of anxiety never seen before in the St. Louis operation. The organization had always been growing, and this was the first time that we had ever moved in such a direct way to cut costs. CWH's general policy is that layoffs are a last resort, but DeltaAg management went directly to this solution—and they implemented the changes brutally. Moreover, we added another layer of management at a time when most companies were trying to reduce their management hierarchy.

In an effort to restore morale following the layoffs, a team of consultants was employed to involve employees in an exercise to identify the core values within the organization. One of the consultants explained:

> We tried to create a common culture in the business and to heal some of the wounds caused by the 1988 reorganization. We got everyone at St. Louis into groups and worked with them to identify the key success factors in the business and their role in delivering them. We thought that ideas would flow back and forth and people would talk about where they were and where they wanted to be as an organization. There was a lot of cynicism, however, and it became clear that the vice-presidents had not really bought into the exercise. The president, who was committed, was reluctant to push the others very hard because the groups said "this exercise is about trust—so trust us." The end result was that some people signed on, but a lot did not.

1991—ANOTHER LOOK AT THE ORGANIZATION

By early 1991, it was clear that the previous year had not been a financial success for DeltaAg. Virtually all measures of profitability had fallen from previous years, and as shown in Exhibit 2, all were far below budget. David Jans, the Vice-President of Finance for DeltaAg explained the situation:

> The 1988 strategy looked great on paper, but we never implemented it. Since then, we have built in even more fixed costs—probably hitting a billion in 1990. Last year we delivered to CWH only 50 per cent of the cash that they were expecting! It does not take a genius to figure out that our absolute priority now has to be to cut costs. We cannot go before CWH management this summer without a cost cutting plan already being implemented.
>
> At the instigation of John Finlayson, we recently looked at cutting the number of active ingredients that we produce by 50 per cent and selling through distributors in about half of the 45 or so countries in which we currently maintain company operations. At the outset this looked very attractive, because like most organizations we make 80 per cent of our total gross margin with 20 per cent of our products and in about 20 per cent of our markets. However, the study was very disappointing. Our country managers indicated that they could not cut their number of employees very much if they dropped their worst selling products. And we would not be able to save much on the production side either. The net result was that eliminating the bottom half of our product line and markets served would actually reduce our return on capital.
>
> But we still need to do something. Corporate is not happy with us.

In early 1991, DeltaAg management instituted a 13 per cent cost cut across the board. All departments were to comply. Also, John Finlayson was asked to begin a study of the organization to see how it could be streamlined. He believed that DeltaAg needed lower costs, fewer people doing more rewarding jobs, clearer accountabilities, and better coordination between the functional departments in St. Louis. He explained:

> We need to change this organization to get rid of the duplication and cross-functional boundaries. My approach is to begin by trying to determine exactly what transactions are necessary to the successful functioning of the organization. Once we know that, we will be in a position to decide how to organize, and we will know where we can cut, and where we cannot.
>
> To do this, I have set up two task forces. One is to examine the product supply chain within the company, the other is to study the new product introduction chain. These are both lateral processes that cut across the functional departments. Each task force is to identify the key interactions and figure out how they could be performed more efficiently—I am sure that there is room for great improvement. I may also set up a group to look at the role of head office here in St. Louis vis-à-vis the national organizations around the world. They say that we collect too much information from them, and do nothing with it. They also complain that we exercise too much control over their strategies. Are they right? We need to find out the minimum required to manage this company, not the "nice to have." Let's push decision-making down to the lowest possible level, stop the second-guessing, and make decisions only once.
>
> We do not have the kind of performance measures you'd expect in a company this well established. Personal reward and gain have to be more direct.

An employee who had been working in the development department at St. Louis for two years (after spending four years in another part of CWH) applauded the organizational review. She commented:

> My job is to help get the technical resources in this company applied to real world projects where they are needed most—for the product areas that I cover. I am a coordinator—I have no direct power—and to be successful, I have to influence people in different parts of the organization to work together. Working up the hierarchy is not effective because I don't get a quick enough response, and often the information that does come back is not useful. It seems like there are eternal gripes between the people who make things and the people who sell things. There are endless circles going up and nothing going across. For the past 18 months, I have been trying to get $80 000 of formulation time devoted to a product that could give us an immediate $10 million return in the market. I can't get the time, and I can't figure out why not. Right now, the project is in limbo and I've run out of options to move it forward. It's unbelievably frustrating.

THE 1991 STRATEGY REVIEW

CWH's management system called for a comprehensive strategy review of each of its businesses every third year. DeltaAg's review was due in the summer of 1991, and in April, Alan Jemison called a management meeting to discuss the DeltaAg submission. After the meeting, he commented:

> This strategy review is a major event and I hope we can take advantage of it. There is no doubt that the business needs to be more profitable—even if that means making it smaller. We should probably cut the product line a little and step out of some markets. We also need to change our R&D strategy to concentrate on fewer, larger product developments. Our strategy of incrementalism has worked well, but with the rising cost of registration, it is getting too expensive to maintain. Finally, we need to devolve headquarter's functions to the national companies—we must learn to stop doing things for them. The trouble is that a lot of our people here don't feel right unless they are out in the field selling something.
>
> My challenge is to get people to buy into the strategy-making process—to take it seriously. I will be retiring in 24 months and no one knows whether my successor will be appointed from inside DeltaAg or from another part of CWH. There is a lot of speculation, and not enough emphasis on improving the business.
>
> I do not believe that we need to change the organization. We have had a lot of organizational changes, and we now need stability. I hear people saying that we need to get rid of the vice-presidential

layer—I don't think so. What we do need is to turn the managers at the top of this company into a team—a committed team with a common objective.

Other senior DeltaAg executives commented on the situation facing the business in 1991.

Senior Vice-President of Research and Development

This is a technically-driven business, and the success of any company in it depends on its ability to create new, high margin, active ingredients. In the short-term, we could cut our research spending and it would improve the bottom line—but we would be giving away our future. We need to preserve our research skills, and work toward developing more significant new products. At the moment, we have too many marginal products and too many marginal territories. What we need to do is identify the key product/territory combinations and focus on them.

Vice-President of Human Resources

I came from the chemicals subsidiary of an American oil company to join this business in 1990. I see my role as being a change agent. This business is too complex, and people seem to revel in its complexity. Managers make their careers here by winning arguments. A decision is the starting point for a debate rather than a move to action. I heard that Alan once gave a clear instruction that a product under development was to be cancelled. When this happened the researchers began to work on it secretly, and even introduced it to the market a few years later. It failed.

To take this organization forward we need to do two things:

1. We need to create horizontal business processes that will increase communication between the functional areas. As well, we need a flatter organization. The middle level and junior employees see this vice-presidential layer and it drives them crazy. Until senior management gets its act together, they say, why should we behave any differently?
2. We need to reduce the number of products that we produce and markets that we serve. We need to create the mix that will produce the most cash in the short term, and growth for the longer term.

Senior Vice-President of Marketing

I have discussed the situation with my vice-presidents and we agree that we should not cut back our product line or reduce our territorial coverage. Our customers need our full line, and every product that we sell makes money. There is no point in throwing away gross margin. Of course, we can improve our efficiency, and we are already doing this. We have moved from 18 operating units in Europe down to 8, and we're looking at a plan that would bring us down to only three formulation plants for the whole region.

To increase profitability, we need to reduce fixed manufacturing costs. We are using a lot of old manufacturing equipment that requires a lot of maintenance. We could get some of our formulation manufacturing done by outside companies—it certainly would be cheaper and we would not need these far flung plants all over the world.

Vice-President of Operations

In the mid-1980s, at the insistence of CWH senior management, we introduced MRP 2 into this business, and it has made a tremendous difference. Our manufacturing performance has increased dramatically over the past few years.

If our priority is to cut costs, we need to look first at cutting back our research. Research has two major laboratories, one in California and the other in the U.K. that came with one of the acquisitions. That British lab is costing in the neighbourhood of $75 million per year. I believe that we should shut it down and fold its operations into our U.S. operation. British researchers are difficult to control, and the British management team has a tendency to use the lab for their own pet projects; they're also duplicating some of the work that we are doing here.

We also need to reduce the complexity of the business. In spite of what the marketing people say, we do have too many marginal products and too many marginal territories.

JOHN FINLAYSON'S DECISION

At the end of May 1991, John Finlayson was reviewing his situation. He felt that he could not continue to manage Westec and spend so much time working on DeltaAg issues. It was time to make a decision.

I have to move one way or the other. I am concerned that without my full time presence in DeltaAg, some of the things that we are doing, like the task forces, will not have any impact. I am already worried that they are losing their way and are just going through the motions. Whether I join the company or not, I think that we should create a vice-president of planning position and give that person the job of managing the change that has to happen. Everyone else is just too busy to give it the time it needs.

The other thing that makes me think that I should move into DeltaAg is the impending strategy review. Alan sent me a draft of their first attempt at a strategy and I found it too conservative—too much business as usual. In the past week, I have put together something stronger—what I call a focused strategy. It clearly separates our winning territories and products, and specifies different levels of service for them than for our more marginal products and areas. I've shown it to a few people in DeltaAg and they seem to like it. Some say it is obvious and what we are already doing—but no one has said it does not make sense.

On a personal level, I don't think that Alan has strong feelings either way about the possibility of my moving over there. We have discussed it, and it's pretty clear that the decision is mine to make. I might be able to move into one of the senior vice-president spots, or perhaps we could create a new one.

EXHIBIT 1   **Partial Organization Chart**

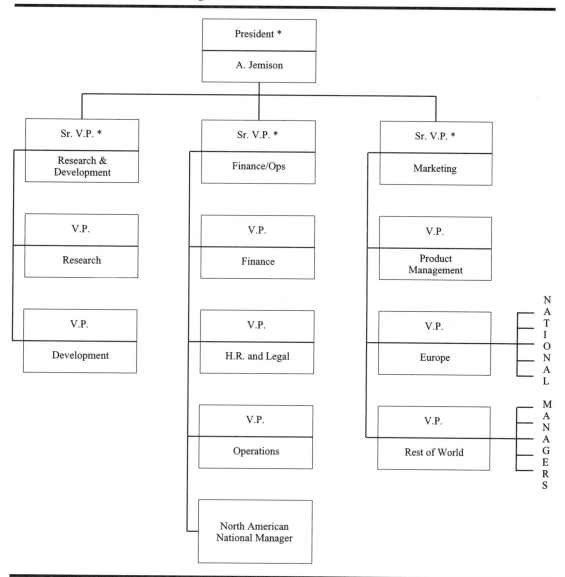

* These four executives plus John Finlayson comprised the Delta Agrochemicals, Inc. management board, responsible for overseeing the company's activities.

EXHIBIT 2 **Financial Performance**

(millions of dollars)

	1986	1987	1988	1989	Actual 1990	Budget 1990
Sales	1 350	1 610	2 160	2 452	2 485	2 570
Gross Margin	665	815	1195	1360	1392	1445
% of Sales	49%	51%	55%	55%	56%	56%
R&D, Sales, Admin	548	564	830	942	1000	980
Depreciation	32	36	60	70	82	80
Other	4	20	26	24	40	28
Operating Profit	81	195	279	324	270	357
	—	—	—	—	—	—
Cash Flow						
Operating Profit	81	195	279	324	270	357
Depreciation	32	36	60	70	82	80
Capital Investment	(114)	(74)	(128)	(176)	(152)	(152)
Acquisition Reorganization			(30)			
Working Capital Changes	(48)	28	(22)	(145)	(42)	42
Cash to Consolidated Western Holdings	(49)	185	159	73	158	327

THE GE ENERGY MANAGEMENT INITIATIVE (A)

case

36

*Julian Birkinshaw
and Joseph N. Fry*

In August 1992, Raj Bhatt, Business Development Manager for GE Canada, met with executives from GE Supply, a U.S.-based distribution arm of GE. The purpose of the meeting was to discuss new business opportunities in Energy Efficiency, an industry that focused on the reduction of energy usage through the installation of energy-efficient technologies. Bhatt had recently gained prequalification for GE Canada to bid in a $1 billion program to install energy-efficient technologies in all federal government buildings. He was confident that GE's expertise in lighting, motors, appliances and financing was sufficient to win

IVEY

Julian Birkinshaw prepared this case under the supervision of Professor Joseph N. Fry solely to provide material for class discussion. The authors do not intend to illustrate either effective or ineffective handling of a managerial situation. The authors may have disguised certain names and other identifying information to protect confidentiality.

at least some of the contracts. Furthermore, he saw the program as a stepping stone to building a new GE business to service the Energy Efficiency needs of a range of clients.

The GE Supply executives informed Bhatt that they had already established a position in the U.S. Energy Efficiency industry, through a joint venture with a new Energy Service Company (ESCo), and had retained the services of a full-time consultant to develop the business. They were interested in the Federal Buildings Program that Bhatt had been working on, but felt that it would be more efficiently run as a division of GE Supply, rather than as a locally managed Canadian venture. The meeting posed a dilemma for Bhatt. He was encouraged by the level of interest that already existed for Energy Efficiency within GE, but at the same time held certain misgivings about folding the Federal Buildings Program into GE Supply's nascent business. Specifically, he was concerned that a lot of interesting Energy Efficiency opportunities existed in Canada which a U.S.-focused business would not be in a position to exploit. Bhatt left the meeting uncertain how to proceed.

GENERAL ELECTRIC (GE)

GE, with $60 billion in revenues in 1991, was among the top ten industrial corporations in the world. From the early days of Thomas Edison, it had grown to be a diversified 54-business corporation by the early eighties. With 400 000 employees and a very strong corporate planning division, it exemplified the traditional strategic planning oriented corporation of the 1970s.

In 1980, Jack Welch, the incoming CEO, made a series of sweeping changes. The corporate planning department was eliminated, layers of management were eliminated and the concepts of empowerment and customer focus became the new drivers behind GE's activities.

GE's many businesses were restructured into 13 autonomous groups,[1] which were further subdivided into a number of operating divisions. In the course of a series of divestments, acquisitions and amalgamations, Welch declared that a major criterion for holding on to a business was that it was number one or number two worldwide in its chosen industry.

Each business group worked from a U.S. head office and was charged with global responsibility for its operations. This move, which by-passed the traditional country organizations, was intended to give priority to the global demands of the businesses, rather than to national interests. International operations, which accounted for about 25 per cent of GE's revenues, were structured under a Vice Chairman, International, but the reality under a so-called direct-connect model was that the operating authority in each country was held by the relevant business unit. Typically, this meant that general management roles in country operations were eliminated and that business leaders or functional managers of specific businesses reported to their headquarters in the U.S., rather than through their country organization. For example, the marketing manager of GE Lighting's Canadian operations reported directly to the GE Lighting grouped headquarters marketing manager in Cleveland, Ohio.

GE Canada

The shift to global management had a major impact on GE's Canadian business. In the 1970s, GE Canada operated as a "miniature replica" of its parent company; most businesses and all functions were represented in Canada, and typically a full line of products was made, primarily for the Canadian market but with some exporting possibilities. The Canadian CEO was fully responsible for the profitability of the Canadian

---

[1] The thirteen groups were: GE Aerospace, Aircraft Engines, Appliances, Communications and Services, Electrical Distribution and Control, Financial Services, Industrial and Power Systems, Lighting, Mechanical Systems, Motors, Plastics, Transportation Systems and NBC.

operating divisions. This changed dramatically under direct-connect structure implemented in the late 1980s.

In 1992, Matthew Meyer, CEO of GE Canada, had a vastly different role from his predecessors. With all operations reporting straight to their U.S. divisional bosses, Meyer was directly responsible only for the activities of a very small number of employees. He had vice-presidents in finance, environmental affairs, legal, human resources and government affairs. These managers were responsible for all the uniquely Canadian issues that cropped up, such as new legislation, tax accounting, government grants and so on. In addition, there was a small business development group, consisting of three managers. Traditionally, this group had been involved in feasibility studies and new market development for the business units in Canada. Following the shift to a "direct-connect" structure, the role had become primarily one of looking for opportunities to leverage the strengths of Canadian activities on a global basis. They were also concerned with identifying new business opportunities in Canada. Bhatt, one of the business development managers, explained:

> Canada is a relatively small marketplace. Consequently, most U.S.-based business leaders have a limited awareness of the opportunities here because they have either a U.S. or a global focus. The role of business development is to attempt to identify investment or market opportunities here that they might find valuable.

There was some discussion among business development managers over the extent to which they should actively "sell" business opportunities to the GE businesses. Some felt that a proactive strategy of promoting Canadian opportunities was appropriate; others preferred to investigate only those cases where business development's involvement had been solicited. The recent decision to promote the Vice-President of Business Development, but not replace him, added further to the uncertainty over the group's role.

Raj Bhatt

Bhatt was only 29. He had worked at GE for just one year, following a successful period at Northern Telecom and an MBA at the University of Western Ontario.

> Business development is quite a challenging experience. There are lots of good opportunities in Canada, but it is sometimes difficult to achieve the level of interest and buy-in necessary to attract the appropriate attention. The Oakville lighting plant, a global manufacturing mandate, is a planned $144 million investment and is certainly our biggest success so far, but there have been a lot of ideas that failed to materialize.

The business development manager typically held that post for only two years, after which he or she was expected to take a line position in one of the businesses. Bhatt had been given a number of attractive options, but had turned them down because he was afraid that his involvement was critical to a number of projects. Specifically, he was concerned that the Energy Efficiency business opportunity he had championed up to now would die because no one else had the knowledge of, or the enthusiasm for, that particular opportunity.

ENERGY EFFICIENCY

Energy Efficiency covered the multitude of ways that energy usage could be optimized, including conservation, use of efficient appliances and off-peak usage. Energy Efficiency was originally conceived in the early 1970s as a response to rising oil prices. It recently saw a resurgence due to the environmental movement and the increasing need for cost competitiveness in the late eighties. Although strongly motivated by public opinion and government pressure, Energy Efficiency initiatives were usually sponsored by the energy supply utilities. They recognized that they could more effectively keep their investment down by reducing demand than by building expensive new power stations. There were also obvious benefits to consumers (in reduced costs) and to the environment.

The growth in utility-sponsored programs for Energy Efficiency was responsible for the formation of many Energy Service Companies (ESCos). These companies aimed to meet the demands and needs of their customers by utilizing these programs. Under the most common arrangement (called a performance contract), the ESCo would install energy efficient technologies at no upfront cost to the client. The costs would be recouped from the savings realized. Such an arrangement could be very lucrative, but the ESCo bore all the risk in the event that the promised savings never materialized.

Th ESCo Industry in Canada

The Canadian ESCo industry was among the most advanced in the world. Both federal and provincial governments had active energy-management programs to promote "green" issues, and had targeted Energy Efficiency as a critical industry. Ontario Hydro and Quebec Hydro had budgets for Energy Efficiency of $800 million and $300 million respectively, in comparison to the C$1.5 billion budget for all U.S. utilities combined.

As a result of the utilities' involvement, the Canadian ESCo industry was growing very rapidly; 1989 revenues of $20 million had grown to $100 million by 1992, and one estimate put the total market potential in the billions of dollars. Three major segments could be identified, each accounting for approximately one third of the total volume. They were commercial, which consisted primarily of office buildings, hospitals and other public buildings; industrial, which consisted of factories and production plants; and residential, which consisted of single-family dwellings. So far the commercial sector had been the most rewarding to ESCos, largely due to the similarities between (for example) one hospital and another. Industrial also had potential, but required knowledge of the specific process technology used in each case.

Over the past decade, the ESCo industry in Canada had experienced mixed fortunes, as companies struggled to understand the dynamics of the market. Lack of technical and risk management experience, flawed contracts, lack of financial strength and energy price collapses had all led to very low levels of profitability among major players. The recent upsurge of interest in Energy Efficiency, however, had pushed the industry onto a more steady footing. Furthermore, a shake-out had occurred, leaving between five and ten serious competitors in Canada.

ESCo Strategies

ESCos saw themselves as undertaking three useful functions with commercial and industrial customers. First, they could undertake energy audits of client sites and advise what forms of energy management were most appropriate. Second, they could engineer and provide access to a wide range of energy-efficient technologies that would normally be hard to get hold of. Third, they could install new energy-efficient equipment, under a performance contract or similar. In the Canadian industry, there were several hundred consulting engineers that participated in energy audits, but only seven "full-service" ESCos that undertook all three functions.

Of the three functions, programs such as performance contracting offered the greatest potential return to ESCos, but also the highest degree of risk. Following an installation, it took between five and ten years before the financial benefits were realized. ESCos were paid at the time of installation by their financing partners, who recovered their costs over the lifetime of the project, but in the event that the project was badly estimated, the shortfall in revenue would have to be made up by the ESCo. Access to capital at a reasonable cost was thus critical. Some ESCos had parent companies with deep pockets. The audit and supply functions, while less lucrative, were important elements of the ESCo's business because they established legitimacy in the eyes of the customer. Many commercial clients were extremely sceptical of the estimated energy savings provided by ESCos, but if they agreed to an energy audit, there was a greater likelihood they could be sold on the merits of an installation. The credibility of the guarantee provided by the ESCo was thus of great importance.

THE GE ENERGY MANAGEMENT INITIATIVE

The Initial Opportunity

As GE Business Development Manager, Raj Bhatt received a communication from the federal government inviting ESCos to seek to be prequalified for the implementation of performance contracts in 50 000 federal buildings in Canada. The program had a potential total value of $1 billion, which was to be split into a number of smaller contracts. Bhatt was struck by the potential fit between GE's areas of expertise and the requirements of the program. ESCos had to be able to provide energy-efficient lighting, motors and controls and provide financing for the project; GE was a leading supplier of many of the required products and had a large financing division. Unlike rival firms that would have to form consortia between electrical and financing companies, GE could do many things in-house.

Bhatt submitted a proposal for the Federal Buildings Program and, along with a number of other consortia, achieved "prequalification," meaning the right to bid on subsequent contracts that fell under the Federal Buildings umbrella. This success underlines the magnitude of the opportunity that GE was facing in the ESCo industry. Rather than limiting GE's involvement to the one-off Federal Buildings Program, Bhatt thought there was potential for an ongoing GE business to meet the expected surge in demand for energy management services. He began to think through the best way of proceeding.

The GE Canada Executive Meeting

Bhatt's first move was to meet with the GE Canada executive group and get their reaction to his idea for an Energy Management Business. Attending were Matthew Meyer, Chairman & CEO, Mike Kozinsky, Vice-President of Finance, and Scott Larwood, Vice-President of Government Relations. Larwood had already been heavily involved in the Federal Buildings Program and was in favour of Bhatt's proposal.

Bhatt:	GE Canada is very well-positioned to start an Energy Management business. We have a broader range of relevant products and services than any other ESCo, and the Ontario and Quebec Hydro programs are among the most advanced in the world.
Kozinsky:	But this is a systems business. We have never been very good at systems implementation.
Bhatt:	I realize that we may have to find partners. We are working with a small ESCo on the Federal Buildings project, which will do all the installation work. We can identify suitable future partners as things progress.
Kozinsky:	But what is our experience in being a prime contractor? This seems to be very different from any business we have been involved with before.
Larwood :	That's not quite true. The Apparatus Technical Service (ATS) business in Power Systems manages service contracts, and there is a lot of project experience in the States.
Meyer:	But there seems to be a considerable risk here. What happens if we pull down a load of asbestos when we're changing a lighting system? GE is an obvious target for legal action.

Kozinsky:	And you stated earlier that there is some downside financial risk if the performance contract does not yield the expected savings.
Bhatt:	True, but the estimates are conservative. The overall financial projections are very promising, and involve very little up-front cost. Apart from the salaries of three or four employees, most costs are on a contract-by-contract basis.
Meyer:	Have you given any thought as to how this business would fit into the GE structure?
Bhatt:	One of the strengths of GE Canada is that it already taps into all the different businesses. I would like to see the Energy Management business based in Canada, and drawing from the other GE businesses as required.

Bhatt received a lot of questioning and cautioning on various aspects of the proposal, but there was consensus at the end that the project was worth pursuing. Meyer recommended that Bhatt investigate the level of interest in the U.S. businesses and at the corporate level before any formal proposal was put together.

The GE Supply Opportunity

In discussion with U.S. colleagues, Bhatt discovered that three U.S. divisions were attempting to establish their own ESCo-like initiatives. Two of them were at about the same stage of development as Bhatt. The third, GE Supply, which was a division of GE Industrial and Power Systems, was more advanced. They had been working with an ESCo for a number of months, and had retained a well-connected consultant to advise them. Up to now, the ESCo had assumed all the risk, with GE providing their name, their products and some servicing expertise, but the division was planning to create a joint venture with the ESCo in the near future.

On hearing about the GE Supply initiative, Bhatt went to Connecticut to visit the GE Supply executives to discuss their respective plans. Present at the meeting were Bhatt, Doug Taylor, CEO of GE Supply, and Fred Allen, manager of the Energy Management business.

Taylor:	Last week we signed a formal alliance agreement with Wetherwell Inc. to run for 18 months. We are now actively looking for contracts.
Allen :	But the U.S. market requires some education. How is the market in Canada?
Bhatt:	There is a very promising opportunity that we are working on right now. Basically, the federal government is looking for bidders on a $1 billion program, and we have already gained prequalification.
Allen :	That beats anything we've got down here. I think there could be some real opportunities for us to work together. We have gained quite a lot of experience over the past 12 months, and combined with your market, we could have a winning combination.
Bhatt:	I am certainly interested in exploring opportunities. How do you see a Canadian Energy Management business fitting with your business?
Taylor:	We could manage the Canadian business out of our office here.
Bhatt:	That causes me some concern. The business relies on close coordination with utilities and government bodies, and a strong local presence would definitely be necessary. I must admit, we considered that management of at least part of the business should be in Canada. The opportunities in Canada are unmatched.
Taylor:	Well, there is some strength to your argument, but I don't see why this business should not fit the normal model.

EXHIBIT 1   GE Structure (North America)

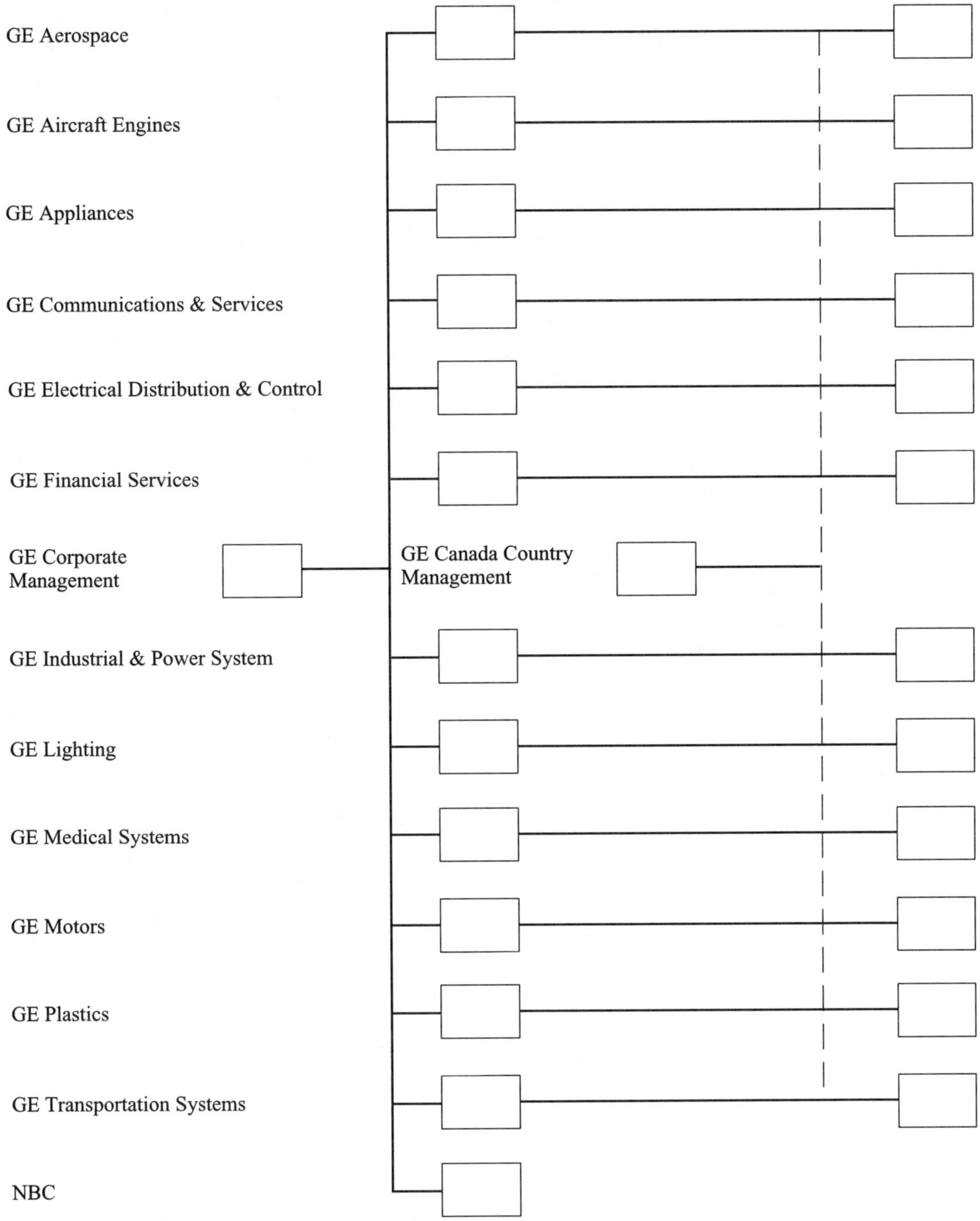

GE Aerospace

GE Aircraft Engines

GE Appliances

GE Communications & Services

GE Electrical Distribution & Control

GE Financial Services

GE Corporate
Management

GE Canada Country
Management

GE Industrial & Power System

GE Lighting

GE Medical Systems

GE Motors

GE Plastics

GE Transportation Systems

NBC

NESTLÉ-ROWNTREE (A)

c a s e

37

J a m e s   C.   E l l e r t,
J.   P e t e r   K i l l i n g
a n d   D a n a   G.   H y d e

Wednesday, April 13, 1988, 10.30 a.m.

"Our offer to help remains open, Mr. Dixon, and I urge you to reconsider our proposals. Please keep in touch." Mr. Helmut Maucher, Managing Director of Nestlé S.A., replaced the receiver and shook his head regretfully as he looked out from his office over Lake Geneva. On receiving the news of Jacobs Suchard's dawn raid on Rowntree plc, Mr. Maucher had called Mr. Kenneth Dixon, Rowntree's Chairman, to offer Nestlé's help and renew Nestlé's earlier proposal to purchase a stake in Rowntree.

Rowntree had been an attractive takeover target for some time, and Mr. Maucher and his colleagues had often discussed the possibility of making a bid. However, it was clear that Rowntree would aggressively contest any takeover attempt and, as Nestlé had never engaged in a hostile takeover, Mr. Maucher had done nothing more than initiate talks with the British-based confectioner. But as he prepared for the meeting with his Comité du Conseil that afternoon, Mr. Maucher worried about Rowntree falling into the hands of one of Nestlé's major competitors.

THE CHOCOLATE INDUSTRY

"Confectionery" was conventionally divided into "chocolate" confectionery and "sugar" confectionery. "Chocolate" confectionery included products made with chocolate; "sugar" confectionery included boiled sweets, toffees, chewing gum and other gums and jellies. Chocolate consumption represented a stable 54 per cent of the total volume of confectionery consumption in the major world markets between 1982 and 1987.

Markets

In value terms, more chocolate was consumed than any other manufactured food product in the world. In 1987 the population of the world's eight major markets consumed more than 2.7 million tonnes of chocolate (the equivalent of over 100 billion Kit Kats), with a retail value of over $19.5 billion (Exhibit 1). In volume terms, chocolate consumption in the eight major markets represented 61 per cent of total world chocolate consumption in 1987. Average per capita consumption in these markets was 4.3 kg per annum, with an annual per capita expenditure of $31. Between 1982 and 1987, volume growth averaged 2.8 per cent per annum in the eight major markets. Future growth was estimated at 2.2 per cent per annum for the next five years, with some variations across individual markets (Exhibit 2).

Product Types

Within chocolate confectionery there were three major product types[1]:

Blocks:	generally molded blocks of chocolate, with or without additional ingredients (Hershey's Chocolate Bar, Nestlé Cailler, Suchard's Toblerone);
Countlines:	generally chocolate-covered products, sold by count rather than weight (Mars' Mars Bar and Snickers, Rowntree's Kit Kat and Smarties);
Boxed chocolates:	included assortments (Cadbury's Milk Tray, Rowntree's Black Magic) and also products such as Rowntree's After Eights.

A few manufacturers had succeeded in branding *block chocolate*, but in many markets block chocolate was considered a commodity product. Each manufacturer's range included a standard variety of block chocolate (milk, dark, white, etc.), and additional ingredients (nuts, fruit, etc.) sold in standard sizes (usually 100g and 200g). Block chocolate was sold mainly through grocery outlets, where it was displayed by manufacturer's range; all of the Nestlé block chocolate products would be grouped on one section of the store shelf, with the other manufacturers' ranges displayed in adjacent sections.

In contrast to block chocolate, *countlines* comprised a wide range of branded products, which were physically distinct from each other in size, shape, weight, and composition. Countlines had wider distribution than the other two product types, with a higher proportion sold through non-grocery outlets including confectioneries, news agents, and kiosks.

Boxed chocolates comprised a wide range of individually branded products, although in some markets boxed chocolates were marketed under the manufacturer's name, and displayed by manufacturer's range. Because boxed chocolates were regarded as a "gift/occasion" purchase, sales were very seasonal.

---

[1] Product definitions varied widely by country. For the purposes of this case, British product definitions have been used.

Approximately 80 per cent of sales took place at Christmas and Easter, a high proportion through grocery outlets; steady sales through the remainder of the year were made through non-grocery outlets.

The popularity of the three product types varied by market. In 1987, for example, Europe consumed approximately twice as much block chocolate and four times as many boxed chocolates as North America. The British and French together accounted for about 70 per cent of European boxed chocolate consumption; North Americans consumed 44 per cent of the world's countline consumption, followed by the British at 20 per cent.

At 7 per cent average annual growth between 1982 and 1987, countlines was the fastest-growing segment of the world chocolate market. Block chocolate sales showed an average annual volume increase of 1 per cent over the same period, while sales of boxed chocolates had declined by an average of 1 per cent per year. By 1987 countlines represented 46 per cent of the world chocolate market by volume, up from 38 per cent in 1982; block chocolate had declined to 30 per cent from 33 per cent, and boxed chocolates to 24 per cent from 29 per cent. In addition to growing demand for countline products, future growth was expected from "indulgence" products such as chocolate truffles, and from specialist branded chocolate retailing.

Industry Structure and Performance

In 1987, there were six major producers in the world chocolate industry: Mars, Hershey, Cadbury-Schweppes, Jacobs Suchard, Rowntree and Nestlé. With individual world market shares ranging from 18 per cent (Mars) to 4 per cent (Nestlé), these six companies accounted for 50 per cent of the total world volume of chocolate confectionery. With the exception of Jacobs Suchard and Nestlé, countline production represented the largest proportion of the chocolate confectionery portfolios of the major confectionery producers (Exhibit 3; additional detail on the product segment and geographic positioning of each company is outlined in Exhibits 4, 5 and 6).

The next tier of competitors included Ferrero, George Weston Ltd., Nabisco, and United Biscuits, each of which sold 2 per cent or less of the total world volume of chocolate confectionery. The remainder of the market was supplied by a large number of smaller (largely national) companies.

The major industry competitors had healthy rates of profitability. Because Mars was a privately held U.S. company, it did not publish sales and profit figures. For the other major competitors, trading profit on sales averaged 9.3 per cent over the five-year period ending in 1987; trading profit on assets averaged 16.1 per cent, and the rate of return on stockholders' equity averaged 16.1 per cent (Exhibit 7; Exhibits 8–12 provide additional financial information for these companies).

Over the past five years, several major producers had acquired a number of smaller, national chocolate companies. Between 1986 and 1988 Jacobs Suchard acquired six confectioners, including E.J. Brach (the third largest confectioner in the U.S., behind Mars and Hershey), Van Houten (Holland), and Cote d'Or (a famous Belgian chocolatier, which Nestlé had also considered acquiring). In 1987 Hersey purchased the Canadian confectionery assets of RJR Nabisco. In early 1988 Cadbury acquired Chocolats Poulain, a famous French chocolatier, and Nestlé was negotiating the purchase of Buitoni, an Italian food group which included the leading chocolatier Perugina.

Business System

Chocolate was made from kernels of fermented and roasted cocoa beans. The kernels were roasted and ground to form a paste, which was hardened in molds to make bitter (baking) chocolate, pressed to reduce the cocoa butter content, and then pulverized to make cocoa powder, or mixed with sugar and additional cocoa butter to make sweet (eating) chocolate. Sweet chocolate was the basic semi-finished product used in the manufacture of block, countline, and boxed chocolate products.

Average costs for a representative portfolio of all three product types of sweet chocolate could be broken down as follows:

Raw material	35%
Packaging	10
Production	20
Distribution	5
Marketing/sales	20
Trading profit	10
Total	100% (of manufacturer's selling price)

For countline products, raw material costs were proportionately lower because a smaller amount of cocoa was used. For boxed chocolates, packaging costs were proportionately higher.

RESEARCH AND DEVELOPMENT

Research and development (R&D) generally focused on making a better chocolate, and on developing new products, although one executive related, "there is never really anything brand new in the confectionery market, just different ways of presenting combinations of the same ingredients." There were minor differences in R&D across the product types, although R&D in the countline segment tended to emphasize applied technology.

RAW MATERIALS

The major ingredient in chocolate confectionery was cocoa, followed by sugar and milk. Although Jacobs Suchard claimed to benefit from large purchase hedging, some manufacturers purchased cocoa supplies as needed at the spot price quoted on the major cocoa exchanges, while others purchased cocoa a year or two in advance to obtain the "best price" and to ensure long-term supplies. Between 1977 and 1988, the international cartel of cocoa producers had fallen into disarray; the price of cocoa had fallen by 50 per cent ($US terms), and surplus cocoa stocks continued to accumulate.

Industry practice was for manufacturers to absorb raw material price changes internally to smooth extreme changes in consumer prices. However, Mars had made an unprecedented move in taking advantage of the falling cocoa price to stimulate volume demand. The company held the price of its Mars Bar and increased the product weight in the late 1970s by 10 per cent, and then by another 15 per cent in the early 1980s, enabling Mars to gain market share.

PRODUCTION

In general, it was difficult to sustain a competitive advantage based on manufacturing process, or on product features due to the lack of proprietary technology. However, some manufacturers had developed countline products which were difficult to duplicate (e.g., Rowntree's After Eights and Kit Kat). The major manufacturers tried to be low-cost producers through increased scale economies. Scale economies were more easily achieved in the production of block chocolate and countlines (both relatively capital intensive), and less easily in the production of boxed chocolates (which was more labour intensive). While minimum efficient scale varied by product, most major producers were moving toward fewer and more concentrated production plants, some dedicated to one or two products.

DISTRIBUTION

Confectionery had the widest distribution of any consumer product. In the U.K., for example, wholesalers serving thousands of small "Confectionery-Tobacco-Newsagent" (CTN) outlets accounted for 50 per cent of total confectionery sales, with multiple grocery stores accounting for 30 per cent, and department stores and multiple confectionery stores the remainder. While distribution patterns and the balance of power between manufacturers and distributors varied across markets, retail concentration was on the increase. Canada and Western Europe (in particular the U.K., France and West Germany) were noted for high levels of retail concentration. Manufacturers' trading margins in these countries averaged 8–12 per cent, compared to U.S. averages of 14–16 per cent.

In general, European multiple retailers tended to stock narrower ranges of competing products than their U.S. counterparts. As one industry executive commented, "In Europe you pay more of a premium to get shelf space in a store. In addition, many of the (multiple) retailers stock only the leading brand and the Number Two. If you are third, you lose visibility, and this damages brand reputation."

MARKETING Consumers displayed considerable brand loyalty. As one industry executive explained, "Most people have a 'menu' of products they like and know. They will buy a new product perhaps once or twice, but the tendency is to go back to the 'old familiars,' the popular established brands." The most popular brands of chocolate were over 50 years old; Mars Bar, for example, was introduced in 1932, and Kit Kat in 1935.

In 1987 the six largest producers spent over $750 million per year on chocolate advertising. In recent years, manufacturers had dramatically increased their overall level of marketing spending, particularly with respect to launching new products. By 1988 one manufacturer estimated that new products, which generally had a much shorter life span than established brands, would have to generate at least $25 million in sales over the first two years to cover product development and marketing costs. Manufacturers therefore tended to focus on brand extensions into new product segments and particularly into new geographic markets.

MAJOR COMPETITORS

Mars

With the world's best selling chocolate bar, and other famous global brands such as Snickers, M&Ms, Twix and Milky Way, Mars was the world leader in chocolate confectionery. In 1987 confectionery was estimated to account for $4 billion of Mars' $7 billion total turnover of confectionery, pet food and electronics products.

With 38 per cent market share, Mars dominated the world countline sector, with particular strength in North America and Europe (Exhibit 4). In 1987, Mars held the largest share of the European chocolate market, and was a close third to Cadbury Rowntree in the U.K. (Exhibit 5). Like Rowntree and Cadbury, Mars spent approximately £25 million annually on advertising in the U.K. In 1987 Mars was one of the top 30 U.S. advertisers ($300 million), and had five of the top ten best-selling chocolate bars in the U.S.

The 1986 introduction of Kudos, a chocolate-covered granola bar, was Mars' first new product in over ten years. Since 1986, however, Mars had mounted a major effort to acquire and develop new products, particularly those which would capitalize on the Mars brand name. Recent product launches included a Mars milk drink and Mars ice cream.

Mars' strategy was consistent across all brands: produce high quality, technologically simple products at very high volumes on automated equipment dedicated to the production of either "layered" (Mars, Snickers) or "planned" (M&Ms, Maltesers) products; and support the brands with heavy marketing spending and aggressive sales organizations and retailing policies. The company's future strategy focused on building and strengthening Mars' global brands. In 1987, for example, Mars had dropped Treets, a £15 million U.K. brand, and repositioned Minstrels under the Galaxy label, both in order to strengthen the 1988 launch of M&Ms into the U.K. market.

Hershey Foods

Founded as chocolate company in 1893, by 1987 Hershey was a diversified food group with total turnover of $2.4 billion. More than 90 per cent of that turnover was in the U.S. (Exhibit 6); confectionery accounted for 66 per cent of total turnover and 80 per cent of trading profit. Although Hershey was a quoted company, it could not be taken over easily because 77 per cent of the company's voting stock was owned by a charitable trust.

Hershey's strength was in block chocolate in North America, where it held a 62 per cent market share. With Hershey's Chocolate Bar, Reese's Peanut Butter Cup and Hershey's Kisses all in the 1987 U.S. "top ten," Hershey was second only to Mars in the U.S. chocolate market. Hershey also produced major Rowntree brands under licence in the U.S.

Between 1981 and 1987, Hershey had increased its advertising and promotion spending from 8.5 per cent to 11.5 per cent of total turnover to "consolidate market share." Hershey's chocolate production was concentrated in Hershey, Pennsylvania, which supplied export markets in Japan, South Korea and Australia. The company also licensed some production in the Far East, Sweden and Mexico, normally under joint venture agreements.

Hershey's corporate strategy was to reduce exposure to cocoa price volatility by diversifying within the confectionery and snack businesses. The company had expanded into branded sugar confectionery, pasta products and ice cream restaurants, largely through acquisitions. By 1987, only 45 per cent of Hershey's sales came from products composed of at least 70 per cent chocolate, down from 80 per cent in 1963.

Cadbury Schweppes

Cadbury Schweppes plc was founded in 1969 with the merger of the Cadbury Group plc and Schweppes Ltd. In 1987, confectionery represented 43 per cent of Cadbury's total turnover of £2 031 million.

With 7 per cent of the world chocolate market and brands such as Dairy Milk, Creme Eggs, Crunchie, Flake and Milk Tray, Cadbury was a major world name in chocolate. Cadbury was the market leader in Australia, and three Cadbury brands (Mounds, Almond Joy and Peppermint Patties) were in the U.S. "Top 20." However, Cadbury's main business was in the U.K., where it held 30 per cent of the market, and had five of the top ten best-selling chocolate products. In 1986 and 1987, Cadbury had launched nine new U.K. brands.

During the late 1970s, Cadbury expanded overseas, and diversified within and beyond the food sector. However, with the appointment of Mr. Dominic Cadbury as Chief Executive in 1983, Cadbury Schweppes embarked on a more focused product and market strategy. Mr. Cadbury announced a restructuring of the Group "to concentrate resources behind (our) leading beverage and confectionery brands in those markets which offer the best opportunities for their development."

Major divestments were made, involving secondary activities in the food and nonfood sectors, and the assets of some under-performing core businesses. Acquisitions were made to strengthen the mainstream branded product lines, and to gain access to new geographic markets. The acquisition of Chocolats Poulain, for example, provided Cadbury's first manufacturing facility in Europe. In January 1987, General Cinema Corporation (which controlled the largest U.S. Pepsi bottling operation) announced the acquisition of an 8.5 per cent shareholding in Cadbury Schweppes and, in November 1987, increased that holding to 18.2 per cent. While General Cinema was less than half the size of Cadbury in market capitalization, industry observers speculated that the company was planning a leveraged buyout of Cadbury Schweppes.

Jacobs Suchard

Controlled by the Jacobs family and based in Zurich, the Jacobs Suchard Group was formed in 1982 in a reverse takeover by Jacobs (a West German coffee company) of Interfood, the parent company of the Suchard and Tobler chocolate firms. In 1987, Suchard's principal businesses were still coffee and confectionery, which accounted for 57 per cent and 43 per cent respectively of Suchard's 1987 turnover of SF6.1 billion.

Europe was Suchard's largest market, accounting for 83 per cent of 1987 turnover. However, Jacobs Suchard operated in more than 20 countries, represented by subsidiaries and licensees, and exported its products to over 100 countries. The Group also had substantial operations in the trading of raw materials for coffee and chocolate production.

Jacobs Suchard held 23 per cent of the European block chocolate market. Leading brands included Toblerone, Suchard, Milka and Cote d'Or. Developing and expanding its portfolio of global brands was of primary importance to the Group; as Mr. Klaus Jacobs, the entrepreneurial Chairman of the Board, stated, "We firmly believe that global brands are the wave of the future." An increasing number of Jacobs Suchard's brands were marketed globally, under the sponsorship of global brand managers.

Since 1984 Suchard had been concentrating production of individual brands in fewer and larger plants in an effort to gain absolute cost leadership. In 1987, European production of chocolate and confectionery took place in 17 plants; Suchard planned to reduce this number to 7 by 1991, as improvements were made in its cross-border distribution system.

Rowntree

Rowntree was founded in York in 1725 by a cocoa and chocolate vendor who sold the business to the Rowntree family in 1862. In 1970, Rowntree merged with John Mackintosh & Sons, Ltd., a British confectioner nearly half the size of Rowntree. In 1988, Rowntree's headquarters were still in York and, with 5 500 workers, the company was by far York's largest employer. Many of the traditions of the Rowntree family, including a strong concern for employee and community welfare, had been preserved; many of the current employees' parents and grandparents had also worked for Rowntree.

In 1987, Rowntree was primarily a confectionery company (Exhibit 13), with major strengths in the countline and boxed chocolate segments. Rowntree's major market was the U.K. where, with a 26 per cent market share, it was second only to Cadbury. Rowntree's Kit Kat was the best-selling confectionery brand in the U.K. (where 40 Kit Kats were consumed per second), and number five in both the U.S. and Japan. Kit Kat was part of a portfolio of leading global brands; many of these brands—Kit Kat, Quality Street, Smarties, Rolo, Aero, Black Magic—were launched in the 1930s; After Eights in 1962; and Yorkie and Lion in 1976. Since 1981 Rowntree had launched seven new brands in the U.K., including Novo, a chocolate cereal bar.

In 1987 Rowntree operated 25 factories in nine countries and employed 33 000 people around the world, including close to 16 000 in its eight U.K. operations. Group turnover was £1.4 billion, with the U.K. and Ireland accounting for 40 per cent of total turnover (Exhibit 14).

Rowntree was headed by Mr. Kenneth Dixon, age 58, who had been with Rowntree for 32 years, and was appointed as Chairman and Chief Executive in 1981. In the words of a long-time senior Rowntree executive, "Mr. Dixon fostered a real sense of positive change in the company."

During the late 1970s, Rowntree's operating performance had shown significant deterioration (Exhibit 15). To reverse this trend, Mr. Dixon initiated a long-term program to improve the efficiency of the U.K. core business, and led diversifications into related businesses, principally through the acquisition and development of brand names. Mr. Dixon also delegated more responsibility to the operating levels of the company, while maintaining a central brand and product strategy.

Branding was the essence of Rowntree's strategy. According to Mr. Dixon, "The fundamental idea which drives Rowntree is branding, the creation of distinct, differentiated, positively identifiable and market-positioned goods. Rowntree seeks to build brands by marketing products and services at competitive prices, positioning them accurately in the markets they serve, and giving them clear identity and character."

In the 1960s, Rowntree granted Hershey a long-term license to manufacture and sell Rowntree products in the U.S. With its expansion into continental Europe underway at the time, Rowntree believed that it lacked the resources to develop an effective marketing presence in both continental Europe and the U.S. In 1978 the agreement with Hershey was renegotiated, giving Hershey rights in perpetuity to the Kit Kat and Rolo brand names in the U.S., which would be retained by Hershey in the event of a change in Rowntree ownership. Rowntree was still free to enter the U.S. market with its other brand names. In 1987 royalties from this agreement contributed about £2 million toward Rowntree Group profits.

Between 1982 and 1987, Rowntree invested nearly £400 million to upgrade manufacturing facilities, and develop high-volume, product-dedicated equipment for several of the company's leading global brands, including Kit Kat, After Eights and Smarties. Products produced on this equipment had a consistent formulation, and were sold all over the world; the Hamburg After Eights plant, for example, shipped to 16 countries. By 1987 Rowntree's investment program for rationalizing capacity was well underway. The associated productivity gains were expected to continue to accumulate over the next few years.

In 1987 Rowntree's £100 million investment in continental Europe was still showing modest financial returns. Rowntree had entered the continental European market in the 1960s, establishing production facilities at Hamburg, Dijon, Elst (Holland) and Noisiel (France). Although advertising and promotion spending (as a percentage of sales) was double that of the U.K., volume growth had not met Rowntree's expectations; as one manager explained, "Kit Kats go well with a cup of tea, but not with wine and beer!"

The trading margin on the Continental European business had inched up very slowly, from 1.0 per cent in 1985 to 3.7 per cent in 1987. However, in early 1988 Rowntree believed that the long-term brand building strategy was finally beginning to pay off, with Lion Bar the second-best selling chocolate bar in France and with more After Eights sold in West Germany than in the U.K. Between 1983 and 1987, Rowntree spent nearly £400 million on acquisitions (Exhibit 16). The acquired companies expanded the company's presence in some traditional businesses, and also provided new activities, particularly in the area of branded retailing of specialist confectionery products. The retail shops acquired by Rowntree were viewed not as outlets for Rowntree brands, but rather as acquisitions of brands in their own right. Because of these acquisitions, a significant stream of Rowntree's profits were being earned in North America. While Rowntree had hedged its foreign exchange risk exposure on the balance sheet, it took a long-term view with respect to foreign exchange risk exposure on the income statement. The resulting transactions exposure concerned some financial analysts.

By 1987 Rowntree's capital investments were beginning to pay off. Over the past five years, the number of U.K. personnel had been reduced from 19 700 to 15 600, and productivity improvements were running at 9 per cent per annum. Trading margins had nearly recovered to the high level previously achieved in 1977, and Rowntree executives were confident that 1988 trading margins would continue to show improvement.

In a highly competitive U.S. market, Rowntree's snack food acquisitions were not generating trading margins consistent with other company activities (Exhibit 13). In January of 1988, Rowntree announced its intention to divest its major snack food businesses to concentrate on confectionery, retailing, and U.K. grocery activities where the potential to develop distinct consumer brands was considered more promising.

Although Rowntree's overall operating performance continued to improve, the company's common share price performance between 1986 and early 1988 was weaker than that achieved by the Financial Times "All Share" and Food Manufacturing Indexes on the London Stock Exchange (Exhibit 17). In early 1988,

London's financial analysts published mixed opinions regarding Rowntree's immediate prospects (Exhibit 18). Mr. Nightingale, Rowntree's Company Secretary, recalled, "For years we have been trying to get the value of our brands reflected in our share price, but without much success. As a consequence, there have always been takeover rumours."

Nestlé

The Nestlé Group grew from the 1905 merger of the Anglo-Swiss condensed Milk Co., a milk processing firm founded in 1866, and Henri Nestlé, a Swiss infant food company founded in 1867 in Vevey. In 1988 the Nestlé headquarters were still in Vevey, and the Group operated 383 factories in 59 countries. In 1988 Nestlé employed 163 000 people, 10 000 in the U.K.

Nestlé was the world's largest food company, and the world's largest producer of coffee, powdered milk, and frozen dinners. In 1987, drinks, dairy products, culinary products, frozen foods, and confectionery products accounted for 79 per cent of Nestlé turnover of SF35.2 billion; other food products accounted for 18 per cent, and non-food products 3 per cent. Only 2 per cent of the Group's turnover came from sales within Switzerland. The 20 companies acquired between 1983 and 1985 (at a total purchase price of $5 billion) added new brands of coffee, chocolates and fruit juice to Nestlé's lineup of strong world brands such as Nescafé, Stouffer's, Maggi and Findus. In 1985 Nestlé increased its U.S. presence through the $2.9 billion purchase of Carnation and, in early April 1988, was finalizing the $1.3 billion purchase of Buitoni-Perugina.

This series of acquisitions had been spurred by Mr. Helmut Maucher, age 60, who joined Nestlé as an apprentice in 1948, and who was appointed Managing Director of Nestlé S.A. in 1981. Under Mr. Maucher's direction, Nestlé had cut costs and divested less profitable operations, including the $180 million Libby's U.S. canned food business.

Mr. Maucher explained Nestlé's approach to acquisitions. "At Nestlé we are not portfolio managers. Acquisitions must fit into our corporate and marketing policy. In other words, they must strengthen our position in individual countries or product groups, or enable us to enter new fields where we have not so far been represented. Acquisitions are part of an overall development strategy. That's why we cannot leave acquisition decisions purely to financial considerations. Of course, you must have some figures to evaluate an acquisition, but more important is the feel you have about why you can do with the brands."

Mr. Maucher was a strong believer in the importance of a long-term outlook. On his appointment as Managing Director, he had banned monthly 25-page reports and quarterly profit and loss statements in favour of a monthly one-page report, which highlighted key numbers such as turnover, working capital and inventories. As Mr. Maucher explained, "With quarterly reports all managers care about is the next three months, and they manage for the next quarter instead of for the next five years." For this reason, Mr. Maucher was reluctant to list Nestlé's shares on any stock exchange which required the disclosure of quarterly reports.

Nestlé entered the chocolate market in 1929 with the purchase of Peter-Cailler-Kohler, a Swiss chocolate group originally founded in 1819. Since 1981, confectionery sales had represented approximately 8 per cent of annual turnover, and in 1987 confectionery was Nestlé's fifth largest business. Nestlé's main product strength was in block chocolate, where it held 15 per cent and 14 per cent respectively of the European and American markets (Exhibit 4). Nestlé's leading brands included Milkybar in the U.S. and Crunch in the U.K. Recent research into the new generation of chocolate and confectionery products had produced "Yes," a pastry snack product, and "Sundy," a cereal bar.

As a result of Nestlé's market-oriented organization structure, Nestlé's block chocolate products were generally produced and positioned according to the tastes of local markets. For example, Nestlé's white block chocolate products, often produced in the same plants as coffee and other food products, were made from several recipes and marketed under several brand names. In the U.K., Nestlé's white chocolate brand, "Milkybar," was positioned as a children's chocolate, whereas in the U.S., it was called "Alpine White" and was oriented toward the "female indulgence" market. "Block chocolate is a traditional product with traditional tastes," Mr. Maucher explained. "A local market orientation is particularly important, because this kind of chocolate must taste the way you got it as a child from your grandmother, whether you are French or Italian or German, and so on. This is true for the traditional chocolate products, not so much for the new generation of products such as countlines."

During the 1970s, Nestlé's confectionery operations had been among the smaller and often relatively less profitable businesses in the company. However, Mr. Maucher saw opportunities in the confectionery business: "The key success factors in confectionery are technology, quality, creativity, and marketing skills, and Nestlé has all of those. If Nestlé cannot be successful at this business, then there is something wrong with Nestlé!"

NESTLÉ–ROWNTREE

In the early 1980s, Mr. Maucher made confectionery a strategic priority. Nestlé increased investment in research and development, and acquired two small U.S. confectionery companies. Nestlé then began to analyze the possibilities for significant expansion in the world confectionery market. "It will take 25 years to develop a major stake in this industry," Mr. Maucher said, "so we are looking at acquisitions to accelerate that development." According to Mr. Ramon Masip, Executive Vice-President in charge of the European market, "For some time we have discussed making a 'big move' into the confectionery business, and Rowntree has always been the number one choice."

"We have always seen Rowntree as a 'perfect fit,'" Mr. Masip continued, "because its strengths would complement Nestlé's." Rowntree's strong position in the growing countlines segment would complement Nestlé's strength in block chocolate. In addition, Rowntree's strong position in the non-grocery outlets such as CTNs would complement Nestlé's strong contacts with the multiple grocery retailers. Rowntree also held a stronger position in the U.K. and in some markets in continental Europe.

Although Nestlé was interested in Rowntree's recent success in launching new products such as the Lion bar, "We are much more concerned with the brands that Rowntree already has in the market!" Mr. Masip exclaimed. Rowntree's strong, well-established world brands were the key reason for Nestlé's interest. "There are very, very few companies in the world with their brands and with their skills in this particular business," Mr. Masip concluded.

Nestlé believed that, should the opportunity to acquire Rowntree arise, additional operating synergies could be achieved in research and development, administration and the sales force. With the potential acquisition, it was estimated that substantial savings—perhaps 5–15 per cent of Rowntree's fixed overhead expenses—could be realized from combining the two companies' operations.

November 1987

In November of 1987, Mr. Maucher and Mr. Masip met in Paris with Mr. Dixon and Mr. Masip's counterpart in Rowntree, Mr. Guerin. The proposal for this meeting had stemmed from quiet discussions between Messrs. Masip and Guerin regarding possible Nestlé-Rowntree cooperation in continental Europe. For over a year, Mr. Maucher had wanted to arrange a meeting with Mr. Dixon to discuss possible forms of cooperation between Nestlé and Rowntree. In fact, some of Mr. Maucher's external financial advisors had advised him to take a position in Rowntree stock, but Mr. Maucher had always replied, "That is not our policy. We do not do anything behind any company's back and, as I have told Mr. Dixon, we will not do anything that would be perceived as unfriendly to Rowntree."

The Paris meeting in November 1987 began with Mr. Dixon advising Mr. Maucher, "Nestlé does not appear to be interested in confectionery, and Rowntree is prepared to buy Nestlé's confectionery business on a worldwide basis." Mr. Maucher exclaimed, "We propose just the opposite!" The ensuing discussion explored possibilities for cooperation in production, marketing, distribution, or in various geographic markets, in order to optimize the situation for both companies. To facilitate development of long-term commitment and cooperation, Mr. Maucher suggested purchasing a 10–25 per cent stake in Rowntree.

After a lengthy and amicable discussion, Mr. Dixon promised to examine Nestlé's suggestions and take them to the Rowntree Board for consideration. According to Mr. Dixon, Rowntree had already considered cooperation with several parties as a basis for market development, particularly in Europe, but "we felt at Rowntree that we could proceed on our own and would prefer to do so." After making this reply to Mr. Maucher in February 1988, he added, "Unfortunately, any sort of association with a company of your size can only have one ending, and at this time we don't feel we need to make that kind of commitment to anyone." Mr. Dixon, responding to Mr. Maucher's grave concerns regarding the persistent takeover rumours, admitted, "This does not mean that we do not recognize there is a risk."

April 13, 1988

At 8:30 on the morning of Wednesday, April 13, 1988, Rowntree was advised that there was significant activity in the trading of Rowntree shares. By 9:15 a.m., Jacobs Suchard held 14.9 per cent of Rowntree plc. While the firm had made no contact with Rowntree, Suchard had begun acquiring Rowntree stock in mid-March, and by April 12th held just under 5 per cent of Rowntree shares. At the start of trading on the London Stock Exchange on April 13th, Suchard's intermediary telephoned major institutional holders of Rowntree shares, offering a 30 per cent premium on the opening share price of 477p[2] if they sold immediately. The shareholders did not know to whom they were selling their shares, but in less than 45 minutes Suchard increased its holding to 14.9 per cent, the maximum allowable under the City Code[3] for such a transaction. When the news of Suchard's raid reached the markets, Rowntree's share price jumped to over 700p.

In what was later described as a "tactical error" by some City observers, on the morning of April 13th, S.G. Warburg issued the following press release on behalf of its client, Jacob Suchard:

> We have acquired a 14.9% investment stake in Rowntree. The stake is a strategic investment in that Rowntree is a company with a great potential based on its excellent global brands. We intend to acquire not more than 25%, at a maximum price of 630p. As you know, we are only permitted to take our holding to 15% today. We hope to buy the remaining 10%, but at no more than the price we are currently offering. This is not a prelude to a full bid and there is no intention of increasing the holding beyond this 25% figure for at least a year although we reserve the right to do so if there is a full bid from a third party in the meantime.

Exercising its interpretive responsibility, the City Takeover Panel swiftly ruled that Warburg's statement prevented Suchard from purchasing any further Rowntree shares for the next 12 months, provided that the Rowntree share price stayed above 630p, unless a full bid for control came in from another party during that time period.

Reaction from the City of London Financial Community

After years of persistent rumours of a Rowntree takeover, Suchard's move ignited speculation on potential counter-bidders. Hershey was identified by City analysts as a leading candidate; purchasing Rowntree would make it second only to Mars in world confectionery. Other rumoured candidates included RJR Nabisco, Philip Morris, Unilever and United Biscuits.

---

[2] 1£ = 100 pence (p).

[3] Refer to Exhibit 19 for a description of the City Code rules which regulated takeover activity in the U.K.

As external financial advisor to Rowntree, Mr. David Challen, a Director of J. Henry Schroder Wagg, was encouraged by the Takeover Panel's ruling. As he explained, "The ruling puts Jacobs in a box. Provided that Rowntree's share price stays above 630p, he cannot purchase additional shares for at least a year. This gives Rowntree the necessary time to prepare an effective takeover defence." Mr. Challen argued that it would be "madness" for another bidder to enter the battle now, as the new bidder would be restricted to accumulating shares (beyond 15 per cent) at the price of its initial offer. However, the entry of another bidder would free Suchard to bid above this price to accumulate more shares. In the scenario predicted by Mr. Challen, Suchard would ultimately emerge with 30 per cent of the shares and be poised to make an offer for the remaining shares. The second bidder would be restricted by the City Code to accumulating 15 per cent of the shares and would always be behind Suchard in share accumulation terms. Thus the second bidder would face a "mega disadvantage" in gaining effective control. Mr. Challen concluded that the situation facing Rowntree was not urgent: "The real challenge for Rowntree is to keep the stock price above 630p so that Suchard cannot accumulate more shares."

Mr. Peter St. George, a Director of County Natwest (Nestlé's financial advisor), recalled discussions with Nestlé in the summer of 1987 regarding a possible takeover bid for Rowntree: "We were in a raging bull market then; paper, not cash, was king; and the takeover bid premium required to purchase Rowntree could not be justified on the fundamentals. Besides, any takeover attempt would have been viewed as hostile by Rowntree."

County NatWest had approached Nestlé in early 1988, advising a raid on Rowntree. "Since the October 1987 crash, the world had changed," Mr. St. George explained. "Share prices had fallen to reasonable levels where one could justify paying takeover premiums. The market no longer wanted paper; cash was king now, and Nestlé had cash. However, Mr. Maucher demurred, stating that hostile raids were not in Nestlé's style."

"Suchard's raid put Rowntree 'in play,'" Mr. St. George concluded. "We contacted Nestlé as soon as we heard the news and encouraged them to make a counter bid for Rowntree. We advised them to act quickly and go into the market with a credible price to test (the fundraising capability of) Jacobs Suchard. We cautioned Nestlé, however, that a successful bid would require a substantial premium on the current Rowntree share price." (See Exhibit 19 for a description of the size of recent takeover bid premiums; Exhibit 20 contains financial market reference data.)

Rowntree's Reaction

The dawn raid came as a complete surprise to Rowntree, and reaction was swift. Mr. Dixon stated in a press release that morning:

> Rowntree does not need Jacobs. We regard the acquisition of a stake by Jacobs as wholly unwelcome and believe that the price at which Jacobs acquired its shares is wholly inadequate for obtaining a major stake in the Group. Rowntree has one of the best portfolios of brand names of any confectionery company in the world, far better known than Jacobs' own. We do not believe that it is in the interests of Rowntree, its shareholders, or its employees that a Swiss company with nothing like the breadth of Rowntree's brands should have a shareholding in the Group. Jacobs may need Rowntree, but Rowntree does not need Jacobs.

Nestlé's Reaction

Suchard's dawn raid also came as a surprise to Nestlé. Mr. Maucher's first reaction was to contact Mr. Dixon; in his telephone phone call that morning Mr. Maucher said, "I am sorry that what I warned you about has happened. I repeat our offer to help." He urged Mr. Dixon to reconsider Nestlé's earlier proposal to acquire a stake in Rowntree.

Mr. Dixon thanked Mr. Maucher for his offer of help, but replied that he did not expect Suchard to make any further moves in the short term. "According to the Takeover Panel, Jacobs cannot move for 12 months," he told Mr. Maucher, "and while I know that Suchard will try to become more involved with Rowntree, we have no intention of having any form of cooperation with Suchard. We fully intend to remain independent. It is our hope and belief that the situation will calm down and that nothing more will come of it." However, Mr. Dixon promised that he and his Board would nonetheless consider Mr. Maucher's proposal.

Mr. Maucher concluded the discussion by saying, "Our offer stands, and I hope you will reconsider and keep in touch. However, I fear that because of Suchard's move your independence is now an illusion. I must now feel free to act in Nestlé's best interests."

Average Currency Equivalents, 1983–88

(SF = Swiss Franc; $ = U.S. Dollar; £ = British Pound)

	1 Swiss Franc equals		*1 British Pound equals*		*US$1 equals*	
1983	$0.48	£0.31	SF 3.23	$1.55	SF2.08	£0.65
1984	0.43	0.32	3.13	1.34	2.33	0.75
1985	0.41	0.32	3.13	1.28	2.44	0.78
1986	0.56	0.38	2.63	1.47	1.79	0.68
1987	0.67	0.41	2.44	1.63	1.49	0.61
1988*	0.71	0.39	2.57	1.83	1.41	0.55

* As of April 1, 1988.

Source: Schweizerische Nationalbank.

E X H I B I T 1 Major Chocolate Confectionery Markets Consumption and Expenditure Per Capita, 1987

	*Chocolate Consumption (000 tonnes)**	*Chocolate Expenditure (US$ millions)*	*Population Mid-1987 (millions)*	*per Capita (kg/annum)*	*Expenditure Consumption per Capita ($/annum)*
U.S.	1 189	5 202	243.8	4.9	21
U.K.	455	3 480	56.9	8.0	61
W.Germany	409	3 387	61.2	6.7	55
France	233	2 750	55.6	4.2	49
Japan	157	1 867	122.1	1.3	15
Canada	101	464	25.9	3.9	18
Italy	106	1 813	57.4	1.8	32
Australia	80	576	16.2	4.9	36
Total	2 730	19 539	639.1	4.3	31

* One metric tonne = 1000 kilograms.

Sources: *UNIDO Handbook of Industrial Statistics,* Vienna, 1988; World Bank; National Trade Associations; Trade Estimates.

E X H I B I T 2   **Actual and Forecasted Chocolate Consumption in Major Markets**

	Consumption (000 tonnes)			Compound Average Annual Growth Rate (per cent)	
	1982 Actual	*1987 Actual*	*1992 Forecast*	*1982–87*	*1987–92*
U.S.	1 003	1 189	1 364	3.5%	2.8%
U.K.	411	455	469	2.0	0.6
W. Germany	401	409	412	0.4	0.1
France	192	233	251	3.9	1.5
Japan	148	157	166	1.2	1.1
Italy	83	106	127	5.0	3.7
Canada	99	101	106	0.4	1.0
Australia	63	80	95	4.9	3.5
Above 8 Markets	2 400	2 730	2 990	2.6	1.8
Rest of World	1 495	1 740	1 990	3.1	2.7
Total	3 895	4 470	4 980	2.8%	2.2%

Sources: Joint International Statistics Committee of IOCCC; *Euromonitor*; *United Nations Industrial Statistics Yearbook*; IMEDE.

E X H I B I T 3   **Chocolate Product Portfolios of Major Confectionery Companies, 1987**

	Mars	*Hershey*	*Cadbury*	*Rowntree*	*Suchard*	*Nestlé*	*Others*
Tonnes (000s)	800	400	320	300	220	190	2 240
World Market Share	18%	9%	7%	7%	5%	4%	50%
Companies' Turnover by Product Type:*							
Block	1%	46%	46%	11%	81%	73%	29%
Countline	99	54	36	55	8	17	32
Boxed	—	—	18	34	11	10	39
Total	100%	100%	100%	100%	100%	100%	100%

* For example, countline sales represented 99% of Mars' total chocolate confectionery turnover in 1987; block chocolate sales represented 1 per cent of Mars' total chocolate turnover.

Sources: International Chocolate Workshop, *Vevey*, 1988; Trade Estimates; IMEDE.

EXHIBIT 4   **Market Shares of Major Competitors by Product Type and Region, 1987**

	Total Market*	Percentage Market Shares						
		Mars	Hershey	Cadbury	Rowntree	Suchard	Nestlé	Others
North America								
Block	280	—	62%	16%	2%	3%	14%	3%
Countline	898	53%	23	5	2	—	1	16
Boxed	112	—	—	11	17	1	5	66
Total	1 290	53%	29%	8%	2%	—	4%	18%
EEC								
Block	541	1%	—	9%	4%	23%	14%	49%
Countline	611	49	—	8	19	2	1	21
Boxed	437	—	—	7	14	4	2	73
Total	1 589	19%	—	8%	12%	10%	6%	45%
Rest of World								
Block	521	—	2%	10%	1%	9%	4%	74%
Countline	544	4%	1	4	6	1	3	80
Boxed	526	—	—	3	4	1	1	91
Total	1 591	1%	1%	6%	4%	4%	3%	81%
World								
Block	1 342	1%	14%	11%	2%	13%	10%	49%
Countline	2 053	39	10	6	8	1	2	34
Boxed	1 075	—	—	6	9	2	2	81
Total	4 470	18%	9%	7%	7%	5%	4%	50%

* In tonnes (000s).

Sources: International Chocolate Workshop, *Vevey*, 1988; Trade Estimates; IMEDE.

EXHIBIT 5   **European Chocolate Market Shares by Major Competitor, 1988**

	Mars	Suchard	Rowntree	Ferrero	Cadbury	Nestlé	Others
U.K.	24%	2%	26%	2%	30%	3%	13%
Austria	4	73	—	—	—	5	18
Belgium	6	82	2	5	—	3	2
France	11	13	17	6	8	10	35
Italy	1	—	—	4	—	5	60
Netherlands	23	—	13	—	—	—	64
Switzerland	9	17	—	—	—	17	57
W. Germany	22	15	3	6	—	8	36
Total	17%	13%	11%	10%	8%	9%	32%

Source: Henderson Crossthwaite.

EXHIBIT 6 **Percentage Breakdown of Total Turnover by Region for Major Confectionery Competitors, 1987**

	Nestlé	*Rowntree*	*Jacobs Suchard*	*Cadbury Schweppes*	*Hershey*
Europe	43%	61%[1]	83%[2]	63%[3]	
N. America	29	29	17	18	> 90%
Asia	13				
Oceana	2	4		19	<10
Others	3	6	1		
Total	100%	100%	101%[4]	100%	100%

[1] U.K. and Ireland = 40% of total turnover.
[2] West Germany and France = 58% of total turnover.
[3] U.K. = 47% of total turnover.
[4] Does not add up to 100% due to rounding errors.

Source: Company accounts.

EXHIBIT 7 **Operating Financial Performance of Major Competitors, 1983–87**

	Confectionery Turnover as % of Total Turnover[1]	*Total Trading Profit*[2] *as % of Total Turnover*	*Total Trading Profit*[2] *as % of Average*[3] *Assets*	*Net Income as % of Average*[3] *Shareholders' Equity*
	1987	*Average 1983–87*		
Hershey Foods	76%	14.7%	15.8%	17.2%
Cadbury Schweppes	43	7.5	20.5	17.1
Rowntree	76	8.3	25.5	16.8
Jacobs Suchard	57	5.9	12.3	16.3
Nestlé	8	10.2	14.3	13.1

Note: As a measure of relative risk, the "beta" values for the common stocks of publicly traded confectionery companies generally clustered around a value of 1.0.
[1] Turnover = Net sales.
[2] Trading profit = Operating profit before interest and taxes.
[3] Average of beginning and end of year.

Source: Company accounts.

EXHIBIT 8 Hershey Foods Corp.—Selected Financial Data, 1984–87

A. Financial Statement Data ($ millions)	1984	1985	1986	1987
1 Turnover (Sales)	1 848.5	1 996.2	2 169.6	2 433.8
2 Gross Profit	578.7	640.4	716.2	821.7
3 Trading Profit	222.8	244.8	270.6	294.1
4 Net Income	108.7	120.7	132.8	148.2
5 Depreciation	45.2	52.4	59.0	70.6
6 Liquid Assets	87.9	110.6	27.6	15.0
7 Current Assets	385.3	412.3	393.4	484.9
8 Fixed Assets	727.3	785.1	962.9	1 160.3
9 Total Assets	1 122.6	1 197.4	1 356.3	1 645.2
10 Current Liabilities	203.0	195.3	222.2	299.8
11 Long-term Liabilities	258.7	274.2	406.2	513.0
12 Stockholders' Equity	660.9	727.9	727.9	832.4
B. Per Share Data ($)				
13 Earnings	1.16	1.19	1.42	1.64
14 Dividends	0.41	0.48	0.52	0.58
15 Stock Price (Average)	11.60	15.00	22.80	29.30
16 Price-Earnings (Average)	10.00	9.70	16.10	17.90
17 Equity Book Value	7.00	7.70	8.10	9.20

Source: Company accounts.

EXHIBIT 9 Cadbury Schweppes PLC—Selected Financial Data, 1984–87

A. Financial Statement Data (£ millions)	1984	1985	1986	1987
1 Turnover (Sales)	2 016.2	1 873.8	1 839.9	2 031.0
2 Gross Profit	746.8	683.0	739.9	853.8
3 Trading Profit	154.4	113.0	140.4	180.6
4a Net Income[1]	72.5	47.8	76.1	112.1
4b Net Income[2]	65.1	41.9	102.0	110.7
5 Depreciation	55.9	54.7	60.4	63.3
6 Liquid Assets	36.6	47.1	177.4	139.9
7 Current Assets	710.7	618.9	723.4	795.5
8 Fixed Assets	627.5	594.0	555.4	603.5
9 Total Assets	1 338.2	1 212.9	1 278.8	1 399.0
10 Current Liabilities	531.2	479.3	536.7	688.7
11 Long-term Liabilities	288.3	262.6	278.9	233.6
12 Share Capital & Reserves	518.7	417.0	463.2	476.7
B. Per Share Data (pence)				
13 Earnings[1]	15.7	9.3	14.3	19.1
14 Dividends	5.9	5.9	6.7	8.0
15 Stock Price (Average)	137.0	153.0	170.0	238.0
16 Price-Earnings (Average)	8.7	16.5	11.9	12.5
17 Equity Book Value	112.0	92.0	87.0	83.0
18 Employees (000s)	35.5	33.8	27.7	27.5

[1] Earnings before Extraordinary Items.
[2] Earnings after Extraordinary Items.

Source: Company accounts.

EXHIBIT 10 **Jacobs Suchard Group—Selected Financial Data, 1984–87**

A. Financial Statement Data (SF millions)	1984	1985	1986	1987
1 Turnover (Sales)	5 111	5 382	5 236	6 104
2 Gross Profit	1 104	1 156	1 304	1 955
3 Trading Profit	244	265	338	471
4 Net Income	120	150	191	265
5 Depreciation	84	092	103	128
6 Liquid Assets	230	788	1470	705
7 Current Assets	1 390	2 008	2 920	2 206
8 Fixed Assets	666	674	832	886
9 Total Assets	2 056	2 682	3 752	3 092
10 Current Liabilities	796	843	1 417	1 120
11 Long-term Liabilities	483	487	885	829
12 Shareholders' Equity	777	1 352	1 450	1 143*

B. Per Share Data (SF per bearer share)				
13 Earnings	351.0	353.0	414.0	19.1
14 Dividends	150.0	155.0	160.0	8.0
15 Stock Price (Average)	5 028.0	6 101.0	7 324.0	238.0
16 Price-Earnings (Average)	14.3	17.3	17.7	12.5
17 Employees (000s)	10.6	9.3	10.0	27.5

* It is normal accounting practice for Swiss companies to write off "goodwill" when acquiring businesses. Nestlé wrote off SF3.2 million of share-holders' equity on its purchase of Carnation in 1985. Jacobs Suchard reduced equity by SF1.1 million in 1987 due to depreciation of goodwill.

Source: Company accounts.

EXHIBIT 11 **Nestlé S.A.—Selected Financial Data, 1984–87**

A. Financial Statement Data (SF millions)	1984	1985	1986	1987
1 Turnover (Sales)	31 141	42 225	38 050	35 241
2 Gross Profit	11 301	14 926	13 603	13 616
3 Trading Profit	3 206	4 315	3 671	3 651
4 Net Income	1 487	1 750	1 789	1 827
5 Depreciation	1 004	1 331	1 157	1 184
6 Liquid Assets	6 168	3 853	5 619	6 961
7 Current Assets	16 407	15 236	15 820	16 241
8 Fixed Assets	8 067	9 952	9 275	8 902
9 Total Assets	24 474	25 188	25 095	25 143
10 Current Liabilities	7 651	8 858	8 119	7 547
11 Long-term Liabilities	3 834	5 092	4 775	4 939
12 Shareholders' Equity	12 989	11 238*	12 201	12 657

B. Per Share Data (SF per bearer share)				
13 Earnings	480.0	515.0	526.0	537.0
14 Dividends	136.0	145.0	145.0	150.0
15 Stock Price (Average)	5 062.0	7 400.0	8 600.0	9 325.0
16 Price-Earnings (Average)	10.5	14.4	16.4	17.4
17 Employees (000s)	138.0	154.8	162.1	163.0

* It is normal accounting practice for Swiss companies to write off "goodwill" when acquiring businesses. Nestlé wrote off SF3.2 million of share-holders' equity on its purchase of Carnation in 1985. Jacobs Suchard reduced equity by SF1.1 million in 1987 due to depreciation of goodwill.

Source: Company accounts.

EXHIBIT 12 Rowntree plc—Selected Financial Data, 1983–87

A. Income Statement Data (£ millions)		1983	1984	1985	1986	1987
1	Turnover (Sales)	951.9	1 156.5	1 205.2	1 290.4	1 427.6
1a	Cost Of Sales	617.9	739.0	759.4	790.2	837.1
2	Gross Profit (1–1a)	334.0	417.5	445.8	500.2	590.5
2a	Fixed Overhead Expenses	265.6	328.3	350	400.5	465.8
2b	Other Operating Income	4.2	4.6	6.0	6.0	5.4
3	Trading Profit (2–2a+2b)	72.6	93.8	101.3	105.7	130.1
3a	Interest	12.2	19.3	22.0	21.7	18.0
4a	Profit After Tax	46.3	58.0	60.7	66.2	87.9
4b	Extraordinary Items	13.5	11.5	16.5	11.3	0.0
4c	Net Profit After Tax	32.8	46.5	44.2	54.9	87.9
5	Depreciation (£m)	28.6	36.2	39.1	43.7	51.0

B. Balance Sheet Data (£ millions)						
6	Liquid Assets	25.1	55.7	41.8	69.2	96.7
6a	Debtors (Receivables)	145.9	171.1	178.7	208.5	214.9
6b	Stocks (Inventories)	159.1	172.9	170.2	176.9	163.2
7	Current Assets	330.1	399.7	390.7	454.6	475.1
8	Fixed Assets	359.7	408.5	403.1	475.1	463.2
9	Total Assets	689.8	808.2	793.8	929.7	938.3
10	Current Liabilities	217.8	229.3	242.4	310.2	270.1
11	Long-term Liabilities	123.0	186.3	177.0	228.1	259.6
12a	Preferred Stock	2.7	2.7	2.7	2.7	2.7
12b	Share Capital & Reserves	346.3	389.9	371.7	388.7	405.9

C. Per Share Data (pence)						
13	Earnings*	31.0	36.0	34.8	35.0	40.8
14	Dividends	9.8	11.0	12.2	13.6	15.5
15a	Common Stock Price (High)	258.0	392.0	450.0	545.0	590.0
15b	Common Stock Price (Low)	200.0	212.0	337.0	363.0	367.0
16	Average Price-Earnings*	7.4	8.4	11.3	13.0	11.7
17	Equity Book Value (12b/19)	233.0	243.0	214.0	206.0	189.0

D. Other Data						
18a	Employees, U.K. (000s)	19.7	18.9	17.7	16.4	15.6
18b	Employees, World (000s)	31.2	32.4	32.0	32.5	33.1
19	Ordinary Shares (000 000s)	149.5	160.6	173.9	188.7	215.0
20	Cash Flow (4a+5)	74.9	94.2	99.8	109.9	138.9
21	Capital Expenditures (£m)	59.9	59.9	71.5	76.2	82.5
22	Business Acquisitions (£m)	159.6	3.3	34.2	189.9	14.2
23	Asset Divestitures (£m)	4.0	3.1	4.5	4.2	5.2

* Earnings based on line 4a (net profit after tax but before extraordinary items) minus preferred dividends. Average of high and low stock prices.

Source: Company accounts.

E X H I B I T   1 3   **Rowntree plc—Breakdown by Activity, 1987 (£ millions)**

Activity	Turnover	% of Total Turnover	Trading Profit	% of Total Trading Profit	Trading Margin
Confectionery	1 088.5	76.2%	101.0	77.6%	9.3%
Snack Foods	191.8	13.4	14.5	11.1	7.6
Retailing	97.3	6.8	8.1	6.2	8.3
Grocery (U.K.)	50.0	3.5	6.5	5.0	13.0
Total	1 427.6	100.0%	130.1	100.0%	9.1%

Source: Company accounts.

E X H I B I T   1 4   **Rowntree plc—Breakdown by Region, 1987**

Region	Turnover	% of Total Turnover	Trading Profit	% of Total Trading Profit	Trading Margin
U.K. & Ireland	566.4	40%	61.7	47%	10.9%
Cont'l Europe	300.4	21	11.0	8	3.7
North America	416.1	29	41.0	31	9.8
Australasia	57.1	4	4.7	4	8.2
Rest of World	87.6	6	11.7	9	13.4
Total	1 427.6	100%	130.1	100%	9.1%

Source: Company accounts.

E X H I B I T   1 5   **Rowntree plc—Operating and Financial Performance, 1976–81**

(£ millions)

	1976	1977	1978	1979	1980	1981
Turnover	340.90	469.20	562.70	601.30	629.80	688.00
Trading Profit	36.80	46.90	51.70	46.60	44.80	48.00
Net Profit[1]	16.90	30.40	34.40	27.20	17.50	29.10
Average[2]	194.90	246.80	332.50	396.60	412.50	448.60
Average Owner's[2] Equity	77.30	120.60	182.30	218.40	231.80	278.90
Trading Margin per cent	9.60	10.00	9.20	7.80	7.10	7.20
Trading Profit/Assets per cent	18.90	19.00	15.60	11.80	10.90	10.70
Turnover/Assets	1.83	1.66	1.47	1.46	1.52	1.38
Net Profit/Equity per cent	21.80	25.20	18.90	12.50	7.60	10.30

[1] Net after-tax profit attributable to ordinary common shares.
[2] Average of beginning and end of year.

Source: Company accounts.

E X H I B I T   1 6   Rowntree plc—Major Business Acquisitions, 1983–87

Company	Location	Primary Area of Business Activity	Year of Purchase	Purchase Price (£m)
Tom's Foods	U.S.	Snack foods	1983	£138
Laura Secord	Canada	Branded retailing	1983	19
Original Cookie Co.	U.S.	Branded retailing	1985	32
Hot Sam	U.S.	Branded retailing	1986	14
Sunmark	U.S.	Branded confectionery	1986	154
Gales	U.S.	Honey products	1986	1
Smaller Acquisitions	U.S., U.K., France, Australia	Snack foods, Confectionery, Branded retailing	1983–87	29
				£399

Source: Company Accounts.

E X H I B I T   1 7   Rowntree plc—Share Price Performance, 1980–87

Rowntree Share Price Performance compared to the Financial Times' Market and Food Manufacturer's Price Indexes on the London Stock Exchange (01/01/80 to 31/21/87, weekly).

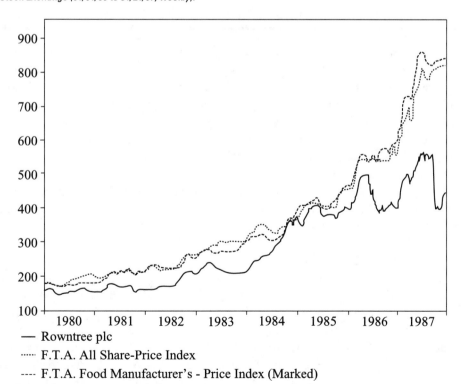

— Rowntree plc

····· F.T.A. All Share-Price Index

---- F.T.A. Food Manufacturer's - Price Index (Marked)

Source: *Financial Times.*

E X H I B I T 1 8 **Stockbrokers' Comments on Rowntree**

Name of Broker	Date of Report	Forecast of 1988	Summary of Major Comments and Recommendations
County Natwest	01/21/88	125	Sell — Dollar weakness limits prospects for 1988.
BZW	01/25/88	127	Decision to sell snack food business correct but unable to give final verdict until consideration is known.
County Natwest	01/26/88	125	Surprise disposals, but good move.
BZW	02/24/88	127	Buy—Current rating of shares is not expensive with absence of bid premium.
Warburg Securities	03/17/88	128	Hold—Core business performed well but reversal in snacks and slowdown in retailing leaves strategy looking threadbare.
Hoare Govett	03/17/88	127	Over-valued in short term. Longer term outlook remaining clouded by current divestment/acquisition plans.
BZW	03/17/88	129	Hold—Lower consideration for disposals than expected would lead to downgrading of forecast. Share price will be susceptible to strengthening of sterling.
County Natwest	03/18/88	125	Good results. Disposal of snack business an excellent move.
Kleinwart Grievson	03/18/88	129	Hold—Fully valued.

Source: Stock brokerage reports.

E X H I B I T 1 9 **The City Code and the U.K. Takeover Climate**

Takeover bids for public companies in the U.K. were conducted according to a complex set of formal rules contained in the City Code on Takeovers and Mergers. The City Code was designed to ensure fair and similar treatment for all shareholders of the same class, mainly through responsible, detailed disclosure and the absence of stock price manipulation. The City Code was administered by the Takeover Panel, a self-regulatory body whose members included Bank of England appointees and representatives of participants in the U.K. securities markets. The Panel was authorized to make rulings and interpretations on novel points arising during the course of a takeover attempt.

The City Code identified consequences associated with the acquisition of certain benchmark percentages of the equity of a takeover target. For example, within 5 days of acquiring 5 per cent or more of the capital of a company, the purchaser was required to inform the target company of its interest; the target company was then required to make an immediate announcement of this fact to the London Stock Exchange.

A purchaser could not acquire 10 per cent or more of the capital of the target within any period of 7 days if these purchases would bring its total interest above 15 per cent of the voting rights in the target company. Between 15 per cent and 30 per cent interest, the purchaser could accumulate shares by tender offer or by a series of share purchases; however, each series of share purchases could not result in the acquisition of more than 10 per cent of the total equity of the target during any 7-day period. Once acquiring an interest totalling 30 per cent, the bidder was obliged to make a general offer for the remaining 70 per cent of the voting capital (at the highest price previously paid by the bidder). After a bidder had obtained 90 per cent ownership of a class of shares, it could compulsorily acquire the outstanding shares from the minority shareholders; similarly, any remaining minority shareholders could require the bidder to purchase their shares at the highest price previously paid by the bidder.

E X H I B I T 1 9 (continued)

Proposed acquisitions could also be reviewed by the Office of Fair Trading (OFT), a sub-section of the Department of Trade and Industry. The OFT had responsibility for deciding whether the competitive implications of the merger warranted investigation. The OFT could refer merger cases to the Mergers and Monopolies Commission (MMC), an independent tribunal which ruled on whether the merger should be blocked in the interests of national competition policy. Referral to the MMC was often prized by managements of takeover targets. Aside from allowing the possibility of a referral decision favouring the target, the referral process gave the takeover target additional time (3–7 months) to mount a more effective takeover defence.

Takeovers of U.K. public companies were either recommended by the Board of the target company or contested. Action by the Board of a target to frustrate an offer for the target company was prohibited without the approval, in a General Meeting, of the shareholders. Recommended offers in the U.K. were generally restricted to smaller companies; they were relatively rare for companies with market capitalization in excess of £200 million.

Between 1985 and 1987, takeover bids were initiated for 14 large U.K. companies, each with individual market capitalizations in excess of £1 billion. Only one of these bids was recommended; the rest were contested. Ultimately, four of these bids were successful while ten failed. For the three successful cash bids, the average share price premium paid was 60 per cent; the individual premiums paid ranged from 40 per cent to 80 per cent.*

More recent acquisition activity in France and the U.K. provided reference points for the value of brand names. During 1987 and 1988, Seagrams (a Canadian drinks group) and Grand Metropolitan (a U.K. drinks and hotel group) waged a fierce takeover battle to acquire Martell (the second largest French cognac house). In February 1988, Seagrams emerged the victor, but only after bidding an estimated 40x the 1987 earnings of Martell. In March 1988, United Biscuits paid a price-earnings multiple of 25x to purchase the frozen and chilled foods division of Hanson Trust. At that time, the average price-earnings ratio for five comparable U.K. food companies was 11.9x.

---

* Share price premiums were calculated by comparing final bid offer prices against the share prices of the target companies two months prior to the date of the final offer.

EXHIBIT 20 Selected Financial Market Rates, 1984–87

	1984	1985	1986	1987	1988 (1st quart. annualized)
Inflation*(%)					
Switzerland	3.0	1.0	0.8	1.4	3.5
U.K.	5.0	6.0	3.4	4.3	1.8
U.S.	4.3	3.5	2.0	3.6	2.6
Long-Term Government Bond Yield (%)					
Switzerland	4.7	4.8	4.3	4.1	4.1
U.K.	10.7	10.6	9.9	9.5	9.4
U.S.	12.5	10.6	7.7	8.4	8.4

* Based on the Consumer Price Index.

Source: International Monetary Fund.